Popular Sovereignty in Hist

M000267730

This collaborative volume offers the first historical reconstruction of the concept of popular sovereignty from antiquity to the twentieth century. First formulated between the late sixteenth and mid-seventeenth centuries, the various early modern conceptions of the doctrine were heavily indebted to Roman reflection on forms of government and Athenian ideas of popular power. This study, edited by Richard Bourke and Quentin Skinner, traces successive transformations of the doctrine, rather than narrating a linear development. It examines critical moments in the career of popular sovereignty, spanning antiquity, medieval Europe, the early modern wars of religion, the revolutions of the eighteenth century and their aftermath, decolonisation and mass democracy. Featuring original work by an international team of scholars, the book offers a reconsideration of one of the formative principles of contemporary politics by exploring its descent from classical city-states to the advent of the modern state.

RICHARD BOURKE is Professor in the History of Political Thought and co-director of the Centre for the Study of the History of Political Thought at Queen Mary University of London. His books include *Peace in Ireland: The War of Ideas* (2003, 2012) and *Empire and Revolution: The Political Life of Edmund Burke* (2015).

QUENTIN SKINNER is Barber Beaumont Professor of the Humanities at Queen Mary University of London. His books include *The Foundations of Modern Political Thought* (2 vols., 1978), *Reason and Rhetoric in the Philosophy of Hobbes* (1996), *Liberty before Liberalism* (1998), *Hobbes and Republican Liberty* (2008), *Forensic Shakespeare* (2014) and a three-volume collection of essays, *Visions of Politics* (2002).

Popular Sovereignty in Historical Perspective

Edited by

Richard Bourke

Queen Mary University of London

and

Quentin Skinner

Queen Mary University of London

CAMBRIDGE
UNIVERSITY PRESS

CAMBRIDGE
UNIVERSITY PRESS

University Printing House, Cambridge CB2 8BS, United Kingdom

One Liberty Plaza, 20th Floor, New York, NY 10006, USA

477 Williamstown Road, Port Melbourne, VIC 3207, Australia

4843/24, 2nd Floor, Ansari Road, Daryaganj, Delhi - 110002, India

79 Anson Road, #06-04/06, Singapore 079906

Cambridge University Press is part of the University of Cambridge.

It furthers the University's mission by disseminating knowledge in the pursuit of education, learning and research at the highest international levels of excellence.

www.cambridge.org
Information on this title: www.cambridge.org/9781107571396

© Richard Bourke and Quentin Skinner 2016

First published 2016
First paperback edition 2017

A catalogue record for this publication is available from the British Library

ISBN 978-1-107-13040-1 Hardback
ISBN 978-1-107-57139-6 Paperback

Contents

Figures

Acknowledgements

This volume began life as a series of conferences held at Queen Mary University of London devoted to tracing the history of popular sovereignty. The editors are grateful to Queen Mary for hosting these events in such a congenial environment. The conferences were made possible by a research networking grant funded by the United Kingdom's Arts and Humanities Research Council. We should like to thank the AHRC for its generosity in supporting the project, and Emma Yates in the School of History at Queen Mary University of London for her help in administering the grant. We are also particularly indebted to Joanne Paul for the major role she played in organising the conferences and disseminating the conclusions of our research. The editors would also like to express their thanks to Richard Fisher and Elizabeth Friend-Smith for commissioning the work on behalf of Cambridge University Press, and Rebecca Taylor, Rosalyn Scott and Christina Sarigiannidou for seeing it through the production process. Finally, we are grateful to Sarah Lambert for her help in compiling the bibliographies, and to the anonymous readers commissioned by Cambridge University Press for their very helpful reports on the penultimate version of the typescript. As our book goes to press, we are very pleased to learn that there is still time to add our thanks to Mary Starkey, our copy-editor, who calmly and efficiently sorted out a considerable number of last-minute difficulties.

Contributors

VALENTINA ARENA is Lecturer in Roman History in the Department of History at University College London. She has published extensively on Roman oratory and political thought and is the author of *Libertas and the Practice of Politics in the Late Roman Republic* (2012).

RICHARD BOURKE is Professor in the History of Political Thought at Queen Mary University of London. His publications include the co-edited volume *Political Judgement* (2009) and *Empire and Revolution: The Political Life of Edmund Burke* (2015).

ALAN CROMARTIE is Professor in the Department of Politics and International Relations at the University of Reading. He is the author of *Sir Matthew Hale: Law, Religion, and Natural Philosophy* (1995) and *The Constitutionalist Revolution: An Essay on the History of England* (2006).

SERENA FERENTE is Senior Lecturer in Medieval and European History at King's College London. She is the author of *La sfortuna di Jacopo Piccinino: storia dei bracceschi in Italia, 1423–1465* (2005) and is currently working on a book on partisan identities in Italy between 1450 and 1500.

BRYAN GARSTEN is Professor of Political Science and Humanities in the Department of Political Science at Yale University. Among his publications is *Saving Persuasion: A Defense of Rhetoric and Judgment* (2006). He is currently completing a monograph on nineteenth-century liberalism titled *The Heart of a Heartless World*.

KINCH HOEKSTRA is Chancellor's Professor of Political Science and Law at the University of California, Berkeley. He writes about ancient and early modern political thought.

DUNCAN KELLY is Reader in Political Thought and a Fellow of Jesus College, Cambridge. His publications include *The State of the Political: Conceptions of Politics and the State in the Thought of Max Weber,*

Carl Schmitt and Franz Neumann (2003) and *The Propriety of Liberty: Persons, Passions and Judgement in Modern Political Thought* (2010).

MELISSA LANE is Class of 1943 Professor of Politics at Princeton University. Her books include *Method and Politics in Plato's Statesman* (1998) and *Greek and Roman Political Ideas* (2014).

KARUNA MANTENA is Associate Professor of Political Science at Yale University. She is the author of *Alibis of Empire: Henry Maine and the Ends of Liberal Imperialism* (2010) and is currently completing a monograph on the political thought of M. K. Gandhi.

ERIC NELSON is Robert M. Beren Professor of Government in the Department of Government at Harvard University. His books include *The Greek Tradition in Republican Thought* (2004) and *The Royalist Revolution: Monarchy and the American Founding* (2014).

LORENZO SABBADINI specialises in seventeenth-century political thought, with a particular focus on ideas of liberty and property in the 1640s and 1650s.

QUENTIN SKINNER is Barber Beaumont Professor of the Humanities at Queen Mary University of London. His books include *The Foundations of Modern Political Thought*, 2 vols. (1978) and *Forensic Shakespeare* (2014).

TIMOTHY STANTON is Senior Lecturer in the Department of Politics at the University of York. He has published widely on the moral and political thought of the seventeenth century and the history of liberalism.

RICHARD TUCK is Frank G. Thomson Professor of Government in the Department of Government at Harvard University. His books include *Philosophy and Government, 1572–1651* (1993) and *The Rights of War and Peace: Political Thought and International Order from Grotius to Kant* (1999).

Introduction

Richard Bourke

Popular sovereignty is a key component of modern political thinking, yet a history of the concept has not previously been attempted. This volume does not pretend to offer a comprehensive treatment. It arises from a collaborative project involving scholars specialising across a range of periods – spanning ancient, medieval, early modern and modern political thought. What has emerged is not a continuous and exhaustive account but a series of chapters that analyse some of the principal developments that reshaped the history of the doctrine.

The term 'sovereignty' came into English from the old French word *souveraineté*, itself derived from the medieval Latin name for a superior, *superanus*. Etymology, however, is not a sufficient guide to meaning. For early modern writers trying to explicate the concept, it seemed necessary to place it within a constellation of terms stretching back into the Graeco-Roman past. For instance, in Chapter 8 of Book I of the 1583 French edition of *Les six livres de la République*, Jean Bodin renders *souveraineté* by the Latin noun *maiestas*.[1] In its most basic sense, this Latin word connotes grandeur or authority. For example, in Livy's history of Rome, in the process of recounting a conflict over the nature of dictatorial authority, the author refers to the 'standing' (*maiestas*) of the Roman senate.[2] Furthermore Cicero, in defining the crime of *lèse-majesté* in his manual on oratory, *De inventione*, emphasised that injury to *maiestas* involved a diminution of greatness (*amplitudo*), authority (*potestas*) and dignity (*dignitas*).[3] Majesty combined dignity with dominion in this context. Dignity could also connote ultimate status, as in the invocation of the supreme authority of the Roman people (*per maiestatem populi Romani*) in Sallust's account of the conflict leading to the Jugurthine war.[4] Sallust's description appears as part of a speech by the Numidian prince Adherbal, who was seeking assistance from the Roman senate.

---

[1] Jean Bodin, *Les six livres de la République* (Paris: Jacques du Puys, 1576; Paris: n.p., 1583), p. 122. (All page numbers cited in this introduction are from the 1583 edition unless otherwise indicated.)

[2] Livy, *Ab urbe condita* VIII, 34.   [3] Cicero, *De inventione* II, xvii, 53.

[4] Sallust, *Iugurtha* XIV, 25.

1

Adherbal stressed his position as an administrative deputy (*procurator*) under the superior authority of Rome. Explaining the implications of his subjection, he ascribed right (*ius*) and control (*imperium*) to the Roman people.[5] Thus in the Latin of republican and early imperial Rome, *maiestas* could be defined in terms of *potestas, ius* and *imperium*. Unsurprisingly, therefore, as early modern humanists such as Bodin set out to develop their own ideas about the nature of authority they became interested in the range of classical usage.

Bodin's approach to understanding the nature of sovereignty was philological and analytical at the same time. His interest in philology prompted him to explore the varieties of past idioms while his faith in analysis impelled him to add precision to previous conceptions.[6] He claimed that sovereignty was a feature of all political communities although its precise character had never been properly understood before. For that reason the notion could be found in all languages – in Hebrew, Greek and Italian, for example – although earlier jurists had failed to unravel the implications of its meaning.[7] It was important to Bodin to emphasise that the Greeks had employed the concept, though like other cultures they had failed to use it with perfect consistency. Phrases such as *akra exousia* (supreme power) and *kurion archē* (authoritative rule), which frequently appear in the texts of the ancient Athenians, seemed to Bodin to point to the idea of sovereignty. But while the Greeks had the idea, he went on to observe, they lacked a complete understanding of how to apply it consistently. As Richard Tuck has pointed out, the thought of Aristotle best exemplified Bodin's criticism: as Bodin tells us in the *Methodus ad facilem historiarum cognitionem*, Aristotle's *Politics* had a name for sovereignty or *summum imperium* although the author 'nowhere defines' it.[8] It therefore fell to Bodin to supply a definition. Towards that end, he explained the concept of *maiestas* (or *summum imperium*) in terms of four universally requisite traits: such power had to be supreme, absolute, indivisible and perpetual.[9] Then, in chapter 10 of Book I of *Les six livres de la République*, he presented the 'marks' (*marques*) or attributes of sovereignty as necessary entailments of these basic traits.

[5] Ibid., XIV, 1–2.
[6] J. Franklin, *Jean Bodin and the Sixteenth-Century Revolution in the Methodology of Law and History* (New York and London: Columbia University Press, 1963); D. R. Kelley, *Foundations of Modern Historical Scholarship: Language, Law, and History in the French Renaissance* (New York and London: Columbia University Press, 1970).
[7] Bodin, *Six livres*, p. 122.
[8] Jean Bodin, *Methodus ad facilem historiarum cognitionem* (Paris: n.p., 1566), p. 181; R. Tuck, *The Sleeping Sovereign* (Cambridge: Cambridge University Press, forthcoming), chap. 1.
[9] Bodin, *Six livres*, p. 122. Cf. Jean Bodin, *De republica libri sex* (Paris: n.p., 1786), p. 345.

There was one attribute above all others that Bodin insisted on ascribing to the bearer of sovereignty, and that was the right of making laws. This right, however, required clarification since it did not stop at legislation as such, but included the privilege of declaring war and concluding peace, as well as the right of selecting the highest magistrates in the state. Bodin's principal objective in setting out the attributes of sovereignty in this way was to elucidate the defining characteristics of princely rule. Thus neither democracies nor aristocracies were his primary concern. Nonetheless, he believed that the accuracy of his account of monarchical sovereignty could be tested against examples of other regime forms. According to an important passage in *Les six livres de la République*, the idea of supreme authority was founded on the distinction between subject and sovereign.[10] This meant that a sovereign could not exhibit any characteristics of subjection without reducing the idea of sovereignty to absurdity. Given the pervasiveness of subordinate jurisdictions in monarchies such as France, sovereignty was above all evident in the subjection of these subordinate powers to the ultimate jurisdiction of the king. Bodin believed that this claim could be reinforced by comparing the relatively simple case of supreme authority under a monarchy with the operation of sovereignty in popular regimes. He therefore turned his attention to Athens and Rome, the two 'plus grandes Républiques populaires' that had ever existed, in order to show that the characteristics of supreme power were as applicable in the case of democratic regimes as they were in kingdoms.[11]

The identification of popular sovereignty with democracy therefore begins with Bodin. Nonetheless, it is important to recognise that key elements of the modern concept were constructed out of classical materials. As Kinch Hoekstra makes clear in his chapter on fifth-century BCE Athens that opens this volume, writers such as Aristophanes and Herodotus had a clear conception of supreme unaccountable rule residing in the people. For Aristophanes in particular, if the *dēmos* were not to be overmastered by their leaders, they had to possess what he dubbed 'tyrannical' power. Tyranny might almost be thought to serve as a synonym for sovereignty here since it is understood as unitary, supreme and unaccountable at once. Yet later, when Bodin came to consider the rights of supreme power, he was careful to distinguish the legitimate use of sovereign authority from the practice of tyrannical government. Sovereignty, unlike tyranny, was a supreme *right*. Bodin proceeded to explain his argument by criticising Philipp Melanchthon on the nature of tyrannical power. According to Bodin, Melanchthon had confused the

---

[10] Bodin, *Six livres*, pp. 214–15.   [11] Ibid., p. 224.

'rights' of sovereignty with the abuse of magisterial power. Sovereignty, Bodin argued, unlike tyranny, was bound by the laws of nature prescribed by God. While sovereignty was therefore juridically absolute it remained a morally subordinate power. That meant that while *summum imperium* was legally unaccountable it was nonetheless answerable for its conduct to the moral law.[12]

If sovereignty was obliged to act under moral constraints while nonetheless enjoying juridical supremacy, Bodin had yet to clarify whether it was subject to political control. A control on power in this sense could take one of two forms, as Bodin saw it: either the people could thwart the will of their ruler, thus restraining sovereignty by popular resistance; or else the exercise of sovereignty could be divided among distinct powers. Bodin firmly set his face against both options. In the first case, if the people claimed a right of appeal against sovereign authority, they were in effect ascribing supreme jurisdiction to themselves. This appeared to Bodin to involve a confusion of roles whereby the subject mistook its status as ultimately supreme. For the people to assert their supremacy was to claim their right as *summum imperium*. It might of course be the case, in a popular regime, that the people were indeed legitimately sovereign. But then, as with monarchical sovereignty, there could be no appeal against their final authority. For supremacy to function it had to be supreme.

Bodin was equally sceptical about dividing the powers of sovereignty, thereby subjecting supreme jurisdiction to practical restraints. Here he focused on criticising the views of Aristotle, Polybius and Dionysius of Halicarnassus. These writers distinguished among different 'parts' of sovereignty, with the implication that one part could limit the power of another. For Bodin, Aristotle was the most serious culprit in this regard since he went so far as to identify the parts of sovereignty inaccurately. Yet Polybius and Dionysius of Halicarnassus were equally misguided in so far as they built their constitutional theory on the false assumption that the parts of sovereignty could also be divided among different powers. Bodin accepted that legislation, the selection and control of officials, and the rights of war and peace could in principle be identified as distinct attributes of supreme power, yet he denied that these prerogatives could reside in distinct political bodies. How could one coherently deprive legislative power of the right to decide on matters of war and peace? In the same vein, how could the legislature not control the means of administration?

---

[12] Ibid., p. 211.

Once again, Bodin was anxious to take issue with Aristotelian claims in particular. Above all, he disputed the idea that different parts of the state could somehow 'share' (*metechein*) in its sovereignty.[13] For instance, if the attributes of sovereignty under a monarchy were diversely located, 'there would be no sovereign prince'.[14] The same applied to the other principal forms of constitution: in a democracy or an aristocracy the marks of supreme authority could not be distributed among different parts of the constitution. Certain attributes of rule, such as administration and deliberation, might be exercised by distinct branches of government, but the supreme functions, like legislation and the control of magistracy, could not plausibly be held separately among distinct agents in the state. Thus, from Bodin's perspective, Aristotle was right to say in Book III of the *Politics* that supreme power (*to kurion*) must be in the hands of either the one, the many or the few.[15] Yet he was mistaken when he argued in Book IV of the same work that its attributes could be variously shared.

Aristotle's argument was based on a division of the city into constitutive components. Every polity, he wrote, is composed of many 'elements' (*mere*).[16] These elements consisted of social divisions within the communality – between rich and poor; oarsmen and hoplites; farmers and traders. Different regimes variously reflected these distinctions, giving rise to assorted forms of government: democracy, aristocracy, oligarchy, monarchy and so forth. As Melissa Lane shows in her chapter on Aristotle's conception of democracy, constitutional forms can in part be defined in terms of two significant criteria: access to office on the one hand, and selection to office on the other. Aristotle recognised that deliberative councils, popular assemblies and the judiciary were essential to the operation of virtually every city-state. But he also emphasised the distribution of offices (*archai*) as a pivotal means of categorising regime forms. In one of the more extreme forms of democracy, which Aristotle describes in Book IV of the *Politics*, all power resides in the commerce between the assembly (*ekklēsia*) and its demagogues (*demagōgoi*): decrees (*psephismata*) supplant laws (*nomoi*) and the authority of offices declines.[17] Yet in Book III Aristotle also argues that the multitude (*to plēthos*) might be given prominence without such unfortunate consequences. This is where they are given access to power sufficient to pacify their ambition

---

[13] The idea of sharing or participating in power is pervasive in Aristotle, *Politics*, Books III and IV. For Bodin's critique see *Six livres*, p. 212.

[14] Ibid.   [15] Aristotle, *Politics* 1279a25–30.

[16] Ibid., 1289b30. On this theme in ancient and early modern political thought, see P. Pasquino, 'Machiavelli and Aristotle: The Anatomies of the City', *History of European Ideas* 35 (2009), pp. 397–407.

[17] Aristotle, *Politics* 1292a1–10.

without investing them with political control over all aspects of the polity. Specifically, they can be trusted with the power of electing governors to offices and holding them to account without allowing them to occupy the highest offices themselves.[18]

Earlier in Book III Aristotle made plain that the exclusive predominance of the common people (*to plēthos*) in the city subverted constitutional government altogether. Legitimate government, he believed, was a system of rule designed to promote the ideal of justice in the polity. That goal could only be served by catering to the general advantage (*to koinon sumpheron*).[19] Correspondingly, it was undermined by the pursuit of factional or partial interests. Where the majority population (*to plēthos*) ruled for its own benefit, the welfare of the people (*ho dēmos*) as a whole was undermined. As Valentina Arena shows in her chapter on the political thought of Cicero, the Platonic–Aristotelian conception of the republic (*politeia*) as an arrangement of offices shared among different constituencies in the city underlies much of the analysis in *De re publica* and *De legibus*. In the latter work, Plato's *Laws* is singled out as the best guide to understanding the problems of legitimate rule. The Stoics, Cicero conceded, had also applied themselves to political philosophy, but not as a practical science. The empirical study of the forms of government was confined to Plato and his disciples, Aristotle being the most distinguished example.[20] The centrepiece of the fourth-century BCE Athenian analysis was the mixed constitution, which blended the need for prudent or wise deliberation with the popular desire for equality. Aspects of that ideal were later adapted by the Romans.[21] As Cicero put it in *De re publica*, the *civitas* is made harmonious by establishing consensus between different orders.[22] Arena shows how Cicero revised what he took to be the appropriate terms of that consensus between his work on *De re publica* and the completion of *De legibus*. That involved reconsidering how the commonwealth (*res publica*) could best benefit the affairs of the people (*res populi*). This reconsideration led Cicero to develop a series of criticisms of populist provisions under the Roman constitution, including the process of election, the role of the censors and the status of the tribunes. Nonetheless, in both *De re publica* and *De legibus* the welfare of the *populus* as a whole is assumed to depend on constitutionally modified power. Moderation, based on some kind of accommodation between the

---

[18] Ibid., 1281b30–35, and Lane, Chapter 2 below.
[19] Aristotle, *Politics* 1279a25–30.   [20] Cicero, *De legibus* III, 14.
[21] For discussion of mixed regimes in classical and early modern thought see W. Nippel, *Mischverfassungstheorie und Verfassungsrealität in Antike und der Früher Neuzeit* (Stuttgart: Klett-Cotta, 1980).
[22] Cicero, *De re publica* I, 45.

liberty of the people and the authority of the senate, is the guiding ideal in both works.[23]

Much of the moral framework standardly employed among classical conceptions of constitutional government was adopted by political commentators in the northern Italian city-states between the twelfth and fourteenth centuries.[24] Marsilius of Padua's *Defender of the Peace* stands out as a rich example. Written, as Serena Ferente emphasises in her chapter, at a time when popular regimes in the *Regnum Italicum* were succumbing to oligarchical manipulation and being squeezed by the rival claims of powerful overlords and the papacy, Marsilius turned back to Aristotle's *Politics*, translated into Latin in the preceding century by William of Moerbeke, in order to develop a conception of legitimate regime formation. According to the scheme developed in *The Defender of the Peace*, just rule was only possible under well-tempered constitutions. These should be based on consent and cater to the general advantage.[25] According to Marsilius, both these criteria were commonly observed in three distinct forms of government, corresponding to Aristotle's 'correct' constitutions. Amongst these correct forms was Aristotle's republic or polity (*politeia*) in which, as Marsilius described it, 'every citizen had some share' in the system of government.[26] Participation, he noted, was by turns; and also according to rank. This last point implied that different orders in the city could divide the governing authority between themselves. We have been emphasising that it was this kind of understanding that provoked Bodin into disputing the viability of mixed regimes. If sovereignty is 'indivisible', he asked, 'how could it be shared by a prince, the nobles, and the people at the same time?'[27]

As Richard Tuck shows in his chapter on the idea of the sleeping sovereign in early modern political thought, Bodin's rhetorical question was made possible by a distinction between sovereignty and government. The distinction seems to be absent in the philosophical commentary of the Greeks. In a famous passage in the *Politics*, Aristotle had written that a constitution should be understood in terms of the 'organisation of the city in respect of its various offices, and especially of the most authoritative of all' (ἔστιν δὲ πολιτεία πόλεως τάξις τῶν τε ἄλλων καὶ μάλιστα τῆς κυρίας πάντων). He went on: 'For the government is everwhere supreme over the city' (κύριον μὴν γὰρ πανταχοῦ τὸ πολίτευμα τῆς πόλεως).[28] For Bodin, on

---

[23] Cicero, *De legibus* III, 17.

[24] Q. Skinner, *The Foundations of Modern Political Thought*, 2 vols. (Cambridge: Cambridge University Press, 1978), I, pp. 3–22.

[25] Marsilius of Padua, *The Defender of the Peace*, trans. Annabel Brett (Cambridge: Cambridge University Press, 2005), pp. 40–1, 47.

[26] Ibid., p. 41.   [27] Bodin, *Six livres*, p. 254.   [28] Aristotle, *Politics* 1278b9–13.

the other hand, it was important to recognise that sovereignty rather than government (*politeuma*) was supreme. As Tuck goes on to show, Bodin's analysis proved fruitful: in Rousseau the distinction between sovereignty and government was still pivotal, being used to differentiate between legitimately sovereign will (*summum imperium*) and specific acts of power (*administratio*). Such acts were by no means insignificant manifestations of authority. Magistracy was the quotidian means of policy implementation. Nonetheless, as Bodin, Hobbes and Rousseau emphasised, these acts of government were authorised by an underlying power which they called sovereignty. As Bodin first formulated the idea, an agent should be distinguished from the authority that empowered it, with the result that the authorising sovereignty had to be distinguished from the governning agents acting in its name: 'the act of an agent (*procureur*) may be disavowed if he has transacted even the slightest matter for another without express permission (*charge*)'.[29]

The idea that political magistracy was ultimately answerable to democratic sovereignty had a complex career ahead of it. It would prove highly controversial during the constitutional debates that divided various partisans during the French Revolution. Many of the terms in which this later controversy was conducted were not, however, without precedent. In the 1640s, for example, the role of the people in relation to government in England was heavily contested in the context of disputes between Parliament and the Crown. As Alan Cromartie argues in his chapter, opponents of the Crown could draw on a tradition of common-law thinking to vindicate the adjudicative role of Parliament in securing the rights of the subject. For advocates of parliamentary privilege such as Henry Parker the defence of popular rights supplanted an older humanistic emphasis on the role of government in the promotion of public virtue. From Parker's vantage point, a desirable system of rule should secure the liberty of the citizen rather than advance the moral perfection of the community. This outcome was best achieved by the operation of representation. Parliament, on Parker's understanding, encapsulated the population at large. It was therefore seen as a virtual approximation of the people and in that capacity entitled to supreme power: Parliament was not a proxy but the embodiment of popular sovereignty. As Lorenzo Sabbadini clarifies the point in his chapter, any initiative by Parliament was a justifiable act of authority, even when opposed by the bulk of the population. Parliament rather than the 'universality' whom it represented was the bearer of popular sovereignty.[30] As Sabbadini emphasises, it was

---

[29] Bodin, *Six livres*, p. 227.
[30] [Henry Parker], *Jus Populi* (London: Robert Bostock, 1644), pp. 18–19.

this claim that Levellers such as John Lilburne and Richard Overton were determined to contest by challenging the authority of parliament in the name of the actual people.

Leveller publicists began by accepting Parliament as a vehicle for popular sovereignty, only to end up objecting to the 'absolutism' of the Lords and Commons. Their anxiety about the tendency among representatives to betray the desires of the population whose interests they were entrusted with protecting encouraged them to champion self-ownership among citizens in opposition to the unrestrained privilges of Parliament. At the same time, they helped to entrench a growing uneasiness through the 1640s about the practicality of mixed regimes. Doubts about the viability of dividing supreme power were entertained on both the Republican and Royalist sides. In *De Cive*, Hobbes had been adamant that a 'mixed state' was a contradiction in terms.[31] Yet to many European observers the establishment of a mixed system of government in Britain after 1688 seemed to point to the possibility of just such an arrangement. It has been influentially argued that the idea of absolute sovereignty was then 'blunted' in the eighteenth century as polemicists strove to justify the principle of moderate government.[32] Between Montesquieu and the Federalists the ideal of a *respublica mixta* became a potent political norm. It is nonetheless a mistake to see this widespread commitment to mixed government as antithetical to the principle of *summum imperium*. In the 1766 version of his *Lectures on Jurisprudence*, Adam Smith was happy to distribute the rights of sovereignty among distinct organs of government: 'With regard to governments where the supreme power is divided amongst different persons, there is no great difficulty in ascertaining when any one transgresses the limits of his power.'[33] In the same vein, in the mid-1790s Immanuel Kant could distinguish between *forma imperii*, whose powers were necessarily absolute, and *forma regiminis*, under which the powers of government could be beneficially divided.[34] Absolute sovereignty, it seemed, could be exercised between different branches of government.

A preoccupation with sovereignty in the eighteenth century arose in two distinct contexts. In the first place it emerged in connection with the tribulations of imperial politics. From the late seventeenth century,

---

[31] Thomas Hobbes, *De Cive: The Latin Version*, ed. H. Warrender (Oxford: Clarendon Press, 1983), pp. 151–2.

[32] F. H. Hinsley, *Sovereignty* (Cambridge: Cambridge University Press, 1986 [1966]), p. 152.

[33] Adam Smith, *Lectures on Jurisprudence*, ed. R. L. Meek et al. (Indianapolis: Liberty Fund, 1982), p. 325.

[34] Immanuel Kant, 'Towards Perpetual Peace: A Philosophical Project', in *Practical Philosophy*, ed. M. J. Gregor (Cambridge: Cambridge University Press, 1999 [1996]), p. 324.

the European balance of states was increasingly understood in terms of a balance of empires. Domestic power was usually seen as a function of the colonial and provincial assets appended by conquest or acquisition to the dominant political players in Europe. The extension of European government both eastwards and westwards into agricultural and trading settlements brought with it a range of subordinate jurisdictions. After the Seven Years War in particular, as subordinate authorities in India and America came into conflict with metropolitan powers, the rights of sovereignty emerged once more as a contentious topic in the politics of the period. In the second place, sovereignty was debated from around the middle of the eighteenth century in the context of disputes about the role of the people in relation to established powers. In Britain these debates intensified from around the middle of the 1760s as parties in Parliament began to mobilise opinion out of doors. The issues involved became still more pressing as insurgency in America after 1775 encouraged a posture of resistance among extra-parliamentary agitators and publicists in the metropole.

It has frequently been noted that popular sovereignty in America helped to inspire the language of opposition in Britain. However, as Eric Nelson argues in his contribution, popular sovereignty in the colonies could take a variety of forms, prominent amongst them being Patriot attempts to reconcile popular authorisation with the prerogatives of the Crown. For many who took issue with the Stamp Act and then the Intolerable Acts, the Revolution was a rebellion against the tyranny of the Westminster Parliament. As James Wilson, Benjamin Franklin, Alexander Hamilton and John Adams made plain in the 1760s and 1770s, Patriots in the colonies were openly alarmed by the British Parliament's claims to bind the will of subordinate legisatures in the Empire. This led to the denial that Parliament represented the Americans merely on account of 'virtually' securing their interests. Instead it was argued that representation had to be authorised by popular consent, whatever the form of government to which the people might pledge themselves. In accordance with this stipulation, the 1787 constitution of the United States combined a mixed system of government with a doctrine of popular sovereignty.

For this reason, when the ratification of the constitution was retrospectively discussed in the British House of Commons during the debate on the Quebec Bill of 1791, Whigs as diverse as Edmund Burke and Charles James Fox were happy to endorse its provisions.[35] For both

---

[35] *The Parliamentary History of England from the Norman Conquest in 1066 to the Year 1803*, ed. William Cobbett (London: n.p., 1806–20), 36 vols., XXIX, cols. 359 ff.

of them, the Americans had blended republican government with the sovereignty of the people. 'Republican', in this context, meant constitutional rule organised under a partition of civil powers. As Burke commented, with his mind increasingly distracted by contemporary developments in France, the British heritage in North America meant that the former colonists were better suited to the establishment of a republican constitution than the French.[36] In his contribution to this volume, Richard Bourke argues that Burke's analysis was heir to a Whig tradition of understanding that viewed the British people as having tacitly authorised the Crown-in-Parliament as the sovereign representatitve of the nation. Burke employed this conception through various attempts over a thirty-year period to reconcile parliamentary monarchy with imperial justice in the provinces. The ferocity of his response to the French Revolution needs to be seen in terms of his fundamental hostility to a rival doctrine of popular sovereignty. As Burke saw it, this doctrine had two characteristic components: it confused the sovereignty of the people with the supremacy of the multitude; and it preferred the unitary power of government to the norms of *respublica mixta*. But as Burke condemned what he saw as a newfangled conception of the authority of the people, a succession of French polemicists strove to reconcile this idea with effective government in a sizeable state.

To achieve this, opponents of the Jacobin republic in particular returned to the distinction between sovereignty and government. As Bryan Garsten shows in his treatment of this theme in post-Revolutionary France, critics of the committee of public safety such as Pierre-Louis Roederer sought to reanimate the ideas of Rousseau and Hobbes on the relationship between public administration and democratic sovereignty. The aim here was to reconceptualise the people's supremacy in terms of the popular authorisation of government rather than the immediate retention of power in the hands of the multitude. In adopting this perspective, Roederer was building on the thought of Emmanuel Joseph Sieyès, for whom legitimate represenatives united the people in virtue of their own unified decision-making activity. On Sieyès' understanding, the devolution of power from the legislature to the populace by means of mandates or sectional agitation risked resuscitating the factionalism that he associated with the coporate structure of *ancien régime* France. Yet for Roederer, as Garsten shows, Sieyès' preference for concentrating effective power in the hands of representative authority was in danger of reducing the flesh-and-blood membership of the state to the role of spectators under a nominally popular despotism. Roederer's solution was

[36] Ibid., col. 365.

to ground popular authority in the procedures of electoral ratification. However, as nineteenth- and twentieth-century experience would show, plebiscitary endorsement was as compatible with Caesarism as it was with liberal constitutionalism.

In the aftermath of the French Revolution, as ideological preferences continued to proliferate, debate about popular sovereignty was conducted under a variety of headings. As Duncan Kelly argues in his chapter on theories of the state in nineteenth-century Germany, from the 1820s the legitimating authority of the people was examined in connection with a range of issues, including national sovereignty, representative government and self-determination. It is clear that the ideas of 1789 did not constitute a radically new beginning – instead, the Revolution recycled older controversies in unfamiliar guises. Nonetheless, in being debated in the shadow of Revolution the old quarrels were prone to exacerbate the polarities out of which they first arose. In the ensuing atmosphere of recrimination across Europe, the idea of 'national' or popular sovereignty threatened empires with dissolution. At the same time, opposition to the principle of government by estates promised constitutional upheaval. Yet increasingly, both the partisans of established government and the adherents of Revolutionary republicanism advanced their cause under the banner of popular sovereignty, while subjecting its significance to divergent interpretations. At the same time there was a degree of common ground: for Tocqueville and Saint-Simon alike, political centralisation compromised self-government; for both again, equality was an unstoppable *telos* of modern development. Yet the question remained of how government power could be made responsible to the community, and how the ideal of equality could be reconciled with existing social reality.

These questions were extended globally in the twentieth century by the process of European decolonisation. As Karuna Mantena observes in her contribution on theories of anti-imperial sovereignty, there has been a problematic tendency in the historical and political science literature to see this extension as a kind of ideologial consummation. This teleological assumption has taken two principal forms: it has either been based on the idea that the modern nation-state represents the logical culmination of all previous regime types; or else, as in the writings of Elie Kedourie, it has been seen as an artificial norm imposed by an intellectual elite that was peculiarly ill-adapted to conditions in the colonial world.[37] In this second case, while popular sovereignty is interpreted as a kind of hoax, the nation-state is nonetheless construed as a historical

---

[37] Elie Kedourie, 'Introduction', in *Nationalism in Asia and Africa* (New York: New American Library, 1970).

norm. As Mantena shows, however, the idea that popular sovereignty in the provinces replicated developments in metropolitan centres occludes the range of alternative visions that played important roles in the struggle for colonial self-government. In India, as elsewhere, these included the image of empire as a collaborative enterprise rather than an edifice of alien rule. On this model, *sawaraj* (self-rule) might take the form of civil equality protected under the kind of federal superstructure that had been advocated in the settler dominions from the middle of the nineteenth century. Yet while this preference prospered in India in the late nineteenth and early twentieth centuries, it was gradually compromised by adverse reactions among imperial officials. As the attractions of liberal imperialism receded, commentators like the West Bengal academic Radhakamal Mukerjee began to associate self-government with local self-rule based on the diminutive structures of village and caste. This approach, which would also win the support of Mohandas K. Gandhi, was avowedly indebted to British pluralism. Congress, however, preferred to conquer the state rather than empower the peasant commune. As that ambition soared from the late 1930s, alarm about the fate of minorities under a prospectively majoritarian regime steadily rose, above all among Muslim activists and publicists.

That alarm reached its apogee in inter-communal strife leading to the Partition of India in 1947. Electoral majoritarianism under a centralised democratic state had bred conflict rather than consensus. As Timothy Stanton shows in his account of popular sovereignty in the age of mass democracy, debate about the capacity of liberal democracy to guarantee consensus intensified in the early decades of the twentieth century. In Germany, Max Weber's sobering claim that democratic politics remained in the last instance a relationship of ruling and being ruled served to focus attention on the dynamics of popular rule. The juridical fiction of a 'national' state might serve to foreground the duty of politics to serve the welfare of the people, yet it left unexplained how the common interest could best be practically served. For Weber, Hans Kelsen and Carl Schmitt alike, the political party was the prime instrument of popular government in the age of mass enfranchisement. For each of these observers, parties were certainly vehicles for expressing popular sentiment. Yet they also saw that rival parties embodied competing interests in society. Under Weimar, the intensity of the competition bred successive constitutional crises. For Kelsen it seemed that this fact should serve to foster the ideal of compromise in democracies. Yet for Schmitt it showed that parliamentarism could not deliver a stable representation of the people. This conclusion serves to remind us that the twentieth century was not characterised by the steady ascent of liberal democracy, but by competing visions of popular sovereignty embracing Caesarism, state socialism, libertarianism and welfare liberalism.

Despite Schmitt's dire prognostications, parliaments and parties since the Second World War have for the most part provided stable frameworks under which the opposing interests of capitalist democracies can compete. Can this competition be said to yield the common interest? The only plausible tribunal entitled to answer this question has to be the people themselves. Yet how should the people be organised politically to deliver an impartial response? The people's power remains a form of power and is therefore open to abuse. How can such abuses be curtailed? This question was first posed in explicitly philosophical terms in Athens in the fifth century BCE. As the chapters in this volume cumulatively demostrate, it lost none of its urgency for political thought over the suceeding two-and-a-half-thousand years.

1   Athenian democracy and popular tyranny

Kinch Hoekstra

I

An account of popular sovereignty that begins with the fifth century BCE may seem to be off to a false start. Foundational works in the history of political thought have taught us that the very notion of sovereignty, and thus of popular sovereignty, emerged from the particular historical circumstances of the early modern era. One might thus believe that fifth-century Greeks could not be discussing popular sovereignty some two thousand years before this concept's emergence.[1] Leading ancient historians and classicists have adopted this view, deeming 'sovereignty' a misleadingly anachronistic way of thinking about Athenian democracy in the classical period.[2] For the concept of sovereignty seems embedded in a later historical context, in which the dominant political unit is the

By agreement, my primary focus is on the fifth century BCE (especially its second half) and Melissa Lane's in her contribution is on the fourth. Earlier versions of this chapter were presented at Queen Mary University of London (Popular Sovereignty Project); Stanford University (Workshop on Ethics and Politics, Ancient and Modern); and UCLA (a combined meeting of the Legal Theory Workshop and the Political Theory Workshop). I am grateful to the audiences on each of these occasions, and for comments from Mark Greenberg, Amanda Greene, Tim Hoekstra, Kathryn Morgan, Seana Shiffrin and Quentin Skinner. For critical counsel I am especially indebted to Mark Fisher, Melissa Lane, Derin McLeod and Josh Ober.

[1] To apply 'popular' to classical Athenian politics is even more contentious than to apply 'sovereignty', as we are sensitive to some of the limitations on who counted as part of the political people, or who was included in or excluded from the body of citizen-rulers. This issue may be set aside here, as the present question is about how the Athenian democracy was understood, not whether it was in fact an instance of popular sovereignty (an empirical question once we have defined what we mean by that term). I also largely set aside discussion of how the ontology of the *dēmos* was understood and how that compares with later understandings of 'the people'.

[2] A point of agreement in the long-running argument between Mogens Herman Hansen and Josiah Ober is that referring to sovereignty in classical Athens is an anachronism. So: 'Historians who speak of the sovereign *ekklesia* [assembly] avail themselves of a constitutional concept developed in sixteenth-century Europe to support monarchy. The correct statement: *The ekklesia was the most important body of government* is transformed into the erroneous and anachronistic statement: *The ekklesia was sovereign*' (M. H. Hansen, *The Athenian Assembly in the Age of Demosthenes* (Oxford: Blackwell, 1987), p. 105). And: 'The concept of sovereignty was developed in the sixteenth and seventeenth centuries by

state, the paradigmatic religion is Christian monotheism, and the term emerged – to simplify – from an attempt to articulate and reinforce the supreme authority of the monarch, and was then transferred to the people who depose him. The logic of sovereignty as initially formulated applies to a unitary, supreme and absolute political authority that has been thought to be alien to Athenian conceptions.[3] This view has been reinforced by recent scholars who have aspired to reject or moderate a simplistic understanding of Athens as a direct democracy and bring it closer to a more palatable constitutionalist system replete with constraints on all political power.[4]

I wish to offer a reconsideration. I will first argue that we have misunderstood the relationship between early modern theorists of sovereignty

Western European political theorists writing on the institution of monarchy. Monarchical power is by definition unitary, since it is located in the person of the monarch . . . these theorists conceived of sovereignty, properly so called, as unitary state power that resided, preferably, either in the person of the monarch or in a representative assembly. The traditional theory of sovereignty does not encompass the idea that legitimate power could reside with an abstraction such as "the People"; consequently it is of very limited utility in explaining democracy' (J. Ober, *The Athenian Revolution: Essays on Ancient Greek Democracy and Political Theory* (Princeton: Princeton University Press, 1996), pp. 120–1; cf. p. 30). Ryan K. Balot reflects a recent consensus when he censures 'scholars [who] have anachronistically imported the modern language of sovereignty' (in R. K. Balot (ed.), *A Companion to Greek and Roman Political Thought* (Oxford: Blackwell, 2009), p. 6); see also A. W. Saxonhouse, *Athenian Democracy: Modern Mythmakers and Ancient Theorists* (Notre Dame: University of Notre Dame Press, 1996), esp. pp. 4–7.

My disagreement with Hansen and Ober here ultimately has more to do with their reading of early modern than ancient theory. Moreover, despite their reservations, and despite those who have appealed to their authority in labelling any such claims anachronistic, both have made clear claims for the sovereignty of the *dēmos* understood as the entire body of Athenian citizens: M. H. Hansen, *Athenian Assembly*, pp. 97, 106 (and see M. H. Hansen, *Polis and City-State: An Ancient Concept and its Modern Equivalent* (Copenhagen: Munksgaard, 1998)); Ober, *Athenian Revolution*, pp. 119, 121 (and see J. Ober, *Mass and Elite in Democratic Athens: Rhetoric, Ideology, and the Power of the People* (Princeton: Princeton University Press, 1989), esp. pp. 299–304). Hansen now rejects 'sovereignty' in favour of 'κύριος πάντων' (M. H. Hansen, 'The Concepts of *Demos, Ekklesia*, and *Dikasterion* in Classical Athens', *Greek, Roman, and Byzantine Studies* 50 (2010), pp. 499–536, esp. p. 500 n. 5), but this is to pull back under his shield.

[3] E.g. by F. H. Hinsley, who states that in classical Greece 'there was no modern conception of law as positive lawmaking without restraint', for an insuperable obstacle to any formulation of the idea of sovereignty – or 'a final and absolute political authority in the community' without any such authority elsewhere – was that 'the *polis* was conceived of as a community that was rightly ruled by the law and not by men' (F. H. Hinsley, *Sovereignty*, 2nd edn. (Cambridge: Cambridge University Press, 1986), pp. 30, 26, 29). It will be more fruitful to recognise the ancient ideas of unrestrained lawmaking, for we can then explore how they are different from early modern ideas in scope, conception and purpose. Conversation has instead been stalled by a thinly contextualised understanding of sovereignty as inextricably early modern, leading to easy claims of its inapplicability to ancient or contemporary situations.

[4] For a variation on this scholarship see n. 105 below.

and ancient political thought. If we pay close attention to seminal articulations of this idea, we do not find a simple break between ancients
and moderns, but see instead that sovereignty is routinely characterised by early modern thinkers in Greek terms (and in Roman terms,
but that is not my theme here). In particular, writers such as Bodin,
Grotius, Hobbes and Pufendorf appeal to the essential *unaccountability*
of sovereignty, which must be immune from review, veto or punishment.
Some explicitly cast their theories of sovereignty in terms of the Greek
notion of being *anupeuthunos*, unaccountable to any authority. Significantly, being *anupeuthunos* (or *aneuthunos*) was for ancient writers a
characteristic feature of tyranny; and I want to suggest that these early
modern writers had ancient characterisations of tyranny in mind when
they set out to articulate their modern theories of sovereignty.

It would thus turn out that there is an ancient Greek concept that
meaningfully resembles and historically influences the early modern idea
of sovereignty: tyranny. Given the Athenians' opposition to tyranny and
their use of it as the antithesis of their democracy, we might think that
we have hereby found a different reason why it is impossible to locate
a conception of *popular* sovereignty in fifth-century Athens. However
paradoxical it may seem to us, there is nonetheless ample evidence that
the Athenians frequently thought of their democracy in terms of tyranny,
not only identifying Athens as a *polis turannos*, but also characterising the
power of the Athenian people as *anupeuthunos*, and even referring to the
authority of the *dēmos* as tyrannical and despotic. Advocates of Athenian
democracy, like the early modern writers on sovereignty discussed briefly
in the next section, arrestingly illustrate just how much power is required
when they insist that it is tantamount to that of a tyrant.[5] Drawing on
history, philosophy, tragedy, comedy and visual art, subsequent sections
provide support for the idea that the *dēmos* or people was understood by
fifth-century democrats as properly holding tyrannical authority.

As will become clear, I believe that there is evidence that a strong
version of 'the *control* thesis',[6] according to which the people had power
by exercising a significant measure of control over government officials,
was already developed in the fifth century; and also that it was seen by

---

[5] It is frequently claimed that no pro-democratic theory is extant from fifth-century Athens.
Certainly the pieces of such a theory have to be carefully excavated, sometimes from an
anti-democratic matrix; but I hope to indicate in what follows that such an operation is
to some extent feasible.

[6] This thesis is advanced by Melissa Lane in her contribution in this volume (Chapter 2),
where she considers the selection and review of magistrates as Aristotle's solution for
how the *dēmos* could safely be given a limited measure of control. Despite this limitation,
she suggests that Aristotle's proposal is that the people can thereby be *kurios*, which she
interprets as a kind of popular sovereignty.

democrats (though not by Aristotle) to be necessarily paired with what I would call 'the *out of control* thesis'. On the democratic view, it is a prerequisite of the people's control of the powerful that the powerful not be in control of the people. Or, to put it differently, neither to be in control nor to be uncontrolled is by itself sufficient for sovereignty, but they are jointly sufficient. This also indicates an analytic advantage of the dramatic comparison of sovereign with *turannos*, rather than with *kurios*, the Greek word most commonly referred to when translators write 'sovereign'. The one who is *kurios* is in control of people or things, but the Greek term does not imply that no one is in turn in control of him; rather, the reference is generally to an authority whose status is guaranteed and limited by a higher legal and political authority.[7] One may be *kurios* of some people or in some respect and still be under another's control; so too there can be multiple *kurioi* (e.g. with specific authority over distinct functions, or over distinct sub-groups) within a given domain.[8] By contrast, the sovereign, like the tyrant, is supreme.

  While it may seem odd to begin the story of popular sovereignty in the ancient world, it may seem wilfully perverse to begin with ancient understandings of tyranny. This is only part of the story, of course, but it may help us to reconsider familiar yet false narratives about ancient and modern political thought. By thinking with the Greeks about popular sovereignty as analogous to tyranny, we may also gain useful, if perhaps discomforting, insights into our own conceptions of democracy and popular sovereignty.

---

[7] For example, a male Athenian citizen was the *kurios* of his wife and minor children; but this certainly did not mean that he had full discretionary powers to do to them as he wished. The legal authority of the polis prohibited a wide range of actions towards such wards (who were not slaves, *douloi*), and indeed imposed obligations for their care. As they both can signify 'master', sometimes *kurios* is used as a synonym for *despotēs*, but the latter ultimately has substantially greater discretionary power. On *kurieia* or guardianship see e.g. D. M. MacDowell, *The Law in Classical Athens* (Ithaca: Cornell University Press, 1978), pp. 84–94; S. C. Todd, *The Shape of Athenian Law* (Oxford: Clarendon Press, 1993), pp. 206–10; and A. R. W. Harrison, *The Law of Athens*, 2nd edn., 2 vols. (London: Duckworth, 1998), I, 97–121.

[8] This limitation and accountability undermine *kurieia* (or *to kurion*) as a proposed *equivalent* of sovereignty, though in particular instances such a translation may be warranted by context. There is an obvious way around this, which is parallel to the familiar Latin equivalents for sovereignty, *summa potestas* and *summum imperium* (cf. the Greek equivalents cited by Jean Bodin (n. 17 below), all of which are word pairs that specify and intensify). And authors did occasionally invoke the idea of an authority that was most *kurios*, *kurios* over all, or *kurios* in or over the polis, the regime or the citizens. Options include *kurion tēs poleōs*, *to kurion tēs politeias*, *to kurion hena pantōn einai tōn politōn* or a more general construction such as *ho pantōn kurios*, as Pindar says of Zeus in *Isthmian* 5.53. Not least, the superlative form *kuriōtatos* can simply mean the supreme or highest authority. For Aristotle's use of such superlatives, see section VII below.

II

The argument that the concept of sovereignty does not fit the Athenian democracy has targeted the suitability of the early modern conception articulated by Jean Bodin and taken up by thinkers like Hugo Grotius, Thomas Hobbes, and Samuel Pufendorf.[9] No one appears to have noticed, however, that these thinkers characterise their essential understanding of sovereignty in language strikingly similar to, and even directly borrowed from, classical Greek descriptions of tyranny.

A *locus classicus* of how tyranny is characterised and contrasted with democracy is the 'constitutional debate' in Herodotus, which has sometimes been seen as establishing or reflecting a paradigm of fifth-century political thought. In this debate about whether rule by one, few or many is best, Otanes assimilates monarchy to tyranny, and describes it as rule that 'is unaccountable [*aneuthunos*] and can do what it wishes'.[10] This is contrasted with rule by the many, wherein every magistrate is *hupeuthunos*, subject to account.[11] *Aneuthunos* here (like *anupeuthunos*, the generally later form of the word) means 'unaccountable', and so even 'irresponsible': the meaning can be narrower (not being liable to the judicial examination of a magistrate's performance and finances upon demitting office) or more extended (having impunity). In the Athenian democracy all officials, most of whom were chosen by lot from the citizen body, were subject to audit or *euthunai*; in principle, no one was powerful enough to escape this check and review.[12] The administrative

---

9 See n. 2 above. The challenge to interpreting Athens in terms of sovereignty has been posed in these terms (perhaps oddly, given recurrent claims that the early modern model is inadequate), which I therefore adopt here. A different approach would be to explain the applicability of a later view of sovereignty, or a less absolutist early modern formulation (see e.g. K. Hoekstra, 'Early Modern Absolutism and Constitutionalism', *Cardozo Law Review* 34 (2013), pp. 1079–98).

Note that while recent discussions focus on legitimacy as a criterion of sovereignty, this receives little theoretical articulation in extant fifth-century materials and will not be emphasised here. It may be worth acknowledging the obvious general point that early modern concerns and contexts were different from those of fifth-century Athens, and that this leads to different inflections of the range of political concepts. Indeed, I mean to argue that we should allow ourselves to think about the values and imperatives animating the idea that the people must be sovereign apart from the commitments, contexts and connotations of the early modern theories of absolute sovereignty.

10 Herodotus 3.80.3: μουναρχίη, τῇ ἔξεστι ἀνευθύνῳ ποιέειν τὰ βούλεται. Assimilation at 3.80.4. All translations mine unless noted otherwise.

11 Herodotus 3.80.6 (ὑπεύθυνον).

12 P. Fröhlich, *Les Cités grecques et le contrôle des magistrats (IVe–Ier siècle avant J.-C.)* (Geneva: Droz, 2004), provides a thorough account of the sources, practices and relevant vocabulary. Despite its title, this study does treat fifth-century sources; for the earlier period see also M. Piérart, 'Les εὔθυνοι athéniens', *L'Antiquité Classique* 40 (1971), pp. 526–73; and E. M. Carawan, '*Eisangelia* and *Euthyna*: The Trials of Miltiades,

associations of the word *hupeuthunos*, accountable, were above all with the Athenian democracy, whereas the tyrant (as Otanes suggests) was the one who was unaccountable. The opposition between rule by tyrant and rule by *dēmos* is frequently drawn; so Alcibiades in Thucydides, to take just one example, says that 'what is contrary to a tyrant is called the people'.[13] Aristotle later appears to confirm the nature of an established dichotomy when, in concluding his taxonomy of the different kinds of constitutions or regimes, his first characterisation of 'tyranny in the highest degree' is that 'the monarch rules in an unaccountable fashion [*anupeuthunos*]'.[14]

Against this backdrop, it is remarkable that Bodin and his followers insist that the sovereign is necessarily unaccountable, above all but divine review and punishment. As Bodin puts it in his *Six livres*, the sovereign 'is not held to render an account to anyone except God'.[15] He states the basic criterion of sovereignty in very similar terms: 'the true marks of sovereignty are included under the power of giving law to all in

Themistocles, and Cimon', *Greek, Roman, and Byzantine Studies* 28 (1987), pp. 167–208. See also J. T. Roberts, *Accountability in Athenian Government* (Madison: University of Wisconsin Press, 1982); and P. J. Rhodes, Euthynai *(Accounting): A Valedictory Lecture Delivered before the University of Durham* (n.p.: n.p., 2005). Note that while the grammatical singular is *euthuna* (from *euthus*, straight, and *euthunein*, to correct or steer straight, govern, examine or call to account), the ancient sources usually refer to the process of review and accounting (even one iteration for a single magistrate) in the plural, *euthunai*. This process of accounting upon completion of annual office is but one of several mechanisms used in Athens to hold accountable those chosen to exercise power, and cognate vocabulary was also used in the fifth century to refer to accountability more generally or without specification of the mechanism.

13 Thucydides 6.89.4, as translated by Thomas Hobbes. Like most subsequent translators, Hobbes simplifies somewhat in rendering the parenthetical here: τοῖς γὰρ τυράννοις αἰεί ποτε διάφοροί ἐσμεν (πᾶν δὲ τὸ ἐναντιούμενον τῷ δυναστεύοντι δῆμος ὠνόμασται). Cf. e.g. Andocides 1.106. Because of the range of sources considered, I have to give short shrift throughout to offering interpretation of such passages according to speaker, occasion, author, etc.

14 Aristotle, *Politics* IV 1295a17–20, trans. C. D. C. Reeve: τρίτον δὲ εἶδος τυραννίδος, ἥπερ μάλιστ᾽ εἶναι δοκεῖ τυραννίς, ἀντίστροφος οὖσα τῇ παμβασιλείᾳ. τοιαύτην δ᾽ ἀναγκαῖον εἶναι τυραννίδα τὴν μοναρχίαν ἥτις ἀνυπεύθυνος ἄρχει. . . .

15 Jean Bodin, *Les six livres de la République* (Paris: Jacques du Puys, 1576), 1.9, p. 127 (= 1583 edn. 1.8, p. 125): 'n'est tenu rendre conte qu'à Dieu'. This language of unaccountability is taken up by Thomas Hobbes, e.g. when he says that sovereigns are 'to give account to none but God' (*The Questions Concerning Liberty, Necessity, and Chance* (London: n.p., 1656), p. 135; cf. e.g. the 1640 *Elements of Law* 2.2.10 for the ability of a sovereign people to call even a king to account). This characterisation may thus be used without qualification for the power of God himself, as Leibniz does in equating his unaccountability and his supremacy. Arguing that God is essentially independent while all things depend on him, Leibniz states: 'he is *anupeuthunos*, that is, he has no superior' (est ἀνυπεύθυνος, seu superiorem non habet). [Gottfried Wilhelm Leibniz], *Causa Dei asserta per justitiam ejus* (Amsterdam: n.p., 1710), p. 5; Leibniz fleshes out his view of God as *anupeuthunos* in his 1706 *Monita*.

general and each in particular, and not receiving it but from God.'[16] Bodin and his followers insist that sovereignty is unified, supreme and unlimited; within the commonwealth, all are subject to the sovereign and the sovereign is subject to no one.[17] Directly addressing the Bodinian view in 1625, Grotius writes that 'sovereignty [is] something singular and in itself undivided, consisting of those parts enumerated here above, with the addition of the highest part, i.e. *tōi anupeuthunōi*, unaccountability'.[18] And in the second edition of *De iure belli ac pacis*, published in 1631, Grotius inserts the following passage: 'In Herodotus, Otanes describes the rule of one thus: *aneuthunos poieein ta bouletai, to do what one wishes, without rendering an account to another.* And thus Dio Chrysostom defines kingship: *epitattein anthrōpois anupeuthunon onta,* to rule in such a way as not to render an account to another.'[19]

[16] Bodin, *Six livres* (1576), 1.11, p. 199 (= 1583 edn. 1.10, pp. 223–4): 'qui son les vrayes marques de souueraineté, comprises soubs la puissance de donner la loy à touts en general, & à chacun en particulier: & ne la receuoir que de Dieu.' ('Soubs cest mesme puissance . . . sont compris touts les autres droicts, & marques de souueraineté: de sorte qu'à parler proprement on peut dire qu'il n'y a que ceste seule marque de souueraineté'.)

[17] Bodin relies heavily on Greek sources and language in expressing these ideas. Thus, in the opening of his first attempt to give an account of sovereignty in *Six livres*, he writes: 'Sovereignty is the absolute and perpetual power of a Commonwealth, which the Latins call *maiestatem*, the Greeks *akran exousian* [highest authority], *kurian archēn* [authoritative rule], and *kurion politeuma* [authoritative governing body]' ('La souueraineté est la puissance absoluë & perpetuelle d'vne Republique, que les Latins appellent maiestatem, les Grecs ἄκραν ἐξουσίαν, & κυρίαν ἀρχήν, & κύριον πολίτευμα' (Bodin, *Six livres*, 1.9 (DE LA SOVVERAINETE), p. 125 ['152'], with minor correction adopted from edn. of 1583, 1.8, p. 122). There are many hundreds of references to Greek sources in this work, and Ioannis Evrigenis, director of the Bodin Project at Tufts University, tells me that Bodin gives words or phrases in the Greek language 212 times in the first Latin edition of this work (1586).

[18] Hugo Grotius, *De ivre belli ac pacis libri tres* (Paris: n.p., 1625), 1.3.17, pp. 82–3 (summum imperium vnum quiddam [est] ac per se indiuisum, constans ex illis partibus quas supra enumerauimus, addita summitate, id est τῳ ἀνυπευθύνῳ). Bodin articulates the criterion of the indivisible unity of sovereignty in, for example, *Six livres* 2.1.

[19] Hugo Grotius, *De ivre belli ac pacis libri tres* (Amsterdam: n.p., 1631), 1.3.8, p. 51 (& apud Herodotum Otanes singulare imperium sic describit: ἀνευθύνως [*sic*] ποιέειν τὰ βούλεται: *facere quod vis velit, ita ut alii rationem non reddat.* Dioni quoque Prusaeensi regnum definitur: ἐπιτάττειν ἀνθρώποις ἀνυπεύθυνον ὄντα ita imperare ut alii ratio non reddatur.) In a formulation that may have influenced Pufendorf and others, Grotius says that to command unaccountably is Dio's definition of *regnum*, a word that can simply mean rule, dominion or sovereignty (whereas Dio had offered this as a student's definition of kingship, which he then refutes). Grotius gets the quotation of Dio from 56.5 (*Agamemnon, or on Kingship*): ἡ ἀρχὴ αὕτη ἣν λέγεις τὸ καθόλου ἀνθρώπων ἄρχειν καὶ ἐπιτάττειν ἀνθρώποις ἀνυπεύθυνον ὄντα βασιλεία καλεῖται. A version of this is restated (as having been refuted) in 56.16; the definition is similar to that offered in Dio's *On Kingship III* (3.43).

That sovereignty is in its essence *anupeuthunos* continued to be force-fully maintained by other early modern theorists.[20] Turning in his 1672 opus to an analysis 'Of the characteristics of supreme sovereignty', Pufendorf writes:

Among the characteristics of sovereignty we encounter, first of all, the fact that it is, and is said to be, *supreme*. . . because sovereignty is supreme, or not dependent on any superior man on this earth, its acts cannot be nullified by the decision of another human will. For a person's ability to alter the decisions of his own will is, itself, a consequence of his freedom. One who holds the supreme sovereignty will for the same reason be unaccountable [*anupeuthunos*]; that is, he will neither have to give reasons nor be subject to human punishment. For both of these presuppose a superior, something that cannot be understood here without a contradiction.[21]

---

[20] For example, Isaac Barrow (1630–77) maintains: 'It is the privilege of a Soveraigne, that he cannot be called to accompt, or judged, or deposed. . . or anywise censured and punished; for this implyeth a contradiction or confusion in degrees, subjecting the superiour to inferiours; this were making a river run backwards; this were to damme up the fountaine of justice; to behead the State; to expose Majesty to contempt.' He then denies that the Pope holds such an *archē anupeuthunos* (*A Treatise of the Pope's Supremacy* (London: n.p., 1680), pp. 388–9). This theme of sovereign unaccountability was at the heart of the debate over the authority of the king vs. the parliament at the time of the trial and execution of Charles I: see e.g. John Goodwin, Ὑβριστοδίκαι, *The Obstrvctovrs of Justice, or A Defence of the Honourable Sentence passed upon the late King, by the High Court of Justice* (London: n.p., 1649), pp. 5–7, 81–6, *contra* Henry Hammond, *To the Right Honourable, the Lord Fairfax, and His Councell of Warre* (London: n.p., 1649), pp. 5, 12–14; and cf. the following note.

[21] *De jure naturae et gentium libri octo* (Lund: n.p., 1672), p. 952 (7.6.1–2), as translated by M. J. Seidler in *The Political Writings of Samuel Pufendorf*, ed. C. L. Carr (New York: Oxford University Press, 1994), p. 72. Pufendorf may have picked this up from other early modern sources. So Salmasius, in his attack on the regicide, quotes from the same sentence of Herodotus on monarchy being *aneuthunos* as Grotius had, and asserts that 'nothing whatsoever is so proper to royal majesty as *to anupeuthunon*, to depend on no one, to be answerable to no one, to be liable to judgement by no one' (pp. 233 and 80 of *Defensio regia, pro Carolo I* (n.p.: n.p., 1649 =Madan 2): 'nihil omnino tam proprium regiae majestati quam τό ἀνυπεύθυνον, à nemine pendere, nemini esse obnoxium, à nemine judicari posse'). John Milton in his attack on Salmasius and his defence of the regicide retorts: 'But that *anupeuthunon*, i.e. *to depend on no one, to render account to no mortal*, which you say is most proper to royal Majesty, Aristotle (*Politics* 4.10) affirms is most tyrannical, and least to be tolerated in a free nation' (*Pro populo anglicano defensio* (London: n.p., 1651 =Madan 1), p. 28: 'Illud autem ἀνυπεύθυνον, id est *a nemine pendere, nulli mortalium rationem reddere*, quod tu regiae Majestatis maximè proprium esse ais, Aristotelis Polit. 4. C. 10. Maximè tyrannicum, & in libera natione minimè ferendum esse affirmat'). Pufendorf had in his library the 1631 Grotius, the 1649 Salmasius, and the 1652 edition of Milton's *Pro populo*, as well as most of the classical works referred to here (F. Palladini (ed.), *La biblioteca di Samuel Pufendorf: catalogo dell'asta di Berlin del settembre 1697* (Wiesbaden: Harrassowitz, 1999), pp. 172, 343, 276).

Sovereignty is necessarily supreme, unaccountable and above human law.[22] The Athenians were familiar with the conjunction of these criteria, but it might seem paradoxical to suggest that they defined their democracy thereby, as if the tyrant could serve as the proper measure of a free state.[23] Thus, even if we locate an important classical element in early modern theories of sovereignty, we might doubt that anything like the idea of *popular* sovereignty was present in Athenian political thought.

III

It is true that in Athens the tyrannicides were lionised, distinctive practices such as ostracism were thought of as warding off the evil of tyranny, and encroachments on the democracy were denounced as tyrannical. But tyranny had an ambivalent legacy. Early denunciations of tyranny or monarchy were generally articulated by or for conservative aristocrats, and a monarch could correspondingly be seen as a *euthunos* of *hubris*, one who could overpower these elites and make straight and restore justice to the city suffering from the crooked ways of its leaders.[24] The tyrant is certainly sometimes set up as a foil in the fifth century, yet the selection and construction of such a foil can reveal much about that to which it is contrasted. And although the democracy set up tyranny as an antithesis, we should not assume that this means that the tyrant's unity, supremacy and ultimate discretionary power imply democratic repudiations of these

---

[22] Pufendorf, *De jure naturae et gentium*, pp. 951–3 (the respective section headings of 7.6.1–3 are 'Imperium in civitate quare summum dicatur', 'Illud qui habet est ἀνυ-πεύθυνος', 'Et legibus humanis superior'). As Pufendorf makes clear, supremacy proper was understood to entail impunity and superiority to law.

[23] Resistance should not, however, come from an idea that an early modern conception of absolute sovereignty is inapplicable to democracy per se (see n. 2 above), for Bodin, Hobbes and others insisted that there could be an absolute democratic sovereign.

[24] So Theognis, anticipating a *monarchos* who will be an *anēr euthuntēr* (lines 39–40). On this and the *euthunos* or corrector in Aeschylus who comes to enforce divine justice, see J. F. McGlew, *Tyranny and Political Culture in Ancient Greece* (Ithaca and London: Cornell University Press, 1993), p. 66. As Leslie Kurke has noted, there is a struggle over how to construe tyrannical power in this period, and there are 'remnants in Herodotus (as elsewhere) of a competing portrait of the tyrant as champion of egalitarian justice and opponent of aristocratic overreaching' (L. Kurke, *Coins, Bodies, Games, and Gold: The Politics of Meaning in Archaic Greece* (Princeton: Princeton University Press, 1999), p. 67). The paradigmatic tyranny for the fifth century was the earlier tyranny of the Peisistratids, which could readily be understood as allied with the *dēmos* against the oligarchs. This is still echoed for example in the account of the tyrant as champion of the people in Plato, *Republic* VIII 565c–566e, or in the listing of Peisistratus with Solon and Cleisthenes as champions of the *dēmos* rather than the elite in 'Aristotle', *Constitution of the Athenians* 28.2.

characteristics. Indeed, there is considerable evidence that these features of the tyrant were seen to be basic features of the ruling *dēmos*.[25]

Thucydides provides a good starting point. Addressing the assembly in 427 BCE, Diodotus complains in familiar terms about the irresponsible authority of the *dēmos*. He chafes at the constraints placed on the leaders in the Athenian democracy, and suggests that the deciding *dēmos* should be likewise reined in by being held responsible for their decisions:

> We who offer recommendations are held to account [*hupeuthunon*] while you who hearken are unaccountable [*aneuthunon*]. If those who gave advice and those who followed it were similarly held in check, you would make more moderate decisions. But as it is, in the anger of the moment, when things go wrong you punish the single judgement of your adviser and not the many judgements of your own that were involved in the shared error.[26]

Although the members of the *dēmos* in the Athenian assembly would not have taken seriously Diodotus' suggestion that they should be liable to constraint and punishment (which is thus best read as a way of exhorting the assemblymen to correct their own error), there is no reason to think that they would have questioned or disliked his characterisation of them as *aneuthunos*.[27] The Athenians' own account of the rise of democracy

[25] An objection here may be that if the advocates of the rule of the *dēmos* were to compare it to or see it as a kind of sole rule, they would compare or identify it with kingship rather than tyranny. This assumes that kingship was available as an effective model in the fifth century, while this has been denied: drawing on the work of Matthias Haake, Nino Luraghi maintains that in this period the conception of the *turannos* is primary, while the image of the good king is a subsequent idealised conception (N. Luraghi, 'Ruling Alone: Monarchy in Greek Politics and Thought', in N. Luraghi (ed.), *The Splendors and Miseries of Ruling Alone: Encounters with Monarchy from Archaic Greece to the Hellenistic Mediterranean* (Stuttgart: Franz Steiner Verlag, 2013), pp. 11–24, at pp. 18–19). However that may be, to appropriate a moralised discourse of the wise *basileus* would have caused difficulties for democrats, as the emphasis on virtue was a usual anti-democratic platform. To focus the demand on ultimate popular discretionary power is to hold off the elite philosophical view that virtue and/or knowledge are required to rule.

[26] Thucydides 3.43.4–5: ἄλλως τε καὶ ὑπεύθυνον τὴν παραίνεσιν ἔχοντας πρὸς ἀνεύθυνον τὴν ὑμετέραν ἀκρόασιν. εἰ γὰρ ὅ τε πείσας καὶ ὁ ἐπισπόμενος ὁμοίως ἐβλάπτοντο, σωφρονέστερον ἂν ἐκρίνετε· νῦν δὲ πρὸς ὀργὴν ἥντινα τύχητε ἔστιν ὅτε σφαλέντες τὴν τοῦ πείσαντος μίαν γνώμην ζημιοῦτε καὶ οὐ τὰς ὑμετέρας αὐτῶν, εἰ πολλαὶ οὖσαι ξυνεξήμαρτον. Cf. Thucydides' own remark at 8.1.1. The use of *hupeuthunon* here (despite M. Ostwald, *Language and History in Ancient Greek Culture* (Philadelphia: University of Pennsylvania Press, 2009), pp. 205–13) is extended: Diodotus refers to the rhetors who served as leaders of the people especially in the assembly without necessarily holding concomitant office. These rhetors could be subject to other forms of accountability for advice that led to failure or otherwise came to be repudiated, but could not be subject to *euthunai* as such.

[27] Nor is this an unusual characterisation. See 'Old Oligarch' (ps.-Xenophon), *Constitution of the Athenians* 2.17, and cf. Praxagora's complaint that the people hold the rhetors to account for their proposals, but are not themselves held to account even though the proposals are only enacted because of the people's support (Aristophanes, *Ecclesiazusae* 193–6).

in response to tyranny has been plausibly interpreted as an account of the seizure by the *dēmos* of the supremacy and total arbitrary power that the *dēmos* was seen to have replaced, rather than as a repudiation of such supremacy and authority.[28] That the power is in this sense tyrannical does not mean that it could not be understood as democratic: what Otanes had singled out as the democratic characteristic that officials be *hupeuthunos* is presented by Diodotus as part of the same Athenian system that makes the *dēmos*, like the tyrant, *aneuthunos*.[29] The basic tenet here is that the *dēmos* is the uncontrolled controller: from Diodotus' objection to it, we can glean the Athenian democratic principle that it is essential to the authority of the *dēmos* both that it holds all other powers to account *and* that it is itself unaccountable.

It may be objected, following Otanes (Herodotus 3.80), that if it is the people who seize sovereignty, then that is enough to change the character of sovereignty essentially. The tyrant is singular, and that is much of the problem, whereas the people is necessarily multiple and diverse, and so in taking over supreme power no longer holds it in a single locus. It is striking, however, how ready Athenian writers were to treat the *dēmos* as singular, willing as they were to attribute characteristics of an individual or personality to a polis, or to personify the people as a whole.

The Athenians were quick to identify *dēmos* and polis, and in some ways of course it is *easier* to understand how we might consider a whole people, rather than one individual like a monarch, as a sovereign equivalent of the state. In Greek it is especially easy to see, given that in political contexts what we refer to as Athens was commonly referred to as *hoi Athēnaioi*: the Athenians. This was apparently tied to the ultimate power of decision in classical Athens being in the hands of the citizen body as a whole. For example, when Thucydides writes of actions and decisions, he overwhelmingly chooses to characterise those done or made by Athens as undertaken by 'the Athenians', for that captures the responsible agent; but when he talks about Persians or Macedonians, they are not the subject but the object of action (or description), whereas the subject of action is generally the autocrat who ruled them.[30]

---

[28] See McGlew, *Tyranny and Political Culture*. Cf. C. de Oliveira Gomes, *La Cité tyrannique: histoire politique de la Grèce archaïque* (Rennes: Presses Universitaires de Rennes, 2007), pp. 114–16.

[29] Diodotus' arguments 'make plain the unconditioned power of the *demos*. Like the tyrant, it is afraid or suspicious of everyone and accountable to no-one . . . Diodotus (like Aristophanes in the *Knights*) sees the *demos* as a tyrant at home no less than abroad.' (C. W. Macleod, 'Reason and Necessity: Thucydides III 9–14, 37–48', *Journal of Hellenic Studies* 98 (1978), pp. 64–78, at p. 74.)

[30] M. Pope, 'Thucydides and Democracy', *Historia: Zeitschrift für Alte Geschichte* 37 (1988), pp. 276–96. P. J. Rhodes replies that we have evidence of individual political agency in

It is also worth noting that the Athenians were more prone than most moderns to understand 'the people' as a unified entity, and were much more inclined to identify the people with the polity itself.[31] Understanding 'the people' as singular is facilitated by the language: *ho dēmos* is masculine singular, so while the Greeks would have regarded the referent as a collective, they were simultaneously primed to think of the people as having the unity and other characteristics of a man.[32] The ready identification of the Athenian people with their polity can be seen in the language of surviving treaties that refer to the entity making the interstate agreement as *ho dēmos ho Athēnaiōn*, the people of the Athenians. It is also seen in the opening language of decisions of the assembly, found on inscriptions and in many literary sources: *edoxe tōi dēmōi*, it seemed good to the people that . . . .[33]

Many Greek writers were ready to characterise poleis and their peoples as bearing the traits of individuals, including their passions, attitudes and capacity or incapacity for prudential calculation. Although we may particularly identify the move of talking about poleis as if they were people with Plato in the *Republic*, Thucydides and other earlier writers provide many examples. In some of these cases the polis is cast as a tyrant, a figure who in normal language is always a single person. So the Corinthian envoys in Book I of Thucydides, mobilising a striking contrast with Athenian democratic valorisations of liberty and equality, say that 'a tyrant polis set up in Greece is set up alike over all and rules over some already and the rest in intention', and thus recommend action: 'Let us attack it and bring it to terms, and let us henceforth live our own lives in safety and set free those Greeks who are already enslaved.'[34] The Corinthians put themselves in the role of resisting a

---

the recording with each Athenian decree of the chairman, the speaker who proposed it, and those who proposed amendments ('The "Acephalous" Polis?' *Historia: Zeitschrift für Alte Geschichte* 44 (1995), pp. 153–67); but the decree remains that of the *dēmos*, and recording and publicising those who promoted it likely serves to ensure that they are controlled (or at least held responsible) *by* the *dēmos*.

[31] I largely set aside the use of *dēmos* to refer exclusively to the poor, which is primarily a fourth-century anti-democratic use (though it is relevant to understanding some authors discussed below, especially the Old Oligarch).

[32] The great Gildersleeve gives *dēmos* as his primary example of this special exception to concord ('Organized number is singular'): B. L. Gildersleeve, *Syntax of Classical Greek from Homer to Demosthenes* (New York: American Book Co., 1900), p. 54.

[33] See M. H. Hansen, 'The *Polis* as a Citizen-State', *Historisk-filosofiske Meddelelser* 67 (1993), pp. 7–29, at pp. 8–9: 'In modern states, even democracies, there is a tendency to identify the state with the executive and the government rather than with the people, but in a democratic *polis*, especially Athens . . . the dominant ideology was that the *polis* was the people (*demos*).'

[34] Thucydides 1.124.3 (first clause based on Hobbes trans.; second is Mynott's trans.). Cf. 1.122.3.

tyrant who is enslaving Greece as a master, where that tyrant and master is the Athenians. The Athenians here are treated as an individual: the Athenians are the polis, and the polis, however democratic, is a tyrant.

Thucydides also shows the Athenians embracing this description of their position. As the war takes an early bad turn and the people begin to lose heart and consider treating for peace, Pericles insists: 'You cannot now give up possession of your rule [archē], should anyone be frightened by the present situation and try to make a manly virtue of non-involvement. For you already hold your rule [archē] like a tyranny.'[35] The Athenians (Pericles would have them believe) can be likened to a tyrant because they are unified as a polis that has relations with its allies that are akin to those of a tyrant over his subjects. In the following book, Cleon upbraids the dēmos in the Athenian assembly in similar but less tentative terms: 'You do not see that the rule [archē] you hold is a tyranny, and one imposed on unwilling subjects.'[36] And in Book VI, Euphemus, the Athenian envoy at Camarina, asserts that both tyrant and ruling polis follow the same logic: 'For a tyrant man or a polis that holds rule [archē], nothing is unreasonable that is advantageous.'[37] The emphasis here is on the rule of the Athenians over other poleis, but it is worth bringing out two points. First, if the Athenians were ready to understand themselves as holding a tyranny over others, then, because of the identification of the polis and the dēmos in Athens, the dēmos could see itself as a tyrant. Second, and relatedly, the vocabulary of tyranny here is not simply negative.

The recent discussion of the polis turannos is peculiar, focusing as it does on rebutting Robert Connor's answer to the puzzle of why Athenians such as Pericles and Cleon use terms similar to those of the critics of Athens, like the Corinthians.[38] If 'tyrant' is a term of abuse in Athens, why do the Athenians apply it to themselves? Connor's answer is that it was a negative term when deployed by those under or threatened by something describable as tyrannical, whereas it was a positive term from the point of view of the tyrant or would-be tyrant, and that Pericles and Cleon are

---

[35] Thucydides 2.63.2 (Mynott trans., modified). Note that archē means rule, first power/authority; as it has a clear connotation of primacy, translators sometimes render it as 'sovereignty'. When its primary referent is the rule of one polis over others, it is sometimes translated as 'empire' (for which there is no ready Greek equivalent).

[36] Thucydides 3.37.2 (Mynott trans., modified).

[37] Thucydides 6.85.1: ἀνδρὶ δὲ τυράννῳ ἢ πόλει ἀρχὴν ἐχούσῃ οὐδὲν ἄλογον ὅτι ξυμφέρον.

[38] W. R. Connor, 'Tyrannis [sic] Polis', in J. H. D'Arms and J. W. Eadie (eds.), Ancient and Modern: Essays in Honor of Gerald F. Else (Ann Arbor: Center for Coordination of Ancient and Modern Studies, 1977), pp. 95–109. See also L. Kallet, 'Demos Tyrannos: Wealth, Power and Economic Patronage', in K. A. Morgan (ed.), Popular Tyranny: Sovereignty and its Discontents in Ancient Greece (Austin: University of Texas Press, 2003), pp. 117–53.

here flattering the *dēmos*. Connor's critics, by contrast, argue that tyranny never has a positive significance in Athenian political rhetoric.[39] But to limit analysis of the term to either positive or negative uses is to disable an adequate answer to the question of how the term is deployed.

For Pericles and Cleon in the above passages surely depend on (while not being limited to) both positive and negative connotations of the term. Each uses the stark comparison to urge the Athenians to recognise that they have to proceed as one does who rules in the face of resistance. Pericles himself had been frequently portrayed as a tyrant, a king, or even as Zeus himself by the comic poets, including Cratinus, Telecleides and Aristophanes.[40] He is effectively telling the same people who would have laughed at these barbs that they themselves – that all of them together – are in effect a kind of tyrant. To tell or remind the Athenians that they hold the reins of power like a tyrant is to focus on what are claimed to be the realities of their power, to tell them that they have to be tough and clear-eyed about the imperatives of action in a context of resentment and hostility. Connor misses this, presenting the matter too simply as a kind of flattery. But those who differ tend instead to overlook just how pervasive are the indications of the attractions of tyranny in the sources of the day, and how this inflects political uses of the vocabulary by Pericles, Cleon and others.[41]

---

[39] Kurt Raaflaub has been the most influential of these critics. 'From a position outside and opposed to democracy, tyranny could be represented as positive. From a position within and identifying with democracy, especially in political discourse and ideology, it was seen as entirely negative . . . It helped the Athenians define what they were not and did not want to be: the hostile Other, which helped them confirm, by contrast, what they were or did want to be . . . Hence "tyranny" encompassed everything that was hostile to democracy . . . In addition, and partly because of this broad antithetical function, the ideology of antityrannicism was the glue needed to hold together a large and complex community that virtually from the fall of tyranny in the late sixth century, embarked on a new and uncharted course' (K. A. Raaflaub, 'Stick and Glue: The Function of Tyranny in Fifth-Century Athenian Democracy', in Morgan (ed.), *Popular Tyranny*, pp. 59–93, at 82–3; see also K. Raaflaub, *The Discovery of Freedom in Ancient Greece* (Chicago: University of Chicago Press, 2004), pp. 120–34).

[40] For discussion see J. Schwarze, *Die Beurteilung des Perikles durch die attische Komödie und ihre historische und historiographische Bedeutung* (Munich: C. H. Beck, 1971).

[41] Contrast e.g. Raaflaub, who argues (*Discovery of Freedom*, p. 134) that in Thucydides' time the term 'tyranny' to describe the rule of Athens 'was used almost exclusively either to evoke negative associations in polemics and propaganda against Athens or by the Athenians themselves to emphasise dramatically, by drawing on these same associations, certain problematic traits of their rule and so to underscore criticism and warning or to justify the need for drastic political measures'. Jeffrey Henderson ('Demos, Demagogue, Tyrant in Attic Old Comedy', in Morgan (ed.), *Popular Tyranny*, pp. 155–79, at 155) characterises the consensus that has emerged around this view: 'It is generally agreed that in imperial Athens, the people's perception of tyranny was entirely negative.'

Such earlier writers as Archilochus, Solon and Pindar express or report some of the attractions of tyranny. The widespread and powerful appeal of tyranny comes across most clearly, however, in the reactions of the Socratics to its attractions (and particularly in their accounts of the views of fifth-century figures). '*Everyone* envies tyrants', according to Simonides in Xenophon.[42] It may seem that Polus and Callicles in Plato's *Gorgias*, or Thrasymachus in the *Republic*, are extreme figures whose praise of tyranny should not be seen as representative. It is worth noting, however, the extraordinary language that they use in praise of tyranny: those who praise it (or are represented as praising it) do so in the language of obviousness (*of course everyone* would choose tyranny as a good), and in the language of exaltation (tyranny is not merely a good to be wished for, but is something especially good, and even uniquely fine and choiceworthy). Other Platonic figures use such language, including Alcibiades and Theages, who says: 'For my part I would pray, I suppose, to become tyrant – preferably over all human beings and, if not, over as many as possible, and so would you, I suppose, and all other human beings – or, probably even better, to become a god.'[43] We might suspect that these figures, too, are being represented as unusually wicked, but it is clear that Plato presents his fifth-century characters as believing that this envy of the tyrant's lot is altogether commonplace. In *Republic* Glaucon says, and Socrates agrees, that 'most people' believe that a tyranny such as that of Gyges' ancestor is desirable and provides for the full range of human goods.[44] The Athenian in the *Laws* begins a list of what are commonly regarded as the highest goods with 'health and wealth and lasting tyranny'.[45]

This is not a mere artifact of a Socratic theory about the hidden impulses of the depraved. The Socratics portray fifth-century characters as perfectly willing to endorse tyranny as a good, and have them cite fifth-century evidence. Thus Plato's Socrates observes that the tragedians express admiration for tyranny, and Adeimantus notes that Euripides and the other poets praise it as godlike.[46] In the extant plays, this matches Euripides' *Trojan Women* of 415 BCE, where Hecuba ranks tyranny as

---

[42] Xenophon, *On Government* 1.9: πάντες ἐζήλουν ἂν τοὺς τυράννους (cf. 1.14, 2.2–2.5, 7.1–7.4, 11.15; cf. also Plato, *Protagoras* 346bc). Cf. Isocrates 9.40.

[43] [Plato?], *Theages* 125e–126a (εὐξαίμην μὲν ἂν οἶμαι ἔγωγε τύραννος γενέσθαι, μάλιστα μὲν πάντων ἀνθρώπων, εἰ δὲ μή, ὡς πλείστων: καὶ σύ γ᾽ ἂν οἶμαι καὶ οἱ ἄλλοι πάντες ἄνθρωποι – ἔτι δέ γε ἴσως μᾶλλον θεὸς γενέσθαι).

[44] Plato, *Republic* II 358a4 and 358a7 with II 362b2–c8 and 360c8–d7.

[45] Plato, *Laws* II 661d: ἆρ᾽ οὖν ὑγίειάν τε κεκτημένον καὶ πλοῦτον καὶ τυραννίδα διὰ τέλους.

[46] Plato, *Republic* VIII 568b.

the highest of human blessings, one equal to the gods.[47] A fragment from Euripides' *Archelaus* reads similarly, marking this out as a common view: 'Tyranny is esteemed [*nomizetai*] second to the gods. For it does not provide immortality, but it provides everything else.'[48] It is impossible to be sure what an average citizen of this time would have thought, or even what they would have openly avowed, but the evidence suggests that when, for example, Plato's Socrates presents it as inevitable that the one who has the first choice of lives will choose the greatest tyranny, this reflects a common view during Socrates' lifetime.[49]

So when Pericles and Cleon tell the Athenians that they are a tyrant, we have reason to believe that they were invoking these aspirational associations along with some harsher ones. Presumably Pericles himself did not find being called a tyrant wholly unwelcome, as the very jest depended on recognition of his pre-eminent power. This appeal to a range of semantic associations makes best sense in the rhetorical contexts. Pericles and Cleon are telling the people that they are in a position of the greatest political power, and that they have to live up to the hard necessities of that position; the related claim that the *dēmos* is a tyrant within the polis can similarly weld together congratulation and caution into a pointed exhortation to do what it takes to retain rule. The tyrant may be both hated and envied by those he rules, who can be assumed to want to displace or diminish his power. This is not an unalloyed blessing and requires vigilance, but it is a tribute to the tyrant's supremacy.

IV

We are used to thinking of the classical Greek constitutional division being that between rule by one, few and many, and according to whether each of these is virtuous or vicious. To think of the *dēmos* as a tyrant is instead

---

[47] Euripides, *Trōades* 1169; cf. *Orestes* 1167–9. A similar view is taken by Eteocles in *Phoenissae* 506 (probably dating to 411–409), but he is upbraided for his selfish ambition by Jocasta (who would have him pursue equality and the good of the city rather than individual tyranny: 528–67) and the chorus.

[48] *Tragicorum Graecorum Fragmenta*, vol. V, part 1, ed. R. Kannicht (Göttingen: Vandenhoeck & Ruprecht, 2004), p. 326. (Fr. 250 (Stobaeus 4.6.5): τυραννίδ᾽ ἢ θεῶν δευτέρα νομίζεται· / τὸ μὴ θανεῖν γὰρ οὐκ ἔχει, τὰ δ᾽ ἄλλ᾽ ἔχει.) Tyrannising is sometimes used positively elsewhere in Euripides, e.g. in *Electra* 876–9 and *Orestes* 1155–6. The figure of the tyrant fits into Mark Griffith's characterisation of tragedy's 'dynastic leaders (including the gods)' who 'become alternately objects of the audience's admiration and sympathy, and of their disapproval and disgust' (M. Griffith, 'Extended Families, Marriage, and Inter-City Relations in (Later) Athenian Tragedy: Dynasts II', in D. M. Carter (ed.), *Why Athens? A Reappraisal of Tragic Politics* (Oxford: Oxford University Press, 2011), pp. 175–208, at 176–7).

[49] Plato, *Republic* X 619b.

to treat the many as if it were one; to think of this as the democratic view is to see in it approval rather than pure opprobrium. While the archetypal and indelible image of early modern sovereignty is that of the crowned figure constituted by the people on the illustrated title page of Hobbes's *Leviathan*, such a portrait of political personality and unity out of multiplicity might seem to be inconceivable by ancients who did not think of political authority in terms of a relation of representation.[50] Among the most famous images from Athenian political theory are instead Plato's verbal portraits of the rabble, in which even the democratic individual, like the democratic polis, is a riot of inconsistency, seething multiplicity and disorder.[51] That the Athenian people did see themselves in the figure of a single ruler may be discerned on the Greek stage; and before glancing at just a few of the many evocative tragic reflections on this topic, it is worth looking at an example from the visual arts.

Dēmos appears to have been a popular subject for both painters and sculptors. In the surviving representations he is invariably portrayed as an individual man, though a man of nearly divine stature, sometimes towering over a meritorious citizen who is being rewarded or recognised. Among the images no longer extant was a famous painting of Dēmos by Parrhasius, active during the last decades of the fifth century; and Pausanias reports that there were sculptures of Zeus, Apollo and Dēmos in the Athenian council chamber.[52] Pausanias also describes a public colonnade with pictures of the twelve gods on one wall, and (undated) paintings of Theseus, Democracy and Dēmos on the other (the first tied in to the others by the tradition that Theseus gave political equality and government to the Athenian people).[53]

The images of Dēmos that have survived are not paintings or sculptures in the round, but stone reliefs. A few of the figures are labelled as Dēmos, while identification of others depends on similarity to labelled figures or descriptions of lost depictions. There are a score or more of likely candidates extant, often paired with a god or goddess (usually Athena), and sometimes either honouring a smaller-scale citizen or watching him

---

[50] See the claims in n. 2, above, that the unitariness of sovereignty is specifically early modern.

[51] See e.g. Plato, *Republic* VIII 561a–563e.

[52] For the *demos atheniensium* painted by Parrhasius see Pliny the Elder's *Naturalis historia* 35.69; for his dates see Xenophon, *Memorabilia* 3.10.1–5 and Quintilian, *Institutio oratoria* 12.10.4. For the bronze *Dēmos Boulaiou* by Lyson (undated) see Pausanias, *Description of Greece* 1.3.5. For another painting of Dēmos see Pliny 35.137, and for another sculpture, Pausanias 1.1.3.

[53] Pausanias 1.3.3; see Euripides' *Suppliants* (c. 424–420 BCE) for Theseus in this role.

being honoured by the divinity.[54] The figure of Dēmos is always a mature male, perhaps modelled on Zeus, and most commonly adorns decrees of the assembly. Although dating is often highly uncertain, it is clear that the great majority of extant figures are from the fourth century. At least two strong fifth-century candidates survive. Especially spectacular is the Choiseul Marble of 409 BCE, from the Athenian Acropolis and now in the Louvre.[55] Although some scholars have maintained that the figures are Athena and Erechtheus, a mythical king of Athens, most have identified them as Athena and Dēmos.[56]

The placement of Dēmos (if it is he) on this stele erected for public viewing on the Acropolis is significant: he stands nearly on a level with the patron goddess of the polis and over a detailed listing of the accounts of the treasurers (*tamiai*) of Athena for the preceding year (410–409 BCE). These include the names of officials, precise amounts (of 32 disbursements, from more than 57 talents down to 91 drachmas and

---

[54] For discussions, catalogues and illustrations see C. L. Lawton, *Attic Document Reliefs: Art and Politics in Ancient Athens* (Oxford: Clarendon Press, 1995), pp. 30–3, 55–8, 86–7; W. Messerschmidt, *Prosopopoiia: Personifikationen politischen Charakters in spätklassischer und hellenistischer Kunst* (Cologne: Böhlau, 2003), pp. 5–47, 166–80, 207–30, and plates 1–13; K. Glowacki, 'A Personification of Demos on a New Attic Document Relief', *Hesperia* 72 (2003), pp. 447–66; and A. C. Smith, *Polis and Personification in Classical Athenian Art* (Leiden: Brill, 2011), pp. 91–107.

[55] Louvre Ma 831 = *IG* I³ 375 (*Inscriptiones Graecae*, vol. I, fasc. 1, 3rd edn., ed. D. Lewis (Berlin: Walter de Gruyter, 1981), pp. 349–50). Two tabulations of annual accounts of a similar kind (probably for 408/7 and 407/6 BCE) are inscribed on the reverse side (*IG* I³ 377).

[56] See n. 54. The difficulty of distinguishing whether the figure is Dēmos or a legendary Athenian king is itself suggestive, and in any case the figure is meant to stand for Athens. The likelihood that the figure is Dēmos is further increased if his stick can be identified with the 'citizen's stick' or 'Bürgerstock' (the iconography of which is discussed e.g. in H.-G. Hollein, *Bürgerbild und Bildwelt der attischen Demokratie auf den rotfigurigen Vasen des 6.-4. Jahrhunderts v. Chr.* (Frankfurt am Main: Peter Lang, 1988), pp. 11–49; and B. Fehr, *Becoming Good Democrats and Wives: Civic Education and Female Socialization on the Parthenon Frieze*, trans. U. Hoffmann et al. (Münster and Zürich: LIT Verlag, 2011), pp. 84–91.

The figures stand on either side of an olive tree, and Dēmos may be collecting its fruit or indicating its (painted) leaves. (The evergreen olive, which replaced its leaves as they dropped, was thus like the polis, according to Plutarch, *Sumposiaka problēmata* 723f, 8.4.) The olive was the legendary gift of Athena to the Athenians, the benefits of which secured her position as their patron divinity. Marcel Detienne observes that the tree of Athena is referred to in Greek sources as 'the olive tree of the city', in the sense of the tree of all of the citizens ('L'Olivier, un mythe politico-religieux', *Revue de l'histoire des religions* 178:1 (1970), pp. 5–23, at p. 11, with references). The antiquary Varro reported that when all citizens of both sexes (ciues omnes utriusque sexus) were called to vote between Athena and Poseidon, the women all voted for Athena and the (less numerous) men voted for Poseidon. The polis thus chose the support of Athena and became Athens, but to appease the rage of Poseidon the women were thenceforth deprived of their vote and their civic identity. See Augustine, *De civitate Dei* 18.9.

Figure 1.1 Stele, called Marble of Choiseul, with Greek inscriptions, *c.* 410/409 BCE. Ma 831. Musée du Louvre, Paris, France. © Musée du Louvre, Dist. RMN-Grand Palais/Daniel Lebée and Carine Déambrosis/Art Resource, NY.

3¼ obols, and including an annual total), funding sources, dates of payment and the public purposes of the expenditures. The inscription makes clear that although the treasurers are responsible for managing the money, the authority for this management comes from the *dēmos*, and it is to them that the officials are held to account. The inscription begins by stating that *the Athenians* have undertaken these expenditures (the first words are *Athenaioi anelosan*), and that Kallistratos of Marathon and his fellow treasurers have transmitted (*paredosan*) the following amounts from the annual revenues in accordance with the decree (or vote) of the people (*phsephisameno to demo*).[57] Observing this figure above these accounts set up on the Acropolis, the people of Athens witnessed both a public statement of and a public representation of the controlling supremacy of the people, and at the same time they were invited to effect that control by examining the accounts themselves. Knowing as they did about the formal process of *euthunai*, citizens who examined these records took up the stance of those who held all magistrates accountable without being held accountable themselves as citizens. Citizens examining this stele mirrored and enacted the position of the controlling Dēmos.

Another place on the Acropolis where the people of Athens could see themselves represented was at the theatre of Dionysus Eleuthereus, where they went to see both tragic and comic performances. This becomes most explicit in comedy, but it is worth at least a mention of tragedy, the audience of which was called to reflect on its own identity while watching the unfolding fates of both good and bad monarchs.

While several extant tragedies focus on this theme, the most famous *turannos* is Sophocles' Oedipus. Among the multiple layers of meaning in this play, one central concern is how vexed it is for one to stand for the many. 'One cannot be equal to many', Oedipus muses.[58] Throughout the action he nonetheless identifies himself with his people and his polis, and yet comes to recognise the costs of this identification.[59] Bernard Knox influentially suggested that Sophocles presents the tyrant standing for Thebes, and takes care to make Thebes parallel to Athens; thus the Athenians in the audience are asked to identify with the tyrant.[60] Froma Zeitlin has argued that the stage Thebes is instead 'the mirror opposite of Athens' whose representation instructs the Athenians 'how their city might refrain from imitating the other's negative example'.[61] On either view (and the audience may well have contained some people

---

[57] Lines 1, 2–3 of the inscription (ΑΘΕΝΑΙΟΙ ΑΝΕΛΟΣΑΝ . . . ΤΑΜΙΑΙ ΗΙΕΡΟΓ ΧΡΕΜΑΤΟΝ ΤΕΣ ΑΘΕΝΑΙΑΣ ΚΑΛΛΙΣΤΡΑΤΟΣ ΜΑΡΑΘΟΝΙΟΣ ΚΑΙ ΧΣΥΝΑΡΧΟ[Ν]ΤΕΣ ΠΑΡΕΔΟΣΑΝ ΕΚ ΤΟΝ ΕΠΕΤΕΙΟΝ ΦΣΕΦΙΣΑΜΕΝΟ ΤΟ ΔΕΜΟ . . .). Referring to the verbs *anelosan* and *paredosan*, an early student of Greek inscriptions in the Louvre noted that the authorisation of expenditure by the Athenian people is 'générale et préparatoire', whereas that of the officials has 'un sens plus restreint et déterminé' (W. Froehner, *Les Inscriptions Grecques* (Paris: Charles de Mourgues Frères, 1865), p. 90).

[58] Sophocles, *Oedipus Turannos* 845: οὐ γὰρ γένοιτ' ἂν εἷς γε τοῖς πολλοῖς ἴσος.

[59] Lines 62–4, 93–4, etc. Sophocles emphasises the ready slide between the ruler and the city from the first line of the play, as R. D. Dawe notes in his commentary *ad loc*.

[60] B. Knox, *Oedipus at Thebes: Sophocles' Tragic Hero and his Time*, 2nd edn. (New Haven: Yale University Press, 1998 [1957]). See esp. the programmatic statements at pp. 77 and 99 (in watching the vices and virtues of the tyrant, the democratic Athenian audience was watching itself).

[61] F. I. Zeitlin, 'Thebes: Theater of Self and Society in Athenian Drama', in J. J. Winkler and F. I. Zeitlin (eds.), *Nothing to Do with Dionysos? Athenian Drama in its Social Context* (Princeton: Princeton University Press, 1992), pp. 130–67, at 144, 145.

who adopted views akin to each), the Athenian audience is supposed to reflect on itself when observing the tyrant, even as it is enjoined to resist his flaws and his fate. The tragic poets, Euripides says in Aristophanes, are to be admired for their warnings, by which they make people better in their poleis; and surely the tragic monarchs are generally the ones through whom these warnings are made manifest.[62] It has been said of Sophocles' heroes that 'they will not be ruled, no one shall have power over them, or treat them as a slave, they are free' – a characterisation that also fits the imperial and democratic Athenian people for whom he wrote.[63] Tragedy presents the *dēmos* with the effects of powerful rulers making both good and bad political judgements, and it is surely meant to learn thereby about its own exercise of authority; but there is little evidence that it is supposed to learn to lessen its power or freedom.[64]

The festival of the Great Dionysia was itself a public commemoration of Athenian power. Once the tragic theatre was full, and even before the plays began, the Athenian people saw the extent and the peril of their rule evoked on the stage. The annual tribute of silver from the subjects of the Athenians was divided into talents and laid out on the stage, for example; at the same time, the sons of those citizens who had been slain in the war (and who were now wards of the *dēmos*) were led onto the stage.[65] What may make it hard to believe that the *dēmos* saw itself in

---

[62] Aristophanes, *Frogs* 1009–10, on why the poet is to be admired: δεξιότητος καὶ νουθεσίας, ὅτι βελτίους τε ποιοῦμεν / τοὺς ἀνθρώπους ἐν ταῖς πόλεσιν.

[63] B. M. W. Knox, *The Heroic Temper: Studies in Sophoclean Tragedy* (Berkeley and Los Angeles: University of California Press, 1983 [1964]), p. 40, cited approvingly in Zeitlin, 'Thebes', p. 158 n. 35.

[64] Jon Hesk spells out the first part of this argument for some Euripidean plays ('Euripidean *euboulia* and the problem of "tragic politics"', in Carter (ed.), *Why Athens?*, pp. 119–43), but the point could as readily be made for the audience watching, for example, Creon's refusal to listen to counsel and his subsequent cascade of errors in Sophocles' *Antigone*. After pointing out that in most extant tragedies the figures of the chorus 'were marginal to the city', Pierre Vidal-Naquet observes: 'In Athens . . . the assembly made decisions; in the tragedies the chorus never makes decisions, or if it does they are derided. As a general rule, it is the hero . . . who commits himself to the irrevocable resolutions upon which every tragedy is based' (P. Vidal-Naquet, 'Oedipus in Athens' [1973], in J.-P. Vernant and P. Vidal-Naquet, *Myth and Tragedy in Ancient Greece*, trans. J. Lloyd (New York: Zone Books, 1990), pp. 301–27, at 312).

[65] See e.g. S. Goldhill, 'The Great Dionysia and Civic Ideology', in Winkler and Zeitlin (eds.), *Nothing to Do with Dionysos?*, pp. 97–129, at 100–2 (quoting a scholion to Aristophanes' *Acharnians* and Isocrates' retrospective account of the practice during the Peloponnesian war). The legal and financial details of how provision of tragic performances harnessed the private resources of powerful elites to democratic control is laid out in P. Wilson, *The Athenian Institution of the Khoregia: The Chorus, the City and the Stage* (Cambridge: Cambridge University Press, 2003). For an argument that the tragic audience represents the body politic of democratic citizens see S. Goldhill, 'The Audience of Athenian Tragedy', in P. E. Easterling (ed.), *The Cambridge Companion to Greek Tragedy* (Cambridge: Cambridge University Press, 1997), pp. 54–68; and esp. J. J. Winkler, 'The

the monarch once the dramatic action was under way is a traditional view that the citizen body would have seen itself instead in the chorus. Despite prominent advocates from Schlegel to Vernant, such a view fits ill with the language or content of many extant odes, relies on a doubtful view of the psychology of the classical audience, and ignores the fact that tragedies usually featured choruses of women, foreigners or slaves.[66]

The tragic monarch does not only serve as a foil against which the Athenians' democracy shines all the brighter, but could also serve to exhibit its virtues or to warn the Athenians about the hazards of their own power. The most complex explorations of democratic virtues via their endorsement by a tragic monarch are found in Aeschylus' *Suppliants* (where Pelasgus is the first of the extant 'democratic kings' of tragedy) and Euripides' *Suppliants* (where Theseus insists both that Athens is free because not ruled by one man, and also that the Athenian *dēmos* is itself a monarch).[67] Yet the Athenian stage also presented the vices of tyrants opposed to Athens or to someone standing for or allied with Athens.

Consider Aeschylus' presentation of two such tyrants: Xerxes, says Atossa, is not accountable to the polis (*ouch hupeuthunos polei*); and Zeus, according to Okeanos, is a harsh monarch who rules without being accountable (*oud' hupeuthunos*).[68] Neither case is animated by the simple idea that rule by one is unacceptable because unaccountable. In *Persians* Darius is presented as a moderate monarch who is as constitutionally unfettered as his son Xerxes; in *Prometheus Bound* there is a strong suggestion that Zeus should choose to moderate his actions and behave justly, but no suggestion that he can or should be checked by the power of others. Each case presents to the ascendant power of Athens, the *dēmos*

Ephebes' Song: *Tragōidia* and *Polis*', in Winkler and Zeitlin (eds.), *Nothing to Do with Dionysos?*, pp. 20–62 (62: the tragic festival is a political 'festival of self-representation').

[66] Or even foreign slave women (though played by men, generally citizens). For criticism of the idea that the *dēmos* would identify with the chorus see esp. J. Gould, 'Tragedy and Collective Experience', in M. S. Silk (ed.), *Tragedy and the Tragic: Greek Theatre and Beyond* (Oxford: Clarendon Press, 1996), pp. 217–43. David Carter discusses this argument and adds that even choruses of citizens were restricted to a narrow part of the citizen body, e.g. those from a particular age group, location or faction (D. M. Carter, 'The Demos in Greek Tragedy', *Cambridge Classical Journal* 56 (2010), pp. 47–94, at 63–9). For more detail see H. Foley, 'Choral Identity in Greek Tragedy', *Classical Philology* 98:1 (2003), pp. 1–30, esp. 26–7.

[67] Euripides, *Supplices* 404–5, 352 (cf. 406); cf. the democratic characteristics of Theseus, esp. in Sophocles' *Oedipus at Colonus*. See S. Mills, *Theseus, Tragedy, and the Athenian Empire* (Oxford: Clarendon Press, 1997). Mills argues that 'technical problems concerning Theseus as king of a democracy fade if he is seen as a personification of the ideal democratic city' (p. 101).

[68] Aeschylus, *Persae* 213; [Aeschylus?], *Prometheus Bound* 324 (a work in which Zeus is frequently called a tyrant). Note that we know little about the latter play outside its text, and cannot be sure that it was written for an Athenian audience.

of the audience, a vivid warning about the tyrant's fall. The fate of the good and prudent Darius is better than the destruction of Xerxes; Zeus would have been overthrown, but heeds the warnings of Prometheus and goes on to reign supreme. Xerxes is presented as the hated enemy and opposite of Athens, but his dramatic fall serves as a multi-layered exhortation to the audience.[69] Both the wiser Zeus and the wiser Darius are unlimited monarchs, and their tyrannical power is admirable; the rash and imperious Zeus would have been deposed, and the hubristic Xerxes was destroyed. Assembled together, the *dēmos* simultaneously observed the wonderful power of the tyrant, and the terrible vices that would lead to ruin.

I cannot here explore the reflective surface that tragedy provides for the Athenian *dēmos*, as these tragedies were written over many decades, had varying purposes and heterogeneous audiences, and should not be reduced to mere political allegories. I wish only to point out that the *dēmos* could see itself in the tragic tyrant, in myriad and challenging ways. The most explicit confrontation of the *dēmos* with an image of itself as a tyrant occurred not in tragedy, however, but in comedy.

V

The Athenian *dēmos* could conceive of itself as a tyrant over other poleis, so it was not a far step to see itself as a tyrant within the polis, where the *dēmos* held ultimate power; and this tyrannical control was associated with control of those who aspired to lead or control the *dēmos* itself. This is indicated by Diodotus, and is woven into tragedies by Aeschylus, Sophocles and Euripides; but Aristophanes does something striking in *Knights*, which the citizen-judges awarded first prize at the Lenaea of 424: he brings Dēmos on stage as a character.[70] Aristophanes first presents Dēmos as the master (*despotēs*) in a household and lord over slaves.[71] The slaves are recognisable Athenian leaders (Cleon and – very probably – Demosthenes and Nicias, all of whom then held the highest elected office of *stratēgos*), and the context from the outset is domestic: the mastery of Dēmos is a mastery of the people as a body over Athens, especially its

---

[69] See D. Rosenbloom, *Aeschylus: Persians* (London: Duckworth, 2006). For a quick catalogue of the relevant plays see M. West, 'King and Demos in Aeschylus', in D. Cairns and V. Liapis (eds.), *Dionysalexandros: Essays on Aeschylus and his Fellow Tragedians in Honour of Alexander F. Garvie* (Swansea: Classical Press of Wales, 2006), pp. 31–40.

[70] For one substantial study see P. Reinders, *Demos Pyknites: Untersuchungen zur Darstellung des Demos in der Alten Komödie* (Stuttgart: J. B. Metzler, 2001).

[71] Aristophanes, *Knights* 40: δεσπότης, a title used for Dēmos during the remainder of the play by Cleon and others.

most powerful individuals. Dēmos is then shown to be a tyrant as well.[72]
Rather than being asked to contemplate its likeness in the mask of a
tragic tyrant or king, the *dēmos* is here presented with an inescapable
and politically freighted comic caricature of itself as tyrant and king. Yet
it is an image presented to the *dēmos* for their approval in a dramatic
competition, and ends up presenting Dēmos using his tyrannical power
for good democratic ends.[73]

It may seem that the *dēmos* cannot be a tyrant *within* the city – for whom
would the body of the people rule *over*? The play suggests a twofold
answer. First, the analogy is meant to highlight the necessary power
of the *dēmos*, understood in terms of its power to act intelligently and
effectively. This focus is on those who do hold power (the *dēmos* in the
place of the tyrants). Second, in so far as the ruling power of the *dēmos*
is understood as power over someone else, it is in the first instance over
those who aspire to rule over the *dēmos*, especially the leading politicians
and powerful officials who are of the citizen body but always threaten to
stand above it. So the chorus warns Dēmos against being manipulated
by the politicians: 'Dēmos, the rule [*archē*] you bear is fine indeed, when
all humankind fears you like a tyrant [*hōsper andra turannon*]. But you are
easily led about, you enjoy being flattered and beguiled, and the orators
always leave you with your mouth hanging open.'[74]

Aristophanes plays a careful game, poking fun at the laziness, gluttony,
gullibility and insatiable desire for praise that characterise Dēmos, and
that thus characterise the *dēmos* of Athens who constitutes his audience.

---

[72] See esp. *Knights* 1111–14.
[73] Cf. Dio Chrysostom 33.10: 'For the comic poets, being suspicious and fearful of the
people [*ton dēmon*], flattered them as a slave flatters a master [*despotēn*], chiding them
gently and with a smile.' In *Knights* we do indeed see Aristophanes chiding and yet
flattering the *dēmos* as a master (and tyrant). Yet Dio also emphasises that the *dēmos*
goes to the comic performances expecting to be criticised (33.9), and commends the
Athenian *dēmos* of the classical democracy for encouraging frank criticisms of itself
despite its power of life and death over any critic (32.6, citing *Knights* 42–3). Cf.
Henderson's argument that 'one constant and central theme of the comic take on
tyranny is this: the Athenian demos held and deserved to hold arguably tyrannical
power at home and abroad' ('Demos, Demagogue, Tyrant', pp. 155–79, at 158).
[74] *Knights* 1111–19:

> ὦ Δῆμε, καλήν γ᾽ ἔχεις
> ἀρχήν, ὅτε πάντες ἄν-
> θρωποι δεδίασί σ᾽ ὥσ-
> περ ἄνδρα τύραννον.
> ἀλλ᾽ εὐπαράγωγος εἶ,
> θωπευόμενός τε χαί-
> ρεις κἀξαπατώμενος,
> πρὸς τόν τε λέγοντ᾽ ἀεὶ
> κέχηνας.

But the lazy life of pleasure that Dēmos leads is not one that Aristophanes was likely to have thought his audience would have regarded as altogether without its attractions. A particularly attractive feature is that Dēmos is presented as having, so long as he grasps it, total power over those who are normally considered most powerful in the polis. This is the power we have seen Diodotus lament. Moreover, the transformation of Dēmos at the end of the play would also appeal to the audience, though more to their aspirations than their immediate desires. And the implicit exhortation of the *dēmos* comes not as an insistence that it should have less power or be guided by others, but on the contrary that it should insist on wielding its full powers of judgement and action wisely and effectively. The rule of Dēmos is praised by the chorus as fine (*kalēn . . . archēn*), a judgement justified by the observation that Dēmos rules like a tyrant man (lines 1111–14). The criticisms of the rule of Dēmos that follow are not complaints about the strength of that rule; rather, they are expressed as concerns about characteristics that tend to weaken it. The admirable excellence of tyrannical rule is particularly at risk from the tendency of Dēmos to be swayed by seductive speakers, and thus to put the politicians rather than the people in charge.[75]

Dēmos retorts that he acts foolishly on purpose, reassuring the chorus (and both reassuring and exhorting the *dēmos* of the audience) that Dēmos always remains in control, using the political leaders to serve his interests rather than being used by them to serve theirs.[76] The chorus makes clear that this is the right course of action: 'Indeed, in this way you would do well, should there be as much shrewdness in your character as you say.'[77] Tyrannical rule is fine; the *dēmos* rules like a tyrant *in* the

---

[75] 'Comic poets particularly wanted the *dēmos* to look through the lies, compromises, self-interest, and general arrogance of their leaders and to remember who was ultimately in charge' (J. Henderson, 'The *Dēmos* and the Comic Competition', in Winkler and Zeitlin (eds.), *Nothing to Do with Dionysos?*, pp. 271–313, at 312). See Aristophanes, *Acharnians* 628–59.

[76] *Knights* 1123–4, 1121–30, 1141–50. 'Leaders' here translates *prostatai* [viz., *tou dēmou*]; as these are those who stand before the people, this is an apt translation; but in so far as the matter in question is who controls whom, 'politician' is in some ways a more apt rendering of *prostatēs*. The language also has connotations of one who sets himself up as champion of the people in order eventually to rule over them (as in Herodotus 3.82.4). Wilfred Major notes that in line 325 the chorus presents Cleon not as 'Protector of the People' (*prostatēs tou dēmou*), but as 'Protector of the Politicians' (*prostatei rhētorōn*) (W. E. Major, *The Court of Comedy: Aristophanes, Rhetoric, and Democracy in Fifth-Century Athens* (Columbus: Ohio State University Press, 2013), pp. 70–1).

[77] *Knights* 1131–3:

χοὖτω μὲν ἂν εὖ ποιοῖς,
εἴ σοι πυκνότης ἔνεστ'
ἐν τῷ τρόπῳ, ὡς λέγεις.

polis; what the *dēmos* needs to be on guard against is unwittingly ceding
any of its ultimate power of judgement or action to the political leaders,
who should not be the masters but the servants, slaves or subjects of the
dēmos.[78] If resources are accumulated or policies developed away from
the direct supervision of the *dēmos*, they will inexorably tend to benefit
one or a few individuals at the expense of the people.[79] The *dēmos* is
hereby urged to pursue its true interests, to avoid the blandishments of
flatterers, to resist easy policies of public handouts, to avoid and prevent
corruption, to pay the naval oarsmen what they are owed, and above all to
enter into a peace treaty.[80] While the *dēmos* should live up to its capacity
for shrewdness in order to do these things, it would be self-destructive to
follow the policies of political leaders or officials, or to allow itself to be
hemmed in by institutional constraints.[81] Rather, the *dēmos* is urged to
do all these things by its own judgement, as monarch (*monarchos*) of the
polis and of all Greece.[82] Aristophanes presents Dēmos as having what
were later formulated as hallmarks of sovereignty: Dēmos is unitary, of
course, this unity being built into the presentation of Dēmos as an individual character; and as a master and especially as a tyrant or monarch
he is supreme and accountable to no one.[83]

Orators would later identify this tyranny and mastery of the *dēmos*
over the political leaders as a magnificent and distinguishing ideal of
fifth-century Athenian democracy. So Isocrates in his *Areopagiticus* says
that in the democracy of Cleisthenes (and of Solon) the *dēmos* was not

[78] Cf. Lysias' speech against Nicomachus (399 BCE). Lysias (30.9, 30.3–6) maintains
that Nicomachus, who had wished to subvert the power of the *dēmos*, was as an official
guilty of hubris for attempting to treat what belonged to the polis as his by avoiding
euthunai, when in fact he was the one who properly belonged to the people (*dēmosios*).

[79] E.g. *Knights* 1207–26, 1388–96.

[80] Flatterers/*erastai*: 1340–46; state pay: 1350–5; corruption: 1358–63, 1369–71; naval
pay: 1366–8; peace treaty: 1332, 1388–95; cf. 794–8 and 805–6. This is not simply
a utopian wish-list exaggerated for comic effect, for many in the audience would have
recognised the feasibility and desirability of these measures (see e.g. Thucydides 4.41
re. the feasibility of a peace treaty at this time).

[81] Dēmos as *dexiōtatos*: *Knights* 753. Dēmos certainly does not always live up to this
capacity (see 754–5, 1349), but these passages and others (see 1115–50) support the
idea that he is consistently presented as capable of such intelligence.

[82] *Knights* 1330; cf. 1333: ὦ βασιλεῦ τῶν Ἑλλήνων. See also Aristophanes' *Birds*, which
ends with the main character Peisetaerus marrying Basileia and being hailed as *turannos*
(1708) – which Major argues is appropriate because he is by that point 'fully identified
with the Demos' (Major, *The Court of Comedy*, p. 131).

[83] Noteworthy are explicit denunciations of Cleon for attempting to divide the Athenians
(*Knights* 817–18) or divide the *dēmos* (*Wasps* 41), and the characterisation of Dēmos
as *monarchos* (*Knights* 1330). Further references to the rule of Dēmos are at *Knights*
965–6 (Dēmos will rule everywhere) and 1086–9 and 1333 (Dēmos rules as a king).
Thucydides' famous remark that under Pericles what was in name a democracy was
in fact government by the first man (2.65.9) may be a twist of the paradox that the
democracy was like rule by a monarch.

only *kurios* but like a *turannos*, while the magistrates were like the slaves of the public.[84] In the *Panathenaicus* he describes this earlier tyrant-like *dēmos* as embodying the truest democracy.[85] Around the same time, Demosthenes in the Third Olynthiac sets up a sharp contrast between the fifth-century situation of popular authority over the leaders (including particular *prostatai* pilloried by Aristophanes) and its reversal in his own day.[86]

> What is the cause of all this, and why did everything go well before but awry now? Because then, having the courage to manage affairs and take the field, the *dēmos* was master [*despotēs*] of the politicians [*hoi politeuomenoi*] and had control [*kurios*] over all its goods, and everyone was happy to receive from the *dēmos* their share of honour, office or reward. Now, on the contrary, the politicians have control [*kurioi*] over goods and through these manage everything, whereas you the *dēmos*... have in turn become an underling and adjunct.[87]

Both Aristophanes and Isocrates suggest that the *dēmos* should be like a *turannos* over the political elite; both Aristophanes and Demosthenes exhort the *dēmos* to be *despotēs*, to ensure that it controls the politicians rather than being controlled by them. The *dēmos* should be (and be understood to be) the fountainhead of power and goods, with the officials and politicians dependent for them on the people; the democracy is fundamentally compromised if the people instead see themselves as dependent on handouts from the leaders and officials.[88] The choice is presented starkly: the *dēmos* either rules as a master within the polis and

---

84 Isocrates 7.16, 7.26–7 (a work usually dated to the 350s). I do not mean to suggest that Isocrates is a radical democrat; his constitutional suggestions for a restoration to an earlier form are animated by aristocratic ideals. The speech is written, however, as an address to the assembly, and integral to its rhetorical prowess is delivering an argument for a more conservative constitution while promoting it as the restoration of an earlier programme of control by the *dēmos* (despite amounting for the people to little more than Aristotle's roughly contemporary proposal that the people be *kurios* only in the sense of voting in elite electoral competitions and punishing officials' malfeasance). It is nonetheless revealing that what Isocrates chooses to appropriate as a slogan of the fifth-century 'true democracy' is that the *dēmos* should exercise tyranny and mastery over the political elite.

85 Isocrates 12.147 (*dēmokratia alēthestera*).

86 Demosthenes 3.21 (Nicias, the earlier Demosthenes, and Pericles) and 3.26 (earlier leaders) (3.27: προστάταις). Demosthenes delivered this speech in Athens in 349 BCE.

87 Demosthenes 3.30–1: τί δὴ τὸ πάντων αἴτιον τούτων, καὶ τί δή ποθ᾽ ἅπαντ᾽ εἶχε καλῶς τότε, καὶ νῦν οὐκ ὀρθῶς; ὅτι τότε μὲν πράττειν καὶ στρατεύεσθαι τολμῶν αὐτὸς ὁ δῆμος δεσπότης τῶν πολιτευομένων ἦν καὶ κύριος αὐτὸς ἁπάντων τῶν ἀγαθῶν, καὶ ἀγαπητὸν ἦν παρὰ τοῦ δήμου τῶν ἄλλων ἑκάστῳ καὶ τιμῆς καὶ ἀρχῆς καὶ ἀγαθοῦ τινος μεταλαβεῖν· νῦν δὲ τοὐναντίον κύριοι μὲν οἱ πολιτευόμενοι τῶν ἀγαθῶν, καὶ διὰ τούτων ἅπαντα πράττεται, ὑμεῖς δ᾽ ὁ δῆμος... ἐν ὑπηρέτου καὶ προσθήκης μέρει γεγένησθε. Cf. Demosthenes 2.30 and 23.209 (τότε μὲν γὰρ ὁ δῆμος ἦν δεσπότης τῶν πολιτευομένων, νῦν δ᾽ ὑπηρέτης), and 'Demosthenes' 13.31.

88 See, e.g., Aristophanes, *Wasps* 689–712.

controls the politicians, or will be subjected to them. Any talk of a moderate position seems to be treated as a dangerous illusion, and most likely a pointed deception.

The two main political incarnations of the *dēmos* are as an assembly and as a jury (or as members of the assembly, *ekklēsiastai*, and judges or jurors, *dikastai*). Whereas the *dēmos* of the *Knights* is especially identified with the power of the people as wielded in the assembly, in the *Wasps*, performed in 422, Aristophanes turns to the popular power of the jury.[89] The story follows Bdelycleon's attempt to convince and, in the event, compel his father Philocleon to refrain from his zealous participation on juries. The angry chorus of wasps, or jurors, repeatedly complains that this attempt to remove his father is tantamount to tyranny, as it undermines the democracy. 'Tyranny has stealthily overpowered us', they say, preventing them from taking up their position of judgement, without justification and 'as the sole ruler himself'.[90] Accused of tyrannising for interfering with the jurymen, Bdelycleon complains:

How everything is tyranny and conspirators with you, whether the accusation is large or small! I haven't heard the word [tyranny] for fifty years, but now it's far more common than dried fish, such that the name itself is tossed around in the marketplace. If one buys a wreckfish but doesn't care for anchovies, the nearby monger of anchovies immediately says 'this person is buying fish fitting for a tyranny!'[91]

Tyranny is used here as an epithet for what is perceived or presented as an arrogation of power or privilege at the expense of the Athenian people — whether undermining the jurors or committing a symbolic

---

[89] For the primary association of Dēmos in *Knights* with the assembly, see lines 40–3, 746–55 (and presumably what follows was staged as an argument in the assembly with *prostatai* arguing each side and Dēmos sitting in judgement as to which politician better serves him), 1109, 1127–40, and 1340–53. That this in no way precludes the association of Dēmos with the jury *as well* is suggested at 46–51, 255–7, 797–800, 1145–50, and 1357–61.

[90] Aristophanes, *Wasps* 464–5, 470:

ἡ τυραννὶς ὡς λάθρᾳ γ᾽ ἐ-
λάμβαν᾽ ὑπιοῦσά με,

. . . αὐτὸς ἄρχων μόνος;

[91] *Wasps* 488–95:

ὡς ἅπανθ᾽ ὑμῖν τυραννίς ἐστι καὶ ξυνωμόται,
ἢν τε μεῖζον ἢν τ᾽ ἔλαττον πρᾶγμά τις κατηγορῇ,
ἧς ἐγὼ οὐκ ἤκουσα τοὔνομ᾽ οὐδὲ πεντήκοντ᾽ ἐτῶν:
νῦν δὲ πολλῷ τοῦ ταρίχους ἐστὶν ἀξιωτέρα,
ὥστε καὶ δὴ τοὔνομ᾽ αὐτῆς ἐν ἀγορᾷ κυλίνδεται.
ἢν μὲν ὠνῆταί τις ὀρφὼς μεμβράδας δὲ μὴ ᾽θέλῃ,
εὐθέως εἴρηχ᾽ ὁ πωλῶν πλησίον τὰς μεμβράδας:
'οὗτος ὀψωνεῖν ἔοιχ᾽ ἄνθρωπος ἐπὶ τυραννίδι'.

offence, the comic version here being to opt for one large solitary fish (the wreckfish) over a group of little schooling ones.[92] The complaints about tyranny may set up a modern audience for surprise when a claim to exercise tyranny is made from the same quarter. For Philocleon the democratic juror goes on to present himself and his fellow jurors in all the trappings of a tyrant, arguing that as a juror he is 'overall ruler'.[93] Tyrannical power is seen not only as what would put down or restrain the power of the people – though in that form it meets with popular outrage – but also as the fullness of the people's power itself. 'As far as our power is concerned', Philocleon tells his son, 'it is nothing less than a kingship [basileias]. What creature is there today more happy and enviable, or more pampered, or more to be feared, than a juror?'[94] The jurors are supplicated to give certain verdicts, but Philocleon insists that they are able to decide whatever they want, as their power is entirely discretionary. Thus everyone fears them and they fear no one.[95] 'Do I not wield great rule [megalēn archēn archō], in no way inferior even to that of Zeus?'[96] What Philocleon does with this great power is what Dēmos initially does with his in Knights: he goes in for gluttony, drinking, sexual activities and the joy of wielding power unaccountably. This position of being unaccountable is integral to the jurors' supremacy: they engage in scrutiny of the magistrates, but – crucially – no magistrates can scrutinise or punish them.[97] Philocleon emphasises the total discretionary power that jurors have over magistrates as they submit to their euthunai

---

[92] See also Aristophanes, Lysistrata 614–35.

[93] Ruler of all, or ruler in all things: ἄρχω τῶν ἀπάντων (Wasps 518). Aristotle notes the view that Solon put the popular jury in complete control, such that the favour of the dēmos was courted like a tyrant (hōsper turannōi tōi dēmōi), and demagogues such as Ephialtes and Pericles were encouraged to propose their further democratic reforms (Politics II 1274a1–10). Cf. the description by Aristotle (or his follower) of the suppression of the democracy by the Thirty in 404: they 'put down the authority that was in the jurors' (τὸ κῦρος ὃ ἦν ἐν τοῖς δικασταῖς κατέλυσαν: 'Aristotle', Constitution of the Athenians 35.2; cf. 41.2).

[94] Wasps 548–51 (trans. Sommerstein, modified); cf. 546 re. the kingly power of the jurors.

[95] Wasps 628–30. Cf. 'Old Oligarch', Constitution of the Athenians 1.18.

[96] Wasps 619 (trans. Sommerstein, modified).

[97] Of course, individuals are still subject to being tried and sentenced by a jury for a crime, but their public actions as jurors (or assemblymen) are immune. Matthew Landauer has recently provided pertinent readings of a range of the texts discussed here, and has concluded that the warrant for this immunity is the powerlessness of the juror or assemblyman. See M. Landauer, 'The Idiōtēs and the Tyrant: Two Faces of Unaccountability in Democratic Athens', Political Theory 42:2 (2014), pp. 139–66 (p. 145: 'The demos may be unaccountable less because it is above the law than because its characteristic political activities are almost beneath the law's notice'). I instead defend here the 'sovereigntist' reading that Landauer calls into question. 'The sovereigntist view is not without merit,' he argues (p. 143), 'but it coheres uneasily with the Athenian emphasis on the need for power to be exercised accountably.' I argue that

or audits, comparing it to the power of a god.[98] The jurors hold all others to account, but they are themselves unaccountable: 'And for doing this we cannot be called to account [*anupeuthunoi*] – which is true of no other public authority [*archē*].'[99] As in *Knights*, this picture of total control is contested, as Bdelycleon charges his father the juror with being a slave rather than the master he ought to be.[100] This is again because the politicians act as if they are serving the people's interest, but instead are using them to serve their own.[101] Revealingly, being *anupeuthunoi* is the one point on which Bdelycleon concedes that the jurors are majestic.[102] He holds that the people do exercise a vast rule, but that the deceptive and self-serving politicians have kept them from benefiting from it.[103]

VI

The unaccountability of the *dēmos* may promise the people freedom and other benefits,[104] but it also opens up the possibility that they will take on characteristics for which the monarchical tyrant was notorious, including greed, cruelty and arrogance. The democratic challenge, articulated in the *Knights* and elsewhere, was for the *dēmos* to avoid these self-destructive excesses through *self*-control rather than through allowing itself to be controlled. Although unaccountable supremacy could lead to tragic reversal, to weaken the unaccountability of assemblymen and jurors is to compromise democratic control, to render the polis vulnerable to insidiation or takeover by anti-democratic forces. Some interpreters have understood the use of mechanisms of accountability or what we might call constitutional checks to be the form of that self-control, but this is not warranted by the fifth-century sources.[105] Such mechanisms as *euthunai*

---

the sovereignty of the *dēmos* simultaneously explains why it must be unaccountable *and* why all those who carry out public functions or manage public funds must be held accountable by it. See also n. 105.

[98] Aristophanes, *Wasps* 570–1.

[99] *Wasps* 587 (trans. Sommerstein): καὶ ταῦτ' ἀνυπεύθυνοι δρῶμεν, τῶν δ' ἄλλων οὐδεμί' ἀρχή. The meaning above apparently depends on assuming that τῶν δ' ἄλλων refers to an implied ἀρχῶν.

[100] See *Wasps* 512–20, 601–2, 653–4, 681–6.   [101] *Wasps* 655–718.

[102] *Wasps* 588 (reading σεμνόν).

[103] Cf. *Wasps* 700. See Aristophanes' account of his own political counsel at *Acharnians* 628–64.

[104] The identification of rule and freedom is common: see, e.g., [Aeschylus?], *Prometheus Bound* 50; Euripides, *Helen* 276; Critias DK 88B37.

[105] See esp. J. P. Euben, *Corrupting Youth: Political Education, Democratic Culture, and Political Theory* (Princeton: Princeton University Press, 1997), pp. 91–108. Euben argues that there was in Athens a shared culture of mutual accountability throughout the citizen body, where unaccountability was seen to be anti-democratic and indeed anti-political. 'Accountability is more than elites being held accountable by the people;

were aimed at individuals, not at the people as such: the *dēmos* was the source rather than the object of review. Although they were drawn from the body of the people by lot or election, the magistrates were always the object of strict control as potential usurpers of the people's ultimate authority.[106] Some scholars have thus identified an elemental Athenian distinction between sovereignty, which inhered in the *dēmos* as a whole, and government, which was undertaken by officials accountable to the sovereign *dēmos*.[107]

One of the best sources for understanding the justification for the unaccountability of the *dēmos* comes from the work of an author who is sometimes called the 'Old Oligarch', and who was probably (though this is much disputed) writing about 424, around the same time as Aristophanes' *Knights*.[108] He declares his contempt for the *dēmos*, and contends that what is truly good furthers the best men, whereas what furthers the worthless men is bad. And yet, implicitly contesting an aristocratic dismissal of the rule of the people as stupid and self-destructive, he offers a penetrating account of the intrinsic intelligence of Athenian democracy as a set of institutions, policies and practices designed to ensure that the *dēmos* rules and is not ruled.[109] In writing to an audience of aristocrats, he draws on an interest-based version of radical democratic ideas:

it is the people being accountable to each other and to themselves' (p. 97). See also E. Markovits, *The Politics of Sincerity: Plato, Frank Speech, and Democratic Judgment* (University Park: Pennsylvania State University Press, 2008), esp. pp. 47–61; and Melissa Lane's contribution to this volume (Chapter 2).

[106] Although the democratic concern was to control elites of all kinds, I have been able to focus here only on the accountability of magistrates. The growth in power of a magistracy was seen as a potent cause of anti-democratic revolution (see Aristotle, *Politics* V 1304a18–22).

[107] See esp. M. Ostwald, 'Popular Sovereignty and the Control of Government', in *From Popular Sovereignty to the Sovereignty of Law: Law, Society, and Politics in Fifth-Century Athens* (Berkeley and Los Angeles: University of California Press, 1986), pp. 3–83; and R. K. Sinclair, *Democracy and Participation in Athens* (Cambridge: Cambridge University Press, 1988). While Plato's allegory of the democratic ship of state in the *Republic* illustrates a low estimate of the intelligence of the system, it does reflect a democratic distinction between sovereignty and government when it portrays the *dēmos* not as the one who steers the ship (*kubernētēs*, the pilot or governor), but as the on-board ship owner (*nauklēros*) to whom the pilot is accountable (*Republic* VI 488ae, following the reading of Aristotle in *Rhetoric* III 4, 1406b35).

[108] See 'Xenophon', *The 'Old Oligarch': The 'Constitution of the Athenians' Attributed to Xenophon*, ed. J. L. Marr and P. J. Rhodes (Oxford: Aris & Phillips, 2008), pp. 31–2 for a catalogue of the dates that scholars have assigned to the work. Marr and Rhodes join those who argue for a date of 425–424, in part because of the possibility that the work refers to plays of Aristophanes, including *Knights* (pp. 3–6, 131–5).

[109] Vivienne Gray thus contends that the text is 'the only analysis of democracy from the point of view of the *dēmos*' (Xenophon, *On Government*, ed. V. J. Gray (Cambridge: Cambridge University Press, 2007), p. 1), and at the least it does seem to borrow heavily from that point of view, or the point of view of some theoretical advocates of the *dēmos*.

[1.6] Someone might say that they ought not to allow everyone in turn the right to speak or to deliberate, but only the cleverest and the best men. However, on this point too, their policy, of allowing even the worthless to speak, is best. For if only the valuable were to speak and deliberate, it would be good for the likes of themselves, but not good for the common people [*dēmotikois*]. As things are, any worthless person who wishes can stand up in the assembly and procure what is good for himself and those like him.

[1.7] Someone might say, 'How could such a person recognise what is good for himself and the *dēmos*?' But they know that this man's ignorance and worthlessness and good will [*eunoia*] are more advantageous to them than are the excellence and wisdom and ill will [*kakonoia*] of the valuable man [*tou chrestou*].

[1.8] It is true that a polis would not be the best on the basis of such practices, but the fact is that the democracy would most securely preserve itself by these means. For the *dēmos* does not wish the polis to be governed well [*eunomoumenēs*] while it is enslaved, but rather to be free and to rule, and so it is not concerned about bad government [*kakonomias*]. The *dēmos* actually derives its strength and its freedom precisely from what you consider not to be good government [*ouk eunomeisthai*].

[1.9] If you are looking for good government [*eunomian*], you will find that, first, the cleverest men draw up the laws for them. After that, the valuable men will punish the worthless ones; they will be the ones who make policy for the polis, and they will not allow wild persons to deliberate or to speak or to attend meetings of the assembly. So, as a result of these good measures, the *dēmos* would very quickly be reduced to slavery.[110]

How can the *dēmos* ensure that, like the tyrant, it is able 'to be free and to rule'? By making all others accountable to it, while being accountable to no one.[111] Granting some people greater influence – such as greater access to speech, agenda setting, legislation, power to punish, or control over membership – on the basis of their intelligence, judgement or ethical or social standing, will lead to those who have been granted greater influence using that influence to procure power and benefits for themselves. Once the people invest powers in an epistemic, ethical, economic, political or social elite, they slip from mastery into slavery. Again, the view is that there is no other option: delegation to those who are wiser and better, or reputed to be so, will not effectively meet the people's aims or

---

110   Marr and Rhodes trans., modified.

111   Aristotle (*Politics* II 1274a15–18) endorses the idea that without the power to elect officials and hold them accountable, the *dēmos* would be enslaved. (Far from considering the *dēmos* sovereign because of these powers of election and review, Aristotle here states that in yielding these powers Solon gave the *dēmos* the minimum power necessary; this measure of control was necessary because without it the *dēmos* would have been enslaved and hostile (*mēde gar toutou kurios ōn ho dēmos doulos an eiē kai polemios*). When Aristotle writes about sovereignty in a way that meets the conditions of the likes of Bodin and Hobbes, he typically makes this clear by using locutions like those in n. 8, above; and he uses these locutions especially about tyranny and the democracy that is like a tyranny.) For Aristotle's assessment of the unaccountability of the *dēmos*, see the final section below.

realise their interests, but will inevitably subvert those aims and interests. The only way to avoid this is to retain rule and mastery.

In the late fifth century, *eunomia*, good order according to law, is an anti-democratic watchword. Critics of democracy praise the constitutional constraints of aristocracy or oligarchy according to law, and lament Athenian democratic lawlessness. As the Old Oligarch observes, however, the people understand that if the constraints of law are applied to them, then they no longer have supreme authority: to be in control, they must be uncontrolled. We can see vociferous insistence on this tenet in Xenophon's report of a notorious meeting of the assembly in 406 BCE for the collective trial of the generals who were at the naval battle of Arginusae. When Euryptolemus tries to block the proceeding on the grounds that it is *paranomos* or against the law, which would have suspended the assembly and the trial until its legality was approved, 'the majority shouted that it would be outrageous if someone were to prevent the *dēmos* from doing whatever it wished'.[112] This episode has frequently been seen to illustrate the descent of direct democracy into (or its ultimate identity with) mob rule. But it can instead be read as a potent expression of the democratic conviction that the *dēmos* must be able to direct and judge even the most powerful officials as it wishes, while not being itself hemmed in by laws or officials.[113]

VII

I should like to return in conclusion to Aristotle. Although he is a fourth-century figure, I wish to consider a famous passage that has often been read as analysing the late fifth-century Athenian democracy.[114] First,

---

[112] Xenophon, *Hellenica* 1.7.12: τὸ δὲ πλῆθος ἐβόα δεινὸν εἶναι εἰ μή τις ἐάσει [i.e. if someone were not to allow] τὸν δῆμον πράττειν ὃ ἂν βούληται. Cf. the Herodotus passage in n. 10 (and Antigone's characterisation of tyranny in Sophocles' *Antigone*, 506–7) for relevantly similar language; and cf. *Hellenica* 1.7.13–14 for the further shouted insistence of the assembly members. The *graphē paranomōn* has often been regarded as a kind of judicial review brought in to curb the excesses of Athenian popular sovereignty, but the reaction of the majority here may be to such a use as instead an attempt to co-opt the mechanism. Intended as a democratic tool against elite takeover (see 'Demosthenes' 58.34; Aeschines 3.191), it would be seen here as having been commandeered to constrain the *dēmos* (and in particular to deny the people's authority to punish members of the political elite as they judged best).

[113] See the reconsideration by D. Gish, 'Defending *Dēmokratia*: Athenian Justice and the Trial of the Arginusae Generals in Xenophon's *Hellenica*', in F. Hobden and C. Tuplin (eds.), *Xenophon: Ethical Principles and Historical Enquiry* (Leiden: Brill, 2012), pp. 161–212.

[114] For the applicability of the model of 'extreme democracy' to the Athenian democracy of the fifth century see e.g. Aristotle, *Politics* II 1274a4–10 and VI 1319b20–1. For an argument that it applies less well to the democracy of Athens in the fourth century see B. S. Strauss, 'On Aristotle's Critique of Athenian Democracy', in C. Lord and D. K.

however, two preliminary passages, one ignored in these contexts and the other well known. Consider first *Rhetoric* I 8, where Aristotle distinguishes constitutions according to the controlling and deciding power:[115] 'In a monarchy, as its name indicates, one alone is supreme over all [*hapantōn kurios*]: that which is according to some ordering is a kingdom, whereas that which is unlimited is a tyranny [*hē d' aoristos turannis*].'[116] A monarchy is a kingship if it is subject to some regulation or right ordering (*kata taxin*); it is a tyranny, however, if it is *aoristos*, without a boundary, unlimited (from *horos*, boundary; *horistos*, limited).

Aristotle's definition of tyranny as *aoristos* has been overlooked in favour of the one that he emphasises in the *Politics*, that tyranny is rule by one in the interest of the ruler (whereas kingship is rule by one in the interest of the ruled or in the common interest). To define tyranny as rule by one without limitation is related to this, but distinct and intriguing; it is, I believe, at work in the *Politics* too.[117]

In the *Politics* Aristotle repeatedly characterises tyranny as similar to the rule of a master (a similarity played upon to great effect in Aristophanes' *Knights*). So he argues that a form of rule that participated in some way in kingly rule was also 'tyrannical, in as much as the monarchs ruled like masters [*despotikōs*] in accordance with their own judgment [*kata tēn hautōn gnōmēn*]'.[118] This conception of the tyrant as following his own *gnōmē* (judgement, inclination or will) fits with Aristotle's characterisation of a kind of tyranny that is no longer kingly at all, but 'tyranny in the highest degree': 'Any monarchy is necessarily a tyranny of this kind if the monarch rules unaccountably [*anupeuthunos archei*] over people who are similar to him or better than him, with an eye to his own benefit, not that of the ruled.'[119] The last of these criteria has received the most attention, and is often offered as Aristotle's definition of tyranny; but it is worth focusing on the first, cast in the language of Otanes' characterisation of

O'Connor (eds.), *Essays on the Foundations of Aristotelian Political Science* (Berkeley and Los Angeles: University of California Press, 1991), pp. 212–33.

[115] τὸ κύριον / τὸ κρῖνον.

[116] Aristotle, *Rhetoric* 1365b37–66a2: μοναρχία δ᾽ ἐστὶν κατὰ τοὔνομα ἐν ᾗ εἷς ἁπάντων κύριός ἐστιν· τούτων δὲ ἡ μὲν κατὰ τάξιν τινὰ βασιλεία, ἡ δ᾽ ἀόριστος τυραννίς.

[117] The proper connection between the Aristotelian characteristics of or criteria for tyranny would seem to put the unlimitedness and unaccountability of the power first, the idea being that having unlimited power leads to being narrowly self-serving (the doubtful reliability of the converse being readily observable). To ensure that the ruling power is not wielded solely for the ruler's benefit requires the capacity to limit that power. A further implication of what Aristotle says here may be that to require a polis to have a certain *taxis* or order is inherently to limit the ruling power.

[118] Aristotle, *Politics* IV 1295a16–17 (trans. Reeve); see III 1285b1–2, 1285b24–5.

[119] Aristotle, *Politics* IV 1295a18–21 (trans. Reeve): τοιαύτην δ᾽ ἀναγκαῖον εἶναι τυραννίδα τὴν μοναρχίαν ἥτις ἀνυπεύθυνος ἄρχει τῶν ὁμοίων καὶ βελτιόνων πάντων πρὸς τὸ σφέτερον αὐτῆς συμφέρον, ἀλλὰ μὴ πρὸς τὸ τῶν ἀρχομένων.

tyranny, Diodotus' account of the power of the people in assembly and Philocleon's self-portrait of the power of the people's juries.

Aristotle's view of extreme tyranny as a form of rule that is unaccountable (*anupeuthunos*) fits well with his view of tyranny as unlimited (*aoristos*). For the introduction of accountability would render the rule *horistos*, limited; and any true limitation would come with some kind of accountability. It also brings out the similarity to early modern theories of sovereignty as discussed in the second section, above. The tendency to focus on a Greek (particularly Aristotelian) view of tyranny as rule for the ruler's own interest may have obscured the connection between an ancient understanding of tyranny and a modern concept of sovereignty. For example, according to the influential Hobbesian analysis, forms of commonwealth cannot properly be distinguished (as Hobbes takes Aristotle and his followers to have done) according to whether the aim is the ruler's benefit or the common benefit. This distinction, he holds, is nothing more than a misconception 'that the Government is of one kind, when they like it, and another, when they mislike it'.[120] By contrast, what Hobbes insists on is that any sovereign must be unlimited and unaccountable – incorporating into his account of sovereignty one part of Aristotle's definition of tyranny even as he vehemently rejects another.

This account of Aristotle on unlimited or indefinite rule may seem odd, as the best-known passage about such rule has been taken to be about something different and more limited. In Book III of the *Politics*, according to the best English translation of that work, Aristotle writes:

Another person, however, holds office indefinitely [*ho d' aoristos*], such as the juror or assemblyman. Now someone might say that the latter sort are not officials at all, and do not, because of this, participate in any office as such. Yet surely it would be absurd to deprive of office those who have the most authority [*tous kuriōtatous*]. But let this make no difference, since the argument is only about a word. For what a juror and an assemblyman have in common lacks a name that one should call them both. For the sake of definition, let it be 'indefinite office' [*aoristos archē*].[121]

The vocabulary of 'office' in this translation by C. D. C. Reeve is tenable, but there is at least a strong connotation throughout (and even a suitable alternative translation) of 'rule' whenever 'office' is mentioned.[122] Moreover, 'indefinite' can instead be rendered as 'unlimited', such that in discussing their *aoristos archē* Aristotle would be addressing the *unlimited rule* of the members of jury and assembly (putting particular emphasis on the adjective by moving it to an unusual place in front of the substantive).

[120] Thomas Hobbes, *Leviathan*, 19.2 (London: Andrew Crooke, 1651, p. 95).
[121] Aristotle, *Politics* III 1275a25–31 (trans. Reeve).   [122] See n. 35 above.

to what people gave offices limited for Aristotle. —

Aristotle is here especially concerned with one sense of the 'unlimited-ness' of the rule or offices of assemblyman and juror, namely, that they do not have limited or specific terms. And the word has therefore been narrowly construed here as an innovation of Aristotle's in this quite specific way: one serves as a juror or assemblyman without a specific term of office. Indeed, the LSJ lexicon gives this as a distinct meaning ('without limit of time'), citing this one passage as its authority. Although Aristotle is here referring to (because at this point concerned with) one primary aspect of the unlimitedness of the juror and assemblyman, I doubt that this is all there is to it. Even if we are to understand the referent here to be only a limitation in tenure, that is itself central to any question of sovereignty. For whoever may set, enforce or alter the terms of office has a kind of control over those who serve a limited tenure, and (at least according to the likes of Bodin and Hobbes) a time-limited sovereign is no sovereign at all. And the unlimitedness of the authority of jurors and assemblymen is more general (and contrasts sharply with the specified duties, legal restrictions and mechanisms for review of the magistrates), though time is the instant case. If the *dēmos* of Athens in its dominant political functions (as jurors and assemblymen) were regulated, then, as the Old Oligarch forcefully puts it, it would be or would quickly become a slave rather than sovereign. Instead, the *dēmos* in its political incarnations of jury and assembly is 'most authoritative' (*kuriōtatos*) and essentially *aoristos*, like the tyrant.

This brings me to a final extended passage, from Book IV of the *Politics*, in which we may now see Aristotle not merely criticising but also representing the substance of the radical democratic ideal:

Another kind of democracy is the same in other respects, but the multitude has authority, not the law . . . For in poleis that are under a democracy based on law . . . the best citizens preside. Where the laws are not in authority, however, . . . the people become a monarch, one person composed of many, since the many are in authority not as individuals, but all together [*monarchos gar ho dēmos ginetai, sunthetos heis ek pollōn: hoi gar polloi kurioi eisin ouch hōs hekastos alla pantes*] . . . such a *dēmos*, since it is a monarchy, seeks to exercise monarchic rule through not being ruled by the law, and becomes a master [*despotikos*]. The result is . . . that a democracy of this kind is the analogue of tyranny among the monarchies. That is also why their characters are the same: both act like masters toward the better people; the decrees of the one are like the edicts of the other; a popular leader is either the same as a flatterer or analogous. Each of these has special power in his own sphere, flatterers with tyrants, popular leaders with a people of this kind. They are responsible for decrees being in authority rather than laws because they bring everything before the people. This results in their becoming powerful because the people have authority over everything [*dēmon pantōn einai kurion*] . . . Besides, those who make accusations against officials say that the people should judge [*krinein*] them. The suggestion is gladly accepted, so as to put down all the officials [*hai archai*].[123]

It is the democracy where the *dēmos* is sovereign, or authoritative over all, that is like a tyranny.[124] In this democracy, the *dēmos* – like Aristophanes' Dēmos – operates as a tyrant in the polis, yet must always jealously guard control lest it be usurped by officials or other political leaders. It is the tyrannical *dēmos* that judges the magistrates, and any other individuals, without being itself answerable to any authority. Read in light of the evidence above, Aristotle does not appear to be criticising the radical democrats for falling into tyranny unawares, but for their candid commitment to it.

Aristotle does nonetheless suggest an internal critique of the radical view, which is that the sovereignty of the people is illusory because of the dominance of the demagogues. The radical democratic view, which we can see in Aristophanes' *Knights*, is that such dominance is a serious risk and would indeed dethrone the *dēmos*, but that it is not inevitable. On the radical view, the Athenian *dēmos* must be as hostile to the rise of any individual power as it is protective of its own. Thus, the self-conception of popular tyranny not only does not contradict popular antipathy to individuals who would be tyrant, it is a natural source of and response to that antipathy. This recalls the simple answer that the Old Oligarch identifies to the existential challenge to the Athenian democracy: because everyone can be assumed to look out for their own interests, any and every restraint on the authority of the *dēmos* will tend to undercut the democracy, so the strict democratic solution is to allow no restraint.

The Athenians did have a word – fraught, double-edged – for unitary, supreme, unaccountable political power: tyranny. If the *dēmos* was to be able to look after its own interests, it had to be unlimited and unaccountable, and thwart the rise of leaders who would diminish its authority. The materials of sovereignty not being available under that name, the people put on the robes of the tyrant.

---

[123] Aristotle, *Politics* IV 1292a4–29, modifying Reeve's trans. See also e.g. II 1274a4–10.

[124] This probably refers (though not exclusively: cf. Aristotle, *Politics* IV 1298a35 and 'Aristotle', *Constitution of the Athenians*, esp. 41) to the Athenian democracy of the later Peloponnesian war.

2 Popular sovereignty as control of office-holders
Aristotle on Greek democracy

Melissa Lane

I

This chapter identifies in Aristotle an attempt to solve a problem that bedevils all democratic regimes in which office-holders exercise powers that distinguish them from the rest of the citizens. The problem is both conceptual and political. If those doing the ruling (in Greek, *archein*) are those who hold the offices (in Greek, *archai*) – call this the 'standard equation' – how then might the mass of the people nevertheless be in charge or in control? This is a fundamental problem that theories of democracy must solve, and that several fourth-century and later thinkers about Greek democracies recognised. They did so, most of them in passing, by suggesting that the people should be sovereign. Or more precisely, that the popular multitude or *plēthos*–or the *dēmos* understood as under the sway of the mass of the people (*plēthos*), which I will indicate by the term 'the popular *dēmos*' – should be *kurios*, a term drawn from contexts of household or monarchical mastery that I shall argue is justifiably translated as 'sovereign'.[1] It is an under-recognised achievement of Aristotle's *Politics* Book 3, chapter 11 that it offers a fully worked-out analysis of the idea of the mass of the people being *kurios* in a regime that they control – by electing the highest office-holders and holding them accountable –and I will conclude that we have good reason to construe this 'control thesis' as developing a key ingredient in a theory of 'popular sovereignty'.[2]

---

[1] In translating the orators, Mogens Herman Hansen used 'sovereignty' for *to kurion* in his early works, but subsequently began to register caution about doing so: see M. H. Hansen, *The Athenian Assembly in the Age of Demosthenes* (Oxford: Blackwell, 1987), p. 106, with J. Ober, 'Review Article: The Nature of Athenian Democracy', *Classical Philology* 84 (1989), pp. 322–34. Among translators of Aristotle, R. G. Mulgan reported a general consensus that 'the most natural English translation of *kurios* is "sovereign"', even though 'we must beware of importing modern ideas of sovereignty into our reading of Aristotle'. See R. Mulgan, 'Aristotle's Sovereign', *Political Studies* 18 (1970), pp. 518–22 at p. 518 for both quotations.

[2] M. Ostwald, *From Popular Sovereignty to the Sovereignty of Law: Law, Society, and Politics in Fifth-Century Athens* (Berkeley: University of California Press, 1986), broke important

The proposal that this is an important ingredient in popular sovereignty and one theorised in ancient Greece will seem counter-intuitive to those in the grip of two prevalent presumptions:[3] that popular sovereignty is essentially about legislation; and that it is essentially an early modern idea, developed in response to royal absolutism, with 'the people' coming to replace 'the prince' – whether this development is lauded as the linchpin of democracy or reviled as a theological residue.[4] Certainly Jean Bodin, widely credited as the first major modern theorist of sovereignty, included the power of legislation as a fundamental mark of sovereignty in his *Six Livres de la République* (1576 first French edition), and had already highlighted this power in the operations of the ancient republics in his *Methodus ad facilem historiarum cognitionem* (in the first edition of 1566, amplified in the second edition of 1572), while also denying in the earlier work that Aristotle had offered a coherent definition of sovereignty. Yet as this chapter will show, Bodin acknowleged that popular Greek and Roman regimes had *exhibited* popular sovereignty, especially highlighting the people's role in controlling office-holders. Bodin's claim was not that the concept of sovereignty was unavailable to them (or to Aristotle), just that Aristotle had failed to define it well – a claim that I shall contest. I argue that Aristotle articulated a normative version of widespread practices in Greek democracies, in which popular sovereignty is conceived as involving control of office-holders. Thus I seek to overturn both of the prevalent presumptions that have blocked our understanding of this lost history, in which an idea of popular sovereignty originates in addressing a fundamental problematic of democracy.

II

Having rebelled against a family of tyrants, the Athenian *dēmos* at the heart of the new constitutional form that would become known as

ground by describing the Athenian democratic practice of popular control of magistrates (as he calls the office-holders) as 'popular sovereignty'. Beyond a single invocation of Aristotle on *to kurion* (p. xix), however, he did not explore how Aristotle or other Greek thinkers themselves theorised this development in the novel terms of being *kurios*.

[3] There is also a third argument, placing the origins of 'popular sovereignty' in ancient Rome in the form of Cicero's use of categories of Roman law to articulate a legal vocabulary of the rights of the people to control and manage their own affairs: see M. Schofield, 'Cicero's Definition of *Res Publica*', in *Saving the City: Philosopher-Kings and Other Classical Paradigms* (London and New York: Routledge, 1999), pp. 178–94. While this fruitful legal vocabulary is indeed absent from the Greek cases I shall consider, I propose that the core problematic of popular control of office-holders was elsewhere articulated without it.

[4] An influential champion of the view of sovereignty as secularised early modern theology is Carl Schmitt, *Political Theology: Four Chapters on the Concept of Sovereignty*, trans. G. Schwab (Cambridge, MA: MIT Press, 1985).

dēmokratia enjoyed the thought of itself as a tyrant in its stead.[5] But this was an oversimplification of the political arrangements of the new regime. For, like every other Greek constitution, it featured holders of offices who were called *archontes*, the holders of *archai*.[6] In oligarchies and monarchies, both etymology and political history presented these office-holders as the effective holders of power – literally, from the etymological connection, those who ruled (*archein*).[7] The same was true of archaic Athens, governed by nine *archontes* who were chosen from the aristocratic families or *Eupatridae*. However, this tight equation would prove inadequate to make sense of the democratic regimes that emerged in the fifth century.

The emerging democratic regimes featured a new set of the powers of the *dēmos*, as indicated in the very etymological formation of *dēmokratia*,[8] coined not from the word *archē*, but rather from *kratos*, a term 'never used of "office"', as Josiah Ober has observed. Ober has argued that '*kratos*, when it is used as a regime-type suffix, becomes power in the sense of strength, enablement, or "capacity to do things"'.[9] But if the *dēmos*– a term that connoted the whole people, but which in democratic regimes was understood to be dominated by the poor multitude or *plēthos*– enjoyed *kratos* in this novel sense, that still left a theoretical question unanswered: what was, or should, be the relation of this *plēthos*-dominated or popular *dēmos* to the offices (*archai*) that had historically been understood to be identified with ruling (*archein*)? The idea of the popular *dēmos* as *kurios*, and of a specifically democratic political sense of being *kurios*, arises in fourth-century Greek discourse as a way, I suggest, of articulating this relationship.

[5] See Kinch Hoekstra, 'Athenian Democracy and Popular Tyranny', Chapter 1 in this volume.

[6] M. H. Hansen, 'Seven Hundred *Archai* in Classical Athens', *Greek, Roman and Byzantine Studies* 21 (1980), pp. 151–73 at p. 153, gives a succinct definition of an *archē* in fourth-century Athens from Aeschines' *Against Ctesiphon* (3.29) together with other sources: 'we can conclude that an *archē* was (a) a citizen of more than thirty years of age who was (b) elected either by lot or by a show of hands, (c) liable to *dokimasia* before assumption of office, (d) appointed for a period of more than thirty days, (e) empowered to preside over a court . . . (f) empowered to impose minor fines . . . (g) empowered to manage public money and to supervise public works and public buildings, (h) liable to audit on the expiration of his office [*euthunai*]'.

[7] See J. Ober, 'The Original Meaning of Democracy: Capacity to Do Things, Not Majority Rule', *Constellations*, 15 (2008), pp. 3–9, at pp. 5–6.

[8] On the emergence of the term *dēmokratia* in the 460s, see K. A. Raaflaub, 'The Breakthrough of *Demokratia* in Mid-Fifth-Century Athens', in K. A. Raaflaub, J. Ober and R. W. Wallace, *Origins of Democracy in Ancient Greece* (Berkeley: University of California Press, 2007), pp. 105–54, at p. 108.

[9] Ober, 'Original Meaning of Democracy', p. 6, for this quotation and that in the previous sentence.

Kurios as a noun or adjective involves the notion of mastery or control; the noun may be translated 'lord' or 'master', especially in household contexts, where the *kurios* is the master of slaves or of the household generally, and in Athenian law also the legal guardian of a woman.[10] Throughout the fifth century it is used in political contexts primarily to describe kingship, the oldest model of political rule. The Spartan king Agis (one of a pair of kings in the unique Spartan system) is described in these terms in Thucydides and Xenophon,[11] as is Zeus in Pindar.[12] The same usage carries over into the fourth-century authors Isocrates and Demosthenes describing the Persian Great King.[13] Thucydides extends the term from a king to an elected Athenian general, Phrynichus, whom he describes as *kurios* in his capacity to act in virtue of his office,[14] a sense echoed in fourth-century treatments of office-holders as *kurios* in virtue of their offices, for example in Demosthenes.[15]

It is not until the fourth century that we find any developed meditation on collective bodies of the people as being politically *kurios* in democracies – for example, the Council of the Areopagus in Lysias (26.12.1), and the *dēmos* as a whole in Demosthenes (3.30.4 and 3.31.2 pairing *despotēs* with *kurios* in describing the democratic *dēmos*). In the 'Seventh Letter' (330d6), a text that is probably fourth century but not necessarily by Plato (in whose corpus it has been preserved),[16] we find the general possibility that either 'one' or 'many' may be politically *kurios*; and we find a contrast between the Spartan *gerousia* and the Athenian *dēmos* as *kurios* in Demosthenes (20.107.6). In the same period we also find extensive use of the idea of the laws as *kurios* in both the orators and in Plato, showing how far the description of being *kurios* has been linguistically extended by this time, from the prototypical king or individual, to a register accommodating collective political bodies as well as the

---

[10] It is used in household contexts in Xenophon, *Oeconomicus* 9.16, and over a dozen times by the orator Isaeus. There is also a usage of *kurios* to describe an individual agent controlling his or her own action: e.g. Aeschylus, *Agamemnon* 104; Aristophanes, *Frogs* 1276; Aristotle, *Eudemian Ethics* 1223a4–5.

[11] Thucydides 8.5.3; Xenophon, *Hellenica* 2.2.12. In a 2013 Princeton Classical Philosophy Conference paper on 'Teleology and Necessity in Aristotle's Account of the Natural and Moral Imperfections of Women', Mariska Leunissen remarks: 'In the context of Aristotle's psychology of action, the term *kurios* often refers to the factor that has the efficient causal power to enact motion', be it a person or a psychological capacity.

[12] Pindar, *Isthmian* 5.53.

[13] E.g. Isocrates 4 (*Panegyricus*), 121.3; Isocrates 9 (*Evagoras*), 68.3; Demosthenes, *Olynthiaca* 3, 16.5.

[14] Thucydides 8.51.1.   [15] Demosthenes 19 (*De falsa legatione*), 268.8.

[16] On the 'Seventh Letter', see P. A. Brunt, 'Plato's Academy and Politics', in *Studies in Greek History and Thought* (Oxford: Clarendon Press, 1993), pp. 282–342.

abstract ideas of the *dēmos* of a democracy, and of the laws, as potentially *kurios*.[17]

More extensive accounts are given in Plato's *Menexenus*, Isocrates' *Areopagiticus* and a fourth-century rhetorical manual called the *Rhetorica ad Alexandrum*. In the *Menexenus*, Socrates recites a funeral oration that he ascribes to Aspasia, characterising the Athenian *politeia* as one that, whether called by the name *dēmokratia* or by some other name:

> in reality . . . is government by the best men with popular consent (*eudoxias plēthous*). We have always had kings; at one time they were hereditary, later elected [meaning the king-archons[18]]. Yet in most respects the people (*plēthos*) have sovereign power (*egkratēs*) in the city; they grant public offices (*tas . . . archas didōsi*) and power (*kratos*) to those who are thought best by them at a given time. (*Menex.* 238c7–d5)[19]

Here the people are endowed with *kratos* (power), which they then bestow through election. *Didonai tas archas* or 'granting public office' is a standard phrase for election to offices.[20] While the *Menexenus* does not feature the term *kurios*, its focus on the mass of the people exercising this power by 'granting public office' is echoed by Isocrates in an idealising account of the Solonian constitution. He calls this constitution a 'democracy', arguing that the role of the people in electing public officials in this

---

[17] Most analyses of the uses of *kurios* in the fourth century have focused specifically on what Athenian orators meant by describing the *dēmos* as *kurios*, and on whether this was identified with a particular institution in different periods, the debate being summed up in Ober, 'Review Article'; note also D. S. Allen, *The World of Prometheus: The Politics of Punishing in Democratic Athens* (Princeton: Princeton University Press, 2000), pp. 111–12, 172–82, and D. Cammack, 'Rethinking Athenian Democracy' (Ph.D. thesis, Harvard University, 2013).

[18] Plato uses the same phrase (*tas megistas archas*) elsewhere (*Men.* 90b2–3; see also the pseudo-Platonic *Thg.* 127e2), but never defines which offices are meant. *Ath. Pol.* 3.2 calls the three senior archonships the '*megistai*' of the offices; Demosthenes (19.237.8) refers to ambassadorships and generalships as among '*tōn megistōn timōn*'. As we will see, Aristotle also uses the phrase repeatedly without defining which offices are included.

[19] Translations of Plato herein are from Plato, *Complete Works*, ed. J. M. Cooper (Indianapolis: Hackett, 1997), unless otherwise stated. The choice of 'sovereign power' for *egkratēs* is that of the translator Paul Ryan in that volume; this choice is independent of the case made herein for translating *kurios* as 'sovereign'.

[20] It is interesting that Plato accords the *dēmos* a form of *kratos*, only to insist that they immediately give it away to the officials. Cf. Plato's *Statesman*, in which the rule of the many is described simply as *plēthous archē* (291d), as if all that were at stake were the many holding the offices; see M. Lane, 'Political Expertise and Political Office in Plato's *Statesman*: The Statesman's Rule (*Archein*) and the Subordinate Magistracies (*Archai*)', in A. Havlíček, J. Jirsa and K. Thein (eds.), *Plato's* Statesman: *Proceedings of the Eighth Symposium Platonicum Pragense* (Prague: OIKOYMENH, 2013), pp. 51–79, at pp. 78–9. In neither text does Plato explore the possibilities of the concept of being *kurios* as a way of resolving the conundrums of democratic power and popular sovereignty, as Aristotle would do.

constitution is what made them *kurios*, and that election is in fact more democratic than lottery (*Areopag.* 7. 23–7).

A similar role of the people in electing office-holders is canvassed in the *Rhetorica ad Alexandrum*. This is a text preserved in the Aristotelian corpus that is now believed to be probably by Anaximenes of Lampsacus and roughly contemporaneous with Aristotle's *Rhetoric*.[21] In Chapter 2 the author takes up the topic of law and constitutions, and immediately confronts the question of how the law in democracies, as opposed to oligarchies, should govern the distribution of offices:

> In democracies legislation should make the general run of minor offices (*mikras archas*) selected by lot (for that prevents party faction) but the most important offices (*tas . . . megistas*) elected by the vote of the community; under this system the people (*dēmos*) having sovereign power (*kurios*) to bestow the honours (*didonai tas timas*)[22] on whom they choose will not be jealous of those who obtain them, while the men of distinction will the more cultivate nobility of character, knowing that it will be advantageous for them to stand in good repute with their fellow citizens (2.14).[23]

To understand this text, we must correct two common but mistaken ideas about the functioning of ancient Greek democracy. The first is that in democracies such as Athens, all citizens were eligible to hold all offices and generally did. On the contrary, Athenian democracy was 'a system in which considerations of social class continued to play a large part in eligibility to the high executive offices'.[24] As another historian remarks: 'The poor in Athens regularly elected the rich, leisured and well educated to the chief positions in the state. Thus the Athenians expected the most

---

21 According to D. C. Mirhady, 'Aristotle, the *Rhetorica ad Alexandrum* and the *Tria Genera Causarum*', in W. W. Fortenbaugh and D. C. Mirhady (eds.), *Peripatetic Rhetoric after Aristotle* (New Brunswick, NJ: Transaction Publishers, 1994), pp. 54–65, 'this treatise is nearly contemporary with Aristotle – its author is likely to have been Anaximenes of Lampsacus' (p. 54), composed probably soon after 341, certainly not after 300 (p. 55). He adds that the *Rhetorica ad Alexandrum* and Aristotle's *Rhetoric* 'clearly appropriate material from common sources, even if independently. They thus worked from the same background of systematic rhetorical thought,' although 'there is hardly any possibility that the author of the *Rhetorica ad Alexandrum*, whether Anaximenes or someone else, had read Aristotle, even though parts of the text, such as the opening sentence, are likely to have been corrupted subsequently by scribes who were influenced by Aristotelian notions' (pp. 55–6).

22 As in Greek thought and practice generally, holding office is considered and described as enjoying an honour (*timē*, expressed here in the accusative plural as *timas*).

23 The translation is from Anaximenes of Lampsacus, *Rhetorica ad Alexandrum*, ed. and trans. T. W. Benson and M. H. Prosser in *Readings in Classical Rhetoric* (Bloomington: Indiana University Press, 1972), ad loc., except thatI have modified 'elected by lot' to 'selected by lot' to avoid obscuring the important textual contrast between lot and election. The Greek text is in the *Thesaurus Linguae Graecae*.

24 Ostwald, *From Popular Sovereignty*, p. xi.

influential speakers in the assembly and their elected officials to differ in social position from the majority of the citizens.'[25] Similarly, a study of fifty-four democracies outside Athens in the classical period concludes that to be considered a *dēmokratia* in the period did not mean that all citizens had to be eligible to hold all offices; on the contrary, '*dēmokratia* meant access to the assembly and at least some of the offices for all citizens.'[26] When Aristotle himself lists 'democratic features' of constitutions in *Politics* 6.2, what he gives is a list of characteristic features, not of individually necessary ones. It starts with 'Having all choose officials from all' – but goes on to 'Having no property assessment for office, or one as low as possible'.[27] Hence in principle, for a constitution to count as a democracy in classical Greece, not all citizens needed to be eligible to hold all offices.[28]

The second misconception is that sortition or lottery was the sole or most important political mechanism for selection of office-holders in Athens and other classical Greek democracies. Again, on the contrary, the highest officials, those with the most important discretionary powers

---

[25] M. M. Markle III, 'Jury Pay and Assembly Pay at Athens', in P. Cartledge and F. D. Harvey (eds.), *Crux: Essays Presented to G. E. M. de Ste. Croix on his 75th Birthday* (Exeter: Imprint Academic, 1985), pp. 265–97 at p. 283. In Solon's time, according to the fourth-century *Constitution of the Athenians* (which may be attributing to Solon constitutional features that he did not introduce), the poorest of the four property classes was excluded from holding any of the *archai*. Changes were made to the eligibility for various *archai* in the course of the democratisation of the constitution in the fifth century; some new offices were introduced without eligibility restrictions being stated; and it is widely accepted that the poorest citizens must have served on the Council for it to have been fully staffed. Yet it is not clear whether the proscription on the poorest holding office was ever wholly abandoned for the highest offices; fourth-century evidence (the Aristotelian *Athenaion Politeia*, 7.4 and 47.1) that has been taken by several historians to suggest that such proscription was a 'dead letter' by that stage may be read instead to indicate that there was life in it yet. In any case, the technical question of eligibility is separate from the sociological cleavage observed in practice as identified in the main text above.

[26] E. W. Robinson, *Democracy beyond Athens: Popular Government in the Greek Classical Age* (Cambridge: Cambridge University Press, 2011), p. 110, where the positive list of 'commonly attested elements in definitions of *dēmokratia*' also includes 'low property qualifications' and 'use of the lot for some offices'.

[27] Except where indicated, translation of the *Politics* is from Aristotle, *Politika (Politics): Aristotle's Politics*, ed. and trans. C. D. C. Reeve (Indianapolis: Hackett, 1998), apart from avoiding his translation of *kurios* as 'authoritative' in favour of translating it as 'sovereign'. Another relevant passage is in *Pol.* 4.15, 1300a31–4, where Aristotle calls *dēmotikai* those three variations of selecting office-holders that do so 'all . . . from all', whether by election, lot or both. This does not assert that no democracy limits eligibility for office, only that it is most characteristic of popularly inclined regimes not to do so.

[28] The speech of Athenagoras in Thucydides 6.39 is not a counter-example. Having argued that the rich, the wise and the many each have a particular role in a democracy, when he concludes that each of these groups have an equal share (*isomoirein*) in the democracy, he cannot mean that they each have the same share, but rather that each group has a distinct part to play.

beyond the routine conduct of business, were typically elected, as was the case with the board of ten Athenian generals. In the form of democracy prescribed in the *Rhetorica ad Alexandrum*, lottery is to be used for the minor offices.[29] Nevertheless, that text's discussion of the *dēmos* as *kurios* makes no appeal to the *dēmos* getting to serve in the 'minor' offices selected by lot. Instead it focuses on the people's role in electing the holders of the highest offices, while assuming, in keeping with the sociological outlook identified above, that the popular multitude (denoted by *dēmos*, but clearly signifying the popular multitude as opposed to the elite who are candidates for the highest offices) will not in fact be elected to those.

In Plato, Isocrates and in the *Rhetorica ad Alexandrum* we find interpretations of democracy in which the key power of the popular *dēmos* is its role in electing the highest office-holders, and it is this power which according to the latter text makes it right to count the *dēmos* as *kurios*. None of these texts however makes mention of any wider roles the *dēmos* might play in such a democracy in the assembly or in the courts, including in relation to the laws (whether making or interpreting/enforcing them). Instead, their interpretations focus on the problem posed for democracy by the standard equation, a problem that they address by suggesting that the role of the people (*dēmos*, but to be read in light of the pervasive and presupposed class division as the popular multitude) should be not to stand for the highest offices themselves, but rather to grant (*didonai*) the honour of holding such office by means of election.[30] This is a partial version of the control thesis: it affords the people control of office-holders by means of election, to which Aristotle will add a second mechanism, that of holding office-holders to account.

III

In the many excellent discussions of Aristotle's *Politics* Book 3, chapter 11, we find surprisingly little recognition that the central architectonic

---

[29] Lottery too might be interpreted as a mechanism for controlling officials. This is how we might make sense of Herodotus 3.80, where Otanes says that the multitude 'controls offices by lot' (*palō men archas archei*).

[30] This view of the *dēmos* as *kurios* in controlling honours (offices) in the *politeia* by election is found in Polybius' distinctively Greek analysis of the Roman constitution in the second century BCE, which asserts that 'the people (*dēmos*) is sovereign (*kurios*) in the *politeia* over honours and penalties' (6.14, my translation from the Greek text in Polybius, *Histoires*, ed. and trans. É. Foulon, with commentary by M. Molin (Paris: Les Belles Lettres, 2004).) Election to office is certainly the form of 'honour' meant here (and all offices in Rome were elected rather than allotted), though 'penalties' may refer to the popular role in judicial punishments, perhaps especially for malfeasance in office.

question that the chapter inherits from the preceding one[31] – who should be *kurios* in a city, and in particular, should it be the popular multitude? – is answered therein by the thesis that the popular multitude might justifiably be *kurios* in controlling the office-holders.[32] The centrality of the control thesis to the chapter is obscured by Aristotle's immediate dive into a comparison between the epistemic capacities of the few most virtuous men, and of multitudes composed of individuals who have only a share of virtue and practical wisdom, in which context he offers attractive analogies such as the democratic feast that have captured commentators' attention. What must be noted is that Aristotle has a specific theoretical purpose to which he puts these epistemic arguments: it is to argue that a multitude should use whatever epistemic capacity they have, not to serve in the highest offices, but to control those office-holders. In this way he advances the control thesis in order to solve the standard equation, explaining how even though an elite should hold the offices (*archai*), nevertheless the multitude may be *kurios* over them.[33]

In returning his attention in the middle of the chapter to the problem of what, if anything, the multitude (now described in a hendiadys as 'the free and the majority of the citizens', 1281b23–4)[34] should be *kurios* over, Aristotle begins by ruling out their holding the highest (*megistas*) offices – just as the *Rhetorica ad Alexandrum* had done in its prescription for democracies. Aristotle writes that 'it would not be safe to have them share (*metechein*) in the most important (*megistas*) offices'. Holding the *megistas* offices is not a safe way for the multitude to 'share' – a verb that

---

[31]   This is an instance of the more general *aporia* raised in 3.10 as to 'what part of the state [lit. city] is to be *to kurion*', where the multitude (*plēthos*) is proposed as one among a number of possible candidates.

[32]   This section draws on, while condensing and sometimes modifying, M. Lane, 'Claims to Rule: The Case of the Multitude', in M. Deslauriers and P. Destrée (eds.), *The Cambridge Companion to Aristotle's* Politics (Cambridge: Cambridge University Press, 2013), pp. 247–74. There, I followed C. D. C. Reeve's translation, which renders *kurios* as 'authoritative'; here, as noted above, my argument about the best translation of *kurios* leads me to modify Reeve's translation of the term.

[33]   Although many commentators discuss 3.11 as 'Aristotle on democracy', in fact he speaks throughout 3.10 and 3.11 specifically of the *plēthos* rather than the *dēmos*, although earlier in Book 3 (in 3.6) he had already made a related argument using the term *dēmos*, which is the term used for the parallel argument in the *Rhetorica ad Alexandrum*. To accommodate this complex situation, I will speak both of *plēthos* or 'multitude', and of the 'popular *dēmos*', in interpreting the chapter.

[34]   Notice that in returning to his opening *aporia* here, Aristotle now glosses this free multitude as those who 'are not rich and have no claim whatsoever arising from virtue' (1281b24–5), so calling into question the applicability of the general analogies for the wisdom of the multitude explored earlier in 3.11, which characterise the multitude in question (but not all multitudes) as having 'some part of virtue and practical wisdom' (1281b4–5, b15–21). This disjunction in the argument of his chapter deserves more attention.

Aristotle elsewhere links to the idea of 'sharing in the constitution'.[35] Yet some way needs to be found for them to 'share', for 'to give them no share and not to allow them to share (*metechein*) at all would be cause for alarm (for a state in which a large number of people are excluded from office and are poor must of necessity be full of enemies)' (1281b28–30, modifying Reeve's punctuation). Asking how such enmity may be mitigated or avoided while the poor multitude is excluded from office, Aristotle must identify some other way in which the multitude may be given a 'share'.

He does so in a full-blown account of the control thesis, invoking the idea of the popular multitude being *kurios*:

> The remaining alternative, then, is to have them participate in deliberation and judgment (*bouleuesthai kai krinein*), which is precisely why Solon and some other legislators arrange to have them participate in election (*tas archairesias*) and inspection (*tas euthunas*) of officials (*tōn archontōn*), but prevent them from holding office (*archein*) alone. (1281b31–34)[36]

In the *Rhetorica ad Alexandrum*, the prescribed role of the *dēmos* in democracies in relation to offices was that of electing the highest office-holders. Speaking of the *plēthos*, Aristotle repeats the emphasis on their role in election: *tas archairesias* means assemblies for election, and was the term used for example in Athens for 'the meeting of the Assembly at which the election of (military) officials was the most important item on the agenda'.[37] He adds a second role for the multitude, that of inspecting officials or (in other words) holding them to account: *tas euthunas* is the term for institutional procedures for holding office-holders to account, which existed both in Athens and in other Greek cities, especially democracies.[38] Together, these two roles constitute an expanded version of the control thesis, outlining an institutional structure by which the popular *dēmos* may with at least some safety and justifiability be made *kurios*. By asking the question 'who is *kurios*?', Aristotle deploys a new category that allows

---

[35] For example, 4.3, 1290a7–13. For the general expression and idea in Aristotle, see Schofield, 'Sharing in the Constitution', in *Saving the City*, pp. 141–59.

[36] Since writing Lane, 'Claims to Rule', I have been persuaded that 'deliberation and judgment' in the first part of this sentence should be interpreted broadly; it is only in the second part of the sentence that Aristotle goes on to apply them specifically to the case of controlling officials.

[37] Hansen, *Athenian Assembly*, p. 349 (Glossary, *archairesia*, q.v.).

[38] Involving a rendering of financial accounts and sometimes an opportunity for investigating other abuses of office, *euthuna* was 'not a uniquely democratic feature ... [but it was] especially associated with democracy': Robinson, *Democracy beyond Athens*, p. 226. For institutions of *euthuna* outside Athens see ibid., pp. 18, 21 on Argos, p. 37 on Mantinea, p. 44 on the Arcadian federation, p. 110 on Croton. See also P. Fröhlich, *Les Cités grecques et le contrôle des magistrats (IVe–Ier siècle avant J.-C.)* (Geneva: Droz, 2004).

him to break free of the confines of the standard equation, explaining how a popular *dēmos* can control the office-holders who would otherwise monopolise rule.

IV

The only example Aristotle gives in 3.11 of the kind of constitution that could meet this standard is the one that Solon introduced in late sixth-century Athens. Why Solon? We can learn more about how Aristotle may have regarded the Solonian constitution from the *Constitution of the Athenians* (*Ath. Pol.*), which if not written by Aristotle himself is widely held to have issued from within his Lyceum circle.[39] There we learn that in the two successive forms of oligarchic constitution prior to Solon's intervention – the 'primitive constitution' and the constitution introduced by Draco – the people 'had virtually no share (*metechontes*)' in the 'constitution' (2.3).[40] In the primitive constitution 'eligibility for office depended on birth and wealth' (3.1); similarly, under Draco no one under the property status of *zeugites* (the third of the fourth property classes) was eligible for office.

According to this text, Solon like Draco restricted all offices to those of the classes of *zeugites* and above, with some offices restricted to the highest or second-highest classes only. This gave the poor multitude in the lowest property class (*thētes*) no eligibility for offices at all. But unlike the preceding constitutions, Solon's constitution did give them something. It accorded them the right to participate in the assembly and the juries – two roles that did not in Athens technically count as 'offices'. As the *Ath. Pol.* says: 'The *thētes* received [from Solon] only the right to sit in the *Ekklēsia* and the *dikasteria*,' contrasting in the context with the offices that were variously distributed among the higher classes (7.3). From the contrast drawn between him and his predecessors, the *Ath. Pol.* implies that Solon can be understood as having given the *thētes* a share in the constitution which did not consist of sharing in (holding) the offices. If Solon did give the multitude a share, however, he certainly did not do so with the aim of making them *kurios*; in the sixth century neither

[39] The question of the authorship of the *Ath. Pol.* is reviewed in the 'Introduction' in P. J. Rhodes, *A Commentary on the Aristotelian Athenaion Politeia* (Oxford: Oxford University Press, 1981), esp. pp. 61–3, reaching this conclusion: 'On the evidence which we have, Aristotle could have written this work himself, but I do not believe he did' (p. 63).

[40] 'Constitution' is supplied as the object of *metechontes*, having been mentioned two lines earlier. Translation of the *Ath. Pol.* is from Aristotle, *The Politics and the Constitution of Athens*, ed. and trans. Stephen Everson (Cambridge: Cambridge University Press, 1996).

dēmokratia as a regime form nor the extension of *kurios* to collective or abstract bodies was yet thinkable.

Return now to Aristotle's *Politics*. We saw that in 3.11 he recommends a version of the Solonian constitution that accords closely with its institutional arrangements as described in the *Ath. Pol.*: the popular multitude are to elect the office-holders and hold them to account, but not hold the highest offices themselves.[41] Aristotle's understanding of the Solonian constitution is fleshed out further elsewhere in the *Politics*, where what he calls the oldest and 'best of the democracies' (1319a4; this is the first of four kinds of democracy in a scheme laid out in 4.4, 4.6 and 6.4) shares in these respects the same institutional arrangements as the Solonian constitution described in 3.11 and in the *Ath. Pol.*, and is characterised with unmistakable verbal resonances of those passages. In this oldest and best democracy, in which the bulk of the citizens are farmers:

it is both beneficial and customary for all the citizens to elect (*haireisthai*) and inspect (*euthunein*) officials (*tas archas*) and sit on juries, but for the holders of the most important (*tas megistas*) offices to be elected from those with a certain amount of assessed property (the higher the office, the higher the assessment), or alternatively for officials not to be elected on the basis of property assessments at all, but on the basis of ability. (1318b27–32)[42]

He explains that this beneficial arrangement, in which the multitude 'elect' and 'inspect' or hold accountable the highest officials – the exact roles accorded them by the control thesis of 3.11 – was not resented by this particular multitude, whom he characterises as finding 'working more pleasant than engaging in politics and holding office, where no great profit is to be had from office, since the many seek money more than honour' (1318b14–17). The fact that they collectively constitute the body 'which is sovereign (*to kurious*) over the election (*elesthai*) and inspection of officials (*euthunein*) will give them what they need, if they do have any love of honour' (1318b21–2, Reeve trans. modified).

That is, this democracy's multitude primarily seek money rather than honour, but if they do seek honour, they can now find it by controlling the *archai* instead of through the traditional route of holding them (*tas*

---

41   The *Politics* and the *Ath. Pol.* disagree on other aspects of the Solonian constitution, such whether Solon instituted selection of magistrates by lottery or by election (in either case from a pre-elected group). M. H. Hansen, 'Solonian Democracy in Fourth-Century Athens', in W. R. Connor, M. H. Hansen, K. A. Raaflaub and B. S. Strauss, *Aspects of Athenian Democracy* (Copenhagen: Museum Tusculanum Press, 1990), pp. 71–99, reviews these differences, while highlighting the theoretical interest of Aristotle's (and Isocrates') accounts.

42   The mention of 'ability' instead of wealth is characteristic of Aristotle's unwillingness to take any given criterion for political power at face value, other than virtue.

timas, or the honours, being another word for *tas archas*, as noted earlier).
This enables Aristotle to resolve an earlier *aporia*, from 3.10, where he
had raised the worry that if the 'decent people' (*tous epieikeis*) should be
kurios in 3.10, that seemed there to run the risk of depriving everyone
else of honours (rendering them *atimous*) (1281a28–32). Now that 'honour' has been attached to controlling the *archai* as well as to its original
sense of holding them, that *aporia* can be resolved. Aristotle sums up
accordingly that in the best kind of democracy, if 'the decent people rule
(*tous epieikeis archein*)' – that is, hold the offices – 'the multitude (*plēthous*)
are in no way shortchanged' (1319a2–4) because they are nevertheless
kurios.

Appeal to the Solonian or 'ancient constitution' by fourth-century
Athenian writers is widely understood as having been an ideologically
charged manoeuvre, critical of the more radical and full-fledged forms
of the democracy that succeeded Solon's regime. It is therefore striking
to find Aristotle deploying this appeal to Solon in the context of a conceptually innovative account of how the popular multitude can be *kurios*
in a democratic regime. On the one hand, the appeal to Solon should
lead us to scrutinise more closely than is often done whether Aristotle is
defending democracy in general in 3.11, or only a certain and perhaps
more conservative institutional manifestation of democracy. On the other
hand, the fact that he is willing to interpret even the storied Solonian constitution as a genuine instance of popular sovereignty, of the multitude
as *kurios*, is a sign that he is not a slave to a single ideological agenda. He
is grappling with the standard equation, allowing that the individually
elected *archontes* continue to do the work of *archein*,[43] while loosening
its constraints by according a pivotal role in controlling office-holders to
the popular multitude, a role sufficient to make them count as *kurios* or
sovereign.

V

The control thesis should be understood as Aristotle's best shot at a safe
way to make a multitude *kurios* in a democracy. His analysis in 3.11 offers
a normative account of how rule by the multitude might be acceptably
instituted, though it does not valorise that account as an absolutely good
ideal (the 'best constitution' is rather that described in Books 7 and 8

---

[43] At a later point in 3.11 Aristotle appears to flirt with a second sense of *archein* belonging
to the multitude. See Lane, 'Claims to Rule', pp. 268–9, though the interpretative
analysis of *Pol.* 3.11, 1282a34–6, on which this claim depends, is controversial. Cf. 3.7,
1275a25–31, where Aristotle is not careful to draw a distinction between who is *kurios*
and who is doing the *archein*.

as the '*polis* of our prayers'). The chapter is not a descriptive analysis of rule by the multitude, as if it were a justification of any and every kind, or aspect, of a democratic regime. It is better understood as a regulative model that can meet an acceptable theoretical as well as practical ('safe') threshold in answering these questions.

Nothing in the control thesis, however, implies that Aristotle held that election and inspection of office-holders should be the sole roles played by the multitude in such a regime, or that these roles exhaust their being *kurios*. Thus we must consider the control thesis in the context of the wider set of discussions of what or who is *kurios* in a constitution (*politeia*) that occupies Books 3–6 of the *Politics* in particular. These discussions apply to all kinds of constitution, and develop what we might consider a broader sociological, or socio-political, account of being *kurios* within which the institutional account of 3.11 must be situated. In other words, the control thesis is a skeleton – responding to the standard equation, which was also a skeleton. It needs flesh on its bones. And much of that flesh may be found in Aristotle's analyses of the *politeuma* – an entity that we can at first approximation understand here as the preponderant political group or, in a loose sense, the governing class – as *kurios*.

The most important passage is found in 3.6, where Aristotle gives his first definition of a *politeia*:

the constitution (*politeia*) of a *polis* is the order (*taxis*) of its various offices (*archōn*), and of that which is sovereign (*kurias*) over all matters (*pantōn*).[44] For what is *kurion* over everything (*pantachou*) is the *politeuma* of the *polis*, and the *politeuma* is the *politeia*. So I say for instance that in democracies the *dēmos* is *kurios*, but in oligarchies by contrast it is the *oligoi*, and we say that the *politeia* is different in these cases. (1278b8–12, translation mine)[45]

---

[44] There is a long-standing controversy over how to translate the phrase *kurias pantōn* here. The reading that I accept, taking *pantōn* as a neuter plural referring to 'all matters' rather than back to all 'offices', finds support in a parallel construction in 3.10 at 1281a29, where *kurious einai pantōn* clearly means '*kurious* over all matters'; this reading stretches back to Piccart and others in the Renaissance and has notable modern English, German and Italian adherents. The alternative reading, taking *pantōn* as if it were functioning as a feminine plural picking up 'offices', likewise has Renaissance roots (in the commentaries of Vettori and Le Roy) as well as notable modern adherents in Spanish, French, German and English. For the Renaissance debates see A. Brett, '"The Matter, Forme, and Power of a Common-Wealth": Thomas Hobbes and Late Renaissance Commentary on Aristotle's *Politics*', *Hobbes Studies* 23 (2010), pp. 72–102, at pp. 90–1, and S. Smith, 'Nature, Knowledge and the City in John Case and the Aristotelian Tradition' (Ph.D. thesis, University of Cambridge, 2014).

[45] Smith, 'Nature', identifies two related traditions in the medieval and Renaissance Aristotelian commentators in interpreting Aristotle's claim that the *politeuma* is the *politeia*. The first tradition follows Moerbeke and Albert the Great in maintaining some distinction between the two ideas, while the second tends to identify them by reading *politeuma* as 'sovereignty' and identifying this with the *respublica*.

The passage seems to imply that the *politeuma* is itself (or itself holds) an office, one that is *kurias* 'over all matters'. If it is an office, it must be so in an extended and plural sense, one that may include particular institutions but is not exhausted by them. In the case of democracies, we can interpret the idea of the *politeuma* as an office in terms of Aristotle's extension in *Politics* 3.1 of the concept of 'office' defined by specific competencies and term limits, to include what he names there the 'indefinite offices' of assemblymen and jurors.[46] It is in the assembly, after all, that officials were generally elected in various democratic regimes, while it is in the courts and council as well as the assembly that the various mechanisms for holding them to account were exercised. But both the *dēmos* of a democracy and the *oligoi* of an oligarchy[47] exercise more general forms of hegemony beyond those identified with any single office or institution. It is fundamentally because the *politeuma* dominates socially and economically that it also dominates politically, and so determines the nature of the constitution, resulting in Aristotle's pithy formulation that 'the *politeuma* is the *politeia*'.[48]

Describing the first kind of democracy in Book 4, chapter 4, Aristotle had offered an evocative account of this broader form of socio-political dominance: 'since the people (*dēmos*) are more, and majority opinion (*doxa*) is *kurion*, this is necessarily a democracy'.[49] He makes the same point about democracies generally, defined as regimes in which 'the poor are *kuriōterous* over the rich' (1317b8–9), elsewhere in Book 6: in such democracies, the opinions (*doxa*) of the majority (*pleious*– the more) will be *kurios* (1317b9–10). The suggestion that the opinions of the governing class are what is *kurios* – not the determination of any particular institution, but the general ideological sway of their views or opinions – expresses an idea of discursive hegemony that is not limited to any single institutional form. Josiah Ober has highlighted discursive hegemony

---

[46]   See Kinch Hoekstra's contribution to this volume (Chapter 1).

[47]   At 1306a14–19 Aristotle points out that in some oligarchies, 'though the entire governing class [*tou pantos politeumatos*] consists of only a few people, not all of them participate in the most important offices [*tōn megistōn archōn*]', giving an example from Elis. I owe this reference to Aristotle, The *Politics* of Aristotle, ed. W. L. Newman (Oxford: Clarendon Press, 1887), note to 1278b10 *ad loc.*

[48]   The Greek can be read so as to make either *politeuma* or *politeia* the subject of the sentence; I follow Aubonnet and Jowett among others (against, e.g., Susemihl and Hicks) in making the former choice. On the general sentiment, compare Isocrates, who twice calls the *politeia* the *psuchē* (soul) of the city (12.138, 15.14); Paul Cartledge glosses these passages nicely, reading the *politeia* as *psuchē* of the city in the sense of its '"life and soul" or "beating heart"', in his The *Greeks: A Portrait of Self and Others*, 2nd edn. (Oxford: Oxford University Press, 2002), p. 107. Aristotle elsewhere describes the *politeia* as the 'life' (*bios*) of the city (*poleōs*) (1295a40–1295b1).

[49]   1291b37–8 (my translation).

as an alternative to overly narrow institutionalist accounts of Athenian democracy,[50] and we find it here already articulated by Aristotle. The discursive hegemony of the dominant group – that thereby becomes the governing class – offers a broader extra-institutional context and complement to the institutional focus of the control thesis in 3.11 (the latter asserting that the *plēthos* or popular *dēmos* can be *kurios* in controlling the offices). That combination of institutional and extra-institutional analysis is central to Aristotle's grappling with the problematic of popular power and its relation to office-holders in a democracy.

VI

We have identified Aristotle's articulation of the control thesis: his case that the *plēthos* or popular *dēmos* can safely be made *kurios* in relation to the *archai* by controlling the most important ones through election and inspection. We must now return to ask: is this role for the popular *dēmos* justifiably construed as 'popular sovereignty'? As we have noted, throughout 3.10–11, Aristotle consistently speaks of the *plēthos*, not the *dēmos*. Nevertheless, while we can justify construing *plēthos* in the control thesis in the light of his and others' use of *dēmos* in related contexts elsewhere, his chosen vocabulary raises a potential objection to the interpretation of his thesis as one of 'popular sovereignty'. For Aristotle's focus is on a conception of the 'people' that is essentially socio-politically and socio-economically differentiated – the popular multitude contrasting with the economic elite – rather than unitary and uniform. If 'popular sovereignty' must mean in the modern context the sovereignty of an undifferentiated people, to that extent the translation and interpretation of the multitude as *kurios* as 'popular sovereignty' will be infelicitous.

But is it the case that the modern idea of 'popular sovereignty' inherently refers to a wholly undifferentiated people? I would argue that on the contrary, some distinction between people and office-holders or (in late Roman and early modern parlance) princes is normally implied. 'Popular sovereignty' is a potential solution to the problem of the relation between the people and those who would normally be called the sovereign ruler or rulers. Thus even if the sociological gap characteristic of Greek democracies between the *plēthos* and those holding the *archai* diminishes in later centuries (though it nowhere disappears entirely), nevertheless the institutional gap between those who choose the office-holders and those who serve in such capacities always remains.

[50] J. Ober, *Mass and Elite in Democratic Athens: Rhetoric, Ideology, and the Power of the People* (Princeton: Princeton University Press, 1989).

As for the translation of *kurios* as 'sovereign': to employ this concept in the context of this volume requires satisfying a test that involves both translation and conceptualisation. On the one hand, we must ask how justifiable is 'sovereign' as a translation of *kurios* in the light of the merits and demerits of rival possible translations of the Greek written at the time. On the other hand, we must judge all such translations in the light of subsequent intertemporal and interconceptual translations among multiple languages – asking how appropriate is 'sovereign' as a translation of ancient Greek political thinking given its loading in Latin, English, French and other languages in the hundreds of years since, especially in early modern European discussions. I suggest that this intertwined test can be passed at a high standard. The merits of 'sovereign' as a translation of *kurios* – picking up its primitive and focal idea of mastery or lordship – are at once linguistic, historical and conceptual. While it is not the sole defensible translation of the Greek (no translation is perfect, so it will remain important to understand the nuances that alternatives better capture), it is both defensible in narrow terms and also for the vista of understanding in political theory that it opens up.

The most serious objection to translating *kurios* as 'sovereign', and understanding Aristotle to be discussing 'popular sovereignty', comes from an influential understanding, or as I shall argue misunderstanding, of Jean Bodin's criticism of Aristotle. In chapter 6 of his *Methodus*, Bodin criticised Aristotle on three counts: not having 'defined' sovereignty properly; not having identified the key distinction between sovereignty and government; and arguing that 'sovereignty' can be 'mixed' rather than singular. But he never denied that Aristotle actually discussed the idea of 'sovereignty' and had a term for it. On the contrary, Bodin acknowledged that what he called *summum imperium* is precisely what Aristotle 'called' the 'κυρίαν πολίτευμα . . . and κυρίαν ἀρχῶν'.[51] His complaint was that Aristotle failed to give a correct definition of such 'sovereignty'. To justify his complaint, however, rather than canvassing the full range of passages that we have considered (*Politics* 3.6, 3.7, 3.10–11, 4.1), Bodin referred in this criticism only to a single passage in *Politics* Book 4, chapter 14 (1297b37–1298a3), a passage that then governs the remaining

---

[51] In transliteration, '*kurian politeuma* . . . and *kurian archōn*'. I cite the Latin text of the *Methodus* (Paris: n.p., 1572 [1566]) from the new variorum edition, indicating additions and deletions in the 1572 edition. See Jean Bodin, *Methodus ad facilem historiarum cognitionem*, ed. and trans. S. Miglietti (Pisa: Edizioni della Normale, 2013). I quote the English translation in Jean Bodin, *Method for the Easy Comprehension of History*, trans. B. Reynolds (New York: Columbia University Press, 1945) which conflates the two editions, and note clarifications as necessary. For the sentence in the text above, Miglietti trans., p. 356, Reynolds trans., p. 156; there is a similar statement on Miglietti trans., p. 389, Reynolds trans., p. 172.

chapters of Book 4. There Aristotle identifies three parts of each constitution, each of which (the deliberative part, the part of choosing magistrates, and the part of jurisdiction or deciding lawsuits) is described in turn as being *kurios*. Having raised objections that both deliberation and jurisdiction may be exercised by private citizens and so do not define sovereignty, Bodin concluded that by treating all three parts of the constitution on a par, Aristotle failed to give a clear and correct definition of sovereignty.

This conclusion is arguably unfair to Aristotle. But even if one is persuaded by Bodin's selective complaint that Aristotle fails to define (though he does discuss) what is 'sovereignty', two important points remain beyond dispute. First, the election of magistrates – central to Aristotle's control thesis – is the (only) one of the three constitutional parts mentioned by Aristotle in 4.14 that Bodin counts in the *Methodus* as a function of sovereignty. Thus Bodin concurs with Aristotle that electing magistrates is the function of 'the highest majesty of power' in any constitution, whether belonging 'to the prince alone or to the people or to the optimates, according to the type of each state'.[52]

It should be said that by 1566, and even more so in 1572, Bodin adverted to other sovereign powers as well. At one point in the 1566 text he names five such powers, including the power of 'proclaiming or annulling laws'. Still, in this list too 'the first, and the most important' is 'creating the most important magistrates, and defining the offices of each one'.[53] In his criticism of Polybius, Bodin in 1566 contended (as Richard Tuck describes in this volume) that the 'right of sovereignty' is 'chiefly displayed' by 'those who can give authority to magistrates, who can take it away', while adding in 1572 an immediate subsequent clause: 'who can make or repeal laws'.[54] Yet even in making the latter addition, he continued to accord the power of choosing magistrates or officials a centrality in his understanding of sovereignty. For he maintained the

---

[52] Bodin, *Methodus*: Miglietti trans., p. 356; Reynolds trans., p. 156.

[53] Bodin, *Methodus*: Miglietti trans., p. 389; Reynolds trans., p. 172. Miglietti's edition shows that 'most important' (*summis*) was added by Bodin in the 1572 edition. In her introduction (p. 33) Miglietti singles this out as one of the most important emendations of that edition to his earlier jurisdictional and constitutionalist view of sovereignty, that in her view is closer to what Bodin's view of sovereignty in the 1576 *République* would become. I would venture however that it may simply reflect Bodin's effort to adhere more closely to Aristotle's focus on the 'greatest' offices or magistracies.

[54] Bodin, *Methodus*: Miglietti trans., p. 400; Reynolds trans., p. 178. This passage is also discussed by Miglietti in her introduction (pp. 34–5), where again she treats the 1572 emendation as a stage in the development of the 'teorizzazione propriamente originale' of the *République*. While Miglietti cautions in her introduction against too teleological a view of authorial modifications to texts over time, her discussion of particular passages often approximates such a view.

conclusion that a people, even 'while they have no powers but the creation of magistrates, still have the sovereignty'.[55]

Second, Bodin in the *Methodus* nowhere claimed that the Greeks and Romans had no actual locus of sovereignty in the proper sense in their constitutions. On the contrary: for Bodin, popular sovereignty was an indisputable and indeed paradigmatic case of sovereignty, on display in multiple constitutions of classical antiquity. As he observed, 'the type of state of the Romans in the age of Polybius, and much more in the time of Dionysius and Cicero, was entirely popular'.[56] While the popular Greek and Roman constitutions lacked a single supreme magistrate or prince as *kurios*, they had a sovereign people, one that was *kurios* precisely in the power to control their magistrates by choosing them.

The same holds true in the *Six Livres de la République*, the first version of which was published in France in 1576, leaving aside the question of whether there are other and broader shifts in Bodin's views between the various French and Latin editions of this work and between all these and the two editions of the *Methodus*.[57] In the 1576 *République*, in analysing the magistracies (offices) in Rome, Sparta, Salonica, Malta, Florence and Athens, he argued that in none of these popular constitutions were any of the magistrates 'sovereign', because in all cases their powers were granted to them only for a limited period. And by whom were they granted? By the people. Wherever a people have a right to choose their magistrates but do not divest themselves of their own sovereign power and right by transferring it to them altogether, Bodin asserts that it is the people who are 'sovereign'.[58] He spelled this out in the case of the king–*archon* in archaic and early classical Athens: 'I still maintain that he was not a prince and did not have sovereignty, but was rather a sovereign magistrate who was accountable to the people for his actions after his time in office had expired'; 'sovereignty thus remained in the people' there as among the Cnidians who granted absolute power to their magistrates but only for a limited time period.[59]

---

[55] Bodin, *Methodus*: Miglietti trans., p. 402; Reynolds trans., p. 179: the 1572 edition changes 'habeant' to 'habeat', which does not affect the broader sense.

[56] Bodin, *Methodus*: Miglietti trans., p. 402; Reynolds trans., p. 179.

[57] On these questions, see Richard Tuck, this volume (Chapter 5).

[58] Bodin, *Six livres*, Book I chapter 8, as translated in Jean Bodin, *On Sovereignty: Four Chapters from the Six Books of the Commonwealth*, ed. and trans. J. H. Franklin (Cambridge: Cambridge University Press, 1992), pp. 6–7; in the standard English edition, reproducing the English translation by Richard Knolles of 1606, Jean Bodin, *The Six Bookes of a Commonweale*, ed. K. D. McRae (Cambridge, MA: Harvard University Press, 1962), p. 88. For lack of space in treating what for me is a secondary issue, I do not cite the French and Latin original editions of this text.

[59] Bodin, *Six livres*, Book I chapter 8: Franklin trans., pp. 6–7; McRae edn., p. 88.

Thus Bodin himself acknowledged a form of what he called 'sovereignty' belonging to the people in popular constitutions whose role was to select magistrates and hold them accountable. His quarrel in the *Methodus* was not with the conceivability of popular sovereignty, but with the conceivability of mixed sovereignty, while in the *République* he was concerned to show what must belong to princes if they are to be truly sovereign, not to show that nobody but a prince could conceivably be sovereign.[60] Construing Aristotle's control thesis of how a multitude might safely be *kurios* as a case for popular sovereignty is entirely compatible with Bodin's reading of Aristotle as having identified, although not theoretically defined, the concept of sovereignty that both men saw as pre-eminently on display in the popular constitutions of ancient Greece (and for Bodin their later heirs).

VII

To read the control thesis advanced by Aristotle – and anticipated in part by Plato and Anaximenes of Lampsacus, who are followed by Polybius – as an articulation of a certain version of popular sovereignty, making the popular *dēmos* or *plēthos kurios* over the office-holders by means of election and accountability, is to identify a submerged tradition in the history of popular sovereignty. This tradition stresses the socio-political dominance of the people, and their concomitant institutional role, in controlling the officials they elect and hold to account, as opposed to the formulation of the people as a corporate body possessing legal rights that they can alienate or entrust to others in the better-known tradition derived from Cicero and Roman law. Strikingly, despite his quarrels with Aristotle's precise formulations, it is exactly election and accountability that Jean Bodin invoked in insisting that certain ancient Greek and Roman (as well as medieval and Renaissance) constitutions had manifested popular sovereignty. Far from treating popular sovereignty as an oxymoron, Bodin took these Greek and Roman manifestations of control through election and accountability to be paradigmatic of the very concept of sovereignty itself.

This claim should not be taken to advocate either a historical or a normative reduction of popular sovereignty to the control thesis alone. Indeed, as we have seen in Aristotle, discursive hegemony and a broad sense of sociological weight is as important in his broader understanding of what it is for the *dēmos* to be *kurios* – recalling the primitive sense of

---

[60] On offices in the latter text see D. Lee, '"Office Is a Thing Borrowed": Jean Bodin on Offices and Seigneurial Government', *Political Theory* 41 (2013), pp. 409–40.

kurios as mastery – as is the control thesis alone. Nevertheless, Aristotle's thesis lays out a certain ingredient in popular sovereignty that persists into (without exhausting) modern normative accounts of democracy. If the people cannot control their office-holders, or as we might say, if they cannot dominate the erstwhile dominators – the elites who had previously monopolised and largely continued to monopolise the highest offices – they cannot enjoy either democracy or sovereignty.[61]

Conceiving of itself as unaccountable (*anupeuthunos*), more than one ancient Greek *dēmos* imposed *euthuna* – a practice of accountability – and elections on these highest office-holders.[62] In so constitutionalising the office-holders' powers, however, the *dēmos* also imposed discipline upon itself. No actual tyrant exercised powers in a regular and periodic fashion – annual elections and *euthuna* – as the Athenian *dēmos* came to do. The constitutional control of office-holders required a self-disciplining of the *dēmos* at the same time that it imposed a discipline on the political elite who typically held the highest offices. Rooted in the practice of as well as the theorising about ancient Greek democracies, popular sovereignty as the multitude's power to control office-holders is a democratic achievement in both senses.[63]

[61] For a modern theory of democracy as control, P. Pettit, *On the People's Terms: A Republican Theory and Model of Democracy* (Cambridge: Cambridge University Press, 2012). Joanna Innes reminded me that a focus on scrutiny and accountability was also a feature of many eighteenth- and early nineteenth-century discussions of democracy.

[62] See Kinch Hoekstra in this volume (Chapter 1), and M. Landauer, 'The *Idiōtēs* and the Tyrant: Two Faces of Unaccountability in Democratic Athens', *Political Theory* 42 (2014), pp. 139–66.

[63] Earlier versions of this chapter were helpfully discussed in workshops held by the AHRC Popular Sovereignty Network and at UCLA (with comments by Roni Hirsch), the New School for Social Research, Ben-Gurion University, Princeton University, the University of Florida, Brown University, the University of Hull and the American Political Science Association 2014 Annual Meeting. Outside these settings, valuable comments were provided by the volume editors; my research assistant Neil Hannan; and Danielle Allen, Paul Cartledge, David Ciepley, Dani Filc, Alex Gourevitch, Kinch Hoekstra, Susan James, Demetra Kasimis, Derin McLeod, Sara Monoson, Josiah Ober, Paulina Ochoa Espejo, Philip Pettit, Elisabetta Poddighe, Arlene Saxonhouse, Malcolm Schofield, Richard Seaford, Matthew Simonton, Sophie Smith and Richard Tuck.

3 Popular sovereignty in the late Roman Republic

Cicero and the will of the people

Valentina Arena

I

This chapter is concerned with the development of Cicero's conception of the relationship between popular sovereignty and aristocratic government from the *De re publica* to the *De legibus*. When placed in its political and intellectual contexts, this development represents a significant strengthening of its aristocratic bias – specifically when considering Cicero's proposed reforms to the institutions of the senate and censorship as well as to the right to vote and the tribunate. The most striking conceptual outcome of this development is a transformation, to use Cicero's own terms, of real liberty into an empty '*species libertatis*'.

While some modern commentators have interpreted these two theoretical works as complementing one another, others have described the form of government resulting from Book 3 of the *De legibus* as a 'strengthened control from the top', to use Dyck's expression, often denouncing Cicero's blind conservatism and the resulting political system as almost an anecdotal curiosity.[1]

I would like to thank Richard Bourke and Quentin Skinner for inviting me to take part in this project as well as for their very perceptive comments on my contribution. Many thanks also to the other participants, and in particular to Melissa Lane, for penetrating observations and important suggestions on this chapter.

[1] Among representatives of the first group see C. W. Keyes, 'Original Elements in Cicero's Ideal Constitution', *American Journal of Philology* 42 (1921), pp. 309–23; E. Rawson, 'The Interpretation of Cicero's De Legibus', *Aufstieg und Niedergang der römischen Welt* 1.4 (1973), pp. 334–56 = E. Rawson, *Roman Culture and Society* (Oxford: Oxford University Press, 1991), pp. 125–48; J.-L. Ferrary, 'The Statesman and the Law in the Political Philosophy of Cicero', in A. Laks and M. Schofield (eds.), *Justice and Generosity: Studies in in Hellenistic Social and Political Philosophy* (Cambridge: Cambridge University Press, 1995), pp. 48–73; and E. M. Atkins, 'Cicero', in C. Rowe and M. Schofield (eds.), *The Cambridge History of Greek and Roman Political Thought* (Cambridge: Cambridge University Press, 2000), pp. 489–98. For the opposing view see L. Perelli, *Il pensiero politico di Cicerone* (Florence: La Nuova Italia, 1990), pp. 113–36; A. Grilli, 'L'idea di stato dal *de re publica al de legibus*', *Ciceroniana* 7 (1990), pp. 249–62; and A. Grilli,

Intervening in the contemporary political and intellectual debate on the censorship and in dialogue with his Platonic model, Cicero re-elaborates the notion of popular sovereignty as formulated in the *De re publica*. In the *De legibus* he advances not only an institutional reordering of the commonwealth, but rather a different conception of the commonwealth, characterised by a 'quasi-alienation' of the people's sovereignty.

II

In the *De re publica* Cicero argues that a *res publica* is a legitimate form of commonwealth if, and only if, the people are the sovereign power and entrust their sovereignty into the capable hands of the elite.[2] At the beginning of the constitutional debate, in response to Laelius' question ('What, then, is the *res publica*?'), Scipio begins by providing a definition of the object under investigation. '*Res publica*, then, is the property of a people (*res populi*). A people, further, is not just any gathering of humans assembled in any way at all; it is a gathering of people in large number associated into a partnership with one another by a common agreement on law (*iuris consensu*) and a sharing of benefits (*utilitatis communione*)' (1.39).

The construction of the definition of a *res publica* as *res populi* in terms of a property metaphor, fully exploited by Cicero in Book 3, allows him to state that in any legitimate form of government the *populus* should own its own *res*.[3] It follows that, for the *populus* to possess its own *res* in any meaningful way, it is necessary that it should also possess the right over its management and administration; this, in turn, is tantamount to the possession of the value of liberty and the ability to exercise it. This notion is expressed in negative terms in Book 3 of the *De re publica*, where Scipio shows that a *populus* has no liberty if its *res* is taken into the possession of a tyrant or a faction. When, in the light of the discussion of justice, Scipio refines and slightly alters his definition of a commonwealth, Laelius agrees with him that neither under a tyranny nor under an oligarchy could a commonwealth be considered as a 'property of the people', since in both constitutional forms those in power, either a tyrant

---

'Populus in Cicerone', in G. Urso (ed.), *Popolo e potere nel mondo antico* (Pisa: ETS, 2005), pp. 123–39.

[2] On which the seminal work by M. Schofield, 'Cicero's definition of *res publica*', in *Saving the City: Philosopher-Kings and Other Classical Paradigms* (London and New York: Routledge, 1999), pp. 178–229.

[3] On the metaphors attracted by the notion of *res publica* see H. Dexter, 'Res Publica', *Maia* 9 (1957), pp. 247–81 and 10 (1958), pp. 3–37.

or a faction, do not adequately consult and take into account the interests of the people, but rather conduct the people's affairs as if they were their own. Under the tyrant Dionysius of Syracuse 'nothing belonged to the people and the people itself belonged to a single man' (3.43), and when the Thirty Tyrants governed Athens most unjustly (*iniustissime*), the 'property of the Athenian people' was nowhere to be found. It could also not be found, Scipio proceeds, when the *decem viri* ruled Rome and the people rose in revolt to recover their property and with it their liberty (3.43–4). In the speech in favour of democracy, its supporters claim that only when the *populus* is the master of the laws, courts, peace, war, treaties, the life or death of an individual and money, is it possible to talk about a true *res publica*. This is the only case, they are said to claim, when the *res* belongs truly to the people and the citizens are endowed with true political liberty:

If the people would maintain their rights (*ius suum populi teneant*), they say no form of government would be superior either in liberty or happiness (*liberius, beatius*) for they themselves would be masters of the laws and the courts, of war and peace, of international agreements, and of every citizen's life and property; this government alone, they believe, can rightly be called a commonwealth, that is 'property of the people'. . . they indeed claim that . . . when a sovereign people is pervaded by the spirit of harmony and tests every measure by the standard of their own safety and liberty, no form of government is less subject to change or more stable. (1.48)

It follows that, according to Cicero, a certain degree of liberty was necessary for any legitimate form of government to function properly, that is for the *populus* to possess its own *res*, hence to be the repository of sovereign power in the commonwealth.

In Book 2, tracing the development of the Roman constitution as the historical incarnation of the best form of government, the mixed and balanced constitution described in the previous book by Scipio, Cicero shows how through a process of trial and error Rome had come to acquire that matrix of civic and political rights (such as the citizens' right to *provocatio*, to *suffragium*, and the set of rights subsumed under the powers of the tribunes of the plebs, *auxilium, intercessio* and *ius agendi cum plebe*) that were essential to the establishment of the citizens' status of liberty (that is, the ability to pursue one's own wishes without being subjected to the arbitrary will of anybody else).[4]

In this historical account, alongside the right to *provocatio* – which 'forbade any magistrate to execute or scourge a Roman citizen in the

---

[4] V. Arena, *Libertas and the Practice of Politics in the Late Roman Republic* (Cambridge: Cambridge University Press, 2012), pp. 48–72.

face of an appeal',[5] and which, Cicero reports, had already been in place in monarchical time according to the *libri pontificales* and *augurales* – the people are reported to have progressively gained a certain degree of political participation in virtue of the establishment of the tribunate of the plebs. Under the consulship of Postimius Cominius and Spurius Cassius, Cicero's account continues, 'the people, freed from the domination of kings, claimed a somewhat greater measure of rights (*plusculum sibi iuris*)', and through two consecutive secessions –first to the Sacred Mount and then to the Aventine Hill – obtained the establishment of the tribunate of the plebs. This magistracy, Cicero shows, came to represent the people's liberty, as it was purposely set up to counterbalance the power of the consuls as well as to diminish the supremacy of the senate, in the active pursuit of the people's interests (as, initially, by the enactment of legislation that alleviated the pressure of debt on the people).[6] This allowed the commonwealth to achieve that balance of rights, duties and functions that provided the magistrates with enough power, the counsel of the eminent citizens with enough influence, and the people with enough liberty, to render the commonwealth stable.[7]

It follows that in the *De re publica* Cicero assigns an essential function to the tribunate of the plebs as one of the institutional tools whereby the people were enabled to exercise a certain degree of political participation. It was this participation, however constrained by the numerous limitations inherent in the very nature of the magistracy (such as its collegiality, its temporary limit to one year and, most of all, the people's entrusting the enactment of their wishes to the good will of an individual), that acted as *conditio sine qua non* for the preservation of the citizens' liberty, and as such provided the people with the institutional means to exercise their rights of management of their own property, the commonwealth. Since, at their most basic level, the powers of the tribunate were universally understood as a necessary means to guarantee the status of liberty, even the fiercest denouncers of its ills never proposed the abolition of this magistracy *tout court*. As I shall discuss later, they debated the limitations that should be imposed on its powers, but never its very existence.

The third and most important means to guarantee the liberty of the citizens as well as that of the commonwealth is the right to *suffragium*. Considering Scipio's definition of *res publica* in Book 1 and his constitutional considerations in Book 3, it is apparent that, by providing the people with a certain degree of political participation, the citizens' right to vote guaranteed that the people were de facto owners of their own

---

[5] Cic. *rep.* 2.53–4.   [6] Cic. *rep.* 2.57–8.   [7] Cic. *rep.* 2.58.

property, which they could administer as they wished – in other words, were the sovereign power in the commonwealth.

Claiming that the mixed and balanced constitution was the best form of government, as it preserved the liberty and the splendour of the commonwealth, Cicero attributes the reason for its superiority to two main factors. First, this form of government is the only one that is truly fair; and second, by virtue of its very fairness, it is the most stable: 'for there should be a supreme and royal element in the commonwealth, some power also ought to be granted to the leading citizens, and certain matters should be left to the judgment and desires of the masses. Such a constitution, in the first place, offers in a high decree a sort of equality (*aequabilitatem quandam magnam*), which is the thing free men can hardly do without for any considerable length of time, and, secondly, it has stability.'[8]

This stability, Scipio continues, finds its roots in the very notion of *aequabilitas*, since 'there is no reason for a change when every citizen is firmly established in his own station (*in suo quisque est gradu firmiter collocatus*)' (1.69). This is best exemplified by the description of the Servian centuriate system, which divided the people into five classes of census in such a way as to ensure that 'the greatest number of votes belonged not to the common people, but to the rich' – upholding the principle, which ought always to be adhered to in a commonwealth, that 'the greatest number should not have the greatest power' (2.39). However, Scipio underlines that in this system it was very important that the large majority of citizens was not deprived of their right to vote, as this would have been tyrannical – that is, it would have deprived them of their liberty.[9] Servius' organisation should therefore be praised, since, on the one hand, it guaranteed that 'no one was deprived of the suffrage, [while, on the other, it ensured that] the majority of votes was in the hands of those to whom the highest welfare of the commonwealth was the most

---

[8] Cic. *rep.* 1.69. On *aequabilitas* see E. Fantham, '*Aequabilitas* in Cicero's Political Theory and the Greek Tradition of Proportional Justice', *Classical Quarterly* 23 (1973), pp. 285–90, who interprets *aequitas* as equality that falls short of a higher concept of fairness. A. R. Dyck, 'On the Interpretation of Cicero *De re publica*', *Classical Quarterly* 48 (1998), pp. 564–8, underlines that what distinguishes *aequitas* from *aequabilitas* is not a higher or lower concept of fairness, but rather that the former is the description of a specific situation (*aequitas* [*sc. honorum*]), while the latter is a principle of governance. Contrast the commentary of J. E. Zetzel (ed.), *Cicero De re publica: Selections* (Cambridge: Cambridge University Press, 1995) ad loc. Later references to *aequabilitas* in the *De re publica* (1.69, 2.42, 2.43, 2.57, 2.62) clearly suggest the proportional equality of the mixed constitution.

[9] *Superbus* is the typical quality of a tyrant that often refers to him almost by metonymy. See Y. Baraz, 'From Vice to Virtue: The Denigration and Rehabilitation of *Superbia* in Ancient Rome', in I. Sluiter and R. M. Rosen (eds.), *Kakos: Badness and Anti-Value in Classical Antiquity* (Leiden and Boston: Brill, 2008), pp. 365–97.

important'.[10] Informed by the Pythagorean ideal of *logismos* as elaborated by Archytas of Tarantum, Scipio's ideal form of government embodied the ideal of both corrective and distributive justice. On the one hand, geometric equality guaranteed that those who had more at stake in the commonwealth were also in a position of political predominance. On the other, arithmetic proportion ensured that everyone was equally entitled to vote – that is, everyone possessed equally the most basic political right, which allows them to play a role in the management and administration of the people's property, the commonwealth.[11]

By virtue of this combination of corrective and distributive justice, Cicero guarantees that at the heart of the best form of commonwealth lies a fundamental recognition of popular sovereignty. The powers of this sovereignty are to be entrusted to an elected aristocracy, which will conduct the affairs of the people whilst keeping in mind the common advantage and in accordance with a common sense of justice – Scipio's requirements for the formation of a *populus* (1.41–3).[12] As in Polybius, therefore, in Cicero's *De re publica* the best form of government is a mixed and balanced constitution whose equilibrium favours the preponderance of the aristocratic element, as it confers upon the senate, its institutional body, the administration and management of its own property.[13] In this form of government, the people, the ultimate repository of sovereignty, choose those to whom they entrust the management of their own property, whose duty will be to administer it on behalf and in the interests of the people (1.42).[14]

In the *De legibus*, which Cicero had begun if not to compose, then at least to conceive, in the late 50s,[15] Cicero had set himself the task of providing the code of law that should govern the best form of government

---

[10] Cic. *rep.* 2.40. Similarly Livy 1.43.10; Dion. Hal. *Ant. Rom.* 4.19.3.

[11] Even in the monarchical period, the people are described as playing a crucial role in electing the kings: see Cic. *rep.* 2.25, 31, 33, 35, 37–8; cf. 2.23, 43. On the historical development of Book 2 see T. J. Cornell, 'Cicero on the Origins of Rome', in J. A. North and J. G. F. Powell (eds.), *Cicero's Republic* (London: Institute of Classical Studies, 2001), pp. 41–56.

[12] Schofield, 'Cicero's definition of *res publica*'; Atkins, 'Cicero', pp. 492–3.

[13] On Polybius see Arena, *Libertas*, pp. 89–97.

[14] The most explicit notion of the people entrusting the administration of their own property to a group of people is in the passage in support of aristocracy as the best form of government at 1.51. Cf. Cic. *Sest.* 137.

[15] On the date of composition see P. L. Schmidt, *Die Abfassungzeit der Ciceros Schrift über die Gesetze* (Rome: Centro di Studi Ciceroniani, 1969); A. Grilli, 'Data e senso del *De legibus* di Cicerone', *Parola del Passato* 45 (1990), pp. 175–87; A. R. Dyck, *A Commentary on Cicero, De legibus* (Ann Arbor: University of Michigan Press, 2004), pp. 5–7; and S. Pittia, 'La Dimension utopique du traité Cicéronien *De legibus*', in C. Carsana and M. T. Schettino (eds.), *Utopia e utopie nel pensiero storico antico* (Rome: L'Erma di Bretschneider, 2008), pp. 27–48.

described by Scipio in the *De re publica*. As Ferrary notes, Cicero's explicit intention in the *De legibus* is to provide the complementary treatment which Tubero requests from Scipio at the end of the second book of the *De re publica*, to describe 'by what training, customs or laws (*qua disciplina, quibus moribus aut legibus*) we shall be able to establish or to preserve the kind of commonwealth you yourself recommend' (2.64).[16]

In the *De legibus*, Cicero replies to Quintus' comments that his law code concerning religion (Book 2) and magistracies (Book 3) almost coincide with the actual laws of Rome – albeit with a few innovations. He responds that 'since Scipio in my former work on the Republic offered a convincing proof that our early commonwealth was the best in the world, we must provide that ideal commonwealth with laws that are in harmony with its character' (2.23).[17] As a result it is natural to infer that those institutional provisions that Cicero lays out in Book 3 of the *De legibus*, usually referred to as *de magistratibus*, are those necessary to implement and maintain aristocratic prevalence in the mixed and balanced constitution delineated by Scipio in the *De re publica*. It is therefore surprising to observe that, of those rights considered essential to the preservation of the liberty of the citizens as well as of the commonwealth, those belonging to the tribunes of the plebs and the citizens' right to *suffragium* come to be the subject of significant reforms which ultimately altered their deepest political significance. In addition, Cicero introduces a number of very important reforms concerning the censors and senate that strengthen further the political power of the elite. To understand these reforms, we must first turn to Cicero's intellectual debt to Plato as well as the immediate intellectual and political context of contemporary Roman debates about the censorship.

III

In seeking to understand how Cicero transformed the mixed and balanced constitution described by Scipio, it is useful to observe the role played by Plato's *Laws* as a model for Cicero's *De legibus*. Cicero openly declares that he is following Plato's example: 'I think I should follow the same course as Plato, who was at the same time a very learned man and the greatest of all philosophers, and who wrote a book about the Republic

[16] Ferrary, 'The Statesman'. On the relation between the two theoretical works see J. G. F. Powell, 'Were Cicero's Laws the Laws of Cicero's *Republic*?' in North and Powell (eds.), *Cicero's Republic*, pp. 17–40.

[17] See also Cic. *leg.* 3.12 on the laws *de magistratibus* as a reflection of the commonwealth described by Scipio in the *De re publica*.

first, and then in a separate treatise described its Laws' (2.14).[18] When also declaring his independence from Plato (*plave esse vellem meus*) (2.17), Cicero de facto declares that he adopted Plato's *Laws* as a source of inspiration and point of reference but did not follow it slavishly.[19] As Annas clearly shows, despite the obvious differences between the two texts, not only does Cicero refer to Plato's *Laws* for points of detail, but also has it in the background all the way through his work. Alongside other influences, it inspires some of the most fundamental assumptions of the *De legibus*.[20]

It follows that it will not be surprising that the reform of the right to *suffragium*, which plays a vital role in the reconfiguration of the mixed and balanced constitution with aristocratic predominance into a different constitutional entity, and which has long puzzled commentators, may have its inspirational origin in Plato's elaborate system of election of the *nomophulakes*, the guardians of the laws.[21] To elect them, Plato establishes a rather complicated method which combines a written vote with one that is publicly known. It is worth reporting Plato's text in full:

The election shall be held in whatever temple the state deems most venerable, and every one shall carry his vote to the altar of the God, writing down on a tablet the name of the person for whom he votes, and his father's name, and his tribe, and ward; and at the side he shall write his own name in like manner. Anyone who pleases may take away any tablet which he does not think properly filled up, and exhibit it in the Agora for a period of not less than thirty days. The tablets which are judged to be first, to the number of 300, shall be shown by the magistrates to the whole city, and the citizens shall in like manner select from these the candidates whom they prefer; and this second selection, to the number of 100, shall be again exhibited to the citizens; in the third, let anyone who pleases select whom he pleases out of the 100, passing between slain victims,

---

[18]   The other places where Plato is mentioned in *De legibus* are 1.15; 2.6, 14, 16, 38, 39, 41, 67, 68; 3.1, 5, 32. See J. Galbiati[us], *De fontibus M. Tulii Ciceronis librorum qui manserunt de R.P. et de legibus quaestiones* (Milan: U. Hoepli, 1916), esp. pp. 263–87; T. B. De Graff, 'Plato in Cicero', *Classical Philology* 35 (1940), pp. 143–53 for the complete list in Cicero's works. See also P. Boyancé, 'Le Platonisme à Rome: Platon et Cicéron', in *Actes du Congrès de Tours et de Poitiers* (Paris: Les Belles Lettres, 1954), pp. 195–221 and A. A. Long, 'Cicero's Plato and Aristotle', in J. G. F. Powell (ed.), *Cicero the Philosopher* (Oxford: Oxford University Press, 1995) pp. 37–62 for Cicero's attitude towards Plato.

[19]   On the relationship between Plato's *Laws* and Cicero's *De legibus* see more recently J. Annas, 'Plato's *Laws* and Cicero's *De legibus*', in M. Schofield (ed.), *Aristotle, Plato and Pythagoreanism in the First Century BC* (Cambridge: Cambridge University Press, 2013), pp. 206–24 and I. Gildenhardt, 'Of Cicero's Plato: Fictions, Forms, Foundations', in ibid., pp. 225–75.

[20]   Cic. *leg.* 2.45 and Pl. *Laws* 955e–956b; Cic. *leg.* 2.67–8 and Pl. *Laws* 958d–e; Cic. *leg.* 3.5 and Pl. *Laws* 701b–c; Cic. *leg.* 2.41 and Pl. *Laws* 716d–717a. See Annas, 'Plato's *Laws*'. *Contra* Rawson, 'Interpretation', p. 343.

[21]   C. Nicolet, 'Cicéron, Platon et le vote secret', *Historia* 19 (1970), pp. 39–66. *Contra* Rawson, 'Interpretation', pp. 351–2 and Ferrary, 'The Statesman'.

and let them choose for magistrates and proclaim the seven and thirty who have the greatest number of votes.[22]

As Nicolet emphasises, the most remarkable aspect of this complex system is not so much its three stages, criticised by Aristotle,[23] as the adoption of a voting tablet on which the names of the candidate as well as the name of the voter should appear, and the publicity to which the tablet, placed on the altar for a month, should be exposed to allow its full examination. This Platonic passage and Cicero's reform in *De legibus* are the only two instances of this peculiar combination of written and public vote. More importantly here, though, the justification that Plato adduces for this system of election is echoed in Cicero's reasoning for his institutional adaptations. Plato claims that 'the mode of election which has been described is in a mean between monarchy and democracy, and such a mean the state ought always to observe' (756b). This mean, which alone preserves cities from civil seditions, Plato continues, can be achieved by combining two different notions of equality, the arithmetic, which apportions honours on the basis of number, and the geometric, 'which is better and of a higher kind . . . and it gives to the greater more, and to the inferior less and in proportion to the nature of each; and, above all, greater honour always to the greater virtue, and to the less less . . . And this is justice, and is ever the true principle of states.' However, Plato laments, although the legislator should always follow this latter notion of equality, in order to avoid internal dissension it is necessary, at times, for the law-giver to grant some concessions to the ideal of arithmetic equality, which 'although it is an infraction of the perfect and strict rule of justice' will nevertheless preserve harmony, *philia*, within the commonwealth. Given the concession of the equality of lot, associated with liberty, and the recognition of virtue, associated with wisdom, this political system will achieve its goal of implementing the harmonious mean between a monarchical and a democratic constitution.

These are indeed the principles of *politeia* construction that Plato has previously argued, in his historical survey of Book 3, are necessarily to be maintained if a political community wants to achieve health and stability.[24] In his historical excursus, whose function is to show the kind of

---

[22] Pl. *Laws* 753c–d. On *nomophulakes* and other institutional arrangements see G. R. Morrow, *Plato's Cretan City: A Historical Interpretation of the* Laws (Princeton: Princeton University Press 1960), esp. pp. 195–214, and R. F. Stalley, *An Introduction to Plato's* Laws (Oxford: Blackwell, 1983), esp. pp. 112–20.

[23] Arist. *Pol.* 1266a 1–30.

[24] M. Schofield, 'The *Laws*' Two Projects', in C. Bobonich (ed.), *Plato's Laws: A Critical Guide* (Cambridge: Cambridge University Press, 2010), pp. 12–28.

constitutional system that could be applied generally to political communities, Plato shows that when Sparta, Persia and Athens were most successful (Sparta at the time of Lycurgus, Persia under Cyrus and Athens at the time of the Persian invasion), each had a political system that embodied wisdom, liberty and friendship in a balanced manner. Although they differed in the way in which each system mixed wisdom and liberty, these three historical examples attest that the success of a political community in any historical circumstance is attained when its constitution succeeds in achieving social harmony (*philia*) by virtue of its balance between wise authority (*phronesis*) and popular liberty (*eleutheria*).[25]

The idea that in a political organisation that gives prominence to the wisdom of the senate it is necessary to concede something to the notion of arithmetic equality in order to preserve social harmony is paralleled in Cicero's justification for his compliance with the use of the *tabella* and the preservation of the tribunate of the plebs.[26] Both institutions are ultimately tolerated as a necessary concession to the liberty of the people. The reforms *de magistratibus* of Book 3 of the *De legibus* allow Cicero to find a form of conciliation between the values of *auctoritas* and *libertas*, identified respectively in the *De re publica* as the aristocratic and the democratic element. As he says, commenting on the aim of his reform of voting rights, this measure aims at reconciling the *auctoritas* of the *boni*, the members of the elite, and the granting of liberty(or at least an appearance of *libertas*) to the people, so as to eliminate any reason for *contentio* (3.38).

Discussing his law concerning the legislative power of the senate, Cicero makes an important statement: 'If the senate is recognised as the leader of public policy (*senatus dominus sit publici consilii*), and all other orders defend its decrees, and are willing to allow the highest order to conduct the government by its wisdom, then this compromise, by which supreme power is granted to the people (*potestas in populo*) and actual authority to the senate (*auctoritas in senatu*) will make possible

---

[25] On Sparta, Pl. *Laws* 3.691d–2b and 693b–4b, and cf. 701d; on Athens, Pl. *Laws* 698a–9d and 700a; on Persia, Pl. *Laws* 3.694b–6b and 3.697c–8a. The most interesting parallel with Rome is given by Athens, or at least Plato's representation of Athens here: see Cic. *Cluent.* 146: 'We are slaves of the laws so that we may be free.' For an analysis of this historical excursus as a response to Thucydides see the illuminating piece by C. Farrar, 'Plato, Thucydides, and the Athenian Politeia', in M. Lane and V. Harte (eds.), *Politeia in Greek and Roman Philosophy* (Cambridge: Cambridge University Press, 2013), pp. 32–56.

[26] On the issue of necessity for these institutions see J. L. Ferrary, 'L'Archéologie du *De re publica* (2.2.4–37.63): Cicéron entre Polybe et Platon', *Journal of Roman Studies* 74 (1984), pp. 87–98.

the maintenance of that balanced and harmonious constitution (*moderatus et concors civitatis status*) which I have described.'[27] Through his reforms he has transformed Scipio's mixed and balanced constitution based on 'an equitable balance in the state of rights and duties and responsibilities (*aequabilis compensatio iuris et officii et muneris*) so that there is enough power in the hands of the magistrates (*potestatis satis in magistratibus*), enough authority in the judgement of the aristocrats (*auctoritatis in principum consilio*) and enough liberty in the people (*libertatis in populo*)',[28] and thereby produced a commonwealth where there must be a compromise which guarantees that *potestas* is granted to the people (*potestas in populo*) and actual authority to the senate (*auctoritas in senatu*), as this will make possible the maintenance of the balanced and harmonious constitution (*moderatus et concors civitatis status*).

Although both passages refer to the same ideal form of commonwealth,[29] in the *De legibus* the third pole (the magistrates) of the trinomial of senate, assembly and magistrates in the *De re publica* disappears. The notion of *potestas* originally associated with the magistrates is reassigned to the people, whose ideal of *libertas*, in turn, is subsumed under this heading.[30] Although commentators have often interpreted this as Cicero abandoning Polybius' tripartite model to embrace the binomial form *populus-senatus* much more in line with Roman political reality, when read in its full political and intellectual context this binary reading of the Roman mixed and balanced constitution is better interpreted as a product of Cicero's debt to Plato. Through a system of calibrated reforms that attempts to recapture the spirit and informing principles of Plato's institutional arrangements in the *Laws*, Cicero is trying to establish a form of government that embodies Plato's idea of the necessary principles for a healthy and stable commonwealth in the *Laws*: wisdom, liberty and friendship.[31]

Accordingly, and in line with the principles that for Plato in the *Laws* should be active to ensure the greatest success to a constitution, Cicero claims that the best possible form of government is preserved in harmony (*concordia/philia*) when it takes the form of a mixed constitution, where the *auctoritas* of the senate, as the repository of public wisdom

---

[27] Cic. *leg.* 3.28.   [28] Cic. *rep.* 2.57.

[29] *Temperatio, moderatus* and *concors* (Cic. *leg.* 3.28) are also all qualifying traits of Scipio's ideal form of commonwealth, see Cic. *rep.* 1.45, 2.69. Cf. 1.69.

[30] Ferrary, 'L'Archéologie', p. 92.

[31] Pl. *Laws* 693b. M. Schofield, 'Friendship and Justice in the *Laws*', in G. Boys-Stones, D. El Murr and C. Gill (eds.),*The Platonic Art of Philosophy* (Cambridge: Cambridge University Press, 2013), pp. 283–98.

(*consilium/phronesis*), and the *potestas* of the people (that is, expression of the active sense of *libertas/eleutheria*) are in balance with one another.

However, the concessions to the democratic notion of liberty and arithmetic equality in Plato's *Laws* constitute a genuine compromise, as nearly all magistrates were chosen through elections involving the whole citizen body. The elaborate system of election, especially with regard to the selection of the *nomophulakes* mentioned above and of those responsible for auditing the accounts, is a sign of the importance that Plato attaches to the problem of political participation and his commitment to it.[32] Although in Plato's *Laws* the people are not sovereign, as only the *nous* could count as such, and do not administer power, in the Platonic political system the citizens are nevertheless responsible for the selection of those considered competent to hold a magistracy. As we shall discuss later, in Cicero any concession made to the people's liberty is immediately deprived of any practical significance. Thus, whilst the *politeia* of Plato's *Laws* could be fairly described as 'an aristocracy with the approval of the people', borrowing Plato's expression from the *Menexenus*,[33] the institutional arrangements described in Cicero's *De legibus* implement an aristocracy with a formal, but ultimately specious, popular approval, since the aristocracy preserves the right to interfere with the people's choice. If Cicero could show, as he emphasises at 3.28, that the people gladly accept this interference, and that they spontaneously grant and support the leadership of the senate, it would follow that the institutional arrangements of the *De legibus* would represent a tighter aristocracy in essence still in line with the political system described in the *De re publica*.

However, as is apparent from the discussion of the role of the tribunate and the right to vote, which we shall discuss later, the people were not prepared to renounce willingly those rights that guaranteed their true liberty. Hence Cicero elaborated an institutional escamotage to ensure an appearance of this value to appease the people in the hope of preserving social cohesion. The form of government that resulted from the implementation of Cicero's reforms *de magistratibus* was no longer Scipio's mixed and balanced constitution of the *De re publica*.

IV

In trying to assess why Cicero modified the institutional structures of his ideal commonwealth, it is important to consider the condition of

---

[32] A. Laks, 'The Laws', in Rowe and Schofield (eds.), *Cambridge History of Greek and Roman Political Thought*, pp. 278–84.

[33] Ibid., p. 281 emphasises that citizens choose their magistrates.

political chaos, violence and anarchy of the late 50s in Rome. At the very beginning of 52 BC Clodius, Cicero's personal and political enemy, had been murdered and Milo, a representative of the traditional aristocracy, was accused of his assassination by means of violent gangs; the curia had been burnt; no consuls had been elected and no interrex appointed; as a result, no meeting of the senate had been convened and no regular political transactions had been carried out. It was a situation of actual anarchy.[34] It is not implausible to imagine that within this political climate Cicero, who at that time was writing the *De legibus* and meditating on Plato's *Laws*, was induced to elaborate, at least theoretically, a political system that could guarantee the curbing of popular forces.

However, Cicero's elaboration in the *De legibus* of a very intricate institutional framework that guarantees the prevalence of the aristocratic component of the commonwealth is not merely an ideological reflex of his senatorial prejudice before the mob violence of the 50s.[35] Despite the limitations caused by its fragmentary state, the *De legibus* stands out as a rather complex theoretical work that actively intervenes in the political and intellectual debates of the time. It appears evident that by the 50s many members of the Roman elite shared a general perception of the decline of the traditional *res publica*. One of the main points of concern, which was the subject of extensive debate and attempted reforms at the time, was the function of the censorship – in Cicero's own words, the most illustrious of Roman magistracies. In the 80s Sulla had seriously weakened its role, not only by introducing a certain number of members in the senate at his own will, but also by increasing the number of quaestors and praetors, that is ultimately of ex-magistrates who were customarily accorded a seat in the senate. Given the traditionally capped number of senatorial seats, the increased total of magistrates, therefore, accentuated the automatic mechanism of accession to the senate, while in the process further curbed the censors' powers. If the censorship of 70 BC tried to reassert its role by implementing an unprecedented severity that resulted in the expulsion of sixty-four senators and, in the process, terrified the elite, the censorships that followed were either particularly problematic or ineffectual, to the extent that the successful elections of the censors in 50 BC was hailed as a return to the *mos maiorum*.[36]

---

[34] For a detailed account of the events of 52 BC see J. Ruebel, 'The Trial of Milo in 52 BC: A Chronological Study', *Transactions of the American Philological Association* 109 (1979), pp. 231–49.

[35] On mob violence in Rome see J. L. David, 'Les Règles de la violence dans les assemblées populaires de la République romaine', *Politica Antica* 3 (2013), pp. 11–29.

[36] A. E. Astin, 'Censorship in the Late Republic', *Historia* 34 (1984), pp. 175–99; G. Clemente, 'Cicerone, Clodio e la censura: la politica e l'ideale', in E. Dovere (ed.)

It is therefore relatively unsurprising that, in an attempt to address a situation of perceived institutional decline, Clodius presented a law concerned with a reform of the censorship during his tribunate in 58 BC. This law, known as the *lex Clodia de notione censoria*, imposed a limitation on the discretionary powers of the censors regarding the *lectio senatus* by establishing the requirement of a formal accusation (or a preliminary sentence) on the part of both censors, who were explicitly required to act in concert with one another.[37] According to Tatum's interpretation, this innovative reform established for the first time the senators' right to hear charges against them and provided them with an opportunity to defend themselves before the censors could strike them out of the *album senatorium*. Acting like a 'prudent legislator carrying a timely practical scheme',[38] in 58 BC Clodius addressed the same concerns about the censorship that Cicero had voiced in his defence of Cluentius in 66 BC.[39]

It may well be that, as Tatum argues, Clodius' first and more immediate aim was to win over political support amongst the senators who were anxious at the excessive powers of the censors and might feel threatened by a potential expulsion. The law undoubtedly diminished the *censoria potestas* by asking the censors to articulate a full justification for their decision on a senatorial expulsion and by forcing them to sit through the defendant's arguments and the reactions of the public, which attended these newly instituted *iudicia*. However, at least in ideological terms, this reform also established a very important principle, whose importance did not escape Cicero. By severely curbing the censors' power over the composition of the senate (*lectio senatus*), Clodius' measure reinforced a principle that in the first century BC had become, at least partially, a reality: the idea that the senate had to be, and actually was, composed of individuals who had acquired the right to sit through popular elections to their magistracy.[40] From Clodius' measure it followed that exclusions from the senate had to be justified and could no longer be left in the hands of those magistrates, the censors, who were traditionally perceived

---

Munuscula: Scritti in ricordo di Luigi Almirante (Naples: Edizioni Scientifiche Italiane, 2010), pp. 51–73.

[37] On Clodius' law: Asc. *Pis.* 8; cf. Sch. Bob. 132 St and Dio Cass. 38.13. See also J. Tatum, 'The *Lex Clodia de censoria notione*', *Classical Philology* 85 (1990), pp. 34–43; J. Tatum, *The Patrician Tribune: Publius Clodius Pulcher* (Chapel Hill and London: University of North Carolina Press, 1999), pp 133–5; Clemente, 'Cicerone, Clodio e la censura'.

[38] Tatum, 'The Lex Clodia', p. 41.

[39] On the analogy between Cicero's arguments in the *pro Cluentio* and Clodius' reform see Clemente, 'Cicerone, Clodio e la censura'.

[40] For a conceptualisation of magistracies as a *beneficium* received from the people see J. L. Ferrary, 'Le idee politiche a Roma nell'epoca repubblicana', in L. Firpo (ed.), *Storia delle idee politiche economiche e sociali* (Turin: Unione Tipografico Edizione Torinese, 1982), pp. 724–804 and Arena, *Libertas*, pp. 61–2.

as the repository of the most aristocratic values.[41] In other words, the underlining principle behind Clodius' reform was an affirmation of the fundamental ideal of popular sovereignty.[42] Cicero was aware that the working of the censorship had been severely hampered by Sulla's reforms as well as by those laws that in the late second century had established the loss of senatorial *dignitas* and exclusion from the list of judges as a result of a conviction in a *iudicium publicum*.[43] Most of all, he fully understood that, if the abolition of the censorial *lectio senatus* was now a matter of fact, Clodius' measure, and those institutional developments of which it was a result, conceptually placed an emphasis on the notion of popular sovereignty to the detriment of traditional aristocratic values. This is the reason why in his code of law he inserts the initially puzzling law according to which 'the senate should be composed of ex-magistrates' (3.27), while immediately registering his displeasure at such a measure. It is a *popularis* law, he claims, that establishes the principle that political power lies with the people who confer it on individuals through elections. It is manifest that here Cicero is intervening in a contemporary debate that is concerned not only with the institutional nature of the powers of the censors, but also with different ways of conceptualising the *res publica*.

By making the censorship the magistracy subject to the most innovative reforms in the *De legibus*, Cicero is clearly responding to a state of affairs concerned with the malfunctioning of the censorship, while also directly opposing Clodius' law on the censors, which was rather revealingly repealed in 52 BC, the time when Cicero was at work on the *De legibus*.[44]

However, although 'some of the major innovations Cicero proposes can be seen as a direct response to Clodius' program',[45] behind the personal animosity of Cicero's personal relationship with Clodius, manifested in the hyperbolic comments against his measure,[46] lay the conceptualisation of deeply different notions of *res publica*. Opposed to the notion of the prevalence of the popular will within the commonwealth expressed

---

[41] Astin, 'Censorship'; J. Suolahti, *The Roman Censors: A Study on Social Structure* (Helsinki: Suomalainen Tiedeakatemia, 1963).

[42] For a discussion of this tradition of thought in Rome see Arena, *Libertas*, pp. 116–68.

[43] See M. H. Crawford (ed.), *Roman Statutes*, 2 vols. (London: Institute of Classical Studies, 1996), I, 98 ff. on the Gracchan *lex repetundarum*. See Asc. *Corn.* 69C on the *lex Cassia* of 104 BC that established the ineligibility of those condemned in a *iudicium populi* or of those whose *imperium* had been abrogated by popular vote.

[44] On Cicero's concerns over the functioning of this magistracy see Cic. *Cluent.* 119–35 and *rep.* 4.6. On the reasons for its repeal see Dio 40.57.1–3; Cic. *Att.* 4.16.14. Cf. Cic *Att.* 4.9.1 and 6.1.17.

[45] Dyck, *Commentary*, p. 17.

[46] Cic. *Sest.* 55; *Pis.* 9; *Dom.* 130; *Har. Resp.* 58; *Prov. Cons.* 46.

through elections, in the *De legibus* Cicero tries to re-establish the idea of the aristocratic *mos* as the guiding principle of moral nature that should govern the senators and the magistrates, and hence the *res publica*. It follows that, in trying to counteract the censors' loss of the *lectio senatus* based on the *cura morum*, Cicero implements a series of reforms whose aim is to re-establish firmly the censors' duty of assessment of senators.[47]

V

Having examined the political and intellectual context of Cicero's reforms of Book 3 of the *De legibus*, I now turn to analyse their nature and political significance.

Whilst in the *De legibus* the right to *provocatio* remained essentially unaltered from the *De re publica* and very much in line with Roman practices,[48] the tribunate of the plebs was the subject of a rather more complex treatment in the *De legibus*. In terms of constitutional prerogatives, strictly speaking, this magistracy does not seem to differ from its traditional functions, adumbrated also in the *De re publica*.[49] However, replying to Quintus, who is represented reciting the traditional arguments against the evils of the tribunate of the plebs, Cicero (apparently out of character) defends this magistracy on two grounds: first, the tribunate is not evil in itself, but rather its nature depends on the individuals who assume it; second, it is so dear to the people that it could not be combated (*nec perniciosam et ita popularem, ut non posset obsisti*) (3.26). Additionally, he claims that this magistracy serves the function of restraining the more cruel and violent power of the people (*vis populi multo saevior multoque vehementior*), by providing it with an institutional channel that will inevitably deprive it of its revolutionary force (3.23). However, provided

---

[47] A. E. Astin, 'Cicero and the Censorship', *Classical Philology* 30 (1985), pp. 233–9, esp. p. 236.

[48] Cic. *leg.* 3.9 and 27. On the suspension of this right *domi militiae* see A. H. M. Jones, *The Criminal Courts of the Roman Republic and Principate* (Oxford: Blackwell, 1972), p. 2; A. W. Lintott, 'Provocatio: From the Struggle of the Orders to the Principate', *Aufstieg und Niedergang der römischen Welt* 1.2 (1972), pp. 226–67, at pp. 251 ff.; A. W. Lintott, *The Roman Constitution* (Oxford: Clarendon Press, 1999), pp. 225–32; and F. Fontanella, 'Introduzione al *De legibus* di Cicerone.II', *Athenaeum* 86 (1998), pp. 181–208, esp. pp. 191–5.

[49] Cic. *leg.* 3.9. On Cicero's analysis of the tribunate of the plebs see L. Perelli, 'Note sul tribunato della plebe nella riflessione ciceroniana', *Quaderni di Storia* 10 (1979), pp. 285–303; Perelli, *Il pensiero politico di Cicerone*, pp. 78 ff.; K. M. Girardet, 'Ciceros Urteil über die Entstehung des Tribunates als Instituion der römischen Verfassung', in A. Lippold (ed.), *Festgabe J. Straub* (Bonn: Nikolaus Himmelmman, 1977), pp. 179–200; Ferrary, 'L'Archéologie du *De re publica*', pp. 87 ff.; and Fontanella, 'Introduzione al *De legibus*', pp. 205–7.

that there are institutional means to restrain this magistracy's power – such as the tribunate's collegiality and the power of *intercessio* that any tribune could use to halt any measure perceived to be detrimental to the commonwealth – the true reason why the tribunate should be accepted is because it provides 'a measure of compromise which made the more humble believe that they were accorded equality with the nobility (*temperamentum, quo tenuiores cum principibus aequari se putarent*), and such a compromise was the only salvation of the commonwealth' (3.24). The tribunate, in Cicero's opinion, fulfilled three functions: first, it provided the people with the impression that they possessed the same amount of rights as the nobility, thereby guaranteeing that the people no longer fought for their rights (*plebes de suo iure periculosas contentiones nullas facit* 3.25). Second, it provided the people with a certain amount of liberty, necessary de facto and not only in words (*re non verbo*) for any constitution that was not a monarchy. Third, and very importantly, it ensured that 'this liberty was granted in such a manner that the people were induced by many excellent provisions (*multis institutis*) to yield to the authority of the nobles (*quae tamen sic data est, ut multis institutis praeclarissimis adduceretur, ut auctoritati principum cederet*)' (3.25). Thus, whilst in the *De re publica* the tribunate of the plebs is represented as a plebeian conquest which constituted an important step towards the creation of a mixed and balanced constitution, by providing an essential counterbalance to the power of the senate and the consuls, in the *De legibus* the same magistracy is perceived as the necessary means (*quid necessarium*, 3.26) for providing the people with the bare minimum of liberty required in any non-monarchical commonwealth, whose effective outcome is the people's yielding to the *auctoritas* of the nobility.[50]

Most interestingly, Cicero uses the same argument in support of his reform regarding the citizens' right to vote: 'when elective, judicial, and legislative acts of the people are performed by vote, the voting shall not be concealed from citizens of high rank, and shall be free to the common people (*nota esse optumatibus, populo libera*)' (3.10). As previously in the discussion of the tribunate of the plebs, although initially Cicero appears to disagree with his interlocutors in the dialogue, Quintus and Atticus, he then claims to share their view that the introduction of the secret ballot has undermined the *auctoritas* of the nobility, and that 'no method of voting could be better than that of open declaration (*nihil ut fuerit in suffragiis voce melius*)' (3.33).[51]

---

[50] On the provisions that deprive the tribunes of their powers see Ferrary, 'Le idee politiche a Roma', p. 785.
[51] On the debate about secret voting see Arena, *Libertas*, pp. 56–60. See also C. Wirszubski, *Libertas as a Political Idea at Rome* (Cambridge: Cambridge University Press, 1950),

However, Cicero argues that since the people hold the *tabella* so dear, the best possible voting measure is that 'the people have their ballots as safeguard of their liberty, but with the provision that these ballots are to be shown and voluntarily exhibited to any of our best and most eminent citizens, so that the people may enjoy liberty also in this very privilege of honourably winning the favour of the aristocracy (*habeat sane populus tabellam quasi vindicem libertatis. . . ut in eo sit ipso libertas, in quo populo potestas honeste bonis gratificandi datur*) (3.39).[52] By this system Cicero guarantees that a certain amount of *libertas* is granted to the people, but that this is done in such a way as to ensure that the aristocracy shall have great influence and the opportunity to use it (*ita libertatem istam largior populo, ut auctoritate et valeant et utantur boni*) (3.38). The aim of the reform is, on the one hand, to provide that people retain the written vote of which they cannot be deprived, since they find great satisfaction in possessing it; and, on the other, to ensure that at the same time they are governed by the influence and favour of the nobility (*auctoritas et gratia*) to which, once free from bribery, they will submit (3.39). 'Hence this law grants the appearance of liberty, preserves the influence of the aristocracy, and removes the causes of dispute within the commonwealth (*quam ob rem lege nostra libertatis species datur, auctoritas bonorum retinetur, contentionis causa tollitur*)' (3.39). Hence, as in the case of the tribunate, in the discussion of the reform of the right to vote the *De legibus* maintains that a certain amount of *libertas* has to be granted. However, this liberty will consist in gratifying the members of the nobility and following their *auctoritas*.

The significance of liberty in the *De legibus* is very different from that articulated in *De re publica*. Although even in the *De legibus* liberty still implies an active participation by the people in the commonwealth, such participation ought to take the form of a submission to the senatorial nobility, regardless of the actual wishes of the people. Thus, as Cicero himself is prepared to admit, when the ideal of liberty contains a form of submission, it is robbed of its core meaning, the ability to live according to one's own wishes unimpaired by the arbitrary will or interference of

---

p. 50. On this passage R. F. Vishnia, 'Written Ballot, Secret Ballot and the *Iudicia Publica*: A Note on the *Leges Tabellariae* (Cicero, *De Legibus* 3.33–39)', *Klio* 90.2 (2008), pp. 334–46. For an overview on the *leges tabellariae* see F. Salerno, *Tacita Libertas: l'introduzione del voto segreto nella Roma repubblicana* (Naples: Edizioni Scientifiche Italiane, 1999).

[52] An interesting, but ultimately unconvincing, reading of this law draws a distinction between the votes of the *optimates*, which should be publicly known, and the voting of the people, which should instead be taken in secrecy: L. Troiani, 'Sulla *lex de suffragiis* in Cicerone *De legibus* III.10', *Athenaeum* 59 (1981), pp. 180–4; L. Troiani, 'Alcune considerazioni sul voto nell'antica Roma a proposito di Cic. *Leg.* III.10', *Athenaeum* 65 (1987), pp. 493–9.

someone else. What is left is simply an appearance of liberty, a *species libertatis*.

If Cicero could show that these reforms were not imposed on the people, but rather upheld by the people's own accord – that is, if he could show that the people spontaneously submitted to the *optimates* – and also that these reforms were enough to ensure that those in command adequately consulted the people's interests, then the form of commonwealth depicted in the *De legibus* would be a variation of the best form of government described by Scipio in the *De re publica*. This is to say that, if Cicero could show that his reforms *de magistratibus* would not abuse or infringe the rights of the people to administer their own property, the form of commonwealth resulting from their implementation could still be described as a mixed and balanced constitution, albeit with an even sharper aristocratic bias, 'a strengthened control from the top', in Dyck's formulation.[53]

However, it appears that Cicero is at odds with himself. He is forced to admit that the people were not favourable to any reform that interfered with these rights, to the extent that they are represented as being not only deeply attached to the tribunate of the plebs – a magistracy which, he claims, they would never let go – but that they were also unprepared to accept any reversal of the method of the written ballot to a system of oral voting.

As in the discussion of the right to vote, the difference in this regard with the *De re publica* is striking, and concerns not only the political rights of citizens. In order to strengthen the political power of the elite further, Cicero also introduces a number of important reforms concerning the censors and senate.[54] If overall these are mainly a formal implementation of the de facto situation in Rome at the time, the most innovative institutional change that he advances in the *De legibus*, which alters traditional republican practices significantly, regards the role of the censors.[55]

Alongside a reiteration of the traditional duties of the censors – such as compiling the list of citizens, and taking charge of temples, streets, aqueducts and the public treasury – Cicero makes some significant alterations, which, he claims, are necessary for the *res publica* (*rei publicae*

[53] Dyck, *Commentary*, p. 15.
[54] Alongside those discussed here see also Cic. *leg.* 3.11 and 40.
[55] It is possible that, alongside the most immediate political context, Cicero's enhanced role of the censors may have found inspiration in the role Plato assigns to the *nomophulakes* given their function of registering citizens according to their property qualifications and overseeing their moral fibre: Pl. *Laws* 6.745d–e. On the presence of this institution in many Hellenistic contemporary cities see E. Ziebarth, 'Nomophylakes', *Realencyclopädie der classischen Altertumswissenschaft* XVII.1 (1936), pp. 832–3 at p. 832.

necessariae).[56] First of all, as opposed to the customary eighteen months, 'the censors shall be in office for five years, [whilst] the other magistrates shall hold office for one year' (3.7).[57] In addition to their customary duties, 'the censors shall have charge of the official text of the laws (*censoris fidem legum custodiunto*). When officials leave office, they will refer their official acts to the censors, but will not receive exception from prosecution thereby' (3.11). The first of these two provisions is rather cryptic (*custodire fidem legum*) and seems to require that the censors should act as the Roman equivalent of the Greek *nomophulakes*, and hence not only supervise the text of the laws, as was formerly the case at Rome, but also observe men's acts and recall them to obedience to the laws (3.46). According to Cicero, at Rome there is 'no guardianship of the laws, and therefore they are whatever our clerks want them to be; we get them from the commonwealth copyists, but have no official records'. Since in Rome laws were kept both in the *Atrium Libertatis* and in the *aerarium*, it seems that Cicero places the censors in charge of the *aerarium* and refers to the need for the circulation amongst the magistrates of the official copies of laws consistent with those held in the official archives.[58] Since the Roman censors, apparently like the Greek *nomophulakes*, have to oversee the actions of individuals, it is possible to infer that Cicero is granting them the function to check the legality of the acts of the magistrates while they are in office.[59] If this were the case, the provision that poses a check on the magistrates in office would naturally lead to the next one, according to which the censors will act as preliminary auditors concerning the acts of retiring magistrates, an institutional practice of accountability calibrated along the lines of the Greek *euthune*.[60] 'Magistrates, after completing their terms, are to report and explain their official acts to these same censors, who are to render a preliminary decision in regard to them. In Greece this is attended to by publicly appointed prosecutors, but as a matter of fact it is unreasonable to expect real severity

---

[56] Cic. *leg*. 3.46. For a list of traditional duties see 3.7. See Fontanella, 'Introduzione al *De legibus*', pp. 185–6 and Dyck, *Commentary*, ad loc.

[57] On an ancient precedent within Roman tradition see Livy 4.24.5, 9.33.6; Zon. 7.19; and Suolahti, *Roman Censors*, p. 27.

[58] Rawson, 'Interpretation', pp. 353 ff. See also C. Nicolet, *La Mémoire perdue: à la recherche des archives oubliées, publiques et privées, de la Rome antique* (Paris: La Sorbonne, 1994).

[59] Fontanella, 'Introduzione al *De legibus*', p. 187 attributes the innovation to Philochorus Jacoby, *F. Gr. Hist.* 328F 64b.

[60] On Demetrius of Phalerus as Cicero's source on this institution see Keyes, 'Original Elements', p. 316. Rawson, 'Interpretation', p. 352 discusses the potential influence of Theophrastus, Aristotle and Zaleucus. For a list of Greek philosophical influence on Cicero's *de legibus* Book 3 see Cic. *leg*. 3.14.

from accusers unless they act voluntarily. For that reason it seems prefer-
able for official acts to be explained and defended before the censors,
but for the official to remain liable to the law, and to prosecution before
a regular court' (3.47). Through what appears to be a series of minor
adjustments, then, Cicero strongly reinforces the role of the censors as
an instrument of the elite's self-regulation, once again moving to deprive
the people of any real power.

As far as the reforms of the senate are concerned, the most important measure establishes the principle that 'its decrees shall be binding
(*eius decreta rata sunto*). But when an equal or higher authority than the
presiding officer shall veto a decree of the senate, it shall nevertheless
be written out and preserved' (3.10). Not only were all decisions concerning foreign policies assigned to the senate and expected to be ratified
by the people, as was traditional practice in the Republic, and all minor
magistrates expected to 'do whatsoever the senate shall decree',[61] but
also, and most importantly, all senatorial decrees were expected to have a
legally binding force on the whole community. Although it seems that, at
least in part, this was already the practice in the late Republic in matters
of religion, finance and international relations (where the content of the
senatus consulta became the subject of popular laws),[62] Cicero seems to
be more innovative and appears to grant actual legislative power to the
senate – power that could be subjected, in standard Roman practice, to
the *intercessio* of magistrates of *par* or *minor potestas* and the tribunes.[63]
Nor would this measure be significantly counterbalanced by the provision
according to which 'the senate is to consist exclusively of ex-magistrates'
(3.10 and 27). Although apparently new and *popularis* in character, in
so far as it requires that 'no one shall enter that exalted order except
by popular election' and deprives the censors of their right to choose
senators (*adlectio senatus*), this measure not only established *de iure* a de
facto state of affairs,[64] but, within the context of Cicero's legal code, was
also based on the premise that such a popular election would operate
by means of an elaborate system that, by preserving the written vote but
making it publicly known to the aristocracy, ensured the influence of the
nobility within the commonwealth (3.27). Ultimately, all the measures
concerning the senate that Cicero presents in the *De legibus* aim at

[61] Cic.*leg.* 3.10 and 6 respectively.
[62] G. Crifó, 'Attivitá normative del senato in etá repubblicana', *Bullettino dell'Istituto di Diritto Romano* 71 (1968), pp. 31–115, at pp. 52 ff. and Y. Thomas, 'Cicéron, le Sénat et les tribuns de la plebe', *Revue Historique de Droit Français et Étranger* 1.5 (1977), pp. 189–210.
[63] *Contra* Fontanella, 'Introduzione al *De legibus*', pp. 200–1 underlines Cicero's continuity with Republican customs.
[64] See Suolahti, *Censors*, pp. 25 ff. and Astin, 'Cicero and the Censorship', pp. 233 ff.

strengthening its role and rendering it the dominant power in the commonwealth.

Thus, whereas in the *De re publica* liberty is an essential means to establish a mixed and balanced constitution that is the best form of commonwealth, in the *De legibus*, through proposals for the reform of the citizens' rights to *suffragium*, the reductive interpretation of the powers of the tribunate and an enhancement of the powers of the senate and censors, Cicero transforms the value of liberty into what he himself calls 'an appearance of liberty'. It follows that not only is this form of commonwealth less stable, but it also does not uphold the ideal of *aequabilitas*, as it deprives some people of their rights in the administration of their property – in other words, it deprives them of some of the essential means to achieve and secure their status of liberty. In fact, adapting the formula used in Plato's *Menexenus* to describe the ancestral constitution of Athens, this form of commonwealth could be described as an aristocracy with (formal) approval of the people.[65] However, if one emphasises the reduction of the value of liberty to only an appearance of it, what Cicero calls the *species libertatis*, rather than the preservation of a form of *libertas*, then it is a rather short step from reading the form of government depicted in the third book of the *De legibus* as an aristocracy with (formal) approval of the people to seeing it as an outright aristocracy, if not an actual oligarchy. Nevertheless, according to Scipio's discussion in the third book of the *De re publica*, an oligarchy is not a corrupt form of government; rather, it is not a commonwealth at all. An oligarchy is not a legitimate form of commonwealth for two main reasons: because under this form of government those who rule do not adequately consult and take into account the affairs of the people, the *res populi*; and because the society under an oligarchy does not contain the shared sense of justice that should be mirrored in its institutional arrangements. Coming very close to depriving citizens of the rights that guarantee their status of liberty, the form of commonwealth that would result from Cicero's legal code in Book 3 of the *De legibus* is a 'quasi-oligarchy', that is, a 'quasi-illegitimate' form of government.

VI

To conclude, whilst in the *De re publica* the powers of the community lie in the senate and are exercised by its magistrates to whom the community has entrusted them, in the *De legibus* these political powers are

[65] On the use of this label to describe Plato's *Laws* see Morrow, *Plato's Cretan City*, pp. 229–32.

not delegated in any meaningful manner, but rather involve a form of 'quasi-alienation' of popular sovereignty.

By depriving the people's judgement of their autonomy and imposing on them an attitude of submission to the *optimates*, Cicero ultimately abused if not infringed the right of the people to administer their own property. In other words, he curbed the liberty of Roman citizens, so that in a commonwealth regulated by the laws *de magistratibus* of the *De legibus*, the citizens would no longer be able to enjoy a status in which they could live according to their own wishes without being subject to others' whims or preferences.[66]

It seems that Cicero never finished the *De legibus*, and he certainly never published it. It is not inconceivable that one of the reasons for his dissatisfaction with the work lay in the perception that his law code, originally formulated for the mixed and balanced constitution at aristocratic preponderance, had come to create an aristocracy with only the formal approval of the people. This new political entity did not consist of a community where sovereignty lay entirely with the people, but one where popular sovereignty is 'quasi-transferred' to the members of the senate. This new conception of the commonwealth creates, at least theoretically, the first signs of a gap between the powers of the people, understood as the members of the community at large, and those of the members of the political elite, now conceived as almost a distinct authority, although not yet in impersonal terms.

[66] Arena, *Libertas*, pp. 14–44.

4 *Popolo* and law

Late medieval sovereignty in Marsilius and the jurists

Serena Ferente

The decades between 1280 and 1350 are a crucial era in Italy for both the practice and the concept of popular sovereignty. The formula 'popular sovereignty' does not belong to those years but its constituent elements do, and they existed in a political landscape rife with experimentation. The study of those constitutent elements offers more than a genealogy of later ideas: it reveals the extent to which the order imposed onto the lush variety and plurality of 'the political' by the successful fiction of the sovereign state is in fact just that, a fiction of words believed by many and accompanied by a great deal of coercive power.

The awareness of the importance of this period for the study of ideas of popular sovereignty is hardly recent; the theme is a well-trodden historiographical path, whose travellers are interesting in their own right. From Otto von Gierke to Francesco Ercole and Walter Ullmann, the best historians of medieval notions of popular sovereignty were very involved in the politics of their own times; indeed (perhaps most evidently in the case of Ercole, who became a minister of the fascist government in Italy) the historiographical fortunes or misfortunes of their interpretations may have less to do with the fourteenth century than the twentieth.[1]

---

[1] Otto von Gierke's *Das deutsche Genossenschaftrecht* was published in four volumes (Berlin: Weidmannsche Buchhandlung, 1868–1913), and part of volume III was translated into English by F. W. Maitland as *Political Theories of the Middle Age* (Cambridge: Cambridge University Press, 1900); Gierke was a strong supporter of Bismarck's Reich and in his old age vocally opposed the Weimar constitution of 1919; on the impact of Gierke's nineteenth-century preoccupations on his theory of medieval corporations see the introduction to S. Reynolds, *Kingdom and Communities in Western Europe, 300–1300* (Oxford: Oxford University Press, 1986). Francesco Ercole adhered to the fascist regime in Italy in 1925 and was later a member of the Camera dei Deputati for the Fascist Party and education minister in the Mussolini government; although his first major works on medieval political thought date from the 1910s (essays later included in *Dal Comune al Principato* (Florence: Vallecchi, 1929) and *Da Bartolo all'Altusio* (Florence: Vallecchi, 1932)), his theories on the popular bases of *signorie* have long been connected with his fascist allegiance; for a recent review of the reception of Ercole's scholarship see the introduction to R. Rao, *Signorie di popolo: signoria cittadina e società comunale nell'Italia nord-occidentale, 1250–1350* (Milan: Franco Angeli, 2012). Walter Ullmann, an Austrian

One author, in a period relatively and blissfully free from an established canon of 'great thinkers', can nevertheless function as the gravitational centre of the whole debate, for a number of reasons. Marsilius or Marsilio Mainardini of Padua (b. before 1287; d. *c.* 1343),[2] and his extraordinary book *Defensor Pacis*, finished in 1324, are situated geographically and theoretically at a crossroads. Padua, Paris, Rome, Munich, scholastic Aristotelianism, civil law jurisprudence, spiritual Franciscanism, early humanism are all pertinent contexts for the understanding of Marsilius and his work, and all contributed concepts and vocabulary to the debate over popular sovereignty.[3] Marsilius was personally involved in major political events, particularly during his maturity. It is an unusual trait of his biography that, unlike so many other writers on political things, Marsilius's masterpiece is also his first work, and pre-dates and informs his better-documented involvement in high politcs rather than following it. His youth and education, unfortunately, are sparsely documented if compared with his later years. The problem of Marsilius's sources is still open[4] and his long-lasting relationship with his friend and companion John of Jandun, an Aristotelian philosopher in his own right, further complicates the interpretation of the *Defensor Pacis* and the sharp differences in tone between its first and second Discourses.[5] It seems important to

Jewish emigré to England, illustrated his vision of 'ascending' and 'descending' theories of government in the Middle Ages in *Principles of Government and Politics in the Middle Ages* (New York: Barnes & Noble, 1961), and several subsequent works; F. Oakley, 'Celestial Hierarchies Revisited: Walter Ullmann's Vision of Medieval Politics', *Past and Present* 60 (1973), pp. 3–48, reprising some of Ernst Kantorowicz's criticisms in a review published in 1964, suggested that Ullmann's 'liberal-democratic' sympathies, as well as his background in legal history, explained the 'inadequacy' of his theoretical framework for an understanding of medieval political thought.

2 On Marsilius's biography see C. Pincin, *Marsilio* (Turin: Giappichelli, 1967); C. Dolcini, *Introduzione a Marsilio da Padova* (Rome-Bari: Laterza, 1995); and the recent thorough review of the extant evidence by F. Godthardt, 'The Life of Marsilius of Padua', in G. Moreno-Riaño and C. J. Nederman (eds.), *Companion to Marsilius of Padua* (Leiden: Brill, 2012), pp. 13–55.

3 The literature on Marsilius is vast: Moreno-Riaño and Nederman (eds.), *Companion to Marsilius*, is useful for a bibliographical overview, and references the works of N. Rubinstein (insisting on Marsilius's Italian background), J. Quillet (on Marsilius's scholasticism), J. Coleman (on Franciscan debates), G. Piaia (on Marsilius's reception during the Reformation), G. Garnett (on Marsilius's philosophy of history), among many others. The critical edition of the text is Marsilius von Padua, *Defensor Pacis*, ed. R. Scholz (Hanover: n.p., 1933). The most recent English is Marsilius of Padua, *The Defender of the Peace*, trans. A. Brett (Cambridge: Cambridge University Press, 2005), and will be used throughout this chapter (abbreviated as DP).

4 See the most recent attempt to map Marsilius's sources in V. Syros, *Marsilius of Padua at the Intersection of Ancient and Medieval Traditions of Political Thought* (Toronto: University of Toronto Press, 2012).

5 The debate over the possible joint authorship of the *Defensor Pacis* continues even after A. Gewirth, 'John of Jandun and the *Defensor Pacis*', *Speculum* 23 (1948), pp. 267–72. All

highlight that the first Discourse, which is of particular interest to us, ostensibly provides simply the philosophical foundation for the virulent anti-papal and anti-ecclesiastical polemic of the second Discourse: it is the latter that earned Marsilius and John of Jandun their excommunication in 1327.[6]

One concept in the *Defensor Pacis* has been central for students of popular sovereignty, that of the *legislator humanus*, the human legislator. Marsilius was a *physicus*, a physician versed in the natural sciences, and it is quite easy to see the extensive organic metaphor he famously uses to structure his description of the political community as a reflex of his expertise:[7] a body metaphor, of course, can serve a variety of political purposes, but all such metaphors imply the fundamental unity and interdependence of the thing that the body represents. The *Defensor Pacis* is indeed written to combat division in general, and the particular type of civil division generated by what Marsilius saw as unhealthy pretensions of the priestly part of the body politic. Within this metaphorical framework, Marsilius presents a broadly Aristotelian theory of the origin and types of political communities and clearly asserts that, whereas of course there are examples of divine institution of a *regnum*, in most cases it is through human agency that governments or polities are established. Collective human agency manifests itself most fundamentally through election, and Marsilius establishes election as the primary way of instituting what he calls the princely part (*pars principans*) of a political community, since 'election can never fail' and only election lasts as long as the human race itself.[8] Even in the case of dynastic monarchies, where the principle governing the choice of the *pars principans* is apparently hereditary, it is to election that the multitude must ultimately revert for a new political beginning, if for example the line of succession is interrupted, or subjects find the government intolerable and overthrow it. The ultimate *efficient cause* of each political institution, however, is not election itself, since election is merely a procedure determined by rules or law, and therefore it is to the efficient cause of law that one must look to find that ultimate *auctoritas*, the originator of political power that so much resembles our idea of sovereign, and which is for Marsilius, precisely, the legislator.

---

the manuscripts cite Marsilius as the sole author, and I.1 contains Marsilius's 'signature' as 'son of Antenor' (i.e. Paduan); on the other hand, Pope John XXII's condemnation of *Defensor Pacis* of 23 October 1327 cites both Marsilius and John of Jandun.

[6] C. Dolcini and R. Lambertini, 'Mainardini Marsilio', in *Dizionario Biografico degli Italiani*, vol. LXIII (Rome: Istituto dell'Enciclopedia Italiana, 2007), pp. 569–76.

[7] The body metaphor appears in DP I, 2. See also T. Shogimen, 'Medicine and the Body Politic in Marsilius of Padua's *Defensor Pacis*', in Moreno-Riaño and Nederman (eds.), *Companion to Marsilius*, pp. 71–115.

[8] DP I, 12.7.

Let us say, then, in accordance with both the truth and the counsel of Aristotle, Politics III chapter 6, that the 'legislator', i.e. the primary and proper efficient cause of the law, is the people or the universal body of the citizens or else its prevailing part, when, by means of an election or will expressed in speech in a general assembly of the citizens, it commands or determines, subject to temporal penalty or punishment, that something should be done or omitted in respect of human civil acts. (I say 'prevailing part' taking into consideration both the quantity and the quality of persons in the community upon which the law is passed.) This is so whether the said body of citizens or its prevailing part does this directly of itself, or commits the task to another or others who are not and cannot be the legislator in an unqualified sense but only in a certain respect and at a certain time and in accordance with the authority of the primary legislator.

And in consequence of this I say that laws and anything else instituted by election must receive their necessary approval from the same primary authority and no other: whatever may be the situation concerning various ceremonies or solemnities, which are not required for the results of an election to stand but for their good standing, and even without which the election would be no less valid. I say further that it is by the same authority that laws and anything else instituted by election must receive any addition or subtraction or even total overhaul, any interpretation and any suspension: depending on the demands of time and place and other circumstances that might make one of these measures opportune for the sake of the common advantage in such matters. It is by the same authority, too, that laws must be promulgated after their institution, so that no citizen or stranger who commits an offence against them can be excused on grounds of ignorance.[9]

It is around some elements of Marsilius's definition of the human legislator that one can organise the late medieval polyphony of popular sovereignty. The first element of the phrase that needs specific attention is *populus*, the people. A definition of *populus* in Marsilius's Italy would immediately incur a crucial ambiguity, which to an extent persists in Western political languages of later eras: *populus* is the whole, but *populus* is also, de facto, a part, which has a tendency to think of itself as a whole. Starting with the 1230s, but most visibly in the 1280s and 1290s, a number of self-governing urban communities in Italy were ruled by so-called *regimi di popolo* and had, as it was said, *stato popolare*. The establishment of *popolo* regimes came as a result of vigorous political struggles and brought about governments that were socially more inclusive than earlier ones and marked by the presence of men enrolled in the city guilds (*arti*) – some of them fabulously rich merchants, others small artisans.[10] Marsilius came from a uniquely important professional subset of the *popolo*,

---

[9] DP I, 12.3.

[10] On the *popolo* in Italy see the brief introductory overview by A. Zorzi, 'The Popolo', in J. M. Najemy (ed.), *Italy in the Age of the Renaissance, 1300–1550* (Oxford: Oxford University Press, 2004), pp. 145–64, and attached bibliography.

since his father had been a notary in Padua – Marsilius's good friend, the humanist Albertino Mussato, echoes ancient Roman categories in calling him a *civis Paduanus plebeius*.[11] Guild membership and an ideology that emphasised peace and an anti-aristocratic notion of justice became indeed the common traits of *popolo* regimes in Italy, recognisable even when the socio-economic make-up of *popolo* governments looked not so dissimilar from the aristocratic groups it sought to marginalise. One of the distinctive features of the few durable *regimi di popolo* was their claim to represent an entirely different political culture, one that was peaceful (as opposed to the bellicose traditions of the aristocracy of *magnates*), organised around work (as opposed to lineage identity and land ownership) and egalitarian – the latter principle exemplified by highly symbolic urban-planning initiatives, new legislative and electoral practices, and new judicial apparati, such as the *capitani del popolo*, conceived as a safeguard against the violence and intimidation generated by social rank.

In its institution-building efforts, however, the successful *popolo* of cities such as Florence or Bologna formally defined itself against a class of eminent families, branded as *magnates* and penalised with legal exclusion from some or all magistracies and a specific criminal law status. The *popolo* was thus distinct from the nobility; it was also distinct from those lower on the social ladder – for example, those who were too poor to pay taxes – but the distinction at the lower end was far less prominent, legally and ideologically, than that at the top. Undoubtedly some of the members of the *popolo* were socially and culturally quite similar to some of the *magnates*, but by the end of the thirteenth century to be a member of the *popolo* meant to be part of a specific legal, and therefore political, category, which nevertheless claimed for itself the all-encompassing potential carried by the word *populus*.

One of the few clear acknowledgements of the ambiguity of the language of *populus* in late medieval Italy comes, unsurprisingly, from a jurist. Slightly older than Marsilius, Cino da Pistoia was a professor of civil law, a fine vernacular poet and a good friend of Dante Alighieri – like Dante he was exiled from his city during a wave of partisan proscriptions. In a legal opinion (*consilium*) preserved in a Vatican manuscript, Cino is

---

[11] Albertino Mussato, 'Ludovicus Bavarus', in *Fontes Rerum Germanicarum*, ed. J. F. Boehmer, vol. I (Stuttgart: n.p., 1843), p. 175: 'In iis Italici duo erant, qui Ludovici productioni operas multas dederant, eiusque lateri sese adiunxerant, quorum consilii potissimum fruebatur: Marsilius de Raymundinis [*sic*], civis Paduanus plebeius, philosophiae gnarus et ore disertus, et Ubertinus de Casali Ianuensis, monachus, vir similiter astutus et ingeniosus.'

compelled to make an interesting conceptual premise before getting down to the business of examining the details of his clients' case:

Although according to Civil Law the name 'people' includes also noble magnates, according to the customary laws of nearly all of Italy the name 'people' only contains the plebeians. And this is why we said 'commune and people', because the name 'commune' also signifies the magnates, whereas 'people' only the plebeians. Hence the councils and orders of the cities, and the decrees of their priors (*decuriones*) are distinct. For one thing is the council and decree of the commune and another the council and decree of the people.[12]

Although in Roman law *populus* includes the nobility, in virtually the whole of Italy in Cino's times the name *populus* by custom excludes the *magnates*, while the name *commune* includes them. For Cino, therefore (and there is an ideological stance behind the legal interpretation here, since Cino came from a family of *magnates*), the subject of the powers that Roman law assigns to the *populus* is in Italy not the *popolo* but the *commune*.

Historians of medieval civil jurisprudence have traditionally traced a theory of sovereignty in legal thought via the fortune of two formulae: 'rex imperator in regno suo' (the king is emperor in his own kingdom) and 'civitas sibi princeps' (a city that is its own prince).[13] Both formulae encapsulate the same conceptual procedure: fullness of powers in Roman law only belongs to the emperor, or *princeps*, and any assertion of sovereignty on the part of other political actors (kings and cities, respectively, in these two cases) must consist in appropriating the powers of the Roman law prince and exercising them within the limits of a given jurisdiction. The powers of the *princeps* implied absolute superiority/sovereignty (*superioritas, superanitas*), which translated into a rejection of any other overlordship (those kings and cities, indeed, *superiorem non recognoscent*). Such powers, however, conceptually if not politically, depended on the overarching hierarchy of empire, which underpinned

---

[12] Partially edited in M. Bellomo, *Questiones in iure civili disputatae: didattica e prassi colta nel sistema del diritto comune fra Duecento e Trecento* (Rome: Istituto storico italiano per il Medio Evo 2008), p. 299: 'Licet de iure communi appellatio populi etiam magnates nobiles conpletatur, de iure tamen consuetudinario quasi totius Italiae appellatio "populi" non continet nisi plebeios. Et hic venit quid dicemus "commune et populo", quia appellatio "communis" significat etiam "magnates", et "populi" plebeios tantum. Hinc destincta sunt consilia civitatum et ordines, decreta decurionum. Nam aliud consilium et decretum communis et aliud consilium et decretum populi. Nec mirum, quia usus hoc ita declarare potest, ut ff. de verborum significatione. l. anniculus (D.50.16.132 *vel* 134) ... Hic premissis veniamus ad narrationem facti.'

[13] See for example W. Ullmann, 'The Development of the Medieval Idea of Sovereignty', *English Historical Review* 64 (1949), pp. 1–33; F. Calasso, *I glossatori e la teoria della sovranità* (Milan: Giuffrè, 1951); J. Canning, *The Political Thought of Baldus de Ubaldis* (Cambridge: Cambridge University Press, 1987).

the continued validity of the *Corpus Iuris Civilis*, even when the imperial throne was vacant, the emperor absent, unable or unwilling to assert his authority.

It was in the late thirteenth and early fourteenth centuries, in coincidence with a prolonged imperial vacancy (between the death of the twice-excommunicated Frederick II in 1250 and the coronation of Henry VII of Luxembourg in 1312) that jurists became more interested in the problem of the origins of imperial power and intensified the debate around the *lex regia*, the act by which the Roman *populus* had transferred its powers to the emperor. Notoriously, the original *lex* does not survive in the body of Roman law, although a handful of passages from the *Institutions* and the *Digest* refer to it and to the transfer of powers. That the transfer had actually happened was not in contention, but jurists intensely debated the issue of its revocability, and therefore the continuing capacity of the Roman people (however expansively defined) to create princely powers. Whereas in the thirteenth century there was a consensus around the revocable nature of the grant, virtually all the great jurists of the fourteenth century – Cino among them – considered the grant largely irrevocable and carefully avoided a theory of popular sovereignty based on the *lex regia*.[14]

Much more impressive than any written passage of the *Corpus Iuris*, however, was a great bronze table inscribed with *litterae antiquae*, ancient epigraphic lettering, which one can still admire in the Capitoline Museums today (Figure 4.1).[15] This epigraph, known as the *lex de imperio Vespasiani*, reports the content of a *senatusconsultum* of late December 69 CE, defining the powers of Emperor Vespasian. The history of this object is still in part obscure. It was 'discovered' around 1347 by the Roman notary Cola di Rienzo, who removed it from its previous location and exposed it on a wall behind the choir of the Lateran basilica, as the chronicle of the so-called Anonimo Romano reports. Cola di Rienzo, who was at the time leading the institution of a *regime di popolo* in Rome and had resurrected for himself the title of tribune, commissioned a series of paintings, now lost, showing the senators granting imperial powers to Vespasian. The chronicler noted that Cola had wooden stalls built in the same location, so that he could mount on a pedestal and read aloud to his fellow Roman citizens the content of the the epigraph, which he was able to decipher and understand correctly, making the

---

14 See on the early debate B. Tierney, '"The Prince is Not Bound by the Laws": Accursius and the Origins of the Modern State', *Comparative Studies in Society and History* 5 (1963), pp. 378–400; on later developments Canning, *The Political Thought*, pp. 55–63.

15 *Lex de imperio Vespasiani*, text in *Corpus Inscriptionum Latinarum*, vol. VI: *Inscriptiones urbis Romae Latinae*, ed. E. Bosmann and G. Henzen (Berlin: n.p., 1876), n. 930.

Figure 4.1 *Lex de imperio Vespasiani* (CIL VI 930; ILS 244), Capitoline Museum, Rome. © Steve Kershaw, licensed under (CC) BY-NC-SA.

greatest impression on his contemporaries: '*Signori*, such was the majesty of the Roman people that it could grant authority to the Emperor. Now we have lost that authority.'[16] As with the *lex regia* it is quite possible to read the *lex de imperio Vespasiani* as a definitive and complete transfer of sovereignty, with no mention of revocability, but this is not the lesson that Cola and his listeners drew from it.

The inscription on the table as it exists today is incomplete, and begins in the middle of a list of prerogatives introduced by 'utique'; there has been a great deal of controversy among classicists around the missing portion of the table and whether it was still complete in Cola di Rienzo's times. Very little is known of the table's placement before its rediscovery in 1347.[17] Cola himself, in one of his epistles to the Archbishop of Prague, explains that the table had been turned upside down and used by Pope Boniface VIII (therefore before 1303) to make an altar, probably in the

---

[16] Anonimo Romano, *Cronica*, ed. G. Porta (Milan: Adelphi, 1979): 'Non moito tiempo passao che ammonio lo puopolo per uno bello sermone vulgare lo quale fece in Santo Ianni de Laterani. Dereto dallo coro, nello muro, fece ficcare una granne e mannifica tavola de metallo con lettere antique scritta, la quale nullo sapeva leiere né interpretare, se non solo esso. Intorno a quella tavola fece pegnere figure, como lo senato romano concedeva la autoritate a Vespasiano imperatore. Là, in miezo della chiesia, fece fare uno parlatorio de tavole e fece fare gradi de lename assai aiti per sedere. E fece ponere ornamenta de tappiti e de celoni. E congregao moiti potienti de Roma, fra li quali fu Stefano della Colonna e Ianni Colonna sio figlio, lo quale era delli più scaitriti e mannifichi de Roma. Anche ce fuoro moiti uomini savii, iudici e decretalisti, moita aitra iente de autoritate. Sallio in sio pulpito Cola de Rienzi fra tanta bona iente. Vestuto era con una guarnaccia e cappa alamanna e cappuccio alle gote de fino panno bianco. In capo aveva uno capelletto bianco. Nella rota dello capelletto stavano corone de aoro, fra le quale ne stava denanti una la quale era partuta per mieso. Dalla parte de sopra dello capelletto veniva una spada d'ariento nuda, e la sia ponta feriva in quella corona e si·lla partiva per mieso. Audacemente sallio. Fatto silenzio, fece sio bello sermone, bella diceria, e disse ca Roma iaceva abattuta in terra e non poteva vedere dove iacessi, ca li erano cavati li uocchi fòra dello capo. L'uocchi erano lo papa e lo imperatore, li quali aveva Roma perduti per la iniquitate de loro citatini. Puoi disse: "Vedete quanta era la mannificenzia dello senato, ca la autoritate dava allo imperio." Puoi fece leiere una carta nella quale erano scritti li capitoli colla autoritate che·llo puopolo de Roma concedeva a Vespasiano imperatore. In prima, che Vespasiano potessi fare a sio benepiacito leie e confederazione con quale iente o puopolo volessi; anche che potessi mancare e accrescere lo ogliardino de Roma, cioène Italia; potessi dare contado più e meno, come volessi; anche potessi promovere uomini a stato de duca e de regi e deponere e degradare; anco potessi disfare citate e refare; anco potessi guastare lietti de fiumi e trasmutarli aitrove; anche potessi imponere gravezze e deponere allo benepiacito. Tutte queste cose consentio lo puopolo de Roma a Vespasiano imperatore in quella fermezza che avea consentuto a Tiberio Cesari. Lessa questa carta, questi capitoli, disse: "Signori, tanta era la maieste dello puopolo de Roma, che allo imperatore dava la autoritate. Ora l'avemo perduta."'

[17] See, for a detailed overview of the late medieval evidence, and some hypotheses, L. Calvelli, '*Pociora legis precepta*: considerazioni sull'epigrafia giuridica esposta in Laterano fra Medioevo e Rinascimento', in J.-L. Ferrary (ed.), *Leges publicae: la legge nell'esperienza giuridica romana* (Pavia: IUSS Press, 2012), pp. 593–625.

same Lateran basilica, so that the inscription was hidden from view.[18] The Pope did so 'in odium imperii', 'in hatred of empire', believed Cola, which suggests (if Cola's information on the Pope's intention is correct) that Boniface understood at least in elementary fashion the meaning of the inscription. The late medieval protocol of imperial coronation powerfully highlighted the divine origin of the emperor's office, and prescribed the mediation of Christ's representative on earth, the Pope. The ritual did contemplate an active role for the Roman people, called to witness and acclaim – these ritual vestiges of a durable notion of popular consent, however, were only pale reflections of the kind of power implied by the *lex de imperio*. There are good reasons to believe that, before being hidden away by Boniface VIII, the table and its inscription were visible somewhere in the immediate vicinity of the Lateran complex, perhaps in the portico near the entrance of the Lateran palace, where an English pilgrim, Magister Gregorius, saw in the early thirteenth century a bronze table containing many laws but too difficult for him to read.[19]

Among the very few who would have had the interest and the ability to read such an inscription before Boniface's initiative were the Paduan friends of Marsilius, a circle of notaries, judges and university professors gathered around Lovato Lovati and better known as the Paduan early humanists.[20] One of them, Rolando da Piazzola, sent to Rome on a diplomatic mission around 1300, saw a marble stone near the basilica of St Paul with an inscription he believed to refer to the poet Lucan and transcribed it in 1304 on the last page of a codex containing, among other texts, Seneca's tragedies – Rolando's transcription of an ancient epigraph is the very first example of such an exquisitely humanist practice.[21] Marsilius was very close to this circle, as Albertino Mussato's metric letters to him prove, and it is also subtly indicated by Marsilius's choice to introduce himself in the *Defensor Pacis* as 'Antenorides ego': 'I, son of Antenor', the Trojan founder of Padua, whose myth Lovato Lovati had been cultivating.[22]

[18] Cola di Rienzo, *Epistolario di Cola di Rienzo*, ed. A. Gabrielli (Rome: n.p., 1890), p. 165.
[19] Calvelli, '*Pociora legis precepta*'.
[20] On the Paduan early humanists see the pioneering lecture by R. Weiss, *The Dawn of Humanism in Italy* (London: Haskell House, 1947); G. Billanovich, 'Il preumanesimo padovano,' in *Storia della cultura veneta*, vol. II: *Il Trecento* (Vicenza: Neri Pizza editore, 1976), pp. 19–110; and R. Witt, *In the Footsteps of the Ancients: The Origins of Humanism from Lovato to Bruni* (Leiden: Brill, 2000).
[21] Billanovich, 'Il preumanesimo', pp. 99–106.
[22] P. Marangon, 'Marsilio fra preumanesimo e cultura delle arti', *Medioevo: Rivista di storia della filosofia medievale* 3 (1977), pp. 89–119. Mussato's metric epistles have been recently re-edited in J. Miethke, 'Die Briefgedichte des Albertino Mussato an Marsilius von Padua', *Pensiero Politico Medievale* 6 (2008), pp. 49–65.

There is no hard evidence connecting Marsilius or any of the Paduan humanists to the *lex de imperio Vespasiani*. We know, of course, that Marsilius followed his protector and patron Ludwig of Bavaria to Rome in 1328, and might have helped to orchestrate the unique ceremony of the imperial coronation of Ludwig, who received crown, sceptre and orb not from the Pope but from the hands of four Roman citizens representing the *populus romanus*.[23] Almost twenty years before Cola di Rienzo, this was a powerful representation of popular sovereignty, enacted as a ritual before the people of Rome themselves. Perfectly coherent with Marsilius's theories in the *Defensor Pacis*, Ludwig's act of 18 April 1328, known as *Gloriosus Deus*, which Marsilius probably co-wrote following the coronation, draws from the authority of the 'Roman people and clergy' the power to depose Pope John XXII, declaring him heretical and guilty of *crimen laesae maiestatis*.[24]

Two other episodes, however, which took place before the composition of *Defensor Pacis*, could have offered analogous symbolic representations of popular sovereignty in the very act of instituting a *pars principans*. One was the first imperial coronation to take place in Rome after 1220 – in many ways an underwhelming affair. Henry of Luxembourg, elected King of the Romans by the German princes in 1308, undertook his journey to the Italian lands of the Holy Roman Empire only in 1310, aiming to receive the imperial crown in Rome from the hands of Pope Clement V, and generating on his way a political ebullience in Italy that could only be compared to the times of Charles of Anjou's expedition to the kingdom of Sicily in the 1260s. Henry became Dante's ideal champion and the foe of the Black Guelfs of Florence: his promise of imperial renewal energised the Ghibelline factions of many Italian cities, and greatly stimulated the political and juridical debate, giving the notion of empire and imperial powers an urgency and immediacy that had long seemed lost.[25] After an initial period of relative concord with the Pope, Henry's quest for the imperial crown ran into the hostility of Clement and his Italian allies,

---

[23] F. Godthardt, 'The Life of Marsilius of Padua', argues that Marsilius reached Rome only after the coronation.

[24] The text is in *Monumenta Germaniae Historica, Constitutiones* VI.1, ed. J. Schwalm (Hanover: n.p., 1927), no. 436.

[25] W. M. Bowsky, *Henry VII in Italy: The Conflict of Empire and City-State, 1310–1313* (Lincoln: University of Nebraska Press, 1960). Henry VII issued in Pisa new constitutions that defined the status of 'rebellion', and sparked juridical reflection on the crime of *lèse-majesté*: see M. Sbriccoli, *Crimen laesae maiestatis: il problema del reato politico alle soglie della scienza penalistica moderna* (Milan: n.p., 1974). Henry's Italian years also constituted the immediate context for the elaboration of Guelf and anti-Guelf ideologies of *libertas*: S. Ferente, 'The Liberty of Italian City-States', in Q. Skinner and M. Van Gelderen (eds.), *Freedom and the Construction of Europe*, 2 vols. (Cambridge: Cambridge University Press, 2013), vol. I, pp. 157–75.

and the coronation ceremony became an object of dispute. The cardinals authorised by Avignon to act on behalf of the Pope refused to perform the coronation, while Henry's armed following barely controlled a portion of the city of Rome.

> Since the Cardinals denied their consent, Cesar summoned in council the Roman people, or rather, those who supported his party, relating the difficulties of the case and consulting on whatever was expedient. By decree of the people (*plebiscito*) it was decided that the Cardinals should crown [Henry] following the exhortations and prayers of the republic; if, however, they refused, they would be forced to do it by the tribunes and the Roman people.[26]

This account of Henry VII's 1312 coronation – the only one that refers to the role of the Roman people – was written in Padua immediately after the events by Marsilius's friend Albertino Mussato; manuscripts of the *Historia Augusta*, of which the account is part, circulated in Paduan circles even before the work's completion in 1315.[27] Henry VII's choice to rely on a popular assembly to resolve his impasse was more innovative in principle than in practice: the consent, or at the very least the acquiescence, of the Romans and their representatives (senators, here called *tribuni*, who were the equivalent of *podestà*, as well as party leaders) were the necessary condition for the success of any ceremonial event taking place within the city. In Mussato's narrative, however, the 'Roman people', assembled in a council, become an alternative source of authority that can compel by law (*plebiscitum*) the cardinals to perform the coronation in the name of the *respublica*, using coercion if necessary: the ecclesiastical mediation is not eliminated from the ritual, but is subjected to an entirely lay and popular command. Mussato's reliance on classical vocabulary was a conscious and deliberate choice, intended to evoke political parallels with ancient Rome, even if it is Mussato himself who insinuates that Henry's coronation depended on partisan support rather than a fictionally unanimous popular mandate.

A second episode that has failed to attract sufficient attention within Marsilian scholarship took place in 1318, when Marsilius, having concluded his rectorate at the Faculty of Arts in Paris, was back in his native Veneto and actively involved in politics, most prominently on behalf of

---

[26] Albertino Mussato, *De gestis Henrici VII. Caesaris*, in *Rerum Italicarum Scriptores*, vol. X (Milan: n.p., 1727), p. 114: 'Cardinalibus vero non assentientibus, Caesar populum romanum, illum videlicet qui suas partes fovebat, in concilium evocavit has proponens facti angustias, quidque expediat consultans. Ex plebiscito itaque obtentum est cardinales reipublicae suasionibus precibusque coronam dare; sin autem coercendos per tribunos populumque romanum.'

[27] M. Zabbia, 'Albertino Mussato', in *Dizionario Biografico degli Italiani*, vol. LXXVII (Rome: Istituto dell'Enciclopedia Italiana, 2012), pp. 520–4.

the Ghibelline party. The city of Padua was under military threat from the lord of Verona, Cangrande della Scala; it was divided between Guelphs and Ghibellines, and seemed unable to produce swift decisions about the conduct of the war and the return of its exiles through the normal channels of republican deliberation and vote.[28] It was in such a context of political emergency that the same Rolando da Piazzola who copied the inscription in Rome, a highly regarded citizen and several times an elected magistrate, rose from his seat during a crucial popular assembly and made a speech: with a very mixed body metaphor he explained to his fellow citizens that limbs must obey a head, and that since all animals in nature have a leader, the Paduans should create a prince from their bosom, by transferring all the political power to one in their midst, the much-admired nobleman Jacopo da Carrara, who was a Guelf with Ghibelline friends.[29] Rolando's speech succeeded in persuading the Paduans (indeed, its echo was so strong that it was recorded in a history written in the neighbouring city of Vicenza), Jacopo da Carrara was elected *signore*, and the Ghibelline exiles were readmitted in the name of a pacification between the parties.

The election of 25 July 1318 marks the beginning of the Carrara lordship over Padua, which would later become hereditary and last, with only brief interruptions, until 1402, when Venice annexed Padua and its territory to the dominion of the *Serenissima*. The text of the public act that sanctioned the election of the new lord has been preserved:

In the name of the Holy and Individual Trinity. On the Election and Primacy of the Noble and Illustrious Man Lord Jacopo of Carrara as Protector, Defender, Governor and General Captain of the City and District of Padua and of the whole People of Padua . . .

We decree and order that for the honour and reverence of Our Lord Jesus Christ, and His glorious mother the Blessed Mary always Virgin, and the Holy Bodies

---

[28] On Paduan history in this period see J. K. Hyde, *Padua in the Age of Dante* (Manchester: Manchester University Press, 1966), which, however, does not cover this episode in much detail.

[29] Ferreto Ferreti, *Le opere di Ferreto de' Ferreti Vicentino*, ed. C. Cipolla, vol. II (Rome: n.p., 1914), p. 255: 'Cum variis animorum iudiciis hesitarent, eloquens vir Rolandus de Placiola, qua pridem sepe vehementia ductus fuerat, in medium constitit. "Et quid opus est verbis, cives? Habemus", infit, "presto salubre nobis patrieque remedium. Experti namque plebiscitis abutimur, resque nostra in ruinam cedit, nisi previsa nos meditatio relevet. Experiamur namque, si privatis legibus melior sors futura sit. Et quidem omnia principem sibi decernunt. Capiti enim cetera membra deserviunt. Animalia ducem habent, orbis terre, si iusto regi pareat, cedes, bella, rapine et feda queque relatu desinerent. Iam et nos moniti hec sequamur exempla. Decernamus igitur e gremio nostro nobis principem, qui solus omnium curas exsolvat, qui suo rempublicam moderetur arbitrio, leges statuat, edicta innovet, vetusta destruat, rerumque nostrarum fiat dominus et protector."'

of the Blessed Prosdocimus, Justina the Martyr, Anthony the Confessor, and Daniel the Martyr, who are the Protectors and Defenders of the Commune of Padua; and especially for the reverence and praise of the Most Blessed and Holy Jacob the Apostle, in whose festive and solemn day the Lord God has enlightened the hearts and minds of the men of the city of Padua, and the whole People, as well as the Nobles of the said City, in appointing as their Rector and Governor the Noble Man Lord Jacopo of Carrara, and for the honour and reverence of all the Saints of God, and for the good, pacific and tranquil state of the City and the People of Padua, and so that homicides, robberies and all other crimes that occurred and were committed in Padua and the Paduan District cease, and so that everyone can live of his own:

That the Nobleman Lord Jacopo of Carrara, born of the late Nobleman Lord Marsilio of Carrara, be, must be, and be understood to be, by the authority of the present Law and Statute and according to the best procedure and right, Defender, Protector, and Governor of the Paduan People, City and District, and General Captain of the inhabitants of those; and that he have and must have pure and mixed authority, and all full and fullest jurisdiction in criminal and civil matters, and in all cases and affairs, and have each and all of the powers that belong to the whole Commune and the whole People of the City and District of Padua, and to him and onto him all the authority and all the power of the People and Commune of Padua are granted and transferred.[30]

Several aspects of this document deserve to be noted, in addition to its possible influence on Marsilius's ideas about the power of the human

---

[30] F. M. Colle, *Storia scientifico-letteraria dello studio di Padova*, vol. I (Padua: Minerva, 1824), pp. 29–33: 'In nomine Sanctae et Individuae Trinitatis: de electione et Praefectura Nobilis et Incliti Viri Domini Jacobi de Carraria in Protectorem, Defensorem, Gubernatorem et Capitaneum Generalem Civitatis Paduae et Districtus et totius Populi Paduani, et ipsius potestate et officio ... Statuimus, et ordinamus quod ad honorem et reverentiam Domini Nostri Jesu Christi, et Beatae Marine semper Virginis ejus gloriosae Matris, et Sanctorum Corporum Beatorum Prosdocimi, et Justinae virginis, Antonii Confessoris, et Danielis Martiris, qui sunt Protectores et Defensores Comunis Paduae; et praecipue ad reverentiam et laudem Beatissimi et Sanctissimi Jacobi Apostoli, in cujus festivitate et solempnitate Dominus Deus noster illuminavit corda et mentes hominum civitatis Paduae, et universum Populum, ac etiam Nobiles ipsius Civitatis in praeficiendo sibi in Rectorem et Gubernatorem Nobilem Virum Dominum Jacobum de Carraria, et ad honorem et reverentiam omnium Sanctorum et Sanctarum Dei, et ad bonum pacificum et tranquillum statum Civitatis et Populi Paduani, et ad hoc ut homicidia, robariae, et caetera maleficia, quae fiebant et committebantur in Padua et Paduano Districtu, cessent, et ut quilibet possit vivere de suo: Quod Nobilis Vir Dominus Jacobus de Carraria, natus quondam Nobilis Viri Domini Marsilii de Carraria, sit et esse debeat, et esse intelligatur auctoritate praesentis Legis et Statuti, et omni modo et jure quo melius esse poterit, Defensor, Protector, et Gubernator Populi Paduani, et Civitatis et Districtus, et in eis habitantium Capitaneus Generalis; et habeat et habere debeat merum et mixtum imperium, et omnem jurisdictionem plenam et plenissimam in criminalibus et civilibus, et in omni casu et negotio, et omnia et singula possit, quaecumque posset totum Comune, et universus Populus Paduanae Civitatis et Districtus Paduae; et ei, et in eum omne imperium, et omnis potestas Populi et Comunis Paduae concessa et translata sint ... '

legislator to elect a *pars principans*. The text is one of the earliest examples of a procedure that, with local variations, underpins the institution of *signorie* in many Italian city-communes. God having enlightened the hearts and minds of the men of the city of Padua, of the people as well as the nobles (propitiously, on the day of the Apostle named Jacob), Jacopo da Carrara is created Defender, Protector and Governor of the People of Padua, of the city and its district and General Captain of its inhabitants for the sake of the peaceful and tranquil state of the city and the people of Padua. The new lord must also take a solemn oath *in arengo*, during a public political assembly. To him 'all *imperium* and all *potestas* of the Commune and the People of Padua are granted and transferred'. Jacopo will excercise this authority in the fullest form, including the power to make laws, and will do so in perpetuity, according to the will (*voluntas*) of the Commune and People of Padua, although the document doesn't specify how the popular will is to be expressed and interpreted. The transfer of authority is irrevocable through ordinary legislative means, but can be modified or reversed if a new statute is promulgated, in the solemn form that specifically abrogates the previous one.

The lack of any reference in the document to the imperial authority, under whose ultimate jurisdiction Padua lay, is noticeable. Equally noticeable is the insisted dyad 'People and Commune', whose full *imperium et potestas* are being transferred to Jacopo: we know from Cino da Pistoia that mention of the Commune was necessary in order to encompass the nobles or magnates in the act of transfer, while mention of the People evoked the fullness of the original power the *lex regia* recognised as belonging to the *populus romanus*. It is at the very moment when that power and that authority are transferred to an individual that their juridical and political attribution to the *popolo* and the *commune* is stated and defined explicitly.

The legislative enactment instituting the new lordship was a statute and, as such, it emanated from the community itself. While it invoked the protection of a populated Christian pantheon and employed strategically the vocabulary of Roman law, a statute remained, in essence, a form of *lex* strongly related to customary law.[31] Indeed, if jurists such as Cino da Pistoia or his pupil Bartolus of Saxoferrato failed to use the *lex regia* as a conceptual anchor for a theory of popular sovereignty, nevertheless another category, that of *consuetudo* or custom, demanded a sustained reflection on the nature of the constant legislative power

---

[31] See Baldus de Ubaldis's phrase 'consuetudo et statutum ambulant pari passu' and a wide overview of the debate in late medieval Italian jurisprudence in R. Garré, *Consuetudo: Das Gewohnheitsrecht in der Rechtsquellen- und Methodenlehre des späten ius commune in Italien (16.–18. Jahrhundert)* (Frankfurt am Main: Vittorio Klostermann, 2005).

residing in the *populus*,[32] neither transferred nor transferrable to a prince. The context for such sustained reflection was the debate on *consuetudo*, and particularly commentaries on Code, 8, 52, the rubric 'Quae sit longa consuetudo', which nearly all the eminent jurists of the period examined at length.

In its rationalising pursuit of a hiearchy of the varied forms of law in existence, civilistic juridical opinion in the fourteenth century was inclined to weaken the force of customary law vis-à-vis other kinds of law. The source of *consuetudo* for Roman law commentators, however, remained the *consensus populi*, the consent of the people; indeed, custom differs from *lex* only because in custom the consent is tacit, whereas in *lex* it is expressed. Cino da Pistoia, for example, insisted that while repetition and time are necessary to prove the existence of a custom, neither repetition nor time per se, but only the tacit consent of the people that they reveal can create law. It is in discussions on this form of law-making by the people that jurists resorted most frequently to the formula *voluntas populi*, the will of the people. And it is in the same commentaries on *consuetudo* that jurists were confronted with the need to explicitly define the boundaries of the *populus*, a group that normally excluded children, mentally impaired and mad people, as well as women. Women's exclusion, as usual, presented some conceptual challenges: it was true, for example, that women were capable of creating custom, for example when they consented, among themselves, that a certain type of property would be by custom transmitted from mother to daughter; Cino and Bartolus, however, in admitting the validity of this creation of custom, skirted around the issue of women's active law-making capacity by saying that custom produced by women was ultimately due to the tacit consent of men, who approved it by refraining from opposing it.[33]

A further feature of fourteenth-century juridical commentary on *consuetudo* is that the consent needed to generate law is always that of 'totus populus vel maior pars eius', the whole people or its greater part. The commentary on *consuetudo* is one of the very few instances in Roman law jurisprudence where the *maior pars* is systematically added to the 'whole of the people' as the legitimate legislator. Much has been written on Marsilius's concept of the *valentior* or prevailing part,[34] which he says must

---

[32] See a brief mention of custom as law of the people in D. Kelley, 'Civil Science in the Renaissance: The Problem of Interpretation', in A. Pagden (ed.), *The Languages of Political Theory in Early-Modern Europe* (Cambridge: Cambridge University Press, 1987), pp. 57–78, at p. 66.

[33] Cinus de Pistorio, *Lectura super Codice* (Venice: n.p., 1493), cc. 362r–366v; Bartolus a Saxoferrato, *In Secundam Codicis Partem* (Venice: n.p., 1570), fols. 113v–116r.

[34] See J. Quillet, 'Community, Counsel and Representation', in J. H. Burns (ed.), *The Cambridge History of Medieval Political Thought, c. 350–1450* (Cambridge: Cambridge

be understood with respect to both quantity and quality. The choice of the adjective *valentior* to define that portion of the whole people that can sufficiently act as the legislator reveals Marsilius's desire to comprehend under the label numerical majorities of the kind envisaged by commentaries on *consuetudo* and republican voting practices, as well as qualitative representation, such as the one embodied by the German Princes Electors, or perhaps those syndics of the Roman people who would crown Ludwig of Bavaria in 1328.

The constant capacity of the people tacitly to produce law is not the only non-transferrable property of the human legislator. Indeed, the issue of the revocability of the transfer of authority can be interpreted as the extreme instance of another general property that Marsilius clearly attributes to the human legislator: the power to hold the prince accountable. One of the concluding chapters of Discourse I of *Defensor Pacis* is devoted to the issue of the correction of the *pars principans*.

However, because the prince, being human, has an intellect and a desire which can take on different forms – such as a false conception or a perverted desire or both – it is possible for him, if he follows them, to do things contrary to what is laid down by law. For this reason the prince is, in these actions, rendered subject to measurement by something else that has the authority to measure or regulate him (or those actions of his that transgress the law) according to the law; for otherwise any principate would become tyrannical, and the life of the citizens slavish and insufficient. And this is an evil to be avoided, as was apparent from what we determined in chapters 5 and 11 of this discourse.

Now the judgement, command and execution of any arraignment of the prince for his demerit or transgression should take place through the legislator, or through a person or persons established for this purpose by the authority of the legislator, as demonstrated in chapters 2 and 5 of this discourse. It is also appropriate to suspend for a period of time the office of the prince who is subject to correction, especially in relation to the person or persons who must judge his transgression so that faction, commotion and fighting do not break out in the community because of the resulting plurality of principates; and also because he is not being corrected as the prince, but as a subject who has transgressed the law.[35]

This famous passage and the whole chapter give special prominence to accountability (here specifically expressed as *mensura*, measurement, and *regula*, regulation), if the princely part is not to become, in

University Press, 1988), pp. 520–71. Quillet suggests a proximity between Marsilius's *pars valentior* and the *maior* and *sanior pars* often mentioned in canon law.
[35] DP I, 18.

Aristotelian terms, despotic (*despoticus*) and cause the citizens to lose their self-sufficiency and live like slaves (*vita servilis et insufficiens*) – the election of the lord Jacopo da Carrara, too, was taking place so that 'quilibet possit vivere de suo', 'anyone can live of his own'. The need for regulated mechanisms of correction of the prince, and particularly Marsilius's recommendation that the prince be suspended from his office while being judged, have reminded historians of one institution in particular, the *sindacato*, which in late medieval Italy existed in city-communes as well as the Kingdom of Sicily.[36]

Sindacato guaranteed that the tenure of temporary officials would be followed, as a matter of procedure, by comprehensive audit trials, where anonymous denunciations were often admissible. In communes ruled by *popolo* regimes the highest ruling officials, including the *podestà*, were routinely subject to *sindacato* and syndicators (*sindacatori*) were appointed by the main political councils, so that syndication could be envisaged, in principle if not in practice, as a systematic form of accountability controlled by the sovereign people (in the kingdom it was the king who appointed syndicators). In Padua and elsewhere the transition from communal to seignorial government, because it was framed as a transfer of the prerogatives of popular and communal authority, left no room for a form of routine accountability of the lord himself. 'Lordly' prerogatives of exemption from syndication became indeed increasingly common even in those city-states that maintained republican forms of government into the fifteenth and sixteenth centuries. There, citizen magistrates progressively replaced and subordinated foreign officials in crucial executive functions, and systematically exempted themselves from syndication.[37] The concentration of political powers into fewer and higher institutional loci, although never a linear process, was generally accompanied by the restriction or loss of traditional, procedural accountability measures.

Late medieval ideas of popular sovereignty emerged from a season of partial but authentic democratisation of politics in city-communes, which gave rise to languages and institutions of popular authority echoing in name and imagery Roman republican models. It is perhaps a familiar

---

[36] On *sindacato* see now M. Isenmann, *Legalität und Herrschaftskontrolle (1200–1600). Eine vergleichende Studie zum Syndikatsprozess: Florenz, Kastilien und Valencia* (Frankfurt: Klostermann Vittorio GmbH, 2010). On the republic of Genoa, which is particularly interesting because of the presumed persistence of medieval constitutional traits in the early modern period, see R. Ferrante, *La difesa della legalità: i sindacatori della Repubblica di Genova* (Turin: Giappichelli, 2005).

[37] On such a process in Florence see M. Isenmann, 'From Rule of Law to Emergency Rule in Renaissance Florence', in L. Armstrong and J. Kirshner (eds.), *The Politics of Law in Late Medieval and Renaissance Italy: Essays in Honour of Lauro Martines* (Toronto: University of Toronto Press, 2011), pp. 55–76.

paradox, however, that popular sovereignty should be first described in theoretical terms precisely at the moment when popular authority was being transferred or alienated to someone or something distinct from the political community itself, and invoked as the juridical and ideological foundation of a variety of forms of monarchic power, imperial or seignorial. Indeed, those communities that succeeded in adapting their republican institutions to the new landscape of concentrated state powers ultimately rejected the popular model and resorted to oligarchic constitutional principles – to be part of the *popolo* in early modern Venice implied nearly total political disenfranchisement[38] – even if experiments with more or less radical forms of popular government continued throughout the early modern period. The absolute and original nature of popular authority had certainly shown its potential to validate comparably absolute and arbitrary forms of power. Yet it could serve that purpose only if deprived of some of its essential properties – the constant, non-transferrable legislative capacity of the people, and the people's power to hold the prince accountable.

---

[38] See now a reconsideration of the role of the Venetian *popolo* in C. Judde de la Rivière and R. Salzberg, 'Le Peuple est la cité: l'idée de popolo et la condition des popolani à Venise (XVe–XVIe siècles)', *Annales HSS* 68 (2013), pp. 1113–40.

Democratic sovereignty and democratic
    government
    The sleeping sovereign

Richard Tuck

In his Eighth *Letter from the Mountain*, written in 1764 in defence of
his *Social Contract* and *Emile* against attacks made on them in Geneva,
Rousseau declared: 'Up to the present the democratic Constitution has
been poorly examined. All those who have spoken about it either did not
know it, or took too little interest in it, or had an interest in presenting it in a false light. None of them have sufficiently distinguished the
Sovereign from the Government.'[1] What he meant by this, as he made
clear both in the *Social Contract* and elsewhere in the *Letters from the
Mountain*, was that the ancient democracies, in which the citizens gathered in an assembly on a regular basis to administer their societies and
make judgements of policy about all matters of concern to them, were
not an appropriate model for the kind of democracy that he advocated.
They had not distinguished between 'government' and 'sovereignty', and
had treated both day-to-day policy questions and fundamental decisions
about the organisation of their societies as falling within the scope of

This chapter is based on the Seeley Lectures which I gave in the University of Cambridge
in May 2012 under the title 'The Sleeping Sovereign'. I would like to thank the History
Faculty of the University of Cambridge and Cambridge University Press for the invitation
to deliver the lectures.
[1] Jean-Jacques Rousseau, *Oeuvres completes*, ed. M. Launay, 3 vols. (Paris: Éditions du
    Seuil, 1971), III, p. 465; for translation see Jean-Jacques Rousseau, *Letter to Beaumont,
    Letters Written from the Mountain, and Related Writings*, trans. C. Kelly and J. Bush, ed.
    C. Kelly and E. Grace (Hanover, NH: University Press of New England, 2001), p. 257.
    He drew the distinction first in his article for the *Encyclopédie* entitled 'Économie', seven
    years before the *Social Contract*: 'I invite my readers also clearly to distinguish *public
    economy*, which is my topic, and which I call *government*, from the supreme authority,
    which I call *sovereignty*; a distinction which consists in this, that the one has the legislative
    right and in some cases obligates the very body of the nation, while the other has only the
    executive power, and can only obligate individuals' (Jean-Jacques Rousseau, *The Social
    Contract and Other Later Political Writings*, ed. V. Gourevitch (Cambridge: Cambridge
    University Press, 1997), p. 6; Rousseau, *Oeuvres complètes*, II, p. 278; and see p. 294 for
    an early draft of this passage, to be found in MS R.16 of the Bibliothèque Publique et
    Universitaire of Neuchâtel. It may be significant that most of the references to Bodin in
    Rousseau's works are to be found in 'Économie'.

the democratic assembly. Against this view, Rousseau insisted that his democracy would be restricted to acts of sovereignty, acts affecting the fundamental legal structure, and that government – including even such things as decisions on going to war – would not ideally be democratic in character (his own preference was for aristocracy). In the *Social Contract* he described this kind of democracy as a 'republic', partly in order precisely to avoid the implication in the familiar notion of a democracy that it must have a democratic *government*; but in the *Letters from the Mountain* he was happy to apply the term 'democracy' to his kind of republic, and in the Ninth *Letter* he made clear (much clearer, in fact, than he had done in the *Social Contract*) that a distinction of this kind permitted the reappearance of democracy in the modern world, a world in which citizens simply could not give the time and attention to government that had been possible for their ancient predecessors. Even in a city the size of Geneva, he wrote, ancient politics could not be revived.

Ancient Peoples are no longer a model for modern ones; they are too alien to them in every respect . . . You are neither Romans, nor Spartans; you are not even Athenians. Leave aside these great names that do not suit you. You are Merchants, Artisans, Bourgeois, always occupied with their private interests, with their work, with their trafficking, with their gain; people for whom even liberty is only a means for acquiring without obstacle and for possessing in safety.

This situation demands maxims particular to you. Not being idle as ancient Peoples were, you cannot ceaselessly occupy yourselves with the Government as they did.[2]

In his *Considerations on the Government of Poland* (1772) he used the same distinction between sovereign and government to recommend a constitutional restructuring for a large modern state in which it was physically impossible for the citizens to meet together.[3] It is clear that in his eyes the distinction was absolutely essential if democratic politics were to be reintroduced to a world of large commercial states.

Two innovations were needed before a theory of this kind could be put forward, a theory which (as we shall see) corresponds to what has become the default constitutional structure of most modern states, in which a procedure such as a plebiscite is used to ratify fundamental

---

[2] Rousseau, *Oeuvres complètes*, III, p. 483; Rousseau, *Letter to Beaumont*, pp. 292–3. The 'beneficent Philosopher' is Stanislas Leszczynski, and the quotation is from his *La Voix libre du citoyen, ou Observations sur le gouvernement de Pologne* (n.p., 1749), part I, p. 195.

[3] E.g. 'One of the vices of the Polish constitution is that it fails to distinguish sufficiently clearly between legislation and administration, and that in the course of exercising legislative power, the Diet mixes in bits of administration, performing indifferently acts of sovereignty and acts of government, often even mixed acts in which its members are simultaneously magistrates and legislators' (Chapter IX: *The Social Contract*, in *Later Political Writings*, p. 217). See *Oeuvres complètes*, III, p. 546.

constitutional legislation, while an elected assembly or set of assemblies legislate on less fundamental matters. Both are to be found in Rousseau. One was the idea that sovereignty and government can be distinguished, and that different kinds of legislation are appropriate to the different levels, and this idea is going to be the principal subject of this chapter. The other is less obvious, but it warrants a brief discussion before I turn to the main issue. It was that it is possible or even desirable to restrict democratic action to a final judgement about what should be binding on the society, and to exclude from democracy to a great extent the process of *collective deliberation*. That exclusion seems surprising to many modern theorists of democracy, for whom (following an idealised and in many ways unhistorical picture of an ancient assembly) the activity of citizens conferring and arguing about their collective decisions is central to the nature of democratic politics. But part of Rousseau's claim that modern states can be democratic was that the principal act of the democratic citizen is the vote, and not the discussion; indeed, he strikingly remarked in the *Social Contract* that the ideal democratic moment would be 'if, when an adequately informed people deliberates, the Citizens had no communication among themselves', and went on to say that it was the activity of communicating with one another that gave rise eventually to what he called 'partial societies' and the eventual corruption of the state.[4] Like much in Rousseau, it should be said, this looked back to Hobbes, who had denounced deliberative assemblies, but was willing to concede that non-deliberative democracy could be a reasonable means of organising a state.[5]

The relevance of the attack on deliberation as the prime democratic activity was that the objection to ancient democracy in a modern state had, before Rousseau, always been presented as largely (so to speak) logistical, in that the citizens of a modern state could not physically gather together, or could not find the time to do so. Implicit in this as an objection was however the belief that the gathering would be to *discuss* legislation, and that there could not be legislation without deliberation. This was why the election of representatives (which had after all been part of the basic structure of government in most Western states for five hundred years or more) was not seen normally as the act of a democracy,

---

[4] Rousseau, *The Social Contract*, Book II Chapter III, in *Later Political Writings*, p. 60; Rousseau, *Oeuvres complètes*, II, p. 527.

[5] He said this clearly in *De Cive*: 'If in a *Democracy* the *people* chose to concentrate deliberations about war and peace and legislation in the hands of just one man or a very small number of men, content themselves with the appointment of magistrates and public ministers, content, that is, to have authority without executive function [*authoritate sine ministerio*], then it must be admitted that *Democracy* and *Monarchy* would be equal in this matter' (X.15).

for the deliberative and legislative activity of the society was restricted to those representatives.[6] Once it was recognised that the element of discussion in their activity could be slight or even non-existent, and once it was recognised that the important acts of democratic sovereignty were by their very nature infrequent, the way was open to recreate democracy in a modern setting and get the citizens as a whole to legislate as well as to elect.

While in the *Letters* Rousseau claimed that no one had used the distinction between sovereign and government in order to interpret democratic constitutions, and while in the *Social Contract* he warned that his long discussion of the distinction in Book III 'requires careful reading' (with the implication that it was unfamiliar and difficult to follow), he must in fact have been well aware that he was not the first person to use it, and furthermore that he was not even the first person to apply it to the question of democracy. But (as we shall see later) for more or less a century the distinction had been either disregarded or expressly repudiated by the principal European political theorists other than Hobbes, so that it was not unreasonable for Rousseau to present his own extensive use of it as an innovation.

The first person to insist on the importance of a distinction of this kind, as his contemporaries and successors well understood, had in fact been Jean Bodin, writing in the 1560s and 1570s. It is a central feature of his theory of sovereignty, something which should have puzzled Bodin's modern readers more than it generally has done: for, as Rousseau's use of the distinction illustrates, it seems to fit more naturally into a defence of modern democratic politics than into the kind of 'absolutist' theory commonly ascribed to Bodin. But while Bodin's principal objective in formulating the distinction was of course not to defend democratic politics of a Rousseaian kind, he was more sympathetic to them than one might have expected; and furthermore his actual objective was much less 'absolutist' than we have been led to think.[7]

The distinction made its first appearance in Chapter 6 of his *Methodus ad facilem historiarum cognitionem* of 1566, a long chapter devoted to the *status Rerumpublicarum*. Though this has, I think, not been observed before, the chapter is structured as a fairly methodical and radical critique of Aristotle's *Politics* Books III–VIII in which Bodin moved through the various arguments of Aristotle about the nature of states,

---

[6] See for a full discussion of this N. Urbinati, *Representative Democracy: Principles and Genealogy* (Chicago: Chicago University Press 2006).

[7] Bodin's use of the distinction is beginning to attract the attention of scholars after many years of neglect; see in particular D. Lee, '"Office Is a Thing Borrowed": Jean Bodin on Offices and Seigneurial Government', *Political Theory* 41 (2013) 409–40.

systematically refuting them.[8] Near the beginning of the critique in Chapter 6 Bodin accused Aristotle of failing to see the distinction between *summum imperium* and *Reipublicae administratio* or *gubernatio*, and consequently going astray in the fundamentals of his politics. Bodin observed that Aristotle had said that 'there are altogether three parts to a *Respublica*; one being deliberation, another choosing magistrates, and the last jurisdiction'.[9] But neither deliberation (which is what Aristotle called κύριον or the supreme power when he referred at 1299a1 to 'the deliberative, that is, the supreme element in states') nor jurisdiction could be seen as parts of sovereignty, Bodin believed, since they were both powers frequently exercised by private citizens – as in a council or parliament under an early modern monarch. Government (*gubernatio* or *administratio*), Bodin continued, was anything concerned with 'decrees, edicts, and their execution'. But these activities were not examples of specifically *sovereign* power; that, Bodin argued in the *Methodus*, consisted in *the right to choose* magistrates and other members of a government, together with the power of ultimate legislation. 'In every state one ought to investigate who can give authority to magistrates, who can take it away, who can make or repeal laws – whether one citizen or a small part of the citizens or a greater part. When this has been ascertained, the type of government is easily understood.'[10] Though it is often said that the *Methodus* did not display the same concentration on legislative sovereignty as the

---

[8] One can see this particularly clearly if one compares the sequence of discussions in Chapter 6 with Jacques Lefèvre d'Étaples's *In Politica Aristotelis Introductio* (1506, but regularly reprinted in the early sixteenth century), with which Bodin was no doubt extremely familiar. This was a précis of the *Politics* which highlighted exactly the topics Bodin dealt with in Chapter 6, in the order in which he dealt with them. Only the first part of the *Introductio*, on the household, and the last part, on education, were not used in Bodin's critique (though there is a brief discussion of the household in the *Methodus*).

[9] There are important differences between the first and second editions of Bodin's *Methodus*, which have recently been clarified in Sara Miglietti's critical edition of the work: see Jean Bodin, *Methodus ad facilem historiarum cognitionem*, ed. and trans. (into Italian) S. Miglietti (Pisa: Edizioni della Normale, 2013). The passage quoted is on p. 356 of Miglietti's edition, p. 181 of the first edition (Paris: n.p., 1566), p. 234 of the second edition (Paris: 1572), and p. 156 of the English translation by Beatrice Reynolds (*Method for the Easy Comprehension of History*, trans. B. Reynolds (New York: Columbia University Press, 1945). The Aristotle reference is to Book IV.14 of the *Politics*, 1297b38.

[10] *quis imperium magistratibus dare & adimere, quis leges iubere aut abrogare possit*: Bodin, *Methodus*, trans. Miglietti, pp. 401–2; Bodin, *Methodus*, 1572 edn., p. 271; Bodin, *Method*, trans. Reynolds, pp. 178–9. The 1566 edn. (p. 207) has simply *quis imperium magistratibus dare & adimere possit* – a good example of the way he seems to have brought the 1572 edition fully in line with the *Republic* (see below). Melissa Lane draws attention in her contribution to this volume to the fact that Bodin's account of Aristotle may be misleading, and rests heavily on a reading of Book IV of the *Politics*, in isolation from other parts of the work where choosing magistrates appears to have been as important to Aristotle as it was to be to Bodin. This is true; the explanation may be that Bodin was tracking the humanist interpretation of Aristotle.

Republic[11] ten years later, in fact both works treated the principal powers of a sovereign as the right to legislate and the right to choose magistrates. Bodin indeed more or less repeated verbatim this definition in Book II Chapter VII of the *Republic*: 'to decide on the type of state (*iuger un estat*), the question is not to know who have the magistracies or offices: but solely who has the sovereignty, and all the power to appoint and dismiss the officers, and to give laws to every one'.[12]

In the *Republic* he also made even clearer than in the *Methodus* that he believed this to be an entirely original discovery in political science. 'There is a clear distinction between the state and the government, a principle of politics [*secret de police* in French] which no one [the Latin adds,

---

[11] I use this translation of the title of Bodin's great work to cover both the French version, published under the name *Les six livres de la République* (first edition 1576, revised editions issued at intervals down to 1587), and the (often quite different) Latin version, published under the name *De Republica libri sex* in 1586, and not significantly revised in subsequent editions. The only complete English translation, of a conflation of the two texts (see McRae's Introduction to his edition, p. A38), appeared in 1606 as *The Six Bookes of a Commonweale*, translated by Richard Knolles; a photographic reprint of this with scholarly introduction and apparatus, produced by K. D. McRae (Cambridge, MA: Harvard University Press, 1962), is still the standard English edition. There is no modern edition which tracks the many variants in the texts. But there is an excellent critical bibliography of Bodin's works by R. Crahay, M.-T. Isaac and M.-T. Lenger, *Bibliographie critique des éditions anciennes de Jean Bodin* (Gembloux: Académie Royale de Belgique, 1992). I have chosen to give page references to the French editions of 1576 (Paris: Jacques du Puys), the first edition, and 1579 (Lyons: Jacques du Puys), the sixth edition, of which Crahay, Isaac and Lenger say that 'pratiquement, le texte atteint ici son stade définitif' (*Bibliographie critique*, p. 111); I also give references to the 1586 Latin edition, *De Republica libri sex* (Paris: Jacques de Puy, 1586) and the McRae edition. All translations from Bodin are my own unless otherwise stated.

[12] *Republique* 1576, p. 281; 1579, p. 235. The last phrase is a translation of 'donner loy à chacun', which Knolles (*Six Bookes*, p. 249) translated 'give lawes unto every man'; but it is noteworthy that the Latin version does not include this phrase, reading simply that we should establish the type of state 'ex eorum persona, qui iura maiestatis habent', and not from the distribution of its magistracies (*Republica* 1586, p. 233). So, intriguingly, the Latin version is closer here to the 1566 edition of the *Methodus*, and the French to the 1572 edition (above, n. 12). For the standard view that the *Methodus* and the *Republic* are significantly different, see J. Franklin, *Jean Bodin and the Rise of Absolutist Theory* (Cambridge: Cambridge University Press, 1973), p. vii; see also p. 23. Franklin's view of the relationship between the two works was shared to some extent by Beatrice Reynolds in her translation of the *Methodus*, describing it as his 'earlier and more liberal work' (*Method*, trans. Reynolds, p. x), but it was not present in the first, and most careful analysis of the *Methodus*, by John L. Brown in his *The 'Methodus ad facilem historiarum cognitionem' of John Bodin: A Critical Study* (Washington, DC: Catholic University of America Press, 1939), and it does not seem to have been a common view earlier. There are sensible remarks about the relationship in R. E. Giesey, 'Medieval Jurisprudence in Bodin's Concept of Sovereignty', in H. Denzer (ed.), *Verhandlungen Der Internationalen Bodin Tagung in München* (Munich: C. H. Beck, 1973), pp. 167–86, at pp. 178–9, and Sara Miglietti in her edition of the text agrees that there is not a clear distinction between the *Methodus* and the *Republic* (pp. 31–48).

'as far as I can tell', *quantum intelligere potuimus*] has hitherto observed.'[13] He also made clear how the distinction enabled one to have a much richer account of constitutional possibilities than the Aristotelian scheme had allowed.

The state can be a monarchy, and nevertheless be governed as a democracy [*gouverné populairement*] if the prince opens up the Estates, magistracies, offices and rewards equally to everyone, without regard to their nobility, wealth or virtue. A monarchy can also be governed aristocratically . . . Similarly an aristocratic state [*seigneurie*] can be governed democratically . . . [And] If the majority of citizens [*pluspart des citoyens*] hold the sovereignty, and if the people give the honorable offices, the rewards and the benefices only to noblemen . . . the state will be democratic, but governed aristocratically.[14]

These situations were the true arrangements which had traditionally been misinterpreted as mixed constitutions: 'this variation in government has misled those who have thought Republics can be mixed, without seeing that the state of a Republic is different from its government and administration'.[15]

Not only did this central theme in Bodin's discussion of sovereignty, the impossibility of mixed government, depend in his eyes on understanding the distinction between sovereign and government; so did another critical feature of sovereignty, its *perpetual* character. At the start of his discussion of sovereignty, in Book I Chapter 8,[16] he was concerned to define it as *perpetual*, and consequently to distinguish between the underlying location of sovereignty and the form that governmental power might take at any particular moment. As he said there,

I have said that this power is perpetual, because it can happen that one or more people have absolute power given to them for some certain period of time, upon the expiration of which they are no more than private subjects. And even while they are in power, they cannot call themselves sovereign princes. They are but trustees and custodians of that power until such time as it pleases the people or the prince to take it back, for the latter always remains in lawful possession.[17]

---

[13] *Republique* 1576, p. 233; 1579, p. 189; *Republica* 1586, p. 189; *Six Bookes*, p. 199.

[14] *Republique* 1576, pp. 233–4; 1579, pp. 189–90; *Republica* 1586, p. 189; *Six Bookes*, pp. 199–200. The last sentence comes later in the same Book, at *Republique* 1576, p. 282; 1579, p. 235; *Republica* 1586, pp. 233–4; *Six Bookes*, p. 249.

[15] *Republique* 1576, p. 234; 1579, p. 190; *Republica* 1586, p. 189; *Six Bookes*, p. 200.

[16] This was in fact Chapter 9 in the first French edition; it became Chapter 8 in the second authorised edition (Paris: du Puys, 1577), when Bodin moved the former Chapter 8 to become Chapter 6 of Book V, and remained in that position for subsequent editions (Crahay et al., *Bibliographie critique*, pp. 101–2). In the Latin version it was Chapter 8 from the beginning.

[17] Translation from J. Franklin (ed.), *Bodin on Sovereignty* (Cambridge: Cambridge University Press, 1992), pp. 1–2. *Republique* 1576, p. '152' (*recte* 125); 1579, p. 85; *Republica* 1586, p. 79; *Six Bookes*, p. 84.

The most eye-catching example of this, and the one to which Bodin immediately moved, was the Roman dictator.

Having laid down these maxims as the foundations of sovereignty, we may conclude that neither the Roman dictator, nor the Spartan harmoste... any other commissioner or magistrate who had absolute power for a limited time to dispose of the affairs of the commonwealth, had sovereignty. This holds even though the early dictators had full power [*summum ius*] and had it in the best possible form, or *optima lege* as the ancient Latins called it. For there was no appeal [from a dictator] in those days, and all the other offices were suspended... It thus appears that the dictator was neither a prince nor a sovereign magistrate [*summum magistratum*], as many have thought [*ut plerique putarunt*].[18]

The *pleri* included Pomponius in the Digest itself, who said that the dictator possessed *summa potestas*,[19] but also many Renaissance writers – for example Sir Thomas Elyot in *The Governour* described the dictator as 'soveraine' and as possessing 'the pristinate authorite and maiestie of a king".[20] But no doubt uppermost in Bodin's mind was Josse Clichtove's commentary on Jacques Lefèvre's *In Politica Aristotelis Introductio*, which listed the dictatorship as one of the five *modi regni*, possessing *totius rei summam authoritatem* and differing from others kinds of kingship only in that it was temporary.[21] From the perspective of the later use of the sovereignty–government distinction, Bodin's argument about the dictator was particularly ominous, for it raised the possibility that a ruler possessing untrammelled monarchical power – precisely 'the pristine authority and majesty of a king' – might not in fact be the sovereign, but instead might be subordinate to a democratic power.

Moreover, Bodin's own defence of monarchy in this context was clearly hard to maintain. He was committed to the proposition that sovereignty had to be perpetual, and that a time-limited ruler such as the dictator could not be sovereign, however extensive his powers, and however minimal the temporal limits were on his office – so that even the archons of the

---

[18] Translation from Franklin (ed.), *Bodin on Sovereignty*, pp. 1–2. *Republique* 1576, pp. 125–6; 1579, p. 85–6; *Republica* 1586, p. 79; *Six Bookes*, p. 85. This is a list based initially on the observations about the dictatorship and the *aisymnetai* in Dionysius of Halicarnassus V.73, though Dionysius treats them both as 'elective tyrants'. See also Bodin's remarks in II.3, attacking Aristotle for calling those magistrates 'kings' who were the equivalent of this Dionysian list (*Republique* 1576, pp. 242–3; 1579, pp. 197–8; *Republica* 1586, pp. 196–7; *Six Bookes*, p. 207).

[19] 'Hunc magistratum, quoniam summam potestatem habebat, non erat fas ultra sextum mensem retineri': *Digest* I.2.2.18.

[20] Thomas Elyot, *The Boke named The Governour*, ed. H. H. S. Croft, 2 vols. (London: Kegan Paul, Trench & Co, 1883), I, pp. 19–20.

[21] Jacques Lefèvre and Josse Clichtove, *In Politica Aristotelis, introductio Iacobi Fabri Stapulensis: adiecto commentario declarata per Iudocum Clichtoveum Neoportuensem* (Paris: n.p., 1535), p. 12r. The commentary was originally published in 1516.

early Athenian republic, who held 'absolute power' for nine or ten years, could not be called sovereign.[22] But Bodin had to recognise that this left monarchy in an awkward position. On the account he gave in Chapter 8 a democratic or aristocratic sovereign was indeed perpetual, in the full sense of the term, as assemblies do not die; but a monarch was perpetual only in the sense that he held power for the term of his life – otherwise, as Bodin acknowledged, 'there would . . . be few sovereign monarchs inasmuch as there are very few that are hereditary. Those especially would not be sovereign who come to the throne by election.'[23] So the difference between an elective dictator and an elective monarch became merely that the expiration date of the former's term of office was known in advance, and that of the latter was not. We shall see in a moment that later readers of Bodin pounced on the unsatisfactory character of his account of perpetuity, and either questioned the whole Bodinian distinction between sovereign and government (as Grotius did) or reworked it to make it more satisfactory, but at the same time more threatening to elective monarchy (as Hobbes did).

Both these aspects of Bodin's theory of sovereignty – that is, the connection between the sovereignty–government distinction and the impossibility of mixed government, and the insistence that sovereignty must be understood as perpetual – had the same effect, to prise apart 'sovereignty' from the actual operation of governmental power. What we had hitherto supposed was political power, Bodin tells us, is not *really* where power lies: it might be the case that on a day-to-day basis we are ordered around by a king or an assembly of some kind, and there may be no recourse to any other institution to protect us from those orders, but hidden underneath those structures, and possibly apparent only at very long intervals, was a different kind of power which gave *legitimacy* to the other institutions.

The most powerful example he gave of this, an example which (again) was to be widely used in defence of democracy, was the Roman constitution both in its republican heyday and under the principate. Bodin insisted, as part of his attack on the mixed constitution, that republican Rome was a democracy; but he also went so far as to say that Rome under the principate down to the time of Vespasian was still a democracy, for 'a principate is nothing other than a democracy or aristocracy in which

---

[22] Franklin (ed.), *Bodin on Sovereignty*, p. 4; *Republique* 1576, p. 127; 1579, p. 87; *Republica* 1586, p. 80; *Six Bookes*, p. 86.

[23] He believed (correctly) that only the French and English monarchies were strictly speaking hereditary. Translation from Franklin (ed.), *Bodin on Sovereignty*, p. 6. *Republique* 1576, p. 128; 1579, p. 88; *Six Bookes*, p. 87. In the Latin version Bodin removed the remark that there are 'few that are hereditary': *Republica* 1586, p. 81.

there is a chief who can give commands to every individual'.[24] Augustus seized the real power in the state, but – Bodin observed in a striking passage –

Here we must inquire into the thing itself [*reipsa*] and not the pretence [*simulatio*]: for he who has most power in the Republic [*plus in Republica potest*] is thought to possess the sovereignty, but if we are concerned with rights [*de iure*], we should look not to what is, but to what ought to be. And therefore a principate is nothing other than an Aristocracy or a Democracy in which one among many is preeminent in dignity; but sovereignty [*maiestas*] is with the people or the optimates.[25]

So the emperor too, like the dictator, could not be seen as a sovereign: Rome remained a democracy in which – in principle – the old legal order could at any time have reasserted itself. If one looks at the use made of Bodin in the late sixteenth and early seventeenth centuries, it was this passage that attracted most attention among his readers, and which proved explosive in the context of the late sixteenth- and seventeenth-century debates about European monarchy.

Obviously, it would be perverse to deny that Bodin's object in writing both the *Methodus* and the *Republic* was to produce a defence of the modern French monarchy against its enemies, and not to put forward a theory of democracy. So the natural question that arises is, why should a project of that kind have led Bodin to invent this distinction and put so much weight on it? I do not want in a volume devoted to popular sovereignty to give a detailed response to this question, but I think the correct answer is along the following lines. We misunderstand Bodin if

[24] Translation from Franklin (ed.), *Bodin on Sovereignty*, p. 107. *Republique* 1576, p. 231; 1579, p. 187; *Republica* 1586, p. 186; *Six Bookes*, p. 196. Vespasian is mentioned in the Latin version, and in the English translation, but not in the French versions, which instead talk about the 'long temps apres' Augustus during which Rome was really a republic. Vespasian was relevant because of the famous *lex de imperio Vespasiani*, an inscription from Rome known since at least the fourteenth century and now in the Capitoline Museum, which appears to confer legislative authority on Vespasian; though since what it clearly says is that Vespasian was to have the same authority as had been conferred on Augustus, Tiberius and Claudius it is not obvious that it made any difference to the legal status of the emperors. Modern scholarship to some extent confirms Bodin's general view of the legal basis of the principate: see P. A. Brunt, 'Lex de Imperio Vespasiani', *Journal of Roman Studies* 67 (1977), pp. 95–116; F. Millar, 'Imperial Ideology in the *Tabula Siarensis*', in J. González and J. Arce (eds.), *Estudios sobre la Tabula Siarensis* (Madrid: CSIC, Centro de Estudios Históricos, 1988), pp. 11–19.

[25] My translation is from the Latin: *Republica* 1586, p. 187, which was followed by the English translation, *Six Bookes*, p. 197. The French is slightly different:'in matters of state [*en matiere d'estat*], he who is master of force, is the master of men, of laws, and of the whole republic: but in terms of right [*en termes de droit*], it is not necessary, says Papinian, to pay attention to what is done at Rome, but properly [*bien*] to what ought to be done': *Republique* 1576, p. 231; 1579, pp. 187–8.

we think that his defence of the French monarchy against particularly its Huguenot critics was a defence of royal absolutism in the sense of an activist monarch. Bodin's governing passion throughout his life was a vindication of the special role of the *parlements* in the government of France. He was accredited as an advocate of the Parlement of Paris in 1561/2, and as he said in the dedication to his *Demonomanie* of 1580 he spent 'the best part of my life' in 'that sovereign school of justice' with 'unbelievable pleasure and profit'.[26] The relationship between the kings of France and their *parlements* was a notoriously complex and subtle one: royal acts had (normally) to be registered by the *parlement* to be treated as valid in the courts, and the registration process could involve a series of remonstrances by the *parlement* back to the king trying to get changes in acts of which they disapproved, remonstrances which characteristically cited general principles of justice but could also draw attention to 'inconveniens' which might arise as a consequence of the royal proposal.[27] The king could in the end force registration against the wishes of the parlement through a *lettre de jussion*, but too frequent a use of this power would have led to the breakdown of the system, and kings were reluctant to do this. But the *parlement* was, in the last analysis, the royal council, and the *parlementaires* (who standardly described themselves as 'representing' the *maiestas* (i.e. the sovereignty, in Bodin's terminology) of the king[28] – not, strikingly, as in England, the people – saw their task as protecting the interests of the monarchy even against the wishes of a particular king. This was most notably expressed in their constant struggle to halt the alienation of the royal domain and to preserve it intact for future monarchs.

Right at the beginning of the *Methodus*, and long before he actually turned to the history of states, Bodin announced that 'it is one thing to declare laws, another to take counsel concerning legislation. The latter is for the senate, the former for the people or the prince or whoever has the sovereignty.'[29] (The Parlement of Paris was standardly described by its admirers as the Senate of France). And when he did turn to the history of France, in Chapter VI, his constant theme was the importance and independence of the Parlement. It is this above all which has traditionally led to the view that the *Methodus* is more 'constitutionalist' than the

---

[26] Jean Bodin, *De la Demononamie des Sorciers* (Paris: Jacque du Puys, 1580), sig. á2r.
[27] A good example is provided by the May 1563 remonstrance on the attempt to abandon the requirement for officers of the Crown to profess the Catholic faith. See S. Daubresse, *Le Parlement de Paris ou La Voix de la Raison (1559–1589)*, Travaux d'Humanisme et Renaissance 398 (Geneva: Librairie Droz, 2005), pp. 490–4.
[28] Ibid., pp. 46 ff.
[29] Bodin, *Methodus*, trans. Miglietti, p. 124; 1566 edn., pp. 29–30; 1572 edn., p. 37; Bodin, *Method*, trans. Reynolds, p. 32.

Republic. But in fact we find just the same defence of the authority and practical independence of the parlements in the *Republic.*[30]

Given Bodin's strenuous defence of *parlements*, which continued even into the period of his adherence to the Catholic League,[31] we can understand the real point of his distinction between sovereign and government, and why it emerged from the distinctive constitutional arrangements of *ancien régime* France. Unlike England, where it might be possible to

---

[30] There are many examples of this, but the most striking and revealing comes in his argument (against the late medieval canonists, in particular) that there is an important difference between *law* and *contract*, and that

> 'a sovereign prince is bound [in the courts, i.e. not merely morally] by the contracts he has made, whether with his subject or with a foreigner. For since he is the guarantor to his subjects of the agreements and mutual obligations that they have entered with one another, there is all the more reason why he must render justice for his own act. Thus the Parlement of Paris wrote to King Charles IX in March 1563 that his majesty could not unilaterally break the contract between himself and the clergy without the clergy's consent, inasmuch as he had a duty to give justice.'

(Translation from Franklin (ed.), *Bodin on Sovereignty* p. 35. *Republique* 1576, pp. 147–8; 1579, p. 106; *Republica* 1586, p. 99; *Six Bookes*, p. 106). This refers to a remonstrance that the Parlement delivered on 11 March 1564, protesting that a payment forced from the Church by Charles IX had not been used for redeeming the royal domain, contrary to the agreement with the Church about its taxation made at Poissy in 1561 (the 'Contrat de Poissy'). Though Bodin was notoriously casual about dates, references etc. (for his casualness, see e.g. the remarks in Giesey, 'Medieval Jurisprudence', p. 168 n.3 and p. 176), his dating of this remonstrance to 1563 is probably not an error. France began to date the new year from 1 January instead of 25 March in 1564 (Charles IX's Edict of Roussillon, issued in January 1563 OS, registered by the Parlement of Paris December 1564 OS and NS). Although the Edict intended that January 1563 OS should be regarded as January 1564 NS, in practice the new dating did not come in until the following year. So when Bodin said March 1563, he will have meant March 1564 NS. Daubresse comments that there is no record of a remonstrance of the kind Bodin describes in March 1563 (*Parlement de Paris*, p. 123 n. 12), but she does not consider the question raised by the change in dating the year, nor link Bodin's remark with the remonstrance of 11 March 1564 she describes on p. 127, which is plainly what Bodin had in mind. But what Bodin did not tell his readers was that a royal *lettre de jussion* of July 1564 replied that the payment had been necessary in order to maintain the Swiss alliance, and that the Parlement gave way and authorised the payment. So in fact the moral of the episode was that the royal will *could* override a contract, a moral Bodin conveniently forbore to draw.

[31] See P. L. Rose, 'The Politique and the Prophet: Bodin and the Catholic League 1589–1594', *The Historical Journal* 21 (1978), pp. 783–808. In the letter (probably to the president of the Paris Parlement, Barnabé Brisson) that Bodin wrote in March 1589 justifying his switch to the League, and which was published anonymously as *Lettre d'un Lieutenant-Général de Province à un des premiers magistrats de France* (Paris: n.p., 1589), Bodin argued that 'une rébellion universelle ne se doyt appeler rébellion. L'union de tant de citez et de peuples que j'ay remarqué ne pouvant être chastiée: veu principalement que tout premièrement tous les parlemens de ce Royaume qui sont les fortes barrières de la France sont uniz' (see J. Moreau-Reibel, *Jean Bodin et le droit public comparé* (Paris: Vrin, 1933), p. 426). In other words, he moved to the League once the Parlement of Paris, and the other *parlements*, split, with most of their members turning to the League.

assert that Parliament (including the queen or king) was both sovereign and government, in France there could be no real plausibility in any claim about the supremacy of the *parlements* – they were patently not sovereign bodies. But on the other hand they were not mere agents of the sovereign monarch, simply implementing his commands, but were able (on Bodin's account) to have a very high degree of autonomy in their decisions – in particular, there was no appeal from their judgments sitting as a high court. The delicate balance between king and *parlements* could not be expressed by saying that the *parlements* were merely the agents of the king, since the whole point of the system was that they were not; but at the same time they could not be regarded as equal to the king, nor as sharers in some sense in his sovereignty. Bodin's great idea was that they were engaged in something different from the activity of the sovereign monarch, and that their relative independence in practice did not call into question the suzerainty of the king. The king's function was to authorise or render legitimate law whose content was (ideally) determined by the *parlements*, and to authorise the punishment of offenders whose guilt had been determined by the judges.

The theoretical structure that Bodin had called into being to capture the idiosyncratic shape of the modern French monarchy proved to be very contentious for the next two hundred years It was above all Hugo Grotius who set the tone for much of what followed with his repudiation of the sovereignty–government distinction. He had always despised Bodin – he described him once as someone who 'knew a great deal but was very confused. His book *De republica* is a great heap of a work, full of falsities'[32] – and as a young man he had already disagreed with Bodin's democratic interpretation of the Roman constitution, remarking in a letter to a friend that

like you I disagree with Bodin . . . I believe that the Roman Republic when it was at its best was an example of those types of aristocracy which Aristotle defines as 'constitutions which incline more than the so-called polity towards oligarchy' . . . For although the highest authority which Bodin calls sovereignty [*ius Maiestatis*] may have been in the people in time of war, there's plenty of

---

[32] R. Pintard, *La Mothe le Vayer – Gassendi – Guy Patin: études de bibliographie et de critique suivies de textes inédits de Guy Patin* (Paris: Boivin, 1943), p. 81. In a letter to his friend Jean De Cordes of 1634 he said that he had always thought of Bodin as 'a man more devoted to things than to words' and as someone 'barely instructed in Greek' (Hugo Grotius, *Briefwisseling van Hugo Grotius*, vol. V, ed. B. L. Meulenbroek (The Hague: Martinus Nijhoff, 1966), p. 279; see also N. Malcolm, 'Jean Bodin and the Authorship of the "Colloquium Heptaplomeres"', *Journal of the Warburg and Courtauld Institutes* 69 (2006), pp. 95–150, at p. 120. Grotius was being rather unfair about Bodin's Greek: Bodin's first publication was a scholarly edition in Greek of Oppian's *De Venatione* (Paris: n.p., 1555).

evidence to show where the administration of government [*rerum administratio*] was to be found ordinarily and – as one might say – on a day-to-day basis. . . . I do not think anyone denies that at Rome that power was with the *optimates*.[33]

So Grotius was already questioning the worth of Bodin's idea that a sovereign might lurk under the superficial apparatus of the day-to day government and be distinguishable from it; as far as he was concerned the actual administration *was* the sovereign.

In his *De Iure Belli ac Pacis* of 1625 he accordingly reasserted something explicitly like Aristotle's account of the *potestas civilis*, repeating Aristotle's analysis of what the various functions involved in *administranda republica* were, without any attempt to distinguish between (for example) legislation and consultation, except that some acts of *potestas* were to do with public things, such as legislation, and some with private, such as judicial decisions (I.3.6).[34] As for Bodin's prime example of the distinction between sovereignty and government, the Roman dictatorship, Grotius was blunt.

We must distinguish between the Thing itself, and the Manner of enjoying it . . . Thus, amongst the *Romans*, the Dictator was Sovereign [*summum imperium . . . habebat*] for a Time . . . Neither can I agree with those, who say the *Roman* Dictator had not the Sovereign Power, because it was not perpetual: For the Nature of moral Things is known by their Operations, wherefore those Powers, which have the same Effects, should be called by the same Name. Now the Dictator, during the whole Time of his Office, exercised all the Acts of civil Government, with as much Authority as the most absolute King; and nothing he had done could be annulled by any other Power. And the Continuance of a Thing alters not the Nature of it. (I.3.11.1; see also I.3.8.1)

Similarly, he rejected any distinction between hereditary and elective kings, observing (again in sharp contradiction to Bodin) that 'the *Roman* Empire, even after all Power was taken from the Senate and People, was conferred by Election' (I.3.10) without this calling the emperor's sovereignty into question.

Strikingly, however, it was Hobbes who came to Bodin's defence against these strictures of Grotius, and indeed pushed Bodin's basic idea even further than Bodin himself had done. He set out his case against

---

[33] Hugo Grotius, *Briefwisseling*, vol. I, ed. P. C. Molhuysen (The Hague: Martinus Nijhoff, 1928), p. 29.

[34] References to and quotations from the *De Iure Belli ac Pacis* are from the 1738 London edition of the English translation, with notes by Jean Barbeyrac, reprinted as *The Rights of War and Peace*, ed. R. Tuck, 3 vols. (Indianapolis: Liberty Fund, 2005). I give the book, chapter and paragraph numbers as is usual with citations from *De Iure Belli ac Pacis*. A critical edition of the Latin text is *De iure belli ac pacis*, ed. B. J. A. De Kanter-van Hettinga Tromp with additional notes by R. Feenstra and C. E. Persenaire (Aalen: Scientia Verlag 1993).

Grotius's account of sovereignty most clearly in Chapter VII of *De Cive*, which contains a remarkable account of democracy as the first and most basic form of a commonwealth, and an extensive discussion of the various forms a democracy can take. Among those forms, Hobbes argued, were all kinds of time-limited monarchies, and he set out his ideas in a long paragraph from which I will quote extensively, as it makes his views entirely clear, and *inter alia* provides the vivid analogy to which I refer in my title.[35] He presumed, of course, that a democracy must involve an actual assembly of citizens, and he considered four possible cases in which a time-limited monarch might be created. The first was when the assembly elected a king without any provision for reassembling on his death; in such a case the democracy had *ipso facto* dissolved itself and transferred sovereignty to the king. The second was when

the *people* leave the assembly after the election of a *time-limited Monarch* with the decision already made to meet at a certain time and place after his death; in this case, on the Monarch's death, power resides firmly in the *people* by their previous right, without any new act on the part of the citizens; for in the whole intervening period *sovereign power* [*summum imperium*] (like *Ownership*) remained with the *people*; only its *use* or *exercise* was enjoyed by the time-limited *Monarch*, as a *usufructuary*.

The third case was

if after the election of a *time-limited Monarch*, the *people* has departed from the council with the understanding that it would hold meetings at fixed times and places while the term set for the Monarch is still running, (as *Dictators* were appointed among the Romans), such a one is not to be regarded as a *Monarch* but as the first minister of the *people*, and the *people* can, if it shall see fit, deprive him of his office [*administratio*] even before his term is finished.

And the fourth was

if the *people* leaves their council after appointing a *time-limited Monarch* without leave to meet again except on the orders of the appointee, the *people* is understood to be thereupon dissolved; and power belongs absolutely to anyone appointed on these terms.[36]

---

[35] Thomas Hobbes, *On the Citizen*, ed. R. Tuck and M. Silverthorne (Cambridge: Cambridge University Press, 1998), pp. 98–100 (VII.16). The Latin text can be found in *De Cive: The Latin Version*, ed. H. Warrender (Oxford: Oxford University Press, 1983), pp. 156–8.

[36] In the *Elements of Law* the distinction between the four cases is less crisp. The dictator is the same as an elected king: 'If this power of the people were not dissolved, at the choosing of their king for life; then is the people sovereign still, and the king a minister thereof only, but so, as to put the whole sovereignty in execution; a great minister, but no otherwise for his time, than a dictator was at Rome' (Thomas Hobbes, *The Elements of Law, Natural and Politic*, ed. F. Tönnies with new introduction by M. Goldsmith

Having set out the four cases, Hobbes enlarged his discussion with the analogy that provided me with the title for this chapter.

If a King without an heir is about to go to sleep and not wake up again, (i.e., is about to die) and hands sovereign power to someone to exercise until he awakes, he is handing him also the succession; likewise if a *people* in choosing a temporary Monarch, at the same time abolishes its own power of reconvening, it is passing dominion over the commonwealth to him. Further, a king who is going to sleep for a while gives sovereign power to someone else to exercise, and takes it back when he wakes up; just so *a people, on the election of a temporary Monarch*, retains the right of meeting again at a certain time and place, and on that day resumes its power. A king who has given his power to someone else to exercise, while he himself stays awake, can resume it again when he wishes; just so a *people* which duly meets throughout the term set for a *time-limited Monarch* can strip him of power if it so wishes. Finally a king who gives the exercise of his power to another person while he sleeps, and can wake up again only with the consent of that person, has lost his life and his power together; just so a *people* which has committed power to a *time-limited Monarch* on the terms that it cannot meet again without his command, is radically dissolved, and its power rests with the person it has elected.

Hobbes thus restated the Bodinian distinction between sovereign and government, using the same terminology of *summum imperium* or *summa potestas* contrasted with *administratio*. But he was willing to go much further. As we saw earlier, Bodin was concerned to insist that monarchs elected for life were significantly different from the dictator – for otherwise, as he said, 'there would . . . be few sovereign monarchs'. Hobbes, however, ruthlessly followed through the logic of the distinction and concluded that elective monarchs were indeed not sovereign: all the elective monarchies of Europe were (by implication) really either aristocracies or democracies. Not even the monarchomachs had gone so far as to say this.

It is worth considering the far-reaching implications of these ideas. On Hobbes's account, a sovereign can be very thoroughly asleep: in the case of an elected monarchy, it might in principle be asleep for sixty or

(London: Frank Cass 1969 [London: Simpkin, Marshall, & Co., 1889]), p. 122 (II.2.9). And the right of the people to assemble during the monarch or dictator's term of office (*De Cive*'s third case) is treated as a general right: 'Though in the election of a king for life, the people grant him the exercise of their sovereignty for that time; yet if they see cause, they may recall the same before the time. As a prince that conferreth an office for life, may nevertheless, upon suspicion of abuse thereof, recall it at his pleasure.' This suggests that at the time Hobbes wrote the *Elements*, while he certainly believed that the critical question with regard to elective kingship was whether the democratic assembly had 'the right of assembling at certain times and places limited and made known' or not (II.2.10), he had not fully focused on the fact that there might be different specifications of the times, some of which would not permit the assembly to exercise its sovereign rights until the death of the incumbent ruler.

seventy years, or even more. Moreover, when awake the sovereign might do nothing more than select a new monarch, and promptly fall asleep again. So all actual legislation to do with the ordinary lives of the citizens, and all actual power exercised over them, would be in the hands of the monarch; yet the monarch would not be sovereign. At the very least this calls into question a naively Austinian view of Hobbes's theory of sovereignty, for it is very clearly not a theory of habitual obedience to a site of *power* in the sense of physical strength (control of an army, say). This point was made by Hobbes himself very clearly in Chapter X of *De Cive*, writing about an infant monarch:

The comparative advantages or disadvantages of different types of common-wealth [do not] result from the fact that sovereignty [*imperium*] itself or the administration of government business [*imperii negotia administranda*] is better entrusted to one man rather than to more than one, or on the other hand to a larger rather than a smaller number. For sovereignty [*imperium*] is a *power* [*potentia*], administration of government [*administratio gubernandi*] is an *act*. *Power* is equal in every kind of commonwealth; what differs are the acts, i.e. the *motions* and *actions* of the commonwealth, depending on whether they originate from the deliberations of many or of a few, of the competent or of the incompetent. This implies that the advantages and disadvantages of a régime do not depend upon him in whom the authority of the commonwealth resides, but upon the ministers of the sovereignty [*ministri imperii*]. Hence it is no obstacle to the good govern-ment of a commonwealth if the *Monarch* is a woman, a boy or an infant, provided that the holders of the ministries and public offices are competent to handle the business. (X.16)[37]

(Kinch Hoekstra has very recently stressed the importance of this fea-ture of Hobbes's theory).[38] Hobbes expressed it in dramatic fashion in *Leviathan* when he asserted (in a passage which has often surprised his readers) that

If a Monarch subdued by war, render himself Subject to the Victor; his Subjects are delivered from their former obligation, and become obliged to the Victor. But if he be held prisoner, or have not the liberty of his own Body; he is not understood to have given away the Right of Soveraigntie; and therefore his Subjects are obliged to yield obedience to the Magistrates formerly placed, governing not in their own name, but in his. For, his Right remaining, the question is only of the Administration; that is to say, of the Magistrates and Officers; which, if he

---

[37] Our edition of *On the Citizen* for Cambridge University Press translates *imperium* in this passage as 'government' (p. 125), but I have now come to realise that this is misleading, and that it should be contrasted with *gubernatio*, *administratio* or the other terms that in this tradition meant government as distinct from sovereignty.

[38] See K. Hoekstra, 'Early Modern Absolutism and Constitutionalism', *Cardozo Law Review* 34 (2012–13), pp. 1079–98, esp. pp. 1095–7.

have not means to name, he is supposed to approve those, which he himself had formerly appointed.[39]

This was an important practical issue when Hobbes was writing, for the king was (or had recently been) in prison, but royal governors were still in office in many places of great strategic significance for the Royalists, including the Channel Islands, Virginia and – above all – Ireland. And on Hobbes's account it was entirely reasonable to suppose that the imprisoned king was still sovereign, as he remained sovereign until his death even if he could do nothing – just as he would if he were similarly inert while asleep. Hobbes provided a startling analogy to this thought in Chapter XIII of *De Cive*:

We must distinguish between the *right* and the *exercise* of sovereign power; for they can be separated; for instance, he who has the *right* may be unwilling or unable to play a personal role in conducting trials or deliberating issues. For there are occasions when kings cannot manage affairs because of their age, or when even though they can, they judge it more correct to content themselves with choosing ministers and counsellors, and to exercise their power through them. When *right* and *exercise* [*jus & exercitium*] are separated, the government [*regimen*] of the commonwealth is like the ordinary government of the world, in which God the first mover of all things, produces natural effects through the order of secondary causes. But when he who has the right to reign wishes to participate himself in all judgements, consultations and public actions, it is a way of running things comparable to God's attending directly to every thing himself, contrary to the order of nature.[40]

God too is a sleeping sovereign.

The political implications of Hobbes's ideas, especially as expressed in *De Cive*, and in particular of his remarks about elective monarchy, were very clear to contemporaries, and they occasioned some of the sharpest criticism which Samuel Pufendorf delivered to Hobbes in his *De Iure Naturae et Gentium* of 1672. Referring to the second of Hobbes's cases of time-limited monarchy, in which the people agreed to meet on the monarch's death, but in the mean time '*sovereign power* (like *Ownership*) remained with the people', Pufendorf expostulated that

we utterly dislike the Assertion of Mr. *Hobbes*, which we meet with in his Book *De Cive* . . . This Notion, if taken in the gross Sense in which it is deliver'd, we cannot but look upon as highly dangerous and prejudicial to all those limited Princes, who are ordain'd by the voluntary Donation of the People, and bound up to certain fundamental Laws. And the rather, because, as he hath taken the Liberty to call

---

[39] Thomas Hobbes, *Leviathan*, rev. edn., ed. R. Tuck (Cambridge: Cambridge University Press, 1996), p. 154 ((London: n.p., 1651), pp. 114–15, Chapter XXI).

[40] Hobbes, *On the Citizen*, pp. 142–3 (XIII.1).

a King for Life a *temporary Monarch*, others may, with as much Reason, extend the Name to those who receive the Sovereignty, with the Privilege of transmitting it by Inheritance, yet so as to keep it within their own Line and Family. Besides, since Mr. *Hobbes* hath not determin'd how far he would stretch the Parallel which he useth, he may easily be intangled in a Train of very pernicious Consequences. For since Property, consider'd in itself, is a much more noble Right, than that of temporary Use; some Men may, on these Principles, conclude that the People are superior to the Prince, and have a Power of bringing him to Correction, in case he doth not govern, according to their Pleasure and Humour.[41]

(This was indeed Hobbes's third case – and Pufendorf was right that the distinction between the second and third cases was a fine one.) Pufendorf accused Hobbes of 'breaking and dividing' sovereignty, so that 'the κτῆσις, the Property or real Possession resides in the People, and the χρῆσις only, or the Use in the Prince'.

He was more hesitant about the dictator, but not on any major theoretical grounds. Partly, he believed that the dictator had not in fact had 'all, and each precise Part of the Sovereignty so committed to him together, as that, during the six Months Space, he might exercise it as he pleas'd', and partly he thought that

Tho' the Continuance of a Thing doth not change the Nature of it, yet there is no doubt to be made, but that a temporary Command is in Dignity much inferior to a perpetual one; since Men are wont to respect those with a much more solid Veneration, whom they apprehend to be incapable of returning to a private Condition, than those whom in a little time they are again like to see on the same Level with themselves.[42]

He also admitted that it might be impossible to find an example of a truly time-limited sovereign of this kind. But it is clear that his general theory committed him, just as it had Grotius, to its being at least a conceptual possibility, and Jean Barbeyrac in his extraordinarily influential editions of both Grotius and Pufendorf asserted that the dictator in the early Republic had indeed been as Grotius thought;[43] classical scholarship in the late seventeenth century, in the shape of Johannes Jens's essay *De dictatoribus populi Romani* of 1698, also endorsed the Grotian view.[44] Like Grotius,

---

[41] Samuel Pufendorf, *The Law of Nature and Nations*, 5th edn., ed. Jean Barbeyerac, trans. Basil Kennet (London: n.p., 1749), pp. 704–5; Samuel Pufendorf, *De Jure Naturae et Gentium* (Lund: n.p., 1672), p. 978 (VII.6.17).

[42] Pufendorf, *The Law of Nature and Nations*, p. 702; Pufendorf, *De Jure Naturae et Gentium*, p. 975 (VII.6.15).

[43] Grotius, *The Rights of War and Peace*, I.3.11 nn. 6 and 7. The original text of the notes can be found in Hugo Grotius, *Le Droit de la Guerre, et de la Paix*, 2 vols., trans. Jean Barbeyrac (Amsterdam: Pierre de Coup, 1724), I, pp. 135–6.

[44] This is to be found in Johannes Jens, *Ferculum Literarium* (Leiden: n.p., 1717), pp. 89–130; the essay is dated 1698 on p. 130.

it was the actual governmental structure that interested Pufendorf and Barbeyrac, and not the constitutional authority that might lie behind government, and be used to change it. And the motive for hostility to Bodin and Hobbes in this area is clear enough: in seventeenth-century Europe there were likely to be few people (even, any longer, in France) who wanted to argue for a 'sleeping' constitutional sovereign in a modern state in the form of a *king*: the force of the idea, for obvious reasons, was always going to be (as it had really been, even in Bodin) that a *people* could be thought of as a sleeping sovereign. It was this possibility that Grotius, Pufendorf and Barbeyrac feared and which Hobbes, remarkable as it might seem, was willing to countenance.

So it was of course precisely those three writers whom Rousseau excoriated in both the *Second Discourse* and the *Social Contract*, and his repeated insistence that the sovereignty–government distinction had been ignored, and that it was critical to modern democracy, was above all a response to their writings. Hobbes's view, on the other hand, at least as set out in *De Cive*, was much closer to Rousseau's. This was so not least, as I suggested at the beginning of this chapter, because both Hobbes and Rousseau were hostile to democratic *government*, in the sense of the ancient civic assemblies dominated by orators: 'Athens was in fact not a democracy, but a most tyrannical aristocracy, governed by learned men and orators,' said Rousseau in his *Political Economy*, in words that could have (and possibly did) come straight out of Hobbes.[45] As he made clear in his *Letters from the Mountain*, Rousseauian democracy was not an idyll of an ancient city-state transported to the present day, but a serious attempt at working out how a modern commercial state might genuinely deserve the title of a democracy, and the key to this was both the separation of government from fundamental acts of sovereign power and the full participation of the citizens in these acts.

The obvious institutional expression of this idea was a combination of constitutional referendums or plebiscites, in which an electorate votes on foundational legislation, and a representative government, and this has indeed become the default constitutional structure of the modern world. It did not require any technical innovations: any country that had general elections could also easily organise referendums, and general elections had been a feature of European societies for five hundred years by Rousseau's lifetime. And it was very soon after Rousseau's ideas became widely understood that in two countries, the United States

---

[45] Rousseau, *The Social Contract*, p. 8; Rousseau, *Oeuvres complètes*, II, p. 279. See Hobbes in *De Cive* X.7: 'Where there is *popular control*, there may be as many *Neros* as there are *Orators* who fawn on the *people*' (Hobbes, *On the Citizen*, p. 120).

and France, plebiscitary systems were introduced, often expressly in Rousseau's name. It should be noted, though, that – rather curiously – Rousseau himself did not discuss plebiscites. This is particularly striking, given that in his later works he had explored various ways of giving the people legislative power in a large state, as well (of course) as in the small states that were his preferred option.[46] *In Considerations on the Government of Poland* (drafted in 1772, but not published until his posthumous *Oeuvres* of 1782) he claimed that a system of mandated delegates to an assembly would achieve the objectives he had set out in the *Social Contract*, while in the 1765 *Project* for Corsica (which was not known until it was published in 1861) he seems to have considered the possibility of the sovereign people meeting separately in a number of large assemblies.[47]

---

[46] To the well-known constitutional sketches for Poland and Corsica, and his remarks on the Genevan constitution in *Letters from the Mountain* and the associated *History of Geneva* (in *Letter to Beaumont*, pp. 102–28) we can add his brief suggestions for a new settlement of the Genevan constitution in a letter to his friend François Coindet in February 1768 (Jean-Jacques Rousseau, *Correspondance complète de Jean Jacques Rousseau: édition critique établie et annotée par R. A. Leigh*, 52 vols., ed. R. A. Leigh (Oxford: Voltaire Foundation, 1965–88), vol. XXXV (1980), pp. 91–7) (letter no. 6239). See R. Whatmore, *Against War and Empire: Geneva, Britain, and France in the Eighteenth Century* (New Haven: Yale University Press, 2012), p. 94, where however the letter is dated 1767.

[47] The constitution of Corsica as it already existed in 1765 was praised by contemporaries such as James Boswell as approaching 'to the idea of a Roman comitia' (J. Boswell, *An account of Corsica* (London: n.p., 1769) p. 147), an assessment endorsed by Dorothy Carrington in her study of the Corsican constitution under Paoli ('The Corsican Constitution of Pasquale Paoli (1755–1769)', *English Historical Review* 88 (1973), pp. 481–503); each village elected (by manhood suffrage) a representative to be sent a very large assembly, the Diet, consisting of *c.* 325 members (pp. 495–6). Rousseau appears to have proposed instead that Corsica should be divided into twelve provinces, each of which should send a representative to the government while (apparently) deciding fundamental matters in a general gathering of the province. This seems to be the implication of the fragmentary remarks in the *Project*, that the people should assemble 'by sections rather than as a whole', that there should be twelve equally sized provinces as the basis for the government, and that 'the firm establishment of this form of government will produce two great advantages. First, by confining the work of administration to a small number only, it will permit the choice of enlightened men. Secondly, by requiring the concurrence of all members of the state in the exercise of the supreme authority, it will place all on a plane of perfect equality, thus permitting them to spread throughout the whole extent of the island and to populate it uniformly. This is the fundamental principle of our new constitution' (Jean-Jacques Rousseau, *Political Writings*, ed. and trans. F. M. Watkins (London: Thomas Nelson & Sons, 1953), p. 286; Rousseau, *Oeuvres complètes*, III, p. 496). Since the population of Corsica in 1780 has been estimated at 140,000 (S. Wilson, *Feuding, Conflict and Banditry in Nineteenth-Century Corsica* (Cambridge: Cambridge University Press, 1988), p. 10), Rousseau may have envisaged assemblies of approximately 10,000. So, in line with the importance he gave to the sovereign–government distinction, he was seeking to render the *government* of Corsica *less* democratic (something Paoli was also seeking in these years – see Carrington, 'Corsican Constitution', pp. 498 ff.), but to give a more effective voice to the *sovereign*.

But something like a modern plebiscitary system was undoubtedly a natural extension of Rousseau's ideas.

The first appearance of the system was in the United States – though not at the federal level (where although a formal separation was introduced through a separate mechanism for constitutional change, the bodies charged with ratifying the changes were still representative) but at the state level. The process began in Massachusetts, where the General Court decided in 1777 to draft a new constitution. At the conclusion of its deliberations, in May 1778, it then declared that it was submitting the constitution to the people and would require a two-thirds majority of the freemen for ratification. A statewide referendum was organised – which promptly rejected the proposals by a majority of 9,972 nays against 2,083 yeas (with 129 out of the 298 towns not submitting returns).[48] The General Court responded with a new proposal that there should now be a dedicated constitutional convention to draft a second version of the constitution, but that this version should also be ratified by a referendum. The vote of 1778 was the first general referendum or plebiscite ever mounted in any state anywhere in the world, and it corresponded exactly to the sovereign–government distinction as it had been theorised by Rousseau: the electorate behaved as a sovereign legislator, promulgating a set of fundamental laws, while leaving government in the hands of an elected legislature. By 1830 ten American states had either used plebiscites for constitutional enactments, or prescibed them, and by the beginning of the Civil War only five out of a Union of thirty-four did not do so.[49]

---

[48] R. M. Peters, *The Massachusetts Constitution of 1780: A Social Compact* (Amherst: University of Massachusetts Press, 1978), p. 19 (the total number of towns from O. and M. Handlin, *The Popular Sources of Political Authority* (Cambridge, MA: Harvard University Press, 1966), Appendix, pp. 933 ff.).

[49] Constitutional plebiscites were held or prescribed by 1830 as follows:
Massachusetts 1778; New Hampshire 1779; Mississippi 1817; Connecticut 1818; Alabama 1819 (prescribed in its constitution, but not actually held until its first amendment in 1828 (see T. M. Owen, *History of Alabama and Dictionary of Alabama Biography*, 4 vols. (Chicago: S. J. Clarke, 1921), I, p. 364); Maine 1819; New York 1821; Rhode Island 1824 (the constitution was thrown out by 3,206 to 1,668 and Rhode Island did not receive a written constitution until 1842, when one was passed by another plebiscite); and Virginia 1830. The five states not using plebiscites by 1861 were Arkansas, Delaware, Florida, South Carolina and Vermont; Delaware remains the only state in the Union not to use them for constitutional amendment. For accurate information (surprisingly hard to come by) see F. N. Thorpe (ed.), *The Federal and State Constitutions*, 7 vols. (Washington, DC: Government Printing House, 1909), together with the information on various state government websites. There is a good discussion by C. G. Fritz of the Jacksonian period's move to popular ratification in *American Sovereigns: The People and America's Constitutional Tradition before the Civil War* (Cambridge: Cambridge University Press, 2008), pp. 235–45.

The similarity between this structure and Rousseau's ideas was noted by contemporaries; indeed, Rousseau was cited during the Massachusetts constitutional debates in 1778,[50] while Josiah Tucker, in the course of an attack on what he took to be the modern Lockeans, observed that the English radical writers had not quite provided the theory for the course of action which (he believed) the Americans had taken.

Honest, undissembling Rousseau clearly saw, where the Lockian Hypothesis must necessarily end. And as he was a Man who never boggled at Consequences, however extravagant or absurd, he declared with his usual Frankness, that the People could not transfer their indefeasible Right of voting for themselves to any others ... The Doctors Priestley and Price do not indeed absolutely join Rousseau in condemning the Use of national Representatives; but it is plain, that they admit them with a very ill Grace, and, with great Reluctance.[51]

And when the new American constitutional arrangements were properly theorised for the first time, in the work of the Virginian St George Tucker, their intellectual roots were made clear.

The American revolution seems to have given birth to this new political phenomenon: in every state a written constitution was framed, and adopted by the people, both in their individual and sovereign capacity, and character. By this means, the just distinction between the sovereignty, and the government, was rendered familiar to every intelligent mind; the former was found to reside in the people, and to be unalienable from them; the latter in their servants and agents.[52]

---

[50] See *Result of the convention of delegates holden at Ipswich in the county of Essex, who were deputed to take into consideration the constitution and form of government, proposed by the Convention of the state of Massachusetts-Bay* (Newbury-port, MA: n.p., 1778), pp. 10, 14–15. It is worth observing that Rousseau himself, discussing the American revolution with an English visitor in 1776, fully supported the Americans, and was even prepared to countenance the continued existence of slavery among them, on the presumption that it would prove short-lived; he also expressed great admiration for Benjamin Franklin. See Thomas Bentley, *Journal of a Visit to Paris 1776*, ed. P. France (Brighton: University of Sussex Library, 1977), p. 60.

[51] J. Tucker, *A treatise concerning civil government, in three parts. Part I. The notions of Mr. Locke and his followers, concerning the origin, extent, and end of civil government, examined and confuted* ... (London: n.p., 1781), pp. 39–40. In his *A letter to Edmund Burke, Esq, in Answer to His Printed Speech* (London: n.p., 1775), p. 13 Tucker had already cited Rousseau's remarks in *A Letter from the Mountain* as expressing the colonists' ideas. As Eric Nelson shows in his chapter in this volume (Chapter 8), the heart of the American case against the British was a mistrust of Parliament as then constituted. As he has seen, some of them (at least for a time) were prepared to turn to the king as a protection from a corrupt Parliament (a theme in English radicalism from the early eighteenth century), but other were interested in *popular* checks on an elected body. Both the Massachusetts radicals and the 'patriot royalists' shared in a hostility to the power of an unrestrained and potentially corrupt legislature.

[52] St G. Tucker, *Blackstone's Commentaries: with notes of reference to the Constitution and laws of the federal government of the United States and of the commonwealth of Virginia*, 5 vols. (Philadelphia: n.p., 1803), I, Note D I.5, Appendix, pp. 153–4.

Tucker was scrupulous about the sovereignty–government distinction, remarking that the two things were often wrongly confused,[53] and it is clear from his terminology, such as his description of government potentially 'usurping' sovereignty, that he was drawing upon Rousseau, whom indeed he cited as the authority for some of his basic principles.[54]

The second country to move in this direction was France, where constitutional plebiscites were discussed from the beginning of 1789, and were finally introduced in the (abortive) Girondin constitution of 1793, to be followed by all major constitutional changes down to 1814. They were first suggested as a serious possibility during the debates over the future of the royal veto in September 1789, when a number of future Girondins argued that the use of the veto should trigger a national vote on the proposed measure. One of them, Jean-Baptiste Salle, made clear the theoretical roots of the idea: responding to a work by the liberal monarchist Jean Mounier, which had defended an absolute royal veto on the grounds that popular government was dangerous: the people 'is essentially credulous; and, in its moments of fury, it uses ostracism against a great man. It wishes the death of Socrates, bewails it the next day, and a few days later dresses the altars for him',[55] Salle wrote.

The people does not know how to govern without passion! But who talks here of governing? Government is not sovereignty; to govern is not to legislate [footnote: 'M. Mounier repeatedly confounds these two things in his last work. This is a familiar sophism of his . . . ']; when the people of Athens judged its great men, it was fulfilling the function of magistracy; it had in view a particular object; it governed, it could go wrong, and it often did so. But, when the people of Athens, of those of Sparta, of Rome, etc., exercised sovereignty, that is made law; when they decreed [*stipulaient*] by themselves and for themselves, they did not go wrong.[56]

---

[53] 'The sovereignty, though always potentially existing in the people of every independent nation, or state, is in most of them, usurped by, and confounded with, the government': ibid., Note B, Appendix, p. 10.

[54] 'The right of governing can, therefore, be acquired only by consent, originally; and this consent must be that of at least a majority of the people . . . See Rousseau's Social Compact': ibid., Note B, Appendix, p. 8.

[55] J. Mounier, *Considérations sur les gouvernemens* (Paris: n.p., 1789), p. 6.

[56] *Archives Parlementaires de 1787 à 1860*, Première Série VIII, ed. M. J. Mavidal, E. Laurent and E. Clavel (Paris: Librairie Administrative de Paul Dupont, 1875), pp. 530–1 (my translation). A few lines later, Salle remarked, 'The general will cannot err, said the greatest political theorist [*publiciste*] of the age. Why? Because when a nation makes laws, everyone prescribes for everyone [*tous stipulent pour tous*]: the general interest is necessarily the only one to dominate; and it is as absurd to suppose that a people can make a set of bad laws, as that a man should decide for his own good to scratch out his eyes; this does not mean that a people cannot make thoroughly bad judgements; but, to repeat myself, to govern or to judge is not to legislate' (p. 531).

The Girondin constitution, substantially the work of Condorcet, embodied this principle, since it made a clear distinction between *lois constitutionnelles*, for which it prescribed ratification by plebiscite, and other laws, which were to be enacted by the Assembly. This was the great difference between the Girondin constitution and the Jacobin version which was actually implemented in the Year I; the Jacobin constitution sought instead as far as possible to hand even ordinary legislation over to popular assemblies.[57] Salle attacked it for giving the citizens of France an impossible choice:

A mass of 24 million men, dispersed over a territory of twenty-six thousand square leagues, industrious and commercial, strongly attached to their private interests, have to stir themselves *spontaneously*, in order to deal with public affairs . . . The People are placed by these articles in a choice each of which is equally dangerous, either to occupy themselves ceaselessly with public affairs, and to completely forget their individual interests . . . or to entrust the security of their rights entirely to the Legislature.

He contrasted this with the detailed mechanism provided in Condorcet's draft for the scrutiny of legislation, along the lines (he said) of Rousseau's ideas; under the Jacobins 'the apparent homage rendered in these articles to the sovereignty of the people is nothing but a scandalous derision'.[58] From the point of view of these Girondin theorists, the Jacobins had blurred the distinction between sovereignty and government every bit as much as Grotius or Pufendorf had done, though they had done so (allegedly) in the interests of democratic rather than monarchical rule; they had failed to segregate acts of sovereignty, which determined the basic structures of the society, from acts of government – including, most alarmingly, as Salle pointed out, acts of criminal jurisdiction.[59]

---

[57] The constitution allowed for the recall of any piece of legislation to the primary assemblies for their decision, if at least one tenth of the primary assemblies in at least half of the departments plus one pronounced against the law. Faustin-Adolphe Hélie, writing from the vantage point of the Third Republic, in 1880, captured exactly the significance of the move from the Girondin to the Jacobin constitution in 1793: the provision of a direct vote by the people on the laws confounded 'avec le souveraineté, le pouvoir, qui doit toujours en rester distinct: il diffère essentiellement du système plébiscitaire, dans lequel le peuple, sans délibération, statue seulement sur les bases fondamentales de la Constitution, et règle ainsi le mode de l'exercise de l'autorité, mais ne l'exerce pas lui-même': F.-A. Hélie, *Les Constititutions de la France* (Paris: Mairesq Aîné, 1880), pp. 387–8.

[58] J.-B. Salle, *Examen critique de la constitution de 1793* (Paris: n.p., An IIIe), pp. 14–16.

[59] See, for an earlier example of this Jacobin view, Robespierre's speech to the Assembly on 10 August 1791, in which he insisted that *all* powers had to be retained by the people (*Archives Parlementaires*, Première Série XXIX, p. 326).

The Girondins lost the constitutional struggles of the Year I, and most of them lost their lives in the Terror. In their absence, the political argument in France, and in Europe more generally, was henceforward to be largely between the heirs of the Jacobins and those of the Abbé Sieyès, neither of whom wanted the kind of arrangements the Girondins had advocated. As is well known, Sieyès, despite coining the terms *pouvoir constituant* and *pouvoir constitué*, was a dedicated opponent of the Rousseauian version of the sovereign–government distinction, insisting that even the *pouvoir constituant* had to be *represented* and could not be exercised by the people themselves.

It is not necessary for the members of the society to exercise the constituting power individually; they can put their trust in representatives who assemble specifically for that purpose, without the power to exercise any of the constituted powers. In a numerous People this delegation is forced on them by the very nature of things. So the People ought to restrict itself to exercising by itself the one Power of *commiting* [*commettant*], that is, it ought to restrict itself to choosing and delegating the people who will exercise their *real* rights [*droits réels*], starting with the right to constitute the public establishment [*l'établissement public*].[60]

---

[60] E. J. Sieyès, *Préliminaire de la Constitution: Reconnaissance et exposition raisonée des Droits de l'Homme et du Citoyen*, enlarged edn. (n.p., 1798), p. 36. The last part of this passage, from 'In a numerous People' onwards, was added to his first edition by Sieyès in response to an objection from Jacques-Pierre Brissot that the idea that 'this power of constituting a nation definitively and irrevocably ought to be exercised by representatives assembled solely with that purpose' was 'a capital error' (see J.-P. Brissot, *Le Patriote François* V (1 August 1789), p. 3 and Brissot's reminiscences of his quarrel with Sieyès over this question in his *Mémoires*, 2 vols., ed. C. Perroud (Paris: n.p., [1902]), II, pp. 105–6); as can be seen from this, Sieyès refused to give way. There is no proper edition of this important work. The different editions can be distinguished by their length. The first version of the text appears in editions by Baudouin, the printer to the National Assembly, at Paris (32 pp.) and Pierres, the royal printer, at Versailles (21 pp.). The expanded version is in another edition by Baudoin at Paris containing 51 pp. Brissot reviewed the Versailles edition in *Le Patriote François*, and it seems to have been more widely distributed than the others. Roberto Zapperi reprinted one of the shorter editions in his edition of Sieyès's *Écrits politiques* (Paris: Editions des archives contemporaines, 1985) and Eberhard Schmitt and Rolf Reichardt translated one of them in their edition of Sieyès's *Politische Schriften* (Munich and Vienna: R. Oldenbourg Verlag, 1981). The edition used in the collection of Sieyès's works in F. Furet and R. Halevi (eds.), *Orateurs de la Révolution française*, vol. I (Paris: Gallimard, 1989) is also the short version. But the enlarged version was used in the Pergamon Press *French Revolution Research Collection* microfilm, from a copy in the BN, and it also appears as a photographic reproduction (with no apparatus) in Sieyès's *Oeuvres*, 3 vols., ed. M. Dorigny (Paris: EDHIS, 1989), II, no. 9. Pasquale Pasquino first drew attention to this difference between the editions: *Sieyès et l'invention de la constitution en France* (Paris: Edition Odile Jacob, 1998), p. 47 and n.52.

It is Sieyès who has been most influential among modern constitutional theorists,[61] but it is the Girondin structure that has in fact emerged – in spite of the leading constitutional theories, rather than because of them – as the default constitution of most modern states, in which fundamental laws are prescribed through plebiscites or referendums rather than through representative bodies, and in which the distinction between a sovereign democratic legislator and a representative government is the basic fact of modern politics. And this would not have been possible, I believe, without the theoretical innovations that this chapter has traced.

[61] See for example the use made of him by Martin Loughlin in his *The Idea of Public Law* (Oxford: Oxford University Press, 2003), pp. 61–4 and *Foundations of Public Law* (Oxford: Oxford University Press, 2010), pp. 224–8.

6 Parliamentary sovereignty, popular sovereignty, and Henry Parker's adjudicative standpoint

Alan Cromartie

A common way of thinking about popular sovereignty is to begin by making a distinction between the kind of language that makes claims to 'sovereignty', understood as an unfettered power to alter the law of the land, and language that merely interprets an existing legal system. When this distinction is applied to early Stuart England, it yields an important empirical finding: from the accession of King James in 1603 to the outbreak of the Civil War in 1642, English debates about the way the country should be governed were almost always focused on interpreting the law; to modern eyes, few features of the period are more striking than the pervasive dominance of an appeal to law at the expense of an appeal to powers above or beyond it. In the eventful Parliament of 1628, one member actually remarked that 'the words "sovereign power" are like some words in logic that are in no predicament'[1] – in other words, that 'sovereign' or supra-legal powers had no intelligible place within the form of discourse within which such discussions were conducted. To use a formulation that still shapes most scholarship, public debate was 'legal' or 'constitutional'.

This finding has encouraged (though it does not justify) a further and more questionable judgement: if early Stuart thinking was 'constitutional', it must have been unequal to the intellectual task of grasping what was really at issue; constructive 'political' thinking is sovereignty-focused. Margaret Judson's classic monograph *The Crisis of the Constitution: An Essay in Constitutional and Political Thought in England 1603–45* (1949) is still the best expression of the relevant assumptions: as its subtitle suggests, her book was concerned with the process by which 'political' thought emerged from 'constitutional' confusion. On Judson's view, the powerful state the Tudors had created required that 'the final authority on public questions be clearly known and generally accepted'.[2] But the

---

[1] *Commons Debates 1628*, 4 vols., ed. R. C. Johnson, M. F. Keeler, M. J. Cole and W. B. Bidwell (New Haven: Yale University Press, 1977), III, p. 531.

[2] M. A. Judson, *The Crisis of the Constitution: An Essay in Constitutional and Political Thought in England 1603–45* (New Brunswick, NJ: Rutgers University Press, 1949), p. 7.

142

English were slow to understand their novel situation: 'No Englishman appeared in either the sixteenth or early seventeenth century to grasp the full significance, as Bodin did in France, of the emergence of the sovereign state and the legal sovereignty of its government.'[3] In other words, they did not grasp 'the great constitutional problem . . . That problem we now realise was this: Where was the final legal authority in government? Was it in the king-in-parliament or in the king alone?' If the answer was the king-in-Parliament (that is, a combination of king and Lords and Commons), but the three parties had a disagreement, 'the problem then transcended the law and constitution and became political'.[4]

The effect of such assumptions is to shape a narrative that gives great prominence to Henry Parker, and in particular to his famous pamphlet, the best-known single statement of the case for Parliament, *Observations on some of his Majesties late Answers and Expresses* (1642). On the conventional interpretation, Parker's achievement was to break with constitutional discourse by re-directing attention to the 'Paramount Law that shall give Law to all humane Lawes whatsoever, and that is *Salus Populi*'[5] (the reference is to the well-known tag *salus populi suprema lex esto*: let the safety of the people be the highest law). This rule, implied in the original contract by which the people initially set up a government, allowed departures from the law in an emergency. With a clearsightedness denied to his contemporaries, Parker was happy to confront the royal accusation that he was giving Parliament an 'arbitrary' power. He did so by frankly accepting the need for such a power somewhere: 'That there is an Arbitrary power in every State somewhere, tis true, tis necessary, and no inconvenience follows upon it.'[6] These iconoclastic statements were to have large implications. As Royalists pointed out, they opened the way for further, more subversive arguments, in which the overriding force of *salus populi* was turned, in the name of the people, against Parliament itself. Parker himself was careful to stop short of such a move, to which there is no doubt that he was hostile; the popular sovereignty that he approved of was permanently embodied, without hope of a recall, in the country's representative assembly. But his bold invocation of *salus populi* was nonetheless a source of the true popular sovereignty supported by the Levellers and others.[7]

---

[3] Ibid., p. 9.   [4] Ibid., p. 7.

[5] [Henry Parker], *Observations upon some of his Majesties late Answers and Expresses* (London: n.p., 1642),p. 3. See Judson, *Crisis*, pp. 409–10, 424–6.

[6] Parker, *Observations*, p. 34.

[7] On Parker in relation to the Levellers see R. Foxley, *The Levellers: Radical Political Thought in the English Revolution* (Manchester: Manchester University Press, 2013), esp. pp. 52–8 and Lorenzo Sabbadini's contribution to this volume (Chapter 7).

There is much to be said for this view both of the period as a whole and of the place within it of Henry Parker's propagandist writings. As we shall see, however, the seductive clarity of the constitutional–political distinction obscures the actual messiness of hastily written exchanges. More seriously, it part-obscures the philosophic nature of the position Parker was maintaining. This chapter's contribution to a fuller understanding of popular sovereignty is to detect a somewhat different pattern in the sources. There were some elements in Parker's thinking – elements easily detached and quoted – suggesting marked hostility to legalistic methods. But the Parliamentarian claims that he was trying to justify had been evolved within a 'constitutional' tradition. On this interpretation, Parker's major intellectual achievement was not so much to abandon this existing mode of thought as to offer a theorisation of its most distinctive features.

The argument is complex, but it falls into four sections. The first picks out some features of Tudor political thought, especially beliefs about Parliament's function, from Henry VIII's initial breach with Rome to the first English Parliament of James VI and I. The second discusses the monarchy's relationship with law from 1603 to 1642. The third draws on both of the former to understand Parker's ideas. A fourth and final section draws some tentative conclusions. An important implication of the analysis will be that Parker's notion of 'the people' excluded the arrangements we now call 'democracy'. But the intention is not to discredit the perfectly plausible claim that there were other elements in his political theory that had a clear democratising logic. During the 1640s the English did possess some intellectual resources that made it quite conceivable, for anyone so minded, to formulate demands for rule by popular assemblies on the basis of election by every adult male. This chapter will sketch out how they acquired them.

I

It is uncontroversial that the most important image through which the Tudors thought about the English polity was the traditional picture of a 'body politic'. For much of the sixteenth century the effect of invoking this image was to strengthen monarchy: to use it was to reinforce a monarchist habit of mind that understood subjects as 'members' (that is, of course, as 'limbs') whose position was defined by their relation to the 'head'. In the words of the preamble of the Act in restraint of Appeals (1533),

this realm of England is an empire, and so hath been accepted in the world, governed by one supreme head and king . . . unto whom a body politic, compact of all sorts and degrees of people divided in terms and by names of spiritualty and temporalty, be bounden and owe to bear next to God a natural and humble obedience.[8]

This is an image, plainly, of the sufficiency of a *realm* to act collectively and of the unnatural character of disobedience. The monarch-focused unity it set out encourage was unity out of diversity – the diversity of 'all sorts and degrees of people', all labouring in their separate vocations, but brought by shared allegiance to serve the common good.

The attraction of this picture, from the monarch's point of view, was its capacity to shape concern for the common good in ways that gave a central place to royal agency. The period's reforming regimes had a shifting range of complex motives – including an uncomplicated greed for church possessions – but all of them found reason to associate themselves with the legitimating rhetoric supplied by broadly humanist aspirations for a more disciplined society, in which the private interests of individuals were overridden in the name of the collective good. Such a society would be a true *res publica* (a word or phrase translated by the English word or phrase a 'commonwealth'). The generally recognised high point of the influence of such language was the short-lived regime of Lord Protector Somerset (1547–9), when humanist aspirations encouraged a Vagrancy Act that set out to suppress the social scourge of idleness by turning persistent vagrants into slaves. His articulate supporter the humanist John Hales regarded such improving schemes as an integral part of a programme of religious reformation:

If there be any way or policy of man to make the people receive, embrace, and love God's word, it is only this, – when they shall see it bringeth forth so goodly fruit, that men seek not their own wealth, nor their private commodity, but, as good members, the universal wealth of the whole body.[9]

Somerset's regime ended in disaster, in part because talk of this nature alarmed conservatives, and his Protestant successors were more cautious. But influential scholarship has rightly drawn attention to the persistent strength of broadly humanist conceptions to which the ideal of common-wealth was central.[10]

---

[8] G. R. Elton, *The Tudor Constitution: Documents and Commentary*, 2nd edn. (Cambridge: Cambridge University Press, 1982), p. 353.

[9] D. MacCulloch, *Tudor Church Militant: Edward VI and the Protestant Reformation* (London: Allen Lane, 1999), p. 50.

[10] M. Todd, *Christian Humanism and the Puritan Social Order* (Cambridge: Cambridge University Press, 1987); M. Peltonen, *Classical Humanism and Republicanism in English Political Thought, 1570–1640* (Cambridge: Cambridge University Press, 1995); J. F. McDiarmid (ed.), *The Monarchical Republic of Early Modern England: Essays in Response to Patrick Collinson* (Aldershot: Ashgate, 2007).

This humanist consensus was a most unlikely seedbed for doctrines that laid stress upon the people's sovereignty: if anything, it presupposed an aristocratic commitment, supported (to the extent that support was needed) by reading Cicero and Aristotle, to the control exerted by a minority with the objective of instilling virtue. The chronology is suggestive: talk of commonwealth seems to have peaked at a time when Protestants were few, but died away towards the end of Queen Elizabeth's reign as they became more numerous and secure. But the political needs of this initially small group did nonetheless encourage some populist ideas. The reason was quite simple: the instrument of the changes it collectively achieved during the period in which it was most vulnerable was the country's representative assembly. Parliament was the setting in which the Tudor monarchs (including the reactionary Mary) declared their understanding of the country's religious arrangements; and in which they were increasingly regarded as having the power, quite simply, to alter religion. Deference to the assembly was by no means confined to the more ardent Protestants, but it was true throughout the period that it was the reformers who had the most to gain from a high view of Parliament's legislative competence. At Elizabeth's accession in 1558, such people acquired a new and overwhelmingly strong motive for denying any limits on what Parliament could do: Elizabeth's claim to be monarch at all was based upon a statute; if Parliament did not have power to settle the succession, the rightful queen of England was Mary Queen of Scots.

What they required, in consequence, was an account of parliamentary action that stressed the assembly's capacity to mobilise the forces of the whole community, and in particular to bind the absent. They could draw on medieval resources: a well-known and well-understood medieval principle maintained that the statutes that Parliament made required no proclamation 'because parliament represents the body of the whole realm'.[11] The most extreme expression of this general line of thought was a fiction that the absent were actually present. As the humanist Sir Thomas Smith explained, in a much-quoted passage of his treatise *De republica Anglorum* (written 1565; printed 1583), 'the most high and absolute power of the realm of England is in the parliament'; anything that Parliament did was 'the prince's and the whole realm's deed; whereupon justly no man can complain'. In a helpful clarification, he compared it with the *comitia centuriata*, that is, with actual gatherings of the whole Roman people:

---

[11] 'Car le parliament represent le corps de tout le realme' (Sir Robert Brooke, *La graunde abridgement* (London: n.p., 1586), s.v. 'Parliament', no. 26).

all that ever the people of Rome might do either in *Centuriatis comitiis* or *tributis*, the same may be doone by the parliament of Englande, which representeth and hath the power of the whole realme both the head and the bodie. For everie Englishman is entended to bee there present, either in person or by procuration and attornies . . . And the consent of the Parliament is taken to be everie mans consent.[12]

For legislative purposes, the Houses *were* the body of the nation, making that body fictionally present, with the result that Englishmen who were physically absent could cooperate with the body's 'head', the queen, to do the same things – achieve the same legal effects – as Romans who were actually assembled.

In modern terms, Smith had outlined an 'authorisation' theory: the function of representation, as he conceived of it, was mainly to empower the representative to do things that would bind the represented. Given the royal capacity to influence Parliament, this was a theory that favoured monarchs. But invocation of republican Rome could also, of course, encourage rather different reflections. In 1565, when he wrote *De republica Anglorum*, Smith was serving Protestant England as ambassador in France. Partly, no doubt, in consequence, his treatise struck a note of patriotic self-congratulation. This was not entirely new: he surely knew the famous comparison with France in Sir John Fortescue's *De Laudibus Legum Anglorum*, a panegyric of the laws of England in which the downtrodden condition of the French peasantry is traced to the fact that French monarchs can make laws without consent.[13] But Smith's updating of this theme involved a novel stress upon a concept of 'the people' that was Roman and indeed republican. He reported that 'some men do judge' that the kings of France are tyrants

because that they make and abrogate lawes and edictes, lay on tributes and impositions of their own will, or by their private Counsell and advise of their friends and favourers onely, without the consent of the people. The people I do call that which the word *populus* doth signifie, the whole body and the three estates of the common wealth: and they blame *Lewes* the xi for bringing the administration royall of Fraunce, from the lawful and regulate raigne to this absolute and tyrannicall power and governement. He himself was wont to glory and say, he had brought the crowne of Fraunce *hors de page*, as one would say out of Wardship.[14]

---

[12] Sir Thomas Smith, *De republica Anglorum*, ed. M. Dewar (Cambridge: Cambridge University Press, 1982), pp. 78–9.

[13] Composed *c.* 1469; available in print as Sir John Fortescue, *Prenobilis militis cognomento Forescu* [sic], *qui temporibus Henrici Sexti floruit, de politica administratione, et legibus civilibus florentissimi regni Angliae, commentarius* (London: n.p., ?1543); re-published with English translation 1567.

[14] Smith, *De republica Anglorum*, p. 54.

On this view, a true *populus* – that is, an appropriately ordered people as gathered fictionally in Parliament – deserved to have a major role in national government.

But national self-consciousness was not invariably so complacent. The constitutional history of the next eighty years was shaped by the perception that monarchs everywhere were following in Louis XI's footsteps. In consequence, there was a threat that English monarchs too would work out ways to govern without a parliament. There were indeed grounds for supposing that such a process was inevitable: liberty did not broaden down from precedent to precedent; it was the queen who was well placed to use emergencies to establish her own precedents for extra-legal conduct. If she opted to invoke the indefinitely extensive powers that were variously referred to as 'absolute', 'extraordinary', 'imperial' or 'regal', there was little anyone could do to stop her. As Sir Humphrey Gilbert told the House of Commons during the Parliament of 1580,

> if wee should in any sort meddle with these matters [that is, with what he called 'prerogatives imperiall'], her Majestie might looke to her owne power and thereby finding her validitie to suppresse the strength of the chalenged liberty, and to challenge and to use the same her own power any way, and to doe as did Lewis of Fraunce who delivered the crowne there out of wardshippe . . . He alsoe sayd other kings had absolute power, as Denmarke and Portugall, where, as the Crowne became more free, soe are all the subjectes thereby rather made slaves.[15]

In 1580 no one had a well-developed answer to Gilbert's pessimistic argument: it was quite reasonable to hold that, if matters were pushed to a crisis, the queen would be alerted to the strength of her position. There is room for disagreement about the extent to which answers had started to emerge before the Scot James Stuart succeeded to the throne. It seems beyond question, however, that the union of crowns encouraged more sophisticated and coherent thought about the special character – and therefore, it was generally believed, the special merits – of English constitutional arrangements. From 1603 onwards England was governed by a foreigner. This simple fact was in itself disturbing. As we have seen, the Houses *were* the body of the nation by a fiction that had made the absent present. The living metaphors of 'head' and 'body' implied both that the body was subordinate to the head and also that the body was incapable of action without the leadership the head provided. As soon as James came south, though, the House of Commons in particular could see itself as standing up for England in the face of interventions

---

[15] T. E. Hartley (ed.), *Proceedings in the Parliaments of Elizabeth I*, 3 vols. (Leicester: Leicester University Press, 1981–95), I, pp. 224–5.

by a cultural outsider, a monarch who knew nothing of his people. In consequence, it might have been expected to emphasise those features of its identity that maximised its scope for independent agency.

Exactly such a process can be seen in operation in a document intended to be given to the king – 'the forme of an Apologie and satisfaction to bee presented to his Majestie' – produced by a Commons committee in the session of 1604. The Apology exemplified Gilbert's anxiety about the direction of travel of modern monarchies: 'The prerogatives of Princes may easily and doe daily growe: the priviledges of subjects are for the most parte at an everlasting stand.'[16] More daringly, it insisted that the privileges of the House of Commons 'are our right and due inheritance, no lesse then our very lands and goods, that they cannot bee witheld from us, denyed or ympayred, but with apparrant wrong to the whole state of the realme'.[17] This extension of the concept of an 'inheritance' would have a very influential future. For present purposes, though, the Apology's most important feature was the way that it subtly altered the idea of 'representation'.

The Commons were historically bringers of petitions and their contemporary self-understanding insisted on their function in transmitting grievances: their legitimacy rested, in part, upon the fact that they knew things that the king or queen did not. The tendency of this strand of thought was to privilege the link between the Commons and 'the people': it contrasted with the Smithian theory that treated Parliament *as a whole* (that is, Parliament including the nobles and bishops) as the authoritative making-present of the body of nation *as a whole* (in which, given contemporary assumptions, the lords and the bishops were naturally very prominent); for Smith, as we have seen, it was not the Lower House alone but the 'three estates' together that was the proper analogue of the Roman *populus*. The Apology thus laid stress on the sheer scale of the forces that the Commons represented: 'The sole persons of the higher nobility excepted, they contain the whole flower and power of your kingdome . . . all these amounting to many millions of people are representatively present in us.'[18] More menacingly, James was told that 'the voyce of the people in thinges of their knowledge is said to bee as the voyce of God'.[19]

James recognised the danger. In a speech that referred in general terms to the Apology, he contested the idea that representation implied that the people had authorised what the House of Commons did:

---

[16] Historical Manuscripts Commission, *Calendar of the Manuscripts of the Most Honourable the Marquess of Salisbury*, part XXIII (London: HMSO, 1973), pp. 144–5.
[17] Ibid., p. 143.   [18] Ibid., p. 146.   [19] Ibid., p. 152.

This house doth not so represent the whole commons of the realm as the shadow doth the body, but only representatively. Impossible it was for them to know all that would be propounded here; much more all those answers you would make to all propositions.[20]

In the first years of the English revolution his son would have many occasions to make similar complaints. In the intermediate period, however, the focus of the clashes between Crown and Parliament was not these rival views of what it was to 'represent', but a gradually changing conception of the assembly's role that was in turn connected to a wider transformation of attitudes towards the law of England. As this too fed into the notion of popular sovereignty, it will require separate attention.

II

One of the main anxieties that James's arrival provoked was that the union of crowns might lead to a 'union of laws' in which the protections afforded by the English legal system were diluted by a compromise with less-developed Scottish institutions. The predictable effect of the union of crowns was thus to encourage conceptions of what it was to be English that laid enormous stress on private freedoms. In the course of the next two decades, several creative minds articulated visions of the English common law, the country's distinctively English legal system, that emphasised its nature as a communal response to problems thrown up by peculiarly English conditions.[21] These thinkers did not share a single theory, or indeed a single set of political preferences, but it was important to all of them that common law was in no need of alien supplementation.

Sir Edward Coke, the best known of these thinkers, adopted an extreme view of the kind of tacit wisdom embodied in specifically professional tradition:

Wee are but of yesterdaie (and therefore had need of the wisedome of those that were before us) and had been ignorant (if we had not received light and knowledge from our forefathers) and our daies upon the earth are but as a shadow, in respect of the ould ancient daies and times past, wherein the lawes have been by the wisdom of the most excellent men, in many successions of ages, by long and continual experience (the triall of right and truth) fined and

---

[20]   J. P. Kenyon, *The Stuart Constitution: Documents and Commentary*, 2nd edn. (Cambridge: Cambridge University Press, 1986), p. 36.

[21]   Besides the texts by Coke and Selden referred to below, see esp. the preface to Sir John Davies, *Le primer report des cases et matters en ley resolves et adjudges en les courts del roy en Ireland* (Dublin: n.p., 1615) and Thomas Hedley's speech to the Parliament of 1610 (E. R. Foster (ed.), *Proceedings in Parliament 1610*, 2 vols. (New Haven: Yale University Press, 1966), II, pp. 170–97).

refined, which no one man (beeing of so short a time) albeit he had in his head the wisedome of all the men in the world, in any one age could never [*sic*] have effected or attained unto.[22]

Coke's theory connected the wisdom of the law with an immoderate statement of its antiquity, but his politically important claim was not that the law was ancient, but that it was rational. This claim was easily severed from his bad history. The learned John Selden remarked, with evident reference to his views, that 'All laws in generall are originally equally ancient. All were grounded upon nature, and no nation was that out of it took not their grounds; and nature being the same in all, the beginning of all laws must be the same.'[23] Selden went on to emphasise the variety of legitimate institutions that various nations developed from this shared starting point. But the points about which both men were entirely in agreement were that the common law was in its essence rational and that there was no need for any English politician to look to other countries' institutions.

It was at the very moment that such ideas were starting to develop that the government was tempted to make a bad mistake. In a difficult financial situation, it sought to evade Parliament's control of new taxation by levying supplementary customs duties (referred to at the time as 'impositions'). In 1606 the Crown's right to levy such duties was recognised by the Court of the Exchequer in a judgment that laid stress on royal extraordinary power. This judgment cut two ways. On the one hand, this example of extraordinary power had been upheld by qualified English judges; it had acquired the authority possessed by common law. But this successful use of the authority of judges implied – or strictly speaking could be taken to imply[24] – that the extraordinary power was justiciable, in other words that it existed within the legal sphere. This point was quickly noticed. As an MP was to argue as early as 1610, 'If the judges may judge the imposition by the legall power, then the absolute power is controllable by the legall power. And therefore he may not sett it by his absolute power.'[25] The act of using judges to support the absolute power had the effect of casting doubt upon its absoluteness.

---

[22] Sir Edward Coke, *La sept part des reports* (London: n.p., 1608), fol. 3v.

[23] John Selden, 'Notes on Fortescue', p. 17 in Sir John Fortescue, *De laudibus legum Anglorum* (London: n.p., 1616).

[24] Chief Baron Fleming's judgment explicitly appealed to 'reasons . . . not extracted out of the books of law'; his colleague Baron Clarke's position was more ambiguous (A. Cromartie, *The Constitutionalist Revolution: An Essay on the History of England, 1450–1642* (Cambridge: Cambridge University Press, 2006), p. 201).

[25] S. R. Gardiner (ed.), *Parliamentary debates in 1610*, Camden Society first series 81 (1862), p. 120.

There was a further interesting effect. In the popular estimation, the judges had got the law wrong. It was natural, in consequence, to look for a court of appeal, and such a court could only be the 'court' of Parliament. The result was that people disposed to resist the pretensions of the Crown acquired a clear incentive to think of Parliament as being an authoritative interpreter of law. As another MP put it, again in 1610, 'If a judgment be against this [that is, against the principle that novel customs duties needed Parliament's assent], yet it is reversible by Parliament; so that it is excellent to be observed that, as the laws begynne, so they allways end in Parliament.'[26] This line of thought was open to an obvious objection: it conflated legislation passed by the king himself with other forms of parliamentary action. But it was still politically potent. Thus the tendency of the impositions issue to expand the legal sphere called forth an answering tendency for Parliament itself to claim adjudicative supremacy. The long debate that followed was highly technical, but its political logic is simply summarised: the Crown claimed an absolute power, but did so through the courts, and in so doing diminished its absolute character; in relying on the judges to legitimate its acts, it chose to fight on territory controlled by common lawyers. In consequence, English political debate acquired the 'constitutional' or 'legal' character so many of its historians have remarked on.

The first peak of this constitutionalising tendency was Charles's half-hearted acceptance, in 1628, of the document referred to as the Petition of Right, which was generally seen as an authoritative re-statement of privileges perennially claimed by English subjects. The expression 'of Right' is important; it was asserting rights, not aspirations. In pursuit of this aim it reaffirmed the illegality of extra-parliamentary taxation, but also denounced the infringement of personal liberties by use of arbitrary imprisonment. In this new situation, the privileges of subjects were conceived as absolute; kingship faced rigid boundaries supplied by private rights. One opposition slogan was the resonant common-law maxim that 'the common law hath so admeasured the King's prerogative, as he cannot prejudice any man in his inheritance', a maxim glossed by John Selden by saying that 'the greatest inheritance a man hath is the liberty of his person, for all others are accessory to it'.[27] There were, however, two different ways of conceiving the Petition. On one view – the more conservative view – what remained to the king was in effect a series of private-law rights. As a Commons spokesman put it, 'two manors or lordships lie adjoining together, and perchance intermixed, so as there is

---

[26] Ibid., p. 61.   [27] *Commons Debates 1628*, II, p. 358.

some difficulty to discern the true bounds of either'.[28] In other words, the king's rights and the subject's are metaphorically on the same plane. What makes this view conservative is that the metaphor of adjoining manors implies that the two parties have symmetrical positions. It is of course bad for the monarch to cross the borders of the subject's manor. But it would in principle be just as bad for the subject to encroach upon the monarch: in other words, the subject can also go too far, breaking the bounds presented by the monarch's privileges.

During the 1640s just such a view would dominate the constitutional thought of the more legalistic Royalists. Its natural affinities were with the mainstream claim, which found supporters on both sides of the First Civil War, that England possessed a distinctively mixed constitution. An implication of this view was that some friction was to be expected and that there would be some residual problems to which the law provided no clear answer. Its adherents saw the history of England as the history of a dynamic tension between the monarch and the English people; they saw virtue in what Milton would describe as 'endless tugging' between the subject's liberty and the prerogative.[29] The king's own programmatic manifesto, the *Answer to the Nineteen Propositions* (1642) explained that the House of Commons furnished 'the good of Democracy', which is 'Liberty and the Courage and Industry which Liberty begets'. This theory plainly blocked the way to an unmixed constitution. If the Commons – the democratic element – were not impeded by some other forces, the country would be plagued by the 'ills of Democracy', which were 'Tumults, Violence, and Licentiousness'.[30]

There was, however, an alternative view, in which the situation was not symmetrical. On this view the king was entrusted with powers for the benefit of others; his rights were not analogous to private property because they had been granted for a purpose, which was promotion of the common good. The law, moreover, regulated everything he did in ways informed by that controlling purpose. It followed that any emergency powers that the common good demanded were by their very nature also legal; there was no room for a separate sphere of 'state' considerations. In the debates preceding the Petition, a speaker referred to as 'Mr Browne, a lawyer' insisted 'the common law hath so provided that it needs no addition of state to strengthen it. *Salus populi* belongs only to the law.'[31]

---

[28] Ibid., III, p. 570.

[29] John Milton, *Complete Prose Works of John Milton*, vol. VII, rev. edn., ed. R. W. Ayers (New Haven: Yale University Press, 1980), p. 375.

[30] Edward Husbands, *An exact collection of all remonstrances, declarations[. . .]petitions, messages, answers, and other remarkable passages* (London: n.p., 1643), p. 320.

[31] *Commons Debates 1628*, II, p. 176.

In the later 1630s this general line of thinking was elaborated further by the opposition lawyer Oliver St John when he was arguing against Ship Money. Ship Money was a levy (a financial sum in lieu of the provision of a ship) to which Charles was entitled in emergency conditions; in other words, it was justified by *salus populi*. St John was happy to concede that the monarch possessed, and must possess, this kind of emergency power; the question, he believed, was 'only *de modo*, by what medium or method this supreme power, which is in his Majesty, doth infuse or let out itself into this particular'. His answer was that the only possible vessel of this power was the highest court and council (two concepts that he noticeably conflated), that is to say, the 'court' of Parliament.[32]

St John's argument anticipated Parker. Before discussing Parker's *Observations*, it is, however, worth pausing for a moment to offer a more general comment on what was happening. Any political outlook to which the idea of 'common good' is central is bound to concede that any merely private interests (let alone the private property of individuals) must yield to the collective good, and in particular to the good of the safety of the people. In consequence, the notion of this collective good was not, by any means, a threat to kingship; it offered the king a rhetorical tool to which he could appeal to override the private rights of subjects. Charles doubtless thought that all his acts had the common good in mind and that his enemies were merely selfish; as his ultra-loyal subject Sir Robert Filmer put it, the trouble with the people was that 'each man hath a care of his particular, and thinks basely of the common good'.[33] The threat to his kingship arose when the power to specify that good in its most important form, the people's safety, was asserted by a group of his own subjects. As these subjects treated kingship as a legal institution, they naturally saw kings as instrumental to the priorities discerned within the legal system: if the common law had 'so admeasured the king's prerogative, as he cannot prejudice any man in his inheritance,' if every private liberty was an inheritance, and if the strictly legal sphere was all-encompassing, then it was easy to conclude that the only royal function was to protect the private rights of subjects.

Though few, if any, at the time grasped what was happening, this was an intellectual revolution; indeed, it precisely inverted the humanist ideas that had previously dominated English social thinking. On almost any conventional understanding, the common good was shorthand for public well-being. On almost any understanding shaped by Aristotle, this

---

[32] Cromartie, *Constitutionalist Revolution*, pp. 238–9.

[33] Sir Robert Filmer, *Patriarcha and Other Writings*, ed. J. P. Sommerville (Cambridge: Cambridge University Press, 1991), p. 28.

good at least included promotion of virtue through the ideal of 'government by laws', laws being institutions securing virtuous rule both by imposing curbs upon behaviour and also, more importantly, by shaping moral habits that could be internalised. Within this broad tradition it was self-evident that the liberty of doing whatever you happened to want was actually a degrading form of licence. But early seventeenth-century Englishmen were led by the expansion of the private legal sphere towards some wholly different assumptions. As the common lawyers started to present it, the common good mapped onto the liberties of the subject, which in its turn mapped onto the ideal of rule by laws. In this new intellectual world, laws were ceasing to be social institutions *directly* aimed at cultivating virtue; they were identified with regulations that had the effect of preserving private spaces. There was, to be sure, some discussion of indirect effects: it was a commonplace throughout this period that the English are brave and hardworking because they have avoided the demoralising fate of losing control of the fruits of their own labours; if their inherited liberties were ever to be lost, they would resemble the French peasantry as Fortescue had chosen to describe them. As Thomas Hedley put it, 'they will use little care or industry to get that which they cannot keep and so will grow both poor and base-minded like to the peasants in other countries'.[34] But the interests with which legal thought was primarily concerned did not include an interest in becoming virtuous. As we shall see, this dramatic conceptual upheaval involved a transformation of political ideas that made democracy more thinkable.

III

We are now in a position to turn to Henry Parker's *Observations*, and to examine the extent to which its invocation of the safety of the people was a decisive breach with constitutional tradition. Parker's pamphlet was the product of a moment at which there were grounds for appealing to *salus populi*. On 4 January 1642 the king had botched a military coup. On 10 January he fled from London. Thereafter he moved from place to place in what was clearly an attempt to find himself an army. In this unprecedented situation, the Houses passed a measure – the 'Militia Ordinance' – that vested control of military forces in people they regarded as being trustworthy. It might have been supposed that they would look upon this measure as an authentic act of legislation. It was, however, central to the Parliamentarian case that the Militia Ordinance was not an attempt to make law. As late as 1647 Parker himself would stress that

[34] Foster (ed.), *Parliament 1610*, II, pp. 194–5.

'we admit that no Acts of *Parliament* are compleat or formally binding without the *Kings* assent'.[35] The Ordinance was thus something best conceived of as a somewhat irregular action that Parliament had *judged* appropriate. As the House declared on 19 May (perhaps five weeks before the publication of the *Observations*),[36]

> If the question be whether that bee Law which the Lords and Commons have once declared to be so, who shall be the Iudge? Not his Majesty, for the King judgeth not of matters of Law, but by his Courts, and his Courts, though sitting by his authority, expect not his Assent in matters of Law: not any other courts, for they cannot Iudge in that case because they are Inferiour: no appeale lying to them from Parliament, the Iudgement whereof is in the eye of the Law the King's Iudgement in his highest Court, though the King in his person be neither present nor assenting thereunto.[37]

This may seem a distinction without a difference: the right to interpret the law of the land is surely the same thing as having the right to make laws in the first place. But the difference is in fact non-trivial. The adjudicative standpoint that the Houses had adopted was a development within a legalistic framework. It encouraged a theorisation of socio-political life in terms of an adjudicative structure – in essence, in terms of a structure assigning interests to those who were regarded as their owners.

It is, in part, as evidence of this conceptual point that the works of Henry Parker are important. As we have seen, he is the Parliamentarian propagandist whose works best fit the thesis of a sharp and sudden departure from earlier, basically legal forms of discourse. It would be foolish to deny that there are many passages within his published works that lend support to this interpretation. The man Henry Parker was plainly intensely responsive to the idea of 'state' considerations that went beyond conventional legal ones. In a much-quoted outburst of 1643 he insisted that 'Reason of State is something more sublime and imperiall then Law . . . the Statesman begins where the Lawyer ceaseth'; it was a pity, he believed, that Parliament's military leader, the Earl of Essex, was not, in the strict Roman sense, a military dictator.[38] Such claims were, of

---

[35] H[enry] P[arker], *An answer to the poysonous sedicious paper of Mr. David Jenkins* (London: n.p., 1647), p. 6.

[36] The bookseller George Thomason, a personal friend of Parker's, acquired his copy on 2 July.

[37] Husbands, *Exact collection*, pp. 206–7.

[38] Henry Parker, *The Contra-Replicant, His Complaint To His Majestie* (London: n.p., 1643), pp. 16, 19. This passage is the most extreme expression of Parker's anti-legal animus. See M. Mendle, *Henry Parker and the English Civil War: The Political Thought of the Public's 'Privado'* (Cambridge: Cambridge University Press, 1995), p. 119 for helpful contextualisation of the pamphlet as a response to legalistic royal propaganda and biographical remarks on its 'anger, lack of reserve, and nervous energy'.

course, polemical gifts to Royalists and Levellers: they invited accusations that he was substituting the arbitrary rule of an oligarchic clique for the arbitrary rule of Charles Stuart and his cronies. As the Parliamentarian Philip Hunton put it, people who thought like Parker were ready to 'give all that to the two Houses which erewhile they would not suffer when the Judges in the case of Ship-money had given it to the King'.[39]

But the spirit of Parker's theory is more ambiguous than his more extravagant comments might suggest; even when he is most extreme, it is difficult to decide if his fundamental doctrine is that reason of state trumps law or if it simply constitutes a higher kind of law that Parliament is able to interpret.[40] His statement that 'Reason of State is something more sublime and imperiall then Law' was closely followed by the counter-statement that 'Policy is to bee observed as the only true Law'.[41] Later in the same passage he could revert from saying that 'the representative body of the Kingdome is a Counsell of State, rather then a Court of Justice' to saying on the next page that 'the Law is cleare enough that the King cannot pardon Royalism'.[42]

These uncertainties are pervasive, but for present purposes it is unnecessary to resolve them. If the focus is shifted from real or imagined sovereignty-claims to other features of his publications, he emerges as a theorist and defender of Parliament's adjudicative standpoint. In this capacity he followed St John in conflating the activity of judgment with the activity of giving counsel. As his *Observations* put it, 'In inferiour Courts, the Judges are so Councellors for the King, as that the King may not countermand their judgements . . . and in Parliament, where the Lords and Commons represent the whole Kingdome . . . the case is far stronger.'[43] In justifying the Houses' claim to offer binding counsel, he resorted to a theory that recalls Sir Thomas Smith. It was the Lords and Commons' role in *representing* England that justified their title to their supremacy; and representation was understood – as Smith had understood it – as fictionally securing complete identity: 'the whole Kingdome is not so properly the Author as the essence itselfe of Parliaments'.[44] For Parker, 'the representative body of the nation' meant 'the nation as embodied by representation'.

It should be stressed that one important purpose of this theory was to empower Parliament – the representative – at the expense of those it represented. Parker was no enthusiast for popular involvement if such

---

[39] Philip Hunton, *A Treatise of Monarchie* (London: n.p., 1643), p. 70.
[40] For helpful remarks on this theme see G. Burgess, *British Political Thought, 1500–1600: The Politics of the Post-Reformation* (Basingstoke: Palgrave Macmillan, 2009), pp. 194–5.
[41] Parker, *Contra-Replicant*, p. 19.   [42] Ibid., pp. 19–20.
[43] Parker, *Observations*, p. 9.   [44] Ibid., p. 5.

involvement was a threat to social order as he understood it; he was critical of the '*Tributa Comitia* managed only by the *Plebeians*' as being 'too adverse to the *Patritian Order*' and '[not] anything else commonly but a vast, rude, confused, indigested heap of the vulgar'.[45] But he thought that the procedures (and the gentry membership) of parliaments and similar assemblies supplied a way of shaping a healthy *populus* that could in fact be trusted with political control:

> till some way was invented to regulate the motions of the peoples moliminous body, I think arbitrary rule was most safe for the world, but now since most Countries have found out an Art and peaceable Order for Publique Assemblies, whereby the people may assume its own power to do itselfe right . . . the whole community in its underived Majesty shall convene to do justice.[46]

The crucial claim is once again that Parliament quite simply *is* the people. The idea that secured this curious fictional identity was not that the House of Commons was elected – still less that (in some cases) a vote had been involved – but that the *interests* of both the Houses coincided with the *interests* of the community. As the *Observations* put it, Parliament had two purposes: 'first that the interest of the people might be satisfied; secondly that Kings might be the better counsailed.'[47] To allow the king unfettered power was 'so to resigne its owne interest to the will of one Lord, as that that Lord may destroy it without injury'.[48] Consistently with the instincts that he had inherited from English constitutional tradition, he held that the most convenient term for every kind of interest was the inclusive term 'propriety': 'Our Kings cannot be sayd to have so unconditionate and high a proprietie in all our lives, liberties and possessions or in any thing else to the Crowne appertayning, as we have in their dignity, or in ourselves.'[49]

Another kind of writer might have left the matter there. But Parker had a genuinely philosophic mind – it was his greatest weakness as a polemicist – and showed a remarkable appetite for spelling out his own presuppositions. The result was a tract, *Ius Populi* (1644), that worked out, in some detail, his concept of representation secured by interests:

> Tis true, in my understanding, the Parliament differs many ways from the rude bulk of the universality, but in power, in honour, in majestie, in commission, it ought not at all to be divided, or accounted different as to any legall purpose. And thus it is not with the King, the King does not represent the people, but only in such and such cases: *viz.* in pleas of a common nature betwixt Subject and Subject. Wherein he can have no particular ends; and at such or such times,

---

[45] Henry Parker, *Ius Populi* (London: n.p., 1644), pp. 58–9 (mispaginated as pp. 60–1).
[46] Parker, *Observations*, pp. 14–15.
[47] Ibid., p. 5.   [48] Ibid., p. 8.   [49] Ibid., p. 5.

viz. when there is not a more full and neer representation by the Parliament. And hereupon the supreme reason or Judicature of this State, from whence no appeale lies, is placed in that representative convention, which either can have no interests different from the people represented, or at least very few, and those not considerable.[50]

It will be noted that this was a passage in which the identity that he asserted was said to exist for 'any *legal* purpose'.

But Parker also addressed some deeper questions by working out a detailed political theory within which rulers were in essence judges. By his own account, *Ius populi* defended three assertions:

1. Princes derive their power, and prerogatives from the people. Secondly, Princes have their investitures meerly for the people's benefit. Thirdly, In all well-formed States, the Laws, by which Princes claim, do declare themselves more in favour of liberty then Prerogative.[51]

It was axiomatic, he thought, that '*salus Populi* is *suprema Lex*: and that *bonum Publicum* is that which must give Law, and check to all pretences, or disputes of Princes whatsoever'.[52] The position of supreme rulers is so wholly instrumental, 'so meerly subservient, and subordinate to the publick good, that to compasse that at any time, nay or to adde any scruple of weight unto the same, it is bound wholly to postpone or deny itself'.[53] Good government was thus defined by reference to the interests of the governed. The most extreme form of bad government, slavery, was defined by its denial that slaves have interests. In some suggestive phrases, Parker noted that 'the very definition of it leaves the slave utterly disinherited of himself'; it is 'iniurious and violent [i.e. unnatural]' in 'devesting the propriety of those which are subjected to it, but also the more publike and sublime propriety; which the Common-wealth, the Society of Mankinde, nay God himself has in the parties enslaved'.[54]

There is, to be sure, some uncertainty created by the notion of 'more public and sublime propriety', but the idea that others (the common-wealth, the society of mankind, God) might have interests in the slave is being used to reinforce, and not to qualify, the idea of the slave's inheritance of freedom. The same can be said of the numerous occasions on which Parker refers to a somewhat nebulous 'public good'; the notion appears to possess little identifiable content beyond the judicial function of assigning each his own. His working definition of the term 'government' was 'that discipline or method which we exercise in promoting, inabling, rewarding persons of good desert in the State, and

---

[50] Parker, *Ius Populi*, pp. 18–19. [51] Ibid., p. 1. [52] Ibid., p. 2.
[53] Ibid., p. 20. [54] Ibid., p. 37.

whereby we prevent, suppresse, punish such as are contrarily affected'. Given the Fall, this would require coercion, which he described as 'formall Jurisdiction'.[55] The master–slave relation is not an instance of such jurisdiction: it 'cannot be called Jurisdiction, because it proposeth no ends of Justice in itselfe'; it is different from 'that Jurisdiction which intends Publique good, and the distributing to every man that which is his own'.[56] Unlike the Aristotelian conceptions this chapter has imputed to the Tudor humanists, Parker's idea of government/jurisdiction is reactive: it responds to human beings as they are, as opposed to shaping character to mould them for the better. In a passage meditating on the depravity of sociable but fallen human beings, he consciously rejected Aristotle:

When *Aristotle* says, that *Men doe associate by instinct of Nature, for ends of honestie, as they are communicative creatures, as well as necessitie and safetie,* He rather intimates *what we should be, than what we are . . .* We must insist upon necessitie therefore, as the main ground and end of Policie.[57]

It is hard not to be struck by this proto-liberal narrowing of government's concerns; a politics focused on property and on self-preservation had visibly replaced an older kind of politics that principally focused upon virtue.

IV

All Parker's writings are ambiguous. On the traditional reading, which is not implausible and which can be supported by quotation, the form of Parliamentarianism that he articulates was both a clear breach with tradition and a penultimate step towards a Bodinian assertion of the people's sovereignty. This chapter has, however, read his works quite differently, suggesting that they can be placed within another story: not so much the abandonment as the final realisation of an appeal to English legal values. On this view, the important implication of the adjudicative supremacy on which the rebel Houses based their constitutional case was not that it disguised their legislative sovereignty, but that it forced them to take up an adjudicative standpoint: a standpoint whose natural perspective on freeborn English adults was that of a tribunal assigning interests.

The effects of adopting this standpoint were far-reaching. The thrust of Parker's theory was anti-populist; in the context of his thinking, the most important function of the idea of representation was to explain

[55] Ibid., p. 3.   [56] Ibid., p. 36.   [57] Ibid., p. 43.

why Parliament could bind the represented in spite of the fact that so many of the latter were fighting in a civil war against it. This view was well adapted to the requirements of a small virtuous minority, and was indeed exploited by the Rump Parliament when that minority regime was first in control of the country.[58] As Milton remembered, 'they knew the people of *England* to be a free people, themselves the representers of that freedom'.[59] But the image of the people as interest-bearers had three democratising implications. First, the assertion that Parliament's title to resolve the situation depended on its having the same interests as the people was consistent with the notion in the Apology that 'the voyce of the people in the thinges of their knowledge is said to be as the voyce of God'.[60] Its tendency was to favour the Commons over the Lords, if only because the former clearly had more interests. More broadly, it was consistent with a form of politics in which political knowledge could be aggregated from subjective impressions about which even simple folk could be authorities. As Harrington was to argue, 'the people do not see, but they can feel';[61] Nedham would prefer the pithier expression, 'they onely know where the shooe wrings'.[62]

Secondly, the primacy of legally protected interests that could be summarised as 'property' could be understood in two quite different ways. It might be said that it implied a gentry-dominated politics: that those with the most interests – and consequently the largest stake in preservation of the legal system – would be appropriately dominant in a Parliament whose purpose was to epitomise the aggregated interests of the nation. But it could equally be said that everybody had some property: as Sir John Selden had put it, 'The greatest inheritance a man hath is the liberty of his person, for all others are but accessory to it.'[63] This point was naturally made by the Leveller spokesmen at Putney. As Edward Sexby complained on that occasion, 'there are many thousands of us soldiers that have ventured our lives; we have had little propriety in the kingdom as to our estates, yet we have had a birthright. But it seems now, except a man hath a fixed estate in this kingdom, he hath no right in this kingdom. I wonder we were so much deceived.'[64]

---

[58] Kenyon, *Stuart Constitution*, p. 292.

[59] Milton, *Complete Prose Works*, vol. VII, p. 411.

[60] Historical Manuscripts Commission, *Calendar of Salisbury MSS*, p. 152.

[61] James Harrington, *The Political Works of James Harrington*, ed. J. G. A. Pocock (Cambridge: Cambridge University Press, 1977), p. 762.

[62] Marchamont Nedham, *The excellency of a free state* (London: n.p., 1656), p. 36.

[63] *Commons Debates 1628*, II, p. 358.

[64] A. S. P. Woodhouse, *Puritanism and Liberty: Being the Army Debates from the Clarke Manuscripts*, 2nd edn. (London: J. M. Dent, 1974), p. 69.

A third effect is subtler, but when fully understood supplies the key to a perplexing problem. Without obvious exception, those writers of the revolution period who could, with a bit of licence, be described as democrats were favourers of religious toleration. In most cases, indeed, their commitment to some kind of toleration appears to have been their strongest political feeling. But religious toleration was not a majority cause; nor was it a majority position within the broadly speaking Puritan community. As a speaker at Putney demanded, in the context of attempts to make a right to toleration a part of the Agreement of the people, 'how can we terme that to bee an Agreement of the People which is neither an Agreement of the major parte of the people, and truly for anything I can perceive . . . nott the major parte of the honest partie of the Kingdome'.[65] Twelve years later, after a decade of tolerant republican rule, the basic situation was unaltered. The tolerationist Henry Stubbe believed that 'they who are for a *free Toleration* are the lesse numerous, beyond all proportion'.[66] It might be thought, in other words, that rational proponents of religious toleration had every reason to agree with Milton's preference for a long-term commitment to aristocracy.

The solution to the problem is found in the conceptual revolution dividing Henry Parker from the Tudor humanists (and also from John Milton – the English republican writer whose views departed least from older humanist ideas). Within the legal discourse that this chapter has discussed, the interests secured by representation boiled down to private rights enjoyed by individuals; the activity of government boiled down to making sure that such interests were properly assigned. But this mode of political thinking was largely secular; moreover, it was not concerned with shaping character. Thus the individual 'interests' it set out to secure did not include an interest in being brought to hold salvific theological opinions. Democracy was an option for these writers because the view of politics that made them democrats was also a support for a quite radical distinction between the secular and the religious.

This point may seem unduly speculative. But there is in fact a remarkable late Interregnum tract – Henry Stubbe's *An Essay In Defence of the Good Old Cause* (1659) – that illustrates precisely those hidden tendencies. Henry Stubbe was a supporter of 'democracy' (his word) because he had acquired a faith in aggregated knowledge, probably largely from James Harrington: 'We ought not to think it so easy to delude a *multitude*,

---

[65] I. Gentles, 'The *Agreements of the people* and their Political Contexts', in M. Mendle (ed.), *The Putney Debates of 1647: The Army, the Levellers, and the English State* (Cambridge: Cambridge University Press, 2001), pp. 148–74, at p.165.

[66] Henry Stubbe, *An Essay In Defence of the Good Old Cause* (London: n.p., 1659), sig.**4+4r.–v.

as a *few*.[67] In the short term, however (rather inconsistently), he recognised that 'the universality of this nation is not to be trusted with liberty at present'[68] and therefore that full citizenship would have to be restricted to the 'honest and faithfull party'.[69] But even this honest and faithful group was not permitted to enforce its own religious views; the purposes of government, when correctly understood, ruled out the possibility of any such form of coercion.

The interest of Stubbe's pamphlet is that he is a self-declared example of a convinced republican who stressed the continuities with constitutional thinking: he believed that 'the *Petition of right* and other laws in being had already deposed *Monarchy*, and we were only to *improve*, not *create* a *Republick*'.[70] As might have been expected, his other attitudes were very similar to Henry Parker's. He had exactly the same tendency to treat the protection of property, the promotion of a common or public good and preservation of the public safety as being roughly equivalent expressions. We find, for example, the following formulations:

[Magistracy] is erected and established for the compassing of their good.[71]

The general *end* men aim at in the erecting *Magistracy* is the *preserving Society*: and . . . Magistrates are constituted for *their good*, and not they for the a*dvantages* of *Magistrates*.[72]

The most *obvious* and *universall end* is the upholding *society and entercourse* by *securing* each in their *property* and *manage of commerce* betwixt one another for mutuall supply of things necessary.[73]

Their *safety* is the *end* aimed at in the institution of *Magistracy*.[74]

It is far from clear if Stubbe intended subtle shades of meaning or if he saw these statements as identical in force. What is, however, crystal clear is the intended payoff: the ultimate purpose of magistracy is radically distinct from the project, which cannot be delegated, of trying to work out one's own salvation: '*Men embody* under *Magistrates* for upholding *civill commerce*, but they gather into *Churches* to maintain a *spirituall communion*.'[75] The adjudicative standpoint had the effect of setting a sharply defined limit to the role of government. Precisely the same payoff was obtained by the same means in the political writings of John Locke.

---

[67] Ibid., sig.***4+4v.   [68] Ibid., sig.**2v–3.   [69] Ibid., sig.**4+1.
[70] Ibid., *4+1.   [71] Ibid., p. 11.   [72] Ibid., p. 17.   [73] Ibid., p. 12.
[74] Ibid., p. 20.   [75] Ibid., p. 26.

7 Popular sovereignty and representation in the English Civil War

Lorenzo Sabbadini

I

The English Civil War has long been recognised as a period as intellectually creative as it was militarily destructive. It is celebrated for giving rise to powerful arguments in favour of religious toleration, for putting forward a distinctive account of political liberty rooted in Roman republican thought, and for developing – in the political philosophy of Thomas Hobbes – an innovative and influential theory of the state. Scarcely less significant, though less widely discussed, is the emergence of the language of popular sovereignty. This was first articulated during the so-called paper war of the 1640s by Parliamentarian pamphleteers anxious not merely to condemn Charles I's policies as a violation of the 'ancient constitution' but also to provide a robust defence of Parliament's own unprecedented actions. It was then appropriated by the Levellers to make a starkly different case: not to vindicate Parliament in its conflict with the king but to protect the people from Parliament.

At the root of the concept of popular sovereignty, as articulated by both Parliamentarians and Levellers, was the idea that all just political authority originates in the people. This yielded two conclusions, both again shared by Parliamentarians and Levellers: that any political actor other than the people holds power by way of trust; and that, if the terms of the trust are violated, this power may be revoked. To this extent, our authors were merely echoing earlier discussions of popular sovereignty, most notably those of the (Calvinist) resistance theorists of the sixteenth century.[1] But for the English writers of the 1640s popular sovereignty was a theory not only about the *origin* of political authority but also, and more

---

[1] On these authors see R. M. Kingdon, 'Calvinism and Resistance Theory, 1550–1580', in J. H. Burns and M. Goldie (eds.), *The Cambridge History of Political Thought, 1450–1700* (Cambridge: Cambridge University Press, 1991), pp. 193–218. On their influence during the English Civil War see J. H. M. Salmon, *The French Religious Wars in English Political Thought* (Oxford: Clarendon Press, 1959).

importantly, about its *exercise*. By contrast with the 'monarchomachs', the English pamphleteers of the 1640s did not conceive of or justify Parliament's stance as an act of resistance by an 'inferior magistrate', even though it could certainly be thought of as such. Instead, they appealed to the principle of popular sovereignty to claim that Parliament – either as it was then constituted or as it ideally might be – was the vehicle through which the people could at all times exercise their sovereign power within the political sphere.

At this general level, Parliamentarians and Levellers were broadly in agreement. Where they came apart was in their understanding of 'the people' and how its sovereignty ought to be exercised in practice. While the Parliamentarians recognised that the people could be thought of *divisim*, they held that it was in the people taken *conjunctim* and thus as a corporation that sovereignty resided.[2] According to what might be thought of as an early theory of 'virtual' representation,[3] Parliament was understood as a physical manifestation of this body. No identifiable act of authorisation was required; representation was instead thought of in terms of a picturing of something, a 're-presentation'. Thus, any action carried out by Parliament, even when opposed by a large section of the population, could be justified in the name of popular sovereignty.

It was as a reaction to this alarming proposition that the Levellers began to unpick the Parliamentarians' argument, turning the language of popular sovereignty on its head, and against Parliament. Since the collective body of the people could only be thought of as an aggregation of the distinct wills of its individual members, sovereignty was not a property of the people as a whole but of every individual – an idea conveyed through the novel language of 'selfe propriety'. The Levellers continued to think of representation largely in descriptive or symbolic terms, but in order for Parliament to constitute a likeness of the people some kind of process of authorisation was required. Parliament as it was then constituted was not a truly representative institution, and the concept of popular sovereignty was transformed from being a means of legitimating an existing authority to serving as the basis for a radical programme of popular reform.

---

[2] See Q. Skinner, 'Hobbes on Persons, Authors and Representatives', in P. Springborg (ed.), *The Cambridge Companion to Hobbes's* Leviathan (Cambridge: Cambridge University Press, 2007), pp. 157–80, at pp. 162–3.

[3] As Eric Nelson shows in Chapter 8 of this volume, Parker was an important source for the concept of virtual representation developed in the eighteenth century by the Whigs in order to vindicate Britain's rule over its American colonies.

II

The idea that power originates in the people had a long and distinguished history, featuring particularly prominently in the religious wars that had recently devastated much of Europe. What is striking, however, is its almost complete absence from the English constitutional debates of the early decades of the seventeenth century. Deploying instead the common-law idiom of the 'ancient constitution',[4] the Stuarts' early opponents in the Parliaments of the 1610s–20s accused them of undermining the precarious equilibrium between the king's prerogative and the subject's liberties. In doing so, they emphatically avoided all discussion of sovereignty, popular or otherwise: their objective was not to specify where authority ultimately resided but to provide a model for reconciling the exercise of executive power with the protection of individual rights.

It is often argued that the principal innovation made in the debates of the 1640s was the introduction of the classical theory of mixed government.[5] Having previously occupied a somewhat shadowy position in English constitutional thought,[6] this theory first entered the limelight in *His Majesties Answer To The Nineteen Propositions* (1642). Identifying in the king, House of Lords and House of Commons the three constitutional forms of monarchy, aristocracy and democracy, the *Answer* drew on Polybius' view that the only way to prevent the natural cycle of instability was to forge a constitution out of a mixture of all three.[7] Although this argument failed to gain much traction among Royalists, it is often claimed that it was widely adopted by their opponents, enabling them to transcend the terms of the ancient constitution

---

[4] See J. G. A. Pocock, *The Ancient Constitution and the Feudal Law: A Study of English Historical Thought in the Seventeenth Century*, 2nd edn. (Cambridge: Cambridge University Press, 1987 [1957]); G. Burgess, *The Politics of the Ancient Constitution: An Introduction to English Political Thought 1603–1642* (Basingstoke: Macmillan, 1992); and A. Cromartie, *The Constitutionalist Revolution: An Essay on the History of England, 1450–1642* (Cambridge: Cambridge University Press, 2006).

[5] C. C. Weston, 'English Constitutional Doctrines from the Fifteenth Century to the Seventeenth: II. The Theory of Mixed Monarchy under Charles I and after', *The English Historical Review* 75 (1960), pp. 426–43; C. C. Weston and J. R. Greenberg, *Subjects and Sovereigns: The Grand Controversy over Legal Sovereignty in Stuart England* (Cambridge: Cambridge University Press, 1981); A. Fukuda, *Sovereignty and the Sword: Harrington, Hobbes, and Mixed Government in the English Civil Wars* (Oxford: Clarendon Press, 1997).

[6] See M. Mendle, *Dangerous Positions: Mixed Government, the Estates of the Realm, and the Making of the Answer to the XIX Propositions* (Tuscaloosa: University of Alabama Press, 1985).

[7] *His Majesties Answer To The Nineteen Propositions* (Cambridge: n.p., 1642), pp. 11–12.

and paving the way for the more fully fledged republicanism of the Interregnum.[8]

The real significance of the *Answer* lay, however, not in the arguments that it introduced into the debates of the 1640s but in those that it prompted its enemies to put forward to rebut it. Although the *Answer* seemed like a concession too far for many Royalists, its aim was to deprive the notion of mixed government of its polemical force by showing how, even within a mixed constitution, the king's prerogative could remain untouched.[9] Moreover, the events of early 1642 began to make the mixed constitution, even if conceived of in less Royalist terms, seem inadequate to the task of justifying Parliament's unprecedented actions. Parliament's seizure of the munitions store at Hull and its passing of the Militia Ordinance suggested that it was not merely claiming shared sovereignty with the king but positioning itself as the highest political authority in the realm.

For Henry Parker,[10] whose *Observations upon some of His Majesties late Answers and Expresses* (1642) was the most influential of the Parliamentarian responses to the *Answer*, it became clear that a new and more radical line of argument was required.[11] At the heart of Parker's political thought lies the idea that 'Power is originally in the people, and it is nothing else but that might and vigour which such or such a societie of men contains in it selfe.'[12] This passage immediately alerts us to what is distinctive about Parker's understanding of popular sovereignty: it refers not only to where power originates but also to where it resides. The whole problem of balancing the royal prerogative with subjects' liberties (as in the ancient constitution) or with the powers of the other two estates (as in the mixed constitution) is cast aside. The solution to England's constitutional crisis lies instead in ensuring that the people are able to exercise their innate sovereignty without undue interference from the king.

---

[8] J. G. A. Pocock, *The Machiavellian Moment: Florentine Political Thought and the Atlantic Republican Tradition* (Princeton: Princeton University Press, 1975), pp. 361–71; Weston and Greenberg, *Subjects and Sovereigns*, pp. 35–53. Richard Tuck, *Philosophy and Government, 1572–1651* (Cambridge: Cambridge University Press, 1993), p. 222 challenges the conflation of the mixed constitution and republicanism.

[9] *His Majesties Answer*, p. 12.

[10] For the sake of simplicity of exposition, I focus exclusively on Parker. His arguments were, however, widely taken up during the 1640s. See e.g. John Marsh, *An Argument Or, Debate In Law* (London: n.p., 1642); *A Political Catechism* (London: n.p., 1643); and *A New Plea For The Parliament* (London: n.p., 1643).

[11] See, however, Chapter 6 in this volume for a revisionist reading of Parker that places him squarely in the common-law tradition.

[12] [Henry Parker], *Observations upon some of His Majesties late Answers and Expresses* (London: n.p., 1642), p. 1.

If, as Parker argued, the king lacked any innate prerogative, then his authority must simply have been entrusted to him by the people. His power was, as Parker put it, 'fiduciary' in character. The contractual nature of monarchical rule was not, of course, in itself a safeguard against absolutism, as Parker would have been aware from his reading of Grotius and possibly also of Hobbes.[13] For Parker, however, the contract by which the people entrusted their power to the king was not an absolute relinquishing of natural right but a conditional, limited and revocable grant:

> power is but secondary and derivative in Princes, the fountaine and efficient cause is the people, and from hence the inference is just, the King, though he be *singulis Major*, yet he is *universis minor*, for if the people be the true efficient cause of power, it is a rule in nature *quicquid efficit tale, est magis tale*.[14]

Unlike Hobbes, Parker believed that the people existed as a corporate entity prior to the establishment of political society, and it was this body that, delegating (some of) its natural power to the king, generated monarchical authority. The people were not only the source of political power but retained it in their own hands even after the establishment of monarchical government.

Parker was particularly anxious to resist the suggestion that a people might be able to relinquish their innate power completely and endow the king with absolute authority. A contract containing such a provision would, according to Parker, amount to an act of voluntary enslavement and would thus violate natural law. As he argues in *Ius Populi* (1644), it might be possible for a nation to 'submit to the will of a Prince absolutely, affirmatively reserving no priviledges, but tacitly renouncing all immunities except onely at discretion'. Yet

> such agreements are not the effects of Nature, and tis not easie to imagine how right reason should ever mingle with such a morall principle, as gave being to such an agreement, especially when it renders the Prince, who for honour and power has his perpetuall dependence upon the people, yet more honourable and

---

[13] For Grotius's influence on Parker see M. Mendle, *Henry Parker and the English Civil War: The Political Thought of the Public's 'Privado'* (Cambridge: Cambridge University Press, 1995), pp. 131–2 and Tuck, *Philosophy and Government*, pp. 204, 228–9. Although there is no conclusive evidence that Parker had read Hobbes by the time he wrote the *Observations*, the responses that it elicited by Royalists such as Dudley Digges and John Bramhall certainly brought him into close contact with Hobbesian ideas. See J. Parkin, *Taming the Leviathan: The Reception of the Political and Religious Ideas of Thomas Hobbes in England, 1640–1700* (Cambridge: Cambridge University Press, 2007), pp. 23–32, 43–7. R. Zaller, 'Henry Parker and the Regiment of True Government', *Proceedings of the American Philosophical Society* 135 (1991), pp. 255–85, at pp. 282–4, identifies some interesting parallels between Hobbes and Parker.

[14] Parker, *Observations*, p. 2.

powerfull in reputation of others then the people, and that by expresse grant of the people.[15]

What this suggests is that the social contract by which a sovereign people entrusts power to its rulers is less a historical fact than a heuristic device for establishing normative principles about legitimate government; it describes not what the people actually did in order to set up political authority but what kind of government would be consistent with principles of natural law.

Although Parker condemned Charles I's policies on the grounds that they violated the terms of any legitimate social contract, his purpose was not – as has sometimes been argued – merely to justify resistance to them.[16] The resistance theorists of the sixteenth century had generally presented the people as passive political actors, able at most to stand up to governments when they abused their trust, and even then only by acting through 'inferior magistrates'. Parker, by contrast, held that the people were at all times politically active: it was not by virtue of a latent right of resistance that they could overcome Charles's tyranny, but through their perennial power of self-government.

The question is how such a body, which is too 'combersome' to congregate, could exercise its sovereignty. Parker's answer is that this is achieved through Parliament, the invention of this institution having made it possible to 'regulate the motions of the peoples moliminous body', such that 'the whole community in its underived Majesty' may 'convene'.[17] By contrast with the king, who is merely entrusted with his power, Parliament bears the people's sovereignty directly. It is therefore justified in standing up to the king and assuming all political power in its own hands, even when doing so puts it at odds with a significant section of the population.

Parker's remarkable claim about the nature of Parliament's power rests on his account of representation as 'standing for' another.[18] This eschews the idea that to represent somebody is to have been authorised by him in the way in which, for example, a lawyer might be said to represent his client. What Parker instead means is that Parliament constitutes a likeness of the people, re-presents them in the sense of appearing to make present something that is in fact absent. The people, Parker declares in the *Observations*, 'is not so properly the Author as the essence it selfe of

[15] [Henry Parker], *Ius Populi* (London: n.p., 1644), pp. 17–18.
[16] See e.g. J. Sanderson, *'But the People's Creatures': The Philosophical Basis of the English Civil War* (Manchester: Manchester University Press, 1989), pp. 33–7.
[17] Parker, *Observations*, pp. 14–15.
[18] On the descriptive and symbolic aspects of representation see H. F. Pitkin, *The Concept of Representation* (Berkeley: University of California Press, 1967), and M. B. Vieira and D. Runciman, *Representation* (Cambridge: Polity Press, 2008).

Parliaments'.[19] Just as a figurative painting might be said to bring to life a particular landscape present only in the artist's imagination or existing only at a particular moment in time, Parliament enables the corporate but incorporeal people to take on a physical form.

What is it about Parliament – by contrast with, say, the king – that gives it this remarkable quality of being able to bring the body of the people to life? Parker's initial answer is that 'we have ever found enmity and antipathy betwixt the Court and the countrey, but never any till now betwixt the Representatives, and the Body, of the Kingdome represented'.[20] Because the people and Parliament have the same interests, Parker suggests, the one can simply be taken as equivalent to the other.

Later, however, Parker offers a different solution that rests not on what the people and Parliament have in common but on what sets them apart:

that this convention [of the people] may not be without intelligence, certaine-times and places and formes shall be appointed for its regliment, and that the vastnesse of its owne bulke may not breed confusion, by vertue of election and representation: a few shall act for many, the wise shall consent for the simple, the vertue of all shall redound to some, and the prudence of some shall redound to all.[21]

It is by artifice, by arranging paints on a canvas in a particular way and with a great deal of skill, that a painter brings his landscape into being, not simply by constructing an exact replica. Likewise, Parliament's re-presentative capacity is contingent on its possession of distinctive attributes, in this case the qualities of wisdom and prudence that channel the virtue of the people in such a way as to make it politically efficacious.

With the outbreak of civil war highlighting and exacerbating the divisions within the English populace, Parker's claims about the relationship between Parliament and people may have begun to look increasingly problematic. Parker, however, became only more strident in his later works, insisting in *The Contra-Replicant* (1643) that

The Parliament is nothing else but the whole Nation of *England* by its owne free choice, and by vertue of representation united in a more narrow roome, and better regulated and qualified for consultation then the collective body without this art and order could be. The Lords and Commons make but one entire Court, and this Court is vertually the whole Nation.[22]

---

[19] Parker, *Observations*, p. 5.   [20] Ibid., p. 11.   [21] Ibid., p. 15.
[22] [Henry Parker], *The Contra-Replicant, His Complaint To His Majestie* (London: n.p., 1643), p. 16.

In *Ius Populi* Parker goes further still. Responding to the objection raised by his critics that '*if the peoples power be not totally involved* [i.e. transferred to the king], *then they remain still, as well superior to the Parliament as to the King*', he argues:

tis not rightly supposed that the people and the Parliament are severall in this case: for the Parliament is indeed nothing else, but the very people it self artificially congregated, or reduced by an orderly election, and representation, into such a Senate, or proportionable body.[23]

It may be true that 'Parliament differs many wayes from the rude bulk of the universality', Parker admits, but 'in honour, in majestie, in commission, it ought not at all to be divided, or accounted different as to any legall purpose'.[24] Parliament's actions, however unprecedented and incompatible with the principles of the ancient constitution, are simply the actions of a sovereign people and thus by definition legitimate.

Parker's primary intention may have been to assert Parliament's supremacy over the king, but his theory of popular sovereignty also enabled him to proclaim its power over individual subjects, thus serving as the basis for what Michael Mendle has labelled a theory of 'parliamentary absolutism'.[25] In response to Royalist accusations that Parliament has become an arbitrary power, Parker claims:

That there is an Arbitrary power in every State somewhere tis true, tis necessary, and no inconvenience follows upon it; every man has an absolute power over himself; but because no man can hate himself, this power is not dangerous, nor need to be restrayned: So every State has an Arbitrary power over it self, and there is no danger for the same reason. If the State intrusts this to one man, or few, there may be danger in it; but the Parliament is neither one nor few, it is indeed the State it self.[26]

Rather than resisting the Royalists' attacks on Parliament, Parker neutralises them by claiming that they involve merely restating the point that he had himself been making all along. To describe an action as arbitrary is no more than to say that it proceeds from the will; Parliament's 'arbitrary' power then simply refers to its capacity to will and thus act on behalf of the people. Far from evincing Parliament's authoritarian character, measures such as the Militia Ordinance turn out to be acts of popular self-government.

---

[23] Parker, *Ius Populi*, p. 18. [24] Ibid., pp. 18–19.

[25] Mendle, *Henry Parker*, p. 70. See also M. Mendle, 'Parliamentary Sovereignty: A Very English Absolutism', in N. Phillipson and Q. Skinner (eds.), *Political Discourse in Early Modern Britain* (Cambridge: Cambridge University Press, 1992), pp. 97–119.

[26] Parker, *Observations*, p. 34.

From early 1643 Parliament had begun to place charges on those living in the territories it controlled, most notably in the form of the deeply unpopular excise tax. In order to legitimate such policies, and defend Parliament from the Royalists' inevitable accusations of hypocrisy, Parker offers a still more forceful defence of Parliament's 'arbitrary' power. Noting derisively in *The Contra-Replicant* that, 'were it not for this great noise and boast of Arbitrary power, our Academians would want matter to stuffe their innumerable pamphlets withall', he insists that 'Arbitrary power is only dangerous in one man or in a few men, and cannot be so in Parliaments'. As such, there were simply no limits to what Parliament could do in the name of popular sovereignty:

The House of Commons without the other States hath had an arbitrary power at all times, to dispose of the treasure of the Kingdome, and where they give away one subsidy, they may give 20 and where they give 50000*l* at one subsidy they may give fifty times so much, and all this whether war or peace be.[27]

As the highest authority in the realm, Parliament was entirely within its rights to demand whatever charges it deemed appropriate from those living within its dominion.

What is particularly striking about *The Contra-Replicant* is the self-consciousness with which it subverts the dichotomy of prerogative and liberties contained in the common-law paradigm:

both Houses have an arbitrary power to abridge the freedom of the Subject, and to inlarge the Kings prerogative, beyond a measure; they may repeale our great Charter, the Charter of Forrests, and the petition of right if they please, they may if they please subject the whole Kingdom for ever to the same arbitrary rule as *France* groanes under.[28]

Having jettisoned the vocabulary of the ancient constitution in the *Observations*, Parker is now redeploying it for his own ends. The balance between prerogative and liberties is so far from being the animating force of the English constitution that both of these are merely the product of Parliament's 'arbitrary' power. It is as if, with his own rhetorical coup over the common-law tradition, Parker is signalling the collapse of the ancient constitution and the triumph of a Parliament that wields the power of a sovereign people.

Not every pamphleteer writing on behalf of Parliament during the paper war took up Parker's uncompromising stance. Philip Hunton, a Presbyterian noted for his even-handed and conciliatory approach to the constitutional crisis of the 1640s, took up the idea of popular sovereignty in *A Treatise of Monarchie* (1643) to put forward a line of argument very

---

[27] Parker, *The Contra-Replicant*, pp. 29–30.   [28] Ibid., p. 30.

different from Parker's. He agreed with Parker that power came from below, claiming that 'the consent of the People, either by themselves or their Ancestors is the only mean in ordinary providence by which soveraignty is conferred on any Person or Family'.[29] But beneath this superficial resemblance lie two fundamental differences: first, Hunton rejects Parker's attempt to derive arguments in favour of parliamentary absolutism from popular sovereignty; second, he offers a radically different account of, and solution to, the conflict then afflicting England.

Hunton's view was that the most effective vehicle for the exercise of popular sovereignty was the mixed constitution. It was, moreover, crucial for Hunton that the three estates of king, Lords and Commons should wield equal power, 'so that one must not hold his power from the other, but all equally from the fundamentall Constitution'.[30] The problem for Hunton was that, if each of the three estates held an equal share of sovereign power, 'there can be no Constituted, Legall, Authoritative Judge of the fundamentall Controversies arising betwixt the three Estates. If such doe arise, it is the fatall disease of these Governments, for which no salve can be prescribed.'[31] For any constitutional body to claim a right to adjudicate between the three estates would be '*ipso facto* [to] overthrow the Frame, and turne it into absoluteness'.[32] In place of – indeed, in reaction to – Parker's disquieting vindication of parliamentary absolutism, Hunton seemed to be accepting England's descent into anarchy.

However, there was for Hunton a possible way out of the abyss. The 'people' responsible for erecting the now perilously unstable constitutional structure turn out on closer inspection to be not a corporate entity such as Parker's but a multitude of individuals, each with a distinct will and a distinct conscience. When this edifice begins to collapse, power reverts back to these individuals, who must take it upon themselves to judge which of the estates is in the right and give their support accordingly: 'the Appeale must be to the Community, as if there were no Government; and as by Evidence mens Consciences are convinced, they are bound to give their utmost assistance'.[33] Hunton's vision of popular sovereignty moved beyond Parker's in its attempt to break down the unwieldy body of the people into its constituent parts. By identifying an abstract corporate entity as the locus of sovereign power, Parker had been able to ignore the awkward fact that there appeared to be no direct equivalence between Parliament and the individuals who made up this body. Hunton, by contrast, wanted to expose the sleight of hand involved in

---

[29] Philip Hunton, *A Treatise of Monarchie* (London: n.p., 1643), p. 23.
[30] Ibid., p. 25.   [31] Ibid., p. 28.   [32] Ibid., p. 29.   [33] Ibid., p. 28.

Parker's theory. To speak of popular sovereignty for Hunton meant that, when the constitutional mechanism originally set up by the people broke down, it fell upon every individual to determine how to fix it.

Hunton's argument was certainly designed to thwart the kind of position that Parker was putting forward, but it was not intended as a direct challenge to Parliament's authority. When it came to consulting his own conscience and adjudicating which party was in the right in controversies such as that surrounding the Militia Ordinance, Hunton tended to come down in favour of Parliament.[34] For other pamphleteers, however, the attempt to divorce Parliament and people had a more polemical thrust.

As one might expect, the most far-reaching challenge to Parker's argument came from the Royalists, who were quick to point out that it was far from clear why Parliament's power should be conceived of any differently from the king's. Commenting on Parker's view that 'the Community . . . is to be lookt at in Parliament', one of the earliest Royalist pamphleteers to respond to the *Observations* asks: 'Well, But good Sir, may not the people withdraw the power of representation, which they granted to the Parliament; was their grant so absolute, and so irrevocable, that they dispossest themselves wholly of taking or exercising that power, their owne proper persons?'[35] If the people are the source of all power, then Parliament no less than the king enjoys its power by way of trust and is equally liable to having it revoked in case it is abused.

What is more surprising is that these Royalist arguments should have been echoed by some Parliamentarians, uneasy about the direction their leaders were taking in the early months of the Civil War. Edward Bowles was concerned that 'the Parliament, through the absence of many resolved men, now imployed in particular services for their owne Countries, out of an intolerable wearinesse of this present condition, and feare of the event' would 'agree to the making up of an unsafe unsatisfying Accommodation'. He therefore questioned whether 'in case the representative body cannot, or will not, discharge their trust to the satisfaction, not of fancy, but of reason in the people; they may resume (if ever yet they parted with a power to their manifest undoing) and use their power so farre as conduces to their safety'.[36]

---

[34] Ibid., p. 42.

[35] *Animadversions Upon Those Notes Which The Late Observator hath published* (London: n.p., 1642), p. 12.

[36] [Edward Bowles], *Plaine English* (London: n.p., 1643), p. 21. On the significance of this work within the context of the radicalisation of Parliamentarian thought in the winter of 1642–3 see D. Wootton, 'From Rebellion to Revolution: The Crisis of the Winter of 1642/3 and the Origins of Civil War Radicalism', *The English Historical Review* 105 (1990), pp. 654–69.

For Jeremiah Burroughs, by contrast, the problem with Parliament was not that its leadership was proving itself too ready to compromise with the Royalists but that it was pursuing its cause too fervently, even at the expense of the good of the people. Since Parliament was liable to act tyrannically, he asserted, the people themselves have the right to 'discharge them of that power they had and set up some other'.[37] Samuel Rutherford echoed this view when he wrote that, if the House of Commons abused its power, the people could rightfully 'annul their commissions and rescind their acts'.[38] For both Burroughs and Rutherford, Parker's insistence that any action carried out by Parliament was legitimated by the principle of popular sovereignty was deeply problematic. On the contrary, for those increasingly concerned about Parliament's abuse of its authority, popular sovereignty offered a compelling argument against any form of arbitrary power, whether monarchical or parliamentary.

As we shall now see, it was precisely through this subversive appropriation of Parker's theory that the Levellers developed their radical arguments in favour of a more inclusive and properly representative politics.

III

Although the Levellers ultimately rejected Parker's account of parliamentary power, discovering in Parliament England's 'new chains', they took his account of popular sovereignty as their point of departure.[39] John Lilburne in particular was deeply influenced by Parker, with whom he may even have been personally acquainted from his time in the regiment of the Earl of Essex, Parker's patron. In *Innocency and Truth Justified* (1646) he appeals to the 'principle . . . nobly discussed by the Author of the printed observations upon some of his late Majesties answers and expresses' that 'power is but secondary and derivative in princes', and – Lilburne adds, hinting at a significant point of departure from Parker – 'in counsells likewise'.[40] In *Regall Tyranny discovered* (1647) he quotes Parker's claim

---

[37] Jeremiah Burroughs, *The Glorious Name of God, the Lord of Hosts* (London: n.p., 1643), p. 134.

[38] Samuel Rutherford, *Lex, Rex: The Law of a Prince* (London: n.p., 1644), p. 152.

[39] On the relationship between Leveller and Parliamentarian thought see R. Foxley, *The Levellers: Radical Political Thought in the English Revolution* (Manchester: Manchester University Press, 2013), esp. pp. 27–8, 40–5, 51–83.

[40] [John Lilburne], *Innocency and Truth Justified* (London: n.p., 1646), p. 57. On this passage and on the Levellers' anti-Parliamentarian use of Parliamentarian theory more generally see Sanderson, *'But the People's Creatures'*, p. 105.

that 'Power is originally inherent in the People',[41] later rendering it in his own words: '*the people in generall are the originall sole legislaters, and the true fountain, and earthly well-spring of all just power*'.[42] Like Parker, Lilburne believes that the king's authority has been entrusted to him by the sovereign people, and that 'He that by *contract* and *agreement* receives a *Crowne* or *Kingdome* is bound to that *contract* and *agreement* the violating of which, *absolves* and *disengages* those, (that made it) from him.'[43] Much space is consequently devoted to attacking the king's abuse of his power, in terms reminiscent of Parker.[44]

However, Lilburne was also increasingly concerned about the nature of parliamentary power. Initially his approach was to drive a wedge between the Commons and Lords, appealing to the former as a (potentially) legitimate representative institution, while condemning the latter as agents of the king. In making this distinction, Lilburne was motivated in part by his personal tribulations at the hands of the Lords, but his argument here also reflected the Levellers' more demanding understanding of representation, which could not accommodate a plenary chamber lacking any form of popular endorsement. In *Regall Tyranny discovered* Lilburne accuses the peers of being 'meer usurpers and incroachers', who 'were never intrusted by the people' but instead 'sit by the Kings prerogative, which is meer bable, and shadow, and in truth, in substance is nothing at all, there being no Law-making-power in himselfe, but meerly, and onely at the most, a Law-executing-power'.[45] As such, the Lords are vulnerable to the same accusations that had been levelled against the king. Lilburne describes 'the *Lordly Prerogative* honour it self that they enjoy from the King (which was never given them by *common consent*, as all right, and just honour, and power, ought to be)' as nothing less than a 'boon and gratuity, given them by the *King*, for the helping him to inslave and envassalise the People'.[46] To allow the Lords this power, making 'all the *Freemen* of *England* . . . answerable to their wills', would be to make the people 'as great slaves as the *Pesants* in *France* are (who enjoy propriety neither in life, liberty, nor estate) if they did not make us absolute vassals as the poore *Turks* are to the *Grand Seigneour,* whose lives, and estates he takes away from the greatest of them, when he pleaseth'.[47]

Another Leveller who dedicated much space in his writings to attacking the Upper House is Richard Overton. In *A Defiance Against All Arbitrary Usurpations Or Encroachments* (1646) he argues that, since the Upper

---

[41] [John Lilburne], *Regall Tyrannie discovered* (London: n.p., 1647), pp. 40–1. Cf. Parker, *Observations*, pp. 1–2.

[42] Lilburne, *Regall Tyrannie*, p. 99.   [43] Ibid., p. 9.   [44] See e.g. ibid., p. 34.

[45] Ibid., p. 43.   [46] Ibid., p. 45.   [47] Ibid., p. 65.

House is unelected, 'then are these Lords neither Lords, nor Representers, then at most they cannot be Representers of so much as their own
Tenants, but rather Presenters of themselves in the Land'.[48] Unless there
is some specifiable electoral process by which one person has entrusted
his (and even for the Levellers it was always 'his') innate power to another,
there can be no representation. An individual or institution claiming to
represent another without having been authorised merely 'presents' himself and as such is 'subordinate to those who represent the whole Nation;
for by the rule of right reason, the lesser must needs be subject to the
GREATER'.[49]

In *A Remonstrance Of Many Thousand Citizens* (1646) Overton highlights the potential affinity between the sovereign people and the elected
chamber. However, his principal purpose is now to remind Members of
Parliament, against the claims being made on their behalf by Parker, that
they are not identical with the population as a whole. As Overton puts it
in the opening sentence:

Wee are well assured, yet cannot forget, that the cause of our choosing you to be
Parliament-men, was to deliver us from all kind of Bondage, and to preserve the
Common-wealth in Peace and Happinesse: For effecting whereof, we possessed
you with the same Power that was in our selves without you, if we had thought
it convenient; choosing you (as Persons whom wee thought fitly quallified, and
Faithfull,) for avoiding some inconveniences.[50]

Including himself in the 'people' by using the first-person plural, while
addressing Parliament in the second person, Overton highlights the distinction between the two: representatives and represented are – gram-
matically as well as legally – distinct persons.

Later in the pamphlet the tone of admonition gives way to one first of
remonstration and then threat:

Yee are extreamely altered in demeanour towards us, in the beginning yee seemed
to know what Freedome was; made a distinction of honest men, whether rich or
poor, all were welcome to you, and yee would mix your selves with us in a loving
familiar way void of Courtly observance or behaviour.[51]

But now, Overton claims, the Lower House is behaving 'more like the
House of Peers then the *House of Commons,* such that it is impossible for the

[48] [Richard Overton], *A Defiance Against All Arbitrary Usurpations Or Encroachments*
(London: n.p., 1646), p. 15.
[49] Ibid., p. 15.
[50] [Richard Overton], *A Remonstrance Of Many Thousand Citizens, and other Free-born
People of England To their owne House of Commons* (London: n.p., 1646), p. 3.
[51] Ibid., p. 16.

people to have their petitions heard; indeed, 'the *Kings*, or the *Lords* pretended *Prerogatives* never made a greater noise, nor was made more dreadfull then the Name of the *Priviledge of the House of Commons*'.[52] Overton's objection is that the Members of Parliament have become increasingly aloof and distant from the people, no longer resembling them and thus no longer fit to represent them. Furthermore, since there is a clear distinction between people and Parliament, Overton is anxious to reclaim the revolution for the people: the struggle against the king, he declares, 'is ours, and not your owne, though ye are to be partakers with us in the well or ill doing thereof: and therefore ye must expect to heare more frequently from us then yee have done'.[53]

This was no empty threat. In the months and years that followed, the Levellers became increasingly vocal in their opposition not only to the House of Lords but also to the Commons.[54] In the *Remonstrance*, a brief and occasional pamphlet written to petition for Lilburne's release from Newgate Prison, Overton had limited himself to condemning the personal failings of Members of Parliament. By contrast, in the more ambitious *An Arrow Against All Tyrants And Tyranny*, published a few months later, he offered a systematic critique of the House of Commons that involved a fundamental challenge not merely to Parker's theory of parliamentary absolutism but to the underlying account of popular sovereignty.

Overton's approach in this pamphlet is to move away from the Parliamentarians' corporatist notion of popular sovereignty and to put forward an alternative theory centred on the individual:

To every Individuall in nature, is given an individuall property by nature, not to be invaded or usurped by any; for every one, as he is himselfe, so he has a selfe propriety, else he could not be himselfe; and on this no second may presume to deprive any of, without manifest violation and affront to the very principles of nature, and of the Rules of equity and justice between man and man.[55]

The vocabulary of 'selfe proprietie' with which Overton describes the sphere of rights surrounding each individual has distinct echoes of Parker's claim that it would be 'unnaturall' for a people to 'give away its owne proprietie in it selfe absolutely and to subject it selfe to a condition of servilitie below men'.[56] Overton endorses Parker's account of

---

[52] Ibid., p. 11.   [53] Ibid., p. 16.

[54] See, however, R. Foxley, 'Problems of Sovereignty in Leveller Writings', *History of Political Thought*, 28 (2007), pp. 642–60, at p. 644 for the view that the Levellers never went beyond asserting the supremacy of the Commons over the Lords and thus did not put forward a theory of popular sovereignty at all.

[55] Richard Overton, *An Arrow Against All Tyrants And Tyranny* (London: n.p., 1647), p. 1.

[56] Parker, *Observations*, p. 20.

sovereignty as a natural power residing in the people that can be conceived of as a form of property. He further accepts the view that the bearers of sovereign power cannot themselves be turned into the property of another. But, whereas Parker placed this property in the body of the people, Overton locates it in each individual, whose rights cannot therefore be overridden in the name of popular sovereignty.[57]

As we have seen, Overton's view is not that Parliament exercises the sovereign power of the people directly but that, like the king, it is merely entrusted with its authority. He now adds that it is individuals, not the collective body of the people, who have entrusted their power to Parliament. Only in this way, Overton claims, can legitimate political power arise, for 'every man by nature being a King, Priest and Prophet in his owne naturall circuite and compasse . . . no second may partake, but by deputation, commission, and free consent from him, whose naturall right and freedom it is'.[58] Addressing the Independent Member of Parliament and Leveller sympathiser Henry Marten, Overton writes:

The free people of this Nation, for their better being, discipline, government, propriety and safety, have each of them communicated so much unto you (their *Chosen Ones*) of their naturall rights and powers, that you might thereby become their absolute Commissioners, and lawfull Deputies, but no more; and that by contraction of those their severall Individuall Communications confer'd upon, and united in you, you alone might become their own naturall proper, soveraign power, therewith singly and only impowred for their severall weales, safeties and freedoms, and no otherwise.[59]

Political power is generated, Overton believes, by the amalgamation of the separate acts of authorisation made by each self-owning individual. It would therefore be inconceivable for these individuals to consent to the kind of 'arbitrary' power that Parker was asserting on Parliament's behalf.

Just as Parker had argued that it would have been contrary to nature for a free *people* to sell itself into bondage by accepting Charles I's absolutism, so Overton claims that no *individual* would enslave himself to Parliament:

For as by nature, no man may abuse, beat, torment, or afflict himself; so by nature, no man may give that power to another, seeing he may not doe it himselfe, for no more can be communicated from the generall then is included in the particulars, whereof the generall is compounded.[60]

Self-ownership entails not an absolute right over oneself but requires that one's property in oneself be used according to principles of natural law.

---

[57] See R. Tuck, *Natural Rights Theories: Their Origin and Development* (Cambridge: Cambridge University Press, 1979), pp. 147–51.
[58] Overton, *An Arrow*, p. 4.   [59] Ibid., p. 4.   [60] Ibid., p. 4.

Parliament's power, originating in the voluntary and conditional agreement of individuals, is therefore limited by the normative restrictions inherent in the concept of self-ownership itself.

The question is what happens when Parliament violates the terms of its trust (or of any trust that would be consistent with natural law). Overton's answer in *An Appeale From the degenerate Representative Body* (1647) is that the power 'returneth from whence it came, even to the hands of the *Trusters*'.[61] This, Overton continues, quoting himself, is because 'all iust *humaine powers* are but betrusted, conferr'd and conveyed by ioint and common consent, *for to every individuall in nature, is given an individuall propriety by nature, not to be invaded or usurped by any*'.[62] The Parliamentarians had argued that an abuse of power on the part of the king justified anything that Parliament chose to do in response, even when this involved riding roughshod over individuals' property rights. For Overton, any attempt by Parliament to invade individuals' 'selfe propriety' would likewise be illegitimate and would entitle those individuals to reclaim their power into their own hands.

What this would involve in practice is not something that Overton considers in any detail. For him, as for the other Levellers, the people's sovereignty has to be mediated; what is crucial therefore is ensuring that the political institutions entrusted with it should be truly representative and not so in name only.[63] According to Overton's somewhat idiosyncratic account, this hinges not on Parliament's proportionality – whether in terms of region, class, occupation or some other measure – but on its *qualitative* resemblance to those it represents. The reason why, Overton claims, Members of Parliament have 'devested and degraded themselves from their betrusted authority of the people, and become no longer their representory Deputies, or Trustees' is that 'tyrants and oppressors cannot be the Representers of the Free-men of *England*, for freedom and tyranny are contraries, that which representeth the one, doth not represent the other'.[64] Since the English people are free-born, their representatives 'must be substantial and reall *Actors* for *freedome* and *liberty*':

for such as is the represented, such and no other must the figure of representation be, such as is the proportion, countenance and favour of the man, such and so must be the picture of the man, or else it cannot be the picture of that man, but of some other, or something else, as is the picture of a grim, meagre, frowning

---

[61] Richard Overton, *An Appeale From the degenerate Representative Body the Commons of England assembled at Westminster* (London: n.p., 1647), p. 6.

[62] Ibid.

[63] On what the Levellers did have to say about direct popular engagement in politics see Foxley, 'Problems of Sovereignty', p. 651.

[64] Overton, *An Appeale*, p. 12.

face is, not the picture of an amiable, friendly smiling countenance; so tyranny neither is nor can possibly be the Representor of Freedome.[65]

With this striking language, Overton brings to the fore the descriptive and symbolic aspects of representation. In order to constitute a true representation of the people, Parliament must actually be like the population at large in the sense of standing for the same principles as them, of embodying the same ideals.

The idea of authorisation, which is eschewed in Overton's account of representation, does however feature prominently in other Leveller writings. This is certainly the case in the *Agreement of the People* (issued in three versions between 1647 and 1649), which not only called for an expansion of authorisation through a broader franchise and regular elections but, requiring the consent of the whole political nation, was itself intended to be part of this process.[66] The problem afflicting England is described from the outset as one of ineffective representation, and it is with the task of remedying this deficiency that all of the first *Agreement*'s four articles are concerned. The first, recalling that 'the People of England being at this day very unequally distributed by Counties, Cities, & Burroughs, for the election of their Deputies in Parliament', demands that they be 'more indifferently proportioned, according to the number of the Inhabitants'.[67] The second and third articles deal with the dissolution of the Rump and the establishment of rules for biennial elections.

What is crucial for the Levellers is that the act of authorising one's rulers to act on one's behalf – whether by signing the *Agreement* or through the ordinary process of electoral politics – is not a relinquishing of one's natural powers but a means of exercising them. Although the authors accept that Parliament is the supreme constitutional body in the kingdom, they insist – in the fourth and final article – that 'the power of this, and all future Representatives of this Nation, is inferiour only to theirs who chuse them'.[68] In stressing that Parliament is at all times subordinate to the individuals who entrust their power to it, the *Agreement* rejects the view that Parliament can override individual rights in the name of popular sovereignty.

Moreover, the power of Parliament extends only to 'whatsoever is not expressly, or impliedly reserved by the represented to themselves'.[69] This includes, most importantly, the proviso 'That matters of Religion, and

---

[65] Ibid., p. 12.

[66] That is not to say, however, that the *Agreement* should be viewed, as it often has been, as an original social contract. See Foxley, *The Levellers*, pp. 74–5.

[67] *An Agreement of the People For A firme and present Peace, upon grounds of common-right and freedome* (London: n.p., 1647), p. 2.

[68] Ibid., p. 3.   [69] Ibid., p. 4.

the wayes of Gods Worship, are not at all intrsuted by us to any humane power', as well as a ban on conscription, immunity against prosecution for crimes committed during the civil war, equality before the law and the requirement that all laws should promote the safety of the people.[70] In the second version of the *Agreement*, this section swells from five to eight sub-clauses, with such additional provisos as 'That no *Representative* shall in any wise render up, or give, or take away any the foundations of Common Right, liberty or safety contained in this *Agreement*, nor shall levell mens estates, destroy propriety, or make all things common.'[71] By the time of the third *Agreement*, issued from the Tower, when the Levellers' hopes of forging an alliance with the Independents had been all but abandoned, the question of how to ensure that Parliament is properly representative seems subordinate to that of how to prevent it from abusing its power.

The first *Agreement* concludes with a longer, more discursive section, where once again the problem of representation takes centre stage. By ensuring that Parliaments are 'certainly cal'd and have the time of their sitting & ending certain & their power or trust cleare and unquestionable', they will become a closer approximation, a more realistic likeness of the individuals they represent:

those whom your selves shall chuse, shall have power to restore you to, and secure you in, all your rights; & they shall be in a capacity to tast of subjection, as well as rule; & so shall be equally concerned with yourselves, in all they do. For they must equally suffer with you under any common burdens, & partake with you in any freedoms; & by this they shal be disenabled to defraud or wrong you, when the lawes shall bind all alike, without privilege or exemption; & by this your Consciences shall be free from tyrannie & oppression, & those occasions of endlesse strifes, & bloudy warres, shall be perfectly removed.[72]

Taking up the Aristotelian ideal of ruling and being ruled in turns, the *Agreement* claims that, if Members of Parliament – who presumably cannot but act out of self-interest – are rotated swiftly enough, they will advance the good of the people as a whole. Only by ensuring that those sitting in Parliament are selected from the class of ordinary people, sharing their experiences and hardships, can they possibly represent them.

The first *Agreement* does not offer a detailed account of who exactly should possess the vote, nor do its claims about representation seem to rest on the size of the electorate. But the call in the first article for the

---

[70] Ibid., p. 4.
[71] *Foundations of Freedom; Or An Agreement Of The People: Proposed as a Rule for future Government in the Establishment of a firm and lasting Peace* (London: n.p., 1648), p. 12.
[72] *An Agreement of the People*, p. 8.

electorate to be 'more indifferently proportioned' was treated during the Putney Debates as evidence of the Levellers' desire to introduce universal male suffrage. Whether this was the case remains uncertain, but it is surely a fact of some significance that when Henry Ireton takes the Levellers to be calling for 'every man that is an inhabitant' to be given 'equal voice in the election', none of the Levellers present contradicts him.[73] Instead, they defend manhood suffrage, asserting that 'all inhabitants that have not lost their birthright should have an equal voice in elections' and that 'every man that is to live under a government ought first by his own consent to put himself under that government'.[74]

Although two (relatively obscure) Leveller spokesmen at Putney, Maximilian Petty and Thomas Reade, do eventually accept that servants, apprentices and alms-recipients should be excluded from the franchise,[75] this may have been a tactical concession and should not necessarily be taken as evidence of the Levellers' anti-populist sympathies.[76] The best-known Leveller at Putney, Thomas Rainsborough, remains steadfast in his commitment to giving the 'poorest he' political rights, even if this would result (as Ireton charged) in the overthrow of private property.[77] However, even with Petty's restriction, which made its way into the second version of the *Agreement* (in which Petty almost certainly had a hand) and to a lesser extent the third, the Levellers were calling for a substantial increase in the franchise, and explicitly treating this as a precondition for the legitimacy of Parliament. Only by voting and thus authorising their representatives to act on their behalf can the naturally self-owning individuals who make up the political nation be adequately represented, and only if this is the case can it be said that the English constitution is founded on the ideal of popular sovereignty.

---

[73] A. S. P. Woodhouse (ed.), *Puritanism and Liberty: Being the Army Debates (1647–9) from the Clarke Manuscripts with Supplementary Documents*, 2nd edn. (London: J. M. Dent, 1974), p. 52.

[74] Ibid., p. 53.   [75] Ibid., p. 83.

[76] For the once influential view that the Levellers were never committed to more than an incremental expansion of the franchise see C. B. Macpherson, *The Political Theory of Possessive Individualism: Hobbes to Locke* (Oxford: Oxford University Press, 1962), pp. 107–59. This interpretation has been challenged in K. Thomas, 'The Levellers and the Franchise', in G. E. Aylmer (ed.), *The Interregnum: The Quest for Settlement, 1646–1660* (London: Macmillan, 1974) and I. Hampsher-Monk, 'The Political Theory of the Levellers: Putney, Property and Professor Macpherson', *Political Studies* 24 (1976), pp. 397–422. Quentin Skinner argues in 'Rethinking Political Liberty', *History Workshop Journal* 61 (2006), pp. 156–70, at pp. 161–3 that Petty and Reade's willingness to curtail the franchise did not result from an abandonment of the ideal of manhood suffrage, but simply reflected their more exclusive definition of 'manhood', which was incompatible with the condition of dependence that characterised certain categories of men.

[77] Woodhouse (ed.), *Puritanism and Liberty*, pp. 61–3.

IV

This chapter has traced the emergence and evolution of the idea of popular sovereignty in the English Civil War, focusing on the paper war of the early 1640s and on the writings of the Levellers from the middle of the decade. An idiom that was originally intended to do no more than buttress the position of Parliament in its conflict with the king was turned on its head, giving rise to radical demands for a more inclusive form of politics. While it has long been recognised that the Levellers were drawing on Parliamentarian pamphleteers such as Parker, the diverging discussions of popular sovereignty found in the two bodies of literature have never been placed side by side in the manner attempted in the present study. Doing so has two particularly important payoffs, which I would like to conclude by underlining.

The first is that, by treating the Levellers as responding specifically to Parker's theory of parliamentary absolutism, we are in a better position to understand the nature of their intervention. In particular, their individualist language of 'selfe propriety' turns out to have little to do with justifying the accumulative activities of an emerging capitalist class, as was once supposed.[78] It was instead put forward in opposition to the Parliamentarians' attempt to use the concept of popular sovereignty to justify the subordination of individuals to the body of the people, and to legitimate the most arbitrary exercise of power in its name. Understanding the genesis of self-ownership is particularly important because of its subsequent afterlife in Lockean and thence, in our own time, libertarian thought.[79] If this concept is nowadays most often invoked in support of the right to the untrammelled accumulation of property, it was originally put forward for the contrasting purpose of giving the 'poorest he' political rights.

The second insight that our story affords concerns the relationship between popular sovereignty and representation, which both Parliamentarians and Levellers, in spite of their differing treatments of the two concepts, assume must go hand in hand. According to one approach, popular sovereignty has to be represented because the people, thought of as a corporate entity, are too unwieldy for effective political action. The rival view involves breaking down the body of the people into its constituent parts, each of which would in theory be capable of acting directly but which delegates its power to a representative body in order to prevent the discord that would otherwise take place.

---

[78] Macpherson, *Possessive Individualism*.
[79] See in particular R. Nozick, *Anarchy, State, and Utopia* (New York: Basic Books, 1974).

The problem with the first approach, highlighted by the Levellers, should by now be clear enough: in the absence of any specifiable act of authorisation, the 'representative' character of Parliament loses the normative force that any satisfactory theory of representation should have and instead serves to legitimate – as Parker himself acknowledges – the unchecked exercise of arbitrary power. Yet the second approach is also not without its drawbacks. Even ignoring the problem of the Levellers' apparent willingness to accept a restricted franchise (and their failure even to consider the possibility of women having the vote), there is the problem of what happens when an individual votes for a losing party in an election or chooses to withhold his vote.[80] Such an individual has certainly not authorised his rulers to act on his behalf, so it is difficult to see how he is being represented, according to the Levellers' own account of what this involves. In what sense, then, can a government that has not actually been established with the consent of each individual derive its legitimacy from the individualistic concept of popular sovereignty that the Levellers espoused?

This question may provide an important context for Hobbes's theory of representation and 'personation' in Chapter 16 of *Leviathan* (1651), a discussion that has no precedent in the earlier versions of his political thought.[81] According to Hobbes, the body of the people is generated by virtue of the declarations of consent given by each individual in the state of nature to establish a sovereign power. Every individual has authorised the sovereign. However, the person that the sovereign represents is not every individual but the people, or what Hobbes describes as the 'Leviathan' or 'state'. The individuals whom the Levellers sought to empower give life to the Parliamentarians' 'people' by erecting an absolute sovereign authority that gives unity to a multitude of distinct wills and 'bears the person' of the body thereby created. As Hobbes famously put it, 'A Multitude of men, are made *One* Person, when they are by one man, or one Person, Represented.'[82] In this way, Hobbes could respond to Leveller critiques of the new regime, which his *Leviathan* was in part intended to legitimate, by pointing out that, even if it did not enjoy the consent of every individual, it was nevertheless representative in so far as it represented the body of the people which had been created through the original contract.

---

[80] This is an issue that is treated at greater length by Eric Nelson in Chapter 8 in this volume.

[81] For a fuller discussion of Hobbes's theory of representation and its relationship to that of the Parliamentarians and Levellers see Skinner, 'Hobbes on Persons, Authors and Representatives'.

[82] Thomas Hobbes, *Leviathan*, ed. N. Malcolm (Oxford: Clarendon Press, 2012), p. 248.

With Hobbes we may have strayed far from popular sovereignty.[83] The theory of the state that he produced, intended as it was to legitimate the most absolute form of sovereign power, whether in an individual or an assembly, is certainly not one that either the Parliamentarians or the Levellers would have endorsed. Yet, if it is true that Hobbes's account of representation was intended in part as a response to the Parliamentarian and Leveller theories of popular sovereignty that we have explored in this chapter, then Hobbes may have provided an unlikely conduit for these ideas among later writers who explicitly drew on his work in order to develop theories more recognisably concerned with popular sovereignty.

[83] See, however, Chapter 5 in this volume.

8   Prerogative, popular sovereignty, and the American founding

Eric Nelson

I

Historians have long recognized that the idea of "popular sovereignty" stood at the center of the ideological landscape that produced the American Revolution and, later, the constitution of the United States. As James Wilson of Pennsylvania put the point in a speech to his state's ratifying convention in 1787, since "it has not been, nor I presume, will be denied, that somewhere there is, and of necessity must be, a supreme, absolute and uncontrollable authority" in every state, which "may justly be termed the sovereign power," the only dispute concerns where this power properly resides.[1] Some suppose that it resides in a supreme legislature, such as the British Parliament, while others come "nearer the truth" by insisting that the "constitution" itself should be regarded as the repository of this power. Yet both of these views are mistaken. "The truth," Wilson explains, "is, that the supreme, absolute, and uncontrollable authority remains with the people," and, while "the great and penetrating mind of Locke" had glimpsed this mighty principle, "the practical recognition of this truth was reserved for the honor of this country."[2] The American Revolution, on this account, had been waged under the banner of popular sovereignty, and, with the drafting of the new constitution, the citizens of the United States could at last achieve "the happiness of seeing it carried into practice."[3]

There has been an understandable tendency to regard the principle of popular sovereignty, thus understood, as a democratic principle – and, indeed, Wilson himself stressed that, in a sense, it was. If "democracy" means "rule by the people," then surely "when the body of the people is possessed of the supreme power" the resulting regime should be called a "democracy."[4] On this conception, the American Revolution and the new constitution did indeed seek to advance "the democratic

---

[1] Jonathan Elliot (ed.),*The Debates in the Several State Conventions on the Adoption of the Federal Constitution*, 5 vols. (Washington, DC: n.p., 1836), II, p. 455.
[2] Ibid., p. 456.   [3] Ibid.   [4] ibid., pp. 478, 482.

principle." But what exactly does it mean to say that, under a proper constitution, the people will possess "supreme power?" Here matters become far more complicated. It was, after all, the very same James Wilson who had declared barely six months earlier in the Constitutional Convention that, during the Revolution, "the people of America Did not oppose the British King but the parliament – the opposition was not against an Unity but a corrupt multitude."[5] The Revolution, on Wilson's account, had been a rebellion against a tyrannical popular assembly, not against a monarch. Indeed, it had been an insurrection in favor of royal power. Wilson was not remotely alone in taking this view. Rufus King of Massachusetts, who had recorded Wilson's remarks in the Convention, cautioned a younger colleague years later that the Revolution had come to be badly misunderstood by posterity:

> You young men who have been born since the Revolution, look with horror upon the name of a King, and upon all propositions for a strong government. It was not so with us. We were born the subjects of a King, and were accustomed to subscribe ourselves "His Majesty's most faithful subjects"; and we began the quarrel which ended in the Revolution, not against the King, but against his parliament.[6]

Rufus King was not mistaken. Benjamin Franklin too had explained his opposition to Britain by observing that the Lords and Commons "seem to have been long encroaching on the Rights of their and our Sovereign, assuming too much of his Authority, and betraying his Interests."[7] The young Alexander Hamilton went so far as to declare in 1775 that the king "is the only Sovereign of the empire," such that "the part which the people have in the legislature, may more justly be considered as a limitation of the Sovereign authority."[8] Such an arrangement, on his account, was uniquely favourable to liberty because a monarch "is under no temptation to purchase the favour of one part of his dominions, at the expense of another; but, it is his interest to treat them all, upon the same footing.

---

[5] *The Records of the Federal Convention of 1787*, ed. M. Farrand, 3 vols. (New Haven: n.p., 1911), I, p. 65. An extended version of the argument that follows may be found in E. Nelson, *The Royalist Revolution: Monarchy and the American Founding* (Cambridge, MA: Harvard University Press, 2014).

[6] Thomas Hart Benton, *Thirty Years' View, Or A History of the Working of the American Government for Thirty Years, From 1820–1850*, 2 vols. (New York: n.p., 1858), I, p. 58.

[7] Franklin to Samuel Cooper, June 8, 1770, in Benjamin Franklin, *The Papers of Benjamin Franklin*, ed. W. B. Willcox et al., 39 vols. (New Haven: Yale University Press, 1977–2008; henceforth *PBF*), XVII, p. 163.

[8] [Alexander Hamilton], *The Farmer Refuted: or, A more impartial and comprehensive View of the Dispute between Great-Britain and the Colonies* (New York: n.p., 1775), p. 16. Cf. "Marginalia in *An Inquiry*, an Anonymous Pamphlet," in *PBF*, XVII, p. 345 ("the King . . . alone is the Sovereign").

Very different is the case with regard to the Parliament. The Lords and Commons have a separate interest to pursue."[9] John Adams similarly reflected that, if he had understood the Revolution to embody a campaign against monarchy, he "would never have drawn his sword."[10] Nor was this understanding of the imperial crisis a matter of "high theory" alone. Describing Washington's fateful muster of the Continental Army on Cambridge Common in April 1775, a British officer stationed with General Thomas Gage recorded that "the Rebels have erected the Standard at Cambridge; they call themselves the King's Troops and us the Parliaments. Pretty Burlesque!"[11]

American "Patriots" of the late 1760s and 1770s developed the view that Parliament possessed no jurisdiction whatsoever over British North America; the colonies, they now claimed, were connected to Britain solely through "the person and prerogative of the king."[12] But the late eighteenth-century British monarchy was in no position to function as the "pervading" and "superintending" power of the empire. The constitutional settlement that followed the Glorious Revolution had definitively subjected the king to Parliament, drastically curtailing his prerogatives and recasting him as a pure "executive." Those powers of state that legally remained with the Crown were no longer wielded by the person of the king, but rather by ministers who were required to command a parliamentary majority (and who themselves sat in one of the two Houses). Patriots of the late 1760s and 1770s were effectively proposing to turn back the clock on the English constitution by over a hundred years – to separate the king from his Parliament and his British ministers, and to restore ancient prerogatives of the Crown that had been extinguished by the Whig ascendancy. These theorists wanted more monarchy, not less.

Defenders of the British administration fully recognized the radicalism of the American position. Lord North observed in the House of Commons that the Patriot program could not be described as remotely "Whig": "If he understood the meaning of the words Whig and Tory . . . he conceived that it was characteristic of Whiggism to

---

[9] Hamilton, *Farmer Refuted*, p. 18.

[10] William Maclay, *Journal of William Maclay: United States Senator from Pennsylvania, 1789–1791*, ed. E. S. Maclay (New York: n.p., 1890), p. 10.

[11] John Barker, *The British in Boston: Being the Diary of Lieutenant John Barker of the King's Own Regiment from November 15, 1774 to May 31, 1776*, ed. E. E. Dana (Cambridge, MA: Harvard University Press, 1920), p. 40. See also Lieutenant William Fielding to Major Generals William Howe, John Burgoyne, and Henry Clinton, June 1775, in M. Balderston and D. Syrett (eds.), *The Lost War: Letters from British Officers during the American Revolution* (New York: n.p., 1975), pp. 29–30; and the "Extract of a Letter from the Camp at Cambridge" published in the *New-York Gazette* on July 24, 1775. For a similar incident in New York see *Pennsylvania Evening Post* (March 11, 1775).

[12] Hamilton, *Farmer Refuted*, p. 16.

gain as much for the people as possible, while the aim of Toryism was to increase the prerogative. That in the present case, the administration contended for the right of parliament, while the Americans talked of their belonging to the crown. Their language therefore was that of Toryism."[13] The Americans, Josiah Tucker likewise complained, were either, in effect, oddly "pleading for the Extension of the Prerogative of the Crown... beyond all the Bounds of Law, Reason, and of Common Sense!" in Britain itself, or else adopting the even more "absurd" view that "though the King cannot do these strange things in England, yet he can do them all in America; because his Royal Prerogative, like Wire coiled up in a Box, can be stretched and drawn out to almost any Length, according to the Distance and Extent of his Dominions."[14] William Markham, Archbishop of York, was even more expansive. The Americans, he proclaimed, "have used their best endeavours, to throw the whole weight and power of the colonies into the scale of the crown," and have therefore plainly rejected the settlement of "the glorious revolution."[15] It was simply through "God's good providence, that we had a prince upon the throne, whose magnanimity and justice were superior to such temptations."[16]

The puzzle, for our purposes, is therefore as follows: how can we reconcile the unprecedented American embrace of the royal prerogative with the undeniable fact that Patriots took themselves to be defending the principle of popular sovereignty? How, in other words, could American theorists have supposed that by empowering the monarch they were simultaneously empowering the people? The answer, I shall suggest, is that a great many Patriots quite self-consciously adopted the political and constitutional theory of those who had waged the last great campaign against the "usurpations" of Parliament: the reviled Stuart monarchs of the seventeenth century. English Royalists had grounded their strident defense of prerogative power in a particular theory of

---

[13] *The Parliamentary History of England: From the Earliest Period to the Year 1803*, ed. T. C. Hansard, 36 vols. (London, 1806–1820), XVIII, p. 771. Cf. "A Revolution Whig," *Scots Magazine* 37 (1775), p. 646.

[14] Josiah Tucker, *A Letter from a Merchant in London to His Nephew in North America* (London: n.p., 1766), pp. 7–8.

[15] William Markham, *A sermon preached before the Incorporated Society for the Propagation of the gospel in Foreign Parts* (London: n.p., 1777), pp. 22–3. For a pro-American response to Markham (and to John Stuart, First Marquess of Bute, who had made the same argument) see Willoughby Bertie, Lord Abingdon, *Thoughts on Mr. Burke's Letter to the Sheriffs of Bristol on the Affairs of America* (Dublin: n.p., 1777), pp. 46–7.

[16] On this theme see G. H. Guttridge, *English Whiggism and the American Revolution* (Berkeley: University of California Press, 1966), esp. pp. 61–3; and P. Langford, "New Whigs, Old Tories, and the American Revolution," *Journal of Imperial and Commonwealth History* 2 (1980), pp. 106–130, esp. pp. 110–112.

representation – one that explained how the king could be regarded as the authorized agent of the people as a whole. But if the monarch's power is truly "representative" in this sense, then his subjects can be regarded as self-governing. If, as Thomas Hobbes famously put it, "the King is the people," then it seems to follow that the people are king – even in an absolute monarchy.[17] Patriots, of course, were not defending absolute monarchy, but they were advocating a kind of prerogativist constitutionalism that had been unimaginable in Britain itself for generations. They therefore felt called upon to challenge and repudiate the rival conception of popular sovereignty that had stood at the center of the Parliamentarian and Whig traditions since the 1640s (and that forms the subject of Lorenzo Sabbadini's chapter in the present volume (Chapter 7)): the notion that the people may only be said to be self-governing if they are exclusively subject to laws made by a "representative" popular assembly. The clash between these rival conceptions during the imperial crisis would come to organize American understandings of popular sovereignty in the 1780s.

II

After a number of forensic false starts, Patriots of the late 1760s and early 1770s settled on the view that Parliament possessed no jurisdiction whatsoever over the colonies.[18] North America was now understood to be "outside of the realm," a separate dominion within the British Empire. It did not follow that the colonies were to be regarded as "independent states"; rather, they were to be understood as "dependent" solely on the person of the king, and not upon the "Legislature of Great Britain." But

---

[17] Thomas Hobbes, *On the Citizen*, ed. R. Tuck and M. Silverthorne (Cambridge: Cambridge University Press, 1998), p. 137.

[18] The best account of the broad contours of this "dominion theory" remains C. H. McIlwain, *The American Revolution: A Constitutional Interpretation* (New York: Macmillan, 1923), pp. 114–147. See also A. Lacroix, *The Ideological Origins of American Federalism* (Cambridge, MA: Harvard University Press, 2010), chaps. 2 and 3; B. McConville, *The King's Three Faces: The Rise and Fall of Royal America, 1688–1776* (Chapel Hill: University of North Carolina Press, 2006), pp. 250–261; M. S. Flaherty, "More Apparent than Real: The Revolutionary Commitment to Constitutional Federalism," *Kansas Law Review* 45 (1996–1997), pp. 993–1014; J. C. D. Clark, *The Language of Liberty, 1660–1832: Political Discourse and Social Dynamics in the Anglo-American World* (Cambridge: Cambridge University Press, 1994), pp. 93–110; J. P. Reid, *Constitutional History of the American Revolution: The Authority of Law* (Madison: University of Wisconsin Press, 1993); J. Rakove, *The Beginnings of National Politics: An Interpretive History of the Continental Congress* (New York: Knopf, 1979), pp. 34–41; G. Wood, *The Creation of the American Republic, 1776–1787* (Chapel Hill: University of North Carolina Press, 1969), pp. 344–354; and B. Bailyn, *The Ideological Origins of the American Revolution* (Cambridge, MA: Harvard University Press, 1967), pp. 216–229.

if the king was to play the role of "harmonizing" and "superintending" power in the empire, he would have to be radically unlike any monarch who had reigned in Britain for more than a century. James Wilson offered a definitive early statement of the mature Patriot conception of monarchy:

To the King is entrusted the direction and management of the great machine of government. He therefore is fittest to adjust the different wheels, and to regulate their motions in such a manner as to co-operate in the same general designs. He makes war: He concludes peace: He forms alliances: He regulates domestic trade by his prerogative; and directs foreign commerce by his treaties, with those nations, with whom it is carried on. He names the officers of government; so that he can check every jarring movement in the administration. He has a negative in the different legislatures throughout his dominions, so that he can prevent any repugnancy in their different laws. The connection and harmony between Great-Britain and us, which it is her interest and ours mutually to cultivate; and on which her prosperity, as well as ours, so materially depends; will be better preserved by the operation of the legal prerogatives of the Crown, than by the exertion of an unlimited authority by Parliament.[19]

It was not unusual for English or American Whigs to express devotion to the king, to look upon him as a defender of their liberties, or to assign him what formally remained the constitutional executive powers of the Crown (the right to make war, treaties, etc.), but it was wholly unprecedented in Whig discourse to flee from parliamentary authority and seek safety in the "prerogatives of the Crown."[20] It was equally stunning to include among those prerogatives the dreaded "negative voice" – which had not been exercised by a British monarch over a parliamentary bill since the reign of Anne,[21] and which the king did not even enjoy on paper in several of the American colonies – and the power to "regulate domestic trade" (that is, trade within the Empire) as well as "foreign commerce."[22]

---

[19]   James Wilson, *Considerations on the Nature and Extent of the Legislative Authority of the British Parliament* (Philadelphia: n.p., 1774), p. 33. Wilson's Scottish background may well have predisposed him to think in these terms: between 1603 (the accession of James I and VI) and 1707 (the Act of Union) Scotland and England had been distinct states sharing a common monarch. On this see LaCroix, *Ideological Origins*, pp. 24–9, 86–87. See also T. H. Breen, "Ideology and Nationalism on the Eve of the American Revolution: Revisions Once More in Need of Revising," *Journal of American History* 84 (1997), pp. 13–39, esp. pp. 23–8.

[20]   Wilson's language here echoes that of the New York pamphleteer William Hicks. See [William Hicks], *Considerations upon the Rights of the Colonists to the Privileges of British Subjects* (New York: n.p., 1766), p. 21. For the demonization of prerogative in pre-Revolutionary America see J. P. Greene, *The Constitutional Origins of the American Revolution* (Cambridge: Cambridge University Press, 2010), pp. 32–3, 60–1.

[21]   Anne vetoed the Scottish Militia Bill in 1707. The Hanoverian monarchs had of course used the veto to nullify acts of American colonial legislatures, a practice bitterly opposed by colonists of the earlier period.

[22]   The Crown lacked a negative voice in Rhode Island and Connecticut, which were charter colonies, as well as in proprietary Maryland (see R. J. Spitzer, *The Presidential*

Wilson was particularly conscious of the radicalism of this final claim, but he boldly defended it nonetheless: "If the Commerce of the British Empire must be regulated by a general superintending power, capable of exerting its influence over every part of it, why may not this power be entrusted to the King, as a part of the Royal prerogative?"[23]

This vision of an imperial monarch governing his various dominions by prerogative soon came to be grounded in a revisionist historical understanding of the English seventeenth century. For, despite their impeccably Whig upbringing, Patriots recognized that it was the early Stuarts who had defended the conception of empire to which they were now committed. James I and Charles I had never permitted their parliaments to meddle in colonial affairs. They had regarded the colonies as private dominions of the Crown, to be governed by the royal prerogative, and had emphatically denied that such an arrangement was incompatible with the liberty of their subjects. Patriots consequently traced the origins of the imperial crisis of the 1760s to the defeat of the seventeenth-century Royalist cause. The first parliamentary bill legislating for America, the Navigation Act of 1651, had been passed in the wake of the regicide by the Long Parliament – the very same body that had first declared "all of the Dominions and Territories" of the Crown to be under "the Supreme Authority of this Nation, The Representatives of the People in Parliament."[24] In the words of one American pamphleteer, it was only "after the death of King Charles the First" that "the Commonwealth

---

Veto: Touchstone of the American Presidency (Albany: State University of New York Press, 1988), p. 8). For the centrality of prerogative in the dominion theory see the insightful, albeit brief, discussion in J. G. Marston, *King and Congress: The Transfer of Political Legitimacy, 1774–1776* (Princeton: Princeton University Press, 1987), pp. 36–9. See also J. P. Reid, *Constitutional History of the American Revolution: The Authority of Law* (Madison: University of Wisconsin Press, 1993), pp. 151–162 (whose discussion is indebted to Marston), as well as the suggestive remarks in E. S. Morgan, *Inventing the People: The Rise of Popular Sovereignty in England and America* (New York: Norton, 1988), p. 244.

[23] Wilson, *Considerations*, p. 34. By 1774 most dominion theorists were prepared to argue pragmatically that, although Parliament lacked the right to regulate American trade, such a power might be "conceded" to it by the colonies as a purely discretionary matter (although this power would *not* include a license to impose "external taxes" (i.e. duties)). This was, for example, the position taken by the First Continental Congress in article four of its Declaration of Rights – although even this concession disappeared in its petition to the king of October 1774. The latter document closed with the insistence that "we wish not a diminution of the prerogative," but rather only to be rescued from Parliamentarian tyranny (*Journals of the Continental Congress: 1774–1789*, ed. Worthington Chauncey Ford et al., 34 vols. (Washington, DC: n.p., 1904–1937), I, p. 119.

[24] "An Act declaring and constituting the people of England to be a Commonwealth" (1649), in *Acts and Ordinances of the Interregnum, 1642–1660*, 3 vols., ed. C. H. Firth and R. S. Rait (London: HMSO, 1911), II, p. 122. More technically, it was the "Rump" Parliament that passed this measure.

Parliament, which usurped the rights of the Crown, naturally concluded, that by those rights they had acquired some kind of supremacy over the Colonies of America."[25] This first act of legislative "usurpation" had been allowed to stand even after the Restoration of 1660, thus establishing a nefarious precedent that had been used to justify increasingly brazen encroachments by Parliament on the king's prerogative to govern his possessions in America. In the great constitutional crisis of the seventeenth century, so Patriots came to believe, the Royalists had got it right after all.

At this point, however, a serious problem presented itself. Whig political theory, which had its origins in the Parliamentarian ideology of the 1640s, straightforwardly denied that rule by prerogative was compatible with the liberty of subjects or the sovereignty of the people. A legitimate representative, on the Whig account, must be a good representation, or image, of those represented. Accordingly, this view insisted that only an assembly reflecting the complex composition of the "body of the people" could be said to represent them – and that such an assembly might represent the entire body of the people even if many citizens did not elect members to it. The theory thus conveniently established two vital propositions: that the king could not be the representative of the people; and that the House of Commons could be the representative of the whole people, despite the fact that nine-tenths of the English population did not elect members to Parliament. But if the king was not the representative of the people, it followed that the existence and exercise of his various prerogative powers (particularly the "negative voice") would place Englishmen in a state of servile dependence upon an arbitrary and alien will – that is, in the condition of slavery.

The most sophisticated and elaborate defense of this position was provided by Henry Parker in a series of influential pamphlets from the early 1640s, most notably the *Observations upon some of His Majesties late Answers and Expresses* (1642). Parker begins the *Observations* by endorsing the contractarian piety that political power originates with the people themselves and is then conveyed by them to magistrates "by a special trust of safety and libertie expressly by the people limited."[26] This formulation

---

25 "Edmund Burke" [pseud.], "To the Right Honourable Lord North" (1774), in *American Archives Fourth Series*, 6 vols., ed. Peter Force (Washington, DC: n.p., 1837), I, p. 339. This claim was endlessly repeated in the late 1760s and 1770s.

26 [Henry Parker], *Observations upon some of His Majesties late Answers and Expresses* (London: n.p., 1642), p. 5. My discussion of the 1640s debate over representation is deeply indebted to Q. Skinner, "Hobbes on Representation," *European Journal of Philosophy* 13 (2005), pp. 155–184. For an astute early study of Parker's theory see M. A. Judson, "Henry Parker and the Theory of Parliamentary Sovereignty," in C. Wittke (ed.), *Essays in History and Political Theory: In Honor of Charles Howard McIlwain* (Cambridge, MA: Russell & Russell, 1936), pp. 138–167.

might be taken to imply that the people may entrust their "safety and libertie" to any constellation of magistrates that they desire, but Parker emphatically denies that this is the case. The people in such a situation must act in accordance with reason, and no rational people, he tells us, would entrust political power to any person or agency whose will was not identical to their own – for to do so would be to forfeit their status as free men. The only legitimate representative *for* the people is one who is representative *of* the people. A people must be represented by an "image" or "likeness" of themselves in miniature, one that reflects their unique composition with such exactitude that the interests (and therefore the will) of the "representative body of the people" will be identical to the interests and will of the "natural body of the people." Parker thus straightforwardly imports into political theory the technical vocabulary of the visual arts: a well-poised assembly represents the people in precisely the same sense that a good piece of what we still call "representational" art re-presents its subject.

Having defended this set of propositions about the character of political representation, Parker is able to ague that Parliament has the exclusive right to represent the people – that it justly "claimes the entire rite of all the Gentry and Commonalty of England."[27] The king is one man and, as such, cannot be said to be a good "representation" of a large and manifold people. Parliament, in contrast, is to be regarded as "virtually the whole kingdome it selfe" (that is, possessing its full "virtue," or power) and as the "quintessence" of the people.[28] Indeed, Parker claims revealingly that "in truth the whole Kingdome is not so properly the Author as the essence itselfe of Parliaments."[29] The key point, in other words, is not that Parliament has been "authorized" by the people (i.e. that the kingdom is its "Author"), but rather that Parliament offers such a "geometrically proportionable" image of the people that the "essence" of the kingdom may be said to reside there. Parliament is "nothing else, but the very people it self artificially congregated" in a "Representative Body"[30] – one to which "all the States doe so orderly contribute their due parts therein, that no one can be of any extreame predominance."[31] The perfection of the resulting image produces a unique congruity of interests between the representative and those represented: "that which is the sense of the whole Parliament, is the judgement of the whole Kingdom; and

[27] Parker, *Observations upon Some of His Majesties Late Answers and Expresses*, p. 15.

[28] Henry Parker, *Some Few Observations upon His Majesties Late Answer to the Declaration or Remonstrance of the Lords and Commons of the 19th of May, 1642* (London: n.p., 1642), p. 4; Parker, *Observations upon Some of His Majesties Late Answers and Expresses*, p. 28.

[29] Parker, *Observations upon Some of His Majesties Late Answers and Expresses*, p. 5.

[30] [Henry Parker], *Ius Populi* (London: n.p., 1644), p. 18.

[31] Parker, *Observations upon Some of His Majesties Late Answers and Expresses*, p. 15.

that which is the judgement of the whole Kingdom, is more vigorous, and sacred, and unquestionable, and further beyond all appeal, then that which is the judgement of the King alone, without Councell, or of the King with any other inferiour Clandestine Councell."[32] Parliament, insofar as it simply is the people "by vertue of representation united in a more narrow room,"[33] will never "counsel or consent to any thing, but what is publickely advantageous"; it "is indeed the State it self."[34] The case is entirely different with Charles I: "the King does not represent the people, but onely in such and such cases: viz. in pleas of common nature betwixt subject and subject. Wherein he can have no particular ends; and at such or such times, viz. when there is not a more full and neer representation by the Parliament."[35] The king, unlike Parliament, does not represent the people. He has "particular ends" of his own in most cases, and, because his will is not identical to that of the people, government by his prerogative constitutes enslavement.

It was this Parliamentarian theory that defenders of the British administration in the 1760s and 1770s invoked, under the rubric of "virtual representation," to explain why the American colonists were in fact represented in Parliament. Contemporaries easily recognized the provenance of the British position. "I am well aware," wrote Soame Jenyns in 1765, "that I shall hear Locke, Sidney, Selden, and many other great Names quoted, to prove that every Englishman, whether he has a Right to vote for a Representative, or not, is still represented in the British Parliament; in which Opinion they all agree."[36] The Patriot James Ingersoll likewise explained that, on the British view, the House of Commons "is supposed to represent, or rather to stand in the place of, the Commons, that is, of the great body of the people . . . when it is said they represent the Commons of England, it cannot mean that they do so because those Commons choose them, for in fact by far the greatest part do not, but because by their Constitution they must themselves be Commoners, and not Peers, and so the Equals, or of the same Class of Subjects, with the Commons of the Kingdom."[37] That is, the House of Commons

[32] Parker, *Some Few Observations*, p. 9.

[33] [Henry Parker], *The Contra-Replicant, His Complaint to His Maiestie* (London: n.p., 1643), p. 16.

[34] Parker, *Observations upon Some of His Majesties Late Answers and Expresses*, pp. 9, 34.

[35] Parker, *Ius Populi*, p. 19.

[36] Soame Jenyns, *The Objections to the Taxation of Our American colonies . . . Examined* (London: n.p., 1765), p. 8.

[37] Letter to Governor Thomas Finch, February 11, 1765, Jared Ingersoll, "A Selection from the Correspondence and Miscellaneous Papers of Jared Ingersoll," in F. B. Dexter (ed.), *9 Papers of the New Haven Colony Historical Society* (New Haven: n.p., 1918), pp. 201–472, at p. 307.

represents all English commoners because its members resemble them; it constitutes a good representation of the body of the people.

The next step was simply to extend this argument to embrace all British commoners, whether residing in Great Britain itself or in British dominions overseas.[38] As the loyalist Martin Howard, Jr., explained in 1765, "it is the opinion of the house of commons, and may be considered as a law of parliament, that they are the representatives of every British subject, wheresoever he be."[39] "The freedom and happiness of every British subject depends," Howard insisted, "not upon his share in elections, but upon the sense and virtue of the British parliament, and these depend reciprocally upon the sense and virtue of the whole nation."[40] The Patriot complaint that Americans were not represented in Parliament, on this account, betrayed a straightforward conceptual confusion. Thomas Whately, the administration spokesman who authored the Stamp Act, put it like this:

The Inhabitants of the colonies are represented in Parliament: they do not indeed chuse members of that Assembly; neither are nine tenths of the people of Britain Electors; for the Right of Election is annexed to certain Species of Property, to particular Franchises, and to Inhabitancy in some particular Places; but these Descriptions comprehend only a very small part of the Land, the Property, and the People of this Island . . . all landed Property that is not Freehold, and all monied Property whatsoever are excluded . . . Women and Persons under Age, be their Property ever so large, and all in Freehold, have none . . . none of them chuse their Representatives; and yet are they not represented in Parliament? . . . The Colonies are in exactly the same situation: All British Subjects are really in the same; none are actually, all are virtually represented in Parliament; for every Member of Parliament sits in the House, not as Representative of his own Constituents, but as one of that august Assembly by which all the Commons of Great Britain are represented.[41]

---

[38] Contemporaries understood that *this* was the novel move in the 1760s; the doctrine of virtual representation within Britain itself had been attested for more than a century. See, for example, *The Crisis, Or, a full defence of the colonies* (London: n.p., 1766), pp. 4–6; Maurice Moore, *The Justice and policy of taxing the American Colonies, in Great Britain, Considered* (Wilmington, NC: n.p., 1765), p. 12.

[39] [Martin Howard, Jr.], *A Letter from a Gentleman At Halifax* (Newport, RI: n.p., 1765), p. 11.

[40] Ibid., p. 13.

[41] [Thomas Whately], *The Regulations Lately Made Concerning the Colonies and the Taxes Imposed Upon Them, Considered* (London: n.p., 1765), pp. 108–109. Whately was Grenville's secretary, so this pamphlet clearly embodied a statement of the latter's own view. Note that Whately's position differs from Gray's in one subtle, but important, respect: for Gray, Members of Parliament should be regarded as "direct representatives of their own constituents, and the virtual representatives of every British commoner wherever he inhabits," whereas, for Whately, "all British Subjects are really in the same [situation]; none are actually, all are virtually represented in Parliament." Whately, in other words, endorses the orthodox Parliamentarian theory, according to which we are

Here again we have an orthodox statement of Parker's Parliamentarian theory, suitably adapted to the imperial context. Parliament represents the inhabitants of the empire by virtue of its status as a good representation of the body of the people; because its interests are aligned with their interests, it can justly be regarded as "virtually" the whole people – that is, as possessing their "virtues," or powers.

A second administration pamphleteer, John Lind, was even more emphatic on this point: "It is not essential to the character of a freeman who is to contribute a tax, that he have a right of voting for his representative. The greater part of the subjects of England, though they contribute to taxes, have no right of voting for their representatives."[42] Yet it by no means followed, on his account, that most Englishmen were governed by an alien will and were therefore to be regarded as slaves. One should not suppose that representatives, rightly understood, are agents who act by "the authority of their constituents" – that is, by virtue of having been directly "authorised" in some fashion (e.g. through elections). Quite the contrary, to "represent" a people is simply to "display, set forth – 'the condition of their country,'" and a legitimate representative is "a body of men chosen by a part of the community; but so circumstanced and related to the rest, that they cannot have or think they have any separate interests of their own to pursue, to the prejudice of the rest."[43] Parliament is plainly such a body: "it is the circumstances, it is the particular relation, that body stands in, to the whole community" which ensures that "they cannot have, they cannot think they have, a separate and distinct interest from the rest of the community."[44] Parker's familiar argument that Parliament (and only Parliament) is the English people had become the administration argument that Parliament (and only Parliament) is the British people.

In order to undermine this Whig equation of popular sovereignty with rule by a popular assembly, a great many Patriots turned momentously to the rival theory of representation that had been formulated by English Royalists in the 1640s – one according to which it is authorization, not resemblance (or "representativeness"), that is both necessary and

---

represented ("virtually present") so long as we are adequately "displayed" in a popular assembly – there is, on his account, no other sense in which individuals can be represented (the idea of an "actual," or "non-virtual" kind of representation is incoherent). Gray, in contrast, endorses a distinction between "real" and "virtual" representation, according to which electors are both "actually" and "virtually" represented, whereas nonelectors are only "virtually" represented.

[42] [John Lind], *Remarks on the principal acts of the thirteenth Parliament of Great Britain* (London: n.p., 1775), p. 66.

[43] Ibid., pp. 71, 84.   [44] Ibid., p. 73.

sufficient to establish the legitimacy of a representative. If any authorized agent can be said to speak or act in the name of the people, then plainly a king, no less than a popular assembly, is capable of "representing" his people, from which it follows that the people can be said to be "sovereign" under the rule of a monarch who wields prerogative powers. Sir John Spelman and Dudley Digges had both offered explicit defenses of this position as early as 1643, but the most systematic statement of the Royalist theory was offered by Thomas Hobbes in his *Leviathan* (1651).[45] Hobbes begins his celebrated discussion by offering a definition of the word "person":

A PERSON, is he, whose words or actions are considered, either as his own, or as representing the words or actions of another man, or of any other thing to whom they are attributed, whether Truly or by Fiction. When they are considered as his owne, then is he called a Naturall Person: And when they are considered as representing the words and actions of another, then is he a Feigned or Artificiall person.[46]

Some of these "Persons Artificall" have "their words and actions Owned by those whom they represent"; in such cases,

the Person is the Actor; and he that owneth his words and actions, is the AUTHOR: In which case the Actor acteth by Authority . . . So that by Authority, is always understood a Right of doing any act: and done by Authority, done by Commission, or Licence from him whose right it is. From hence it followeth, that when the Actor maketh a Covenant by Authority, he bindeth thereby the Author, no lesse than if he had made it himselfe; and no lesse subjecteth him to all the consequences of the same.[47]

For Hobbes, to be a representative is simply to have one's words and deeds "owned" by an "author," such that one's actions count as the actions of another. In the political context, a representative is created when a number of individuals

conferre all their power and strength upon one Man, or upon one Assembly of men, that may reduce all their Wills, by plurality of voices, unto one Will: which is as much as to say, to appoint one Man, or Assembly of men, to beare their Person; and every one to owne, and acknowledge himselfe to be Author of whatsoever he that so beareth their Person, shall Act, or cause to be Acted, in those things which concerne the Common Peace and Safetie.[48]

---

[45] See [Sir John Spelman], *A View of a printed book intituled observations upon his Majesties late answers and expresses* (London: n.p., 1643), pp. 7, 25; and Dudley Digges, *The unlawfulness of subjects taking up arms* (London: n.p., 1643), pp. 33, 67, 151–2.

[46] Thomas Hobbes, *Leviathan*, ed. N. Malcolm, 3 vols. (Oxford: Clarendon Press, 2012), II, p. 244.

[47] Ibid., I, pp. 244–6.   [48] Ibid., p. 260.

Again, authorisation is both necessary and sufficient to create a legitimate representative. It follows that a representative can come in any number of shapes and sizes: it can be one man, a few, or many. Hobbes utterly rejects the thought that a representative must resemble, or constitute a good likeness of those represented – that the "representative body" must re-present the "body of the people."[49] Kings are no less capable of representing the people than parliaments; it is authorization through political covenant that allows magistrates, of whatever number or character, to act and speak in the name of the nation as a whole. A king's actions can therefore count as our actions and the subjects of a monarch may be regarded as self-governing.[50]

For Patriot writers who adopted this theory in the 1770s, Parliament did not represent the people of British America because it had not been authorized to speak and act in their name – not because it did not constitute a "good image" of the colonists, or because Americans did not elect members to the House of Commons. At no point had the colonists entrusted political authority to the "legislature of Great Britain," although, counterfactually, they could certainly have done so (Parliament would then have been their legitimate representative, whether or not Americans elected members to it). In contrast, the people of British America had authorized the king and his successors to govern them in conjunction with the various colonial legislatures. This authorization had taken the form of colonial charters, to which

---

[49] Indeed, Hobbes takes considerable pains to insist that there is simply no such thing as the "body of the people" before the creation of the sovereign representative. In the state of nature there is merely a "multitude" of individuals; they become a "people" only in virtue of sharing a common representative.

[50] Hobbes took the view that *any* action of the sovereign must count as the subject's action, such that it is incoherent to say that a subject may be "injured" by his sovereign (Ibid., p. 270). But it was entirely possible to accept Hobbes's theory of representation while still rejecting his view about the open-endedness and unconditionality of the original grant of authority: that is, one could argue that a king should be authorized to act as my representative in some respects, but not in others, or that his authorization should be conditional on good behavior. This is an important point to bear in mind as we turn to the American material. Indeed, it is worth noting that Adams, when discussing the theory of representation in the *Defence*, referred to Hobbes as "a man, however unhappy in his temper, or detestable for his principles, equal in genius and learning to any of his contemporaries" (John Adams, *A Defence of the Constitutions of Government of the United States of America*, 3 vols. (London: C. Dilly, 1787–1788), III, p. 211); he likewise listed "Hobbs" along with Harrington, Sydney, Nedham and Locke as the authors on politics whom he had chiefly consulted before 1776 (John Adams, *Diary and Autobiography of John Adams*, ed. L. H. Butterfield, 3 vols. (Cambridge, MA: Belknap Press of Harvard University Press, 1961), III, p. 359). Hobbes had preached the cause of "simple monarchy and absolute power," but Adams saw that his theory of representation could be detached from these commitments.

succeeding generations of British Americans had tacitly consented.[51] The theory thus delivered the desired result: the king, and not Parliament, acted in the name of British Americans, and his government over them did not constitute enslavement.[52]

The Patriot pamphleteer Edward Bancroft offered a canonical statement of this position in his *Remarks on the Review of the Controversy between Great Britain and her Colonies* (1769). The original settlers of North America, on his account, could certainly have chosen to make Parliament their representative had they wished to do so – this despite the impossibility of electing their own members to the House of Commons. But, as it happens, they did not enter into any such agreement: "not the least Provision is made therein [in the charters] for their Dependence, either on the law or Legislature of England, which are not even named in the Patents."[53] Lacking any such authorization, Parliament now governs the colonists "without their Consent" and for this reason alone cannot be described as "their Constitutional Representative."[54] Allegiance to the Crown and its succession, in contrast, is "provided for by clauses for that Purpose in their Charters."[55] The king has therefore been authorized to govern the colonies in conjunction with their legislatures, and this original authorization is constantly renewed by tacit consent (a Lockean argument that Bancroft endorses unreservedly).[56]

Bancroft's various disciples in the 1770s repeated and refined this analysis. In 1773 the Massachusetts House of Representatives declared in its reply to Thomas Hutchinson that "our Charters reserve great Power to the Crown in its Representative, fully sufficient to balance, analogous to the English Constitution, all the liberties and Privileges granted to the

---

[51] One deep problem with this argument, frequently pointed out by opponents, was that most American colonies did not have charters.

[52] It is important to distinguish this position from the far more orthodox view that the king could be regarded as the "representative" of the "the collective executive power of the whole realm" (see, e.g., Thomas Pownall, *The Administration of the Colonies*, 4th edn. (London: n.p., 1768), p. 134), or that the king, as executive, might be thought of as the "representative" of the legislative power of Great Britain (see, e.g., *Pennsylvania Gazette*, March 8, 1775, in *American Archives: Fourth Series*, I, p. 89; and [Joseph Galloway], *A Candid Examination of the mutual Claims of Great-Britain, and the Colonies* (New York: n.p., 1775), pp. 7–8).

[53] [Edward Bancroft], *Remarks on the Review of the Controversy between Great Britain and her Colonies* (New London, CT: n.p., 1771), p. 21.

[54] Ibid., pp. 19, 42.   [55] Ibid., p. 45.

[56] See, for example, ibid., pp. 46–7. Cf. Arthur Lee, *Observations on the Review of the Controversy between Great-Britain and her Colonies* (London: n.p., 1769), pp. 22–3. Lee writes that he requires only an "*implied* consent by representatives unequally and partially chosen," not that "the people should give their actual consent by deputies equally elected" (as he thinks Locke proposes).

People."[57] But "is any Reservation of Power and Authority to Parliament thus to bind us, expressed or implied in the Charter? It is evident, that king Charles the first, the very Prince who granted it, as well as his Predecessor, had no such idea."[58] In fact, the House concludes, the charters themselves "are repugnant to the Idea of Parliamentary Authority," and, for this reason, "if the Colonies were not annexed to the Realm, at the Time when their Charters were granted, they never could be afterwards, without their own special Consent, which has never since been had, or even asked."[59] Again, it is not the fact that Americans do not elect members to the House of Commons that disqualifies Parliament from governing them; it is rather that they have not, by means of their charters, assigned Parliament the "authority" to govern them (although they might have done so at any time by annexing themselves to the realm). The colonists had, however, authorized the king to govern them, and the "great power" exercised by the Crown in America is therefore not incompatible with their status as free men.[60]

By 1774 this view had become dominant among Patriot pamphleteers. James Iredell of North Carolina cited various statements of James I and Charles I in order to establish that the charters had intentionally "prohibited Parliament from interfering in our concerns, upon the express principle that they had no business with them."[61] In contrast, the charters had fully authorized the king to exercise his prerogative rights over British America. Iredell is thus able to conclude as follows:

We respect and reverence the rights of the king; we owe, and we pay him allegiance, and we will sacredly abide by the terms of our charters. These were purchased by the hard and severe labor of our ancestors, which procured for our Sovereign this fine country. But we will not submit to any alteration of the original terms of the contract, because these were the price for which the service was engaged, and in pleasing consideration of which it was alone performed.[62]

[57] *The Briefs of the American Revolution: Constitutional Arguments Between Thomas Hutchinson, Governor of Massachusetts Bay, and James Bowdoin for the Council and John Adams for the House of Representatives*, ed. J. P. Reid (New York and London: New York University Press, 1981), p. 73.

[58] Ibid., p. 60.   [59] Ibid., pp. 58–9.

[60] Cf. "To the Inhabitants of New York" (October 6, 1774): "Let that august Assembly [Parliament] only relinquish all pretence of right to govern the *British* Colonies in *America*, and leave that to whom it solely and exclusively belongs, namely the King, our lawful Sovereign, with his Parliament in the respective Colonies, and the *Americans* have a Constitution without seeking further" (*American Archives: Fourth Series*, I, p. 826).

[61] James Iredell, *The Life and Correspondence of James Iredell, One of the Associate Justices of the Supreme Court of the United States*, ed. G. J. McRee, 2 vols. (New York, 1857–1858), I, p. 213.

[62] Ibid, p. 214.

An anonymous pamphlet from Virginia, issued in the same year under the pseudonym "Edmund Burke," likewise argued that "from these charters it manifestly appears to have been the Royal intention, to form these Colonies into distinct States . . . dependant on the Crown, but not on the Parliament of England."[63] It followed that, since the charters had not authorized Parliament to govern the colonists, "nothing but an act of union, made with their own consent, can annex them to the Realm, or subject them to its Legislature."

The young Alexander Hamilton offered perhaps the most expansive version of this argument in his *The Farmer Refuted* (1775). George III, he declared, "is King of America, by virtue of a compact between us and the Kings of Great-Britain. These colonies were planted and settled by the Grants, and under the Protection of English Kings, who entered into covenants with us for themselves, their heirs and successors."[64] By means of these covenants, the king had been authorized to exercise his prerogative powers over British America, and these powers were therefore not incompatible with the liberty of American subjects. Parliamentary laws, in contrast, "are subversive of our natural liberty, because an authority is assumed over us, which we by no means assent to."[65] The fact that the king "is the only Sovereign of the empire" was thus fully compatible with the essential, underlying sovereignty of the people.

Yet, despite their insistence that the king had been authorized to govern British America (and that Parliament was not the "constitutional representative" of America, simply because it had not been authorized to act as such), these Patriots of the early 1770s quite noticeably declined to call the king their "representative."[66] The reason is clear enough. In the context of the imperial crisis, to designate the king as the representative of the colonies would have exposed Patriots to the argument that they had in fact never been taxed without their consent: since parliamentary bills could not become law without receiving the royal assent (recall that it was the Patriots themselves who were arguing that the defunct royal veto remained a viable prerogative of the Crown), if the king truly represented the colonists, his agreement to these bills could be construed

---

[63] "Edmund Burke", "To the Right Honourable Lord North," I, p. 338. Cf. [Thomson Mason], "The British American," Letter 6 (July 7, 1774) in *American Archives: Fourth Series*, I, p. 522.

[64] Hamilton, *Farmer Refuted*, p. 9.

[65] Hamilton had made precisely the same argument in a pamphlet published the previous year. See [Alexander Hamilton], *A Full Vindication of the Measures of the Congress* (New York: n.p., 1774), p. 5.

[66] Hamilton, *Farmer Refuted*, p. 7. See, for example, Bancroft, *Remarks*, pp. 19, 90–1. See also the Connecticut Resolution of May 1774 (*American Archives: Fourth Series*, I, p. 356).

as embodying their consent. As one anonymous English pamphlet put it, "no Part of the Property of the People can be taken from them, but by laws which receive the assent of the Sovereign, who has no Interest distinct from the general Interest of all his Subjects."[67] The Patriots, of course, had an answer to this objection: on their account, the king had indeed been authorized to exercise a number prerogative powers over British Americans, but not to tax them without the consent of their colonial legislatures. His assent to a parliamentary tax bill therefore did not express the consent of the colonists to be taxed. But Patriot pamphleteers clearly preferred to avoid this discussion altogether by reserving the term "representative" for the members of their colonial legislatures. This rhetorical sleight of hand, however, amounted to very little in substantive terms. If I can be said to have authorized the king to govern me, such that his actions are to count as my actions, then his government over me is fully compatible with my status as a free man. Once I have accepted this conclusion, it matters not at all that I decline, for semantic or tactical reasons, to call the king my "representative" – for, at this point, to say that the king is not my representative has no normative bite (it is no longer to say that his government over me constitutes rule by an alien will, and thus amounts to slavery).[68]

Not all Patriots, however, adopted this straightforwardly Royalist position on the question of representation. While they were willing to agree that authorization was both necessary and sufficient for representation, some gravitated instead toward the view that authorization could only be conveyed through voting. Only a magistrate for whom I have voted is entitled to claim that he has been authorized to act in my name, and that he is therefore my representative. This argument, periodically advanced but underdeveloped in the first half of the 1760s, would be formulated with increasing sophistication as the conflict progressed. In 1769, John Joachim Zubly's *Humble Enquiry* made the case that "the people have not representatives assigned, but chuse them, and being so chosen, the rights of the people reside now in them."[69] "Every representative in Parliament," Zubly insisted, "is not a representative for the whole nation,

---

[67] *American Resistance Indefensible* (London: n.p., 1776), p. 20.

[68] A number of theorists acknowledged this point after the imperial crisis had passed. See, for example, Zabdiel Adams, "An Election Sermon" (Boston, 1782) in C. S. Hyneman and D. S. Lutz (eds.), *American Political Writing during the Founding Era, 1760–1805*, 2 vols. (Indianapolis: Liberty Fund Inc., 1983), I, pp. 543–5. Adams agrees that "to be deprived of the power of chusing our rulers is to be deprived of self dominion," but he likewise insists that the people may choose a hereditary monarch as their "representative."

[69] [John Joachim Zubly], *An Humble Enquiry into the Nature of the Dependency of the American Colonies* ([Charleston]: n.p., 1769), p. 21.

but only for the particular place for which he hath been chosen ... The electors of Middlesex cannot chuse a representative but for Middlesex, and as the right of sitting depends entirely upon the election, it seems clear to demonstration, that no member can represent any but those by whom he hath been elected; if not elected he cannot represent them, and of course not consent to any thing in their behalf." The implications of this position were quite sweeping, as Zubly himself appreciated:

If representation arises entirely from the free election of the people, it is plain that the elected are not representatives in their own right, but by virtue of their election; and it is no less so, that the electors cannot confer any right on those whom they elect but what is inherent in themselves; the electors of London cannot confer or give any right to their members to lay a tax on Westminster, but the election made of them doubtless empowers them to agree to or differ from any measures they think agreeable or disagreeable to their constituents, or the kingdom in general. If the representatives have no right but what they derive from their electors and election, and if the electors have no right to elect any representatives but for themselves, and if the right of sitting in the House of Commons arises only from the election of those designed to be representatives, it is undeniable, that the power of taxation in the House of Commons cannot extend any further than to those who have delegated them for that purpose; and if none of the electors in England could give a power to those whom they elected to represent or tax any other part of his Majesty's dominions except themselves, it must follow, that when the Commons are met, they represent no other place or part of his Majesty's dominions, and cannot give away the property but of those who have given them a power to do so by choosing them their representatives.[70]

This passage embodies the most complete possible rejection of the Parliamentarian theory of virtual representation, as well as perhaps the boldest single pre-Revolutionary statement of the view that authorization requires voting. On Zubly's account, only a magistrate for whom I have voted can be said to represent me. Those elected by others do not represent me, although they may certainly take it upon themselves to act in my interests once in office.

The most influential elaboration of Zubly's view was offered by Wilson in his 1774 *Considerations* – a pamphlet that established the terms in which Wilson and his acolytes would discuss the theory of representation for the next twenty years. Wilson begins by endorsing both the authorization theory of representation and the election theory of authorization: he insists that a free man must be governed by magistrates whom

---

[70] Ibid., pp. 17–18. Cf. William Drayton, who argued that the consent of "American Freeholders ... is not signified in Parliament, by *a Representation of their own election*" (emphasis in original): William Drayton, *A Letter from a Freeman of South-Carolina, to the Deputies of North-America, Assembled in the High Court of Congress at Philadelphia* (Charleston: n.p., 1774), p. 12.

he himself has authorized, and that authorization must take the form of voting. It follows that the only citizens who may safely be deprived of the franchise are those who are not free men – i.e. those persons who are dependent on the will of others for their livelihoods. "All those are excluded from voting," Wilson explains, "whose poverty is such, that they cannot live independent, and must therefore be subject to the undue influence of their superiors. Such are supposed to have no will of their own; and it is judged improper that they should vote in the representation of a free state."[71] But these are the only exceptions. All free men must be governed by laws to which their representatives have consented, and they may only be represented by agents for whom they have voted. Armed with these arguments, Wilson is prepared to offer a remarkable account of the English constitution and the character of the imperial crisis:

Though the concurrence of all the branches of the Legislature [Parliament] is necessary to every law; yet the same laws bind different persons for different reasons, and on different principles. The King is bound, because he assented to them. The Lords are bound, because they voted for them. The Representatives of the Commons, for the same reason, bind themselves, and those whom they represent. If the Americans are bound neither by the assent of the King, nor by the votes of the Lords to obey Acts of the British Parliament, the sole reason, why they are bound, is, because the representatives of the Commons of Great-Britain have given their suffrages in favor of those Acts. But are the representatives of the commons of Great Britain the representatives of the Americans? Are they elected by the Americans? Are they such as the Americans, if they had the power of election, would probably elect? Do they know the interest of the Americans? Does their own interest prompt them to pursue the interest of the Americans? If they do not pursue it, have the Americans power to punish them? Can the Americans remove unfaithful members at every new election? Can members, whom the Americans do not elect; with whom the Americans are not connected in interest; whom the Americans cannot remove; over whom the Americans have no influence – can such members be styled, with any propriety, the magistrates of the Americans?[72]

Wilson flirts with several different arguments in this passage (his statement that Members of Parliament and British Americans "are not connected in interest" amounts to an internal critique of the Parliamentarian theory[73]), but its basic thrust is unmistakable. Wilson argues that the House of Commons is the only representative of the English people, not (as the Parliamentarians had insisted) because it alone constitutes a good likeness or representation of the people, but because only its members are

---

[71] Wilson, *Considerations*, p. 5.   [72] Ibid., p. 15.   [73] Cf. ibid., pp. 17–18.

elected and, therefore, authorized by the people.[74] The king and Lords are unelected and, therefore, unauthorized to govern Englishmen without the consent of the House of Commons, and the House of Commons is unelected by Americans and therefore unauthorized to govern them. As Wilson explains, "allegiance to the King and obedience to the Parliament are founded on very different principles. The former is founded on protection: The latter, on representation. An inattention to this difference has produced, I apprehend, much uncertainty and confusion in our ideas concerning the connexion, which ought to subsist between Great-Britain and the American Colonies."[75] Representation requires authorization, and authorization requires voting.[76]

Here we see the stark dividing line between Wilson's authorization theory and the Parliamentarian theory of virtual representation. For Wilson, a single first magistrate or a small deliberative body may be said to represent the people, so long as he or they have been elected by the entire population of free men. Wholly absent from this view is the thought that a representative must be a good "representation" of the "body of the people" – i.e. a large assembly. But the line of demarcation between Wilson's theory and the Royalist theory of representation is equally clear: if representation requires authorization, and if authorization requires voting, then a hereditary monarch cannot be said to represent the people (leaving Wilson's defense of the royal prerogative on very shaky ground indeed[77]).

---

[74] Several pages later Wilson states explicitly that the Irish, and by analogy the Americans, are not "represented" in Parliament because they do not "send Members to Parliament" (p. 21).

[75] Ibid., pp. 21–2.

[76] Cf. *Pennsylvania Gazette*, March 8, 1775. The anonymous author of this essay argues, in a Wilsonian vein, that "the whole body of the [English] people" is "represented by the House of Commons" because "there is scarce a free agent in *England* who has not a vote" (*American Archives: Fourth Series*, I, p. 89).

[77] Wilson, as we have seen, tried to make room for an energetic monarchy by arguing that we owe obedience to the king, not because he represents us (he does not, because we have not elected him), but rather because he protects us, and "protection and obedience are the reciprocal bonds, which connect the Prince and his Subjects" (*Considerations*, p. 31). Here Wilson offers a straightforwardly Hobbesian characterization of the nature of political obligation – Hobbes famously declared that he had written *Leviathan* "without other designe, than to set before mens eyes the mutuall Relation between Protection and Obedience" (Hobbes, *Leviathan*, III, p. 1141) – but he refuses to endorse Hobbes's conclusion, namely that by accepting the protection of a sovereign I *thereby make him my representative*. It is for this reason that Wilson gets into trouble: if the king is not my representative, then it follows that he does not have the right to speak and act in my name (recall that, on the authorization theory, a representative *just is* someone who has this right). If I am constrained to obey him notwithstanding this fact, then, by definition, I am dependent on an alien will and am therefore unfree.

Yet, as both loyalists and the more circumspect Patriots quickly realized, this election theory of authorization was a hopeless muddle. John Lind identified its great liability as follows: if it were true of free men

that their own personal consent, or the personal consent of their representative is necessary to render a tax legal . . . it would follow, that no representative could be chosen but by the unanimous consent of every constituent, that no law could pass without the unanimous consent of every representative . . . Yet this principle, pregnant with such fatal consequences, have many of the friends of America chosen as a shield to protect the colonies against the power of the British legislature. This principle has the same extravagance laid down as the corner stone of British freedom.[78]

In other words, the Wilsonian view that representation requires authorization and that authorization requires voting is tantamount to a defense of anarchy. For in every election there are citizens who vote for the losing candidate, and in almost every legislative controversy there are representatives who vote against the eventual law. If it is really the case that one cannot be represented by a magistrate for whom one has not voted, and that one cannot be said to have authorized a law for which one's representative has not voted, then it would appear that there are only two choices: to grant every citizen a veto over the election of representatives, and every representative a veto over the enactment of laws; or to accept the enslavement of large numbers of citizens.[79]

The alternative is to argue that our authorization is conveyed, not by voting per se, but rather by our continuing, tacit consent to be bound by whatever decisions emerge out of the institutional scheme under which we live (a scheme perhaps initially authorized by our forebears at a moment of original contract), whether we agree with these decisions or not – and whether the particular magistrates for whom we ourselves voted happen to support them or not. But if this is the case, then the argument delivers a momentous result: namely, that an unelected monarch might be the representative of the people. For why, on this account, am I more thoroughly "represented" by a majority of legislators for whom I have not voted than I am by a king for whom I have not voted? The Royalist provenance of the authorization argument becomes obvious and inescapable.

III

All of those who supported ratification of the new federal constitution in 1787 – which notably featured a prerogative-wielding chief magistrate

---

[78] Lind, *Remarks*, p. 66.
[79] For precisely the same argument see Tucker, *A Letter from a Merchant*, pp. 66–7. Note that Franklin's response to Tucker on this point begs the question ("Marginalia in a Pamphlet by Josiah Tucker," in *PBF*, XVII, p. 363).

at its center – believed that the new frame of government instantiated the sovereignty of the people. But they believed this for very different reasons. The most emphatic defender of the Royalist conception of the federal and state constitutions was undoubtedly John Adams. For Adams, "in America, the right of sovereignty resides indisputably in the body of the people" simply because the people had authorized the institutions and magistracies of the state to act on their behalf.[80] The people of the United States would have been no less sovereign had they chosen instead to be governed by a hereditary monarch. "If the original and fountain of all power and government is in the people, as undoubtedly it is," Adams argued, then "the people have as clear a right to erect a simple monarchy, aristocracy, or democracy, or an equal mixture, or any other mixture of all three, if they judge it for their liberty, happiness, and prosperity, as they have to erect a democracy... and the wisest nations that ever lived, have preferred such mixtures, and even with such standing powers as ingredients in their compositions."[81] Moreover, "even those nations who choose to reserve in their own hands the periodical choice of the first magistrate, senate, and assembly, at certain stated periods, have as clear a right to appoint a first magistrate for life as for years, and for perpetuity in his descendants as for life."[82]

Adams amplified his argument in a striking passage:

An hereditary limited monarch is the representative of the whole nation, for the management of the executive power, as much as a house of representatives is, as one branch of the legislature, and as guardian of the public purse; and a house of lords, too, or a standing senate, represents the nation for other purposes, namely, as a watch set upon both the representative and the executive power. The people are the fountain and original of the power of kings and lords, governors and senates, as well as the house of commons, or assembly of representatives. And if the people are sufficiently enlightened to see all the dangers that surround them, they will always be represented by a distinct personage to manage the whole executive power.[83]

Rejecting both the Parliamentarian view that only an assembly could represent the people (which he associated above all with Marchamont Nedham) and the election theory of authorization, Adams insists that any agency authorized by the people to act on their behalf is properly called a "representative" – whether elected or not, whether unitary or composite. A single hereditary monarch might be the representative of the people, and, *a fortiori*, if the people are wise enough to parcel out political authority among several "standing powers as ingredients" in

---

[80] Adams, *Defence of the Constitutions*, I, p. 14. Adams offers an additional argument in favor of this claim that focuses instead on the "popular" balance of landed property. See ibid., p. 71.

[81] Ibid., III, pp. 366–7.   [82] Ibid., p. 367.   [83] Ibid., pp. 367–8.

an overarching scheme, a single first magistrate, whether elected for life or "for years," is likewise to be considered as the representative of the people. And if a people is governed exclusively by "representative" power, that people may be said to be self-governing and, hence, sovereign.

James Wilson agreed with Adams that the new constitution was consistent with the requirements of popular sovereignty, but, unsurprisingly, he defended this claim on very different grounds. In his "Lectures on Law," delivered in 1790 at the College of Philadelphia, he offered a comparison between the English constitution and the new constitution of the United States. In England, he explained, the principle of representation extends only to the House of Commons, because only the Commons are elected (and only imperfectly at that, given the restrictions on the franchise that Wilson continued to bemoan).[84] But in the new United States the case was entirely different: "the American States enjoy the glory and the happiness of diffusing this vital principle throughout all the different divisions and departments of the government."[85] In America, all "departments" of government (executive, legislative, and judicial) in all "divisions" (state and federal) may be said to represent the people because all magistrates are elected by the entire population of free men (or are chosen by those who have been so elected) – and have therefore been authorized by the people. "The right of representing," Wilson, explained, "is conferred by the act of electing."[86] It was for this reason that Wilson zealously (and unsuccessfully) advocated the direct election of both senators and the president, whereas Adams and so many others were completely untroubled by the indirect election of these office-holders.[87]

Wilson's distinctive position on the theory of representation, in turn, explains his celebrated claim (with which I began) that "the practical recognition" of the principle of popular sovereignty "was reserved for the honor of this country" (i.e. the United States). The people of Great Britain, on his account, cannot be regarded as sovereign because only one-third of their supreme legislature can claim to represent them. Because a hereditary monarch cannot represent the people, any "original contract" between king and nation must be taken to "exclude, rather than to imply delegated power." In other words, some share of political authority is transferred from the people to the king in Britain, whereas

---

[84] James Wilson, *The Works of James Wilson*, 2 vols., ed. Robert McLoskey (Cambridge, MA: The Belknap Press of Harvard University Press, 1967), I, pp. 311–312.
[85] Ibid., p. 312.   [86] Ibid., p. 364.
[87] *Records*, I, pp. 24, 68. See also Wilson, "Speech on Choosing the Members of the Senate by Electors; Delivered, on the 31st December, 1789, in the Convention of Pennsylvania," in Wilson, *Works*, II, pp. 781–793; "Lectures on Law," in ibid., I, p. 411.

the totality of it is derived from them in the United States.[88] Only when all of those entrusted with the making of law are elected by the people, on Wilson's account, can the people be said to be sovereign.

Few Federalists troubled to make clear exactly which theory of authorization undergirded their claim that the new constitution secured the sovereignty of the people – that is, whether, on their account, the president and senate would represent the people in virtue of being elected by them in some attenuated sense (Wilson's theory), or in virtue of the fact that Americans would authorize all magistrates, however chosen, to act on their behalf by submitting to the constitution (Adams's theory). In the context of the ratification debates there was no need to address this question, since both theories of authorization delivered the desired result: each established that, *pace* the Parliamentarian theory of the anti-Federalists, a single man, or a small group of men, could be said to represent the body of the people. But this strategic ambiguity on the part of the framers would have serious consequences for the future of American political thought. It would efface the crucial fact recognized by Adams and the other veterans of the pamphlet wars of the 1770s: that if popular sovereignty in America does not rest on the Royalist theory of representation, it rests on nothing.

---

[88] Wilson, *Works*, I, pp. 311, 317.

9 Popular sovereignty and political representation
Edmund Burke in the context of eighteenth-century thought

Richard Bourke

I

The story of popular sovereignty is usually told in linear terms that depict the rise of 'the people' to a position of authority in the state.[1] This narrative begins with the apparent defeat of the theory of 'absolutism' as formulated in the writings of Bodin and Hobbes.[2] That defeat is frequently traced to Rousseau's *Contrat social* in so far as it ascribed the right to shape political life directly to the people themselves.[3] Sometimes this development is imagined as a revival of ancient norms of the kind examined in the opening chapters of this volume. In its Rousseauian form, this revival is often supposed to have tied the sovereignty of the people to superannuated principles rooted in the past.[4] Yet still the rebirth of the democratic ideal is normally understood as pointing to the future to the extent that the ancient conception of self-government was adapted to modern circumstances by a succession of thinkers from Richard Price and Thomas Paine to Benjamin Constant.[5] Richard Tuck has already shown (in Chapter 5 in this volume) how this rise-of-the-people narrative begins to come unstuck as soon as we properly analyse the arguments of Rousseau. Yet much of the succeeding story still remains intact. According to this interpretation, the 'Age of Revolutions' reconciled popular

[1] E. S. Morgan, *Inventing the People: The Rise of Popular Sovereignty in England and America* (New York: W. W. Norton, 1988).

[2] For these writers as part of an 'absolutist' tradition see J. P. Sommerville, 'English and European Political Ideas in the Early Seventeenth Century: Revisionism and the Case of Absolutism', *Journal of British Studies* 35.2 (April 1996), pp. 168–94.

[3] See, for example, J. Shklar, *Men and Citizens: A Study of Rousseau's Social Theory* (Cambridge: Cambridge University Press, 1985 [1969]); D. Grimm, *Souveränität: Herkunft und Zukunft eines Schlüsselbegriffs* (Berlin: Berlin University Press, 2009), p. 34.

[4] B. Williams, 'Saint-Just's Illusion', in *Making Sense of Humanity and Other Philosophical Papers, 1982–1993* (Cambridge: Cambridge University Press, 1995), p. 136.

[5] The attempt to connect Rousseau to Price and his British contemporaries in these terms began with Josiah Tucker, *A treatise concerning civil government* (London: n.p., 1781).

sovereignty to the conditions of modern social life.[6] In the process, the values of the old regime were allegedly displaced by the characteristic forms of modern politics. On this reading, figures such as Hume, Smith and Burke are necessarily seen as partisans of a bygone era steeped in the values of subordination and custom.[7] Their vision, it is assumed, was steadily replaced by a contractual ideal of government founded on the sovereignty of the people.

However, the claim that popular sovereignty evolved in line with the progress of history away from political arrangements defended by men such as Smith and Burke has little basis in fact. What is striking, on the contrary, is the extent to which the eighteenth-century British constitution was typically understood as exemplifying popular sovereignty. To take an almost random example: in March 1775, in a fierce attack on the policy of Lord North towards the American colonies, the MP for Milborne Port, Temple Luttrell, asserted that 'supreme sovereignty' in the British state was vested in 'society at large'.[8] In making this claim, Luttrell was appealing to what he saw as the standard conception of British public life. What precisely Luttrell meant in locating authority in the people could prove controversial under circumstances of national upheaval. For instance by 1790, when the British Girondin David Williams declared that national sovereignty was to be found in the people 'itself', he could expect little support from mainstream Whiggism, unsettled by the advent of the Revolution in France.[9] Even so, as late as February 1793, Burke's one-time protégé, Charles James Fox, could declare in Parliament that 'the people are the sovereign in every state'.[10] The doctrine of popular sovereignty was a staple component of Whiggism, not a radically new idea that emerged between Rousseau and the Revolution.

---

[6] R. R. Palmer, *The Age of Democratic Revolution: A Political History of Europe and America, 1760–1800*, 2 vols. (Princeton: Princeton University Press, 1959–64). See also the overarching perspective in J. Innes and M. Philp (eds.), *Re-imagining Democracy in the Age of Revolutions, 1750–1850* (Oxford: Oxford University Press, 2013).

[7] J. C. D. Clark, *English Society, 1688–1832: Ideology, Social Structure and Political Practice during the Ancien Regime* (Cambridge: Cambridge University Press, 2000 [1985]).

[8] Temple Luttrell, Debate on the Bill to Restrain the Trade of the Southern Colonies, 30 March 1775, in *The Parliamentary History of England from the Norman Conquest in 1066 to the Year 1803*, ed. William Cobbett, 36 vols. (London: n.p., 1806–20), XVIII, col. 597.

[9] David Williams, *Lessons to a Young Prince on the Present Disposition in Europe to a General Revolution* (London: n.p., 1790), p. 24. The second edition of the work contained an elaborate attack on Burke.

[10] Charles James Fox, Debate on the King's Message, 1 February 1793, in *Parliamentary History*, XXX, col. 310.

Nonetheless, it is true that rival interpretations of popular sovereignty became increasingly embroiled in controversy as the eighteenth century progressed. This development was substantially driven by domestic power struggles as well as unforeseen events affecting overseas empire. As this chapter will show, Burke provides a convenient vantage from which to view the situation in Britain since his position in Parliament obliged him to comment on affairs as they unfolded. In chronological terms, the British debate about sovereignty began with disputes over the future of the Empire, above all in response to the fear that conditions in the provinces would determine the shape of metropolitan government. This anxiety launched Burke on a sustained assault on what he perceived as attempts on the part of the Crown to cultivate popular opinion as a prelude to subverting the mixed system of government. Reacting to developments in India and America, this resulted in a defence of constitutional politics in opposition to government by popular decree.

In fact, Burke's career as a whole might plausibly be summarised as vindicating the sovereignty of the people in opposition to government by popular decree. This commitment became conspicuous after 1789 as he responded to developments in France. In 'all forms of Government', Burke had written in the 1760s, 'the people is the true Legislator'.[11] The real question was how this legislative function could best be realised in practice. In the pages that follow, I examine how Burke tackled this issue in connection with the Empire after the Seven Years War before turning to how his ideas evolved in response to the French Revolution. Popular sovereignty, he believed, was only compatible with justice under a system of constitutional restraint that reconciled the consent of the people with procedures for deliberation. Yet the actions of the revolutionaries in France eradicated all hope of such reconciliation, first by destroying the possibility of coherent deliberation, and second by insulating representation from any meaningful expression of consent. If the resulting tyranny was re-described as 'souveraineté populaire', then Burke was happy to indict this new invention.[12] Aping the French, it had become common by 1792 for British supporters of the Revolution to champion the original rights of the 'English nation'. Yet Britain, Burke responded, 'knew of no nation as a distinct body from the representative powers'.[13] A

---

[11] Edmund Burke, *Tracts Relating to Popery Laws* (1765) in *The Writings and Speeches of Edmund Burke*, ed. P. Langford, 9 vols. (Oxford: Oxford University Press, 1981–2015), IX, p. 454.

[12] Edmund Burke, Speech on the Aliens Bill, 28 December 1792, in *Parliamentary History*, XXX, cols. 183–4.

[13] Ibid.

genuinely popular form of sovereignty, he was suggesting, was a function of constitutional government.

II

In September 1772, following a financial crash earlier in the summer, the East India Company defaulted on its payments to the British treasury. The event was a significant blow to commerce and public credit, attracting the attention of the ministry under Lord North to the affairs of the trading corporation. This occurred against a backdrop of mounting allegations of malfeasance against the Company, culminating in the publication of William Bolts' *Considerations on Indian Affairs* and the third volume of Alexander Dow's *History of Hindostan*, both of which contributed to the rising tide of opinion that British involvement on the Subcontinent was in need of radical reform.[14] The Company set about pre-empting government interference by deploying its own commission of supervisors to the region, but North's administration resolved to obstruct this move, introducing a measure to halt the Company's efforts to regulate its conduct from within. Opponents of the government were astounded: as one of them put it, the administration was invading the rights of corporate property, striking at 'the very charter and constitution of the Company'.[15] In fact, according to Edmund Burke, the Bill threatened nothing less than a total usurpation. Should it pass, he declared, Parliament would in effect 'become' the East India Company, drawing upon the plenitude of its own sovereignty to abolish a subordinate jurisdiction.[16]

The question of British sovereignty over its possessions on the Indian Subcontinent had been a controversial matter since 1766. In that year the Chatham administration launched an inquiry into the affairs of the Company with a view to resolving disputes over the right to its revenues.[17] This was a subject of immediate concern to the ministry, still afflicted by debt in the wake of the Seven Years War. With the recent repeal of the Stamp Act under the previous administration, the expectations of enrichment that accompanied the East India Company's acquisition of tax-raising

[14] William Bolts, *Considerations on Indian Affairs, Particularly Respecting the Present State of Bengal and Its Dependencies* (London: n.p., 1772); Alexander Dow, *The History of Hindostan from the Earliest Account of Time to the Death of Akbar*, 3 vols. (London: n.p., 1768–72).

[15] William Dempster, Debate on the Bill to Restrain the East India Company from Appointing Supervisors in India, 7 December 1772, in *Parliamentary History*, XVII, col. 560.

[16] Edmund Burke, ibid., col. 567.

[17] H. V. Bowen, 'A Question of Sovereignty? The Bengal Land Revenue Issue, 1765–1767', *Journal of Imperial and Commonwealth History* 16.2 (January 1988), pp. 155–76.

powers in Bengal held out the prospect of financial deliverance to the British government. The grant of *diwani*, or authority over the revenue, had been bestowed upon the Company as part of the Treaty of Allahabad on 16 August 1765. The grant represented an immense dividend to the Company, and completed its transition from a trading concern to a territorial power.[18] The question remained, however, of who was entitled to benefit from this influx of Asian wealth, and on what terms.[19] Chatham intended to settle the controversy in favour of the British government by securing a parliamentary ruling in its favour. His aim was to show that, since the procurement of revenue had been a product of military conquest, the right to manage the income resided in the ministry with the support of the Commons. In a dispatch to Chatham on 16 April 1767, the Company stated its rival claim: the revenues had been granted as a free gift from the Mughal emperor, making them corporate property under the terms of the Company Charter as revised in 1698.[20] This divergence of opinion had not been resolved by the 1770s, turning the disagreement over the Company's plan for sending supervisors to India into a bitter struggle over the implications of parliamentary supremacy over subordinate institutions of government.

Consequently, in December 1772, as Lord North sought to limit the Company's entitlement to regulate its affairs, the issue of jurisdiction raised its head again. On 18 December James Adair and Elijah Impey, both counsel for the Company, were called before the bar of the House of Commons, where they stated that the attempt to prevent the transmission of supervisors was a violation of corporate privilege. No one could deny, they asserted, that the Restraining Bill represented an 'extraordinary' extension of 'parliamentary authority', an intrusion of sovereign right into a corporate jurisdiction.[21] The presumption of the government was all the more remarkable since no 'delinquency' had been established on the part of the East India Company, and no absolute 'necessity' confronted the government.[22] The implication was that both delinquency and necessity constituted sufficient grounds for alleging breach of contract, with the

---

[18] For these developments see H. Dodwell, *Dupleix and Clive: The Beginning of Empire* (London: Frank Cass & Co., 1967 [1920]), pp. 238–43.

[19] For the manner in which the revenues were administered see A. Majed Khan, *The Transition in Bengal, 1756–1775: A Study of Saiyid Muhammad Reza Khan* (Cambridge: Cambridge University Press, 1969), pp. 78–102.

[20] 'Papers Transmitted by the Chairman of the East India Company to the Earl of Chatham, 16th Apr. 1767', Chatham Papers, The National Archives (TNA), PRO 30/8/99, Part III, fols. 188–260.

[21] James Adair and Elijah Impey, Debate on the Bill to Restrain the East India Company from Appointing Supervisors in India, 18 December 1772, in *Parliamentary History*, XVII, col. 652.

[22] Ibid., cols. 651, 652.

result that the privileges of the Company would revert to the Crown. Nonetheless, delinquency and necessity had to be stringently observed criteria since, in the case of the East India Company, the revocation of the corporate rights of a trading corporation involved tampering with its powers of government over a subject population encompassing around thirty million souls.

On the final reading of the Restraining Bill, towards the end of the debate, Burke charged Lord North with seeking to invade the prerogatives of the Company on a pretext for redressing grievances.[23] The true reason for interference was the prospect of increasing the leverage of the court, hoping to employ the spoils of conquest as a means of patronage. Burke cited a Roman maxim – *de re publica non desperandum* – in defence of sustainable balance in the mixed system of government.[24] Through the 1760s, he believed, this had been under threat, and by now the Commons itself was succumbing to corruption. The attitudes of 'passive obedience' and 'non-resistance' were affecting its spirit of independence, rendering Members of Parliament mere tools of the ministry.[25] Burke developed the point into an observation on the constitution in general as being captured by monarchical populism. Government, he argued, was increasingly being executed by decree. He specifically complained that legislation was being passed by *psephismata*, which always, as Aristotle had noted, led to the 'ruin' of the state.[26]

Burke was alluding to Aristotle's discussion of the varieties of democracy in Book IV of the *Politics*. More particularly, he was appropriating the idea of demagogic rule under which partial sentiment reigned instead of law. As Aristotle had put it, under this arrangement, animated by the spirit of equality, the decrees (*psephismata*) of the assembly were authoritative (*kuria*) over law (*nomos*).[27] In practice, this meant domination by the multitude under the tutelage of popular leaders, leading to civil faction instead of political rule. Democracy by decree, Aristotle concluded, was therefore indistinguishable from tyrannical forms of monarchy.[28] For Burke, developing this thought in an eighteenth-century

---

[23] *London Evening Post*, 19 December 1772. See also Edmund Burke, 'Speech on East India Restraining Bill', 18 December 1772, in *Writings and Speeches*, II, pp. 377–81, reproducing the notes for the speech in the Burke Papers, Sheffield Archives, Wentworth Woodhouse Muniments (henceforth WWM), BkP 9: 11–13. Cf. the brief report of the speech in the *Gentleman's Magazine*, 1773, pp. 55–6.

[24] Edmund Burke, Debate on the East India Company from Appointing Supervisors in India, 18 December 1772, *Parliamentary History*, XVII, col. 669, reproducing the report of the speech in the *London Magazine*, 1773, pp. 273–6.

[25] Edmund Burke, Debate on the Bill to Restrain the East India Company from Appointing Supervisors in India, 18 December 1772, *Parliamentary History*, XVII, col. 668.

[26] Ibid., col. 673.   [27] Aristotle, *Politics* 1292a5–7.   [28] Ibid., 1292a15–20.

context, a monarchy that strove to govern without restraint while having to act through a parliamentary system depended on the corruption of the democratic component within the constitution. With unmixed systems of government, bereft of countervailing forces of moderation, monarchy might function as a popular despotism, just as, under pure democracy, tyranny presided in the shape of demagogic rule.[29] Burke was acutely aware that the British constitution had to regulate an imperial structure in which the provinces might determine the mode of government in the metropole. At the back of his mind was the fate of Rome after the subjugation of the affluent East. In Britain, after the victories of Robert Clive, British power had been seduced by the riches of Asia. Ministries had serviced the expansion of court power by exploiting the passivity of Parliament. This passivity had advanced in the absence of party cohesion capable of stiffening the Commons against the ambitions of George III.[30] The process had been facilitated by the social impact of returning nabobs who had stimulated the hostility of public opinion. The nobility resented their upstart wealth while the commons envied their ostentatious display.[31] Ministries, under these circumstances, could play the role of demagogues, increasing the power of the executive by exploiting popular prejudice. The sovereignty of the people meant the dominion of the Crown.

Burke recognised that the government had the power to pursue this course, but he denied that it had a right to do so.[32] What he meant was that the government possessed the sovereign right but not the practical authority to subvert the privileges of a corporation. It lacked the authority, not because the weight of popular opinion was against it, but because an invasion of chartered immunities was an affront to the rights of property, undermining the security of liberty, and thus the very basis of government by consent. The only thing that could license a resort to the sovereignty of Parliament against the rights of the corporation was an appeal to the overall welfare of the people. In general terms, as counsel for the East India Company had indicated during its submissions to the House of Commons in December 1772, this appeal was usually

---

[29] For classical antecedents to this argument see the chapters by Kinch Hoekstra (Chapter 1) and Melissa Lane (Chapter 2) in this volume.

[30] These fears were challenged in the context of Fox's India Bill in William Pulteney, *The Effects Expected from the East India Bill upon the Constitution of Great Britain* (London: n.p., 1783), drawing on Jean-Louis de Lolme, *The Constitution of England; or, an Account of the English government* (London: n.p., 1781).

[31] WWM BkP 9: 40.

[32] Edmund Burke, Debate on the Bill to Restrain the East India Company from Appointing Supervisors in India, 18 December 1772, in *Parliamentary History*, XVII, col. 673.

conducted with reference to two criteria: the delinquency of public officials or the necessity of preserving the state. Already by the early 1770s Burke had begun to recognise the possibility that Company servants had been delinquent in their duties as they plied their trade in South Asia, though he did not credit the administration's declared aim of securing redress. Between 1777 and 1780, however, his sense of the magnitude of the problem had increased exponentially as he investigated the corrupt practices of financiers in Madras in collusion with the Nawab of Arcot.[33] Soon after, on account of his membership of the select committee set up to investigate the affairs of the Company, he became staggered by the levels of British rapacity in India, and the impunity with which it was conducted. This dismay culminated in his drafting of Fox's India Bill of 1783 – destined, of course, to end in failure.

In his notes for his speech on North's Regulating Bill of 1773, Burke had invoked the criterion of delinquency as offering a standard against which the legitimacy of provincial government could be measured, but it was a decade later, in in his speech on Fox's India Bill, that he illustrated in more detail how Company delinquency constituted a breach of contract.[34] He set out four benchmarks in terms of which the scale of delinquency could be ascertained, before convicting the British government in India of malversation.[35] He computed that the East India Company was administering an annual revenue of seven million pounds while presiding over an army of sixty thousand troops.[36] At the same time, it was responsible for a population that was commonly estimated to be in excess of three times the population of Britain. By any reckoning, therefore, the trust invested in the Company was substantial; but it had been betrayed by the systematic turpitude of its servants. As a consequence, it had forfeited the right to exercise the authority invested in it. Fox's India Bill, in recommending a dramatic overhaul of the system of imperial subordination in the East, unsurprisingly met with resistance among defenders of the Company. These inevitably took their stand on the chartered rights of the corporation, as Burke had done when resisting the Crown in the early 1770s. Yet then, as now in 1783, Burke

---

[33] This is usually represented as a dramatic shift in attitude. See, originally, Holden Furber, 'Edmund Burke and India', *Bengal Past and Present: Journal of the Calcutta Historical Society* 76 (1957), pp. 11–21; H. Furber, 'Introduction', in Edmund Burke, *The Correspondence of Edmund Burke*, ed. T. W. Copeland, 10 vols. (Chicago: University of Chicago Press, 1958–78), V, pp. xiii–xxi.

[34] For Burke's position in 1773 see WWM, BkP 9: 17; for 1783 see Edmund Burke, *Speech on Fox's India Bill* (1 December 1783), in Burke, *Writings and Speeches*, V, p. 387.

[35] Burke, *Writings and Speeches*, pp. 389 ff.   [36] Ibid., pp. 384–5.

also saw that a trading monopoly in command of an army, presiding over a sizeable population, was a peculiar kind of corporation: it was in truth a system of government, whose privileges were a creation of human artifice. Political dominion, as Burke put it, was 'wholly artificial', and so it was answerable to those who had generated the artifice.[37] In the event of palpable delinquency, accountability was violated, and so the trust of government could legitimately be revoked.

In describing political power as artificial, Burke was indicating that he saw it as founded on agreement. In other words, it was founded on popular consent. This was a bold assertion in the context of imperial politics. After all, it was open to Burke to argue that Company rule on the Subcontinent was accountable to Parliament at Westminster, and that a breach of trust conferred by the imperial power entailed a reversion of delegated authority into the hands of metropolitan government. Despite this, Burke assessed the obligations of government with reference to the Indian population. He naturally recognised that the trust of imperial rule had been bestowed *de facto* by the British Parliament, but since this transaction had conferred a right of government over a people, it was for the benefit of that people that it had to be exercised. It was, *de iure*, their artifice, and so its authority ceased whenever it significantly deviated from serving the purpose 'for which alone it could have a lawful existence'.[38] Burke was not slow to spell out what the sole purpose for which artificial power could legitimately be instituted over human beings was. It was, he candidly stated, to protect 'the rights of *men*'.[39] Where those rights were violated, legitimate authority ceased, and power became the prerogative of the people.[40] Lest there be any confusion about what his argument meant, he elucidated its meaning for his audience: by the rights of men, he meant 'the natural rights of mankind' which civil society had been instituted to protect.[41] These rights might be officially recognised – say, by a formal contract of government – as they were by the East India Company charter; but in any case they were acknowledged by the primary charter of nature. That charter recognised 'an original right in the subject' which could only be relinquished by subverting the obligations of government, and with that all order in society.[42]

---

[37] Ibid., p. 385.   [38] Ibid.

[39] Ibid., p. 383. The phrase the 'rights of men' was deployed in the debate on the second reading of Fox's India Bill on 27 November 1783 by Archibald Macdonald, in *Parliamentary History*, XXIII, col. 1299, and by Henry Beaufoy, ibid., col. 1398.

[40] The argument was challenged in *Observations on Mr. Burke's Speech on Fox's India Bill* (London: n.p., 1783), pp. 3 ff.

[41] Burke, *Speech on Fox's India Bill* (1 December 1783), in *Writings and Speeches*, V, p, 383.

[42] Ibid., p. 384.

III

Burke's argument as laid out in his speech on Fox's India Bill, delivered just six years before the French Revolution, might seem to diverge significantly from the principles he later articulated in opposition to developments in France. Closer inspection, however, proves this impression to be false, and with it the charge of apostasy against him, first levelled by Charles James Fox in the 1790s.[43] Certainly in 1783 no auditor in the House of Commons could have been surprised by Burke's definition of the rights of sovereignty in terms of the responsibility of power to the people. Three months before the debate on Fox's India Bill, the Treaty of Versailles concluding the war of American independence had been signed. This formality brought to a close nearly two decades of transatlantic struggle over the terms of imperial subjection. It was a struggle that had taken the form of a contest between the jurisdiction of Parliament and the immunities of a people. Anticipating the final outcome of the contest in 1780, between the battle of Saratoga and the siege of Yorktown, Burke wrote that half an empire had been lost over what amounted to an 'idle quarrel'.[44] Nonetheless, it was a quarrel that, in addition to leading to the separation of a colonial people from their fraternal ancestors in Europe, had also divided the parliamentary opposition from the ministry of Lord North as well as the elements of the opposition from each other. The first attempt to mend these divisions by parliamentary legislation had been enacted by the Rockingham Whigs in 1766. Then, in the face of the impossibility of enforcing the Stamp Act against the colonists, the measures of George Grenville were revised. For William Pitt the debate preceding repeal was a national event, the most significant since the Glorious Revolution.[45] As Eric Nelson has reminded us in the previous chapter, it was the sovereignty of Parliament that was at issue, with implications for the administration of the Empire. Pitt's own position on the question drew support from a reading of Locke on the relationship between taxation and representation.[46] In resorting to Locke, he was rejecting the policy of the Rockingham administration, based on facilitating repeal by the passage of a Declaratory Bill.

---

[43] Burke reported the allegation himself: see Edmund Burke to Earl Fitzwilliam, 5 June 1791, in Burke, *Correspondence*, VI, p. 274.

[44] Edmund Burke to Job Watts, 10 August 1780, ibid., IV, p. 261.

[45] William Pitt, Debate on Disturbances in America, 14 January 1766, in *Proceedings and Debates of the British Parliaments Respecting North America, 1754–1783*, ed. R. C. Simmons and P. D. G. Thomas, 6 vols. (Milwood, NY: Kraus International Publications, 1982–), II, p. 86.

[46] See Chatham Papers, TNA, PRO 30/8/74, fol. 436.

Support for a Declaratory resolution was agreed at a series of meetings among the Rockinghamites in late January 1766. That month Burke took his seat in Parliament while acting as secretary to Lord Rockingham. The Declaratory Bill was drafted by the attorney general, Charles Yorke, based on the Irish Dependency Act of 1720, commended by the Earl of Hardwicke, Yorke's father. It stated the right of Parliament to 'bind the Colonies and *People of America* . . . in all Cases whatsoever'.[47] This amounted to an uncompromising claim to sovereignty, asserted as an absolute prerogative. It was accompanied, however, by a series of measures designed to appeal to those opposed to Grenville's regulations. Opposition in America had been impressively demonstrated, but it had also been active in Britain, much of it coordinated by the Rockinghams themselves in an attempt to win endorsement for their programme.[48] In fact, the Rockingham campaign represented one of the earliest attempts in post-Walpolean Britain to raise extra-parliamentary support for government measures.[49] Not once within living memory, *The Annual Register* noted, had the public been so engaged by parliamentary affairs.[50] The idea behind the campaign was to illustrate the responsiveness of the ministry to popular sentiment while asserting the supreme jurisdiction of the king-in-parliament. It was a position that Burke would defend into the late 1770s, beginning with his advocacy in the Commons in February 1766. In the notes for his speech on the Declaratory resolution delivered on 3 February, he declared that the absolute sovereignty of Parliament was undeniable, conferring 'unlimited' power upon 'supreme legislative authority'.[51] It was, however, a purely speculative right, ultimately 'little to the purpose', incapable of enforcing the general will in the absence of compliance. Therefore, in practical terms, ultimate jurisdiction had to command on the basis of authority, not merely on the grounds of theoretical supremacy. Thus, while accepting the substance of the Declaratory Act, Burke was aware of its inadequacy as a foundation for practical government. It identified a final resort for the decision-making process, but it said nothing about how sovereignty should be used.

[47] *Statutes at Large from the Twenty-Sixth Year of the Reign of King George the Second to the Sixth Year of the Reign of King George the Third* (London: n.p., 1786): 6 Geo. III, c. 12.

[48] On this, including remarks on the originality of the strategy, see Edmund Burke, *Short Account of a Late Administration* (1766), in *Writings and Speeches*, II, p. 55.

[49] L. Sutherland, 'Edmund Burke and the First Rockingham Ministry', *English Historical Review* 47.185 (January 1932), pp. 46–72, at p. 54. See also L. Sutherland, 'The City of London in Eighteenth-Century Politics', in R. Pares and A. J. P. Taylor (eds.), *Essays Presented to Sir Lewis Namier* (London: Macmillan, 1956), pp. 49–74, at p. 67.

[50] 'The History of Europe', *The Annual Register for the Year 1766* (London: n.p., 1767), p. 35.

[51] Edmund Burke, Notes for Speech on Declaratory Resolution, 3 February 1766, in *Writings and Speeches*, II, p. 47.

This last point would prove crucial to Burke's ideas about America. After the fall of the Rockingham government in the summer of 1766, their 'system', as Burke thought of it, was abandoned by their successors. As a consequence, the abuse of sovereignty came to exemplify the administration of the Empire for a procession of ministries extending from the Earl of Chatham's to Lord North's. The accompanying tale of woe is well known. Repeated attempts to extract revenue from the colonies to contribute to the expense of imperial establishments provoked consternation followed by escalating resistance. Already in the early stages of that process, enthusiastic declarations of the rights of the colonists led David Hume and Josiah Tucker to long for deliverance in the form of separation from the Atlantic seaboard colonies.[52] Their attitude reflected a wider alarm that improvident constitutional adjustments in the 1760s would replicate on an imperial scale the conflagration of the 1640s. For his part, Burke settled on a policy of conciliation, arguing that this was the only means of avoiding a return of the kind of upheaval that had capsized the British polity in the seventeenth century. Conciliation had to involve accommodating provincial claims to liberty with the representative interest of the Empire. The establishment of such a representative interest required determination in the last instance of the welfare of the whole. The problem was that the bid for colonial freedom staked its claim in terms of the rights of subordinate representation. One solution to this clash of representative wills was the establishment of an incorporating union encompassing the Atlantic Empire, as adumbrated by Adam Smith in 1776. Another, of course, was colonial secession, as advocated by Tucker.

Yet another possibility was to retain the representative function of colonial governments while subordinating them to the supremacy of Parliament. This, it seemed to Burke at least, was the only means of combining effective authority with popular consent. In the absence of subordination, provincial consent would in practice mean colonial sovereignty. Yet without colonial representation deciding upon its own taxation, imperial

---

[52] See, for example, David Hume to Lord Hertford, 27 February 1766, in David Hume, *The Letters of David Hume*, ed. J. Y. T. Greig, 2 vols. (Oxford: Oxford University Press, 1932), II, pp. 18–19. For comment on Hume in this period, see M. Baumstark, 'The End of Empire and the Death of Religion: David Hume's Later Political Thought', in R. Savage (ed.), *Philosophy and Religion in Enlightenment Britain: New Case Studies* (Oxford: Oxford University Press, 2012), pp. 231–57. See also Josiah Tucker, *A Letter to Edmund Burke, Esq., in Answer to His Printed Speech* (London: n.p., 1775), p. 20. For discussion of Tucker and Burke see J. G. A. Pocock, 'Josiah Tucker on Burke, Locke and Price: A Study in the Varieties of Eighteenth-Century Conservatism', in *Virtue, Commerce, and History : Essays on Political Thought and History, Chiefly in the Eighteenth Century* (Cambridge: Cambridge University Press, 1985), pp. 157–92.

sovereignty would be without effect. The right of supremacy would be reduced to a hollow legal claim without any purchase on the dynamics of imperial politics. What had to be reconciled, therefore, was a legal conception of authority with a political conception of power. The former was based on a bureaucratic organisation of decision making terminating in a pre-eminent tribunal, whereas the latter was based on practical accommodation between government and the governed. The administration of a diversified imperial polity unavoidably involved both components. A hierarchy of jurisdictions together with the means of brokerage between rulers and ruled characterised the division of political labour within any complex civil society. When it came to adjudicating between jurisdictions, Burke was clear about what was required in the context of the Empire. As he put it in a manuscript note from the middle of the 1760s: 'I think we have the clearest right imaginable not only to bind them Generally with every Law, but with every mode of Legislative Taxation.'[53] However, as the Rockinghamites in general recognised, there was a distinction between the right of supremacy and the unmitigated use of power. In the end, as Hume had observed, even the management of the Praetorian Guard could not presume on automatic submission.[54] As Burke saw things, it was the idea that the plenitude of sovereign jurisdiction licensed a resort to every reserve of command that led to attempts to enforce the Townshend duties come what may. In due course, with the passage of the 'intolerable' Acts in May 1774, civil administration in Britain wore the appearance of military government in America, kindling resistance into rebellion. The Americans were bridling under a monstrous creation – a 'republican despotism', as Burke termed it, referring to the executive management of pure democracies such as the colony of Massachusetts Bay.[55]

Nonetheless, it remained Burke's view that the preservation of the rights of sovereignty in the hands of Parliament was essential. He was committed to this position for three reasons. He subscribed to it, first of all, for the very general reason that sovereignty by definition was unaccountable, and so it was vital that its location should be publicly identified. 'The sovereign power is in all governments absolute,' as Adam Smith remarked; this meant that it could not be controlled by any

---

[53] Fitzwilliam Manuscripts at the Northamptonshire Record Office (henceforth Northamptonshire MSS), MS. A, XXVII, 55.

[54] David Hume, 'Of the First Principles of Government', in *Essays Moral, Political, and Literary*, ed. E. F. Miller (Indianapolis: Liberty Fund, 1987), pp. 32–3.

[55] WWM, BkP 27: 229.

'regular force'.[56] It also implied that it could be usurped by recourse to 'irregular' force, which was to say that it could be seized by conquest or insurrection. The identification of supremacy within a constitutional order was a means of describing the usual channels of obedience and command, erecting a bulwark against irregular subversion. Secondly, and relatedly, claiming sovereign status supported the exercise of authority, winning allegiance for the bearer of ultimate decision-making powers.[57] Where the seat of empire was remote from the objects of government, this was an important attribute of authority. As Burke remarked in 1769 with reference to the American case, without the assertion of a principle of supreme jurisdiction, British authority would 'vanish into an empty name'.[58] Finally, and more specifically, the sovereignty of Parliament within an imperial context underpinned the Glorious Revolution as well as the Declaration of Right. If subordinate legislatures were permitted to grant taxes independently of the Crown, the Empire would be converted into a composite monarchy, a *dominium politicum et regale*, and the domestic constitution would be undone.[59] Even so, if the colonies could not function as dominions directly subordinate to the monarch without destroying the equipoise of the British constitution, the Empire ought nonetheless to be seen, in Burke's phrase, as 'an aggregate of many States' rather than a unitary body politic.[60] This description was intended as a refutation of Thomas Pownall, who had led the way in pressing for the incorporation of the colonies into the system of British parliamentary representation.[61] Yet in rejecting a unitary system of representation for the Empire, Burke raised the problem of adjudication among this aggregate of communities. Where there was an aggregate,

---

[56] Adam Smith, *Lectures on Jurisprudence*, ed. R. L. Meek, D. D. Raphael and P. G. Stein (Indianapolis: Liberty Fund, 1982), p. 326.

[57] It might equally incite opposition to the claim, as Burke later implicitly conceded. See Edmund Burke to Richard Champion, 19 March 1776, in Burke, *Correspondence*, III, p. 254.

[58] Edmund Burke, *Observation on a Late State of the Nation* (1769), in *Writings and Speeches*, II, p. 196.

[59] On composite monarchy as an early modern political system see H. G. Koenigsberger, 'Monarchies and Parliaments in Early Modern Europe: *Dominium Regale* or *Dominium Politicum et Regale*', *Theory and Society* 5.2 (March 1978), pp. 191–217; for application to the American context see H. G. Koenigsberger, 'Composite States, Representative Institutions and the American Revolution', *Historical Research* 62.148 (June 1989), pp. 135–53.

[60] Edmund Burke, Speech on Conciliation with America, 22 March 1775, in *Writings and Speeches*, III, p. 132.

[61] Thomas Pownall, *The Administration of the Colonies*, 4th edn. (London: n.p., 1768). It was this edition that Burke owned and annotated. His copy can be found in the British Library under reference c. 60. i. 9.

there would be diversity, and with diversity came disputes. The ensuing conflict would require a mechanism for arbitration, terminating in sovereignty.

According to Pufendorf, an aggregate of states on the model that would later be endorsed by Burke was a malformed entity, a *respublica irregularis*, in which sovereignty would be in contention.[62] It was neither a union nor a confederacy, but a hierarchical association in which subordinate communities would dispute the terms of their subjection. Sovereignty in this case was disunited, rendering its constituent elements accountable to one another. This arrangement subverted the basic condition of sovereignty, which was that it be constituted precisely so as to be unaccountable to any power. As Kinch Hoekstra has outlined in his chapter opening this collection, the criterion of unaccountability was derived from Aristotle, transmitted to Pufendorf via Grotius. Aristotle's term, to recapitulate, was *anupeuthunos*, and it was employed to describe the irresponsibility of tyranny in Book IV of the *Politics*.[63] The fullest extent of tyrannical rule was completely unaccountable (*anupeuthunos*) in the sense that it was exempt from every conceivable obligation. Such rule, as Plato had claimed in the *Laws*, was essentially autocratic.[64] This idea of irresponsible rule was indebted to Athenian public law. The concept of being *anupeuthunos* was based on a negation of *euthunos*, an auditor. As Melissa Lane explains in her chapter (Chapter 2 in this volume), an audit described the legal process of *euthuna*, the examination of officials upon the expiry of their office, originally performed by popular inspection, and subsequently by a board of *euthunoi* appointed by the Boulē.[65] Among the characteristics that Otanes in Herodotus's *History* ascribes to democracy, the scrutiny of officials is itemised along with *isonomia* and selection by lot.[66] For Pufendorf, however, sovereignty was unaccountable in every regime, whether it was a monarchy, aristocracy or democracy: in each case, *imperium* was exempt from scrutiny and punishment by a superior.[67] However, under a *respublica irregularis* there was

---

[62] Samuel Pufendorf, *De officio hominis juxta legem naturalem*, 2 vols. (Lund: n.p., 1673), II, viii, 12–15.

[63] Aristotle, *Politics*, 1295a15–20.   [64] Plato, *Laws*, 875b1–5. Cf. ibid., 761e5.

[65] See [Aristotle], *Athenaion Politeia*, XLVIII, 3–4. For comment see P. J. Rhodes, *A Commentary on the* Athenaion Politeia (Oxford: Oxford University Press, 1981), p. 150; for discussion see T. E. Rihll, 'Democracy Denied: Why Ephialtes Attacked the Areiopagus', *Journal of Hellenic Studies* 115 (1995), pp. 87–98. For recent discussion of the history of *euthuna* see D. D. von Dornum, 'The Straight and the Crooked: Legal Accountability in Ancient Greece', *Columbia Law Review* 97.5 (June 1997), pp. 1483–1518.

[66] Herodotus, *Historiae*, III, 80, xi.

[67] Pufendorf, *De officio hominis*, II, ix, 2, citing Thomas Hobbes, *De cive*, IV, §14.

neither a federal union nor uniform subjection to a single head, with the result that *imperium* was distributed among assorted members, and so divided against itself.

In Burke's mind the British Empire down to 1763 disproved these claims. Ever since the issuing of colonial charters, authority had been exercised by disparate communities without detriment to the unity of sovereignty. This judgement conformed to the Grotian observation that *imperium* might remain undivided even when it was wielded by more than one head, as evidenced by the unity of the Roman Empire when it existed under both Eastern and Western governments.[68] As Grotius explicitly stated, sovereignty had to be seen as *anupeuthunos*, but the manner of its exercise permitted a partition of its powers.[69] This included subjecting the head of state to binding precepts originally imposed by the people: here the right of sovereignty remained entire although its functions were shared among contracting parties.[70] Down to the outbreak of hostilities with America, Burke had been keen to defend imperial subjection in terms of an informal arrangement whereby trade was governed by metropolitan regulations while the rights of taxation were conceded to provincial legislatures. On this basis, the unity of sovereignty had been maintained in the midst of a partition of the prerogatives of power. But as negotiation with the colonies was diverted into conflict, Burke proposed the possibility of supplanting informal empire with a contractual distribution of roles. Hitherto, imperial organisation had evolved as circumstance dictated. The time had come for a transatlantic pact.

The situation in America had changed dramatically with the passage of the Prohibitory Act restraining colonial trade on 22 December 1775. Lord North's aim was to use the measure as a means of inducing the rebels to come to terms.[71] In fact, it succeeded in tipping protest into rebellion by threatening the livelihood of Americans with naval blockades. Burke commented that the administration was debating the starvation of thousands with the same detachment with which it might discuss the 'regulations of a Turnpike'.[72] A peace commission was dispatched to negotiate terms with the Americans, which in the event of success would lead to a suspension of restraints on colonial trade. But since the arrival of the commission postdated the resort to blockades, the colonies were

[68] Hugo Grotius, *De iure belli ac pacis libris tres* (Paris: n.p., 1625), I, iii, 17.
[69] Ibid., I, iii, 17–18.   [70] Ibid., I, iii, 17.
[71] P. D. G. Thomas, *Tea Party to Independence: The Third Phase of the American Revolution, 1773–1776* (Oxford: Oxford University Press, 1991), chap. 9.
[72] Edmund Burke to Richard Champion, 9 March 1775, in Burke, *Correspondence*, III, p. 132.

in effect being treated as foreign enemies in war.[73] A unilateral embargo on the means of subsistence, Burke claimed, was an affront to 'the Rights of man'.[74] The American recourse to arms was justified by this violation, as the colonists took up the rights of war in the absence of protection. Even so, as late as 1777, as the Americans confronted the British under conditions of entrenched belligerence, Burke persisted in defending the sovereignty of Parliament. However, he now contended that parliamentary government of the Empire required a charter of agreement delimiting the respective roles of London and the provinces. A 'ratified security' for the liberties of Americans should replace the old colonial system based on improvisation.[75]

IV

In this way, over the course of his engagement with America, Burke came to defend insurrection against the British government on the basis of a right to self-defence. In 1788, in convicting Warren Hastings of despotic practices in Bengal, he again endorsed the right of revolution, this time in the context of the rebellion of Benares against the depredations of the East India Company. Chait Singh, the Raja of Benares, had been forced into 'downright revolt', Burke contended.[76] As he delivered this verdict in February 1788, the *parlement* of Paris was openly resisting Louis XVI. The following November the director-general of finance, Jacques Necker, addressed the Assembly of Notables about the convocation of the Estates General. This would form, he remarked, an 'Assembly of the Nation'.[77] It would not, however, constitute a popularly sovereign body. François Furet has described the resort to an electoral process for selecting membership of the Estates based on proportionality between the population and its electors as a modern procedure subversive of the traditionalism of the monarchy. But if it was 'modern' it was also, he thought, riven by contradiction.[78] Despite these claims, the fact is that the Estates were

---

[73] Edmund Burke, Notes on American Prohibitory Bill, WWM, BkP 6: 119. Cf. Edmund Burke, *Letter to the Sheriffs of Bristol*, 3 April 1777, in Burke *Writings and Speeches*, III, p. 312.

[74] WWM, BkP 27: 230.

[75] Burke, *Address to the Colonists*, January 1777, in *Writings and Speeches*, III, p. 285. Cf. EB, Second Speech on Conciliation, 16 November 1775, ibid., pp. 190–5.

[76] Northamptonshire MS. A, XXII, 56.

[77] *Archives parlementaires de 1787 à 1860, première série (1787–1799)*, ed. M. J. Mavidal (Paris, 1875–), I, p. 394.

[78] F. Furet, *Interpreting the French Revolution* (Cambridge: Cambridge University Press, 1981, 1988 [1978]), pp. 40–4; F. Furet, 'La Monarchie et le règlement électoral de 1789', in K. M. Baker et al. (eds.), *The French Revolution and the Creation of Modern Political Culture*, 4 vols. (Oxford: Pergamon, 1987–94), I, pp. 375–86, at pp. 375 ff.

conceptualised as a delegation of counsellors, not a sovereign representative body. Deputies were mandated on the basis of the *cahiers de doléances* to advise the king and his ministers on a rescue plan for the fiscal crisis. Since the last meeting of this grand council of the nation in 1614, French society, by standard reckonings, had been utterly transformed. As Necker had himself noted in his address to the Assembly of Notables, deficit financing had reconfigured relations between citizens and the state while the spread of trade and manufactures had reformatted the composition of the orders.[79] Mandating the Estates to represent the grievances of all ranks of society can only be described as contradicting popular election after the fact. It is true that the elections to what became the National Assembly inadvertently triggered a contest between popular sovereignty and monarchy, but that was in the future in 1788. The contest was staged in the months following May 1789, and by October the decisive victory had fallen to the Constituent Assembly. According to Burke, it was at this point that France was subjected to a form of national sovereignty, organised under a system of democratic rule. But it was a species of popular government of a peculiarly aberrant kind.

In the *Reflections on the Revolution in France*, which appeared in November 1790, Burke set about describing the organisation of France in terms of the language of classical constitutional thought. For the present, he argued, the country had to be seen as a 'democracy', although it was probable that before long it would take the form of an oligarchy – a 'mischievous and ignoble oligarchy', as he put it.[80] Famously, Burke anticipated that the state would pass through further '"varieties of untried being"' before settling at last into a military monarchy.[81] The overarching course that Burke imputed to the Revolution thus mirrored the trajectory ascribed by Hume to the progress of the English Civil Wars: the attempt to realise a form of democracy was succeeded by oligarchy, which was duly repressed by the monarchy of Cromwell. The independents, Hume argued, had been motivated by a spurious dream of liberty, which in practice meant a desire for dominion. Before long, however, they were faced with 'the rebellion of their own servants', and exposed to the insults of the constituency with whose support they had originally clambered to power.[82] Popular revolution forecast inauspicious results. 'By

---

[79] *Archives parlementaires*, I, p. 393.

[80] Edmund Burke, *Reflections on the Revolution in France*, ed. J. C. D. Clark (Stanford: Stanford University Press, 2001), p. 291.

[81] Ibid., p. 414, citing Joseph Addison, *Cato: A Tragedy* (London: J. Tonson, 1713), V, I, l. 11.

[82] David Hume, *The History of England from the Invasion of Julius Caesar to the Revolution in 1688*, 6 vols. (Indianapolis: Liberty Fund, 1983 [1788]), 6 vols., VI, p. 54.

recent, as well as ancient example,' Hume commented, 'it was become evident, that illegal violence, with whatever pretences [*sic*] it may be covered, and whatever object it may pursue, must inevitably end at last in the arbitrary and despotic government of a single person.'[83] Hume ascribed the descent into demagogic despotism to the captivating yet spurious notion that 'the people are the origin of all just power.' The idea, he thought, had been contradicted 'by all history and experience', and yet again it had been falsified in the 1640s.[84] However, this was not intended as a denial of popular sovereignty, but as a warning against the seizure of power in the name of the populace, which could only succeed by popular oppression. In addition, Hume was disputing the equation of popular government with the common good on the assumption that the will of the populace would administer impartial justice. When Burke revived these positions in the 1790s, he was not reclaiming Hume for post-Revolutionary politics so much as drawing on one aspect of his critique of a Whig fundamentalism that projected its ideological origins on to the militancy of the 1640s. For his own part, Burke was clear that he would not condemn any form of government on the basis of normative prescriptions about its theoretical impossibility. Certainly democracies had previously existed, above all in the ancient world, and they could not be ruled out *a priori* in the modern.[85]

From Burke's perspective, the constitution of the British state was a practical demonstration of the compatibility between popular sovereignty and a mixed system of government. From the same vantage, the Revolution in France was staging a collision between the sovereignty of the nation and democratic forms of representation. As Bryan Garsten makes clear in his chapter in this volume (Chapter 10), this was an outcome that assorted publicists in France had anxiously sought to avoid. Under the circumstances, it seemed wise to consider whether democratic governments had been justly administered in the past, and whether they might plausibly be made to work in the future. The problem with purely popular government had been best captured by Aristotle, Burke maintained. An absolute democracy was no more to be considered a legitimate form of polity than an absolute monarchy. Burke turned to the discussion in Book IV of the *Politics* where, as he recollected, 'Aristotle observes, that a democracy has many striking points of resemblance with a tyranny'.[86] What Aristotle had in mind was that form of popular rule in which decrees (*psephismata*) rather than laws (*nomoi*) were dominant (*kuria*).[87] Under these circumstances, the demagogue

[83] Ibid.   [84] Ibid., V, p. 533.   [85] Burke, *Reflections*, pp. 291–2.
[86] Ibid., p. 292.   [87] Aristotle, *Politics* 1292a5–10.

prospers before an audience of the multitude just as the flatterer (*kolax*) does in the court of a tyrant.[88] In revising the *Reflections*, Burke offered his own translation of this famous passage, rendering a flatterer as a 'court favourite' and despotic commands as 'ordinances and arrêtes [*sic*].'[89] For Aristotle, the key point seems to have been that, under this particular form of democracy, impartiality was sacrificed to the corrupt relationship between the *dēmos* and their leaders, while all magistracies (*archai*) were dissolved.[90]

We have already seen how Burke believed that, in the absence of a mixed system of government, monarchy would take the form of a popular tyranny. Based on the same Aristotelian insight, he now presented pure democracy as liable to degenerate into a demagogic despotism. 'The ruin of the ancient democracies was', he later observed, 'that they ruled, as you do, by occasional decrees, *psephismata*'.[91] For Aristotle, government by decree meant that popular leaders predominated (*einai kurion*) over the *dēmos* from whom they drew their sustenance.[92] By contrast, in Plato's *Gorgias* the relationship between popular rulers and the ruled is described in terms of collusive corruption. Despite the skills of the rhetorician in prevailing over the populace, ultimately the *dēmos* dictates to the demagogue.[93] In this spirit, Burke draws the *Reflections* to a close with a meditation on the theme of popularity. Having dedicated a considerable portion of his pamphlet to excoriating the aptitudes of the deputies to the Assembly, he at last concedes that its leading members might not be as deficient as they appear. Nonetheless, the train of calamitous measures that had been voted by the Assembly, particularly between 4 August and 2 November 1789, called for some kind of explanation. Certainly some of this activity could be attributed to the incompetence of the legislators, along with the social composition of the Assembly. However, still more could be ascribed to the specious claims of the rights of man, and the dynamic that an appeal to these rights had unleashed.

Burke's point was never that these rights did not exist. In fact, we have seen how he invoked them as a resource against oppression. The point was that they legitimated recourse to rebellion, but could not serve as a basis for constructing a civil society. In the last analysis, the rights of man were rights of nature, founded on unqualified equality. They were intrinsically destructive of the justice of the republic, dedicated to safeguarding civil equality on the basis of meritorious proportionality between citizens.

---

[88] Ibid., 1292a20–25.   [89] Burke, *Reflections*, p. 292n.
[90] Aristotle, *Politics* 1292a25–30.   [91] Burke, *Reflections*, p. 377.
[92] Aristotle, *Politics* 1292a25 ff.   [93] Plato, *Gorgias* 481e.

Moreover, the appeal to natural equality as an instrument of statecraft was inevitably an exercise in hypocrisy. Burke illustrated his argument by highlighting Sieyès's concession that every political society was based on stratification.[94] The question for the author of the *Essai sur les privilèges* was why the hegemony of two hundred thousand aristocrats was more offensive than the 'government of five hundred country attornies' who presided in the National Assembly.[95] In making a parade of the rights of man, the deputies in the Assembly were auctioning their popularity, but they would end their days as flatterers, not legislators – instruments of popular prejudice instead of guides to the common good.[96] This subjection of public orators to the whims of popular feeling was not determined by relations within the legislative chamber but by the dependence of the Assembly on the population at large. The violence of mid-July succeeded by the mayhem of the October Days issued a warning. However, Burke also noted the more quotidian pressures to which deliberation was exposed: the threats to Assembly members on the basis of their ideological credentials, the intrusion of the public into the process of debate, the activism of the clubs and the harangues from the Palais Royal all stimulated competition for the opinion of the multitude.[97] The problem did not simply reside with the crowd, Burke admitted: 'I charge these disorders . . . on the Duke of Orleans, and Mirabeau, and Barnave, and Bailly, and Lameth, and La Fayette, and the rest of that faction.'[98]

The pretensions of popularity were best illustrated by the machinations of the Committee of the Constitution established in mid-July 1789. Despite the effective abolition of the Estates General on 27 June, this committee was deliberately formed on the basis of proportionality between the three orders: two places for the clergy, two for the nobility and four from the Third Estate.[99] Champion de Cicé delivered a preliminary report on 27 July, and Nicolas Bergasse presented proposals for the reform of the judiciary on 17 August.[100] The activities of the Committee were conducted against the background of legislative and popular upheaval, including the intimidation of deputies, particularly around the

[94] Emmanuel-Joseph Sieyès, *Essai sur les privilèges*, in R. Zapperi (ed.), *Écrits politiques* (Brussels: Éditions des Archives Contemporaines, 1994), p. 103.

[95] Burke, *Reflections*, p. 209.   [96] Ibid., p. 413.   [97] Ibid., pp. 227–9.

[98] Edmund Burke to Philip Frances, 17 November 1790, in Burke, *Correspondence*, VI, p. 172.

[99] M. P. Fitzsimmons, 'The Committee of the Constitution and the Remaking of France, 1789–1791', *French History* 4.1 (1990), pp. 23–47, at p. 25.

[100] *Archives parlementaires*, VIII, pp. 372 ff., 449 ff.; Nicolas Bergasse, *Rapport du comité de constitution sur l'organisation du pouvoirs judiciare* (Paris: n.p., 1789).

debate concerning the role of the monarchical veto.[101] On 10 September a unicameral legislature was agreed in the Constituent Assembly, and the following day the king was vested with a purely suspensive veto. Faced with the defeat of their preferred provisions, Mounier, Bergasse and Lally-Tollendal resigned from the Committee. On 29 September Jacques-Guillaume Thouret, elected to a newly constituted Committee two weeks earlier, presented proposals for the reconfiguration of the electoral map of France. These proposals were subsequently modified, but originally they comprised the re-division of the territory of France into eighty geometrically equal departments, subdivided into communes and cantons.[102] These divisions were to form the basis for both the administrative and electoral organisation of the state.[103] On that foundation, a 'gouvernement représentatif' was to be formed, the only species of government, Thouret asserted, appropriate to 'un peuple libre'.[104] This could only be achieved, however, on the basis of what Thouret termed 'proportionate equality' in contravention of the radical equality stipulated by the rights of man. The Committee intended to proceed by organising the representation of France on three bases: territorial; personal; and in terms of tax contributions. The territorial reconfiguration was mechanical and straightforward, designed to replace existing haphazard divisions with a uniform arrangement. The provisions for representation based on personal and contributory criteria, however, proved more complex. Density of population would vary between one canton and another, as would the distribution of wealth. A true representation of the polity would therefore have to reconcile these differences on the basis of artificial distinctions. These distinctions would constitute civil privileges, in conflict with natural equality.

Behind the recommendations put before the Assembly on 29 September lay a distinction drawn by Sieyès between passive and active citizenship presented to the Committee of the Constitution on 20 and 21 July 1789.[105] In fact, it seems that Thouret's outline was substantially derived from Sieyès's ideas.[106] A representative system, Sieyès thought,

---

[101] On shifts in the mood and alignments within the Assembly in this context see T. Tackett, 'Nobles and the Third Estate in the Revolutionary Dynamic of the National Assembly, 1789–1790', *American Historical Review* 94.2 (April 1989), pp. 271–301.

[102] M. P. Fitzsimmons, *The Remaking of France: The National Assembly and the Constitution of 1791* (Cambridge: Cambridge University Press, 2002 [1994]), p. 71.

[103] M.-V. Ozouf Marignier, *La Formation des départements: la representation du territoire Français à la fin du 18e siècle* (Paris: EHESS, 1989).

[104] *Archives parlementaires*, IX, p. 202.

[105] Sieyès, *Préliminaire de la constitution*, in Zapperi (ed.), *Écrits politiques*, p. 199.

[106] M. Forsyth, *Reason and Revolution: The Political Thought of the Abbé Sieyes* (New York and Leicester: Holmes & Meier/Leicester University Press, 1987), pp. 151, 159.

was a refinement of 'rude' democracy, based on a division of political labour embodied in a process of electoral filtration.[107] As described by Thouret, this would involve approximately four-and-a-half million active citizens in primary assemblies electing members to secondary bodies from a pool of eligible deputies determined on the basis of their fiscal contributions. From these secondary, or communal, assemblies, eligible representatives would next be deputed to departments, which would then elect to a national legislature.[108] This process was to be combined with the system for allocating representation in terms of the composite ratio between territory, population and wealth already described. Burke complained that, taken together, these provisions encompassed an elaborate system of 'juridical metaphysics' superimposed upon an ideology of arithmetic equality.[109] Political rights were subject to qualifications, as was eligibility to office. The final recommendation of the Committee of the Constitution was that admission to the national legislature should be conditional upon making an annual return of fifty *livres* in taxation.[110] Public responsibility was thus a graduated qualification, as Robespierre vociferously complained: sovereignty resides in the people, 'in every member of the populace', he declared.[111]

Burke noted that the terms of the suffrage under the new electoral proposals tended to the 'utter subversion' of the original 'equalising principle' of the Revolution.[112] At the same time, the qualifications stipulated for public office were hierarchical in spirit. Moreover, the adjustment of voting power in terms of territorial contributions would establish 'an *aristocracy of the rich*'.[113] Finally, the graduated process of election introduced two levels of mediation between the primary voter and the national representative.[114] The consequence of this would be, not the unity of the French republic, but the severance of the polity into secessionist

---

[107] Emmanuel-Joseph Sieyès, *Observations sur le rapport du Comité de constitution sur la nouvelle organisation de la France*, in Zapperi (ed.), *Écrits*, p. 262.

[108] *Archives parlementaires*, IX, pp. 203–5.   [109] Burke, *Reflections*, p. 346.

[110] This is the estimated contemporary value of the *marc d'argent*. See M. Crook, *Elections in the French Revolution* (Cambridge: Cambridge University Press, 2002 [1996]), pp. 36–7. The qualification was abolished on 27 August 1791.

[111] Maximilien Robespierre, *Oeuvres complètes*, ed. M. Bouloiseau, G. Lefebvre and A. Soboul, 10 vols. (Paris: George Thomas, 1910–67), VI, p. 553. The complaint was subsequently echoed by J. Jaurès, *Histoire socialiste de la Révolution française*, 7 vols. (Paris: Éditions sociales, 1968–73), I, pp. 587–8, and A. Soboul, *The French Revolution, 1787–1799* (London: Unwin Hyman, 1989 [1962]), pp. 179–82.

[112] Burke, *Reflections*, p. 347.   [113] Ibid., p. 349.

[114] This was subsequently modified on 22 December 1789 by reducing the intermediate stages between primary assemblies and the legislature, as Burke acknowledged in Edmund Burke, *Letter to a Member of the National Assembly* (1791), in *Writings and Speeches*, VIII, p. 296, responding to François-Louis-Thibault de Menonville to Edmund Burke, in Burke, *Correspondence*, VI, p. 163.

jurisdictions.[115] Taken together, the work of the Committee of the Constitution exemplified for Burke both the ineptitude and the hypocrisy of the leading deputies in the Revolution. They established a system of discrimination as they laboured to dismantle traditional privilege; they destroyed the possibility of popular consent as they sought to create a form of popular sovereignty. In general terms, as Burke understood it, the Revolution was driven by the twin forces of irreligion and populism. The former was soon channelled into a system of persecution while the latter took the form of an aristocracy of *rentiers*, backed up by desperate men of letters. This new-formed government of the few was in thrall to the politics of the street and the square without representing the popular will. The Assembly ruled by *psephismata*, and in the process subverted the means of compliance. Sovereignty was expressed as government by force unsupported by public opinion: 'The state', as Burke would later put is, was 'all in all'.[116]

---

[115] Burke, *Reflections*, pp. 352–3.
[116] Edmund Burke, *Second Letter on a Regicide Peace* (1796), in *Writings and Speeches*, IX, p. 288.

10　From popular sovereignty to civil society in post-revolutionary France

Bryan Garsten

I

The French Revolution did not turn out to be a revolution against the state. Perhaps some of the Jacobins, speaking in the name of "the people" and even of "all mankind," had initially hoped to carry through such a thorough revolution against centralized authority, but if that was their goal, they failed.[1] Instead, as Tocqueville pointed out, the Revolution furthered the state-building program that had been initiated by the modernizing eighteenth-century monarchy.[2] Many writers and politicians in the decades after the Revolution sought to understand what this fact implied about the fate of popular sovereignty in France. Did the revolutionaries' failure to resist administrative and military centralization spell the end of republican dreams of self-rule? Or were the various experiments in constitutionalism that emerged from the Revolution best understood as efforts to use the state to institutionalize popular sovereignty?[3] In France the timing and nature of the Revolution and the immediate military threat from outside the borders conspired to pose in an unusually direct way the question of whether popular sovereignty was compatible with centralized state authority over a large territory.

Leaving the state form behind altogether was not an option for France. Even Benjamin Constant, who was fascinated for a time by William Godwin's anarchism and who wrote well about the importance of decentralization and federalism, asserted the advantages of a large state: Only a strong centralized authority could maintain a military capability sufficient

---

[1] I. Hont, "The Permanent Crisis of a Divided Mankind: 'Nation-State' and 'Nationalism' in Historical Perspective," in *Jealousy of Trade: International Competition and the Nation-State in Historical Perspective* (Cambridge, MA: Harvard University Press, 2005), pp. 447–528, at pp. 516–17.

[2] Alexis de Tocqueville, *The Old Regime and the French Revolution*, trans. S. Gilbert (New York: Anchor, 1955).

[3] "In France . . . the state was the real instigator of popular sovereignty": L. Jaume, *Tocqueville: The Aristocratic Sources of Liberty*, trans. A. Goldhammer (Princeton: Princeton University Press, 2013), p. 41.

to defend France from its neighbors; only a centrally coordinated state could solve the first-mover problem in trying to end unjust practices such as slavery and serfdom; only a large territory contained the variety of human experiences, and allowed enough mobility among them, to encourage the gradual elimination of prejudices and the growth of enlightenment in the public.[4] Among these sorts of considerations, the military one dominated, so much so that according to Germaine de Staël both aristocrats and democrats during the revolutionary period thought that even the modest checks on executive power found in the English arrangements would have been fatal to France's security, which required a large standing army.[5]

If France had to be governed by a state, could that state at least take on a republican form? The reigning assumption, of course, famously endorsed by both Montesquieu and Rousseau, was that republican forms of government were viable only in territories much smaller than France. The idea of a "French republic" was simply not imaginable to most actors, even after the Revolution had begun. Thus the early debates about constitutional questions, from 1789 to 1791, were aimed at finding a form of constitutional monarchy compatible with the revolutionary aspiration for popular sovereignty. The death of the king ended that stage of the debate, but did not answer the fundamental question of how to combine an executive power sufficient to accomplish the goals of the state with some form of popular rule. Everyone knew that "representative government" was supposed to solve these problems, but the devil was in the details of precisely how such a government should be arranged. Obviously the Convention failed when it devolved into Terror, but the Directory that followed also found itself incompetently seizing more emergency powers than many of its early supporters could stomach, and it fell to Napoleon's *coup d'état* in 1799.

Even before the coup, it was easy to conclude from the difficulties of these early experiments that the whole project of representative government – that of institutionalizing popular sovereignty through the agency of a large state – was a misguided one. Joseph de Maistre, scornful of the idea that the Directory had successfully introduced any form of truly popular rule, offered a crude but rhetorically effective calculation in his *Considerations on France*: If every adult male in the country were to receive a single turn serving in the newly created Legislative Assembly, he noted, each

---

[4] Benjamin Constant, *Principles of Politics Applicable to All Governments* (Indianapolis: Liberty Fund, 2003), XV.3, pp. 323–4.
[5] Germaine de Staël, *Considerations on the Principal Events of the French Revolution*, ed. A. Craiutu (Indianapolis: Liberty Fund, 2008), p. 217.

man would be able to serve as a representative once every sixteen thousand years. "The imagination is staggered," he concluded sardonically, "by the prodigious number of 'sovereigns' condemned to die without having reigned."[6] While Maistre made the point as part of his counter-revolutionary argument, he was able to cite favorably the disappointed invective of none other than the proto-communist 'Gracchus' Babeuf, whose "conspiracy of the equals" to violently overthrow the Directory had only recently been foiled, and who had described the new representative government as an aristocratic, usurping, and enslaving force.[7] From both the right and the left sides of the political spectrum, critics of the Directory asserted that hopes of combining democratic–republican ideals with a large and powerful state had proven impossible to realize. "The phrase *large republic*, like *square circle*, is self-contradictory," wrote Maistre.[8]

Maistre's calculation dramatized the fact that most citizens would not actively participate in governing. What he declined to consider was the possibility that the people could be "sovereign" in some meaningful sense even *without* actively participating in governing. That was the strange, almost-but-not-quite-paradoxical thought that became central to one emerging understanding of "representative government." Could that thought be made coherent and satisfying? Thomas Hobbes, a principal theorist of sovereignty, had suggested this possibility. As Richard Tuck emphasizes in his contribution to this volume (Chapter 5), Hobbes had imagined in some detail how a people could appoint a monarch to govern without yielding its sovereignty.[9] Of course, Hobbes clearly preferred monarchical government to democratic institutions; in chapter ten of *De Cive* he elaborated in detail the problems likely to occur in democratic assemblies, from the factionalism and demagoguery they encouraged to the high taxation they tended to enact so as to be able to provide gifts to their many constituencies.[10] He mocked the democratic desire to participate in deliberative assemblies as little more than a longing to display one's eloquence and be praised for it. Still, even in that discussion, Hobbes did concede one way in which a democracy might succeed:

---

[6] Joseph de Maistre, *Considerations on France*, ed. R. Lebrun (Cambridge: Cambridge University Press, 1994), p. 36.

[7] Ibid., p. 37.   [8] Ibid.

[9] See R. Tuck, "Democratic Sovereignty and Democratic Government: The Sleeping Sovereign," in this volume.

[10] Thomas Hobbes, *On the Citizen*, ed. R. Tuck and M. Silverthorne (Cambridge: Cambridge University Press, 1998), 10.6, 10.9–12, pp. 119, 122–4.

But if in a *Democracy* the *people* should choose to concentrate deliberations about war and peace and legislation in the hands of just one man or of a very small number of men, and were happy to appoint magistrates and public ministers, i.e. to have authority without executive power [*auctoritate sine ministerio*], then it must be admitted that *Democracy* and *Monarchy* would be equal in this matter.[11]

Hobbes went on to clarify the importance of the distinction between *auctoritas* and *ministerium*, arguing, "the advantages and disadvantages of a regime do not depend upon him in whom the authority of the commonwealth [*civitatis auctoritas*] resides, but upon the ministers of sovereignty [*imperii ministros*]."[12] The first implication he drew was that sovereign authority could reside in a single person and yet lead to incompetent rule if the administration were too democratic in character. Another implication, however, was the one mentioned in the passage above: sovereign authority could reside in the people without compromising competent rule if the *administration* of government was appropriately centralized – if the people did not actually do the work of governing.[13]

The next section of this chapter will trace this Hobbesian thought into debates about how to institutionalize popular sovereignty after the French Revolution. As we will see, some influential writers and politicians did indeed take up a quasi-Hobbesian strategy for reconciling popular sovereignty and the state, but they soon encountered the limits and dangers of that approach, and a second wave of reflection – that associated with the French liberalism of Benjamin Constant and Alexis de Tocqueville – can be understood as a response to those dangers. While the idea of a people holding authority without administration is not itself incoherent, it came with a set of strong assumptions about what a "people" was, assumptions that made the sort of "sovereignty" retained by the people less substantive and less satisfying than the sort of political engagement that many proponents of popular rule craved. The understanding of civil society that emerged from the later liberals was, in part, an effort to imagine other forms of democratic self-governing that were compatible with, that could survive within, a large state.

The main issue that would arise can be summarized easily enough: The Hobbesian strategy suggested that a "people" could retain sovereignty if it were understood to be an aggregation of separate and equal individuals

---

[11] Ibid., 10.15, p. 125.

[12] Ibid., 10.16, p. 125. I have changed Silverthorne's translation to emphasize that *imperium* refers to sovereign authority, not administrative governance, as Tuck now suggests.

[13] For more on the sovereignty-government distinction see B. Garsten, "Representative Government and Popular Sovereignty," in I. Shapiro et al. (eds.), *Political Representation* (Cambridge: Cambridge University Press, 2010), p. 90–110 and Chapter 5 in this volume.

brought together in acts of voting to produce a majority that would delegate the work of governing. To grant priority to the agency of individuals, as emerging plebiscitary practices did, was to privilege the individuation of wills and their aggregation through voting over other modes of social authority that could be found in communities that existed prior to and outside of the state. In the revolutionary context, asserting the priority of individuals in this way was a kind of liberation; it freed people from the various forms of domination found in family, corporation, guild, and church – in short, from the social–political hierarchies of feudal life. To lodge sovereign authority in a constructed aggregate of individuals was, necessarily, to take authority away from those traditional social entities. Thus the "people" retaining authority in the Hobbesian understanding of popular sovereignty was already an imagined product of the Revolution; it was a vision of the members of society as they appeared through the eyes of someone standing outside any particular standpoint within society – through the eyes of the state, as James Scott might say.[14] However, while this perspective was devised to free people from the grip of churches and guilds and the petty despotisms of local lords, it also often worked against the associations, societies, and localities engaging in popular politics on the ground. Thus for revolutionaries as well as traditionalists in France, the intended liberation of Hobbesian popular sovereignty often *felt* like a rejection of their own concrete forms of community and political practice.

When nineteenth-century liberals such as Constant, Staël, and Tocqueville voiced concerns about "popular sovereignty," they were often expressing worries about the substitution of an aggregate of individuals, an abstract entity whose will could easily be usurped, for the concrete, socially embedded communities that had been traditionally associated with popular rule. When these liberals stood up for "society" they meant to defend an understanding of "the people" not filtered through the sieve of social contract theory. In criticizing the Hobbesian strategy of reconciling popular sovereignty and the state, they contributed to the emergence of a theory of civil society and its virtues that still reigns supreme today both in political science (in the form of Robert Putnam's work on social capital, for example) and in political practice (in the many organizations promoting "civil society institutions"). One task of this chapter is to show that this understanding of civil society arose in part as a correction to the view that popular sovereignty could be realized in large territories only through the agency of state institutions legitimized by plebiscites. The

---

[14] J. C. Scott, *Seeing like a State: How Certain Schemes to Improve the Human Condition Have Failed* (New Haven: Yale University Press, 1999).

state's function was not only to put majority rule at the national level into effect, but also to create background conditions for a richer set of local democratic practices that were more deeply rooted in the actual social life of the people. That, at least, was the hope of the liberal theorists in France who came to prefer the language of civil society to that of popular sovereignty.

II

To follow the trajectory of the Hobbesian view of popular sovereignty in revolutionary France, we can begin with the thought of Pierre-Louis Roederer. Readers who know of Roederer are most likely to be familiar with the important and somewhat dubious roles he played at two moments in revolutionary history. As prefect of Paris during the tumultuous popular uprising on August 10, 1792, Roederer responded to the gathering of crowds by leading King Louis XVI to the hall of the Legislative Assembly. He was probably trying to save the king's life and prevent the country from falling into an unconstitutional form of regime change, but some believe his action unintentionally helped to end the monarch's life. Later in the decade, Roederer joined with Sieyès and Napoleon to help facilitate the *coup d'état* that ended the Republic. He was one of the chief authors of the constitution of the Year VIII, introduced just after the coup, and he worked hard for Napoleon during his rule, claiming that doing so was the best way to secure the protection of liberal rights and reformist goals. Andrew Jainchill has classified Roederer as a proponent of "liberal authoritarianism," which he defines as "not a rejection of liberal principles, but, rather, an attempt to maintain them through the establishment of a Hobbesian sovereign and the concomitant rejection of democratic practices."[15] While Roederer's later Napoleonic activities can easily be labeled "authoritarian," I want here to examine the less simply classified train of thought that he followed during the decade between 1789 and Napoleon's coup, for it turns out that Roederer was exploring something quite close to the Hobbesian approach to popular sovereignty described above.

Roederer was an early enthusiast of the Revolution; he supported the idea of popular sovereignty for which the Revolution had been fought, and he joined the Jacobin club. In time, however, he split with Robespierre and others who dominated the Jacobins, so much so that during the Terror he was forced into hiding. While in hiding he developed his views

[15] A. Jainchill, *Reimagining Politics after the Terror: The Republican Origins of French Liberalism* (Ithaca: Cornell University Press, 2008), 198–9.

on political theory, which he explained in a series of lectures at the Lycée of Paris in 1793 under the title *Cours d'organisation sociale*. It so happens that just as he was writing those lectures he was also occupying himself by translating Hobbes's *De Cive*.[16] He gave as a reason for his interest, "There are several parts in his [Hobbes's] work that are excellent; it is from him that Rousseau took the principle of popular sovereignty."[17]

In his lectures and elsewhere in his writings Roederer demonstrated that he had thought carefully about the tenth chapter of *De Cive*, the one from which the distinction between *auctoritas* and *ministerium* comes, as he was particularly interested in the arguments comparing the benefits of monarchy and democracy.[18] He even closed his consideration of democracy with a gloss on precisely the passage I have quoted above. He positioned himself as disagreeing with Hobbes, but on this point only: he understood Hobbes to be suggesting not only that the people should not be directly involved in administration, but also that they should not have a role in making the laws. This last part, he thought, went too far, and was based on a worst-case understanding of the vices of democratic deliberation. To meaningfully keep "authority" at all, he argued, the people would have to have some role in legislation.[19]

Elsewhere in his course of lectures Roederer put quite a lot of weight on the distinction in book three of Rousseau's *Social Contract* between sovereignty and government, a distinction that parallels Hobbes's between *auctoritas* and *ministerium*. His goal was to show how a Rousseauian understanding of popular sovereignty was, in spite of Rousseau's famous arguments against representation, compatible with elected, constitutional government in France. First, he took Rousseau's distinction between sovereignty and government to imply a justification

---

[16] Pierre-Louis Roederer, *The Spirit of the Revolution of 1789 and Other Writings on the Revolutionary Epoch*, ed. M. Forsyth (Aldershot: Scolar Press, 1989); Hont, "Permanent Crisis of a Divided Mankind," p. 489n.73; K. Margerison, "P.-L. Roederer: Political Thought and Practice during the French Revolution," *Transactions of the American Philosophical Society*, NS, 73.1 (January 1983), pp. 1–166, at p. 114.

[17] Pierre-Louis Roederer, *Œuvres*, 8 vols. (Paris: Firmin Didot, 1853), VIII, p. 306.

[18] The relative advantages of monarchy and democracy – of obvious and immediate interest in the early 1790s – also dominated another work that Roederer composed at this time, an imagined dialogue between Hobbes, Voltaire, Rousseau, Montesquieu, Bayle, Helvétius, and Sieyès – in which he indicated that he believed, with Sieyès, that a wholly new form of government had to be invented, one that had the stability of a Hobbesian monarch and the deliberative virtues of a well-constituted democratic assembly. See R. Scurr, "Pierre-Louis Roederer and the Debate on Forms of Government in Revolutionary France," *Political Studies* 52.2 (June 2004), pp. 251–68. Roederer also quoted from chapter ten of *De Cive* in his account of his experience with the Parisian mobs in 1792. See Pierre-Louis Roederer, *Notice de ma vie pour mes enfants*, in Roederer, *Œuvres*, III. Cf. Roederer, *The Spirit of the Revolution of 1789*, p. 71.

[19] Roederer, *Œuvres*, VIII, p. 301.

for the constitutional separation of legislative and executive powers. Second, and more interestingly, he spotted a way of justifying the fact that a constituent or legislative assembly could *create* laws without taking the ultimate authority to *make* laws away from the people. As he highlighted during his exposition of Rousseau's thought, "the constituent power is not sovereignty."[20] While it was true that the people were too numerous to gather and debate laws for themselves and therefore that they had to appoint representatives, it was crucial not to mistake the representatives for "a governing authority."[21] The assembly that deliberates and votes on laws should be regarded as having merely provisional power. More precisely, its power was that of discussing, deliberating, and voting *on its own final opinion*. Even the "constituent power" that Sieyès made so much of should be understood to include only these functions. "The sovereign [people] can say to whomever it chooses: Debate among yourselves, in my presence, all the questions that interest me, and I will listen to you; vote by plurality one opinion, and I will see if it pleases me."[22] The final authority would remain with the people, thus preserving Rousseau's idea that sovereignty was inalienable.[23]

At the same time, Roederer insisted that his audience pay close attention to what could count as a "law" in Rousseau's argument. Laws had to be wholly *general* in scope and in application, otherwise they lost their particular claim to legitimacy, a claim based entirely on their emergence from the nation as a whole and their equal application to everyone in it. Thus Roederer suggested that much of what the Constituent Assembly had spent time debating had been too specific, essentially executive decrees. He assumed that once the true nature of a law was understood, there would be very few laws proposed by a legislative assembly, and that would make it possible to actually bring them before the people for endorsement. Roederer supported an "obligation to submit the laws to popular sanction."[24] This is consistent with an argument he had made in a 1788 pamphlet on the subject of how to organize the coming meeting of the Estates General, in which he had argued that a nationwide

---

[20] Ibid., p. 259. "Le pouvoir constituant n'est point souveraineté; voilà une première notion sur laquelle il faut se fixer."

[21] Ibid., p. 254.

[22] Ibid., p. 260. "Le pouvoir de discuter et de délibérer une constitution, voilà ce que c'est que le pouvoir constituant."

[23] Roederer may have had in mind here a discussion he heard in the National Assembly on August 10, 1791 about whether to add the word "inalienable" to the description of the general will in the Constitution. See *Archives Parlementaires de 1789 À 1860: Recueil Complet Des Débats Législatifs & Politiques Des Chambres Françaises*, ed. J. Mavidal and E. Laurent (Paris: Librairie administrative de P. Dupont, 1862), XXIX, pp. 327–9.

[24] Roederer, *Œuvres*, VIII, pp. 260–1.

referendum was needed to ascertain the view of a plurality of citizens on the best mode of organization.[25]

Roederer's endorsement of appeals to the people, even if only occasionally and for the most general and fundamental laws, distinguished his point of view from that of Sieyès. As is well known, Sieyès opposed any sort of direct appeal to the people, because he thought there was no unified agent called "the people" to whom anyone could appeal except through properly convened representative assemblies.[26] Sieyès thus followed a different strain of thought in Hobbes, stated most clearly in chapter sixteen of *Leviathan*: that unity could be found only in the *representer* and not the represented.[27] For Sieyès, this meant that consulting the people through plebiscites, or even through assemblies in which each representative presented the local interests of his constituents, failed to yield a single governing authority that could legitimately act for the nation as a whole. The importance of this theoretical point for Sieyès was evident in the fact that he bothered, on June 16, 1789, to resist Mirabeau's motion to name the post-revolutionary version of the Estates General the "Assembly of the People's Representatives." Instead, Sieyès seems to have supported the awkward "Assembly of known and verified representatives," which he then withdrew, proposing instead the simpler title,

---

[25] Ibid., VII, pp. 573–4.

[26] "Only representation is the reunited people, since the ensemble of parties to the association cannot achieve a unity any other way. The integrity of the nation is not anterior to the will of the reunited people, which is only available through its representation. Unity begins in it. Nothing, therefore, is above representation, and it is the only organized body. Dispersed, the people is not an organized body, and has neither a singular will nor a singular mind – indeed, nothing singular at all": Sieyès in the Archives nationales, 284 A.P. 5, folder 1(2), as quoted in P. Rosanvallon, *Democracy Past and Future*, ed. S. Moyn (New York: Columbia University Press, 2006), p. 89. See also K. M. Baker, *Inventing the French Revolution: Essays on French Political Culture in the Eighteenth Century* (Cambridge: Cambridge University Press, 1990), pp. 295–301.

[27] The first to suggest that Sieyès followed Hobbes in this way may have been Dominique Garat, who, before he was interior minister, had reported on the debates in the National Assembly for the *Journal de Paris* from 1789 to 1791. As Michael Sonenscher notes, Garat identified Hobbes, Montesquieu and Rousseau as the philosophical sources of Sieyès's philosophy, calling Hobbes "the only one, among all the political writers, who best understood the true foundations of political societies, the rights of man, and the principles of peace among nations": Dominique Joseph Garat, *Dominique-Joseph Garat, membre de l'Assemblée constituante, à M. Condorcet...* (Paris: Desenne, 1791), 25–6, as cited in M. Sonenscher, "Introduction," in Emmanuel Joseph Sieyès, *Political Writings: Including the Debate between Sieyès and Tom Paine in 1791*, ed. M. Sonenscher (Indianapolis: Hackett Publishing Company, 2003), pp. xlv–xlvi. That Sieyès followed Hobbes in this way is the argument of a number of studies, including M. Forsyth, "Thomas Hobbes and the Constituent Power of the People," *Political Studies* 29. (1981), pp. 191–203; M. Forsyth, *Reason and Revolution: The Political Thought of the Abbé Sieyès* (New York and Leicester: Holmes & Meier/Leicester University Press, 1987); Hont, "Permanent Crisis of a Divided Mankind."

"The National Assembly," which of course won the day.[28] As early as September 7, 1789, speaking to the National Assembly, he followed the line of thought that Roederer would later dismiss:

It is evident that five to six million active citizens, spread over twenty-five thousand square leagues, cannot assemble together; it is certain that they cannot aspire to anything except a representative legislature. Therefore the citizens who name representatives renounce, and should renounce, making the law directly themselves.[29]

Sieyès thus placed a lot of weight on the simple but stubborn fact that it was impossible to gather all citizens together at one time and place. In doing so he was following Hobbes's arguments in *De Cive*. Hobbes had stated quite directly that a people could only be said to hold sovereign authority when they *assembled*. And in the cases when a citizenry wanted to appoint another person or group to do the work of governing, it could only be said to retain its sovereign authority, according to Hobbes, if, while assembled to make the appointment, it also set the next time and place of assembly. Gathering together in meetings was not incidental in Hobbes's account in *De Cive*; it was one of only two announced criteria for what counted as a democracy: "Two things, then, constitute a *Democracy*, of which one (an uninterrupted schedule of meetings) constitutes a Δημος, and the other (which is majority voting) constitutes το κρατος, or authority."[30] When Hobbes later discussed the differences between monarchy, on the one hand, and aristocracy and democracy, on the other, he remarked that the latter forms of government "require specific times and designated places for deliberation and decision . . . *Optimates*, and the *people*, need to assemble, because they are not *one thing by nature*."[31] Once a people transferred sovereign authority to a monarch or to an assembly without making provision for assembling themselves together again, the people as a singular agent "dissolved" and turned again into a "rude multitude" whose authority "vanished."[32] Indeed, when Hobbes outlined the possibility of locating sovereign authority in any number of forms of government, from a monarchy to a democracy, he always seems to have assumed that the options were either to locate it in "*one man*" or in "*one Assembly* or *council* of many men."[33] The interesting inclusion of both

---

[28] See Mirabeau's speech in the Estates General about the name of the assembly, and the recorded motion by Sieyès: *Réimpression de La Moniteur Ancien*, vol. I (Paris: Henri Plon, 1858), pp. 81–2. Cf. Rosanvallon, *Democracy Past and Future*, p. 83; Hont, "Permanent Crisis of a Divided Mankind," p. 477.

[29] *Archives Parlementaires*, VIII, p. 594.

[30] Hobbes, *On the Citizen*, 7.5, p. 94. The Greek words are *demos* (the people) and *to kratos* (rule), the two parts of the word *democracy*.

[31] Ibid., 7.13, p. 97.   [32] Ibid., 7.8, 7.9, 7.11.   [33] Ibid., 7.1, p. 91.

"assembly" and "council" in this formulation, repeated elsewhere in the text, suggests that Hobbes was thinking in concrete terms about gatherings of citizens. It is not plausible to think that Hobbes regarded voting to find a majority as the only important activity undertaken in an assembly; he explained the purpose of an assembly of all men at the beginning of chapter seven in this way: "so that each of them has the right to vote and can participate in debating issues if he so wishes."[34] All the vices of democratic debate that he catalogued so powerfully, the demagoguery and factionalism, were introduced as arguments against democracy and not arguments against the idea that democracy required assembling and debating.[35] Therefore, when Sieyès argued that France could not be a democracy because its citizens could not physically assemble together, he was following Hobbes's definition of democracy in a very straightforward way, according to which it was hard to see how a dispersed multitude of a large state could hold or retain *auctoritas* at all.[36]

Roederer, who was quite close to Sieyès on many points but who still wanted, as we have seen, to identify some notion of popular authority that could persist even through the appointment of an administration, found himself having to think quite carefully about the *kinds* of appeals to the people that were possible in a state as large and diverse as France. How, precisely, would "submitting the laws to public sanction" work in practice? To which assembly, assemblies, or persons would the proposed laws be submitted? In revolutionary France, the question of whether citizens needed to actually gather together to select representatives and vote on referenda was a live one. As Malcolm Crook has noted, the plebiscites on the constitutions in 1793 and 1795 relied on traditional processes in which citizens assembled in meetings at set times and places in their cantons, waiting together through a long process of calling the rolls to register their votes in front of their peers. For Sieyès, the problem in appealing to the people in this way was that when people met in societies or cantonal assemblies or other partial associations, they were more likely to vote for their familial or religious or sectional interests, and they could more easily fall prey to oratorical demagoguery. Sieyès thought that a unified national will could be found or created only if those interests

---

[34] Ibid.

[35] As Richard Tuck points out, the passage I quoted earlier, from 10.15, suggests that Hobbes imagined the possibility of separating deliberation from democracy, delegating deliberation to ministers rather than considering it to be a constituent part of democratic sovereignty: Chapter 5 in this volume, pp. 115–41. Roederer tried to follow this lead by portraying constituent assemblies as delegated deliberations, as I described in the previous section.

[36] "Je soutiens toujours que la France n'est point, ne peut pas être une *démocratie*": *Archives Parlementaires*, VIII, p. 594.

were set aside in favor of the national interest, and he did not imagine it desirable or even possible to ask people to set aside their particular interests themselves as they assembled in small meetings at the local level. It was at the national level that he expected representatives to give priority to the national interest. The Constitution of 1795 summarized his view in its 52nd article: "The members of the Legislative Body are not representatives of the department which has elected them, but of the entire Nation, and they cannot be given any mandate." He opposed federalism and direct elections because he thought they conveyed a confused message on this point.

Sieyès's insistence that sovereignty could not be exercised by any part of the whole was enshrined in the 1791 constitution.[37] He was opposed not only by traditionalists jealously trying to preserve local privileges, but also by revolutionaries who thought that popular sovereignty meant that actually existing, concrete communities should participate in ruling. Robespierre, for example, had forcefully spoken against Sieyès's view in the National Assembly on August 10, 1791. He had brought murmurs from the crowd (according to the transcript in the *Archives parlementaires*) when he had noted that they already implicitly allowed parts of the country to exercise the sovereignty that Sieyès said belonged only to the whole whenever they allowed a region to select representatives to the Assembly; after all, he argued, the selection of representatives was itself an act of sovereignty.[38] In his own proposal for a different version of a *Declaration of Rights of Man and Citizen*, Robespierre included a provision specifically designed to emphasize the respect due not only to the people as a whole, but also to *sections* of the people.[39] The point

---

[37] "La Souveraineté est une, indivisible, inaliénable et imprescriptible. Elle appartient à la Nation; aucune section du peuple, ni aucun individu, ne peut s'en attribuer l'exercice": *Constitution of 1791*, section 1, title 3.

[38] *Archives Parlementaires*, XXIX, pp. 326–7. Sieyès had tried to answer this line of argument two years earlier in a speech on the royal veto on September 7, 1789: "Il faut donc reconnaître et soutenir que toute volonté individuelle est réduite à son unité numérique; et ne croyez pas que l'opinion que nous nous formons d'un représentant, élu par un grand nombre de citoyens, détruise ce principe. Le député d'un bailliage est immédiatement choisi par son bailliage; mais médiatement, il est élu par la totalité des bailliages. Voilà pourquoi tout député est représentant de la nation entière. Sans cela, il y aurait parmi les députés une inégalité politique que rien ne pourrait justifier; et la minorité pourrait faire la loi à la majorité, ainsi que je l'ai démontré ailleurs": ibid., VIII, p. 593.

[39] G. Rudé, *Robespierre* (New York: Prentice Hall, 1967), pp. 55–6, article 19: "No portion of the people may employ the power of the entire people, but the wish which it expresses must be respected as the wish of a portion of the people, which is to concur in forming the general will. Each and every section of the assembled sovereign must enjoy the right to express its will with entire liberty; it is essentially independent of all constituted authorities and master of regulating its police and its deliberations."

was crucial to Robespierre's understanding of the role that clubs and communities should play in self-government.

Roederer may have supported a kind of appeal to the people, but he did not at all follow Robespierre on this fundamental point. He felt a deep unease at the way in which social dynamics within particular localities or societies could intimidate and suffocate individuals and minorities. In his 1788 tract on the Estates General he had introduced a broad argument about how equality should be understood and institutionalized in electoral systems, arguing that voting should be by individuals rather than estates, and also that representatives should not take instructions from their localities or provinces, but should think of themselves as fully national. He specifically remarked that representatives who were only messengers delivering the views of their cantons to the central assembly could never produce an adequate representation of the will of the whole, but would only reproduce "the small divisions of societies in a state of war with one another."[40]

If this argument was conceived initially as an attack on feudal corporations, it nevertheless applied just as well to republican understandings of popular sovereignty through organized bodies smaller than the state as a whole. Roederer's views on the Estates General reappeared in his later hostility to clubs and associations, a hostility intensified after his own experience with the Jacobin club and, most significantly, his time as the Parisian prefect responding to the unrest on the Parisian streets in the summer of 1792. When he later wrote an account of the *journée* of August 10, 1792, he saw the events of that day through the lens provided by Hobbes's account of democratic factionalism and oratory in *De Cive*. He referred to the uprising as "democracy, or, if one prefers, a formidable ochlocracy [mob rule]" and described it in these terms:

Each popular assembly had its own [orator] . . . A swarm of men had arisen in France, men of powerful and barbarous eloquence . . . men who had discovered far better than those in the national assemblies the techniques of persuasion and bewitchment . . . They presented France to the proletarians as a prey which was theirs if they wished to seize it . . . One saw at that time the realization, the revival of what happened in the revolution of 1648 in England. The writer Hobbes who defended, in his work *De Cive*, the monarchical system against the partisans of democracy, said to those who objected that a Caligula or a Nero might come to the throne under a monarchy, [but] '*In democratia, tot possunt esse Nerones, quot*

---

[40] Pierre-Louis Roederer, *De la députation aux Etats-Généraux*, in Roederer, *Œuvres*, VII, pp. 539–74, esp. pp. 542, 562–3. Cf. Roederer, *The Spirit of the Revolution of 1789*, p. xv.

sunt oratores qui populo adulantur. Simul plures sunt in democratia et quotidie novi suboriunter. Suboriunter, which means, others, more base, rise up *from below.*'[41]

When Roederer emerged from hiding, having survived the Terror, one of his first public interventions offered a sharp argument against the claims of sections, clubs, or associations to exercise any sort of legitimate political authority. He published *Des sociétés populaires* in 1794 and then largely recycled it into another pamphlet in August 1799, *Des sociétés particulières, tells que clubs, reunions, etc.*[42] In these pieces he argued in favor of strong laws regulating the activities of clubs and societies, limiting their size to no more than twelve or fifteen people, and shutting some of them down altogether. The purpose of such groups, he argued, should be friendship and instruction; they should aim at the enlightenment of each individual member, but they should not deliberate or vote about political actions or positions to be taken by the group as a singular whole. Against writers who claimed that societies could aid in the surveillance of the government, he argued that surveillance ought to be the work, on the one hand, of individuals exercising their rights, and, on the other, of the nation as a whole, but only as a whole. He rejected the view that clubs could be helpful intermediary bodies between individuals and the constituted authorities; they were accountable only to their members; they were institutionalized in a way that put no checks on their power; and they could therefore tyrannize over both individuals and government officials. In explaining why he opposed letting societies deliberate and vote, he echoed Hobbes's warning about the vanity and ambition of orators, who he said would focus on the contest and so eclipse the possibility of instruction. He recalled that in 1789 and early in 1790 the Jacobin club had been useful and not dangerous; it had not taken votes, but only sparked discussion, leaving each individual freer and more informed as a result.

Roederer's most significant theoretical point in these writings against politicizing societies was that they interfered with the creation of a genuine and legitimate form of "public opinion." Public opinion should come from an aggregation of the separate opinions of individuals, individuals who were not cowed or dominated by the majority within any particular section. He echoed a passage from Rousseau's *Social Contract* claiming that the general will would arise not from shared deliberation but

---

[41] Roederer, *The Spirit of the Revolution,* p. 71. The Latin passage: "In a democracy there may be as many Neros as there are orators who flatter the people. Many exist at the same time in a democracy and each day new ones rise up." This is a slightly altered version of Hobbes's statement in *De Cive* 10.7.

[42] Roederer, *Œuvres,* VII, pp. 17–22, 87–94; Margerison, "P.-L. Roederer," 122–3.

instead from each individual's silent and spontaneous opinion.[43] Voting on a particular group's position, implicitly submitting one's individual will to the will of the group, would interfere with the separate process of opinion formation within each individual, and therefore with the process of forming a genuine public opinion of the whole.[44] The sort of representation that would emerge from the world of clubs and societies and sections was, Roederer argued, a "false image" of public opinion. The true image was the aggregate of separate individual wills.[45]

Thus, in spite of the difference we have noted, Roederer and Sieyès were not so far apart. Neither supported an appeal to people as they were found in their particular communities, whether old regime corporate communities or revolutionary republican ones. In some ways the natural compromise between Sieyès and Roederer on this point seems to have been precisely the change in voting procedures that came when they collaborated on Napoleon's *coup d'état* in 1799. The hastily drafted constitution to support that coup was, in fact, submitted to the people for approval in the plebiscite of January 1800. But the citizens were no longer asked to assemble together at one time and place in their cantons. Instead, they were given longer periods of time during which they could present themselves individually at local polling places to register their votes separately. Roederer was an organizer and proponent of this new system of voting. When he defended it, he remarked not only on its

---

[43] Roederer, *Œuvres*, VII, p. 93: "L'opinion publique, qui ne peut se composer que de la majorité des opinions individuelles des citoyens, et ne peut naître que d'une manière silencieuse et spontanée, nu sein des lumières et de la liberté. Des opinions de confréries, de sectes, de parti, parviendront sans peine à étouffer celle-ci et à l'empêcher de se produire, si des sociétés ont le droit d'émettre leur vœu avec éclat et autorité." Cf. Rousseau, *Social Contract*, book 2, chapter 3: "If, when an adequately informed people deliberate, the citizens were to have no communication among themselves, the general will would always result from the large number of small differences, and the deliberation would always be good. But when factions, partial associations at the expense of the whole, are formed, the will of each of these associations becomes general with reference to its members and particular with reference to the state. One can say, then, that there are no longer as many voters as there are men, but merely as many as there are associations" (Jean-Jacques Rousseau, *The Social Contract: And Other Later Political Writings* (Cambridge: Cambridge University Press, 1997), p. 60).

[44] Roederer, *Œuvres*, VII, p. 21: "Une opinion collective exerce sur les opinions individuelles une sorte d'autorité contraire à la formation de l'opinion publique, qui ne peut naître que spontanément au sein de la liberté et des lumières ; des opinions de *confrérie*, de *corporation* , de *secte*, de *parti*, sont substituées à l'opinion du peuple, qui , livrée à elle-même, ne se réglerait que sur l'intérêt general."

[45] Ibid., p. 20. "Elle donne à chaque individu les connaissances nécessaires pour avoir un vœu ou une opinion particulière, et que c'est de la somme des opinions particulières et individuelles que se forme l'opinion publique. L'opinion des sociétés n'en est que la fausse image, puisque l'opinion de la majorité des sociétés peut n'être pas celle de la majorité des citoyens, ni même celle de la majorité des membres de toutes ces sociétés pris en masse, attendu l'inégalité du nombre dont chacune est composée."

convenience, but also on the fact that it allowed individuals to be free from "the vexations of a political rival or canvassing for his vote . . . no opposition has to be endured."[46] In other words, individual voting freed people from local politics. As Crook notes, "The business of voting thus became an individual rather than a collective gesture, though it also became more susceptible to official rather than communal pressure as a consequence."[47]

For Roederer, the abstraction from social circumstance involved in this way of imagining what it was to be a "people" was a moment of liberation, an attack on the inherited, naturalized, and dominating authority of corporate entities in society. From the perspective of any ordinary part of society, however – from the perspective of a church, a family, an estate, a trade guild, a section or club, and so on – the "liberation" involved in this assertion of popular sovereignty appeared as an attack. Representative government based on this understanding of popular sovereignty seemed, from those perspectives, not a means of making government responsive to society, but rather of freeing government from society's influence, of giving it a new autonomy and authority of its own. To picture "the people" as an entity constructed by individuals through voting was to create a powerful new authority – the state – above and independent of the regular texture of social life. Hobbes himself had never denied this. Even if he had introduced the somewhat disingenuous language of "natural" equality, he had also emphasized the artificiality of the sovereign that recognized that equality and so brought it into actual existence. He had recognized that while he often wrote of individuals as "natural persons" he was actually asking us to regard men "as if they had just emerged from the earth like mushrooms and grown up without any obligation to each other."[48] While the myth of the social contract suggested that we regard sovereignty as arising *from* agreements among individuals, the political reality evident in revolutionary France was that state sovereignty would have to come *before* the real existence of anything resembling a state of nature among individuals; the state is what made it possible to conceive of people as free and equal individuals. Only a sovereign authority separate from all social authorities would be able to free people from social

[46] Pierre-Louis Roederer, *Mémoires D'économie Publique, de Morale, et de Politique*, 2 vols. (Paris: L'imprimerie du journal de Paris, 1799), II, p. 7. as quoted in M. Crook, "The Uses of Democracy: Elections and Plebiscites in Napoleonic France," in M. F. Gross and D. Williams (eds.), *The French Experience from Republic to Monarchy, 1792–1824* (New York: Palgrave Macmillan, 2000), pp. 58–71, at p. 61.

[47] Crook, "The Uses of Democracy," p. 60. M. Crook, "The Plebiscite on the Empire," in P. Dwyer and A. Forrest (eds.), *Napoleon and his Empire: Europe, 1804–1814* (New York: Palgrave Macmillan, 2007), pp. 16–29, at p. 16.

[48] Hobbes, *On the Citizen*, 8.1, p. 102.

hierarchies and so turn simple biological and volitional individuation into a more salient political fact. "Popular sovereignty" understood as an appeal to the people through a plebiscite of individuals was therefore not the coming to power of any previously existing assemblage of people; it was the displacement of all such assemblages by a newly constructed entity given the name "the people." The subsequent history of plebiscitary voting in France would only intensify the question of whether its institution was a moment of liberation or the enabling of a new form of despotism.[49]

III

To better understand the assumptions at work in Roederer's approach and that of his opponents, it will be helpful to turn to another controversy about electoral reform. This was the question of whether the people should elect their representatives directly or through electoral colleges. Sieyès and Roederer, for reasons already alluded to, generally preferred indirect procedures of election and appointment, in which citizens offered lists at the local level, thus selecting a smaller group of communal electors who could offer another set of lists, from which departmental officials would choose a final national list, from which representatives to the national government would be appointed.[50] On this point they ran into opposition from more democratically minded liberals such as Benjamin Constant, who objected to the distance such procedures introduced between the people and their government. Of course, introducing

---

[49] That such a line of thinking could justify the plebiscitary approval of a dictator should be no surprise. Hobbes himself, when he refashioned the *De Cive* passage about *auctoritas* and *ministerium* in *Leviathan*, had moved in just this direction: "There is no great Common-wealth, the Soveraignty whereof is in a great Assembly, which is not, as to consultations of Peace, and Warre, and making of Laws, in the same condition, as if the Government were in a Child ... And as a Child has need of a Tutor, or Protector, to preserve his Person, and Authority: So also (in great Common-wealths,) the Soveraign Assembly, in all great dangers and troubles, have need of *Custodes libertatis;* that is of Dictators, or Protectors of their Authoritie; which are as much as Temporary Monarchs; to whom for a time, they may commit the entire exercise of their Power; and have (at the end of that time) been oftner deprived thereof, than Infant Kings, by their Protectors, Regents, or any other Tutors." Cf. *On the Citizen*, 10.16 with Thomas Hobbes, *Leviathan*, ed. R. Tuck, rev. edn. (Cambridge: Cambridge University Press, 1996), chap. 19, p. 133. While Oliver Cromwell was not yet called "Lord Protector" when Hobbes was writing these words, at least one of Hobbes's readers (Wallis) saw passages such as this one as evidence of his willingness to defend Cromwell, a charge that Hobbes denied. Thomas Hobbes, *The English Works of Thomas Hobbes of Malmesbury*, 11 vols., ed. W. Molesworth (London: John Bohn, 1840), IV, pp. 413–424.

[50] Roederer, *The Spirit of the Revolution*, p. xxvii. Rosanvallon, *Democracy Past and Future*, p. 83; Hont, "Permanent Crisis of a Divided Mankind," p. 477.

this distance was exactly what the Hobbesian strategy followed by Roederer demanded. The people as they existed in their localities needed to demonstrate that they retained sovereign authority without straying too close to the domain of national administration for which they were, by virtue of their localism, ill suited. Pierre Rosanvallon notes that the structure of indirect elections adopted during the revolutionary period, in which the people who participated in the first and most inclusive stage of electing were not even called "electors," served to institutionalize the difference between holding authority as citizens and playing any role in governing or administration: "The distinctive quality of the revolutionary period is to have to a great extent dissociated the register of citizenship from that of the exercise of popular power."[51]

Constant opposed this extent of dissociation when he objected, as he frequently did, to the system of indirect election. An associate of both Sieyès and Roederer, Constant nevertheless publicly broke with them on this point. Much of the material for his later works on political theory, especially *Principles of Politics Applicable to All Representative Governments* (1815), came from a manuscript he had composed earlier and never published, now known under the title *Fragments d'un ouvrage abandonné sur la possibilité d'une constitution républicaine dans un grand pays*. In that work we can see that he specifically had Roederer in mind when he wrote on the topic of direct elections. He wrote of the need to refute a set of "absurd arguments" that had been made in defense of aristocracy, apparently referring to a pamphlet of Roederer's in which the latter had argued that the form of government trumpeted by Constant as new – "representative government" – was simply a form of elective aristocracy.[52] To rebut Roederer's concerns that direct elections would bring the tumult of mob politics, Constant drew upon his own experiences in England watching political campaigns. He admitted that he had witnessed rough-and-tumble local politics during the run-up to direct elections; he conceded the presence of clamors and violent disputes, especially among members of the lower classes. But he insisted that these happenings did not detract from the quality of the people elected and that they did not spill over into ordinary life after the election. On the day after the vote, he recounted, the same people who had been engaged in the disputes became "hardworking, docile and respectful, satisfied with having exercised their rights . . . [and] convinced of their political importance." He condemned the passivity of the French people, attributed it to their long

[51] Rosanvallon, *Democracy Past and Future*, p. 140.
[52] Benjamin Constant, *Fragments D'un Ouvrage Abandonné Sur La Possibilité D'une Constitution Républicaine Dans Un Grand Pays* (Paris: Aubier, 1991), pp. 304, 481 n.56.

oppression, and argued that "in order for the spirit of liberty to penetrate to a people's soul" it was necessary to allow room for the "stormy and noisy" popular forms of participation.[53] He insisted that "citizens are interested in their institutions only when they are called to participate in them with their votes."[54] Germaine de Staël also voiced support for direct elections in some of her writings, arguing that "a choice made directly by the people, and subjected to a fair qualification in point of property, is infinitely more favourable to the energy of a free government. A nation becomes attached to its representatives when it has chosen them itself: but when obliged to confine itself to the electing of those who are to elect in their turn, the artificial combination casts a damp on its interest."[55]

In response to the concern that people voting locally would prioritize their local or sectional interests over the general good, Constant developed several arguments. He first insisted that the reasoning was too "metaphysical."[56] By this he meant that it relied too heavily on the notion of generality, privileging the general interest, general legislation, and so on, assuming that the generality of a sovereign will would guarantee its justice. He denied that the general interest was wholly separate from and opposed to particular interests. "What is the general interest, if not the transactions at work among the particular interests? What is the general representation, if not the representation of all the partial interests that must compromise about objects that are theirs in common?" He argued that general and particular interests were not opposed in a zero-sum game, but instead that the former emerged only from the latter, from both sectional and individual interests as they encountered one another in the assemblies of representatives deliberating together. If one began with an overly abstract notion of unity at the top, instead of allowing a common good to emerge from the bottom, one risked imposing a uniform solution that would not be appropriate to particular situations.[57]

---

[53] Ibid., p. 319. It is relevant to note that Constant had read Machiavelli's *Discourses on Livy* with some attentiveness.

[54] Constant, *Principles of Politics*, book 15, chapter 5, p. 332.

[55] Staël, *Considerations*, part II, chap. 22, p. 278. Staël's use of the word "energy" in this way is striking, and seems similar to the word's usage in Tocqueville's writings. For other examples in Staël, see "The first quality of a nation that begins to weary of exclusive and arbitrary governments is energy. Other virtues can be only the gradual result of institutions which have lasted long enough to form a public spirit" (p. 630) and "that energy of independence which can resist everything upon earth and prostrate itself only before God" (p. 754). For the use of "energy" in Tocqueville see B. Berger, *Attention Deficit Democracy: The Paradox of Civic Engagement* (Princeton: Princeton University Press, 2011), chap. 4.

[56] It is interesting to note that Napoleon also associated Roederer with "metaphysics." By Roederer's own account the emperor would tease him by greeting him with the question, "How goes metaphysics?" See Roederer, *The Spirit of the Revolution*, p. xvi.

[57] Constant, *Fragments D'un Ouvrage Abandonné*, pp. 309–10.

From this perspective Constant defended not only direct elections, but also federalism and, later, the importance of municipalities.[58] Most significantly, however, he developed his own treatment of a theme that his hero, Montesquieu, had touched upon only briefly: the dangers of uniformity.[59] Initially drafted as a part of *Fragments*, the passages that Constant drafted on this topic took on new importance when he included and amplified them in his anti-Napoleonic writings years later, *The Spirit of Conquest and Usurpation* (1814) and *Principles of Politics Applicable to All Representative Governments* (1815). Roederer, while working for Napoleon, had moved in a strongly social-scientific direction, and was ready to view uniformity as a mark of rationality. Similarly, for Sieyès, the most likely alternative to enlightened uniformity was "a chaos of local customs, regulations and prohibitions in each locality."[60] Constant answered this line of thought with a powerful defense of local habits and communities. In no sense reactionary, without a trace of patience for unjust customs and prejudices such as those that supported slavery, Constant nevertheless argued that slow processes of local social development would be, in general, more effective and ultimately more progressive than uniform regulations imposed from above. He remarked upon the greater likelihood of developing a "sentiment of liberty" in communal settings and also noted that more robust forms of patriotism were rooted in local allegiances. His account of the spirit of the commune was not essentially different from Tocqueville's later description of the spirit of the township in America, though it was less developed. In attempting to liberate individuals from local ties and prejudices, Constant argued, the state would be doing harm to one of its own prerequisites:

How bizarre that those who called themselves ardent friends of freedom have worked relentlessly to destroy the natural basis of patriotism, to replace it with a false passion for an abstract being, for a general idea deprived of everything which strikes the imagination and speaks to memory! How bizarre that to build an edifice, they have begun by crushing and reducing to powder all the materials they needed to use . . .

[Individuals,] detached from their native soil, with no contact with the past, living only in a swift-moving present and thrown like atoms on a monotonous plain, take no interest in a fatherland they nowhere perceive and whose totality

---

[58] Benjamin Constant, *Principles of Politics Applicable to All Representative Governments*, in *Political Writings*, ed. B. Fontana (Cambridge: Cambridge University Press, 1988), chap. 12.

[59] Charles de Secondat baron de Montesquieu, *The Spirit of the Laws*, ed. A. M. Cohler, B. C. Miller, and H. S. Stone (Cambridge: Cambridge University Press, 1989), book 29.

[60] *Archives Parlementaires*, VIII, p. 593.

becomes indifferent to them, because their affection cannot rest on any of its parts.[61]

In this passage Constant came upon the link between statist uniformity (based on the notion of a nation as an "abstract being") and the rise of individuals as entities "detached [from one another] . . . like atoms."[62] Thus we find in one of the first liberals the complaint about atomized individualism that has so often been wielded *against* liberalism. Constant's joint condemnation of statism and atomization, implicitly recognizing the link between them, was, however, only the first of his complaints against the kind of indirect popular sovereignty that Roederer introduced.

Constant's second complaint was that establishing too great a distance between a government and its constituents, based on too abstract an understanding of what a "nation" should be, was dangerous because it opened the door to the usurpation of popular sovereignty by particular individuals or groups claiming to speak for the nation as a whole. Maistre had already noted this problem in his *Considerations on France*, when he had remarked, of the 1795 constitution's emphasis on the nation, "a wonderfully convenient word, since one makes of it whatever one wishes."[63] What was a quip in Maistre became, in Constant, a far-reaching argument about the inherent potential for abuse in any understanding of popular sovereignty that was so abstracted from actual communities.[64] Constant readily conceded that the principle of popular sovereignty was not false: Where else could sovereignty lie but in the people?, he asked in chapter one of *Principles of Politics*. But he thought that the notion was most useful in its negative moment, as what he called a "principle of constitutional guarantee," which meant that it aimed "to prevent any individual from seizing the authority which belongs only to the political society as a whole."[65] Once the phrase "popular sovereignty" took on a

[61] Constant, *Principles of Politics*, book 15, chap. 3, p. 326.

[62] Another mention of individuals as atoms occurs in a passage arguing against the concentration of authority in the national capital: "The individuals, lost in an unnatural isolation, strangers to the place of their birth, cut off from all contact with the past, forced to live in a hurried present, scattered like atoms over an immense, flat plain, detach themselves from a fatherland which they can nowhere perceive, and whose whole becomes indifferent to them because they cannot place their affections in any of its parts" (Ibid., chap. 12, p. 255).

[63] Maistre, *Considerations on France*, p. 36.

[64] This should not be taken to imply any general agreement between Maistre and Constant. In fact they were political enemies. Maistre's *Considerations on France* seems to have been written largely in response to Constant's 1797 pamphlet, *De la force du gouvernement actuel*. Constant replied in his 1799 work on the English revolution, *De suites de la contre-révolution de 1660 en Angleterre*. See K. S. Vincent, *Benjamin Constant and the Birth of French Liberalism* (New York: Palgrave Macmillan, 2011), pp. 92–3.

[65] Constant, *Principles of Politics*, book 1, chap. 3, p. 11.

more positive valence – once it was thought to be a "principle of government" – it would be seized upon by all sorts of politicians ambitious for
rule:

When, for example, a mistaken majority oppresses the minority or, which happens
far more often, when a ferocious and noisy minority seizes the name of the
majority to tyrannize society, to what does it lay claim in justification of its
outrages? The sovereignty of the people, the power of society over its members.[66]

Constant remarked that the understanding of popular sovereignty derived
from Hobbes and Rousseau eschewed all external checks on authority.
While Montesquieu had sought to restrain authority with the simple idea
that "justice exists before the laws," the new view of popular sovereignty
insisted on the "total handing over of every aspect of our lives to the
advantage of an abstract entity." We were supposed to be reassured that
this authority would not be abused by seeing that it had to be wholly
general in both its source and its application, that "each person, giving himself to everyone else, gives himself to no one."[67] The purifying
effect of generality was meant to distinguish the sovereign and its actions
from everyday policies advanced by particular people in government, and
to give them special legitimacy. Constant was suspicious of the "metaphysics" of generality and regarded the distinction between sovereignty
and government as "oversubtle."[68] He pointed out that a general concept
of the popular will had no agency until it was represented by some particular person or group. As soon as it was so represented, the sovereign
power lost all the qualities of generality that were supposed to prevent its
being abused:

He [Rousseau] forgets that all the life-preserving properties which he confers on
the abstract being he calls sovereignty, are born in the fact that this being is made
up of all the separate individuals without exception. Now, as soon as the sovereign
body has to use the force it possesses, that is to say, as soon as it is necessary to
establish political authority, since the sovereign body cannot exercise this itself,
it delegates and all its properties disappear. The action carried out in the name
of all, being necessarily willy-nilly in the hands of one individual or a few people,
it follows that in handing yourself over to everyone else, it is certainly not true
that you are giving yourself to no one. On the contrary, it is to surrender yourself
to those who act in the name of all.[69]

---

[66] Ibid., book 17, chap. 1, p. 384.   [67] Ibid., book 1, chaps. 3–4, pp. 10, 15.
[68] Ibid., chap. 4, p. 16. See B. Garsten, "Benjamin Constant's Liberalism and the Political
   Theology of the General Will," in J. Farr and D. L. Williams (eds.), *The General Will: The
   Evolution of a Concept*, (Cambridge: Cambridge University Press, 2015), pp. 382–401.
[69] Constant, *Principles of Politics*, book 1, chap. 4, p. 16.

The fact that sovereignty could not be exercised except through delegation meant that, in practice, any distinction between sovereignty and government was academic, "a chimera." Any part of sovereign power that could not be exercised was not in fact a power at all, and any part that could be exercised was bound to be exercised by particular people, with all of their particularities and faults. The insistence that sovereign authority is unlimited amounted, in practice, to a justification of unlimited *governmental* authority. Constant located in Hobbes the basic argument that "democracy is an absolute sovereignty placed in the hands of everyone" and argued that French authors such as Molé had merely "reproduced" Hobbes's arguments, though with less profundity. The basic error in this whole line of thinking, he asserted, was to imagine that one could give unlimited authority to any entity, even a fictional one, without helping to justify arbitrary rule by particular people claiming to represent that entity.[70]

One might think that well-structured plebiscites could avoid this problem by fixing one authorized means of determining the popular will, thus closing the door on dubious interpretations of public opinion by its self-appointed prophets. However, plebiscites raised problems of their own. First, of course, there was the simple matter of fraud, which seems to have been widespread and quite significant during Napoleon's rule.[71] Second, plebiscites could be, and were, implemented without accompanying guarantees for freedom of association, opposition political parties, and a free press. In fact, such guarantees were often decried as contributors to the distortion of popular opinion for reasons similar to the ones Roederer had raised against clubs. In the absence of an active civil society, the results of plebiscites gave to "public opinion" a uniformity that did not do justice to the actual variety and substance of opinions in the public.[72] And, when police power was in evidence, the apparently free votes of a majority reflected little more than the desires of those who

---

[70] Ibid., chaps. 5–8.   [71] Crook, "The Plebiscite on the Empire."

[72] Hannah Arendt captured the spirit of this objection to plebiscites: "Opinion was discovered by both the French and American revolutions, but only the latter . . . knew how to build a lasting institution for the formation of public views into the very structure of the republic. What the alternative was, we know only too well from the course of the French Revolution and of those that followed it. In all these instances, the chaos of unrepresented and unpurified opinions, because there existed no medium to pass them through, crystalized into a variety of conflicting mass sentiments under the pressure of emergency, waiting for a 'strong man' to mould them into a unanimous 'public opinion,' which spelled death to all opinions. In actual fact, the alternative was the plebiscite, the only institution which corresponds closely to the unbridled rule of public opinion; and just as public opinion is the death of opinions, the plebiscite puts an end to the citizen's right to vote, to choose and to control their government" (H. Arendt, *On Revolution* (New York: Penguin Books, 1963), p. 228).

controlled the power. When Napoleon restricted discussion and the press, noticed Constant, "the nation might have been stunned by that silence." Napoleon's response? "He provided, extorted or paid for acclamation which sounded like the national voice."[73]

Constant thus saw in Napoleon's use of plebiscites the seed of a wholly new form of despotism, one that penetrated more deeply into people's lives precisely because it rested on "the counterfeiting of liberty" in voting. Napoleon's despotism was worse than hereditary rule, Constant argued, because the usurper felt compelled to justify his position and so forced the people to express their support for him. "There is no limit to the tyranny that seeks to exact all the signs of consent," he observed.[74] As Melvin Richter has shown, this analysis was part of the development of a new understanding of illegitimacy in nineteenth-century France, one that culminated in the identification of a type of regime that was called, alternately, "democratic despotism" or "imperialism" or "Caesarism" or, once it had been repeated by Napoleon III, "Bonapartism." Melvin Richter defines the type in this way: "a form of military usurpation historically novel because it based its legitimacy upon plebiscitary approval, and hence popular sovereignty as proclaimed during the French Revolution."[75] When the issue arose again later in the century, Tocqueville repeated the diagnosis in a letter describing the rise of Louis Napoleon to an American. Everyone saw, he wrote, "that in the name of the sovereignty of the nation all public liberties have been destroyed, that the appearance of a popular election has served to establish a despotism which is more absolute than any of those which have appeared in France before."[76]

For the argument of this chapter, the most relevant and theoretical point is that this kind of election fraud and manufacturing of consent were made possible, and perhaps even likely, by the abstractness of the conception of "the people" that plebiscites institutionalized. When the voice of the people was conceived as an aggregate number of votes in support of a leader, rather than more substantive expressions of policy by coherent groups with identifiable perspectives and interests, the precise meaning of any electoral outcome was harder to identify; debates about what an election offered a "mandate" for allowed charismatic leaders

---

[73] Constant, *Political Writings*, p. 163.

[74] Benjamin Constant, *The Spirit of Conquest and Usurpation*, in ibid., chap. 3, pp. 44–169, at p. 95.

[75] M. Richter, "Toward a Concept of Political Illegitimacy: Bonapartist Dictatorship and Democratic Legitimacy," *Political Theory* 10.2 (May 1982), pp. 185–214, at p. 196.

[76] J. Jennings, *Revolution and the Republic: A History of Political Thought in France since the Eighteenth Century* (Oxford: Oxford University Press, 2013), p. 188.

to more easily present themselves as the agents of popular sovereignty. As Istvan Hont points out, the conception of the people as an imagined social contract among hypothesized individuals "undercut . . . traditional notions of popular sovereignty. In 'pre-state' idioms of popular government, it was the actual flesh-and-blood commonality of the people that controlled ultimate decision making . . . The idea of the 'state' destroyed the theory and practice of direct popular legitimation, as upheld previously by republicans and monarchomachs."[77] From Constant's liberal democratic perspective, Roederer's overly "metaphysical" understanding of what qualified a people to be a legitimate sovereign – an understanding rooted in Hobbes's and Rousseau's notions of the difference between popular sovereignty and popular government or administration – had opened the door to the rejection of local practices of republican politics and to the abuse of democratic language and institutions, both central features of Napoleonic despotism.

IV

Even as liberals such as Constant were suggesting that a Hobbesian interpretation of democracy could fuel plebiscitary despotism, they themselves were being attacked for helping to defend other forms of undemocratic politics. In particular, liberals were often described as "aristocratic," a label that has been revived by recent commentators.[78] There is truth in the label, and not just because writers such as de Staël and de Tocqueville were associated with aristocratic families and harbored aristocratic sentiments. The crucial point is that the liberals adopted patterns of argument against the state very similar to those that nobles had used to defend themselves against the Crown. If we were to accept that the state was the best or only way to enact popular sovereignty, then these liberal and anti-statist arguments would indeed be anti-democratic. The best response that can be made on behalf of these liberals from a democratic perspective, therefore, is that they did not accept the notion that the state was a desirable way to institutionalize popular sovereignty. As we shall now see, some liberals sought to escape this frame of thought by showing that a different kind of popular self-rule was possible, within the confines of the state but not solely through its mediation; they sought to show how a society transformed by the state could produce forms of popular self-rule that did not work through the consolidated agency of the state.

---

[77] Hont, "Permanent Crisis of a Divided Mankind," p. 465.

[78] Jaume, *Tocqueville*; A. De Dijn, *French Political Thought from Montesquieu to Tocqueville: Liberty in a Levelled Society?* (Cambridge: Cambridge University Press, 2011 [2008]); A. S. Kahan, *Aristocratic Liberalism: The Social and Political Thought of Jacob Burckhardt, John Stuart Mill, and Alexis de Tocqueville* (New York: Oxford University Press, 1992).

The aristocratic argument that the post-revolutionary liberals took up had its *locus classicus* in Montesquieu's *The Spirit of the Laws*. Montesquieu had advanced a powerful case against the centralization of authority in the royal court. What distinguished a legitimate monarch from a despot, he had famously argued, was that legitimate monarchies did not try to eliminate the intermediary bodies between them and the people, especially the Church and the nobles. As he stipulated near the beginning of his work, "Intermediate, subordinate, and dependent powers constitute the nature of monarchical government, that is, of the government in which one alone governs by fundamental laws."[79] Montesquieu's account of the separation of powers and checks and balances in England reflected the same sympathy for the social world and its authorities, in that it granted distinct places in government to representatives of the various corporate parts of society. Montesquieu had gone so far as to argue that monarchies that incorporated various social authorities into government through complex institutional checks, including the famous separation of powers, would protect freedom better than republics that had centralized authority in one council. "In the Italian republics," he wrote, "where the three powers are united, there is less liberty than in our monarchies."[80]

After the Revolution, habits of resisting the centralization of power in a modernizing monarchy were transferred easily enough into the campaign against the administrative centralization of a modernizing representative state. In making his case for a plurality of authorities, Montesquieu had asked his readers to imagine that they found themselves on the wrong side of the monarchy, and unjustly. To whom would they turn for help, if the monarch were the only authority in the land? The nobility offered at least a source of resistance to the Crown. Constant, in his manuscript on the possibility of a republican government in a large state, had followed the spirit of Montesquieu's original point, remarking that if there had to be a king, it would be better to have a nobility too, "because where a sole individual governs, it is desirable that there are other powerful men to stand up to him."[81] It is interesting to notice that when Constant briefly served under Napoleon during the Hundred Days of his return, he even suggested establishing a new hereditary nobility – a suggestion he later admitted had been ill-considered.[82] The impulse, however fleeting, reveals a deep concern about allowing any centralized authority to

---

[79] Montesquieu, *The Spirit of the Laws*, part 1, book 2, chap. 4, p. 17. Cf. Benjamin Constant, *Usurpation*, chap. 2, p. 88.
[80] Montesquieu, *The Spirit of the Laws*, part 2, book 11, chap. 6, p. 157.
[81] Constant, *Fragments D'un Ouvrage Abandonné*, p. 196.
[82] J. T. Levy, "Montesquieu's Constitutional Legacies," in R. E. Kingston (ed.), *Montesquieu and His Legacy* (New York: State University of New York Press, 2008), pp. 115–138, at pp. 129–30.

be unchecked. While Constant agreed with revolutionary authors who found Montesquieu's approach too closely linked to feudalism, he found a way to adapt the argument to republican contexts. He argued that directly elected local representatives could offer the kind of resistance to centralized state power that nobles had offered. The representatives' authority no longer came from inherited privilege; it came from their "inviolable credentials for opposing the government," i.e. from the fact of having been directly elected.[83] The concrete allegiances of local communal life also created nodes of authority that could resist centralization, he observed: "The interests and memories that arise from local customs contain a germ of resistance that authority is reluctant to tolerate and that it is anxious to eradicate. It can deal more successfully with individuals; it rolls its heavy body effortlessly over them as if they were sand."[84] Constant thus suggested that healthy local politics, especially in cities, could recreate the benefits of feudal social plurality without reinstituting its unjust hierarchies and dominations.[85]

It is not hard to see that Alexis de Tocqueville further adapted the same argument in *Democracy in America*. In speaking of popular sovereignty, Tocqueville depicted the danger of its domination in the Montesquieuian way, asking to whom an individual could turn if there were no authority other than that of the majority.[86] While he was somewhat interested in constitutional issues, he did not have as much faith as Constant did in the institutional arrangements of federalism and checks and balances to resist what he frankly called a "tyranny of the majority." Instead, he pointed to other locations of informal social authority – to lawyers, with their "aristocratic character," to individual rights which are "taken from

---

[83] Constant, *Principles of Politics*, book 15, chap. 5, p. 332. He noted that he was adapting old regime arguments in other ways too, e.g.: "The benefits of feudalism have sometimes been praised for keeping the lord in the midst of his vassals and sharing out the opulence equally between all the parts of the territory. Popular election has the same desirable effect without entailing the same abuses" (p. 330).

[84] Benjamin Constant, *The Spirit of Conquest*, chapter 13 in *Political Writings*, p. 74.

[85] Jacob Levy sums up Constant's stance well: "Constant's constitutional project was one of trying to simulate or recreate the benefits of a Montesquieuian ancient constitution in an age when that constitution's social bases were lost and anachronistic" (Levy, "Montesquieu's Constitutional Legacies," p. 130).

[86] Alexis de Tocqueville, *Democracy in America*, trans. H. C. Mansfield and D. Winthrop (Chicago: University of Chicago Press, 2002), 1.2.7, p. 241: "When a man or party suffers from an injustice in the United States, whom do you want to address? Public opinion? that is what forms the majority; the legislative body? it represents the majority and obeys it blindly; the executive power? it is named by the majority and serves as its passive instrument; the public forces? the public forces are nothing other than the majority in arms; the jury? the jury is the majority vested with the right to pronounce decrees: in certain states, the judges themselves are elected by the majority. Therefore, however iniquitous or unreasonable is the measure that strikes you, you must submit to it."

the English aristocracy," and to religion, which is "the most precious inheritance from aristocratic centuries."[87] In each of these discussions the word "aristocratic" designates a source of possible resistance to the centralization of power. There, in brief, is the case for Tocqueville's "aristocratic" liberalism.[88]

To many revolutionaries, arguments such as these seemed vestiges of the old regime and obstacles to its downfall. During the Revolution Montesquieu had been denounced as a "Gothic" or "feudal" thinker and the English system he praised had been regarded as, at best, a noble effort at republicanism that had stalled halfway through. Montesquieu's arguments, and the versions of them we find in Constant, Tocqueville, and other liberals, seemed merely a return to the apparent justifications of the old regime that could be found in Grotius's and Pufendorf's sympathetic descriptions of "society," and in the compilations of their writings that circulated so widely.[89] The state, after all, was meant to be the agent of revolutionary change, and society remained the realm of aristocratic privilege and religious hierarchy. To argue against the state in the name of society, as liberals often did, could therefore seem to be a very familiar form of aristocratic self-justification. Roederer, for example, had argued against the view that the people needed intermediary bodies to protect them, preferring to put his faith in the enlightenment and democratic sympathies of the central authorities.[90] And if revolutionaries viewed the liberal arguments as old-fashioned, so too did many legitimists; Tocqueville's *Democracy in America* received a warm reaction from some conservatives who focused on its restatement of Montesquieuian themes.[91]

What both revolutionaries and conservatives who saw only the aristocratic aspect of the liberals missed was the fact that Constant and Tocqueville had reconciled themselves to, and in some ways actively welcomed, the coming of democracy. Tocqueville, the less enthusiastic of the two, famously regarded democratization as a "providential fact."[92] His goal was not to return to aristocratic times, nor even to create a government that mixed democratic and aristocratic elements; he described the idea of mixed government as a "chimera."[93] Instead of returning to prerevolutionary politics, he aimed to find a new means of preventing

---

[87] Ibid., 1.2.8, p. 254; 2.4.4, p. 648; 2.2.15, p. 519.

[88] The case for liberalism's aristocratic *sources* is much richer. See Jaume, *Tocqueville*.

[89] The association of these thinkers with the old regime comes mainly from Rousseau, who targeted Grotius in his *Social Contract* and Pufendorf in his *Discourse on the Origins of Inequality*. Rousseau, *The Social Contract*, book 1, chaps. 2–5. See R. Wokler, *Rousseau, the Age of Enlightenment, and their Legacies*, ed. B. Garsten (Princeton: Princeton University Press, 2012), chap. 6.

[90] Roederer, *Œuvres*, VII, p. 20.   [91] Jaume, *Tocqueville*, pp. 15 ff.

[92] Tocqueville, *Democracy in America*, pp. 6–7.   [93] Ibid., 1.2.7, p. 240.

despotism that was appropriate for a democratic age. This is what he meant when he wrote, in a one-sentence paragraph in the introduction to *Democracy in America*, that, "a new political science is needed for a world altogether new."[94]

What Tocqueville claimed to find in America was a situation in which defending "society" did not necessarily mean defending the dominations and hierarchies of feudal life, nor even defending all the new hierarchies of bourgeois life. "Society" was no longer synonymous with "inequality." Tocqueville's entire social science depended on that fact, which is why he announced early on that he had found in America a "democratic social state."[95] He understood a social state to be the "first cause of most of the laws, customs, and ideas that regulate the conduct of nations." Sciences understand first causes, and he announced that to understand America it was above all necessary to see that "the social state of the Americans is eminently democratic" and that "not even the seed of aristocracy was ever deposited" in New England.[96] The phrase "social state" (*l'état social*) in Tocqueville's writings was not new; Roederer, for instance, had used it in his translation of Hobbes's *De Cive* to translate *societas*, the social world in which people found themselves, and Lucien Jaume has found the phrase in Constant and Guizot, among others.[97] It was almost unheard of, however, to speak of a "democratic" social state. Tocqueville's claim that a general "equality of conditions" could be found in American society, and that this equality had emerged developmentally and not only through the revolutionary action of a state, was the crucial and distinctive part of his argument. This is what allowed a defense of society to escape the aristocratic register.

To fully escape the dilemmas about popular sovereignty that had mired Roederer and others in difficulties, however, it was necessary not only to show that equality did not need to be constantly reproduced by a centralized power, but also that democratic self-rule did not always, or even primarily, manifest itself through the consolidated agency of a sovereign representative. In the first volume of *Democracy in America* Tocqueville placed great emphasis on both the religious and associational practices he had seen in New England towns. These two sets of practices had been indissolubly linked together in the Puritan settlements of colonial America, which Tocqueville claimed represented the "point of departure" for understanding American democracy and, even more, constituted "the

---

[94] Ibid., p. 7. See B. Garsten, "Seeing 'Not Differently, but Further, than the Parties,'" in S. R. Krause and M. A. McGrail (eds.), *The Arts of Rule: Essays in Honor of Harvey C. Mansfield* (Lanham, MD: Lexington Books, 2009), pp. 359–76.

[95] Tocqueville, *Democracy in America*, 1.1.5, p. 45.   [96] Ibid., 1.1.3, pp. 45–6.

[97] Roederer, *Œuvres*, p. 306n. (Hobbes's note). Jaume, *Tocqueville*, p. 83.

password to the great social enigma that the United States presents to the world in our day." He was struck by the fact that citizens of colonial Connecticut had legislated *for themselves* but that they had done so *using* religious texts and authorities. This, he thought, was a "strange idea."[98] The strangeness was that the Americans had found a way to combine a social authority (religion) with the political authority of the people without inscribing the social authority into government and thereby politicizing it. Tocqueville's complicated account of American religious authority aimed to show that ordinary citizens wielded authority over themselves directly. They gave the name of "religion" to this self-regulation, and even gave credit to religious texts and leaders, but in fact their practice revealed that they themselves were the active source of restraint on themselves. "If one looks very closely," Tocqueville wrote, "one will see that religion itself reigns there much less as revealed doctrine than as common opinion."[99] No church had political authority, yet religion functioned as an informal "political institution."[100] For Tocqueville religion in America was not, as commentators sometimes suggest, an authority wholly separate from majority rule; nor was it always a check upon it. Instead, religion in America was a manifestation of the way that the people exercised a kind of sovereignty over themselves *within* civil society and through its internal dynamics, rather than through an external tool such as the state.[101]

The other famous location of civil self-regulation in Tocqueville's account was associational life. Associations lived entirely outside the constitutionally mandated structures of government in America; they were voluntary; they came with no obviously hierarchical principles of authority; and yet they offered, Tocqueville thought, some of the benefits that the nobles' secondary bodies had offered in the old regime.[102] They differentiated the otherwise homogeneous landscape of social life into a pluralistic world where someone oppressed by one group or by the state might find refuge and voice opposition. Because they were constituted in a more democratic fashion, however, associations also offered training in democratic habits of mind and action; they offered training in persuasion. Unlike political associations in Europe, which were viewed as "weapons

---

[98] Tocqueville, *Democracy in America*, 1.1.2, p. 104.
[99] Ibid., 2.1.2, p. 404.   [100] Ibid., 1.2.9, pp. 301–2.
[101] Garsten, "Seeing 'Not Differently, but Further.'" See P. Manent, *Tocqueville and the Nature of Democracy* (Lanham, MD: Rowman & Littlefield, 1996).
[102] Tocqueville, *Democracy in America*, 1.2.4, pp. 183–4: "In aristocratic nations, secondary bodies form natural associations that halt abuses of power. In countries where such associations do not exist, if particular persons cannot create artificially and temporarily something that resembles them, I no longer perceive a dike of any sort against tyranny."

of war" through which a group aimed to make its claim to speak for the people as a whole and so gain sovereign authority, associations in America implicitly conceded that they did not speak for the whole; they aimed not to supplant or speak for the majority, but to persuade it. And all of this occurred in a regime of unlimited freedom of association, without the regulations on societies that Roederer had thought necessary. This was possible in America because universal suffrage made it implausible for associations to pretend they represented the national will better than the government, and because the relative homogeneity of public opinion left no group so alienated that they could not imagine persuading others. In Tocqueville's account, associations demonstrated that corporate entities in society could offer a check on the state without standing in the way of democratization. American associations, like American religions, showed that "society" was not always a regressive or aristocratic force.[103]

Tocqueville thought the civil self-regulation evident in religion, in towns, and in associational life had helped to make possible an astonishing administrative decentralization – an apparent absence of the state in everyday life:

> What most strikes the European who travels through the United States is the absence of what is called among us government or administration. In America you see written laws; you perceive their daily execution; everything moves around you and nowhere do you discover the motor. The hand that directs the social machine vanishes at each instant . . .
>
> The administrative power of the United States offers in its constitution nothing central or hierarchical; that is what causes one not to perceive it. Power exists, but one does not know where to find its representative . . .
>
> Thus nowhere does there exist a center at which the spokes of administrative power converge.[104]

Tocqueville went on to raise and answer the questions that he thought any European would have about how such a system works: how are officials held accountable on matters of general concern? (Americans use a combination of electoral accountability from below and judicial authority from the county level, eschewing administrative oversight from the center.) Is there enough authority in the central government to allow the pursuit of a common good? (There is very strong "governmental centralization" even though there is no "administrative centralization," and because the government represents the majority, there is no recognized check on it.) Isn't it the case that a rationalized and centralized government can administer localities more effectively and more justly than localities could manage for themselves? (Not when the people are

---

[103] Ibid., 1.2.4, pp. 184–6.   [104] Ibid., 1.1.5, pp. 67–9.

"enlightened, awakened to their interests, and habituated to thinking about them as they are in America.")[105]

If a Hobbesian understanding of popular sovereignty conceived of the people as "sleeping" during the time they allowed representatives to administer or govern for them, Tocqueville's understanding required a people very much awake, as he thought the Americans were.[106] He admitted to not knowing how to reproduce that wakefulness in France: "It is difficult to point out in a sure manner the means of awakening a people that sleeps," he lamented.[107] He thought the French were passive and despot-prone, in part because they had resorted to the alienated agency of the state to enact their effort at holding sovereignty. Americans, in contrast, did not need to create an artificial authority built upon an abstraction from concrete social life in order to free themselves from social inequality or find a kind of democratic agency. That freedom and agency had come more or less on its own, the product of a seven-hundred year process of historical development and the unique geographical and historical position of the country, and it was preserved in habits and mores. When Tocqueville stated, in his introduction to *Democracy in America*, that "a great democratic revolution is taking place among us," he chose his verb carefully: He did not say, "we are in the midst of accomplishing a great democratic revolution." He thus went one step beyond Constant in his estimation of civil society's potential for self-regulation. In Constant's thought, society could be a lively source of political opinion but did not take on the function of actually governing until it somehow occupied state or municipal institutions, becoming what he referred to as "the social authority." This is why Constant granted more agency to the revolutionaries than Tocqueville did. For Tocqueville, the revolution had come, and the task of politics now was not to accomplish or consolidate it but to grapple with its implications.

Among those implications was the actualization in real life of the atomized individualism that social contract theory had merely hypothesized, an individualism that Tocqueville, like Constant, thought too hospitable to despotic leaders and docile citizens. The structure of political life should aim to balance against, rather than institutionalize, this individualism. A single representation of the nation in government could not do that:

America's lawmakers did not believe that, to cure a malady so natural to the social body in democratic times and so fatal, it was enough to accord to the nation as a whole a representation of itself; they thought that, in addition, it was fitting to

[105] Ibid., 1.1.5, pp. 69–92.   [106] Hobbes, *On the Citizen*, 7.16, pp. 99–100.
[107] Tocqueville, *Democracy in America*, 1.1.5, p. 86.

give political life to each portion of the territory in order to multiply infinitely the occasions for citizens to act together and to make them feel every day that they depend on one another.[108]

The statist model of popular sovereignty relied on the identification of oneself with the national vote or the leaders and policies selected by it. Tocqueville insisted that the classic problem of republicanism – to bring citizens to identify the public good as their own – was better addressed by involving as many citizens as possible in "the administration of small affairs."[109] Voting in elections to demonstrate one's authority was not enough; involvement in administration (*ministerium*) was necessary too.

Tocqueville never suggested that America was not a state or that it should not be one. The mirage of social self-sufficiency never tempted him as it would tempt Karl Marx, who radicalized the liberals' argument for limiting the state into a deeper critique of its very existence.[110] Tocqueville did worry that the tendency of democratic life would make the centralization of administrative authority attractive, perhaps too attractive ultimately for even the Americans to resist. For the time being, however, he thought he spied practices that could, if interpreted correctly, challenge the tendency to always identify popular sovereignty with state authority. The example of America suggested that a modern state could be structured in such a way as to incorporate local practices of self-rule in society. In a letter to his father from America about American towns, he described the achievement he thought he had found: "that is how they made the republic practical. Individual ambition finds within reach everywhere a small focus where it can act without danger to the state."[111]

That, in a nutshell, was the possibility that Hobbes and his followers had denied. American social–political life demonstrated, the young Tocqueville hoped, that self-interest, ambition, and pride could be channeled in productive ways, reinforcing civic habits of mind and action rather than always threatening factional conflict and encouraging demagoguery in the way that Roederer had feared. The crucial implication, and the one that the whole of *Democracy in America* was originally meant to illustrate, was that the concentration of authority in a unitary state structure justified by plebiscite was not the only means by which to bring democracy into being in a large territory, and not the only form that democracy could take there. Tocqueville's liberal vision was not to replace the state with a self-governing society, but to envision the state's

---

[108] Ibid., 2.2.4, pp. 486–7.   [109] Ibid., 2.2.4, p. 481.
[110] Karl Marx, "On the Jewish Question," in *The Marx–Engels Reader*, 2nd edn. (New York: W. W. Norton & Co., 1978), pp. 26–52.
[111] As cited in Jaume, *Tocqueville*, p. 29 n. 36.

role as preserving and facilitating more substantive, local, and concrete forms of self-rule than could be enacted through the voting mechanisms of large-scale plebiscitary democracy.

Of course it is an open question whether the democratic practices that Tocqueville thought he saw in America had come about quite as easily as he suggested; he did not write much about the American Revolution. Nor did he emphasize the role that the state would have to play in continually combating the tendency of society to generate new social inequalities; he may have overestimated the strength of society's movement toward equality. He was a young man when he wrote the first volume, and he had set out for America looking for a way out of the fruitless dichotomies of French politics; by 1840, in the second volume, his focus had already shifted toward the fragility of American democracy. And even if his description of America was more or less accurate, it is another open question whether the practices he saw have lasted, or could last, beyond the particular historical moment of Andrew Jackson's America, a populist period under a weak and decentralized national government, a government that would soon find it could not survive except through a bloody assertion of its sovereignty over the South and a subsequent explosion of centralized administration. A generation earlier, Maistre had responded to writers inspired by America with a dismissively short paragraph: "America is often cited," he wrote. "I know of nothing so provoking as the praises bestowed on this babe-in-arms. Let it grow."[112] Whether America's undeniable growth away from the society and practices that Tocqueville admired indicates a fundamental flaw in the very idea of a democratic social state, or whether it is merely the product of contingencies unrelated to such theoretical questions, is a matter very much worth investigating. Constant and Tocqueville sought an understanding of popular self-rule that did not rely so heavily on the "mortal God" the Hobbesians had tried to construct. They were trying, in their theories of civil society, to find practices that could counteract the drift into despotism and docility that was, and remains, the most obvious danger in any Hobbesian account of democratic sovereignty.

---

[112] Maistre, *Considerations on France*, p. 35.

11   Popular sovereignty as state theory in the nineteenth century

Duncan Kelly

I

Popular sovereignty is more than simply an essentially contested concept, and the sheer range of its compass is amply attested in this volume. Yet even by the time it is assumed to have become foundational for modern politics in the nineteenth century, it still barely had a stable independent meaning or existence. In the celebrated lectures of John Austin, for example, published in 1832 as *The Province of Jurisprudence Determined*, we find the most explicit discussion of his so-called command theory of sovereignty, but his only concession to anything like popular sovereignty is the idea that sovereignty might, on occasion, be checked by popular opinion.[1] Equally, in the catalogues of the British Library (BL) and the Cambridge University Library (CUL), only one English-language book in the entire century bears the formulation as a title. Charles Anthony's *Popular Sovereignty: Being Some Thoughts on Popular Reform* appeared in 1880,but takes the form of a historically minded account of the primacy of a 'democratic tendency' in the English character, which helped develop principles of representative democratic government appropriate to advanced public opinion under modern liberalism.[2]

Anthony's account clearly draws on writers such as J. S. Mill, Alexis de Tocqueville and Henry Maine, but even these canonical sources rarely use the terminology of popular sovereignty. When Tocqueville notes that 'administrative despotism and sovereignty of the people' are fictions, he is hardly saying anything new about the subject, but then he hardly uses the terminology of popular sovereignty at all. He talks instead of democracy.[3]

---

[1] John Austin, *The Province of Jurisprudence Determined* (London: John Murray, 1832), p. viii.

[2] Charles Anthony, *Popular Sovereignty: Being Some Thoughts on Popular Reform* (London: Longmans, 1880), pp. 7, 9; cf. Henry Maine, *Popular Government* (Indianapolis: Liberty Fund, 1976 [1885]), p. 35.

[3] Alexis de Tocqueville, *Democracy in America*, ed. J. P. Mayer (New York: Anchor, 1969 [1835]), p. 693.

270

In fact, it looks as if the nineteenth-century victory of indirect representative sovereignty was inspired by the work of the Abbé Sieyès during the French Revolution. His claims defeated avowedly republican conceptions of popular sovereignty such as those outlined by Jacques Necker, who tied together republican politics and direct electoral authorisation by the people.[4] Sieyès's apparent victory set the tone for later discussions of the subject.

A few instances of German texts with titles including *Volkssouveränität* exist across the nineteenth century, but they are disproportionately if predictably clustered around 1848. Even then, however, most radical claims for popular sovereignty were tempered with some recognition of the validity of the monarchical principle.[5] In America, works discussing popular sovereignty tend to cluster around the 1850s and 1860s, focusing on the rights of federal states and the sovereignty of the nation in civil war and reconstruction, particularly focusing on slavery.[6] There were considerable overlaps between federal–national debates in America, Germany and Switzerland.[7] More studies exist in French considering *la souveraineté du peuple*, but the vast majority of those occur in and around the Revolution during a fecund decade of political debate, before dramatically tailing off. During the nineteenth century, again around 1848, the terminology reappeared, but often only with reference back to a revolutionary spirit of 1789.

By the time one of the most important treatises on the general theory of the state in France was published just after the Great War, Raymond Carré de Malberg's massive two-volume *Contribution à la théorie générale de l'état*, only two pages were devoted to the subject of popular sovereignty. Why? Because the major transition in thinking about sovereignty and the state during the past hundred years had been towards what Malberg sees as 'national sovereignty'.[8] Moving from the constitutional debates of the French Revolution, where the sovereignty of the

[4] M. Sonenscher, *Before the Deluge* (Princeton: Princeton University Press, 2007), p. 352.

[5] M. Hewitson, '"The Old Forms are Breaking up . . . Our New Germany is Rebuilding Itself": Constitutionalism, Nationalism and the Creation of a German Polity during the Revolutions of 1848–49', *English Historical Review* 75.116 (2010), pp. 1173–1214, esp. pp. 1183–90, 1205.

[6] Stephen Arnold Douglas, *Popular Sovereignty in the Territories: The Dividing Line between Federal and Local Authority* (New York: Harper & Brothers, 1859), p. 28; cf. C. Childers, 'Interpreting Popular Sovereignty: A Historiographical Essay', *Civil War History* 57.1 (2011), pp. 48–70.

[7] H. Dippel, 'The Changing Idea of Popular Sovereignty in Early American Constitutionalism: Breaking Away from European Patterns', *Journal of the History of the Early Republic* 16.1 (1996), pp. 21–45.

[8] Raymond Carré de Malberg, *Contribution à la théorie générale de l'état*, 2 vols. (Paris: Siery, 1920), I, esp. pp. 82–7.

nation was asserted, Malberg traces the genealogy of the legal fiction of national sovereignty. He explains that the category of sovereignty as *summa potestas*, originally vested in the monarch, was subsequently applied to the people as nation in post-revolutionary thought. But that had also been a crucial insight behind the critique of sovereignty elaborated by the Abbé Sieyès during Year III of the French Revolution, and like Sieyès, Malberg was keen to show that the sovereignty of the people refers simply to an idea or background constitution, and not to the reality of representative rule. Sovereign action by a state, or indeed by elevated bodies and organs within the state, trumps the general idea of popular sovereignty as the site of sovereign action. Sieyès made this abundantly clear in a provocative note, again written up during Year III, concerning the limits to sovereignty. After having argued that the division of labour and the separation of powers were the natural components of the term 'constitution', and that one must think of the unanimous agreement on the part of the people to be governed as a fundamental law that pre-dates any subsequent constitutional arrangements, Sieyès delivered his major claim. Just as the constitution enshrined the division of labour and a separation of powers, it was a category mistake 'to talk of the sovereignty of the people as if it had no limits'.[9] It has nothing but limits.

These limits are primarily national, and across the nineteenth century we see a move from late eighteenth-century discussions of popular sovereignty as radical democracy to the idea of an indirect sovereignty of the people under a modern national state.[10] The most adept and adroit analysts of this development were historians of the relationship between legal and political theory, many of whom took their cue from Sieyès. But precisely because of the success of this transition, best expressed in Sieyès's defence of sovereignty as indirectly representative, multiply located, and always practically divided even if in principle grounded on the nation as the source of constituent power, hardly anybody in the nineteenth century seems to have used the terminology of popular sovereignty. Instead, they looked to cognates, such as representative government, democracy or national sovereignty. Unsurprisingly, therefore, contemporary historians of the subject as well as legal and political theorists simply note that if popular sovereignty is supposed to mean

---

[9]   Emmanuel-Joseph (Abbé) Sieyès, 'Limites de la souveraineté, An III', in P. Pasquino, *Sieyès et l'invention de la constitution française* (Paris: Odile Jacob, 1998), pp. 177–80, at p. 178: 'On se trompe donc lorsqu'on parle de la souveraineté du peuple comme n'ayant point de bornes.'

[10]   B. Manin, *The Principles of Representative Democracy* (Cambridge: Cambridge University Press, 1997).

self-government in all but executive function, it remains 'an impossible fiction' or a 'dynamic fiction'.[11]

To understand the development of popular sovereignty in the nineteenth century therefore requires us to look in some apparently unusual or inauspicious places, though they are unusual and inauspicious only because of the mainstream accounts of nineteenth-century European political thought that we have become accustomed to. Arguments by writers concerned to delineate the nexus between law and politics through general theories of the state were those that most clearly focused on the problems of popular sovereignty for modern political theory, and in this, few were more important or subsequently foundational than Johann Kaspar Bluntschli (1808–81), whom my discussion will shortly address.

II

As an account of political authority and legitimacy in the later nineteenth century, the conceptual development of popular sovereignty intersects with claims about the intellectual origins of the nation-state. The combination receives an eloquent outline in Hegel's lectures on the *Grundlinien der Philosophie des Rechts*, where the modern rational nation-state (*das Volk als Staat*) is predicated upon a perfect link between people (*Volk*) and state (*Staat*). This would be a technically correct rendering of popular sovereignty. Hegel was nevertheless concerned to show that oppositional republican claims of an opposition between popular sovereignty and the sovereignty of a monarch were based on a 'garbled notion of the people'. Without its monarch, he wrote, the people remained a formless mass (*formlosse Masse*).[12] In German, *Volk* refers to a people who exist within a state, while *Nation* indicates membership of a cultural or ethical community. In English and French the implications are reversed, and the development of nationalism in French political discourse became fundamental in dethroning monarchical absolutism during the Revolution.[13]

The German language distinction, however, indicates the quite severe political implications that follow the choice between *Nation* and *Volk* in

[11] H. Laski, 'The Theory of Popular Sovereignty', *Michigan Law Review* 17.3 (1919), pp. 201–15, at p. 204; cf. E. S. Morgan, *Inventing the People: The Rise of Popular Sovereignty in England and America* (New York: Norton, 1988), p. 306.

[12] G. W. F. Hegel, *Elements of the Philosophy of Right*, ed. A. W. Wood (Cambridge: Cambridge University Press, 1991 [1821]), §§ 331, 279, pp. 366, 318 f.

[13] R. Koselleck, 'Volk, Nation, Nationalismus, Masse', in R. Koselleck and O. Brunner et al. (eds.), *Geschichtliche Grundbegriffe*, 8 vols. (Stuttgart: Klett-Cotta, 1978) VII, pp. 357–62; D. Bell, *The Cult of the Nation in France* (Cambridge, MA: Harvard University Press, 2003).

thinking about popular sovereignty. One might refer to the *Nationalsouveränität* of the *Volk*, or to the popular sovereignty (*Volkssouveränität*) of the *Nation*. Perhaps unsurprisingly, *Volkssourveränität* was the preferred term of art in the nineteenth century because this connection to the *Volk* presumed a politically organised community of people living under a state. Its counterpart, *Nationalsouveränität*, and its proximity to the *Nation* as an ethical or cultural community, signifies a lack of political organisation. Since 1830 Continental lawyers such as Bluntschli had been suggesting that the *Volk* is the material (*Stoff*) of the state, and the state is the form of the *Volk*.[14] In nineteenth-century debates this means at least two things. First, positing an account of post-revolutionary politics in Europe that makes sense of how the distinction became operative during the French Revolution. Second, connecting the idea of indirect popular sovereignty to an account of the dilemmas facing the sovereignty of the state in nineteenth-century Europe. In turn, this requires the re-description of popular sovereignty as fictitious and indirect. Taken together, these requirements help to show how it is not altogether fanciful to say that nineteenth-century developments of the idea of popular sovereignty under the nation-state were attempts to steer through dilemmas of politics that were outlined most effectively by Hobbes and Rousseau, and filtered through the writing of the Abbé Sieyès.

For Hobbes, by means of a complex mechanism of representation the individual members within a multitude, who mutually consent to a sovereign representative, are 'made *One* person' when they are represented by a unitary sovereign. This transition from mere multitude to political union or a civil state is predicated upon the '*Unity* of the Representer'. Here, the sovereign represents a new and '*Artificiall Person*' known as the state. And Hobbes's political theory from *De Cive* to *Leviathan* is very often structured around about this connection between state sovereignty and the production of a unitary collective political will of the people.[15] Each individual ceases to become their own judge in political matters, and instead is governed by this general will. It is almost precisely the same thought that Rousseau would develop, but with his added claim that popular sovereignty is inalienable even if government

---

[14] J. K. Bluntschli, *Das Volk und der Souverän im allgemeinen betrachtet und mit besondere Rücksicht auf die Schweizerischen Verhältnisse* (Zurich: Drell, Füsli & Co., 1834), pp. 6 ff.

[15] Thomas Hobbes, *On the Citizen*, ed. R. Tuck and M. Silverthorne (Cambridge: Cambridge University Press, 1998), chap. 12. 8, p. 137, chap. 13. 2–4, pp. 143 f.; Thomas Hobbes, *Leviathan*, ed. R. Tuck (Cambridge: Cambridge University Press, 1991), chap. 16, esp. pp. 111 f., 114; Q. Skinner, *Visions of Politics*, vol. III: *Hobbes and Civil Science* (Cambridge: Cambridge University Press, 2002), chap. 6.

and executive authority is a delegated form of that sovereign power.[16] Hobbes's initial terminology was also a conceptual breakthrough, relocating the fulcrum of political power (sovereignty) away from both princely rule and the idea of politics as sovereign self-government. It reconfigured the traditional doctrine of *salus populi* into one where absolute protection presupposed absolute obedience, and the boundaries of the state are the boundaries within which that protection holds. As Quentin Skinner suggests, this was little short of a conceptual counter-revolution.[17] And in Max Weber's penetrating elaboration of its trajectory, the transition from princely expropriation to the expropriation of the prince (*Enteignungsprozeßes*) by the modern state parallels politically the ways in which capitalist development gradually expropriates small producers.[18]

If Rousseau saw the force of Hobbes's construction of a homogeneous and unitary political will, he would not countenance the idea that the individual will of each citizen is realised only when represented by a sovereign who stands above, or outside, the body of the people or state. His account of the general will was designed as a means to solving this problem, where 'each man is united yet still obeys only himself'.[19] Such popular sovereignty could only be expressed through radically democratic self-representation or self-government, even though Rousseau knew that such austerely democratic politics was impossible in large modern nation-states. Montesquieu had already shown that.[20] Yet the only alternative to this despotism of the law under a republic was the 'perfect' despotism outlined by Hobbes, and the problem of modern politics was how to navigate around these choices. It was a problem, like squaring the circle, which he found impossible to solve.[21] Squaring the circle, though, is precisely what Sieyès attempted to do when he considered the active members of a nation as the foundation for his theory of indirect representation and limited popular sovereignty.

---

[16] Jean-Jacques Rousseau, *The Social Contract* (1762), in *The Social Contract and Other Later Political Writings*, ed. V. Gourevitch (Cambridge: Cambridge University Press, 1997) pp. 39–162, at book III, chap. 15, pp. 113–18.

[17] Q. Skinner, *Hobbes and Republican Liberty* (Cambridge: Cambridge University Press, 2008).

[18] Max Weber, 'Politik als Beruf' (1919), in *Gesammelte Politische Schriften*, ed. J. Winckelmann 5th edn. (Tübingen: J. C. B. Mohr (Paul Siebeck), 1988 [1921]), pp. 505–60, at pp. 511 f.

[19] Rousseau, *Social Contract*, book I, chap. 6, pp. 49 f.

[20] Charles Louis Secondat, Baron de Montesquieu, *Spirit of the Laws*, ed. A. Cohler et al. (Cambridge: Cambridge University Press, 1988), part I, book 3, chap. 3, pp. 22 ff. and book 5, esp. chaps. 3–7, pp. 43–51; D. Kelly, *The Propriety of Liberty* (Princeton: Princeton University Press, 2010), pp. 96 f.

[21] Rousseau, 'Letter to Mirabeau', 26 July 1767, in *Later Political Writings*, pp. 268–271.

Sieyès effectively made possible a new conceptual combination where the nation is the people exercising their active or constituent power (*pouvoir constituant*), claiming that this connection of people with nation in the modern social state (*état social*) is the best way of understanding the indirect quality of representative sovereignty. Modern democratic politics for Sieyès, and for French liberalism generally, meant the social state.[22] Rallying against the idea of a re-totalisation of society through the renewal of an absolutist model of unitary sovereignty, Sieyès sought instead a complex national system of representation underpinned by the social division of labour. His conceptual innovation was to re-inscribe the qualities of Hobbes's artificial man, or state, into the modern French nation. This was what he called the *ré-publique*, rather than its *ré-totale*, where instead of popular sovereignty as direct popular rule and analogously to Hobbes, Sieyès made the generation of a collective national will dependent upon the unity of a national representative body, the Assemblée Nationale, whose representatives had constituted power (*pouvoir constitué*) to act in the name of the people.[23] The people were again central, but only when represented through the common interest by their sovereign representatives, who were also permanently constrained. What Istvan Hont has called Sieyès's 'Hobbesian constitutionalism' was antithetical to later Jacobin political thought, where popular sovereignty is identical with popular democracy. And after the Jacobin descent into terror, unsurprisingly Sieyès and his works became hugely influential for writers seeking to understand the legacy of the Revolution for modern politics.[24]

When France got its perfect despotism under the tyranny of the Committee of Public Safety, such avowedly perfect Hobbism was nevertheless actually presented as the most austere form of anti-Hobbesian politics. Under Jacobinism state sovereignty was deconstructed and the brotherhood of mankind proclaimed, creating a complicated political and intellectual shadow. In the aftermath of 1848 Alexander Herzen looked back on the half-century since the French Revolution, and sensed how hard it was to reject the motivational force of an earlier sort of anti-political

---

[22] A. de Dijn, *French Political Thought from Montesquieu to Tocqueville: Liberty in a Levelled Society?* (Cambridge: Cambridge University Press, 2008).

[23] Emmanuel Sieyès, *Qu'est-ce que le Tiers État?*, ed. R. Zapperi (Geneva: n.p., 1971 [1789]), pp. 180 f.; Emmanuel Sieyès, 'Bases de l'Ordre Social' (1794/5), in Pasquino, *Sieyès*, pp. 181–91, esp. p. 185; Emmanuel Sieyès, 'Contre la Ré-totale', in ibid., pp. 175–6; Emmanuel Sieyès, 'Fragments Politiques', in C. Fauré (ed.), *Des Manuscrits de Sieyès* (Paris: Champion, 1999), p. 471; M. Forsyth, *Reason and Revolution: The Political Thought of the Abbé Sieyes* (New York and Leicester: Holmes & Meier/Leicester University Press, 1987), pp. 60–3, 74–7, 142 f.

[24] I. Hont, *Jealousy of Trade* (Cambridge, MA: Harvard University Press, 2005), p. 486.

politics that sounded so noble but which ended in terror. Was *salus populi* as much of a crime as *lèse-majesté*, he wondered?[25] If it was, and if modern politics was a system of states or peoples who lived in a world of states governed by an unsocial, commercial sociability just as Hobbes and Sieyès had proposed, was it any better than Jacobin and revolutionary forms of anti-politics based on claims of natural sociability, direct democracy and moral universalism? The conflict between these two competing visions through the nineteenth century was mediated by a reformulation of the idea of popular sovereignty not only as indirect and representative, but as necessarily filtered through the principle of nationality and claims to self-determination. Few were more acutely aware of how the navigation of this series of challenges in the nineteenth century posed particular problems for the history of political and legal thinking than Bluntschli.

III

A major figure in the development of the general theory of law and the state in German-speaking Europe from the middle to the end of the nineteenth century, Bluntschli was a Zurich-born Swiss Protestant. A student of law in his home town, he also trained privately with Friedrich Savigny in Berlin. His first academic appointment came in 1830 when he was called to Zurich, from where he wrote about the codification of Swiss law and democracy in its federal and religiously diverse cantonal system. He was formed politically in the context of the brief civil war of 1847 in Switzerland, known as the *Sonderbundkrieg*, which highlighted to him the need for a unified theory of the state that could cope with the demands of a religiously diverse federal system, and his experience turned him into a firm-minded liberal. Bluntschli's anti-radicalism was certainly straightforward in terms of its rather brusque conflation of radicalism with communism. For example, he wrote a dossier on communism in Switzerland, which was used to indict the revolutionary tailor Wilhelm Weitling, who was subsequently exiled to New York.[26] Though he was against radicalism, Bluntschli also stood firm against ultramontane political absolutism, and his move to incorporate popular sovereignty into a modern state theory is set against both direct democracy and clerical

---

[25] Alexander Herzen, *Selected Philosophical Works* (Moscow: Foreign Languages Publishing, 1956 [1914]), p. 375.

[26] See C. Wittke, *The Utopian Communist: A Biography of Wilhelm Weitling* (Baton Rouge: Louisiana State University Press, 1950); G. Claeys, 'Non-Marxian Socialism', in G. Stedman-Jones and G. Claeys (eds.), *The Cambridge History of Nineteenth-Century Political Thought* (Cambridge: Cambridge University Press, 2011), pp. 521–55.

predominance. It helped make his construction distinctive, for he related these puzzles of popular sovereignty in mid-nineteenth-century Europe back to foundational debates about popular sovereignty in the history of political thought.

Bluntschli suggested that the most adequate terminology for understanding popular sovereignty in the nineteenth century lay in the tradition drawn from Hobbes, Rousseau and Sieyès, because he was interested in thinking about the modern state as the arrangement wherein the members of a *Nation* are politically unified into a *Volk* and hence a state, by virtue of being represented by a sovereign personality. Because the sovereignty of this state is embodied in the figure of its representative, popular sovereignty turns once more towards an argument about the personality of the state (*Staatspersönlichkeit*) and its figural ruler (the monarch), although now it is developed in tandem with claims about national self-determination.[27] In effect, Bluntschli emphasised more clearly than most how the theory of popular sovereignty in the nineteenth century was effectively a form of modern state theory, which perhaps explains why most direct discussions of the concept occur in treatises on that subject, and why canonical texts of political theory treat it only indirectly.

The very indirectness of popular sovereignty means that it is usually relocated into a wider discussion of the tendencies of modern democracy towards despotism, or towards the thought that mass politics is national politics and popular sovereignty is effectively tied to a claim about the increasing politicisation of national differences.[28] Tocqueville, for example, understood the rise of modern democracy and popular sovereignty to be inevitable even as he lamented the binary forms of politics they set in motion, hovering awkwardly between administrative centralisation and social equality. It was a form of politics whose homogenising qualities threatened individual freedom and self-reliance, whose levelling tendencies threatened to bring renewed forms of despotism in its wake, and whose continual short-term failures were paradoxically the foundation of its potential success in the long run.[29] For many liberals, particularly in France, the short-term pathologies were rendered all too obvious when Napoleonic reaction signalled the end of another revolutionary period

---

[27] K. Stein, *Die verantwortlichkeit politischer Akteure* (Tübingen: J. C. B. Mohr (Paul Siebeck), 2009), pp. 9, 18 ff.

[28] B. Yack, 'Popular Sovereignty and Nationalism', *Political Theory* 29.4 (2001), pp. 517–36, at pp. 523 ff.

[29] S. Holmes, 'Saved by Danger/Destroyed by Success: The Argument of Tocqueville's *Souvenirs*', *Archives européennes de sociologie* 50.2 (2009), pp. 171–99, esp. pp. 182–7, 189 f.

around 1851. Marx's analysis is the canonical debunking of this period of avowedly popular sovereignty in action.[30]

In 1848, as revolution swept across Europe under the banner of radicalism and of calls for the popular sovereignty of the people to be established in political institutions more representative than monarchical, Bluntschli moved from Switzerland to Germany. He was called to a position at the University of Munich, which he combined with practical activity in the upper Bavarian Diet and from where he took part in early discussions about German unification. Four years after his arrival he had published a major work of synthesis, the *Allgemeines Staatsrecht, geschichtliche begründet*.[31] And even when he moved into the sphere of international law (*Völkerrecht*) or considered the American Civil War and the laws of war, his *Allgemeines Staatsrecht* remained the foundation for his general theory of the state. It was revised, reiterated and expanded over several years, ultimately appearing as a three-volume *Lehre vom modernen Staat*, or *Theory of the Modern State*, in 1875.[32] Its updates and revisions overlapped with a polemical revisionist history of the recent 'civil war' (*Bürgerkrieg*) over unification in Germany. It was, he suggested, the start of a revolution that would lead to a new order (*Neugestaltung*) for the nation. Both enterprises tried to reconnect German history after 1848 to models of federal and representative nationalism inspired by the Swiss civil war of 1847 on the one hand, and American constitutional debates from both the founding convention to the Civil War, on the other.[33]

His textbooks on state theory (for this is what they are) outlined the threefold character of his argument. The second volume considered the relationship between law and the state, as a series of practical instruments through which the sovereignty of the state might be described (*Staatsrecht*). The third volume outlined the life of the state as vital organism with its own personality, which is given focus through politics (*Politik*). The first volume, though, suggested ways in which a general theory of the state (*Allgemeine Staatslehre*) could be constructed. This required a focus on both politics and law simultaneously, because only in combination can the normative direction and the juristic framework of the state be seen as

---

[30] Karl Marx, 'The 18th Brumaire of Louis Bonaparte' (1851), in *Marx: Surveys from Exile*, ed. D. Fernbach (Harmondsworth: Penguin, 1973), pp. 143–249, esp. pp. 150, 157 f., 162 f., 232, 290.

[31] J. K. Bluntschli, *Allgemeines Staatsrecht, geschichtlich begründet* (Munich: Literarisch-Artistischen Anstalt, 1852).

[32] For the publishing history of these volumes, see E. Loening, 'Vorrede', in J. K. Bluntschli, *Lehre vom modernen Staat*, vol. I: *Allgemeine Staatslehre*, 6th edn. (Stuttgart: J. G. Cotta, 1886 [1876]), pp. v–xiv, at p. xi.

[33] J. K. Bluntschli, *Die Neue Gestaltung von Deutschland und die Schweiz* (Zurich: Orell, Fusli & Co., 1867), pp. 9 ff.

a unity. They are united through the claim that the state is a particular sort of vigorous personality, one that is organic and natural and which represents the people within a nation-state. Crucially, its development is part of a historical elaboration of the principle of human sociability.

Bluntschli's framework clearly chimed with some of the ways in which debates about popular sovereignty were transformed in the wake of both the Frankfurt Parliament and the development of southern German liberalism. Conceptual codification appeared in a hefty series of volumes edited by the parliamentary representatives Carl von Rotteck and Carl Theodor Welcker, entitled the *Staats-lexicon*, which emblematised the new concern with popular sovereignty in post-revolutionary Europe.[34] Just like Tocqueville and Bluntschli, Welcker's liberalism was tempered. For although most writers were happy to suggest that modern politics should necessarily be constrained by public opinion, in parliamentary debates those like Welcker indicated an ambivalence about excessive attempts to grant this opinion excessive force. Thus in 1848, when the subject of discussion in the constituent assembly was the suspensive veto power of the next head of the Reich, public opinion was deemed safe (because distant), whereas public action as direct sovereignty looked like a throwback to Jacobinism.[35] Thereafter, wider support for a *juste milieu* as the basis of a moderate liberalism was derived from Tocqeuville and the French Doctrinaires, and went alongside critical discussions of the conceptual antonym of representative politics, the *Freistaat* of the self-governing republic, with its own historical origins in early modern Europe.[36]

Modern republicanism possessed a genealogy with roots in Machiavelli. The trajectory from Machiavelli to modern republicanism, it was suggested, nevertheless led towards Rousseau, who was the 'father of the Jacobins', and hence ultimately towards terror. Machiavelli's views were also said to lie behind French and Austrian moves to war in 1812.[37] The consequence of Machiavelli's politics for these makers of the modern theory of popular sovereignty was neo-Roman tyranny, and Napoleon

---

[34] Carl Rotteck and Carl Theodor von Welcker (eds.), *Staats-lexicon, oder Encyclopedie der Staatswissenschaft*, 14 vols. (Altona: Hammerlich, 1839–48).

[35] Carl Theodor von Welcker, speech of 13 December 1848, in F. Wigard (ed.), *Stenographischer Bericht über die Verhandlungen der deutschen constituierenden Nationalversammlung*, 9 vols. (Leipzig: Teubner, 1848–9), VI, pp. 4083–4; Hewitson, 'Old Forms', pp. 1188 f.

[36] A. Craiutu, *Liberalism under Siege: The Political Thought of the French Doctrinaires* (Lanham, MD: Lexington Books, 2003).

[37] Carl Theodor von Welcker, s.v. 'Juste-milieu', in Rotteck and Welcker (eds.), *Staats-lexicon*, IX, pp. 3–29; Carl Theodor von Welcker, s.v. 'Moral', in ibid., X, pp. 692–755, at p. 699 (*Freistaat*) and p. 707 (*Vater der Jacobiner*).

was the 'greatest Maestro of Machiavellism'.[38] Therefore, instead of
seeking republican foundations for modern popular sovereignty, new
forms of liberalism would have to be developed to justify a more indirect
form of representative and commercial republic. It had to be a robust
and realistic form of liberalism, rather than simply parading itself as a
grand-standing doctrine of human freedom, or a knee-jerk reaction to
oppression and inequality.[39] For the liberal Rotteck, this required an
understanding of the contrast between historically grounded accounts of
contemporary liberalism and the intellectual origins of liberalism in natural law or 'idealist' forms of politics (*idealer Politik*).[40] For contemporary
critics such as August Rochau, however, liberalism itself was a utopian
form of ideal politics, one that very clearly rejected the principles of
what he self-consciously referred to as *Realpolitik*. Whether realistic or
idealistic, though, post-revolutionary politics had to reconcile a theory
of the state as the embodiment of popular sovereignty with a politics
of indirect representation.[41] Once again, Bluntschli offered a distinctive
path through these requirements by way of his recourse to an alternative genealogy of the history of political thought. On his account, a
new form of political union could be derived from a counter-history
that rejected the politics of Machiavelli, Hobbes and Rousseau, but
whose account of popular sovereignty (*Volkssouveränität*) is unthinkable
without them.

In *Theory of the Modern State* Bluntschli asked a very direct question
about popular sovereignty. In a modern, representative state (typically
that which he and others would call a republic) are the people sovereign
at all? Having previously determined that sovereignty is an attribute of
the state, independent from other forms of authority, possessing majesty
(*maiestas*), plentitude of power and expressing political unity, it seems
unlikely that Bluntschli could think the people might ever be sovereign.
He ran through the standard options in the history of modern political
thinking from the French Revolution onwards, asking who exactly are
the people if they are to be considered sovereign? A multitude of persons, united by membership in the state? If so, he wrote, that would
'contradict the very existence of the state, which is the basis of

---

[38] Welcker, 'Moral', p. 749: Napoleon is the 'größte Meister des Machiavellismus'.
[39] Paul Pfizer, s.v. 'Liberalismus', in Rotteck and Welcker (eds.), *Staats-lexicon*, IX,
pp. 713–30, at pp. 728, 729.
[40] Carl von Rotteck, 'Über den Streit natürlicher Rechtsprinzipien oder idealer Politik
mit historisch begründeten Verhältnissen' [1818], *Sammlung kleinerer Schriften*, 2 vols.
(Stuttgart: Franck, 1829), II, pp. 42–70.
[41] August Rochau, *Grundsätze der Realpolitik* (Stuttgart: Karl Öpel, 1853), p. 41: 'Die
Nation ist ein genealogisch-geschichtlicher, das Volk hingegen ein rein politischer
Begriff.'

sovereignty'.[42] What then of collective voting in assemblies? If democracy really involves citizen control and assembly-based voting and participation, then the sovereignty of the people is to be found there. But of course, he wrote, nobody really thinks that modern democracy is anything other than a representative republic, based on states whose size and scale dwarf any sort of assembly-based democratic project. As he wrote of these two options, 'the first is anarchical, the second absolutely democratical'.[43] But as the author of a synthetic tract on the theory of the state, he wanted to focus on how these ideas were transformed, and claimed that the pure theory of democracy found its most extreme modern manifestation in the French Revolution, where popular sovereignty as absolute equality justified terror.[44] Developing a critique of Jacobin sovereignty, Bluntschli once more noted how the French Doctrinaires, like Royer-Collard and Guizot, tried to ground the idea of equality and popular sovereignty anew by focusing on moderation and the idea of sovereignty based upon reason. Tocqueville added the suggestion that 1848 had shown modern democracy within the nation-state grounded on popular sovereignty to be a providential fact, and Bluntschli hardly disagreed.

For Bluntschli, nevertheless, because ideas only have force when given personality, abstract ideas about sovereignty were little more than legal and political fictions.[45] If personality is to be real rather than artificial, and if personality is to be cultivated through popular sovereignty, then how was this to be achieved? Finally, Bluntschli answered his own question by focusing on the modern representative republic as the political form taken by a nation, whose population (or body) necessarily needs a head (or state). Where the state is the site of political sovereignty, then popular sovereignty is simply the instrumental antecedent to a fully developed account of sovereignty. To speak of sovereignty is always to speak of state sovereignty, because 'certainly the sovereignty of the whole state is superior to the sovereignty of any member of the state'.[46] State sovereignty therefore incorporates and supersedes popular sovereignty understood as the rule of the people, through the idea of political representation. The monarch, or figurehead of the state, represents the entire nation-state. Although he used the illustration of the English king as both Crown-in-Parliament and formal head of the constitution, Bluntschli emphasised that this 'is not a peculiarity of the English constitution, but a fundamental principle of modern representative institutions'. Here, the 'highest

---

[42] J. K. Bluntschli, *The Theory of the State*, 3rd edn., trans. from the 6th German edn. (Oxford: Clarendon Press, 1901 [1885]), pp. 495, 497.
[43] Ibid., p. 498.   [44] Ibid., p. 499.   [45] Ibid., pp. 499 ff.   [46] Ibid., p. 501.

sovereign power, that of legislation, is not entrusted to the head alone, but to the head along with the representative body, that is to say, to the whole body of the state'.[47] He therefore concluded by arguing that 'all the power of the prince is essentially only the concentrated power of the nation', so that 'though princes and dynasties fall, the nation and the State retain their legal existence'.[48] There was therefore no division of sovereignty.

There was therefore also no contradiction between the sovereignty of the state and of the prince. Because of this unity, Bluntschli suggested that both state and monarch were part of a wider organism in which both sides made up the whole. The sovereignty of the state was described in law, while that of the prince or ruler was located in governmental rule and administration. So while there could be 'no peace between the democratic sovereignty of the people and the sovereignty of the prince', there should be a contented peace between the sovereignty of the state and the sovereignty of the prince. Bluntschli, therefore, came not to bury the idea of popular sovereignty for the nineteenth century, but to make it safe for representative politics by noting how popular sovereignty as traditionally understood had required either absolute democracy or else total anarchy. For him these were two sides of the same coin, which is why he tried to re-route his critique of the way in which popular sovereignty was discussed towards a historically sensitive analysis of how the theory of the modern state as a personality had developed. In so doing his view fell into line with the general sense of mid-century liberal–republican politics in Germany, where a federal nationalism gelled relatively easily with an updated form of *Reichspatriotismus*, considered as a form of confederal union between federal nation states.[49] This would, however, only begin to be realised as a new 'revolution in government' during the 1850s and 1860s.[50]

IV

Locating these general problems of state theory in the context of a history of political thought moves Bluntschli into a wider argument about what is missing for modern politics in the historical arguments of Machiavelli, Hobbes and Rousseau. Indeed, Bluntschli was part of a much wider

---

[47] Ibid., p. 502.   [48] Ibid.

[49] M. Hewitson, *Nationalism in Germany, 1848–1866* (Basingstoke: Macmillan, 2010), p. 242.

[50] C. Clark, 'After 1848: The European Revolution in Government', *Transactions of the Royal Historical Society* 22 (2012), pp. 171–97, esp. pp. 195 ff.

move in German-speaking state theory to reject the centrality of natural law for understanding modern politics. Thinking that the history of natural law between Grotius and Kant was of a different age, as well as having been overtaken by new, more 'scientific' theories of politics and sociability, Bluntschli and many others decided to rewrite the history of modern *Staatsrechtslehre*, taking on the mantle of Kant's 'modern' theory of natural law as a starting point.[51] If the humanist idiom of natural law from Grotius to Kant had been concerned to reconcile *honestum* and *utile* through the refutation of scepticism and the development of a science of morality, then the principal use made of Kant by modern legal and political writers was as a theorist of the possibilities of peace and enlightenment in an era of international economic and political competition. *Utile* and *honestum* were thought once more to be capable of combination, but that combination would now have to be understood as a regulative ideal, one that could incorporate a broader cosmopolitan claim about the direction of human history towards its end as an ideal. That end, literally 'humanity' for Bluntschli, was the possible consequence of a move that based a politics of representative nationalism on a federal system of states, a project that bears some relation to much more recent iterations in contemporary political theory today, but which then emerged out of a series of debates about whether European federalism and political union was best understood through the transition from a federation of states (*Staatenbund*) towards a union of federal states (*Bundesstaat*). These unions were entered into for various reasons of force or *fortuna*.[52] Their intellectual history, however, could show how certain ideas about the relationship between political virtue, commercial society and modern history might have prompted ideas that would transform the ways in which the possible futures of such national unions were imagined.[53]

For Bluntschli the answer was to see political union through the lens of a confederation of federally organised nation-states, where popular sovereignty was indirect in each. If the nation has primacy, moreover, the form of union in the political and federal nation needs to be recast, and the form of federal union Bluntschli proposed was designed to

---

[51] Bluntschli, *Lehre vom modernen Staat*, vol. III: *Allgemeines Staatsrecht*, p. 547; cf. R. Tuck, 'The "Modern" Theory of Natural Law', in A. Pagden (ed.), *Languages of Political Theory in Early-Modern Europe* (Cambridge: Cambridge University Press, 1987), pp. 99–122, esp. pp. 116–19.

[52] M. Forsyth, *Unions of States* (Leicester: Leicester University Press, 1981), esp. chaps. 4–6; J. Parent, *Uniting States* (Oxford: Oxford University Press, 2011), esp. pp. 8 f., chaps. 4–5; D. Miller, *National Responsibility and Global Justice* (Oxford: Oxford University Press, 2012).

[53] For example, Bruno Hildebrand, *Die Nationalökonomie der Gegewart und Zukunft* (Frankfurt: J. Rütten, 1848).

incorporate elements of liberalism and republicanism, and thus avoid the twin extremes of pure democracy and Hobbesian absolute unity.[54] Bluntschli's form of political union was less than Hobbesian artificial unity, but more than merely economic or commercial concord. He wrote that a 'union is always imperfect when it is merely personal', but a 'higher unity is to be found in the so-called Real Union, which is related to Federation, as Personal Union is to Confederation'.[55] In his direct focus on the problems of union (*Bund*), the Swiss background to Bluntschli's thinking was clear, and his autobiographical statements noted that the years 1847 in Switzerland and 1848 in Germany had convinced him (as they had convinced Tocqueville) that out of civil war a new and democratic form of politics could emerge.[56] It convinced him too that Switzerland could survive within a new European system of states. Finally, it convinced him of the importance of the federal union (*Bund*) for modern political theory based on popular and national sovereignty.[57] Bluntschli's own anti-Napoleonic 'mediation' of these intensely political moments focused his attention on the question of popular sovereignty in subsequent decades. Furthermore and in line with Tocqueville's insights into the radical difficulties of judging the successes and failures of a democratic politics based on popular sovereignty in the short as opposed to the long term, Bluntschli suggested that these initial disappointments had ultimately made national unification possible.[58]

Bluntschli's liberalism, on this reading, is developmental and can be understood as a linear teleology in a similar way to the development of Kant's liberalism by his successor in Königsberg, Wilhelm Traugott Krug. In Krug's hands, Kant's liberalism became a new form of Christian eschatology.[59] Even so, this linear liberalism also retained the Hobbesian dimensions of Kant's political philosophy drawn from his essay on the relationship between theory and practice. There, Kant had argued that states have to act according to the demands of right and justice first, and could only legislate for welfare or public happiness secondarily.[60] His

---

54 Bluntschli, *Lehre vom modernen Staat*, III, p. 382.
55 Bluntschli, *Theory of the State*, pp. 271, 272.
56 J. K. Bluntschli, *Bemerkungen über die neuesten Vorschläge zur deutschen Verfassung* (Munich: C. Kaster, 1848), p. 9.
57 Carl Welcker, s.v. 'Bund', in Rotteck and Welcker (eds.), *Staats-lexicon*, III, pp. 76–116, at pp. 76, 79.
58 Cf. R. Koselleck, *Futures Past*, trans. K. Tribe (New York: Columbia University Press, 2004 [1979]), pp. 61, 64 ff.
59 Wilhelm Traugott Krug, *Geschichtlicher Darstellung des Liberalismus alter und neuer Zeit* (Leipzig: Brockhaus, 1823), pp. 149 ff.
60 Immanuel Kant, 'On the Common Saying: "This May be True in Theory but it does not Apply in Practice"', in H. Reiss (ed.), *Kant: Political Writings* (Cambridge: Cambridge University Press, 1991), pp. 61–92, at pp. 73–86.

traditional reason of state-inspired argument presumed that sovereignty and *salus populi* remain the guiding principles of politics. A crucial conceptual development, though, of which Bluntschli's analysis was a major part, was the idea that the determination of *salus populi* be understood as coeval with the determination of national welfare. As Bluntschli wrote, the principle of nationality had transformed national welfare (rooted in the people or 'proletariat' as the 'fourth estate', the 'foundation' of politics and the subject of the state's care) into modern reason of state.[61]

This is what Bluntschli meant when he talked about reason in history after Kant. It signified the predominance of a modern principle of nationality directed by a new and organic state person, typically the monarch. In fact, representation of the indirect sovereignty of the people by the organs of government under the overall direction of a virile, organic state person was the crux of Bluntschli's counter-narrative to Hobbes. Where Hobbes offered artifice through representation, Bluntschli countered by naturalising nationality and embodying it in the figure of the sovereign who in turn embodied the spirit of the nation. It was a liberal history of the stages of governmental progress from barbarism to civility, led by great statesmen who filtered the national spirits of different territories. In such a framework, Montesquieu, Mill and Mazzini could collide with Tocqueville, Guizot and Lorenz von Stein. It was also a claim where echoes of eighteenth-century conjectural histories were subsumed under the patina of nineteenth-century liberal republicanism. Under the aegis of a historical interpretation of the law and politics, Bluntschli wove together in synthetic form historical anthropology, historical sociology, stage theories of the economy, histories of Europe, the history of European political and legal thought, abstract theories of politics, time-honoured doctrines concerning the forms of government, modern class analysis and the legal and constitutional theories of modern representative government. His was yet another liberal–republican synthesis.

A crucial issue for Bluntschli concerned the distinctiveness of the modern state. He rejected all conventional foundations, whether in terms of the intellectual development of a concept of the modern state in Hobbes's political theory during the English Revolution or the Glorious Revolution, or the American Declaration of Independence or the French

---

[61] J. K. Bluntschli, s.v. 'Vierter Stand', in J. C. Bluntschli and K. Brater (eds.), *Deutsches Staatswörterbuch*, 11 vols. (Stuttgard and Leipzig: n.p., 1865), XI, pp. 72–5, at p. 75: 'Der vierte Stand ist die Grundlage des modernen Staates und zugleich der Hauptgegenstand seiner Sorge'; J. K. Bluntschli, s.v. 'Nation und Volk, Nationalitätsprincip', in J. K. Bluntschli and K. Brater (eds.), *Staatswörterbuch in drei Bänden*, 3 vols. (Leipzig and Stuttgart: n.p., 1876), II, pp. 651–7, at p. 653: 'Das Volk im vollen höchsten Sinn des Wortes ist die zum Staate geeinigte und staatlich organisirte politische Person.'

Revolution. None were critical in his view. Rather, the key period was the beginning (for him at least) of the Enlightenment in 1740. The inauguration of a distinctively modern state was found in the enlightened despotism of Frederick the Great, allied to administrative and political changes in England that introduced representative, limited, constitutional monarchical government. Here was the beginning of modernity, he wrote, and it was signalled by an explicit rejection of mainstream Machiavellian politics in the *Anti-Machiavel* of Frederick and Voltaire. But it also coincided with a reconsideration of Machiavelli's place in the development of a theory of proto-national sovereignty.

Bluntschli was far from alone in thinking that a reconsideration of Machiavelli for modern German politics was significant. In the 1840s, shortly before Bluntschli started writing, the highly successful German artist Adolph Menzel had already produced some two hundred etchings celebrating Frederick the Great's life, work and army uniforms. One etching in particular is of interest to my argument, an image of Machiavelli as if he were facing trial while nailed on a pillory with rotten edges, framed by an oak and laurel wreath, with two dates of judgement.

Peter Paret has written engagingly about this image, which surely means to show that in 1840 Frederick William IV continues to triumph over Machiavelli just as Frederick the Great had done a century earlier.[62] In fact, as the note to the text in the anniversary edition of these prints makes plain, Machiavelli and his political ideas are dramatically nailed to the pillory and literally damned by the prosecuting judgement of the *Anti-Machiavel* of 'Federic' in 1740. The later date of 1840 signals not only the reign of the new king, but, when allied to the wreath placed above the pilloried image, indicates a century of anti-Machiavellian Enlightenment in Prussia.[63] Yet the defeated Machiavelli was only the purely political operator, the figure who seemed to describe politics as the combination of prudence, cruelty and cunning and who symbolised but one strand of the intellectual history of reason of state. The other side of this history and the other side of Machiavelli, the theorist of proto-national unity, remained very much alive.[64] At this time in Prussia particularly there was a widespread renewal of interest in the political economy of such apparent anti-Machiavellianism, because many hoped that Frederick's reforms and programmes of industrial development would bring order to a fragmented Holy Roman Empire, and redress the balance-of-power deficit

---

[62] P. Paret, *German Encounters with Modernism* (Cambridge: Cambridge University Press, 2001), pp. 11, 13 ff.

[63] Menzel, *Adolph Menzel's Illustrationen*, I, p. 38.

[64] J. K. Bluntschli, s.v. 'Machiavelli', in E. Löning (ed.), *Bluntschli's Staatswörterbuch in drei Bänden*, 3 vols. (Leipzig and Stuttgart: n.p., 1875–6), II, pp. 571–6, at pp. 571, 575.

Figure 11.1 Adolph Menzel, 'Machiavelli', in *Adolph Menzel's Illustrationen zu den Werken Friedrichs der Grossen*, Jubilaeums Ausgabe, 2 vols. (Berlin: R. Wagner, 1886), I, image 66. Image courtesy of the text at the Internet Archive, via the Getty Research Institute, Los Angeles (83-B7391).

with the French monarchy through means other than pacific commercial trade. That meant military and economic competition, and such policies looked more like a Machiavellian form of anti-Machiavellianism in the service of national advancement than their opposite. Robert von Mohl's standard bibliographic guide to the history and literature of the science of the state (*Staatswissenschaft*) has a section on 'Machiavelli Literatur' listing some ten pages of relevant and recent bibliography, indicating the extent of current engagement with Machiavelli. Furthermore, revising the standard view of Machiavelli at this time would also bear considerable fruit at the beginning of the next century, when writers such as Friedrich Meinecke and Carl Schmitt debated Machiavelli's importance for generating an understanding of reason of state into which the quest for German unification could be inserted.[65]

Machiavellianism therefore clearly meant at least two things. First, instrumental Machiavellianism was Caesarism, and Caesarism, for Bluntschli and almost all the post-revolutionary theorists, was analogous with Bonapartism.[66] This is how they understood the neo-Roman legacy of Machiavellian politics, as a form of imperialism. Conversely, like all forms of Caesarism it simultaneously carried within it the seeds of resistance that could be consciously redeployed, whether through the memory of a Brutus or through later eighteenth-century critiques of parliamentary corruption in the English constitution. Machiavellian politics thus understood presupposes a theory of resistance, which increasingly mattered in German-speaking political thought because such a conceptual construction could point towards a way of understanding the importance of the wars of liberation in Prussia in 1812–13, for instance, as prolegomena to later claims about national unification.[67] Resistance both to revolutionary and neo-Roman tyranny, as well as to Catholic and ultramontane reaction and restoration through the principle of nationality in the aftermath of the French Revolution, was hugely significant for Bluntschli. Indeed, we might extend his argument and say that Bluntschli's resistance to the idea of the state as Hobbesian or Rousseauvian in origin leads him to support forms of federal confederation that could counterbalance overbearing sovereignty, and whose distant origins lie in a revised use of Machiavelli's political theory. The two faces of Machiavellian politics combined for Bluntschli in a model of reason of state to be rejected, and a republican account of popular sovereignty and resistance to (national) tyranny that could be updated and retained.

Combining this double-sided vision of the nature and extent of major political theories allowed Bluntschli to present his synthetic and stagist

[65] Friedrich Meinecke, *Die Idee der Staatsräson in der neuere Geschichte* (Berlin: Oldenbourg, 1924); Carl Schmitt, 'Zu Friedrich Meineckes *Idee der Staatsräson*', *Archiv für Sozialwissenschaft und Sozialpolitik* 56 (1926), pp. 226–34.

[66] J. K. Bluntschli, 'Cäsar und Cäsarismus', in Bluntschli and Brater (eds.), *Deutsches Staatswörterbuch*, I, pp. 387–92, esp. p. 391.

[67] C. Clark, 'The Wars of Liberation in Prussian Memory', *Journal of Modern History* 68.3 (1996), pp. 550–76.

theory of the rise of the modern state in a series of developmental cycles and their later iterations. What he provided was a historically informed theory ranging from the ancients to the moderns, underpinned by a narrative of the rise, partial survival and fall of ideas and periods. There were three such cycles in his narrative. First, the ancient communitarian state had no individual rights, was based on a slave economy, and retained an overpowering (imperatorial) government. There were no recognised international rights and no legal limits on state power, so that the state expanded wherever it was militarily possible to do so. Renaissance republicanism was then cast as a revival of this ideological shadow. Second, he presented the medieval state as both legalistic and dualistic, upholding political theories of divine right and the king's two bodies but proposing a separation of church and state. There was no religious toleration here, and only weak administration. The English revolutions became, for Bluntschli, part of the afterlife of this moment, which is to say that they appeared at the end of a cycle that began with the Reformation rather than commencing a new cycle themselves. This was so whether he considered the radical (Hobbesian) or more overtly conservative (Lockean) forms of English political theory. Perhaps not altogether surprisingly, his account is similar to the claim made about the English Revolution by Thomas Hill Green in 1867.[68] Bluntschli's third claim was that modern state theory inaugurated the development of a new cycle, whose proximate origins lay in the Enlightenment and whose initial force could be found in the figure of the enlightened monarch. Bluntschli's modern state image is thereby clearly defined in opposition to these ancient, neo-ancient and medieval state forms. His idea that politics is the vital, living force that moves these cycles in their new directions through the actions of the statesman as the literal as well as figural embodiment of the personality of the state (*Staatspersönlichkeit*) tied in very well with the idea, derived from both Kant and Hegel, that law and politics needed to be 'timely' to be effective. Positive law, whether in the domestic or the international realms, simply could not function if it was not 'vital'.[69] Thus, neither Machiavelli, nor Hobbes, nor Rousseau alone was going to be able to ground Bluntschli's conceptual argument about the modern state.

Additionally, if these earlier cycles and their later revisions or iterations could not provide reliable foundations for the modern state, neither could the French Revolution. For his Enlightenment-inspired theory of national and popular sovereignty (*Volkssouveränität*) to work, Bluntschli

[68] D. Kelly, 'Idealism and Revolution: T. H. Green's *Four Lectures on the English Commonwealth*', *History of Political Thought* 27.3 (2006), pp. 505–42.

[69] B. B. Röben, 'The Method Behind Bluntschli's "Modern" International Law', *Journal of the History of International Law* 4 (2002), pp. 249–92, at p. 270.

had to counteract the idea that the French Revolution was the beginning of the new, by presenting it instead as the partial victory of a series of despotic and radical ideas. In his terms, the defence of the Revolution as the enforcement of a strict and mathematical equality between citizens was a form of Jacobin tyranny. Such tyranny directly led to terror and was directly inspired by Rousseau's account of the general will, because Rousseau's general will was in turn simply an updated version of Hobbes's absolutist political theory of sovereignty.[70] Here, the chain of reasoning was quite straightforward, and quite conventional for much nineteenth-century political theory. The French Revolution was a break from political moderation, a direct assault on privilege and complex representation, and culminated in a form of dictatorship. For Bluntschli, as for many others such as Tocqueville, Edgar Quinet and Mill, that outcome made French revolutionary Jacobinism look altogether like counter-revolution.

In curious ways, this is a view that has had great appeal in more recent interpretations. Not only does the liberal anti-Jacobin revisionist scholarship of writers such as François Furet suggest something similar, so too does the fleeting triumph of what Jonathan Israel has deemed another moment of Radical Enlightenment, where the claims of reason, equality and democracy upheld briefly by Condorcet and Sièyes until late 1793 were toppled by Jacobin Counter-Enlightenment.[71] The revolutionary decline, seen from Robespierre's power grab to Thermidor, turns out to be the counter-revolution. Once more though, this is simply to put the point back into nineteenth-century terms. Furet obviously knew this, when looking back to Tocqueville, August Cochin and Quinet as his nineteenth-century models for how to think critically about the legacy of the revolution, while Bluntschli and the German lawyers and state theorists had already made this quite conventional move of disputing the equation of Jacobinism with political modernity. However, if Jacobinism was a failed revolution how should one understand modern politics in its wake? For Bluntschli, as for Kant, the question turned on his thinking about how a new cycle in an age of Enlightenment might develop. For both, this concerned the reconciliation of nationality with enlightened monarchy. Because of their obvious intellectual connections in the eyes of his contemporaries, Bluntschli was soon located as the logical end point of broad histories of *Staatswissenschaft* that began with

---

[70] Bluntschli, *Lehre vom modernen Staat*, III, p. 601; Bluntschli, *Theory of the State*, pp. 301 ff.

[71] Cf. F. Furet, *Penser la revolution française* (Paris: Gallimard, 1978); J. Israel, *Revolutionary Ideas* (Princeton: Princeton University Press, 2014).

Kant on the general question of Enlightenment.[72] Bluntschli in particular suggested that because the state person or monarch is decisive for moving the political will of the nation, only enlightened nations 'worthy' of development would prosper in the competitive world of nineteenth-century international relations, and constitutional monarchs rather than Napoleonic tyrants would be best placed to succeed.[73]

These overlapping cycles and stages reflected Bluntschli's general idea of the relationship between the state and law. Avowedly following both Aristotle and Bodin, in particular Bodin's distinction between sovereignty and government (the distinction examined by Richard Tuck in Chapter 5 in this volume), Bluntschli suggested that the state was not the same as the constitution, and therefore that law and politics were separate. There was nevertheless a relationship between them, and the nature of that relationship was crucial, for it signals a movement from the ideal or normative dimensions of Blutnschli's analysis towards real politics. In other words, Bluntschli's synthesis of *Staatsrecht* and *Staatslehre* into a form of *Politik* was relational, and required an account of popular sovereignty that could combine in various ways what he (like Bodin, Hobbes, Rousseau and Sieyès) saw as the distinction between the active and passive elements of sovereignty. As he wrote, 'in constitution making and legislation the sovereignty of the State is in active exercise: otherwise, as a rule, it is in repose'. When Bluntschli talked of monarchy, he continued to suggest that 'the nation, as a whole, remains at rest, while its head acts either directly or indirectly by means of magistrates and officials'.[74] This was how he thought the connections between politics and morality should be understood, and so he wondered how Germany could retain a constitutional monarchy that guaranteed union without resort either to Caesarism or patrimonialism. He answered that it could only be guaranteed by the effective adaptation of the statesman to the demands of the nation, in particular by guaranteeing national welfare as the principal reason of state in a system of modern, representative and simultaneously democratic politics. From this domestic perspective, international law was conceived of as 'emergent' rather than merely 'positive', stemming from necessity first but developing in line with the principles of Christian morality that govern 'humanity'.[75] This extra (Protestant) Christian element was supplemented in his gloss on the laws of war and international law, which had in turn developed out of ideas elaborated by

---

[72] G. Mollat, *Lesebuch zur Geschichte der Deutsche Staatswissenschaft von Kant bis Bluntschli* (Osterwieck: Zickfeldt, 1891).

[73] Bluntschli, *Theory of the State*, p. 107.   [74] Bluntschli, *Theory of the State*, p. 509.

[75] Röben, 'Method', p. 269.

his émigré colleague Francis Lieber during the American Civil War.[76] Like Bluntschli, Lieber had developed the thought that modern liberty and popular sovereignty had to avoid both Catholic and socialist-style centralisation (forms of 'imperatorial sovereignty').[77]

V

Bluntschli's work might best be seen as a reflection on the relationship between theory and practice from a post-Kantian perspective. Like Kant, however, his account of what sovereignty generally entailed, and what popular sovereignty as indirect, national and representative particularly required, was shot through with conventional resonances from the history of political thought. He first developed a claim about the need to understand state sovereignty as the reconciliation of *iustitia* with *salus populi*, but where *salus populi* was understood as national welfare (*Wohlfahrt*) moved by the demands of politics (*Politik*). Next, the legitimacy of the state person or *Staatsman* would be judged according to the standards of prudence in maintaining and extending this national welfare, and, as Bluntschli was well aware, this now included the constraints posed by political parties. Like the synthetic *Staats-lexicon*, he understood parties to fulfil complex psychological and representational needs on the part of citizens.[78] Then, to try and keep this intellectual compound stable he differentiated liberalism from alternative ideological forces, especially versions of socialism and clerical reaction.

The 'highest political idea' of liberalism, he wrote, was 'not nationality, but humanity'. True politics was thus always 'liberal' in essence, and his liberal concept of the state had a 'psychological character'.[79] It meant that his work was an attempt to reconcile the principal dualism in the history of political thought, that between justice and reason of state, by describing a psychology of the state with a cosmopolitan purpose. It combined justice and welfare by meeting the demands of the modern principle of nationality, and redefined *salus populi* as the driving and active principle of politics. Just as Kant had suggested, justice provided a regulatory structure, but could not of its own accord motivate political action. For that, an organic state person (rather than the mechanical or

---

[76] J. K. Bluntschli, *Das moderne Völkerrecht der civilisierten Staaten* (Nordlichen: Beck, 1868), esp. pp. 30–44.

[77] Francis Lieber, *On Civil Liberty and Self-Government* (Philadelphia: J. B. Lippincott, 1859), pp. 394–7, 404.

[78] s.v. 'Parteien', in Carl von Rotteck and Carl Welcker (eds.), *Supplemente zur ersten Auflage des Staats-lexicons*, 4 vols. (Altona: Hammerlich, 1848), IV, pp. 209–32, esp. pp. 213–16, 219, 221.

[79] Bluntschli, *Lehre vom modernen Staat*, III, pp. 601, 605 ff.

artificial man of the Hobbesian commonwealth) was required, and the organic state person was for Bluntschli the representative of a new form of politics, a democratic nationalism within a cosmopolitanism of nations.[80] Here, it looks as if Bluntschli could hardly be closer to Mazzini's political theory, which is often taken to be emblematic of a straightforward nineteenth-century theory of popular sovereignty. But that is just to say that they both understood their terms in almost exactly the same way. Popular sovereignty will be the 'logical outcome' of a 'victory of right' according to Mazzini, when the union of 'free' elements within a state are combined and united through the principle of nationality.[81] That was an idea with a lengthy afterlife, filtering through Woodrow Wilson's intellectual formation and into the Great War.[82] Bluntschli's emendation was to make the nationality principle of post-1848 politics operative as something akin to Hegel's *Geist*, within the regulative Kantian boundaries of Enlightenment and cosmopolitan humanity, in order to reconcile state and civil society through a modified account of popular sovereignty.[83]

What both Bluntschli and Mazzini needed was a defensible theory of nationalism in order to produce a coherent theory of representative democracy. They provide more extensive discussion of this principle of nationality than had John Stuart Mill, for example, in his *Considerations on Representative Government*, even though Mill had discussed the different forms of federal union in America and Switzerland both before and after 1848, with sympathy and a certain acknowledgement of their importance to nineteenth-century debates about popular sovereignty. In chapter fifteen of his *Considerations*, Mill noted that 'it is in general a necessary condition of free institutions, that the boundaries of governments should coincide in the main with those of nationalities'.[84] Only then could appropriate relations between ideas of constitutional balance and the dynamism of political liberty be gauged.[85] Equally, Mill had no

---

[80] Bluntschli, *Theory of the State*, p. 482.
[81] Giuseppe Mazzini, 'Against the Foreign Imposition of Domestic Institutions', in S. Recchia and N. Urbinati (eds.), *Mazzini: A Cosmopolitanism of Nations* (Princeton: Princeton University Press, 2010), pp. 136–40, at p. 138.
[82] S. Recchia, 'The Origins of Liberal Wilsonianism: Giuseppe Mazzini on Regime Change and Humanitarian Intervention', in S. Recchia and J. Walsh (eds.), *Just and Unjust Military Intervention* (Cambridge: Cambridge University Press, 2013), pp. 237–62.
[83] Cf. D. Moggach and W. de Ridder, 'Hegelianism in Restoration Prussia, 1841–1848', in L. Herzog (ed.), *Hegel's Thought in Europe* (Basingstoke: Palgrave, 2013), pp. 71–92, at pp. 77 ff.; M. Hardimon, *Hegel's Social Philosophy: The Project of Reconciliation* (Cambridge: Cambridge University Press, 1985).
[84] John Stuart Mill, *Considerations on Representative Government* (1861), in *Collected Works of John Stuart Mill*, ed. J. Robson, 33 vols. (Toronto: University of Toronto Press, 1977), XIX, part 2, chap. 16, p. 547.
[85] J. Burrow, *Whigs and Liberals* (Oxford: Clarendon, 1988), pp. 115, 117, 122.

hesitation claiming that the 'ideally best form of government is that in which the sovereignty, or supreme controlling power in the last resort, is vested in the entire aggregate of the community'.[86] Bluntschli, too, was particularly adept at combining the lessons of these federal nations when framing his discussion of popular sovereignty, even wondering whether Switzerland offered a possible model for the future of Europe, or whether Swiss ideas ultimately lay behind the federalism of the United States of America.[87] He well understood the fiscal limitations upon Switzerland's capacity to wage war on a truly modern scale, however, something the American experience had highlighted. But the principle of nationality and the indirect dimensions of popular sovereignty were as ideally congruent for Bluntschli as they were for Guizot and Tocqueville, and as they remained for Mazzini.

If there is a nineteenth-century theory of popular sovereignty, then, it is concerned with the connections between nationality and indirect sovereignty, and in that sense it is a logical heir to the claims about the nation and popular sovereignty that were elaborated by Sieyès during the brief decade of his major political writing. If Mill's is a much better-known account of the desirability of national popular sovereignty under representative government, it is certainly not the case that he uses the language of popular sovereignty anywhere nearly as extensively as does Bluntschli. Bluntschli's argument proposed a reintroduction into the nineteenth century of principles of peaceful federation on the basis of a revised principle of nationality and a renewed model of popular sovereignty. He sought to reintroduce a peace that had been shattered by the French Revolution. Furthermore, he tried to explain unity in the modern state as the result of a process of deliberation rather than the imposition of a general will. In its tentative ways, this clearly mapped onto the fluid legal and cartographic boundaries of sovereignty in central Europe in the nineteenth century.[88] In fact, Bluntschli might even constitute an unacknowledged foundation for contemporary democratic theory in its attempt to reconnect popular sovereignty with indirect forms of deliberative and federal politics.[89] More likely, though, is Harold Laski's suggestion that ended his discussion of the theory and practice of popular sovereignty after the Great War. There he wrote that 'certainly the history of popular sovereignty will teach

---

[86] Mill, *Considerations*, chap. 3, p. 404.

[87] J. K. Bluntschli, s.v. 'Demokratie und Repräsentativdemokratie', in Löning (ed.), *Bluntschli's Staatswörterbuch in drei Bänden*, I, pp. 464–70.

[88] S. Weichlein, 'Europa und der Föderalismus: Zur Begriffsgeschichte politischer Ordnungsmodelle', *Historisches Jahrbuch* 125 (2005), pp. 133–52.

[89] B. Manin, 'On Legitimacy and Political Deliberation', *Political Theory* 15.3 (1987), pp. 338–68, esp. pp. 346 ff.

its students that the announcement of its desirability in nowise coincides with the attainment of its substance'.[90] If the nineteenth century does have a theory of popular sovereignty, it exists only with reference to the particular development of a new state theory of national, indirect and representative government.

[90] Laski, 'Theory of Popular Sovereignty', p. 215.

12   Popular sovereignty and anti-colonialism

Karuna Mantena

I

In the history of popular sovereignty, the twentieth century marks the moment of its greatest expansion and acceptance.[1] And within this story of expansion, the political processes of decolonisation came to play a defining role. Decolonisation was the pivot whereby self-determination became the dominant principle of political legitimacy – gaining international legal recognition and codification for the first time – and the nation-state became its institutional counterpart. Together, this enabled the simultaneous delegitimisation of empire as a political form and a conclusive rejection of monarchy as a principle of legitimacy. In these terms, decolonisation would appear responsible for the geographic reach of a distinct institutional–ideological nexus, one that in effect marked the political transformation towards popular sovereignty on a truly global scale.

This has come to be a standard view of the historical achievement of decolonisation and the project of anti-colonial nationalism. But while it is compelling and correct in the broadest sense, it also harbours important limitations for historical and critical analysis. First, the spread of popular sovereignty is understood primarily as a story of diffusion, of settled concepts and institutional forms that moved outward from Europe to encompass the globe. Decolonisation here is seen to complete older political trajectories. It serves as the vehicle, on the one hand, for the universalisation of the Westphalian state system and, on the other, the spread of a model of national self-determination, of popular sovereignty in its nationalist form that had come to fruition in nineteenth-century Europe. Secondly, this account often entails a teleology in which the endpoint of decolonisation – the post-war nation-state settlement – is taken to be an

---

[1] Popular sovereignty is here associated most readily with principles of self-determination and democratic legitimacy, though, of course, both terms have been subject to immense interpretative ambiguity. See J. Dunn, *Setting the People Free: The Story of Democracy* (London: Atlantic Books, 2006).

intended and necessary, rather than a contested and contingent, historical outcome. And because anti-colonial nationalism seemingly ended in the proliferation of nation-states, arguing for the nation-state is understood as the main agenda of anti-imperial thought.[2] Both tendencies hide from view the changing contexts and predicaments that propelled the politics of decolonisation and animated the diverse ideological projects of anti-colonialism, especially the varied ways in which of the problem of popular sovereignty was imagined within them.

For a classic diffusionist account from the perspective of international relations, consider the seminal collection *The Expansion of International Society*, edited by Hedley Bull and Adam Watson. This work characterised decolonisation as the entry of non-European states into a pre-existing 'society of states', a cultural–political order whose foundations were primarily if not wholly European in origin and structure.[3] Anti-colonialism appears as a demand for inclusion into a regime of formal sovereign equality as it had already been codified, a view that downplayed the contentious nature of its politics, especially radical critiques of the existing international order that often sustained the political imagination of Third Worldist nationalism.[4] Narratives of successful diffusion of this kind lend themselves to expectations of peaceable accommodation and translation, even perhaps an implicit celebration of Westernisation as the proper *telos* of a now globalised modernity.

But accounts of diffusion can also have a more neutral or critical stance. Indeed, some of the most revealing are those that have used this frame as way to offer more starkly negative assessments of decolonisation. Here, diffusion works to expose the *artificiality* of the process. The spread of nationalism and adoption of the nation-state appear as fraught impositions on societies that lack the requisite sociological characteristics to meet this historical challenge.[5] In a seminal early account, Elie Kedourie provocatively portrayed anti-colonial nationalism as an

[2] See esp. M. Goswami, 'Imaginary Futures and Colonial Internationalisms', *American Historical Review* 117.5 (2012), pp. 1461–85.

[3] H. Bull and A. Watson (eds.), *The Expansion of International Society* (Oxford: Clarendon Press, 1984), pp. 1–9, 117–26.

[4] M. T. Berger, 'After the Third World? History, Destiny and the Fate of Third Worldism', *Third World Quarterly* 25. (2004), pp. 9–39.

[5] The works of Elie Kedourie, Basil Davidson and Robert Jackson, despite important differences in tone and perspective, are exemplary of this genre of analysis. B. Davidson, *The Black Man's Burden: Africa and the Curse of the Nation-State* (New York: Times Books, 1992); E. Kedourie, *Nationalism* (London: Hutchinson & Co. Ltd, 1960); E. Kedourie, 'Introduction', in *Nationalism in Asia and Africa* (New York and Cleveland: New American Library, 1970), pp. 1–152; R. H. Jackson, *Quasi-States: Sovereignty, International Relations and the Third World* (Cambridge: Cambridge University Press, 1990).

inherently self-defeating project. It was a mimetic importation of a European pathology, one whose fundamental flaws had been more severely exposed as it came to be adopted in Asia and Africa.[6] For Kedourie, nationalism was always infused with romantic and revolutionary fantasy, fantasies of uniformity and *tabula rasa* foundings. When such projects were exported, they became ever more untethered from political realities and ever more subject to outright manipulation. In effect, nationalism functioned as an ideology intrumentalised by an alienated, Westernised elite to mobilise mass sentiment towards the capture of state power.[7] Even the anti-modernism of Gandhi, that is, anti-colonial visions that were explicitly formulated as alternatives to Westernisation, are still, for Kedourie, trapped within the logic of imitation, here as a reactionary pastoralism that is equally European/Western in derivation.[8]

Whether seen as curse or a blessing, these diffusionist accounts take the nation-state and nationalism in its European form as the *telos* of anti-colonialism. In so doing, they effectively circumscribe the debate on decolonisation as one in which the historical efficacy of the anti-colonial project stands or falls on its ability to successfully adopt European models. What this misses – in a rather profound sense – is an account of what nationalism in its anti-colonial form was demanding in its own terms and at various moments in its historical emergence and evolution.

This lacuna was sharply brought to light in Partha Chatterjee's seminal work, *Nationalist Thought and the Colonial World*.[9] In his critical view of the then burgeoning scholarly literature on nationalism, Chatterjee noted how this literature was trapped by attempts to distinguish good from bad or pathological nationalisms. Moreover, what was especially prominent and problematic in his view was how – in the case of the non-European world – pathological formations were taken as almost inevitable and explained in terms of sociological differences. For it was something within the character of those societies – their underdevelopment, their demographic pluralism etc. – that was seen to determine the failure of proper instantiation or adoption of Western models of the nation-state. For Chatterjee, this way of conceptualising failure as a kind of deviation from a pre-existing norm allowed for the reinvigoration of the purity and salience of the norm itself, and at the same time it left no effective room to view anti-colonial nationalism as a space of

---

[6] Kedourie, *Nationalism in Asia and Africa*, pp. 29–31.
[7] Kedourie, *Nationalism*, introduction and chap. 6; Kedourie, *Nationalism in Asia and Africa*, pp. 81–92.
[8] Kedourie, *Nationalism in Asia and Africa*, pp. 58–61.
[9] P. Chatterjee, *Nationalist Thought and the Colonial World: A Derivative Discourse?* (London: Zed Books, 1986).

conceptual or institutional innovation. In Chatterjee's terms, there was no space to think the autonomy of nationalist discourse.[10] To be sure, using the term *autonomy* in opposition to conditions of modularity and mimicry can sometimes appear like a plea for the recognition of the authenticity of anti-colonialism. But the stakes of Chatterjee's intervention were different. They had less to do with the authenticity of the politics of decolonisation than a call to understand their *specificity*. That is, it was most importantly a demand to reconstruct the problems and predicaments facing decolonising societies to which anti-colonial nationalism emerged as a distinct response.

This brings us to the second limitation in accepted understandings of decolonisation, namely the problem of teleology. Since decolonisation seemingly concluded in the separation and independence of formal colonial possessions, the nation-state is taken as the logical outcome of the political evolution of anti-colonialism. 'From this perspective', as Manu Goswami notes, 'all anti-imperial struggles were a staging ground for the modular developmental endpoint of a sovereign nation-state rather than an open-ended constellation of contending political futures.'[11] Moreover, as Mrinalini Sinha has argued, this kind of account 'gives an air of inevitability to the trajectory from empire to nation-state'.[12] In such a retrospective view, the British Empire is reconfigured as naturally evolving towards self-government. And, in doing so, for Sinha, we do not adequately attend to the ways in which a dramatically changing imperial landscape itself impinged upon and shaped the political visions and arguments of erstwhile critics of empire.[13] In particular, we miss the broad range of conceptualisations of self-determination, sovereignty and self-rule which in their historical emergence were compatible with and premised upon intensified connection and greater integration with imperial political structures.

Crucially, if we take the nation-state to exhaust the political imagination of anti-colonialism, we are very likely to leave out of view an understanding of projects of sovereignty that were popular and anti-imperial but not necessarily *national* and *statist* as their post-war settlements. Some of the most important projects in this more 'open-ended constellation' that Goswami notes would be the various internationalist

[10] Ibid., pp. 1–36.　[11] Goswami, 'Imaginary Futures', p. 1462.

[12] M. Sinha, 'Whatever Happened to the Third British Empire? Empire, Nation Redux', in A. S. Thompson (ed.), *Writing Imperial Histories* (Manchester: Manchester University Press, 2013), pp. 168–183.

[13] Ibid.; M. Sinha, 'The Strange Death of an Imperial Ideal: The Case of *Civis Britannicus*', in S. Dube (ed.), *Handbook of Modernity in South Asia: Modern Makeovers* (New Delhi: Oxford University Press, 2012), pp. 29–42.

visions of anti-imperialism that explicitly sought ways to build models of solidarity and political modernity beyond the nation-state.[14] Even in its more mainstream form – for instance, in the internationalism of the Bandung declarations – anti-colonial intellectuals and politicians argued for a critical assessment and reconstitution of the international order, but in a manner that did not position nationalism and internationalism as antagonistic ideologies. A second form of non-state and non-national projects of sovereignty, and one I will attend to more closely, can also been found in various arguments for and articulations of models of federation.

With these corrections in mind, this chapter takes the Indian case and charts the evolution of the debate on empire, state and popular sovereignty in anti-imperial thinking. First I consider the conjuncture in the late nineteenth century when Indian nationalism becomes anti-imperial as such. I track how Indian liberalism and anti-colonial criticism developed in tandem through the articulation of a set of demands for the British Empire to fulfil its liberal ideals, demands for *swaraj* (self-rule) that were premised on greater inclusion and representation within a federated imperial structure. I argue that these models break down in the context of external changes in imperial and dominion politics which propelled anti-colonial critique in a more separatist direction. I then examine how the conceptualisation of the problem of empire shifts, and how these shifts come to shape competing views of post-colonial sovereignty. In particular, I draw attention to various arguments and proposals for decentralised and federative forms of sovereignty. I am interested in these alternative models less to raise them as utopias or lost ideals to be recovered than as a means to chart in a more textured way how actors understood the political predicaments they faced and how that assessment changed over time. Most crucially, in the evolution of anti-colonial critique and the politics of decolonisation, I chart how the problem of popular sovereignty shifts from questions of self-rule and overcoming empire towards anxieties about representation in the transition to popular rule.

II

In reconstructing the diverse forms of opposition to empire, I want to begin by marking a key conjuncture in which empire emerged as a political problem that required overcoming. Recent scholarship on the origins and varieties of anti-colonial thought and practice has highlighted the ways in which anti-colonial criticism often began by seeking some

---

[14] Goswami, 'Imaginary Futures'.

kind of framework of participation and equal citizenship *within* imperial frameworks before making any outright claims for independence. This argument has been most forcefully made in the case of the French Empire, in which a republican model of equal citizenship was available as a political ideal towards which imperial reformers and critics alike could orient themselves. In this vein, Gary Wilder has shown that *négritude* – often taken as deep rejection of imperial ideology – had its origins in inter-war projects of imperial reform premised on imperial institutional integration.[15] Fred Cooper has made this case even more insistently vis-à-vis post-war African decolonisation.[16] Cooper has shown how many left-wing movements – labour movements especially – used the egalitarian rhetoric of imperial republicanism, most radically instantiated in the 1946 law of imperial citizenship, to ground assertions of equal social and political rights, rights to equal participation, access to education, wages and social services. Again, extensive claims for equality were tied to arguments for more substantial institutional integration – especially claims for equal representation and voice in an empire that would be effectively transforming into a unified multinational state.[17] These aspirations made a range of claims that, in the end, the metropole found impossible to fulfil within the political form of empire, and thus set the stage for more open demands for separation.

For Cooper, the ways in which African movements navigated and opened up 'internal fissures within imperial structures and ideologies'[18] shows how the trajectory from empire to nation-state, which in retrospect seems natural and inevitable, was in fact a highly conjunctural and contingent outcome. Nineteenth-century empires contained within themselves diverse and competing political tendencies and possibilities, and devolution into autonomous self-governing units was not in any obvious way the dominant tendency. Arguments for more integrated federation – whether as national empires and or imperial nation-states – proved especially attractive. Indeed, what is striking is how arguments for greater self-government could be yoked quite easily with claims for imperial connection. One need only consider here the wide-ranging debate on the idea of Greater Britain, a set of projects whose political momentum and logic could be seen, in part, as the fulfilment of the dominion idea. For many metropolitan and colonial advocates, the idea of Greater Britain

[15]   G. Wilder, *The French Imperial Nation-State: Negritude and Colonial Humanism between the Two World Wars* (Chicago: University of Chicago Press, 2005); G. Wilder, 'Untimely Vision: Aimé Césaire, Decolonisation, Utopia', *Public Culture* 21.1(2009), pp. 101–40.

[16]   See esp. F. Cooper, *Colonialism in Question: Theory, Knowledge, History* (Berkeley: University of California Press, 2005), pp. 153–230.

[17]   Ibid., p. 177.   [18]   Ibid., p. 204.

could reconcile claims for self-government with tighter cooperation in a manner that could allow it to compete effectively with the large national empires/imperial states that dominated world politics.[19]

Though not equivalent to the timing and pattern of African decolonisation, Indian nationalism underwent a similar trajectory. In the latter half of the nineteenth century Indian liberalism began to articulate a critique of empire within the fissures of British imperial structures and discourses of legitimacy. Indian critics in numerous ways called upon Britain to fulfil the liberal imperial ideal that had at various times been overtly articulated as a discourse of legitimacy. This model was most often associated with the idea of British rule as a trusteeship that would oversee education of native subjects towards self-government, offer legal equality and protection as imperial subjects of the Crown, and promote economic freedom and prosperity.[20] The vigour of liberal criticism was closely tied to claims for greater inclusion and representation within a federated imperial structure. The political coordinates that enabled the emergence of anti-colonial criticism of this kind would be imbricated in changing imperial trajectories and horizons (and vice versa). As the avenues for imperial integration along liberal lines became more and more constrained, anti-colonial criticism began to seek political solutions beyond the framework of British rule, and at the same time began to pose the problem of empire in sharper and more radical terms.

The British Empire in the late nineteenth century was marked by two divergent constitutional trajectories. The white settler colonies and future dominions – what Seeley called the true British Empire[21] – were demanding and accruing greater degrees of self-government. By contrast, the dependent empire – colonies and dependencies of predominantly non-white populations – were experiencing growing authoritarianism and aggressive disavowals of the possibility of representative government. In British India, this represented a sharp reversal of the model of liberal empire that had been advocated in the early part of the nineteenth century, and associated with such reformers such as James Mill and T. B. Macaulay. In India, especially after 1857, official rhetoric and policy began to push back against this liberal agenda and its institutional programme – the cornerstone of which was education for

---

[19] D. Bell, *The Idea of Greater Britain: Empire and the Future of World Order, 1860–1900* (Princeton: Princeton University Press, 2007).

[20] T. Metcalf, *Ideologies of the Raj* (Cambridge: Cambridge University Press, 1995), pp. 28–66; E. Stokes, *The English Utilitarians and India* (Oxford: Clarendon Press, 1963); K. Mantena, *Alibis of Empire: Henry Maine and the Ends of Liberal Imperialism* (Princeton: Princeton University Press, 2010), pp. 21–55.

[21] J. R. Seeley, *The Expansion of England* (London: Macmillan, 1883).

self-government.[22] In Macaulay's well-known liberal formulation, British rule in India should promote the production of a class of Anglicised Indians who would mediate the relationship between rulers and subjects and legitimate British rule through affective ties to the regime and its civilisational heritage.[23] Elite education would promote greater investment and participation in British rule, lending security to the imperial enterprise and laying the foundations for eventual self-government. But as the liberal project came to be criticised for its allegedly destabilising effects, members of the Anglicised Indian elite were increasingly portrayed as alienated, dangerous and untrustworthy collaborators in British rule.

The irony was that just as imperial liberalism entered a period of decline, Indian liberalism was reaching a moment of fruition and self-confidence.[24] C. A. Bayly has recently argued that Indian liberalism reaches back at least to the early nineteenth century, and produced a recognisably liberal set of political demands whose appeal continued throughout the century.[25] But its late nineteenth-century ascendency was distinct in that its political agenda was now intimately tied to the experience and claims of a broader class of Indians, a class comprising the direct beneficiaries and descendants of the Macaulayite vision. Indian liberals of this generation were thus inculcated with affective and material investments in the liberal ideal, and saw its fulfilment as part of Britain's historical mission in and for India.[26] Moreover, the concurrent expansion of the dominion ideal – as well as the importance of the Indian empire within the imperial structure as a whole – would raise Indian hopes for some expansion of representative government.

These liberal endeavours, premised upon a continued framework of imperial collaboration, were increasingly rebuffed, sparking deepening disillusionment. Some of the events that galvanised liberal outrage were the setbacks in the instantiation of legal equality, represented by the Ilbert Bill Crisis (1883) within British India and the debate on the status of overseas Indian migrants in South Africa. Racialisation was seemingly

---

[22] Metcalf, *Ideologies of the Raj*, pp. 66–112; Mantena, *Alibis of Empire*, pp. 21–55, 148–78.

[23] T. B. Macaulay, 'Minute on Indian Education', in *Macaulay: Prose and Poetry* (Cambridge, MA: Harvard University Press, 1970), pp. 720–35. See also the 1833 speech on charter renewal, 'Government of India', pp. 688–718 in the same volume.

[24] Theodore Koditschek explores this historical conjuncture very well in relation to key figures of Indian liberalism such as Surendranath Banerjea, Dadabhai Naoroji and R. C. Dutt, in *Liberalism, Imperialism, and the Historical Imagination: Nineteenth-Century Visions of a Greater Britain* (Cambridge: Cambridge University Press, 2011), pp. 286–311.

[25] C. A. Bayly, *Recovering Liberties: Indian Thought in the Age of Liberalism and Empire* (Cambridge: Cambridge University Press, 2011).

[26] Ibid., pp. 131–61; Koditschek, *Liberalism, Imperialism, and the Historical Imagination*, pp. 286–93.

triumphing over the more universal potential of imperial citizenship. The Indian National Congress was founded in 1882, at the moment of this clash between a retreating imperial liberalism and Indian liberal assertion. Its core demands – from greater elected representation on legislative councils to lowering the barriers placed upon Indians in relation to the Indian Civil Service – were closely aligned to the Macaulayite project of education towards self-government. But perhaps the most original and most consequential form of anti-colonial critique to emerge from this milieu was that of Dadabhai Naoroji and R. C. Dutt. It targeted the third pillar of the liberal imperial project in India – the promise of economic prosperity – as the means by which to press claims for representation. Naoroji's *Poverty and Un-British Rule in India* announced in its title its liberal style of critique, charging the British with the 'non-fulfilment of solemn promises' and seeking to impress 'their duty' to realise 'true British rule'.[27]

Naoroji, a scholar, industrialist and statesman from Bombay, was known as the 'Grand Old Man' of Indian politics.[28] He was a leader of the liberal cause for over forty years. One of the founding members of the Indian National Congress, and one of its precursors, the East India Association (1867), which explicitly sought to lobby for the Indian cause in British politics, Naoroji was for much of his later years deeply enmeshed in British Indian politics in London, and was the centre of gravity for Indian students and activists. Famously, Naoroji became the first Indian MP in Britain, as a Liberal for Finsbury Central in the elections of 1892. Throughout his career, Naoroji had been keen to investigate the impact of the government's economic policies in India, and – as an MP – he pushed for a full parliamentary commission on the subject. The papers, speeches and commentary collected as *Poverty and Un-British Rule in India* came to establish the so-called drain theory. This tried to demonstrate a net transfer of wealth from India to Britain, in effect showing that British economic development had been made on the back of Indian exploitation. Naoriji used statistical models to calculate ratio of investments, returns and tax burdens.[29] He argued that the average Indian was subject to drastically higher taxation than their English counterpart, and that this heavy tax burden seemed to only make them poorer. The period of British growth was coincident with a period of decline in per

---

[27] D. Naoroji, *Poverty and Un-British Rule in India* (Delhi: Government of India Press, 1962 [1901]).

[28] M. K. Gandhi, 'The Grand Old Man of India (3–9–1910)' in *The Collected Works of Mahatma Gandhi* (electronic book), 98 vols. (Delhi: Government of India, 1999), XI, pp. 112–13 (henceforth *CWMG*).

[29] Bayly, *Recovering Liberties*, pp. 104–31.

capita income in India. Naoroji's succinct charge was that Indians paid higher taxes with fewer benefits, and that India was an extreme of case of taxation without representation. Dutt extended this analysis to include a longer-term account of colonial maldevelopment.[30]

Theodore Koditschek has referred to Naoroji's argument as a kind of 'radicalized Macaulayism'.[31] Naoroji would often cite Macaulay's argument in his 1833 speech on charter renewal to cement the point that England would benefit more from Indian prosperity than poverty.[32] The references to Macaulay also revealed a structural feature of the argument, which took the form of a petition. The petition form built arguments from a set of citations that functioned like constitutional precedents: from the early liberal pronouncements of Macaulay and Munro, the 1833 charter renewal Act as well as – and most especially – the 1858 Royal Proclamation (which was considered the Magna Carta for India). These citations created a lawyerly case, establishing precedent, so as to demonstrate that imperial practice had gone astray from the avowed ethical and political aims enshrined and promised in these documents. For Naroji and Dutt the argument was framed as a course that could still be corrected and solved within the terms of imperial institutions. The central solution involved greater representation of and consultation with Indians in the development of colonial policy, so that Indian interests would no longer be subordinated to English ones.

The term around which these demands coalesced was the call for *swaraj*, or self-rule. Institutionally, *swaraj* was understood as something like a legislature or parliament in India with substantial native representation, and linked sometimes to a reformed imperial parliament. In the meantime, Congress would be the germ of such a native parliament. Though India was rarely included in Victorian arguments about the forging of a more integrated empire, since arguments for Greater Britain almost always focused on the white settler colonies and dominions, it generated a horizon of expectation in terms of which Indian nationalists could imagine inclusion on equal terms with white dominions. Thus in its emergence *swaraj* was a model of self-rule compatible with

---

[30] R. C. Dutt, *The Economic History of India*, 2 vols. (New York: Ben Franklin, 1970 [1906]).

[31] Koditschek, *Liberalism, Imperialism, and the Historical Imagination*, p. 294.

[32] 'It would be on the most selfish view of the case far better for us that the people of India were well-governed and independent of us, than ill-governed and subject to us – that they were ruled by their own kings, but wearing our broadcloth and working with our cutlery, than they were performing their *salaams* to English collectors and English magistrates, but were too ignorant to value, or too poor to buy, English manufactures. To trade with civilised men is infinitely more profitable than to govern savages': quoted in Naoroji, *Poverty and Un-British Rule*, p. 81.

membership in the Empire. Indeed, ambiguity about what *swaraj* actually meant – slippage between more sovereignty within empire, dominion status, to outright independence – remained at least until the 1929 Congress resolution calling for *purna swaraj* or total independence.

From the vantage point of later nationalist historiography, these liberal forms of critique are often viewed and ridiculed as accommodationist, even sycophantic in their attachment to British ideals and institutions. But at another level it is striking that they began to imagine something like dominion status, or some form of self-government, despite the fact that there was nothing even close to institutions of self-government in place. Here one underrated factor that contributed to this outsized ambition was the sheer importance of the Indian empire in the nineteenth century. British India often functioned as an independent power. It had its own foreign policy (for example, it ran a residency system that extended outwards from Delhi to South-East Asia, Iran and East Africa) and, like the dominions, it had representation at the Treaty of Versailles and a seat at the League of Nations. In fact, it was this legal identity that India would inherit in 1947. This anomalous status of British India – as on par with but yet not equivalent to a dominion – would be the problem that greater imperial integration would continually come up against.

If the late nineteenth century saw the shrinking of the liberal model within British India, a similar kind of reversal was experienced by Indians in the Empire. Perhaps the best-known case that illustrates this dilemma was M. K. Gandhi's famous campaign on behalf of the rights of Indian indentured labourers and migrants in South Africa. Gandhi's political work began with a series of attempts to forestall the disenfranchisement of Indians in Natal and then in the Transvaal. Over time, these manoeuvres became concerted efforts to restrict Asian immigration entirely, with the explicit goal of making residence in South Africa so unattractive as to motivate repatriation. In his early campaigns Gandhi appealed directly to the Crown to protect the equal legal and political status of Indians as their birthright as imperial subjects, and to secure, at a minimum, non-racial criteria for suffrage. In these petitions, as well as in *Hind Swaraj*, Gandhi like Naoroji would refer to a similar set of documents – Macaulay, Munro, the 1833 Charter Act, and the 1858 Proclamation to substantiate claims for citizenship. Gandhi would also add excerpts from Max Muller and Henry Maine to prove that Indians had had experience of representative government.[33] What little Gandhi could secure from

---

[33] M. K. Gandhi, 'Petition to Natal Assembly (28–6–1894)', in *CWMG*, I, pp. 144–8, at p. 145; M. K. Gandhi, *Hind Swaraj*, in *CWMG*, X, pp. 245–325, at pp. 312–15.

London would be increasingly circumscribed by the eventual grant of self-government to the Union of South Africa.

Gandhi had become instantly and dramatically politicised by the South Africa predicament because it was experienced as the loss of the basic privileges of imperial citizenship: mobility across the empire and legal protection. Gandhi often remarked with incredulity that the Crown and Parliament seemed unwilling to protect in South Africa the same basic rights that Indians like himself readily enjoyed in London. This transition, as Sinha argues, marked a radical shift from an imperial idea associated with an enlarged but integrated empire-state to one that was becoming a congeries of national entities. By the inter-war years – after a very brief flirtation with a broad-based citizenship law – the nationalisation of the empire seemingly triumphed, and with it the final abandonment of the imperial model of federation.[34] Gandhi's departure from South Africa for India was in part a recognition that the battle for imperial citizenship was a losing one. Indians could no longer look to the imperial Parliament for protection across the empire, but rather their rights might be better secured via self-government in India.

III

The hope for more integrative models of imperial union and imperial citizenship had begun to lose their purchase for anti-colonial projects as their attempted realisation received little traction either in Parliament or from successive British Indian administrations. Though the idea of accommodating *swaraj* within the British Empire was not explicitly rejected by the call for full independence until 1929, what *swaraj* could mean had begun to shift in the wake of a series of mass mobilisations against British rule, first with the Swadeshi movement in 1905–7, and most spectacularly with the Non-Cooperation/Khilafat movement of 1920–2. Moreover, the move away from notions of an imperial federation or Greater Britain towards a looser model of a commonwealth of nations signalled an important defeat of what Sinha terms 'an erstwhile imperial conception of empire'.[35]

Though all these tendencies seemingly marked the sharp decline of empire as a unified political form, the centralised nation-state did not immediately fill this vacuum as the only available alternative. In the inter-war period, all the way to the very moment of independence, other

---

[34] Sinha, 'Whatever Happened to the Third British Empire?'; Sinha, 'The Strange Death of an Imperial Ideal'.

[35] Sinha, 'Whatever Happened to the Third British Empire?', p. 169.

models of less centralised, federal state forms were envisaged and given some institutional shape. In the next two sections I examine three different attempts to construct alternative federal models for Indian independence. In this section I focus on the Gandhian–*swadeshi* model, arguably the most utopian and thoroughgoing attempt to conceptualise a polity beyond empire and nation. I shall then consider more briefly the aborted princely state federation and the federal proposals made by M. A. Jinnah as leader of the Muslim League. Jinnah's pleas and proposals in particular were driven less by concerns about the problem of empire per se than with the dilemmas posed by the transition to popular sovereignty in a national form. In effect, he was facing up to the challenges and predicaments posed by *decolonisation* in the most direct sense.

The liberal critique of the late nineteenth century began to pose the problem of empire as a problem of alien rule. Alien rule was seen as enabling arbitrary and despotic government, distortions that were undermining India's economic future and constraining social and political evolution. In the first instance it was a problem that required mitigation by greater native representation, i.e. it could be resolved within liberal terms. But metropolitan resistance to reform – the refusal to live up to liberal ideals – opened up a series of claims that the liberal mission might be better and more quickly secured outside the framework of British rule altogether. Indeed, the scale of the liberal critique itself – the unveiling of a wide range of negative consequences of British rule – worked to engender a sense that empire might be unreformable on its own terms. What began as an internal critique of British rule on grounds of exclusion and inequality developed into more critical meditations about pathologies resulting from the very fact of empire.

For Gandhi a truly post-imperial politics would require a more thoroughgoing rejection of imperial cultural and political forms. In South Africa through to the launching of the Non-Cooperation Movement Gandhi would position himself as an internal, liberal critic of empire, arguing for rights as a loyal British subject. But within these early campaigns he began to shift his tactics from a liberal model of petitioning to acts of civil disobedience, eventually moving to mass forms of non-violent resistance, or *satyagraha*; a shift which entailed a new understanding of the problem of empire. This new agenda was first announced in his seminal pamphlet, *Hind Swaraj or Indian Home Rule* (1909), written while he was still enmeshed in South African politics and a full seven years before his return to India.

In *Hind Swaraj* Gandhi famously ridiculed both traditional liberals and their radical critics for conceiving of independence as merely a demand for 'English rule without the Englishman'.[36] If empire is understood as simply a problem of alien rule, Gandhi argued, anti-colonial nationalism seemingly aimed at 'a mere change of personnel',[37] or, more bitingly, 'a change of masters only'.[38] For Gandhi, greater native representation was not altogether insignificant; he thought it would end specifically colonial forms of exploitation (such as the drain of wealth) and check the most egregious abuses of power. At the same time, such an understanding of anti-colonial sovereignty was too limited and could not be equated with true *swaraj*. To simply replace British rule 'by Indian rule based on modern methods' would condemn India to 'become a second or fifth edition of Europe or America'.[39]

In *Hind Swaraj*, Gandhi attempted to demonstrate to the Western-educated elite, the then leaders and activists of the Indian cause, that the nationalism they espoused was not thorough or radical enough precisely because it was overly enamoured of the achievements of modern civilisation. In this respect, *Hind Swaraj* is remembered, and rightly so, as Gandhi's most sustained indictment of modern civilisation as one that degrades and 'de-civilizes'.[40] Gandhi's critique was therefore in part a plea for civilisational revitalisation, but it was one that was also tied to the search for specifically anti- or post-imperial political institutions.

Gandhi posed the problem of empire as the problem of a particular kind of rule, tied to a specific state form. If independence would result in the mere capturing of the state, then it would simply retain, in his words, 'the tiger's nature but not the tiger'.[41] That is, the adoption of the modern state would do nothing to undo institutional tendencies towards militarism, expansion and domination – in other words, imperialism. For Gandhi, true *swaraj* had to challenge the underlying forces that made possible and emboldened imperialism. In its more creative and radical form, Gandhi's proposal involved a series of claims that saw the structure of empire implicated in the nature of the modern state. It asserted that a properly post-imperial political form required a rejection of the state in its modern imperial form and therefore sought a reconfigured state form that could serve as the basis for an alternative to the Eurocentric world order, and perhaps of modernity itself.

These aspects of Gandhi's cultural–political agenda had their most direct roots in the Swadeshi movement of 1905–7, a turning point in

---

[36] Gandhi, *Hind Swaraj*, p. 255.
[37] M. K. Gandhi, 'Letter to *The Times of India* (22–8–1919)',in *CWMG*, XVIII, p. 304.
[38] M. K. Gandhi, 'Speech at Meeting of Deccan Princes (28–7–1946)',in *CWMG*, XCI, p. 371.
[39] M. K. Gandhi, 'Letter to H. S. L. Polak (14–10–1909)', in*CWMG*, X, pp. 168–9.
[40] Gandhi, *Hind Swaraj*, chap. 3.   [41] Ibid., p. 255.

anti-colonial mobilisation.[42] Sparked by the administrative partition of the province of Bengal, the movement galvanised and popularised a more radical ideal of self-rule which – like Gandhi's vision – entailed a more explicit rejection of imperial cultural and political authority. The ideology of *swadeshi* evolved in part as a reaction against what was viewed as the assimilative ideals of late nineteenth-century Indian liberalism. *Swadeshi* can be translated as 'of one's own, of one's own country' – Gandhi saw it as the Indian equivalent of the term *Sinn Fein* – and as such it was characterised by an anti-colonial cultural politics that rejected European/British culture as corrupting, materialist and eviscerating of Indian traditions. But this cultural revivalism could be tied to disparate, inchoate and even contradictory institutional projects – everything from militant statist projects (that, for example, took Japan as their model) to explicitly apolitical agendas of social and spiritual reform.

The strand I want to highlight – and one that I suggest was developed in Gandhian politics –directed its attention to the discovery, revival and reform of specifically Indian political institutions. Just as the cultural politics of *swadeshi* advocated a return to the indigenous and the vernacular, some of the intellectual currents it engendered turned towards unearthing vernacular political forms. At its most innovative moments, these works thought hard about how to modify these traditional political and economic institutions in the direction of alternative – post-imperial and universal – political forms.

The turn to the history of Indian political institutions broadly took two forms.On the one hand, intellectuals looked to specify and reconstruct Hindu political institutions, a tradition which was often taken to lack a theory of politics. In this vein, they revisited a range of ancient texts – such as the epics the *Ramayana* and *Mahabharata* – as well as archaeological evidence to unearth precedents for democratic practices and evidence of republican institutions, from elected kingships and aristocracies to forms of voting in religious orders (the most persuasive of which relied upon the Buddhist Pali canon).[43] A second and sometimes overlapping strand was more sociological/anthropological and focused especially on analysing caste bodies, village societies and local governing institutions as self-regulating social–political orders.

---

[42] S. Sarkar, *The Swadeshi Movement of Bengal 1903–1908* (New Delhi: Oxford University Press, 1973).

[43] The most important works of this historiography were R. C. Majumdar, *Corporate Life in Ancient India* (Calcutta: Firma K. L. Mukhopadhya, 1918); R. Mookerji, *Local Government in Ancient India* (Oxford: Clarendon Press, 1920); B. Prasad, *Theory of Government of Ancient India* (Allahabad: Indian Press, 1927); H. N. Sinha, *Sovereignty in Ancient Indian Polity: A Study in the Evolution of Early Indian State* (London: Luzac, 1938).

Some of this literature was meant simply to prove the existence of democratic institutions as a way to reject the imperial claim that India had no experience of representative institutions and was thus incapable of self-government – one key element in late nineteenth-century justifications of imperial rule. But the most interesting strands were more constructive in purpose, and sought to describe the persistence of these institutions as the potential basis of a new popular, decentralised, post-imperial polity. Radhakamal Mukerjee's *Democracies of the East* was the most accomplished work in this vein.[44] It represented a form of Indian pluralist argument that directly engaged with the debates of the English pluralists and drew upon the imperial sociology of Henry Maine and Alfred Lyall.[45]

This combination made possible – as it did in English pluralist theory – a particular convergence, where village and caste as self-regulating socio-political institutions were posited as alternative forms of association to the centralising structures of the modern state. From Maine especially, the centralising state was seen as necessarily imperialist in its ambition to uniformity and thereby implicated in undermining local associational life. In Indian pluralism Maine's conservative critique of modern sovereignty would be refashioned in a democratic direction, specifically on behalf of a model of decentralised peasant democracy. Here, village societies and caste groups were seen as self-regulating orders (akin to the medieval guild and urban communes) that had resisted incorporation by the state and could therefore form the basis of a new kind of pluralist polity. For Mukerjee the persistence of village communities and caste institutions meant that Asian pluralism was already better placed to reinvigorate new forms of direct democracy and solidarity than Western pluralism, which had to recreate institutions on the ruins of the old medieval guild.

Mukerjee's arguments would coincide with Gandhian attempts to imagine a post-imperial constitution.[46] Like Mukerjee, Gandhi proposed a radically decentralised peasant democracy based upon the revitalised village community at its core as definitive of his conception of *swaraj*. This model offered a genuine contrast to the statist vision of independence associated with Nehru, and entailed a rival understanding of popular sovereignty. For Gandhi and Mukerjee statist sovereignty was associated with dangerous centralisation and hierarchy, and in terms of representation with majoritarianism and elite-driven, constrictive systems

---

[44] R. Mukerjee, *Democracies of the East: A Study in Comparative Politics* (London: P. S. King, 1923).

[45] K. Mantena, 'On Gandhi's Critique of the State: Sources, Contexts, Conjunctures', *Modern Intellectual History* 9.3 (2012), pp. 535–63 at pp. 548–59.

[46] S. N. Agarwal, *Gandhian Constitution for Free India* (Allahabad: Kitabistan, 1946).

of territorial representation. In turning to models of local organisation and functional representation, pluralists were working with a concept of democracy and popular sovereignty defined more by ideals of direct participation and self-rule than by majority rule and the centralised competition of mass democracy.

Within Indian anti-colonialism, the political life of this rival view of empire and sovereignty tended to be restricted to the economic realm. That is, the most important arena for practical implementation and experimentation with the revival of decentralised institutions proved to be the economy, and a whole series of endeavours centred on the rejuvenation of co-operative enterprises at the village level. Mukerjee himself also penned a well-known book, *The Foundations of Indian Economics*,[47] which dovetailed with the large-scale Gandhian programmes in reviving *khadi* and other village industries. At the same time, the more directly political aspects of the project in decentralisation proved to have little traction.

A direct confrontation between statist and anti-statist projects (decentralised vs. centralised visions) never became the main axis of debate within Indian nationalism. On the one hand, Congress's hard investment in centralism was partially shaped by the nature of its confrontation with Britain, where the battle for effective control at the federal centre was seen as key to dislodging British rule (a point I shall come back to). On the other hand, within the Congress, the challenge that Gandhian decentralisation posed was subsumed by a debate about tactics – where *khadi* and constructive work (Gandhi's term for the broad programme of village revitalisation and reform) were understood as primarily programmes of peasant mobilisation and consciousness-raising rather than the groundwork of a new polity. Moreover, when controversy did emerge on the future role of the village (for example, on the eve of independence[48]) the anti-statist or pluralist position was dismissed as backward-looking and traditionalist. In effect, the debate was read as a contest over modernisation. When the constituent assembly met in the late 1940s to fashion the new constitution, the Gandhian imprint was ceremonial at best.

IV

If the nationalisation of empire came to constrain the possibilities of models of federation based upon the imperial form and ideal, nowhere

---

[47] R. Mukerjee, *The Foundations of Indian Economics* (London: Longmans, 1916).

[48] See esp. the Gandhi–Nehru letters of the 1940s which debated the status of the village in a future economy: U. Iyengar and L. Zachariah (eds.), *Together They Fought: Gandhi–Nehru Correspondence, 1921–1948* (New Delhi: Oxford University Press, 2011).

was this reversal felt more sharply than in relation to the fate of India's princely state system and the aborted attempt to build an all-India federation upon it. Britain's concerted efforts to keep India under its political hold, coupled with explicit commitments to the princes – understood as its most powerful and natural of political allies – resulted in strong investments in constitutional frameworks that could secure both aims while effectively resisting the nationalist solution increasingly demanded by Congress. The model of devolution in the British Empire typically took the form of federal unions of self-governing colonies, such as the Union of South Africa, Australia and Canada. In India the princely states – on paper – were perhaps most analogous to these kinds of self-governing units, and so unsurprisingly sought – and were encouraged – to replicate that model of union. But in a rapidly shifting international and domestic political scene around the Second World War and the accelerated pace of post-war devolution, they were soon to discover that their freedom of action was circumscribed and their legal status rendered precarious in the extreme.

This process itself proved to be a protracted and open-ended affair, replete with surprising opportunities and unexpected reversals. From the turn of the century, partly as a reward for their strong allegiance and support as a bulwark against nationalist agitation, Britain had sought ways to create a more permanent institutional structure for princely representation.[49] This effort reached a surprising highpoint in the 1930s, when an all-India Federation was put forward by the Chamber of Princes at the Round Table Conferences (RTC). As Ian Copland notes, despite lacking support from Congress (which had boycotted the initial RTC meetings), the proposal was 'hailed as a grand solution to the Indian dilemma'.[50] With the princely states agreeing to form the backbone of the constitution, in which they could serve as a continuous counterpoise to agitations of the directly ruled territories, the British government for a moment seemed willing to grant a more immediate move to responsible government and dominion status.

This model became the basis of the Government of India Act of 1935, with the majority of provisions being carried forward into the Indian constitution. Despite recognition and anxiety about this deep continuity, the Act's provenance in a princely state system has been rarely remarked upon. The Act established an institutional structure which

---

[49] For example, the Chamber of Princes, which began to function in 1930. I. Copland, *The Princes of India in the Endgame of Empire 1917–1947* (Cambridge: Cambridge University Press, 1997), pp. 35–43.

[50] Ibid., pp. 73–91.

combined provincial autonomy with strong imperial control over 'federal' subjects at the centre. It converted directly ruled territories – the presidencies and the north-west territories – into provinces. Indeed, what was being generalised to all of India was the kind of constricted internal autonomy that the princely states had enjoyed under the structure of British paramountcy. That the princely states might have served as the forerunner to the current logic of provincial autonomy is a striking legacy.

One of the intriguing aspects of the model was its attempt to keep together two contradictory aims: devolution within a hierarchical imperial framework. This paradox was also mirrored in the mixed incentives and strategies that princely states themselves pursued, which were caught between seeking greater connection to imperial supremacy and more autonomy. For decades princes were concerned to renegotiate and clarify treaty terms and obligations, obligations that were understood to lie directly with Crown (and not the government of India). In the 1935 Act this search for imperial guarantees was reiterated in an understanding that the British connection sat at the pinnacle of the federation, and the princely states' accession to it would be via direct negotiation with the Crown.

Why this federation model came undone is the subject of some controversy. The 1937 provincial elections mandated by the Act were the first far-reaching elections in India. They proved to be a stunning victory for Congress, and entailed a marked shift in the balance of power. On the heels of this success, Congress was emboldened to agitate more openly in territories controlled by the princes, and to become more strident in its demands that their accession be conditional on internal political reform. But Copland argues that the federation model was still on track to come into force, despite these disruptions, through to 1939. In his view it came very close to being enacted, but was thwarted by the unpredictable effects of the war, and its impact on a radically accelerated programme of devolution. Whatever its source, the momentum for federation with princely states at its core was abandoned during the war and the British began to disinvest very rapidly in the princely states as their key allies and negotiating partners. The reversal of fortune culminated in the Cabinet Mission Statement of May 1946 in which Britain unilaterally revoked its treaty obligations to the princes (on the contentious grounds of non-fulfilment) and forced them to accede to the successor states of British India.

In the aftermath of the war, and a more concerted interest in finding a final resolution to the Indian question, the princely states' claims were abandoned and overshadowed by dilemmas of devolution. The question that came to dominate discussions of an eventual transfer of power was the communal question, or more specifically that of Muslim representation. It was within the intricate politics around this issue that the idea of federation remained an abiding possibility. But here the question of federation and its appeal emerged in a new way. It was no longer linked to the problem of empire and its overcoming or as part of the lingering hope for imperial citizenship. Rather, federation was proposed to address centrally the predicament of the transition to popular rule, and more specifically, anxieties about majority rule. The princely states were also in effect caught up in this predicament, but their reliance upon older modes of imperial connection underwrote a strategy of resistance to the full implications of electoral democracy on a unified and national scale.

The Gandhian model of radical decentralisation in its own way tried to reckon with the dilemmas of democratic representation. In its scheme, the village was to be vested with primary political authority; it was to be the only body directly elected by the people based upon universal adult suffrage. Part of the argument for direct democracy at the village level was a plea for simplicity. But it was also premised upon a worry about the adverse consequences of centralised structures of democratic competition. On the one hand, if national politics became the more prestigious and consequential arena of political competition it would leave the common man/woman – here the peasant – vulnerable to the ambitions and agendas of elite, urban politicians. On the other hand, centralised competition abstracted groups from local contexts, and in so doing engendered violent forms of antagonism and politicisation. Religion and caste conflict, which had historically been contained or moderated at local levels, could spiral outwards into civil war. Gandhi worried about a kind of militant majoritarianism that equated democracy with the power of numbers. Here, his Victorian anxieties about mass democracy were directed in interesting ways to understand the specific predicaments facing decolonising societies in the transition to popular rule.

In practical terms, it was the question of Muslim representation that brought these issues to the forefront. Representation proved to be the most intractable dilemma of Indian decolonisation, with Partition being its direct and devastating consequence. In many ways it proved to be the Achilles heel of the project of anti-colonial sovereignty. In the 1940s the issue of Muslim representation gave a fillip to the federal imagination. The key figure pressing this claim was M. A. Jinnah, in the name of the demand for 'Pakistan'. As Ayesha Jalal has shown in her landmark study, in the intricate and tortured three-way negotiations between Congress, the Muslim League and the British in the lead-up to independence,

Jinnah pressed for various constitutional formulae and federal arrangements that could protect Muslim interests.[51]

Jinnah vividly sensed that however important a community South Asia's Muslims were –numbering upwards of a hundred million at the time of Partition, and politically strong in many provinces – their political weight in all-India matters would always be undercut by a Hindu majority. Jinnah was explicit that popular sovereignty entailed a new numbers game, one that would always leave Muslims at best ineffective in national politics and at worst permanently vulnerable. One answer repeatedly offered to this dilemma (and the one that was eventually enacted) was the idea of separation, in which Muslim-majority provinces and areas could be consolidated into a separate state.[52] But Jinnah was never drawn to this option, and instead was always trying to work out an alternative all-India resolution. For him the crucial issue was how to ensure Muslim interests in areas of Hindu majority, a problem that neither a loose federalism nor partition could resolve.

In the 1940s Jinnah aimed to secure a form of federation in which provincial autonomy would be linked to a centre in which Muslims were represented as a group. For him, provincial autonomy needed to be offset by strong national parties that could discipline provincial ministries when minorities – either Hindu or Muslim – were threatened. This was why it was so crucial for Jinnah that Muslims have outsized strength at the central level, i.e. that this centre could not just be a reflection of population. Jinnah began to experiment with forms that could retain the principle of majority rule within legislatures but find other mechanisms to guarantee what he termed 'parity' at the centre. In the final negotiations he pressed for separate constituent assemblies that could meet as two nations to negotiate the terms of federation into a unified India.[53]

The Cabinet Mission Plan of 1946 was in many ways the best approximation of the kind of federalism that Jinnah envisioned.[54] It was a scheme that placed provinces into three groups, two of which comprised Muslim-majority provinces. Though provinces would have considerable autonomy they would meet at the centre to make decisions on central subjects. This plan – and various other federal options – was rejected by Congress, and indeed it was Congress who opted for partition as the better alternative to any kind of loose federation or one in which communal representation was built into its structure.

[51] A. Jalal, *The Sole Spokesman: Jinnah, the Muslim League and the Demand for Pakistan* (Cambridge: Cambridge University Press, 1985).
[52] For instance, those proposed by Mohammed Iqbal and Rahmat Chaudhury Ali.
[53] Jalal, *The Sole Spokesman*, pp. 241–87.   [54] Ibid., pp. 174–207.

There were a number of reasons why Congress resisted all of these varied forms of federation. Some of this resistance was principled, and linked
to an investment in a strong, centralised state that could be the agent
of modernisation, promoting rapid development and securing equality.
Resistance was also due to the specific pattern of confrontation and negotiation with the British government, which made the Congress extremely
wary of any attempt to thwart the principle of majority rule. To Congress,
Jinnah's federalism looked as regressive as that of the princely states, since
both schemas seemed to be imperial creations and given imperial support to offset Congress's strength. But despite what may have been its
legitimate objections, what it also meant was that Congress did not take
the issue of representation as seriously as did its opponents (such as Jinnah, and also B. R. Ambedkar). What is surprising is the lack of serious
thinking about the problem of representation – especially majoritarianism – from within the Congress party. And yet, majoritarianism has been
a consistent feature of post-colonial politics, and one that has proved
hard to separate from the inner logic of popular sovereignty. If one of
the central challenges for anti-imperial thought was how to construct an
institutional form (a system of representation and a federal structure)
that could be seen as broadly popular and democratic *and* post-imperial,
it is arguably a challenge that has remained in part unfulfilled.

V

The last decades have witnessed a profound turning away – in post-
colonial societies themselves as well as globally – from the coordinates
and commitments that made anti-colonialism a political possibility. From
many sides there is a sense that the statist vision of sovereignty and self-
determination that animated decolonisation has been in serious crisis
and decline at least since the late 1970s, and so also one that has limited
purchase for galvanising political action and critique.[55] Looking back
now, in hindsight, we might readily agree that the ambitions of post-
colonial/anti-colonial sovereignty were deeply flawed, fantastical or, less
provocatively, seriously unfulfilled. We might even concur with Kedourie
that some of the failures stemmed from inherent contradictions of the
national model of state formation, one that was premised on a kind
a demographic homogeneity and coincidence of political and cultural
boundaries that for the most part are non-existent. We could also take
up this line and join with cosmopolitan critics of the nation-state.

[55] D. Scott, *Refashioning Futures: Criticism after Postcolonialism* (Princeton: Princeton University Press, 1999).

But to do so would be to bypass important questions about how to pose critical diagnoses of the limits of decolonisation. If we want to be freed from a criterion of assessment that still holds out European models as the implicit norm against which deviations and failures are judged, then we must be more attentive to the diverse arguments and projects that comprised anti-colonial visions of popular sovereignty at the time of their emergence and evolution. In so doing, I hope we can find a fruitful manner to assess the successes, failures and future trajectory of post-colonial sovereignty.

13 Popular sovereignty in an age of mass democracy

Politics, parliament and parties in Weber, Kelsen, Schmitt and beyond

Timothy Stanton

I

'In my view', declared Leopold von Ranke in 1854, 'the leading tendency of our time is the conflict between two principles, that of monarchy and that of popular sovereignty. All other conflicts and oppositions are connected to this one.'[1] Ranke proceeded to admonish those who wished too devoutly to see history moving inexorably in the direction of the triumph of the second principle over the first following the revolutions of 1848. This was to misunderstand 'what the bell had struck'. So many destructive tendencies were bound up with the principle of popular sovereignty that both culture and Christendom would be put at risk if it decisively gained the upper hand. Accordingly monarchy – 'hereditary authority from above' as against 'self-government from below'[2] – had to be given its place, being necessary to eradicate those destructive tendencies that popular principles 'swept in with them in a great flood'.[3] The outstanding problem of Europe, he insisted, was how to reconcile these two principles with one another. It was a problem that could not be ignored.[4]

The profound disquiet about popular sovereignty to which Ranke's words gave resounding expression, and the matching desire for a contrary principle to nullify its projected effects, was widespread among Germans of the next generation. Some time after Ranke issued his admonition we find Friedrich Nietzsche considering the same problem in rather more apocalyptic terms. 'I believe', he confided to his notebook in the autumn of 1885, 'that the great, advancing, and unstoppable *democratic* movement of Europe, that which calls itself "progress" . . . fundamentally

[1] Leopold von Ranke, *Uber die Epochen der neueren Geschichte* (Leipzig: Duncker & Humblot, 1906 [1854]), p. 141.
[2] Ibid., p. 139: 'Nationalsouveränität und Monarchie, Erblichkeit von oben, Selbstregierung von unten'.
[3] Ibid., p. 142.   [4] Ibid., p. 143.

signifies only the tremendous, instinctive conspiracy of the whole herd against everything that is shepherd . . . and Caesar, to preserve and elevate all the weak, the oppressed, the mediocre, the hard-done-by, the half-failed; as a long-drawn-out slave revolt, at first secret, then more and more self-confident, against every kind of master, ultimately against the very concept of "master".' In Nietzsche's view, all genuine instances of progress in human life had been 'the work of an aristocratic society which believed in a long ladder of order of rank and difference in value between man and man . . . [for] without the *pathos of distance*, as it arises from the deeply carved differences between the classes, from the ruling caste's constant looking outwards and downwards unto its underlings', the self-development and 'self-overcoming of man' was impossible.[5]

By the time German politicians of the generation after Nietzsche were forced to hastily improvise a new political system under the shadow of Bolshevism and out of the ruins of the second Reich, late in the autumn of 1918, anxiety about popular sovereignty had ripened in many segments of society into open resentment of democracy and parliamentary government. The situation, however, seemed to admit of no alternative. The abdication of the Kaiser was announced on 9 November and the following day the incoming chancellor, Friedrich Ebert, informed the German public that the new government would be a government of the people. Thomas Mann spoke for many who felt themselves forced into a position they had never wished to occupy when he proclaimed, 'I want the monarchy . . . I don't want this parliament and party business that will sour the whole life of the nation with its politics . . . I don't want politics. I want competence, order, and decency.'[6] Max Weber, who had identified himself as 'a resolute follower of democratic institutions' as early as 1905,[7] also chose that moment to speak out in defence of monarchy. Nothing seemed to him less desirable at this critical juncture than 'a radical break from monarchic traditions', even if his 'support for

---

[5] Friedrich Nietzsche, *Writings from the Late Notebooks*, ed. R. Bittner and trans. K. Sturge (Cambridge: Cambridge University Press, 2003), p. 68.

[6] T. Eschenburg, *Die improvisierte Demokratie: gesammelte Aufsätze zur Weimarer Republik* (Munich: R. Piper & Co., 1963), p. 43, as cited in E. Kennedy, 'Carl Schmitt's *Parlamentarismus* in its Historical Context', in Carl Schmitt, *Crisis of Parliamentary Democracy*, trans. E. Kennedy (Cambridge, MA: MIT Press, 1988), pp. xiii–l, at p. xxiv. For Mann's general attitudes in this period see his *Reflections of a Nonpolitical Man*, trans. W. D. Morris (New York: Frederick Ungar, 1983 [1918]), pp. 16–17, which denounced democracy as 'foreign and poisonous to the German character' and suggested that the 'much decried "authoritarian state" is and remains the one that is proper and becoming to the German people, and the one they basically want'.

[7] Max Weber, 'Capitalism and Rural Society', in H. H. Gerth and C. Wright Mills (eds.), *From Max Weber: Essays in Sociology* (New York: Oxford University Press, 1946), pp. 363–85, at p. 370.

the monarchy provoked general headshaking' amongst disbelieving and disapproving friends and colleagues.[8]

These observations bring me to the central problem to be considered in this chapter. Where exactly did Weber position himself in what Ranke called the great movement 'of action and reaction of minds' incited by the problem of popular sovereignty and monarchy,[9] and what was his legacy? This question has been fiercely debated by historians at least since the publication of Wolfgang Mommsen's revisionist work of 1959, *Max Weber and German Politics*, and interest only quickened with the dramatic intervention of the young Jürgen Habermas at a conference at Heidelberg in 1964 to celebrate the centenary of Weber's birth.[10] At issue is not merely the depth of Weber's commitment to democratic institutions but whether he was really committed to them at all. For the views he developed in his later political writings, especially from 1919 onwards, have struck numerous commentators as 'hostile to the very spirit of democracy' as a regime 'uniquely committed' to the realisation of the principle of popular sovereignty.[11] The predilection for 'Caesarian' or 'leader democracy' (*Führerdemokratie*) that those writings evinced, with a directly elected and powerful presidential figure, savoured to many, including Mommsen, of the illiberal nationalism of Wilhelmine Germany, but also looked forward to the decisionism of Carl Schmitt and, beyond that, into the darkness of Nazi dictatorship.[12]

Mommsen argued that Weber's support for the monarchical principle was the result of 'technical considerations about the best form of government'. Monarchy enjoyed a formal advantage over republican and other forms of popular government in that 'the highest position in the state was permanently occupied',[13] thus providing a practical and constitutional limit to both the drive for power of personally ambitious politicians and the desire of the military to extend its power into the political sphere,

---

[8] W. Mommsen, *Max Weber and German Politics, 1890–1920*, trans. M. S. Steinberg (Chicago: University of Chicago Press, 1984 [1959]), p. 291.

[9] Ranke, *Der neueren Geschichte*, p. 142.

[10] See Otto Stammer (ed.), *Max Weber and Sociology*, trans. K. Morris (Oxford: Basil Blackwell, 1971).

[11] J. E. Green, 'Max Weber and the Reinvention of Popular Power', *Max Weber Studies* 8 (2008), pp. 187–224, at p. 188.

[12] See e.g. K. E. Becker, '*Der Römische Cäsar mit Christi Seele*': *Max Webers Charisma-Konzept: Eine systematisch kritische Analyse unter Einbeiziehung biographischer Fakten* (Frankfurt am Main: Peter Lang, 1988); Mommsen, *Max Weber*; and, more guardedly, J. P. McCormick, 'Legal Theory and the Weimar Crisis of Law and Social Change', in P. E. Gordon and J. McCormick (eds.), *Weimar Thought: A Contested Legacy* (Princeton: Princeton University Press, 2013), pp. 55–72; and cf. Green, 'Max Weber'; E. Kilker, 'Max Weber and Plebiscitary Democracy: A Critique of the Mommsen Thesis', *International Journal of Politics, Culture, and Society* 2 (1989), pp. 429–65.

[13] Mommsen, *Max Weber*, p. 289.

averting the threat of 'Caesarian domination [by] military parvenus'.[14] But the 'conservative strain' in Weber's political thought, as Mommsen called it, infected his plans for constitutional reform and emptied his professed commitment to democratic institutions of genuine resolution: it was to military parvenus, not to Caesarian domination, that Weber was opposed.[15] A similar line of criticism was pursued by David Beetham when he objected that Weber's account of democracy 'makes no reference to democratic *values*, much less regards them as worth striving for'. His theory of government, Beetham went on, 'did not seek to justify such government in terms of recognizably democratic values, such as increasing the influence of the people on policies pursued by those who governed'.[16] On the contrary, and as his advocacy for monarchy in 1918 demonstrated, Weber was ambivalent at best about democratic values. In the final analysis his valorisation of charismatic rulership was difficult to square with the democratic ideal of a sovereign people.[17]

As the people took to the streets in the winter of 1918–19, Munich and Berlin became battlegrounds in which rival republics were noisily proclaimed and ruthlessly put down. Germany was engulfed by what Weber famously damned as 'a bloody carnival that does not deserve the honourable name of a revolution'.[18] It is little wonder, therefore, that his later writings could be interpreted as expressing a growing disaffection for popular power and a longing for authority, order and control.[19]

This chapter argues, by contrast, that Weber should not be read as disavowing the principle of self-government in favour of authority, but instead as working towards his own novel response to the problem of

---

[14] Weber, 'Capitalism and Rural Society', p. 370.

[15] Georg Lukács, who had been a member of Weber's circle at the University of Heidelberg before the First World War, suggested in 1954 that Weber's support for the institutions of democracy was a 'technical measure to help achieve a better functioning imperialism'. See Georg Lukács, *Die Zerstörung der Vernunft* (Berlin: Aufbau, 1954), p. 488, cited in Green, 'Max Weber', p. 195.

[16] D. Beetham, *Max Weber and the Theory of Modern Politics* (London: Allen & Unwin, 1974), pp. 101–2.

[17] For a comprehensive and illuminating discussion of the difficulty see J. Derman, *Max Weber in Politics and Social Thought: From Charisma to Canonization* (Cambridge: Cambridge University Press, 2012), pp. 176–98.

[18] Marianne Weber, *Max Weber: Ein Lebensbild* (Heidelberg: Lambert Schneider, 1950 [1926]), p. 642. For the revolution see E. Kolb, *The Weimar Republic*, trans. P. S. Falla (London: Unwin Hyman, 1988), pp. 3–22; H. Mommsen, *The Rise and Fall of Weimar Democracy*, trans. E. Forster and L. E. Jones (Chapel Hill: University of North Carolina Press, 1996 [1989]), pp. 20–50; D. Peukert, *The Weimar Republic: The Crisis of Classical Modernity*, trans. R. Deveson (London: Allen Lane, 1991), pp. 47–51.

[19] See e.g. E. von Kahler, *Der Beruf der Wissenschaft* (Berlin: Georg Bondi, 1920), and cf. the judgement of Max Horkheimer (Stammer (ed.), *Max Weber*, p. 53), who attended Weber's lectures on socialism at the University of Munich in 1920, and came away sadly disappointed, convinced that 'Max Weber must be ultraconservative'.

how to conceive and apply these principles together in an age of mass democracy.[20] His putative solution did not mean asserting one principle over the other, or compromising differences;[21] rather, it meant seeking the proper balance between the competing tendencies they represented. Naturally, this allowed for – indeed, it required – different postures to be adopted at different times. In 1905–6 it meant throwing one's weight behind democratic institutions against the claims of 'aristocracies' and 'authorities' and 'the rule of capitalism'.[22] In 1918–19 it meant re-establishing a balance against an unchecked politics of popular will by revitalising or drawing attention back to the virtues of leadership, individual responsibility and independent judgement. This was as much an imaginative and rhetorical challenge as it was an institutional and political one – not just a matter of offering a theory or propounding a scientific truth, though Weber certainly thought he was doing that, but of trying to exhort his audience to certain modes of thought and action through his example[23] and his words.[24]

The challenge was heightened by the fact that the competing tendencies of thought about the constitution of government for which the principles of popular sovereignty and monarchy stood were given form and content through a political vocabulary that, because common to both, was systematically ambiguous. Democracy, for instance, might suggest both the institutional means of limiting the exercise of political power and a plebiscitary device to legitimise the concentrated and extensive exercise of that power by a single individual. The practical meaning of such terms thus depended – as arguably it still does – on how these different ways of thinking were mediated.

As John Dunn observes, democratic governments, at least presumptively, are governments whose rule is authorised by those whom they rule, and, in presumption again, so authorised not by a single mythical

---

[20] A similar conclusion is developed in a different direction by Jeffrey Edward Green, first in 'Max Weber', and now, more expansively, in *The Eyes of the People: Democracy in an Age of Spectatorship* (Oxford: Oxford University Press, 2011).

[21] See W. J. Mommsen, 'The Antinomian Structure of Max Weber's Political Thought', *Current Perspectives in Social Theory* 4 (1983), pp. 289–311 for this style of thinking as typical of Weber.

[22] Max Weber, 'On the Situation of Constitutional Democracy in Russia' [1906], in P. Lassman and R. Speirs (eds.), *Weber: Political Writings* (Cambridge: Cambridge University Press, 1994), pp. 29–74, at pp. 68–9.

[23] For personality and personal contact as an important contributory element in the formation of Weber's posthumous reputation see J. Derman, 'Skepticism and Faith: Max Weber's Anti-Utopianism in the Eyes of his Contemporaries', *Journal of the History of Ideas* 71 (2010), pp. 481–503, esp. pp. 495–503.

[24] See Max Weber, 'Science as a Vocation' [1918], in Gerth and Wright Mills (eds.), *From Max Weber*, pp. 129–256, at pp. 145–6.

episode in the distant past, but by a series of iterative occasions over time. The point of these occasions is to recast every citizen as subject to democratic laws, 'through some imaginatively accessible and pertinent set of mediations, and hence as part author of the laws to which each is subject'.[25] The difficulty which Weber felt it necessary to confront was that, under the peculiar conditions of mass society, the mediations purporting to provide that authorisation were uniformly disreputable exercises in utopianism or self-deception. Modern democratic institutions and the bureaucracy that governed them operated according to the permeating rationalism and functionalist logic characteristic of modern European civilisation, which, he argued, had brought about the 'disenchantment of the world' (Entzauberung der Welt).[26] They were moved by reasons and forces entirely internal to them. What could democracy, what could popular sovereignty, *mean* in such circumstances as these? It is the answers that Weber gave to this question, and the ways in which two of his successors, Hans Kelsen and Carl Schmitt, responded to those answers, that will be the principal focus of my attention in the remainder of this chapter.[27]

Three statements may be taken together as providing a prospectus for what follows. The first is found in the preamble to the Weimar Constitution of 1919 and runs: 'The German people, united in every branch . . . has given itself this Constitution.' The guiding principle of the new constitution was that the German state was and should be the political organisation of the people: the people were the Reich and (as Article 1 went on to assert) 'The German Reich is a Republic. All state authority emanates from the people.'[28] The second occurs in a letter written in 1908 by Weber to his young friend Robert Michels: 'Any thought of removing the rule of men over men through even the most sophisticated forms of "democracy" is "utopian" . . . concepts such as "the will of the people", the "true will of the people", etc., ceased to exist for me long ago. They are *fictions*.'[29] The third comes from Edmund Morgan's account of

---

[25] See J. Dunn, 'Legitimacy and Democracy in the World Today', in J. Tankebe and A. Liebling (eds.), *Legitimacy and Criminal Justice: An International Exploration* (Oxford: Oxford University Press, 2014), pp. 7–18, at p. 9.

[26] Weber, 'Science as a Vocation', p. 139.

[27] The challenge laid down by Weber was also taken up, in different ways, by Friedrich Meinecke and Ernst Troeltsch to name only two. For Schmitt's response to the former see Carl Schmitt, 'Zu Friedrich Meineckes Idee der Staatsräson', *Archiv für Sozialwissenschaft und Sozialpolitik* 56 (1926), pp. 226–34.

[28] E. M. Hucko (ed.), *The Democratic Tradition: Four German Constitutions* (Oxford: Berg, 1987), p. 149, and cf. p. 50.

[29] M. R. Lepsius and W. Mommsen with B. Rudhard and M. Schön (eds.), *Max Weber: Briefe, 1906–1908* (Tübingen: Mohr Siebeck, 1990), p. 620, cited in Mommsen, *Max Weber*, pp. 394–5 (translation amended).

the origins of self-government in England and the United States, *Inventing the People*. 'Government', Morgan observes there, 'requires make-believe . . . make believe that the voice of the people is the voice of God. Make believe that the people *have* a voice or make believe that the representatives of the people *are* the people.' In order to be effective (Morgan goes on) these 'fiction[s] must bear some resemblance to fact . . . Because fictions are necessary, because we cannot live without them, we often take pains to prevent their collapse by moving the facts to fit the fiction, by making our world conform more closely to what we want it to be . . . the fiction takes command and reshapes reality'.[30]

The principal purpose of the present chapter, then, is to explore the ways in which fact and fiction interacted in Weber's thinking about popular sovereignty, politics and the modern state, and how Hans Kelsen and Carl Schmitt reacted to what they found in Weber. This notable triumvirate has already been discussed at length and with great distinction in many books,[31] and my aim here is simply to analyse Weber's account of democracy and the state as a late contribution to a movement of thought stretching back to Ranke. I hope by this means to put some of the more familiar aspects of the story in a new light, and thence to consider the views of Kelsen and Schmitt anew in that same light, before offering

---

[30] E. S. Morgan, *Inventing the People: The Rise of Popular Sovereignty in England and America* (New York: Norton, 1988), pp. 13–14. For discussion see A. Przeworski, *Democracy and the Limits of Self-Government* (Cambridge: Cambridge University Press, 2010), pp. 11–13.

[31] See, in addition to the works by Derman and Mommsen cited above, S. Baume, *Hans Kelsen and the Case for Democracy*, trans. J. Zvesper (Colchester: ECPR Press, 2012); P. C. Caldwell, *Popular Sovereignty and the Crisis of German Constitutional Law: The Theory and Practice of Weimar Constitutionalism* (Durham, NC: Duke University Press, 1997); M. Caserta, *Democrazia e constituzione in Hans Kelsen e Carl Schmitt* (Rome: Aracne, 2005); D. Diner (ed.), *Hans Kelsen and Carl Schmitt: A Juxtaposition* (Gerlingen: Bleicher, 1999); D. Dyzenhaus, *Legality and Legitimacy: Carl Schmitt, Hans Kelsen, and Hermann Heller in Weimar* (Oxford: Oxford University Press, 1999); M. Eberl, *Die Legitimität der Moderne: Kulturkritik und Herrschaftskonzeption bei Max Weber und bei Carl Schmitt* (Marburg: Tectum, 1994); R. Gross, *Carl Schmitt and the Jews: The 'Jewish Question', the Holocaust, and German Legal Theory*, trans. J. Golb (Madison: University of Wisconsin Press, 2007); C.-M. Herrera (ed.), *Le Droit, le politique: autour de Max Weber, Hans Kelsen, Carl Schmitt* (Paris: L'Harmattan, 1995); A. Kalyvas, *Democracy and the Politics of the Extraordinary: Max Weber, Carl Schmitt, and Hannah Arendt* (Cambridge: Cambridge University Press, 2008); D. Kelly, *The State of the Political: Conceptions of Politics and the State in the Thought of Max Weber, Carl Schmitt, and Franz Neumann* (Oxford: Oxford University Press, 2003); A.-J. Korb, *Kelsens Kritiker: Ein Beitrag zur Geschichte der Rechts- und Staatstheorie (1911–1934)* (Tübingen: Mohr Siebeck, 2010), pp. 135–48; E. Topitsch, *Gottwerdung und Revolution: Beiträge zur Weltanschauungsanalyse und Ideologiekritik* (Munich: Dokumentation, 1973); G. L. Ulmen, *Politischer Mehrwert: eine Studie über Max Weber und Carl Schmitt* (Weinheim: VCH Acta Humaniora, 1991); G. Zarone, *Crisi e critica dello stato: scienza giuridica e trasformazione sociale tra Kelsen e Schmitt* (Naples: Scientifiche Italiane, 1982).

some brief reflections on the subsequent fortunes of those views and the prospects of popular sovereignty and democracy in the present age. But to begin we must turn back to Weber.

II

When Weber first applied his mind to politics it was in a practical context in which the German Reich under Bismarck had striven for several decades to impose a single scheme of law in the empire and, at least by implication, a single source of direction emanating from his will.[32] The pulverising and depoliticising consequences for civil society of this assault were registered at the time by Otto von Gierke, among others, who looked to the medieval period to distil from the practice of the guilds, leagues and corporations a tradition of pluralist thinking about the real personality of groups that had been sidelined and squashed by the modern state.[33] In the process, Gierke had delivered an indirect but astringent commentary on the political situation of late nineteenth-century Germany. Weber's commentary on the consequences of Bismarck's policy, written towards the end of the Great War, which provided a yet more devastating commentary of its own, bespoke the same recognition, but it was more direct.

Weber stated that Bismarck's political legacy was 'a nation *entirely lacking in any kind of political education*'. Above all, Bismarck had bequeathed to the future 'a nation *entirely without any political will*, accustomed to assume that the great statesman at the head of the nation would take care of political matters for them'. Weber continued in words that must be quoted at length:

Furthermore, as a result of his misuse of monarchic sentiment as a cover for his own power interests in the struggle between the political parties, he left behind a nation accustomed to *submit passively* and fatalistically to whatever was decided on its behalf, under the label of 'monarchic government,' without criticising the political qualifications of those who filled the chair left empty by Bismarck

---

[32] For Bismarck and the German Reich cf. F. Darmstaedter, *Bismarck and the Creation of the Second Reich*, new edn. (New Brunswick, NJ: Transaction Books, 2008), pp. 172–408; M. Gross, *The War against Catholicism: Liberalism and the Anti-Catholic Imagination in Nineteenth-Century Germany* (Ann Arbor: University of Michigan Press, 2004), pp. 240–91; P. Pulzer, *Germany, 1870–1945: Politics, State Formation, and War* (Oxford: Oxford University Press, 1997), chapter 2; and, at length, O. P. Pflanze, *Bismarck and the Development of Germany, vol. II: The Period of Consolidation* 1871–1880, 2nd edn. (Princeton: Princeton University Press, 1990). For the Reich constitution of 1871 see Hucko (ed.), *The Democratic Tradition*, pp. 22–38, 119–45.

[33] O. von Gierke, *Das deutsche Genossenschaftsrecht* (Berlin: Weidmannsche Buchhandlung, 1868).

and who seized the reins of government with such an astonishing lack of self-doubt. It was in this area that the most severe damage by far was done... At the same time his enormous prestige had the purely negative consequence of leaving *parliament utterly without power*... The powerlessness of parliament also meant that its intellectual level was very low... [But] whether a parliament is of high or low intellectual quality depends on *whether great problems* are not only *discussed* but are *conclusively decided* there. In other words, it depends on *whether anything happens in parliament* and on *how much depends on what happens there*, or whether it is merely the reluctantly tolerated rubber-stamping machine for a ruling bureaucracy.[34]

Weber's complaint was that Bismarck had created an abyss within the state, between laws and policies that derived their authority from his personal cachet and the ovine acquiescence of the masses. Individual will and judgement had no role to play in this situation except in the severely straitened sense that they could be read off mass obedience to law. Both here and elsewhere in Weber's writings,[35] this complaint was reformulated as a wider statement about the nature of politics in the modern world.

The steel-hard logic of modern politics, as Weber understood it, moved remorselessly towards a reckoning with three fundamental questions. The first was: how is it possible to salvage any remnant of individual freedom worthy of the name in the face of an all-powerful trend towards bureaucratisation in the modern state? The second, we have seen, was: how is democracy possible at all in the same conditions? The third was: what sorts of person could carry the hopes of freedom and democracy responsibly in these conditions?[36] Some of Weber's answers are implicit in the remarks quoted above, but to understand how he arrived at those answers it is necessary to say a little more about his views of the twin crises of modern statehood and modern individuality.

By 1895 Weber had already concluded that it was a grave mistake to ascribe moral or metaphysical grandeur to the state and to think of

[34] Max Weber, 'Parliament and Government in Germany under a New Political Order' [1917], in Lassman and Speirs (eds.), *Political Writings*, pp. 130–271, at pp. 144–5.

[35] For parliament, see e.g. Max Weber, 'Bureaucracy', in Gerth and Wright Mills (eds.), *From Max Weber*, pp. 196–244, at pp. 232–9, 'Suffrage and Democracy in Germany' [1917], in Lassman and Speirs (eds.), *Political Writings*, pp. 80–129, at pp. 81–2, 96–106. For inadequate political education see 'Bureaucracy', pp. 240–4, 'National Character and the Junkers', in Gerth and Wright Mills (eds.), *From Max Weber*, pp. 386–95, at pp. 388–9, and, entire, 'The Profession and Vocation of Politics' [1919], in Lassman and Speirs (eds.), *Political Writings*, pp. 309–69.

[36] Weber, 'Parliament and Government', pp. 159–61. See also 'Constitutional Democracy in Russia', p. 69: 'It is quite ridiculous to attribute to today's high capitalism... any "elective affinity" with "democracy" or indeed "freedom" (in *any* sense of the word), when the only question one can ask is how these things can "possibly" survive at all in the long run under the rule of capitalism.'

it as 'elevated ever higher, the more its nature is shrouded in mystical obscurity'.[37] The state was nothing other than 'the worldly organisation of the nation's power' and must be understood in these terms. It was a bearer of 'economic and political-power interests', not values, and it could not be used to realise ultimate values or 'to impose them on the future'.[38] Still less could it impose them itself. This was first because it was not a 'person' or 'personality'[39] and secondly because modern politics was not a realm of ultimate values: 'The fate of our times', Weber repeated, 'is characterised by rationalization and intellectualization and, above all, by the "disenchantment of the world". Precisely the ultimate and most sublime values have retreated from public life either into the transcendental realm . . . or into the brotherliness of direct and personal human relations.'[40] The ends of life could not be institutionalised and could not be matters of public consensus. When 'ultimate *Weltangschauungen*' collided, as inevitably they did, one had 'eventually to choose between them',[41] a matter of personal, not collective, decision. Every individual living in the 'world' found 'himself subject to the struggle between multiple sets of values, each of which, viewed separately, seems to impose an obligation on him. He has to choose which of these gods he will and should serve, or when he should serve the one and when the other. But at all times he will find himself engaged in a fight against one or other of the gods of this world'.[42] The state was different. By virtue of its 'depersonalization', it operated impartially, according to its own norms and ends, '*sine ira et studio*, without hate and therefore without love', and was impervious to 'substantive ethicization'. Its ends were simply those of power and its distribution.[43]

This conclusion was powerfully affirmed in Weber's casually shocking observation that the modern state was an 'organisation' (*Betrieb*) in

---

[37] Max Weber, 'The Nation State and Economic Policy (Inaugural Lecture)' [1895], in Lassman and Speirs (eds.), *Political Writings*, pp. 1–28, at pp. 16–17. Here Weber surely had in his sights not only Hegel, whose students had recalled him claiming that the state was 'the march of God in the world' but also Ranke, who had referred to states in *Das politische Gesprach* as 'spiritual substances . . . thoughts of God'. Cf. G. W. F. Hegel, *Elements of the Philosophy of Right*, ed. A. W. Wood (Cambridge: Cambridge University Press, 1991) p. 279, and L. von Ranke, *Geschichte und Politik: ausgewählte Aufsätze und Meisterschriften* [1836], ed. H. Hoffman (Stuttgart: A. Kröner, 1942), p. xxii.

[38] Weber, 'The Nation State', pp. 17, 15.

[39] For Weber's rejection of the 'personality' of the state see Kelly, *State of the Political*, chapter 3.

[40] Weber, 'Science as a Vocation', p. 155.

[41] Weber, 'Profession and Vocation', p. 355.

[42] Max Weber, 'Between Two Laws', [1916], in Lassman and Speirs (eds.), *Political Writings*, pp. 75–9, at pp. 78–9. See also Weber, 'Science as a Vocation', pp. 147–8.

[43] Max Weber, 'Religious Rejections of the World and their Directions', in Gerth and Wright Mills (eds.), *From Max Weber*, pp. 267–359, at p. 334.

exactly the same way as a factory. In both cases 'the relations of rule' within the organisation were determined by 'firmly established areas of responsibility, the keeping of files, [and] hierarchical structures of superiority and subordination'.[44] Accordingly, from a social-scientific point of view, the state was differentiated from other enterprises – such as factories – only by its means, being defined as 'a human community which (successfully) lays claim to the *monopoly of legitimate physical violence* within a certain territory', that is to say, a structure of domination.[45]

One upshot of this insight was to enable Weber to argue for the democratisation of the German state against those 'academic littérateurs' who wished to see the Reich constitution of 1871 preserved in perfection. If the state was an organisation that, in principle, functioned in a '*rationally calculable* manner according to stable, general norms', like 'a machine', it could and should be altered, as any machine would be adjusted, in the interests of operational efficiency.[46] But it had disabling consequences too. It became impossible, for one thing, to credit the idea that the state was the outcome of a voluntary and rational agreement, or that it derived its legitimacy from that source: the 'optimistic faith in the natural harmony of interests among free individuals', Weber observed, had 'nowadays been destroyed forever by capitalism',[47] while belief in natural law and objective universal values had gone the same way. Neither was it possible to regard the law of the state as having been authored by the people in any meaningful sense. Law was just one more 'rational, technical apparatus . . . continually transformable in the light of expediential considerations and devoid of all sacredness of content'. One peculiar side effect of this development, Weber noted in passing, was to have promoted 'actual obedience to the power, now viewed solely from an instrumentalist standpoint, of the authorities who claim legitimacy at the moment'.[48]

Weber was formally agnostic about whether what legitimacy those authorities possessed derived from charisma, tradition or law,[49] but his

---

[44] Weber, 'Parliament and Government', p. 146. *Betrieb* has connotations of regularised purposive activity and may be translated into English variously as 'organisation', 'enterprise', 'firm', 'business', 'operation' or the like (see Lassman and Speirs (eds.), *Political Writings*, p. 372). For Weber's own discussion of the term as meaning 'continuous rational activity of a specified kind' see Max Weber, *Economy and Society: An Outline of Interpretative Sociology*, ed. G. Roth and C. Wittich (Berkeley: University of California Press, 1978), pp. 52–3.

[45] Weber, 'Profession and Vocation', pp. 310–11; Weber, 'Religious Rejections', p. 334.

[46] Weber, 'Parliament and Government', pp. 266–71. For discussion, see Derman, *Max Weber*, pp. 105–7.

[47] Weber, 'Constitutional Democracy in Russia', p. 46.

[48] Weber, *Economy and Society*, pp. 895, 875.   [49] Ibid., pp. 212–54, 266–98.

writings left the firm impression that for most people everything turned on a disposition to obedience. Whatever legitimacy the state enjoyed was more a matter of faith or belief, or indeed wishful thinking, on the part of those who obeyed than anything else, and its long-term prospects turned on whether 'mass discipline' would continue to trump periodic 'explosions' of 'undirected mass fury', a question, Weber said, 'of *nerves*'.[50] As he had reprimanded Michels, the fact was that, even in a democratic state, domination of the ruled by the ruler was unavoidable. If the genuine self-rule of the people was impossible – a fiction – what other possibilities remained?

The choice reduced, as Weber saw it, to one between 'leaderless' and 'leadership democracy', which he placed in contrapuntal relationship.[51] The former, which Weber associated with Bolshevism, was the apotheosis of bureaucratisation, the rule of officials in which the mass of citizens were '"administered" like a herd of cattle' and left 'without freedom or rights'.[52] The second responded to what Weber identified as 'the essence of all politics . . . *conflict, the recruitment of allies and a voluntary following*'.[53] What it involved in practice was a different question, to which Weber offered somewhat different answers at different times.

In the end this was a question about where, if anywhere, the leadership he desiderated might be found. Three potential answers seemed to present themselves: the monarch; bureaucrats; or politicians. The second option effectively collapsed the distinction between leaderless and leadership democracy and so could be discounted. The first had some residual appeal, at least rhetorically, because it implied a source of leadership outside the bureaucratic machine and capable of directing it. Weber's avowed support for the principle of monarchy in 1918 reflected that appeal, but *au fond* he was extremely pessimistic about the chances of monarchy escaping bureaucracy's smothering embrace: under 'the conditions of the modern state . . . no monarch . . . has ever been, nor can he be, a counterweight to and a means of controlling the . . . power of *specialised officialdom*'[54] – and withering about the inept dilettantism of the tsar and Wilhelm II and their kind during the First World War. The 'special qualities necessary' for leadership, Weber observed sardonically, 'including the strict *objectivity*, the steady sense of *proportion*, the restrained *self-control*, and the capacity for *unobtrusive* action which it calls

---

[50] Weber, 'Parliament and Government', pp. 231–2.

[51] Weber, 'Profession and Vocation', p. 351; Weber, *Economy and Society*, p. 269.

[52] Weber, 'Suffrage and Democracy', p. 129. Cf. Max Weber, 'Socialism' [1918], in Lassman and Speirs (eds.), *Political Writings*, pp. 272–303, at pp. 291–4.

[53] Weber, 'Parliament and Government', p. 173.   [54] Ibid., p. 163.

for – these are not necessarily inherited along with the crown'.[55] They were, however, qualities that Weber associated with politicians.

In 'Parliament and Government in Germany under a New Political Order', written between April and June of 1917, Weber attributed the formation and cultivation of those qualities to 'the machinations of party struggle' in parliament. Parties (he would note elsewhere) presuppose the recruitment of a following to a cause by a variety of means both coarse and subtle.[56] Parliament provides an institutional framework within which politicians compete for votes and for eminence, develop their own leadership qualities, and in the process create roles of authority, thereby filling the vacuum that had opened under Bismarck. It is not 'the many-headed assembly of parliament' as such that governs or makes policy, but the leader or leaders whose virtuosity in appearing to harmonise competing interests brings success in this competition. '*That is how things should be*', Weber wrote. 'This element of 'Caesarism' is ineradicable (in *mass states*)'.[57] It was this aspect of Weber's thinking that provoked Habermas's outburst that Carl Schmitt, the *Kronjurist* of the Third Reich, was 'a 'legitimate pupil' of Weber's',[58] but Weber presented it as the only meaningful sense in which citizens could be 'integrated into the state by making them its *co-rulers*'.[59]

In two texts of February 1919, 'The Profession and Vocation of Politics' and 'The President of the Reich', Weber offered an alternative analysis. He now suggested that parliament, or parliament alone, could not sufficiently train and discipline prospective leaders.[60] The reasons for this change of emphasis – or change of mind – are not entirely transparent. One probable cause is that the constitution of the Weimar Republic, which would come into effect on 14 August 1919, specified a complicated

55 Max Weber, 'Russia's Transition to Pseudo-democracy' [1917], in G. C. Wells and P. Baehr (eds.), *The Russian Revolutions* (Cambridge: Polity Press, 1997), pp. 241–60, at p. 245.

56 Max Weber, 'Class, Status, Party', in Gerth and Wright Mills (eds.), *From Max Weber*, pp. 180–95, at pp. 194–5.

57 Weber, 'Parliament and Government', p. 174.

58 Stammer (ed.), *Max Weber*, p. 66. Stammer reports that following 'a friendly piece of advice', Habermas decided that, on reflection, 'a natural son' of Weber's was 'a more appropriate expression', presumably because it slyly left open the question of Schmitt's 'legitimacy'.

59 Weber, 'Suffrage and Democracy', p. 127.

60 Green, 'Max Weber', p. 210, sees in this analysis a decisive turn 'against th[e] parliamentary system' Weber had previously advocated. D. Villa, 'The Legacy of Max Weber in Weimar Political and Social Theory', in Gordon and McCormick (eds.), *Weimar Thought*, pp. 73–97, at p. 78, suggests that it is supplementary to, and 'presupposes a continuity with', that system. What Weber had previously argued was that plebiscitary principles would be injurious to 'the role of the party leaders and the responsibility of officials' in parliament. See Weber, 'Parliament and Government', p. 226.

form of proportional representation. Weber had been involved in discussions surrounding the drafting of the constitution and knew what was in the offing. His intense sensitivity to bureaucratisation led him to worry that the party lists would be filled by placemen who regarded 'national politics as "Hecuba"', producing '*a parliament of closed, philistine minds*, in no sense capable of serving as a place where political leaders are selected'. It was therefore essential to find a counterweight to parliament. The counterweight he identified was plebiscitary leader democracy, whereby politicians would be forced to compete directly for the support of a mass electorate, resulting in a '*head of state* resting *unquestionably on the will of the whole people*'.[61]

Weber died of pneumonia in the following year. The posthumous publication of *Economy and Society* revealed that he understood plebiscitary democracy as a device through which the 'basically authoritarian principle of charismatic legitmation' was transformed in a democratic direction. The validity of charismatic authority, Weber contended, rested entirely upon 'recognition by the ruled, on "proof" before their eyes'. The progressive rationalisation of this process brought about a remarkable reversal: 'instead of recognition being treated as a consequence of legitimacy, it is treated as the basis of legitimacy: *democratic legitimacy* . . . the personally legitimated charismatic leader becomes leader by the grace of those who follow him . . . Plebiscitary democracy – the most important type of *Führer-Demokratie* – is a variant of charismatic authority, which hides behind a legitimacy that is *formally* derived from the will of the governed. The leader . . . rules by virtue of the devotion and trust which his political followers have in him personally.'[62] In this way, leadership was formed through the electoral process, as politicians engaged in a fight to win and retain popular attention and acclaim. The deeply ambivalent character of the process in view, in which the personal qualities of politicians were transmuted into charismatic authority through their success in a political contest which appeared to select for what it in fact produced, found its complement in Weber's equally ambiguous language: he wrote of a 'self-selected leader of the masses' (*selbstgewählten Vertrauensmann der Massen*), a phrase which could mean either 'a spokesman elected by the masses themselves'[63] or someone who selected himself as worthy of their confidence by dint of his own 'initiative, effort, and capacity to lead and direct a political machine'.[64]

---

[61] Max Weber, 'The President of the Reich' [1919], in Lassman and Speirs (eds.), *Political Writings*, pp. 304–8, at pp. 306, 304. Cf. Weber, 'Profession and Vocation', pp. 339–51.

[62] Weber, *Economy and Society*, pp. 266–8.

[63] As given in Weber, 'The President of the Reich', p. 305 (italics removed).

[64] The interpretation preferred by Green, 'Max Weber', p. 192.

Weber sweetened this pill by suggesting that electoral competition would draw on talent developed in local, associational life, in the sporting clubs and hobby groups that made up civil society. But it was not clear, if he himself had ever thought it was clear, that this combination of skilful political leadership and low-level pluralism could sustain the disposition to obedience required for stability on terms compatible with individual freedom and democracy as most people understood them: if plebiscitary democracy was the specified means of 'deriving the legitimacy of authority from the confidence of the ruled', Weber nonetheless conceded that 'the voluntary nature of such confidence [was] only formal and fictitious', while 'its real value as an expression of the popular will' was also open to question.[65] Once this was recognised, a further question arose about why anyone should, in the end, regard the results of any modern democratic process as legitimate. An answer to that question was ventured in the writings of Hans Kelsen.

III

Hans Kelsen was born in 1881 in Prague, then in the Austrian part of the Austro-Hungarian Empire. His family moved to Vienna in 1883. After reading for a law degree, Kelsen completed a doctorate on Dante's theory of the state, which was published in 1905.[66] In 1911 he published a second book, originally his *Habilitationsschrift*, a massive study of the theory of public law entitled *Hauptprobleme der Staatsrechtslehre*.[67] During the First World War he acted as an adviser to the military administration and as legal adviser to the War Ministry. After the war he took up a professorship in public and administrative law at the University of Vienna. In 1919 he was invited to draft the new Austrian constitution, which was adopted in 1920. In that document Kelsen gave special importance to the role of the Constitutional Court, to which he was appointed as a member in 1920, remaining a member for ten years until he resigned in protest at political interference with its work.[68] During this period Kelsen continued to publish on many subjects, including sovereignty and the

---

[65] Weber, *Economy and Society*, p. 267.

[66] Hans Kelsen, *Die Staatslehre des Dante Alighieri* (Vienna: Deuticke, 1905). For Kelsen's biography, from which the information provided here is drawn, see N. B. Ladavac, 'Hans Kelsen (1881–1973): Biographical Note and Bibliography', *European Journal of International Law* 9 (1998), pp. 391–400.

[67] Hans Kelsen, *Hauptprobleme der Staatsrechtslehre entwickelt aus der Lehre vom Rechtssatze* (Tübingen: Mohr, 1911).

[68] As Ladavac records, 'despite the fact that Austria's administrative authorities permitted remarriage in Catholic Austria, the lower courts considered these dispensations invalid. Led by Kelsen, the Constitutional Court overturned these rulings, but in the final score

relationship between state and international law, laying the groundwork of the 'pure theory of law' with which his name has come to be inextricably linked.[69] But he also wrote about the nature and prospects of democracy, taking his cue from Weber's diagnosis of the defining characteristics of the modern state, initially in a short essay of 1920,[70] later expanded to book length and published in 1929 under the same title, *On the Essence and Value of Democracy*.[71]

Kelsen began with an observation of fact: 'Not all those belonging to the people as subject to norms or rule can take part in the process of norm creation – the form in which rule is necessarily exercised – or can form the people as ruling subject. Democratic ideologues themselves', he went on, 'often do not realize what an abyss they are concealing when they identify the "people" in the one sense [as a multitude of persons subject to certain norms] with the "people" in the other [as a unified ruling entity]'[72]. A perfect coincidence of individual wills and the provisions of the state was possible only in the imaginary situation of a state of nature in which unanimous agreement in the form of a contract or covenant provided the foundation of political society: since real political life was not like that, a different approach was needed. This meant the replacement of the principle of unanimity implicit in Rousseau's account of the social contract with a principle of majority, as the best available approximation of the ideal of freedom.[73] As Kelsen put it, the idea 'that, if not all, then at least *as many people as possible shall be free*, that is, that as few people as possible should find their wills in opposition to the general will of the social order' leads rationally to 'the majority principle'.[74]

Of course any decision taken by a majority, when understood in these terms, requires a restriction of the freedom of those belonging to the minority. But it was just a fact that in modern mass states this kind of restriction was necessary for any kind of collective self-government to exist in a manner appropriate to the time and place. Since, as Weber had recognised, direct democracy was utterly impractical outside 'the very favourable conditions of the Swiss cantons', democracy had to be

the Christian Social Party won the case. And Kelsen lost his place on the Court'. See Ladavac, 'Hans Kelsen', p. 392.

[69] For which see E. Voegelin, 'Kelsen's Pure Theory of Law', *Political Science Quarterly* 42 (1927), pp. 268–76 and L. Vinx, *Hans Kelsen's Pure Theory of Law: Legitimacy and Legality* (Oxford: Oxford University Press, 2007).

[70] Hans Kelsen, 'Vom Wesen und Wert der Demokratie', *Archiv für Sozialwissenschaft und Sozialpolitik* 47 (1920), pp. 50–85.

[71] Hans Kelsen, *Vom Wesen und Wert der Demokratie*, 2nd edn. (Tübingen: Mohr, 1929).

[72] Hans Kelsen, 'On the Essence and Value of Democracy', in A. Jacobsen and B. Schlink (eds.), *Weimar: A Jurisprudence of Crisis* (Berkeley and Los Angeles: University of California Press, 2000), pp. 84–109, at pp. 90–1 (translation amended).

[73] Ibid., pp. 85–7.   [74] Ibid., p. 87.

representative.[75] For Kelsen this implied a system of parliamentary representation, which enabled '*the formation of the governing will of the state according to the majority principle through a collegiate organ* [meaning a body of representatives authorised to create or execute legal norms] *elected by the people* . . . the state's will is not formed directly by the people itself, but by a parliament created by the people'.[76] Described in this way, parliamentary democracy was a compromise between the demands of freedom and the division of labour characteristic of modern states. The facts of political life in modern industrialised societies were such that the 'people' as such could not rule themselves directly, and must be content severally and collectively with their allotted role in the creation of an 'organ' which then determined the will of the state.

The salient facts were two. The first was that there was no people per se. 'Split by national, religious, and economic conflicts . . . the unity that appears under the name "people" . . . is – according to sociological findings – more a bundle of groups than a coherent mass of one and the same aggregate state.'[77] The second was that in modern conditions, as Weber had once insisted, political parties were crucial. In the 1929 text Kelsen would go so far as to say that modern democracy was impossible without them. He discerned in anti-party views a poorly concealed animus to democracy and hinted at an ideologically driven plot by the supporters of monarchy to prevent its implementation.[78] His own view was that competition for election between parties which reflected the divisions and differences of civil society was the only practicable means of arriving at the united will that the ideal of the social contract represented in thought and image. As he put it, political parties were like 'many underground streams feeding a river that comes to the surface only within the popular assembly or the parliament, where it is directed into a single channel'.[79] Out of this procedure the will of the state is produced.

Kelsen repeatedly emphasised that parliament, not the people, formed that will. The two had been elided, he suggested, by the '*fiction of representation*'. This fiction served 'to legitimize parliamentarianism from the

---

[75] Weber, 'Parliament and Government', pp. 225–7. For discussion, see R. Bellamy, *Liberalism and Modern Society: A Historical Argument* (University Park: Pennsylvania State University Press, 1992), pp. 214–16.

[76] Kelsen, 'Essence and Value', p. 95. For 'collegiate organ', cf. Hans Kelsen, *The Political Theory of Bolshevism: A Critical Analysis* (Berkeley: University of California Press, 1948), p. 7: 'A state is a democracy if the legislative and executive powers are exercised by the people either directly in a public assembly, or indirectly by organs elected by the people on the basis of universal and equal suffrage . . . The principle of majority decisions in collegiate organs represents the maximum of autonomy possible within a social order.'

[77] Kelsen, 'Essence and Value', p. 90.

[78] Ibid., p. 92, and see related notes printed on pp. 350–3.

[79] Ibid., p. 92 (translation amended).

standpoint of *popular sovereignty*'. It had been a powerful force in earlier struggles against autocracy and monarchy, and had held the political movements of the nineteenth and early twentieth centuries 'on a rational middle course' by canalising popular aspirations to self-determination into elected parliaments. But in the long run, Kelsen suggested, it played into the hands of parliament's opponents. For they had seized upon the facts to which Kelsen adverted to argue that the democratic ideal of a free sovereign people had been betrayed in practice and that the modern parliamentary system 'promised something it failed to carry out'.[80] Kelsen retorted with disarming frankness that no such promise had been made. Parliament was not and could not be the voice of a sovereign people. It was a machine, a 'specific, socio-technical means of creating the state's order'.[81] The lubricant that oiled the wheels of this machine was compromise, which Kelsen treated as the corollary of his majority principle.

Kelsen argued that 'the will of the community formed according to the so-called majority principle' was the result of a 'clash of political wills'. The 'entire parliamentary process, with its techniques of dialectic and contradiction, plea and counterplea, argument and counterargument, aims at achieving *compromise*'. All parliamentary procedures therefore aimed at finding a middle line between the opposing views of majority and minority:

Parliamentary procedure creates guarantees that the various interests of the groups represented in parliament can raise their voices and manifest themselves in a public process . . . from the confrontation of thesis and antithesis of political interests a synthesis is somehow created. But that cannot mean a 'higher', absolute truth, an absolute *value* above group interests, with which parliamentarianism is often wrongly saddled by those who confuse its reality with its ideology, but a compromise.[82]

As it happened, Kelsen doubted that there *was* an absolute superior truth to be known, offering his own version of Weber's value pluralism when suggesting that consensus about values could only be arrived at by an analogous method.[83] But the commitment to compromise which his moral and political theory alike required rested at bottom on the Freudian hypothesis of a psychological propensity to engage in compromise peculiar to democratic society.

---

[80] Ibid., pp. 97–8. Article 21 of the Weimar constitution perpetuated this fiction by stating that deputies of the Reichstag were 'representatives of the whole people'. See Hucko (ed.), *The Democratic Tradition*, p. 154.

[81] Kelsen, 'Essence and Value', p. 98.   [82] Ibid., pp. 102–3 (translation amended).

[83] Ibid., pp. 107–9.

Kelsen had enjoyed frequent contacts with Freud and his circle in Vienna, participating in Freud's 'Wednesday Meetings' and joining the Vienna Psychoanalytic Society in 1911. He used Freud's analyses in his discussions of democracy, postulating that the democratic 'character' was typified by a relatively reduced sense of ego, extended sympathy and pacifism, and the tendency to direct aggressive drives inward rather than outwards.[84] Discount this hypothesis, and there may be some reason to doubt that whatever 'general will of the state' emerged from these procedures would readily win the people's assent.

What, though, of the will of the people? For Kelsen, the 'people' was simply a juridical fiction which answered to the fact that a given collection of persons was subject to the same juridical order, to 'the will of a state'.[85] But 'the will of the state', there again, is also a juridical fiction, as, indeed, is the state itself, which is 'a simplifying personification of the legal code which constitutes the social community, which forms the unity of a multiplicity of human conducts'. The idea of the state, Kelsen continued, was like that of substance in natural philosophy – merely an image that gave intuitive immediacy to what upon analysis turned out to be a bounded system of pure relations which 'primitive' minds postulated as something real.[86] It may be unnecessary to add that if the state was a system of relations, sovereignty could not be meaningfully predicated of it. The rule of law meant just that, the *sovereignty* of law as a self-referring norm, the validity of which was found only in procedural consistency.

Carl Schmitt did not think of the state in these terms. In his text of 1923, *The Crisis of Parliamentary Democracy*, he, like Kelsen, took as his starting point Weber's analogy between the state and a modern capitalist enterprise. But he claimed that Kelsen was one of many who had pursued this analogy to conclusions that were potentially catastrophic,[87] developing understandings of politics, parliament and parties that could

---

[84] C. Jabloner, 'Kelsen and his Circle: The Viennese Years', *European Journal of International Law* 9 (1998), pp. 368–85, at pp. 382–4. For the democratic character see Kelsen, 'Essence and Value', p. 108, and, at length, Hans Kelsen, *Staatsform und Weltanschauung* (Tübingen: Mohr, 1933).

[85] Kelsen, 'Essence and Value', p. 90. The idea that a people could give itself a constitution would of course look very odd in this light.

[86] Hans Kelsen, 'The Conception of the State and Social Psychology, with Special Reference to Freud's Group Theory', *International Journal of Psychoanalysis* 5 (1924), pp. 1–38, at pp. 35–6.

[87] Carl Schmitt, *The Crisis of Parliamentary Democracy*, ed. and trans. E. Kennedy (Cambridge, MA: MIT Press, 1988 [1923]), p. 24, which picked out Kelsen's essay of 1920, 'Vom Wesen und Wert', as typifying the way in which this analogy had been used. Cf. Carl Schmitt, *Political Theology: Four Chapters on the Concept of Sovereignty*, ed. and trans. G. Schwab (Cambridge, MA: MIT Press, 1985 [1922]), p. 65: 'The kind of economic-technical thinking that prevails today is no longer capable of perceiving a

neither account for nor generate the substantive values a stable political order required. In a succession of works Schmitt developed positions about all three which put into question almost everything that Kelsen wished to defend.[88]

IV

Schmitt began from the metaphysical assumption that political forms like the state have real existence. He used an analogy between the state and the church, as against a capitalist enterprise, to establish the distinctive character he wished to attribute to the state. According to Schmitt, the state, like the church, was a concrete unity. That unity rested on two principles, which were opposed to one another but which needed to be combined together for unity to be possible. These were, respectively, identity and representation. The archetypal model for their successful combination

political idea. The modern state seems actually to have become what Max Weber envisioned: a huge industrial plant.' For Schmitt's relations to Weber, see K. Englebrekt, 'What Carl Schmitt Picked up in Weber's Seminar: A Historical Controversy Revisited', *The European Legacy* 14 (2009), pp. 667–84; J. P. McCormick, *Carl Schmitt's Critique of Liberalism: Against Politics as Technology* (Cambridge: Cambridge University Press, 1997), pp. 31–82; G. L. Ulmen, 'The Sociology of the State: Carl Schmitt and Max Weber', *State, Culture and Society* 1 (1985), pp. 3–57.

[88] To present the matter in these terms has the (intended) effect of mutually secluding Schmitt and Kelsen from the wider debates and controversies in which they were involved. For that reason the following section says nothing about the sources of Schmitt's thinking or rival figures and schools of thought prominent in his day. This narrowing of attention should not be taken for an uncritical endorsement of the idea that these two thinkers exhaust all conceptual possibilities or were fixated exclusively upon one another. Of the two, Kelsen was by far the better known and more eminent figure in German jurisprudence in the 1920s. To take him as one's opponent, as Schmitt did, was by implication to place oneself on his level. Different purposes were served for Schmitt by the facts that Kelsen was, notwithstanding his eminence, an 'outsider', coming from Prague and owing his intellectual formation to the Austro-Hungarian Empire, and a converted Jew. The difficulty – perhaps the impossibility – of disentangling these purposes from Schmitt's oeuvre as a whole is demonstrated in Gross, *Carl Schmitt and the Jews*. For Kelsen as 'the enemy' see Carl Schmitt, *Dictatorship: From the Origin of the Modern Concept of Sovereignty to Proletarian Class Struggle*, ed. and trans. M. Hoelzl and G. Ward (Cambridge: Polity Press, 2014 [1921]), p. xlv (Kelsen is accused of 'relativistic formalism'); Schmitt, *Political Theology*, pp. 18–22 (where Schmitt finds in Kelsen 'relativistic superiority', 'unproved certainty' and 'methodological conjuring'), p. 29 ('The objectivity that he claim[s] for himself amount[s] to no more than avoiding everything personalistic and tracing the legal order back to the impersonal validity of an impersonal norm'), pp. 42, 49; Carl Schmitt, *Constitutional Theory*, ed. and trans. J. Seitzer (Durham, NC: Duke University Press, 2008 [1928]) pp. 63–5, 106 (Kelsen's state theory is dismissed as an 'empty husk'); Carl Schmitt, *The Concept of the Political*, ed. and trans. G. Schwab (Chicago: University of Chicago Press, 1996 [1932]), pp. 70–3 (which, without naming Kelsen, inveighs against '*pure* . . . individualistic liberalism' [emphasis added] and its appeal to 'abstract . . . norms').

was the medieval Roman Catholic church, which Schmitt described, accordingly, as a *complexio oppositorum*, a complex of opposites.[89]

Identity implied a condition in which a group of people was 'factually and directly capable of political action by virtue of a strong and conscious similarity, as a result of firm natural boundaries, or due to some other reason'. In that case, Schmitt went on, 'a political unity is a genuinely present entity in its unmediated self-identity'.[90] However, this principle could never be realised without its co-operative contrary, since the political unity of a people was neither natural nor spontaneous. It was rather the result of a constitutive sovereign decision about friend and enemy which established who was embraced within that unity and who was not. In every state, therefore, there had to be a person or persons to represent that unity by making present through their public acts the otherwise fictional idea that the people could act as a unit, by taking the decisions and performing the real actions which sustained that people as a real unity.

What this meant was creating 'total peace' within the state and its territory by producing 'tranquility [*sic*], security, and order', and thereby establishing 'the normal situation [which] is the prerequisite for legal norms to be valid. Every norm presupposes a normal situation, and no norm can be valid in an entirely abnormal situation.'[91] Schmitt had no time for those who spoke, as Kelsen had done, of a 'sovereignty of the law'.[92] Law became valid only with the decision that secured the foundational unity of the state, and sovereignty was defined in terms of that decision: 'sovereign is he who decides on the exception'.[93] This definition at once linked sovereignty to an existing order and suggested that a sovereign could act outside the norms of that order, including the provisions of emergency law, to restore the normal situation when the existence of the state was threatened. In 1934 Schmitt made explicit the implied analogy with the medieval papacy: the decisions of the sovereign, like those of the infallible Pope, presume an existing political form. They do not create it *ex nihilo*: 'the infallible decision of the Pope does not

---

[89] Carl Schmitt, *Roman Catholicism and Political Form*, ed. and trans. G. L. Ulmen (Westport, CT: Praeger, 1996 [1923]), pp. 7–8, 14, 18–19.

[90] Schmitt, *Constitutional Theory*, p. 239.

[91] Schmitt, *Concept of the Political*, p. 46. See also Carl Schmitt, *Legality and Legitimacy*, ed. and trans. J. Seitzer (Durham, NC: Duke University Press, 2004 [1932]), p. 71; Carl Schmitt, 'State Ethics and the Pluralist State' [1930], in Jacobsen and Schlink (eds.), *Weimar*, pp. 300–12, at p. 304.

[92] Schmitt, *Political Theology*, pp. 18–19, 29–31; Schmitt, *Constitutional Theory*, p. 187. See also Carl Schmitt, *On the Three Types of Juristic Thought*, trans. J. Bendersky (Westport, CT: Praeger, 2004 [1934]), p. 50, for the same position expressed in fiercely polemical terms: 'Through this "rule of law"...law destroys the concrete kingly or leadership order (*Führerordnung*); the master of *Lex* subdues *Rex*.'

[93] Schmitt, *Political Theology*, p. 5.

establish the order and institution of the church but presupposes them'.[94]
These same views conditioned Schmitt's thinking about the Weimar
constitution.

A democratic constitution, Schmitt claimed, was the result of an exercise of constituent power by a politically united people.[95] If the people
did not already exist, he reasoned, it could not give itself a constitution,
and the same logic bore against treating the constitution as expressing the
principles of some hypothetical contract or covenant between otherwise
disunited individuals. If the constitution was not given by the people to
itself, it would not be a democratic constitution. The Weimar constitution, then, expressed the decision of an *already existing* sovereign people
to give itself the form of a state: and so the essence of the constitution,
Schmitt argued, was contained in its preamble and Article 1, rather than
in its subsequent articles – those that, as it happened, contained provisions for parliamentary government, constitutional courts, individual
rights and freedoms and so forth.[96] This argument was lethally double-
edged, and it had a double effect. Schmitt used one side of the argument
to puncture Kelsen's ambitions for parliament and political parties. He
used the other side to fillet Article 48 of the constitution, which gave
the president of the Reich emergency powers to secure public order and
security, and to stuff it with his own distinctive conception of sovereign
power to validate presidential dictatorship in the name of democracy.[97]

Parliament, Schmitt declared, was no longer a forum where a 'will of
the state' could form. So far from reconciling oppositions to produce a
united will, it had become the forum of a pluralistic division of organised
social powers. Perhaps it had once functioned successfully, in the nineteenth century, when its purpose was to integrate the bourgeoisie into the

---

[94] Schmitt, *On the Three Types*, p. 60. Schmitt had previously claimed that the Weimar
Republic was a continuation of, not a break with, the Reich constitution of 1871, the
insinuation being that similarly dramatic modifications of the current political order
could also be represented as upholding existing constitutional principles. See Carl
Schmitt, 'The Liberal Rule of Law', [1928], in Jacobsen and Schlink (eds.), *Weimar*,
pp. 294–300, at p. 294. For discussion see D. Bates, 'Political Theology and the Nazi
State: Carl Schmitt's Concept of the Institution', *Modern Intellectual History* 3 (2006),
pp. 415–42; S. Baume, 'On Political Theology: A Controversy between Hans Kelsen
and Carl Schmitt', *History of European Ideas* 35 (2009), pp. 369–81'; D. Kelly, 'Carl
Schmitt's Political Theory of Representation', *Journal of the History of Ideas* 65 (2004),
113–34.

[95] Schmitt, *Constitutional Theory*, pp. 75–7, 125–30, 140–6. See Kelly, 'Carl Schmitt's
Theory', pp. 122–34.

[96] In the preface to the second edition of his book on *Dictatorship*, published in 1928,
Schmitt dismissed the idea that the constitution should be identified with each of its
181 Articles. It was necessary, he said, to discriminate between merely *formal* elements
and inalienable ones. See Schmitt, *Dictatorship*, p. xxxiv.

[97] For Article 48, see Hucko (ed.), *The Democratic Tradition*, p. 160.

monarchic state, but in the conditions of mass society 'the apparatuses and machines' that had served that purpose were useless.[98] The present situation was one of 'unpredictable parliamentary majorities, incapable of governing . . . changing from one instance to the next, of . . . innumerable and in all respects heterogeneous political parties [which reflected] the pluralistic division of the state itself', all constantly shifting.[99] Decisions were not taken in parliament at all, but in its committees, in which the interests of economically powerful groups were traded off in secret, resulting in one compromise after another, compromise being a bottomlessly pejorative term in this context. Parliamentarians had become mere delegates of those interest groups, not genuine representatives of the people, and the formal provisions of contemporary parliamentary law concerning the independence of representatives were 'superficial decoration, useless and embarrassing'. It was as if, Schmitt memorably sniped, 'someone had painted the radiator of a modern central heating system with red flames in order to give the appearance of a blazing fire'.[100] Kelsen's 'subterranean streams' were channels of pollution which corrupted parliament and made a mockery of the notion of popular sovereignty.

The Crisis attempted to make this case by turning Kelsen's own reasoning against him. If parliament is no more than an expedient answering to the practical necessity of a political division of labour in the modern state, Schmitt asks, why cannot the will of the people be represented just as effectively by 'a single trusted representative' as an assembly? The argument from expediency, 'without ceasing to be democratic', will also justify 'an antiparliamentary Caesarism'.[101] There has to be, he goes on to argue, a deeper reason for favouring an assembly. Reconstructing Kelsen's steps, he discovers it in a foundational commitment to the principle of government by truth.[102]

Schmitt begins his analysis by fastening on Kelsen's invocation of Weber's analogy between the state and the modern factory. By equating the two, he suggests, Kelsen reduces the political to a shadow of economic reality and treats political problems as if they were 'fundamentally the same' as economic problems. It follows that for Kelsen the solution is likewise the same in both cases: 'free competition', the unrestrained clash of opinions in an assembly in the one case and an unregulated market in

[98]   Schmitt, 'Liberal Rule of Law', p. 297.
[99]   Carl Schmitt, *Der Hüter der Verfassung* (Tübingen: Mohr, 1931), pp. 88–9.
[100] Schmitt, *The Crisis*, p. 6.   [101] Ibid., p. 34.
[102] Ibid., pp. 34–7, 44–50. For critical discussion, see McCormick, *Carl Schmitt's Critique*, pp. 179–86 and, more broadly, B. Manin, 'On Legitimacy and Political Deliberation', *Political Theory* 15 (1987), pp. 338–68.

the other – 'everything must be negotiated in a deliberately complicated process of balancing'.[103] Parliament thus obtains its rationale as the place 'where a relative truth is achieved through discourse, in the discussion of argument and counterargument [between] multiple parties'.[104]

Schmitt contends, however, that this rationale has been vitiated by various changes which began in the nineteenth century and continue to accelerate in the present day.[105] The simulacrum of a *complexio oppositorum* has survived,[106] but the disconnection of structures from deliberation has opened a prospect in which segmental interests battle with one another to control state action via rationalised administrative processes from which contestation is systematically eliminated. In short, an intellectual and practical apparatus sustaining a core of unity has been dissolved and a multiplicity of dissonant voices has taken its place. Modern parliamentary democracy is exposed as a contradiction in terms: it fragments and destroys the popular will that it notionally represents.

One effect of this contention is to draw attention back to the confounding question of unity. In order for a people to be self-governing, Schmitt believes, it is necessary that it should be one, rather than a disorderly heap of many: it must be subject to a single will – its own – in order for the identity of ruler and ruled in which the essence of democracy consists to be realised. Kelsen himself had allowed that this identity was essential to democracy.[107] But he was emphatic that, interpreted literally, it was absurd. As we have already seen, by 'the people' Kelsen meant nothing more than the 'system of the acts of individual human beings determined by the state's legal order'. This made it natural for him to suppose that in reality there was an 'unavoidable distance between the will of the individual and the state order'.[108] Yet this invites an obvious objection: how is that supposition compatible with the claim that the people rule themselves? Kelsen's answer is that precisely *because* the

---

103 Schmitt, *The Crisis*, p. 25, and see also pp. 34–5, esp. p. 35: 'Normally one only discusses the economic line of reasoning that social harmony and the maximization of wealth follow from the free economic competition of individuals, from freedom of contract, freedom of trade, free enterprise. But all this is only an application of a general liberal principle. It is exactly the same: That the truth can be found through an unrestrained clash of opinion and that competition will produce harmony.'

104 Ibid., p. 46.

105 See ibid., pp. 22–50, and cf. Schmitt, *Concept of the Political*, pp. 22–5.

106 See Schmitt, *Roman Catholicism*, p. 26.

107 Schmitt, *The Crisis*, pp. 25–6. Cf. Kelsen, 'Essence and Value', p. 89. Of course Kelsen parted company with Schmitt over the *value* of democracy, which he, unlike Schmitt, located in the preservation of individual freedom and the protection of minorities.

108 Kelsen, 'Essence and Value', pp. 90, 88.

isolated individual has no real political existence, because he can gain no actual influence on forming the will of the state... democracy is possible in earnest only if individuals integrate into associations for the purpose of influencing the common will from the standpoint of their various political goals. Collective groupings which unite the similar interests [wants, wills] of their individual members as political parties have to mediate between the individual and the state... A democracy is necessarily and unavoidably a multi-party state,

for by this means alone the 'normative fiction' of the people is translated into political fact as a single will emerges from the interplay of discrete, separated parts within the state.[109]

Schmitt counters that this is simply impossible. Unity of the relevant kind can never be accomplished through the mere aggregation of private wills. Even the 'unanimous opinion of one hundred million private persons' would not constitute 'the will of the people', because 'the people exist only in the sphere of publicity' as a concrete political entity.[110] Schmitt reads into Kelsen's positions a subversive logic which aims to divide and depoliticise the German people through the insinuation, both open and concealed, of the pathologies of the private individual and his interests into every domain of life and thought.[111] Worse still, it is succeeding. The practical outcome of those positions is a state besieged by rival social and economic forces and the disaggregation of the people into a mess of solipsistic individuals and particular partisan interests.[112]

---

[109] Ibid., p. 92. See also p. 94: 'Irresistible developments lead in all democracies to the organisation of "the people" into political parties; or, rather, since "the people" as a political force does not previously exist, democratic developments integrate the mass of isolated individuals into political parties, thus releasing for the first time social forces that can somehow be described as "the people".'

[110] Schmitt, *The Crisis*, p. 16. Readers will recognise that Schmitt is silently helping himself to something like Rousseau's distinction between the general will and the will of all, which is the sum of every particular will. Cf. Jean-Jacques Rousseau, *The Social Contract* [1762], in V. Gourevitch (ed.), *Rousseau: The Social Contract and Other Later Political Writings* (Cambridge: Cambridge University Press, 1997), pp. 39–152, at p. 60.

[111] Schmitt, *The Crisis*, p. 20. Here and elsewhere Schmitt nests such claims in a wider story about world-historical tendencies which, it is implied, malign forces are seeking to exploit and accelerate. See e.g. ibid., pp. 33–50, and, at length, Schmitt, *Political Theology*; Schmitt, *Concept of the Political*; and Carl Schmitt, 'The Age of Neutralizations and Depoliticizations' [1929], trans. M. Konzett and J. P. McCormick, *Telos* 96 (1993), pp. 130–4. For the meaning of 'malign forces' in this context, see Gross, *Carl Schmitt and the Jews*.

[112] Cf. Rousseau, *Social Contract*, p. 122: 'when the State close to ruin subsists only in an illusory and vain form, when the social bond is broken in all hearts, when the basest interest brazenly assumes the sacred name of public good; then the general will grows mute, everyone, prompted by secret motives, no more states opinions as a Citizen than if the State had never existed, and iniquitous decrees with no other goal than particular interest are falsely passed under the name of Laws'.

V

When Schmitt looked about him in 1928 he claimed to see

> a people . . . divided in many ways – culturally, socially, by class, race, and religion . . . The German Reich is primarily a unity for paying reparations; it appears as such from the outside. However, politically nothing is more necessary than to envision the task of integrating the German people into political unity from the inside.[113]

Such prognostications were scarcely new. In 1919 Weber had drawn a similar inference. 'Particularism', he had declared, 'cries out for a *bearer of the principle of the unity of the Reich.*'[114] Traditionally this had been the monarch. But the age of monarchy, if not the principle that it represented, was gone.[115] Weber's preference, we know, was for the president of the Reich to fill the vacancy, carried into office on a wave of popular support; but popular support cuts both ways: 'Let us ensure that the president of the Reich sees the prospect of the gallows as the reward awaiting any attempt to interfere with the laws or to govern autocratically.'[116] It should also be remembered that his conception of plebiscitary democracy was presented as a counterweight to parliament, not as a replacement for it. Indeed, Weber predicted that the 'mighty current of democratic party life' stirred up by the need to organise election campaigns before a mass public would 'benefit parliament' too. He was certain that, whatever its defects, there were some functions for which 'parliaments are indeed irreplaceable in all democracies'. 'The complete abolition of the parliaments has not yet been demanded seriously by any democrat', ran one especially confident sentence in *Economy and Society*, 'no matter how much he is opposed to their present form'.[117] Enter Carl Schmitt.

---

[113] Schmitt, 'Liberal Rule of Law', p. 300.

[114] Weber, 'The President of the Reich', p. 307.

[115] The Reich constitution of 1871 made the king of Prussia both president and emperor of the Reich and its sole authorised representative. See Hucko (ed.), *The Democratic Tradition*, pp. 119–45. Cf. Weber, 'The President of the Reich', p. 306: 'Let us . . . debar all members of the dynasties from this office in order to prevent any restoration by means of a plebiscite.'

[116] Weber, 'The President of the Reich', p. 306. Marianne Weber records the following conversation between her husband and General Erich Ludendorff, which took place around the time that 'The President of the Reich' was published. 'In a democracy', Weber explains, 'the people choose the leader in whom they place their trust. Then the chosen person says, "Now keep quiet and do as you are told". The people and parties may no longer interfere with him . . . Afterwards the people can judge him – if the leader has made mistakes, then off to the gallows with him!' Ludendorff replies, perhaps rather disconcertingly, 'I could get to like such a "democracy"!' See Weber, *Lebensbild*, p. 703, as cited in Derman, *Max Weber*, p. 184.

[117] Weber, *Economy and Society*, p. 1454. For further discussion see McCormick, *Carl Schmitt's Critique*, pp. 175–9.

Schmitt agrees with Weber that 'monarchy's hour has tolled'.[118] But so too, he indicates, has parliament's. It can contribute nothing to the great task in view, the task of unifying the German people, because it is an instrument of division, a screen for individual self-assertion and sectional interest. It is for the same reason undemocratic. Democratic legitimacy, Schmitt maintains, 'rests on the idea that the state is the political unity of a *people* . . . the state is the political status of a people'.[119] The purest expression of that unity is found in the direct and unmediated expression of the will of a people assembled together, constituting itself as a single entity – 'the self-identity of the genuinely present people' – an ideal that Schmitt, like Kelsen, found in Rousseau.[120] Such purity may be unattainable in the extended territory of the modern nation-state, as Rousseau himself recognised,[121] but it remains for Schmitt the 'natural form' in which a people's will is expressed. In modern conditions, he then asserts, this united will is articulated most effectively in public acclamation, 'saying yes or no', and this acclamation becomes 'all the more simple and elementary, the more it is a fundamental decision on their own existence'; in other words, the more closely it approaches the ideal.[122] But the people can acclaim only what is presented to it or, better yet, re-presented to it by a spokesman capable of incarnating and expressing its own general will. 'Compared to a democracy that is direct', Schmitt concludes, 'not only in the technical sense but also in a vital sense, parliament appears an artificial machinery . . . while dictatorial and Caesaristic methods not only can produce the acclamation of the people but can also be a direct expression of democratic substance and power'.[123] The question Schmitt posed to Kelsen has its answer.

It is true that Schmitt sometimes made enthusiastic noises about Weber's 'democratic ideal of a political leader', an elected president above the party fray and 'borne by the confidence of the entire people',[124] but his own view, that dictatorship is not antithetical to democracy but founded upon it, ought to clarify any vestigial ambiguity on this score.[125] His avowed position was that the state, as a substantive body, was already disintegrating, and the German people and constitution with it: what remained was 'a highly fragmented pluralized *Parteienstaat* [with] clumps of power subject to political influence', each seeking 'to exploit

---

[118] Schmitt, *The Crisis*, p. 8.   [119] Schmitt, *Constitutional Theory*, pp. 138, 131.
[120] Ibid., p. 264.
[121] See Jean-Jacques Rousseau, 'Considerations on the Government of Poland' [1772], in Gourevitch (ed.), *Later Political Writings*, pp. 177–260, at pp. 239–55.
[122] Schmitt, *Constitutional Theory*, p. 131.   [123] Schmitt, *The Crisis*, p. 17.
[124] Schmitt, *Constitutional Theory*, p. 367.
[125] See Schmitt, *Dictatorship*, pp. 180–226. Green, *Eyes of the People*, pp. 169–71, offers a most interesting discussion of Schmitt's 'plebiscitary theory', but the difficulties identified there put question marks against the utility of the chosen description.

the moment of their power' and using 'every type of justification as a weapon in domestic political struggle... Neither parliamentary legality nor plebiscitary legitimacy... can overcome such a degradation to a technical functional tool.' Even 'the constitution itself breaks up into its contradictory components and interpretative possibilities such that no normative fiction of a "unity"' – surely he had Kelsen in his sights – 'can prevent warring factions from making use of that... constitutional text... they believe is best [to] knock... the opposing party to the ground in the name of the constitution'.[126]

State, people and constitution could be restored only by direct recourse to the political in its purest sense: that sovereign decision about friend and enemy which alone makes substantive existence possible. This is why, for Schmitt, the essence of state sovereignty had to be understood 'not as the monopoly to coerce', as Weber had imagined, but 'as the monopoly to decide'.[127] Since Article 48 gave the president whatever power was needed to secure order in an emergency, and since the decision about whether the state exists at all is placed entirely in his hands by Schmitt, the state of emergency becomes permanent and the president is free to act in whatever way he deems necessary to secure the continued existence of state and people. This paradox is captured most vividly in Schmitt's description of the president as 'guardian of the constitution' precisely because his decision, which transcends all constitutional constraints, sustains in existence the people whose will it expresses.[128]

The theoretical reflection Schmitt undertook as part of the great task he envisaged therefore led him finally to a conception of politics and political rule very far removed from Weber's, one in which charisma and the electoral contestation that developed it ultimately had little place: his extraordinary lawgiver combined 'legislative and executive [power]... in his person. [He was free] to intervene in the entire system of existing statutory norms and use it for his own purposes.' The threat of the gallows receded to vanishing point.[129]

---

[126] Schmitt, *Legality and Legitimacy*, p. 93.   [127] Schmitt, *Political Theology*, p. 13.

[128] Schmitt, *Der Hüter*, esp. p. 159. Cf. Schmitt, *The Crisis*, p. 29: 'only political power, which should come from the people's will, can form the people's will in the first place'. For Schmitt's position more generally see Caldwell, *Popular Sovereignty*, pp. 85–199; D. Dyzenhaus, 'Legal Theory in the Collapse of Weimar: Contemporary Lessons?', *American Political Science Review* 91 (1997), pp. 121–34 and Dyzenhaus, *Legality and Legitimacy*, pp. 38–101; E. Kennedy, *Constitutional Failure: Carl Schmitt in Weimar* (Durham, NC: Duke University Press, 2004), pp. 119–53. Kelsen responded to Schmitt's claims directly in *Wer soll der Der Hüter der Verfassung sein?* (Berlin: W. Rothschild, 1931). For discussion see Baume, *Hans Kelsen*, pp. 36–9.

[129] Schmitt, *Legality and Legitimacy*, pp. 68–71; A. Kalyvas, 'Who's Afraid of Carl Schmitt?' *Philosophy and Social Criticism* 25 (1999), pp. 87–125, at p. 92. É. Balibar, *We, the People of Europe? Reflections on Transnational Citizenship* (Princeton: Princeton University

By 1935 that great task had been completed in terms that met with Schmitt's evident approval: 'Today the German people has...become the German people again...The state is now a tool of the people's strength and unity. The German Reich now has a single flag...and this flag is not only composed of colors, but also has a large, true symbol: the symbol of the swastika that conjures up the people.'[130] These claims appeared in an essay with the title 'The Constitution of Freedom'.

Schmitt did not condescend to explain what he meant by freedom in the essay. But his other writings in and after 1933 made clear what previously had been hedged about or disclosed only to the extent that explicit statement was unavoidable to advance the argument in hand: that its meaning included the removal of all existing constitutional protections for the individual and the forcible creation of the people's unity through the dispossession and extrusion of its 'enemies', and excluded parliamentary sovereignty, an independent judiciary, a plurality of political parties and the rule of law.[131]

Kelsen was one of the many casualties of freedom. In 1933 he was removed from his chair at the University of Cologne on account of his Jewish origins. His recently appointed junior colleague, Schmitt, declined to sign a letter of resolution in his support.[132] Kelsen's landmarks may have been crumbling, but his commitment to democracy was unshakeable. Shortly before his dismissal he had addressed himself directly to the acutely pressing question of how democracy should defend itself against enemies who exploited the system to bring it down from the inside – a prospect raised, with cunning dialectical negativity, in Schmitt's 1932 text *Legality and Legitimacy*. Kelsen's response was that the question was answered in the asking: a democracy that seeks to assert itself against the will of the majority by force has already ceased to be a democracy. How, then, should a democrat act when confronted with this eventuality? Kelsen answered emphatically, '[He] must remain true to his colours, even when the ship is sinking, and can take with him into the depths only the hope that the ideal of freedom is indestructible and that the deeper

Press, 2004), p. 137, writes of 'the transfer of full powers of decision to a charismatic leader', but textual support for this gloss is not provided. For a more ambivalent treatment, which narrows the gap between Weber and Schmitt, see Green, *Eyes of the People*, pp. 166–71.

[130] Carl Schmitt, 'The Constitution of Freedom' [1935], in Jacobsen and Schlink (eds.), *Weimar*, pp. 323–5, at p. 325.

[131] See Carl Schmitt, *State, Movement, People: The Triadic Structure of the Political Unity* [1933], [with] *The Question of Legality* [1950], ed. S. Draghici (Corvallis, OR: Plutarch Press, 2001), pp. 10–11, 25–7.

[132] See Gross, *Carl Schmitt and the Jews*, pp. 25–6.

it has sunk, the more passionately it will revive.'[133] Kelsen went down with his ship. He resurfaced first of all in Geneva, where he worked until 1940, returning intermittently to Prague until that, too, became impossible, before emigrating to America, where he would remain until his death in 1973.

In 1955 Kelsen returned again to the question of democracy in a long essay published in the journal *Ethics*. 'Foundations of Democracy' reaffirmed his commitment to a proceduralist vision of democracy, with the majority principle and the protection of the rights of minorities at its centre. He issued stern warnings about those who, invoking the will of the people and the benefits of 'leadership', wished to abandon democracy and bring in autocracy under the disguise of a democratic terminology. A discreet but cutting footnote remarked that a 'typical representative of this doctrine is the one expounded by Carl Schmitt, who enjoyed temporary success as ideologist for National Socialism'.[134] Kelsen would not have relished the sequel. Today Schmitt is celebrated in many circles as one of the most important and penetrating critics of liberal democracy history has produced,[135] while Kelsen's efforts to defend that democracy in an hour of desperate need have been almost forgotten.[136]

---

[133] See Hans Kelsen, 'Verteidigung der Demokratie' [1932], in *Verteidigung der Demokratie: Abhandlungen zur Demokratietheorie* (Tübingen: Mohr Siebeck, 2006), pp. 229–37, at p. 237, as cited in C. Jabloner, 'Hans Kelsen', in Jacobsen and Schlink (eds.), *Weimar*, pp. 67–76, at p. 74.

[134] See Hans Kelsen, 'Foundations of Democracy', *Ethics* 66 (1955), pp. 1–101, at pp. 1–32, with accompanying note on 96. Cf. Schmitt, *State, Movement, People*, p. 37: 'The strength of the National Socialist State resides in the fact that it is dominated and imbued from top to bottom and in every atom of its being by the idea of leadership.'

[135] For the resurgence of interest in Schmitt see A. Koenen, *Der Fall Carl Schmitt: Sein Aufsteig zum 'Kronjuristen des Dritten Reiches'* (Darmstadt: Wissenschaftliche Buchgesellschaft, 1995), pp. 1–24. For a representative instance see e.g. C. Mouffe, *The Return of the Political* (London: Verso, 1993), pp. 117–56, esp. p 118: 'I propose to take as my starting point [for 'a thoroughgoing study of the liberal democratic regime'] the work of one of its most brilliant and intransigent opponents, Carl Schmitt. Though Schmitt's criticisms were developed at the beginning of the [twentieth] century, they are, in fact, still pertinent and it would be superficial to believe that the writer's subsequent membership of the National Socialist Party means that we can simply ignore them.' Schmitt is subsequently praised for his rigour and perspicacity. See also J. Freund, 'Schmitt's Political Thought', *Telos* 102 (1995), pp. 11–42; P. Piccone and G. L. Ulmen, 'Introduction to Carl Schmitt', *Telos* 72 (1987), 3–14.

[136] At least by Anglophone scholars: no complete translation of *Vom Wesen und Wert* appeared in English until 2013 (see Hans Kelsen, *The Essence and Value of Democracy*, trans. B. Graf and ed. N. Urbinati and C. I. Accetti (Lanham, MD: Rowman & Littlefield, 2013)). This situation is beginning to change, however. See esp. Baume, *Hans Kelsen* but also P. Pettit, *On the People's Terms: A Republican Theory and Model of Democracy* (Cambridge: Cambridge University Press, 2012), p. 287; Przeworski, *Democracy*, pp. 24–38; M. P. Saffon and N. Urbinati, 'Procedural Democracy, the Bulwark of Equal Liberty', *Political Theory* 41 (2013), pp. 441–81.

VI

The primary purpose of this chapter has been to explore the way that Max Weber set himself to analyse the contemporary political situation in Germany, to suggest an intellectual context which sheds light on that analysis, and to use the same context to examine a series of oppositions, across a range of issues, between Hans Kelsen and Carl Schmitt. Recent studies of Weber, and the long shadow that his work cast over many aspects of the Weimar Republic's intellectual life, have been much preoccupied with the question of whether his later political writings continued the liberal and democratic lines of thought that his Anglophone admirers especially had discerned in his earlier work, or whether they constitute instead a dramatic volte-face towards decisionism, authority and antiparliamentarianism. Is there, in other words, a direct path from Weber to Kelsen and beyond, or does the path lead from Weber to Schmitt and from there to the pathologies of National Socialism?[137]

Perhaps this is the wrong question to ask. Weber bequeathed to his successors not a set of directions but a set of dilemmas about how to live a meaningful life and conduct politics responsibly in the conditions of the modern world. In working through those dilemmas they developed positions that have exercised a powerful influence on democratic theory down to our own day, establishing parameters that continue at once to circumscribe and to energise the range of internal movement potential in our politics.[138]

Many of Kelsen's most Weberian claims were repeated by Joseph Schumpeter in his *Capitalism, Socialism and Democracy* of 1942.[139] Schumpeter attacked what he called the 'classical doctrine' of democracy, according to which the people itself decides issues through the election of representatives who identify and implement its general will. About this doctrine, Schumpeter made four points. First, that there was no such thing as a general will that 'all people could agree on or could

---

[137] See Villa, 'The Legacy', esp. pp. 74–5, 92–3, which argues against a 'slippery slope' from Weber to Schmitt. Cf. R. Eden, 'Doing without Liberalism: Weber's Regime Politics', *Political Theory* 10 (1982), pp. 379–407; F. Ringer, 'Max Weber's Liberalism', *Central European History* 35 (2002), pp. 379–95; M. Warren, 'Max Weber's Liberalism for a Nietzschean World', *American Political Science Review* 82 (1988), pp. 31–50.

[138] Consider a recent synoptic discussion of the 'main approaches' to democracy in current academic debates, which distinguishes three: (i) the 'epistemic' conception of democracy as a process of truth seeking; (ii) the 'populist' conception of democracy as a mobilising politics that defies procedures; and (iii) the 'minimalist' conception in which democracy is understood as a system in which parties lose elections. The authors seek to reclaim a fourth approach, 'procedural democracy', which they explicitly associate with Kelsen. See Saffon and Urbinati, 'Procedural Democracy'.

[139] Kelsen cited Schumpeter's text approvingly in 'Foundations of Democracy', p. 4.

be made to agree on by the force of rational argument'. Second, that agreement should not be expected because ultimate values could not be decided by rational argument. Third, that even if a general will somehow emerged the agreement that it superficially embodied would necessarily be manufactured rather than natural and lack 'not only rational unity but also rational sanction'. Finally, there was the question of implementation, about which no agreement could be expected either.[140]

As Schumpeter presented it, the political process was completely divorced from the pursuit of truth and the common good. What was good for one individual or group was not so (and not felt to be so) for another, and no amount of deliberation, nor any process of aggregation, would alter this sociological fact. Schumpeter did not share Kelsen's optimism about the likelihood of compromise between parties and had little patience with schemes for proportional representation, not least because he doubted whether any individual was the bearer of interests, preferences or volitions that were sufficiently well defined or known to him for anyone else to represent them.[141] In view of his deep scepticism about the idea that it possessed intrinsic value or could realise any popularly imposed goal, Schumpeter defined democracy by the process it characteristically employed, being 'that institutional arrangement for arriving at political decisions in which individuals acquire the power to decide by means of a competitive struggle for the people's vote', based on the principle that 'the reins of government should be handed to those who command more support than do any of the competing individuals or teams'.[142] In a democracy, the people do not rule: their role is to elect those who do. Schumpeter was moved to wonder how the classical doctrine, which was 'so patently contrary to fact', could have retained its allure for so long, and commended his own theory as 'much truer to life' than its rival.[143]

The thought that democracy, properly understood, was merely a method through which leaders were selected proved irresistibly attractive to political theorists of the 1950s and 1960s entranced – as many were – by the prospect of a purely descriptive social science. This way of thinking enjoyed considerable vogue for a time, providing as it did a decisive and reassuringly simple criterion for distinguishing democratic

---

[140] Joseph Schumpeter, *Capitalism, Socialism and Democracy* (London and New York: Routledge, 1994 [1942]), pp. 250–3.
[141] Ibid., p. 261.   [142] Ibid., pp. 269, 273.
[143] Ibid., pp. 264, 269. This view of democracy is defended on normative grounds in A. Przeworski, 'Minimalist Conception of Democracy: A Defence', in I. Shapiro and C. Hacker-Cordón (eds.), *Democracy's Value* (Cambridge: Cambridge University Press, 1999), pp. 23–55.

arrangements from undemocratic ones, and it spawned in its turn various economic and empirical theories of democracy which genuflected to Schumpeter as a source of inspiration.[144] The possibility of a purely empirical and value-neutral social science soon came under suspicion, however, and with it the pretensions of the empirical theorists of democracy to have eliminated all normative considerations from their analyses. The very act of description involved an implicit appeal to evaluative criteria which, once laid out, led some to question whether the Schumpeterian model salvaged enough of what was conventionally understood by the term 'democracy' to merit the description in the first place. Quite what remained of popular sovereignty on his model, for instance, was obscure;[145] likewise why democrats should or would give their allegiance to a set of procedures which, on Schumpeter's own admission, might be less adept at securing outcomes acceptable to all the competing groups that comprised the people than a dictatorship.[146]

Reflecting on these questions, a number of prominent theorists began to seek new grounds on which to mount a normative defence of democracy. John Rawls initially attempted to vindicate a conception of democracy suitable to a just society on terms that set out from the different wants and interests of real individuals, but came to realise that a bargain among competing groups would not deliver justice:[147] each would 'take a narrow or group-interest standpoint' rather than aiming at a common good.[148] His first response was to impose a common standpoint on all parties through the procedural contrivance of a 'veil of ignorance' which deprived them of knowledge of their own particular circumstances, thereby bracketing the problem of particularism and enabling him to present the principles of justice chosen behind the veil as expressing a general will common to all similarly situated rational agents. In later work he confronted the problem more directly, invoking the principle of public reason to explain how citizens, divided on questions of ultimate value, could nevertheless deliberate together about matters of public concern and sustain over time an 'overlapping consensus' about political justice.

---

[144] Among the former, see esp. A. Downs, *An Economic Theory of Democracy* (New York: Harper & Row, 1957); among the latter, R. Dahl, *A Preface to Democratic Theory* (Chicago: University of Chicago Press, 1956) and *Who Governs?* (New Haven: Yale University Press, 1961). For discussion see Q. Skinner, 'The Empirical Theorists of Democracy and their Critics: A Plague on Both their Houses', *Political Theory* 1 (1973), pp. 287–306.

[145] Skinner, 'Empirical Theorists', 290–303 showed the difficulty of resolving this question in the terms with which the empirical theorists and their critics alike were operating.

[146] Schumpeter, *Capitalism*, pp. 255–6.

[147] See J. Rawls, 'Justice as Reciprocity' [1959, first published 1971], in *Collected Papers*, ed. S. Freeman (Cambridge, MA: Harvard University Press, 1999), pp. 190–224.

[148] J. Rawls, *A Theory of Justice* (New York: Oxford University Press, 1971), pp. 360–1.

Elaborating his position, Rawls recalled the fate of the Weimar Republic which, in his summary account, fell when the members of powerful elites abandoned constitutional politics and gave up on the co-operation needed to make it work. Schmitt was cited in passing;[149] but it soon became evident that Rawls's flanks were vulnerable to lines of criticism that Schmitt had pressed against Kelsen:[150] while Rawls continued to assign priority to the basic rights and freedoms of individuals, not only over procedural rights but also over any collective or common good,[151] self-interested individuality remained 'the *terminus a quo* and *terminus ad quem*' of his conception of democracy and public reason reduced to an ideological instrument which masked its own service to particular interests and the endless bargaining of such interests – of the sort Rawls agreed was incompatible with justice – in a highly moralised and misleading language of consensus.[152] In response, some commentators (unwittingly) marched backwards into positions Kelsen had occupied, defending democratic procedures and institutions as the best guarantors of equal political freedom among individual citizens between whom no consensus should be expected.[153]

A somewhat different approach was developed by Jürgen Habermas. Habermas was as illusionless about Schmitt as he was irreverent,[154] but he shared some of Schmitt's stated doubts about the ability of existing democratic procedures to deliver meaningful outcomes. He proposed to identify the conditions under which they might do so. These turned out to involve the reinvigoration of institutions and principles that Kelsen

[149] J. Rawls, *Political Liberalism*, expanded edn. (New York: Columbia University Press, 1996), pp. lix–lx.

[150] See Schmitt, *Concept of the Political*, pp. 70–1.

[151] For procedural rights as 'subordinate to the other freedoms', see Rawls, *A Theory of Justice*, p. 233; for rights as prior to the common good, see e.g. p. 560.

[152] See P. Johnson, 'Carl Schmitt, Jürgen Habermas, and the Crisis of Politics', *The European Legacy* 3 (1998), 15–32, at p. 20; Dyzenhaus, 'Legal Theory', 132–3; and cf. Mouffe, *The Return of the Political*, pp. 102–34.

[153] See e.g. N. Wolterstorff, *Understanding Liberal Democracy: Essays in Political Philosophy*, ed. T. Cuneo (Oxford: Oxford University Press, 2012), part 2. Cf. p. 295: 'to affirm the liberal democratic polity is to put the shape of our life together at the mercy of votes in which the infidel has an equal voice with the believer'.

[154] See J. Habermas, 'The Horrors of Autonomy: Carl Schmitt in English', in *The New Conservatism: Cultural Criticism and the Historians' Debate*, ed. and trans. S. W. Nicholsen (Cambridge, MA: MIT Press, 1989), pp. 128–39, at p. 129: '[Schmitt] wants to lay the conceptual groundwork for detaching democratic will-formation from the universalist presuppositions of general participation, limiting it to a . . . substratum of the population, and reducing it to argument-free acclamation by the immature masses. Only thus can one envision a caesaristic and ethnically homogeneous *Führerdemokratie*, a democracy under a Führer in which such a thing as "sovereignty" would be embodied.' For irreverence, see note 58 above.

held dearest, including 'the significance of deliberative bodies in democracies, the rationale of parliamentary opposition, the need for a free and independent media and sphere of public opinion, and the rationale for employing majority rule as a decision procedure'.[155] Thus the problem became one of achieving mutual understanding with others about the world of human experience and activity rather than harmonising, neutralising or reconciling competing claims or partisan interests. Habermas used the same logic to hobble the Schmittian critique of public reason before it left the blocks. Democratic principles were not subordinate to, but neither did they seek to trump, basic rights and freedoms. Rather, they were 'equiprimordial' and complicit, rights being understood not as individual possessions but as relations grounded in mutual recognition and interpersonal action.[156]

Popular sovereignty was treated in similarly diffusive terms. 'The people from whom all governmental authority is supposed to derive does not comprise a subject with will and consciousness,' Habermas insisted. 'It only appears in the plural and *as* a people it is capable of neither decision nor action as a whole.'[157] As with Kelsen, so with Habermas it is only through participation in the procedures of democratic decision-making that individuals rule themselves. For Habermas this ideally implies communicative interaction free from coercion, bureaucratic control or socioeconomic subordination. In reality, however, these are always present to some degree, and in recent writings Habermas has acknowledged roles for bargaining, voting and leadership alongside deliberation in the daily life of a democracy.[158]

The attempt to sublimate popular sovereignty into certain specified procedural conditions or discursive processes duly provoked a reaction among writers who wished to reintroduce into political theorising the idea that the people could act as one, possessing a collective will and being capable of expressing it without the mediation of representative institutions. Thus Ernesto Laclau, in a work of 2005, could echo Schmitt in suggesting that the collective will was represented truly only by a figure (or figures) that spoke for the people as a whole, beyond parliament and parties, and so achieved the perfect identity of ruler and ruled which Schmitt

---

[155] See S. Benhabib, 'Deliberative Rationality and Models of Democratic Legitimacy', *Constellations* 1 (1994), pp. 26–53, at p. 42.

[156] J. Habermas, *Between Facts and Norms: Contributions to a Discourse Theory of Law and Democracy*, trans. W. Rehg (Cambridge, MA: MIT Press, 1996), pp. 82–131.

[157] J. Habermas, 'Popular Sovereignty as Procedure', in J. Bohman and W. Rehg (eds.), *Deliberative Democracy: Essays on Reason and Politics* (Cambridge, MA: MIT Press, 1987), pp. 35–65, p. 41.

[158] Habermas, *Between Facts and Norms*, pp. 336–40; J. Habermas, 'Leadership and Leitkultur', *New York Times*, 28 October 2010.

had made the essence of democracy. Laclau likewise bewailed the reduction of the people to a plurality of inconsistent interests and values and its debilitation through strangulation in rules and procedures.[159] He wanted to recover and mobilise the people's potential for revolutionary action. Critics have worried that his way of thinking leaves little scope for opposing or criticising whatever emerges in the realisation of that potential, 'let alone challenging it through effective political contestation'.[160] They also worry about the potential for the people to be demobilised, their participation in politics reduced to a passive spectatorship that presents an even less effective means of contesting political decisions than electoral politics 'or subordination by the hegemonic collective under the representation of a charismatic leader'.[161] In making these points, it is Kelsen's positions these critics claim to be restating.

VII

A recent book announces that we are living in *The Time of Popular Sovereignty*. It tells us that popular sovereignty is the only true ground of democratic legitimacy. At the same time it argues that the people is a series of events, not a collective agent or an aggregation of persons, and so constantly in flux, yet that it is still sovereign; that its decisions are not necessarily right, that it does not embody rationality, and that there is no intrinsic obligation on the part of citizens to obey it.[162] Confronted with a notion of sovereign power that is simultaneously in nobody's possession and in everyone's, and in principle binding on none, our first impulse may well be to heed the advice of Frank Ankersmit, who has suggested that we would do better to 'abandon the doctrine of popular sovereignty just like that of the divine right of kings: in representative democracy . . . no segment of society and no institution . . . can properly be said to "own" the state and the political powers embodied in it'.[163]

Sound reasons for firmly resisting that initial impulse were enunciated many years ago by R. G. Collingwood, when he observed that sovereignty

159 E. Laclau, *On Populist Reason* (London: Verso, 2005), pp. 162–4.
160 Saffon and Urbinati, 'Procedural Democracy', p. 453. The authors note (p. 476, n. 93) Laclau's recent comments about the 'illegitimacy' of opposition to Argentina's 'populist' leader Cristina Kirchner and his belief in the importance of her being re-elected indefinitely to allow her hegemonic project to be consolidated.
161 Saffon and Urbinati, 'Procedural Democracy', pp. 452–3. An attempt is made to address this worry in Green, *Eyes of the People*.
162 P. Ochoa Espejo, *The Time of Popular Sovereignty: Process and the Democratic State* (University Park: Pennsylvania State University Press, 2011), pp. 180–225.
163 F. R. Ankersmit, *Political Representation* (Stanford: Stanford University Press, 2002), p. 118.

'is merely the name for political activity, and those who would banish sovereignty as an outworn fiction are really only trying to shirk the whole problem of politics'.[164] Of course that problem may be understood in many different ways. For Schmitt, the problem presented itself in the form of a question about how political unity could be maintained in the face of an increasingly pluralistic struggle of interests and ideals. On his assumptions, plurality could never be a preface to peaceful coexistence (because plurality implied a variety of positions each of whose claims were total) but, rather, was the prelude to a contest for survival. Kelsen's assumptions led him to another destination. He found value in plurality and thought it possible for civilised people to come together in their differences, giving every political conviction the same chance to be articulated and to compete freely to win the hearts and minds of citizens.

The conceptions of democracy defended by Kelsen and Schmitt complemented their wider positions. Kelsen emphasised the constituted power of the people, understanding by the people the individuals who play their various parts, above all electoral, in establishing their representatives and thus in forming and conditioning the institutions that deliver the laws under which they live. Schmitt dwelt upon the constituent power of the people, understanding by that same term a united body acting as one to give itself constitutional form, receiving its unity at the moment of formation from the sovereign power that decides in its name.

So described, their conceptions mirror almost exactly the two 'diametrically opposed notions' symbolising 'two equally opposed states of affairs' that Sheldon Wolin once identified within democracy: 'One is the settled structure of politics and governmental authority typically called a constitution, and the other is the unsettling political movement typically called revolution. Stated somewhat starkly: constitution signifies the suppression of revolution; revolution the destruction of constitution'.[165] A recent commentator notes that Wolin 'urges us to recognize that authentic democracy takes shape exclusively around the latter pole', that popular sovereignty manifests itself truly only in extraordinary moments of collective disobedience and mass protest.[166] But would we be wise to follow these urgings?

---

[164] R. G. Collingwood, 'Political Action' [1928–9], in *Essays in Political Philosophy*, ed. D. Boucher (Oxford: Clarendon Press, 1989), pp. 92–109, at p. 106.

[165] S. Wolin, 'Norm and Form: The Constitutionalizing of Democracy', in J. P. Euben, J. R. Wallach and J. Ober (eds.), *Athenian Political Thought and the Reconstruction of American Democracy* (Ithaca: Cornell University Press, 1994), pp. 29–58, at pp. 29, 37.

[166] S. Bilakovics, *Democracy without Politics* (Cambridge, MA: Harvard University Press, 2012), pp. 204–5.

My own judgement is that we would not.[167] The two notions Wolin identifies are not, so it seems to me, alternative opposites each giving its own complete understanding of democracy but rather twin poles which, through their partnership and interaction, provide both the limits and the impetus to our thinking about democracy and our attempts to govern ourselves and to shape the course of our common political life, each exerting a pull which makes itself felt over the full range of movement. The limits are not fixed for all time – as we have seen, they are the historical deposits of an intellectual and political contest that is ongoing – but on any given occasion they are relatively fixed and constrain all contesting parties to a certain field of vision and a certain range of opportunity.[168]

At the limit, where the pull of its counterpart is weakest, each notion gains a strength through purity and simplicity which ultimately disposes it to excess and exposes it to self-defeat: the view is unrestricted and the possibilities are sharply polarised. Schmitt saw in the liberal constitutionalist state an empty formalism which encouraged the reign of private interest and with it, or so he feared, the kind of enfeebling lethargy that overtakes a people when it has given up on politics and on the idea of ruling itself. He oriented his theory of democracy around the concrete will of a united people, united in and under a leader with unchallenged authority. Kelsen saw behind Schmitt's invocation of popular will over and against the existing constitutional order, and in all similar attempts to ignore or evade the 'facts' of modern political life, 'the gaping stare of the *Gorgon's naked power*'.[169] He denied that the people had a will, and oriented his rival theory around the protection of the rights of minorities and procedures which assured the possibility that the minority 'may at any time itself become a majority'.[170]

Each theory, whatever else we might think of it, has the merit of illuminating the strengths and weaknesses of its rival; yet each must partake of something of the other to be viable. When democratic procedures and institutions are systematically unaccountable to the people in whose name they operate – when the fact bears no resemblance at all to the fiction – they have little to commend them and little capacity to compel the adhesion of citizens even in times of relatively untroubled stability and security, let alone in times of test; but there is always something

---

[167] For a similar judgement, on contrasting grounds, defended at much greater length, see Pettit, *On the People's Terms*, esp. pp. 252–92.

[168] This image is adapted from M. Oakeshott, *The Politics of Faith and the Politics of Scepticism*, ed. T. Fuller (New Haven: Yale University Press, 1996), p. 116.

[169] Hans Kelsen, 'Ansprache', in *Veröffentlichungen der Vereinigung der Deutschen Staatsrechtslehrer*, vol. III (Berlin: Walter de Gruyter, 1927), pp. 53–5, at pp. 54–5.

[170] Kelsen, 'Essence and Value', p. 108.

to be said for a regime in which, however unsatisfactory it is in other respects, we retain the ability at regular intervals, and without bloodshed, to remove our governors 'when enough of us have had more than enough of them'.[171] It may be that, in the end, in our efforts to realise the ideal of a self-governing people we cannot do better than such a regime.[172] (We can assuredly do appreciably and dismayingly worse.) We cannot doubt, however, that the question of whether and how we *might* do better remains one of the most central questions of contemporary life. To shirk it is to shirk the whole problem of politics.

[171] Dunn, 'Legitimacy and Democracy', p. 16. See also Przeworksi, 'Minimalist Conception'.
[172] For a sustained recent attempt to show how we can do better see Pettit, *On the People's Terms*.

Bibliography

BIBLIOGRAPHY OF PRIMARY SOURCES

MANUSCRIPTS, NEWSPAPERS AND COMPILATIONS

Burke Papers, Sheffield Archives, Wentworth Woodhouse Muniments (WWM).
Fitzwilliam Manuscripts at the Northamptonshire Record Office (Northamptonshire MSS).
Chatham Papers, The National Archives (TNA), PRO 30/8/99.
Gentleman's Magazine.
London Evening Post.
London Magazine.
New-York Gazette.
Pennsylvania Evening Post.
Pennsylvania Gazette.

PRINTED PRIMARY SOURCES

Acts and Ordinances of the Interregnum, 1642–1660. 3 vols. Edited by C. H. Firth and R. S. Rait. London: HMSO, 1911.
Adams, John. *A Defence of the Constitutions of Government of the United States of America*. 3 vols. London: C. Dilly, 1787–8.
　Diary and Autobiography of John Adams. 3 vols. Edited by L. H. Butterfield. Cambridge, MA: The Belknap Press of Harvard University Press, 1961.
Addison, Joseph. *Cato: A Tragedy*. London: J. Tonson, 1713.
Aeschines. *Speeches*. Edited by C. D. Adams. Cambridge, MA: Harvard University Press, 1919.
Aeschylus. *Persae*. Edited by A. F. Garvie. Oxford: Oxford University Press, 2009.
　Prometheus Bound. Edited and translated by A. J. Podlecki. Oxford: Aris & Phillips, 2005.
Agarwal, Shriman Narayan. *Gandhian Constitution for Free India*. Allahabad: Kitabistan, 1946.
Agreement of the People For A firme and present Peace, upon grounds of common right and freedome. London: n.p., 1647.
American Archives: Fourth Series. 6 vols. Edited by Peter Force. Washington, DC: n.p., 1837.
American Resistance Indefensible. London: n.p., 1776.

Anaximenes of Lampsacus. *Rhetorica ad Alexandrum*. Greek text in TLG. Edited and translated by Thomas W. Benson and Michael H. Prosser in *Readings in Classical Rhetoric*. Bloomington: Indiana University Press, 1972.

Animadversions Upon Those Notes Which The Late Observator hath published. London: n.p., 1642.

Annual Register for the Year 1766. London: n.p., 1767.

Anonimo, Romano. *Cronica*. Edited by G. Porta. Milan: Adelphi, 1979.

Anthony, Charles. *Popular Sovereignty: Being Some Thoughts on Popular Reform.* London: Longmans, 1880.

Archives Parlementaires de 1787 à 1860. Première Série VIII. Edited by M. J. Mavidal, E. Laurent and E. Clavel. Paris: Librairie Administrative de Paul Dupont, 1875.

Archives Parlementaires de 1789 à 1860: Recueil Complet Des Débats Législatifs & Politiques Des Chambres Françaises. Edited by J. Mavidal and E. Laurent. Paris: Librairie administrative de P. Dupont, 1862.

Aristophanes. *Ecclesiazusae*. Edited and translated by Alan H. Sommerstein. Warminster: Aris & Phillips, 1998.

  Knights. Edited and translated by Alan H. Sommerstein. Warminster: Aris & Phillips, 1997.

  Wasps. Edited and translated by Alan H. Sommerstein. Oxford: Aris & Phillips, 2004.

Aristotle. *Ars Rhetorica*. Edited by W. D. Ross. Oxford: Clarendon Press, 1959.

  Athenaion Politeia. Edited by John Edwin Sandys. 2nd edn. London: n.p., 1891.

  Athenaion Politeia (Constitution of the Athenians). In P. J. Rhodes, *A Commentary on the Aristotelian* Athenaion Politeia. Oxford: Clarendon Press, 1981.

  Atheniensium Respublica. Edited by Frederic G. Kenyon. Oxford: Clarendon Press, 1937.

  Politica. Edited by W. D. Ross. Oxford: Clarendon Press, 1957.

  Politica (Politics): Aristotle's Politics. Edited and translated by C. D. C. Reeve. Indianapolis: Hackett, 1998.

  Politics. Edited and translated by H. Rackman. Cambridge, MA: Harvard University Press, 1932.

  The Politics *of Aristotle*. Edited by W. L. Newman. Oxford: Clarendon Press, 1887.

  The Politics *and the* Constitution of Athens. Edited and translated by Stephen Everson. Cambridge: Cambridge University Press, 1996.

Asconius. *Orationum Ciceronis Quinque Enarratio*. Edited by Albertus Curtis Clark. Oxford: Oxford University Press, 1907.

Austin, John. *The Province of Jurisprudence Determined*. London: John Murray, 1832.

Balderston, Marion and David Syrett (eds.). *The Lost War: Letters from British Officers during the American Revolution*. New York: n.p., 1975.

Bancroft, Edward. *Remarks on the Review of the Controversy between Great Britain and her Colonies*. New London, CT: n.p., 1771.

Barker, John. *The British in Boston: Being the Diary of Lieutenant John Barker of the King's Own Regiment from November 15, 1774 to May 31, 1776.* Edited by Elizabeth Ellery Dana. Cambridge, MA: Harvard University Press, 1920.

Bartolus de Saxoferrato. *In Secundam Codicis Partem.* Venice: n.p., 1570.

Bentley, Thomas. *Journal of a Visit to Paris 1776.* Edited by Peter France. Brighton: University of Sussex Library, 1977.

Benton, Thomas Hart. *Thirty Years' View, Or A History of the Working of the American Government for Thirty Years, From 1820–1850.* 2 vols. New York: n.p., 1858.

Bergasse, Nicolas. *Rapport du comité de constitution sur l'organisation du pouvoirs judiciare.* Paris: n.p., 1789.

Bertie, Willoughby, Lord Abingdon. *Thoughts on Mr. Burke's Letter to the Sheriffs of Bristol on the Affairs of America.* Dublin: n.p., 1777.

Bluntschli, Johann Caspar. *Allgemeines Staatsrecht, geschichtlichbegründet.* Munich: Literarisch Artistischen Anstalt, 1852.

Bemerkungenüber die neuesten Vorschlägezurdeutschen Verfassung. Munich: C. Kaster, 1848.

'Cäsar und Cäsarismus'. *Deutsches Staatswörterbuch.* 11 vols. Edited by J. C. Bluntschli and K. Brater, vol. I, 387–92. Stuttgart and Leipzig: n.p., 1865.

'Demokratie und Repräsentativ demokratie'. *Bluntschli's Staatswörterbuch in drei Bänden.* 3 vols. Edited by E. Löning, vol. I, 464–70. Leipzig and Stuttgart: n.p., 1875.

Lehre vom modernen Staat. 3 vols. Stuttgart: J. G. Cotta, 1886 [1876].

'Machiavelli'. *Bluntschli's Staatswörterbuch in drei Bänden.* 3 vols. Edited by E. Löning, vol. II, 571–6. Leipzig and Stuttgart: n.p., 1876.

Das modern Völkerrecht der civilisierten Staaten. Nordlichen: Beck, 1868.

'Nation und Volk, Nationalitätsprincip'. *Staatswörterbuch in drei Bänden.* 3 vols. Edited by J. K. Bluntschli and K. Brater, vol. II, 651–7. Leipzig and Stuttgart: n.p., 1876.

Die Neue Gestaltung von Deutschland und die Schweiz. Zurich: Orell, Fusli & Co., 1867.

The Theory of the State. 3rd edn., translated from the 6th German edn. Oxford: Clarendon Press, 1901 [1885].

'Vierter Stand'. *Deutsches Staatswörterbuch.* 11 vols. Edited by J. C. Bluntschli and K. Brater, vol. XI, 72–5. Stuttgart and Leipzig: n.p., 1865.

Das Volk und der Souveränimallgemeinenbetrachtet und mitbesondere Rücksicht auf die Schweizerischen Verhältnisse. Zurich: Drell, Füsli & Co., 1834.

Bodin, Jean. *De la Demononamie des Sorciers.* Paris: Jacque du Puys, 1580.

Lettre d'un Lieutenant-Général de Province à un des premiers magistrats de France. Paris: n.p., 1589.

Method for the Easy Comprehension of History. Translated by Beatrice Reynolds. New York: Columbia University Press, 1945.

Methodus ad facilem historiarum cognitionem. Paris: n.p., 1572 [1566].

Methodus ad facilem historiarum cognitionem. Edited and translated (into Italian) by Sara Miglietti. Pisa: Edizioni della Normale, 2013.

De Republica libri sex. Paris: Jacques de Puy, 1586.

De republica libri sex. Paris: n.p., 1786.

The Six Bookes of a Commonweale. Edited by K. D. McRae and translated by Richard Knolles. Cambridge, MA: Harvard University Press, 1962 [1606].

Les six livres de la Republique. Paris: Jacques du Puys, 1576; 2nd edn. Paris: Jacques du Puys, 1577.

Les six livres de la Republique. Lyons: Jacques du Puys, 1579.

Les six livres de la Republique. Paris: n.p., 1583.

On Sovereignty: Four Chapters from the Six Books of the Commonwealth. Edited and translated by Julian H. Franklin. Cambridge: Cambridge University Press, 1992.

Bolts, William. *Considerations on Indian Affairs, Particularly Respecting the Present State of Bengal and Its Dependencies.* London: n.p., 1772.

Boswell, James. *An account of Corsica.* London: n.p., 1769.

[Bowles, Edward]. *Plaine English.* London: n.p., 1643.

Briefs of the American Revolution: Constitutional Arguments Between Thomas Hutchinson, Governor of Massachusetts Bay, and James Bowdoin for the Council and John Adams for the House of Representatives. Edited by John Phillip Reid. New York and London: New York University Press, 1981.

Brissot, Jacques-Pierre, ed. *Le Patriote François* V. Paris: n.p., 1789.

Mémoires. 2 vols. Edited by C. Perroud. Paris: n.p., [1902].

Brooke, Sir Robert. *La graunde abridgement.* London: n.p., 1586.

Burke, Edmund. *The Correspondence of Edmund Burke.* 10 vols. Edited by Thomas W. Copeland. Chicago: University of Chicago Press, 1958–78.

Reflections on the Revolution in France. Edited by J. C. D. Clark. Stanford: Stanford University Press, 2001.

Writings and Speeches of Edmund Burke. 9 vols. Edited by Paul Langford. Oxford: Oxford University Press, 1981–2015.

Burroughs, Jeremiah. *The Glorious Name of God, the Lord of Hosts.* London: n.p., 1643.

Carré de Malberg, Raymond. *Contribution à la théorie générale de l'état.* 2 vols. Paris: Siery, 1920.

Cicero. *Cicero, On the Commonwealth and On the Laws.* Edited by J. E. Zetzel. Cambridge and New York: Cambridge University Press, 1999.

Cicero De Republica: Selections. Edited by J. E. Zetzel. Cambridge: Cambridge University Press, 1995.

De inventione, De optimo genere oratorum, Topica. Cambridge, MA: Loeb Classical Library, 1949.

De re publica, De legibus. Edited and translated by C. W. Keyes. Cambridge, MA: Harvard University Press, 1943 [1928].

Epistulae ad Atticum. 6 vols. Edited by D. R. Shackleton Bailey. Cambridge: n.p., 1965–8.

In Pisonem. Edited by R. G. M. Nisbet. Oxford: Clarendon Press, 1961.

Pro Archia. Post Reditum in Senatu. Post Reditum ad Quirites. De Domo Sua. De Aruspicum Responsis. Pro Plancio. Edited and translated by N. H. Watts. Cambridge, MA: Harvard University Press, 1923.

Pro Caelio, De Provinciis Consularibus, Pro Balbo. Edited and translated by R. Gardner. Cambridge, MA: Harvard University Press, 1958.

Pro Lege Manilia. Pro Caecina. Pro Cluentio. Pro Rabirio Perduellionis Reo. Edited and translated by H. G. Hodge. Cambridge, MA: Harvard University Press, 1927.

Pro Sestio and In Vatinium. Edited and translated by R. Gardner. Cambridge, MA: Harvard University Press, 1958.

Cinus de Pistorio. *Lectura super Codice.* Venice: n.p., 1493.

Coke, Sir Edward. *La sept part des reports.* London: n.p., 1608.

Cola di Rienzo. *Epistolario di Cola di Rienzo.* Edited by Annibale Gabriell. Rome: n.p., 1890.

Collingwood, R. G. 'Political Action'. (1928–9). *Essays in Political Philosophy.* Edited by D. Boucher, 92–109. Oxford: Clarendon Press, 1989.

Commons Debates 1628. 4 vols. Edited by R. C. Johnson, M. F. Keeler, M. J. Cole and W. B. Bidwell. New Haven: Yale University Press, 1977.

Constant, Benjamin. *Fragments D'un Ouvrage Abandonné Sur La Possibilité D'une Constitution Républicaine Dans Un Grand Pays.* Paris: Aubier, 1991.

    Political Writings. Edited by Biancamaria Fontana. Cambridge: Cambridge University Press, 1988.

    Principles of Politics Applicable to All Governments. Indianapolis: Liberty Fund, 2003.

Crawford, M. H., ed. *Roman Statutes.* 2 vols. London: Institute of Classical Studies, 1996.

The Crisis, Or, a full defence of the colonies. London: n.p., 1766.

Davies, Sir John. *Le primer report des cases et matters en ley resolves et adjudges en les courts del royen Ireland.* Dublin: n.p., 1615.

de Lolme, Jean-Louis. *The Constitution of England; or, an Account of the English government.* London: n.p., 1781.

Debates in the Several State Conventions on the Adoption of the Federal Constitution. 5 vols. Edited by Jonathan Elliot. Washington, DC: n.p., 1836.

Demosthenes. *Demosthenis Orationes.* 4 vols. Edited by M. R. Dilts. Oxford: Clarendon Press, 2002–10.

Digges, Dudley. *The unlawfulness of subjects taking up arms.* London: n.p., 1643.

Dio, Cassius. *Roman History.* 8 vols. Edited and translated by E. Cary and H. B. Foster. Cambridge, MA: Harvard University Press, 1914–27.

Dio, Chrysostom. *Agamemnon, or on Kingship,* in *Discourses 37–60.* Translated by J. W. Cohoon and H. Lamar Crosby. Cambridge, MA: Harvard University Press, 1946.

    Discourse of Kingship, in *Discourses 1–11.* Translated by J. W. Cohoon. Cambridge, MA: Harvard University Press, 1932.

    To the People of Alexandria and *First Tarsic Discourse,* in *Discourses 31–36.* Translated by J. W. Cohoon and H. Lamar Crosby. Cambridge, MA: Harvard University Press, 1940.

Dionysius of Halicarnassus. *Roman Antiquities.* 7 vols. Edited and translated by E. Cary. Cambridge, MA: Harvard University Press, 1937–50.

Douglas, Stephen Arnold. *Popular Sovereignty in the Territories: The Dividing Line between Federal and Local Authority.* New York: Harper & Brothers, 1859.

Dow, Alexander. *The History of Hindostan from the Earliest Account of Time to the Death of Akbar.* 3 vols. London: n.p., 1768–72.

Drayton, William. *A Letter from a Freeman of South-Carolina, to the Deputies of North-America, Assembled in the High Court of Congress at Philadelphia.* Charleston: n.p., 1774.

Dutt, R. C. *The Economic History of India.* 2 vols. New York: Ben Franklin, 1970 [1906].

Elliot, Jonathan, ed. *The Debates in the Several State Conventions on the Adoption of the Federal Constitution.* 5 vols. Washington, DC: n.p., 1836.

Elton, G. R. *The Tudor Constitution: Documents and Commentary.* 2nd edn. Cambridge: Cambridge University Press, 1986 [1982].

Elyot, Thomas. *The Boke named The Governour.* 2 vols. Edited by Henry H. S. Croft. London: Kegan Paul, Trench, & Co., 1883.

Euripides. *Helen*, in *Fabulae*, vol. III. Edited by James Diggle. Oxford: Clarendon Press, 1994.

Trōades, in *Fabulae*, vol. II. Edited by James Diggle. Oxford: Clarendon Press, 1981.

Ferreti, Ferreto. *Le opere di Ferreto de Ferreti Vicentino*, vol. II. Edited by C. Cipolla. Rome: n.p., 1914.

Filmer, Sir Robert. *Patriarcha and other writings.* Edited by Johann P. Sommerville. Cambridge: Cambridge University Press, 1991.

Fortescue, Sir John. *De laudibus legume Anglorum.* London: n.p., 1616.

A learned commendation of the politique laws of Englande. London: n.p., 1567.

Prenobilis militis cognomento Forescu [sic], qui temporibus Henrici Sexti floruit, de politica administratione, et legibus civilibus florentissimi regni Anglia, commentarius. London: n.p., 1543.

Foster, E. R., ed. *Proceedings in parliament 1610.* 2 vols. New Haven: Yale University Press, 1966.

Foundations of Freedom; Or An Agreement Of The People: Proposed as a Rule for future Government in the Establishment of a firm and lasting Peace. London: n.p., 1648.

Franklin, Benjamin. *The Papers of Benjamin Franklin.* 39 vols. Edited by William B. Willcox et al. New Haven: Yale University Press, 1977–2008.

Franklin, Julian, ed. *Bodin on Sovereignty.* Cambridge: Cambridge University Press, 1992.

Furet, François and Ran Halevi, eds. *Orateurs de la Révolution française.* Paris: Gallimard, 1989.

Galbiati[us], J. *De fontibus M. Tulii Ciceronis librorum qui manserunt de R.P. et de legibus quaestiones.* Milan: U. Hoepli, 1916.

[Galloway, Joseph]. *A Candid Examination of the mutual Claims of Great-Britain, and the Colonies.* New York: n.p., 1775.

Gandhi, M. K. *The Collected Works of Mahatma Gandhi.* 98 vols. (electronic book). Delhi: Government of India, 1999.

Garat, Dominique Joseph. *Dominique-Joseph Garat, membre de l'Assemblée constituante, à M. Condorcet . . .* Paris: Desenne, 1791.

Gardiner, S.R., ed. *Parliamentary debates in 1610*, Camden Society first series 81. Camden Society, 1862.

Gierke, O. *Das deutsche Genossenschaftsrecht.* 4 vols. Berlin: Weidmannsche Buchhandlung, 1868.

Gourevitch, V., ed. *Rousseau: The Social Contract and Other Later Political Writings.* Cambridge: Cambridge University Press, 1997.

Grotius, Hugo. *Briefwisseling.* Vol. I, edited by P. C. Molhuysen et al. The Hague: Martinus Nijhoff, 1928.; vol. V, edited by B. L. Meulenbroek. The Hague: Martinus Nijhoff, 1966.

Le Droit de la Guerre, et de la Paix. 2 vols. Translated by Jean Barbeyrac. Amsterdam: Pierre de Coup, 1724.

De iure belli ac pacis. Edited by B. J. A. De Kanter-van Hettinga Tromp, Robert Feenstra and C. E. Persenaire. Aalen: Scientia Verlag, 1993.

De iure belli ac pacis libris tres. Paris: n.p., 1625.

The Rights of War and Peace. 3 vols. Edited by Richard Tuck. Indianapolis: Liberty Fund, 2005.

Hamilton, Alexander. *The Farmer Refuted: or, A more impartial and comprehensive View of the Dispute between Great-Britain and the Colonies.* New York: n.p., 1775.

A Full Vindication of the Measures of the Congress. New York; n.p., 1774.

Harrington, James. *The Political Writings of James Harrington.* Edited by J. G. A. Pocock. Cambridge: Cambridge University Press, 1977.

Hegel, G. W. F. *Elements of the Philosophy of Right.* Edited by Allen W. Wood. Cambridge: Cambridge University Press, 1991 [1821].

Herodotus. *Historiae.* 2 vols. Edited by Karl Hude. Oxford: Oxford University Press, 1927.

Historiae. Vol. I. Edited by Karl Hude. Oxford: Clarendon, 1963.

Herzen, Alexander. *Selected Philosophical Works.* Moscow: Foreign Languages Publishing, 1956 [1914].

Hicks, William. *Considerations upon the Rights of the Colonists to the Privileges of British Subjects.* New York: n.p., 1766.

Hildebrand, Bruno. *Die Nationalökonomie der Gegewart und Zukunft.* Frankfurt: J. Rütten, 1848.

His Majesties Answer To The Nineteen Propositions. Cambridge: n.p., 1642.

Historical Manuscripts Commission. *Calendar of the manuscripts of the most honourable the Marquess of Salisbury.* Part XXIII. London: n.p., 1973.

Hobbes, Thomas. *De Cive: The Latin Version.* Edited by Howard Warrender. Oxford: Clarendon Press, 1983.

The Elements of Law, Natural and Politic. Edited by Ferdinand Tönnies with new introduction by Maurice Goldsmith. London: Frank Cass, 1969.

The English Works of Thomas Hobbes of Malmesbury. 11 vols. Edited by William Molesworth. London: John Bohn, 1840.

Leviathan. London: Andrew Crooke, 1651.

Leviathan. Edited by Richard Tuck. Cambridge: Cambridge University Press, 1991.

Leviathan. Edited by Richard Tuck. Rev. edn. Cambridge: Cambridge University Press, 1996.

Leviathan. Edited by Noel Malcolm. Oxford: Clarendon Press, 2012.

On the Citizen. Edited by Richard Tuck and Michael Silverthorne. Cambridge: Cambridge University Press, 1998.

The Questions Concerning Liberty, Necessity, and Chance. London: n.p., 1656.

Howard, Martin, Jr. *A Letter from a Gentleman At Halifax.* Newport, RI: n.p., 1765.

Hume, David. *Essays Moral, Political, and Literary.* Edited by Eugene F. Miller. Indianapolis: Liberty Fund, 1987.

The History of England from the Invasion of Julius Caesar to the Revolution in 1688. 6 vols. Indianapolis: Liberty Fund, 1983 [1788].

The Letters of David Hume. 2 vols. Edited by J. Y. T. Greig. Oxford: Oxford University Press, 1932.

Hunton, Philip. *A Treatise of Monarchie.* London: n.p., 1643.

Husbands, Edward. *An exact collection of all remonstrances, declarations, petitions, messages, answers, and other remarkable passages.* London: n.p., 1643.

Hyneman, Charles S. and Donald S. Lutz, eds. *American Political Writing during the Founding Era, 1760–1805.* 2 vols. Indianapolis: Liberty Fund Inc., 1983.

Ingersoll, Jared. 'A Selection from the Correspondence and Miscellaneous Papers of Jared Ingersoll'. *9 Papers of the New Haven Colony Historical Society.* Edited by Franklin B. Dexter, 201–472. New Haven: n.p., 1918.

Inscriptiones Graecae. Vol. I, fasc. 1, 3rd edn. Edited by David Lewis. Berlin: Walter de Gruyter, 1981.

Iredell, James. *Life and Correspondence of James Iredell, One of the Associate Justices of the Supreme Court of the United States.* 2 vols. Edited by Griffith John McRee. New York; n.p., 1857–8.

Isocrates. 'Evagoras' and 'Epistle 6: To the Children of Jason'. *Isocrates,* vol. III. Translated by La Rue Van Hook. Cambridge, MA: Harvard University Press, 1945.

Iyengar, Uma and Lalitha Zachariah, eds. *Together They Fought: Gandhi–Nehru Correspondence, 1921–1948.* New Delhi: Oxford University Press, 2011.

Jacobsen, Arthur and Bernard Schlink, eds. *Weimar: A Jurisprudence of Crisis.* Berkeley and Los Angeles: University of California Press, 2000.

Jacoby, F. *Die Fragmente der griechischen Historiker.* 3 vols. Berlin: Wiedmann, 1923–58.

Jens, Johannes. *Ferculum Literarium.* Leiden: n.p., 1717.

Jenyns, Soame. *The Objections to the Taxation of Our American colonies... Examined.* London: n.p., 1765.

Journals of the Continental Congress: 1774–1789. 34 vols. Edited by Worthington Chauncey Ford et al. Washington, DC: n.p., 1904–37.

von Kahler, E. *Der Beruf der Wissenschaft.* Berlin: Georg Bondi, 1920.

Kant, Immanuel. 'On the Common Saying: "This May be True in Theory but it does not Apply in Practice"'. *Kant: Political Writings.* Edited by H. Reiss, 61–92. Cambridge: Cambridge University Press, 1991.

'Towards Perpetual Peace: A Philosophical Project'. *Practical Philosophy.* Edited by Mary J. Gregor. Cambridge: Cambridge University Press, 1999 [1996].

Kelsen, Hans 'Ansprache'. *Veröffentlichungen der Vereinigung der Deutschen Staatsrechtslehrer*. Vol. III, 53–5. Berlin: Walter de Gruyter, 1927.

'The Conception of the State and Social Psychology, with Special Reference to Freud's Group Theory'. *International Journal of Psychoanalysis* 5 (1924): 1–38.

The Essence and Value of Democracy. Edited by N. Urbinati and C. I. Accetti and translated by B. Graf. Lanham, MD: Rowman & Littlefield, 2013.

'Foundations of Democracy'. *Ethics* 66 (1955): 1–101.

Hauptprobleme der Staatsrechtslehre entwickelt aus der Lehre vom Rechtssatze. Tübingen: Mohr, 1911.

'On the Essence and Value of Democracy'. *Weimar*. Edited by Arthur Jacobsen and Bernard Schlink, 84–109. Berkeley and Los Angeles: University of California Press, 2002.

The Political Theory of Bolshevism: A Critical Analysis. Berkeley: University of California Press, 1948.

Staatsform und Weltanschauung. Tübingen: Mohr, 1933.

Die Staatslehre des Dante Alighieri. Vienna: Deuticke, 1905.

'Verteidigung der Demokratie'. *Verteidigung der Demokratie: Abhandlungen zur Demokratietheorie*, 229–37. Tübingen: Mohr Siebeck, 2006 [1932].

'Vom Wesen und Wert der Demokratie'. *Archiv für Sozialwissenschaft und Sozialpolitik* 47 (1920): 50–85.

Vom Wesen und Wert der Demokratie. 2nd edn. Tübingen: Mohr, 1929.

Wer soll der Hüter der Verfassung sein? Berlin: W. Rothschild, 1931.

Kenyon, J. P. *The Stuart Constitution: Documents and Commentary*. Cambridge: Cambridge University Press, 1986 [1966].

Krug, Wilhelm Traugott. *Geschichtlicher Darstellung des Liberalismus alter und neuer Zeit*. Leipzig: Brockhaus, 1823.

Laski, Harold. 'The Theory of Popular Sovereignty'. *Michigan Law Review* 17.3 (1919): 201–15.

Lassman, Peter and Ronald Speirs, eds. *Weber: Political Writings*. Cambridge: Cambridge University Press, 1994.

Lee, Arthur. *Observations on the Review of the Controversy Between Great-Britain and her Colonies*. London: n.p., 1769.

Lefèvre d'Étaples, Jacques. *In Politica Aristotelis Introductio*. Paris: n.p., 1506.

Lefèvre d'Étaples, Jacques and Josse Clichtove. *In Politica Aristotelis, introductio Iacobi Fabri Stapulensis: adiecto commentario declarata per Iudocum Clichtoveum Neoportuensem*. Paris: n.p., 1535.

Leibniz, Gottfried Wilhelm. *Causa Dei asserta per justitiamejus*. Amsterdam: n.p., 1710.

Lepsius, M. R. and W. Mommsen with B. Rudhard and M. Schön, eds. *Max Weber: Briefe, 1906–1908*. Tübingen: Mohr Siebeck, 1990.

Leszczynski, Stanislas. *La voix libre du citoyen, ou Observations sur le gouvernement de Pologne*. n.p., 1749.

Lex de imperio Vespasiani. Corpus Inscriptionum Latinarum, vol. VI: *Inscriptiones urbis Romae Latinae*. Edited by E. Bosmann and G. Henzen. Berlin: n.p., 1876.

Lieber, Francis. *On Civil Liberty and Self-Government*. Philadelphia: J. B. Lippincott, 1859.

Lilburne, John, *Innocency and Truth Justified*. London: n.p., 1646.

Lind, John. *Remarks on the principal acts of the thirteenth Parliament of Great Britain*. London: n.p., 1775.

Livingston, Philip. *The Other Side of the Question*. New York: n.p., 1774.

Livy. *Ab urbe condita*. 5 vols. Edited by W. Weissenborn, M. Müller and W. Heraeus. Leipzig: Teubner, 1887–1908.

History of Rome. 14 vols. Edited and translated by B. O. Foster (I–V), F. G. Moore (VI–VIII), E. T. Sage (IX–XII), A. C. Schlesinger (XII–XIV), J. Obsequens (XIV). Cambridge, MA: Harvard University Press, 1919–59.

Loening, Adolph. 'Vorrede'. In J. K. Bluntschli, *Lehre vom modernen Staat*, vol. I: *Allgemeine Staatslehre*, 6th edn., v–xiv. Stuttgart: J. G. Cotta, 1886.

Lukács, Georg. *Die Zerstörung der Vernunft*. Berlin: Aufbau, 1954.

Macaulay, Thomas B. *Macaulay: Prose and Poetry*. Cambridge, MA: Harvard University Press, 1970.

Maclay, William. *Journal of William Maclay: United States Senator from Pennsylvania, 1789–1791*. Edited by E. S. Maclay. New York: n.p., 1890.

Maine, Henry. *Popular Government*. Indianapolis: Liberty Fund, 1976 [1885].

de Maistre, Joseph. *Considerations on France*. Edited by Richard Lebrun. Cambridge: Cambridge University Press, 1994.

Majumdar, R. C. *Corporate Life in Ancient India*. Calcutta: Firma K. L. Mukhopadhya, 1918.

Mann, T. *Reflections of a Nonpolitical Man*. Translated by W. D. Morris. New York: Frederick Ungar, 1983 [1918].

Markham, William. *A sermon preached before the Incorporated Society for the Propagation of the gospel in Foreign Parts*. London: n.p., 1777.

Marsh, John. *An Argument Or, Debate In Law*. London: n.p., 1642.

Marsilius of Padua. *The Defender of the Peace*. Translated by Annabel Brett. Cambridge: Cambridge University Press, 2005.

Defensor Pacis. Edited by R. Scholz. Hanover: n.p., 1933.

Marx, Karl. 'The 18th Brumaire of Louis Bonaparte' [1851]. *Marx: Surveys from Exile*. Edited by D. Fernbach, 143–249. Harmondsworth: Penguin, 1973.

'On the Jewish Question'. *The Marx–Engels Reader*, 26–52. 2nd edn. New York: W. W. Norton & Co., 1978.

Mazzini, Giuseppe. 'Against the Foreign Imposition of Domestic Institutions' [1851]. *Mazzini: A Cosmopolitanism of Nations*. Edited by S. Recchia and N. Urbinati, 136–40. Princeton: Princeton University Press, 2010.

Meinecke, Friedrich. *Die Idee der Staatsräson in der neuere Geschichte*. Berlin: Oldenbourg, 1924.

Menzel, Adolph. 'Machiavelli'. *Adolph Menzel's Illustrationen zu den Werken Friedrichs der Grossen, Jubilaeums Ausgabe*. 2 vols. Berlin: R. Wagner, 1886, vol. I, Image 66, p. 38.

Mill, John Stuart. *Considerations on Representative Government* (1861). *Collected Works of John Stuart Mill*, 33 vols. Vol. XIX, edited by J. Robson. Toronto: University of Toronto Press, 1977.

Milton, John. *Complete Prose Works of John Milton*, vol. VII, rev. edn. Edited by Robert W. Ayers. New Haven: Yale University Press, 1980.

Pro populo anglicano defensio. London: n.p., 1651.

Mollat, Georg. *Lesebuchzur Geschichte der Deutsche Staatswissenschaft von Kant bis Bluntschli.* Osterwieck: Zickfeldt, 1891.

de Montesquieu, Charles de Secondat, Baron. *The Spirit of the Laws.* Edited by Anne M. Cohler, Basia C. Miller and Harold S. Stone. Cambridge: Cambridge University Press, 1989.

Monumenta Germaniae Historica, Constitutiones, vol. VI.1. Edited by J. Schwalm. Hanover: n.p., 1927.

Mookerji, Radhakumud. *Local Government in Ancient India.* Oxford: Clarendon Press, 1920.

Moore, Maurice. *The Justice and policy of taxing the American Colonies, in Great Britain, Considered.* Wilmington, NC: n.p., 1765.

Mounier, Jean. *Considérations sur les gouvernemens.* Paris: n.p., 1789.

Mukerjee, Radhakamal. *Democracies of the East: A Study in Comparative Politics.* London: P. S. King, 1923.

The Foundations of Indian Economics. London: Longmans, 1916.

Mussato, Albertino. *De gestis Henrici VII. Caesaris.* In *Rerum Italicarum Scriptores*, vol. X. Milan: n.p., 1727.

'Ludovicus Bavarus'. *Fontes Rerum Germanicarum*, vol. I. Edited by J. F. Boehmer. Stuttgart: n.p., 1843.

Naoroji, Dadabhai. *Poverty and Un-British Rule in India.* Delhi: Government of India Press, 1962 [1901].

Nedham, Marchamont. *The excellency of a free state.* London: n.p., 1656.

New Plea For The Parliament. London: Henry Overtone, 1643.

Nietzsche, Friedrich. *Writings from the Late Notebooks.* Edited by R. Bittner and translated by K. Sturge. Cambridge: Cambridge University Press, 2003.

Oakeshott, M. *Observations on Mr. Burke's Speech on Fox's India Bill.* London: n.p., 1783.

The Politics of Faith and the Politics of Scepticism. Edited by T. Fuller. New Haven: Yale University Press, 1996.

Oppian. *De Venatione.* Translated by Jean Bodin. Paris: n.p., 1555.

Overton, Richard. *An Appeale From the degenerate Representative Body the Commons of England assembled at Westminster.* London: n.p., 1647.

An Arrow Against All Tyrants And Tyranny. London: n.p., 1647.

A Defiance Against All Arbitrary Usurpations Or Encroachments. London: n.p., 1646.

A Remonstrance Of Many Thousand Citizens, and other Free-born People of England To their owne House of Commons. London: n.p., 1646.

Parker, Henry. *An answer to the poisonous sedicious paper of Mr. David Jenkins.* London: n.p., 1647.

The Contra-Replicant, His Complaint To His Majestie. London: n.p., 1643.

Ius Populi. London: n.p., 1644.

Observations upon some of His Majesties late Answers and Expresses. London: n.p., 1642.

Some Few Observations upon His Majesties Late Answer to the Declaration or Remonstrance of the Lords and Commons of the 19th of May, 1642. London: n.p., 1642.

Parliamentary History of England: From the Earliest Period to the Year 1803. Edited by Thomas C. Hansard. 36 vols. London: n.p., 1806–20.

Parliamentary History of England from the Norman Conquest in 1066 to the Year 1803. 36 vols. Edited by William Cobbett. London: n.p., 1806–20.

'Parteien'. *Supplement zur ersten Auflage der Staats-lexicons*. 4 vols. Vol. IV, edited by Carl von Rotteck and Carl Welcker, 209–32. Altona: Hammerlich, 1848.

Pausanias. *Description of Greece*. Vol. I. Translated by W. H. S. Jones. Cambridge, MA: Harvard University Press, 1918.

Pfizer, Paul. 'Liberalismus'. *Staats-lexicon, oder Encyclopedie der Staatswissenschaft*, 14 vols. Vol. IX, edited by Carl Rotteck and Carl Theodor von Welcker, 713–30. Altona: Hammerlich, 1839–48.

Plato. *Complete Works*. Edited by John M. Cooper. Indianapolis: Hackett, 1997.

Gorgias. Edited by E. R. Dodds. Oxford: Oxford University Press, 1959.

Laws. *Platonis Opera*. Vol. V, edited by John Burnet. Oxford: Clarendon Press, 1907.

Laws. 2 vols. Edited and translated by R. G. Bury. Cambridge, MA: Harvard University Press, 1952 [1926].

Republic. Edited by S. R. Slings. Oxford: Clarendon Press, 2003.

Symposium. *Platonis Opera*. Vol. II, edited by John Burnet. Oxford: Clarendon Press, 1901.

Theages. *Platonis Opera*. Vol. III, edited by John Burnet. Oxford: Clarendon Press, 1903.

Pliny the Elder. *Naturalis historia liber XXXV*. Edited by Roderich König. Düsseldorf: Artemis & Winkler, 2007.

Political Catechism. London: n.p., 1643.

Polybius. *Histoires*. Edited and translated by Éric Foulon, with commentary by Michel Molin. Paris: Les Belles Lettres, 2004.

Pownall, Thomas. *The Administration of the Colonies*. 4th edn. London: n.p., 1768.

Prasad, Beni. *Theory of Government of Ancient India*. Allahabad: The Indian Press, 1927.

Proceedings and Debates of the British Parliaments Respecting North America, 1754–1783, 6 vols. Edited by R. C. Simmons and P. D. G. Thomas. Milwood, NY: Kraus International Publications, 1982.

Pufendorf, Samuel. *De jure naturae et gentium*. Lund: n.p., 1672.

De officio hominis juxta legem naturalem. 2 vols. Lund: n.p., 1673.

The Law of Nature and Nations. 5th edn. Edited by Jean Barbeyerac and translated by Basil Kennet. London: n.p., 1749.

The Political Writings of Samuel Pufendorf. Edited by C. L. Carr and translated by M. J. Seidler. New York: Oxford University Press, 1994.

Pulteney, William. *The Effects Expected from the East India Bill upon the Constitution of Great Britain*. London: n.p., 1783.

Quintilian. *The Orator's Education, Volume V: Books 10–12*. Translated by Donald A. Russell. Cambridge, MA: Harvard University Press, 2002.

von Ranke, L. *Geschichte und Politik: ausgewählte Aufsätze und Meisterschriften*. Edited by H. Hoffman. Stuttgart: A. Kröner, 1942 [1836].

Über die Epochen neueren Geschichte. Leipzig: Duncker & Humblot, 1906 [1854].

Rawls, John. 'Justice as Reciprocity' [1959]. *Collected Papers*. Edited by S. Freeman, 190–224. Cambridge, MA: Harvard University Press, 1999 [1971].

Political Liberalism, expanded edn. New York: Columbia University Press, 1996.

A Theory of Justice. New York: Oxford University Press, 1971.

Records of the Federal Convention of 1787. 3 vols. Edited by Max Farrand. New Haven: n.p., 1911.

Regall Tyrannie discovered. London: n.p., 1647.

Réimpression de La Moniteur Ancien. Vol. I. Paris: Henri Plon, 1858.

Result of the convention of delegates holden at Ipswich in the county of Essex, who were deputed to take into consideration the constitution and form of government, proposed by the Convention of the state of Massachusetts-Bay. Newbury-port, MA: n.p., 1778.

Robespierre, Maximilien. *Oeuvres complètes*. 10 vols. Edited by Marc Bouloiseau, Georges Lefebvre and Albert Soboul. Paris: George Thomas, 1910–67.

Rochau, August. *Grundsätze der Realpolitik*. Stuttgart: Karl Öpel, 1853.

Roederer, Pierre-Louis. *Mémoires D'économie Publique, de Morale, et de Politique*. 2 vols. Paris: L'imprimerie du journal de Paris, 1799.

Œuvres. 8 vols. Paris: Firmin Didot, 1853.

The Spirit of the Revolution of 1789 and Other Writings on the Revolutionary Epoch. Edited by Murray Forsyth. Aldershot: Scolar Press, 1989.

von Rotteck, Carl. 'Über den Streitnatürlicher Rechtsprinzipien oder idealer Politik mit historisch begründeten Verhältnissen' [1818] *Sammlung kleinerer Schriften*. 2 vols. Vol. II, 42–70. Stuttgart: Franck, 1829.

von Rotteck, Carl and Carl Theodor von Welcker, eds. *Staats-lexicon, oder Encyclopedie der Staatswissenschaft*. 14 vols. Altona: Hammerlich, 1839–48.

Rousseau, Jean-Jacques. 'Considerations on the Government of Poland' [1772]. *The Social Contract and Other Later Political Writings*. Edited by V. Gourevitch, 177–260. Cambridge: Cambridge University Press, 1997.

Correspondance complète de Jean Jacques Rousseau: édition critique établie et annotée par R. A. Leigh. 52 vols. Edited by R. A. Leigh. Geneva and Oxford: Institut Voltaire and Voltaire Foundation, 1965–88.

Letter to Beaumont, Letters Written from the Mountain, and Related Writings. Edited by Christopher Kelly and Eve Grace and translated by Christopher Kelly and Judith Bush. Hanover, NH: University Press of New England, 2001.

'Letter to Mirabeau', 26 July 1767. *The Social Contract and Other Later Political Writings*. Edited by V. Gourevitch, 268–71. Cambridge: Cambridge University Press, 1997.

Oeuvres complètes. Edited by Michel Launay. Paris: Éditions du Seuil, 1971.

Political Writings. Edited and translated by F. M. Watkins. London: Thomas Nelson & Sons, 1953.

The Social Contract (1762). The Social Contract and Other Later Political Writings. Edited by V. Gourevitch, 39–152. Cambridge: Cambridge University Press, 1997.

Rutherford, Samuel. *Lex, Rex: The Law of a Prince.* London: n.p., 1644.

Salle, Jean-Baptiste. *Examen critique de la constitution de 1793.* Paris An IIIe.

Sallust. *Catilina, Iugurtha, Historiarum Fragmenta Selecta.* Edited by L. D. Reynolds. Oxford: Oxford University Press, 1991.

Salmasius. *Defensio regia, pro Carolo I.* N.p: n.p., 1649.

Schmitt, Carl. 'The Age of Neutralizations and Depoliticizations' [1929]. Translated by M. Konzett and John P. McCormick. *Telos* 96 (1993): 130–42.

The Concept of the Political. Edited and translated by George Schwab. Chicago: University of Chicago Press, 1996 [1932].

Constitutional Theory. Edited and translated by J. Seitzer. Durham, NC: Duke University Press, 2008 [1928].

'The Constitution of Freedom' [1935]. *Weimar: A Jurisprudence of Crisis.* Edited by Arthur Jacobsen and Bernard Schlink, 323–5. Berkeley and Los Angeles: University of California Press, 2000.

The Crisis of Parliamentary Democracy [1923]. Edited and translated by E. Kennedy. Cambridge, MA: MIT Press, 1988.

Dictatorship: From the Origin of the Modern Concept of Sovereignty to Proletarian Class Struggle. Edited and translated by Michael Hoelzl and Graham Ward. Cambridge: Polity Press, 2014 [1921].

Der Hüter der Verfassung. Tübingen: Mohr, 1931.

Legality and Legitimacy. Edited and translated by J. Seitzer. Durham, NC: Duke University Press, 2004 [1932].

'The Liberal Rule of Law' [1928]. *Weimar: A Jurisprudence of Crisis.* Edited by Arthur Jacobsen and Bernard Schlink, 294–300. Berkeley and Los Angeles: University of California Press, 2000.

Political Theology: Four Chapters on the Concept of Sovereignty [1922]. Edited and translated by George Schwab. Cambridge, MA: MIT Press, 1985.

Roman Catholicism and Political Form. Edited and translated by G. L. Ulmen. Westport, CT: Praeger, 1996 [1923].

'State Ethics and the Pluralist State' [1930]. *Weimar: A Jurisprudence of Crisis.* Edited by Arthur Jacobsen and Bernard Schlink, 300–12. Berkeley and Los Angeles: University of California Press, 2000.

State, Movement, People: The Triadic Structure of the Political Unity [1933], with *The Question of Legality* (1950). Edited by S. Draghici. Corvallis, OR: Plutarch Press, 2001.

On the Three Types of Juristic Thought. Translated by J. Bendersky. Westport, CT: Praeger, 2004 [1934].

'Zu Friedrich Meineckes Idee der Staatsräson'. *Archiv für Sozialwissenschaft und Sozialpolitik* 56 (1926): 226–34.

Scholia Bobiensia. Edited by T. Stangl. Leipzig: n.p., 1912.

Schumpeter, J. *Capitalism, Socialism and Democracy.* London and New York: Routledge, 1994 [1942].

Seeley, J. R. *The Expansion of England*. London: Macmillan, 1883.

Sieyès, Emmanuel Joseph. 'Bases de l'Ordre Social' [1794/5]. In P. Pasquino, *Sieyès et l'invention de la constitution française*, 181–91. Paris: Odile Jacob, 1998.

'Contre la Ré-totale' [1792]. In P. Pasquino, *Sieyès et l'invention de la constitution française*, 175–6. Paris: Odile Jacob, 1998.

Écrits politiques. Edited by Roberto Zapperi. Paris: Editions des archives contemporaines, 1985.

Essai sur les privilèges, Observations sur le rapport du Comité de constitution sur la nouvelle organisation de la France et Préliminaire de la constitution. Écrits politiques, edited by Roberto Zapperi. Brussels: Éditions des Archives Contemporaines, 1994.

'Fragments Politiques'. *Des Manuscrits de Sieyès*. Edited by Christian Fauré. Paris: Champion, 1999.

'Limites de la souveraineté, An III' [1794/5]. In P. Pasquino, *Sieyès et l'invention de la constitution française*, 177–80. Paris: Odile Jacob, 1998.

Oeuvres. 3 vols. Edited by Marcel Dorigny. Paris: EDHIS 1989.

Political Writings: Including the Debate between Sieyès and Tom Paine in 1791. Edited by Michael Sonenscher. Indianapolis: Hackett Publishing Company, 2003.

Politische Schriften. Edited by Eberhard Schmitt and Rolf Reichardt. Munich and Vienna: R. Oldenbourg Verlag, 1981.

Préliminaire de la Constitution: Reconnaissance et exposition raisonée des Droits de l'Homme et du Citoyen. N.p: n.p., 1789.

Qu'est-ceque le Tiers État? Edited by R. Zapperi. Geneva: n.p., 1971 [1789].

Sinha, HarNarain. *Sovereignty in Ancient Indian Polity: A Study in the Evolution of Early Indian State*. London: Luzac, 1938.

Smith, Adam. *Lectures on Jurisprudence*. Edited by R. L. Meek, D. D. Raphael and P. G. Stein. Indianapolis: Liberty Fund, 1982.

Smith, Sir Thomas. *De republica Anglorum*. Edited by Mary Dewar. Cambridge: Cambridge University Press, 1982.

Sophocles. *Antigone*. Edited by Mark Griffith. Cambridge: Cambridge University Press, 1999.

Oedipus Rex. Edited by R. D. Dawe. Cambridge: Cambridge University Press, 1982.

Spelman, Sir John. *A View of a printed book intituled observations upon his Majesties late answers and expresses*. London: n.p., 1643.

de Staël, Germaine. *Considerations on the Principal Events of the French Revolution*. Edited by Aurelian Craiutu. Indianapolis: Liberty Fund, 2008.

Statutes at Large from the Twenty-Sixth Year of the Reign of King George the Second to the Sixth Year of the Reign of King George the Third. London: n.p., 1786.

Stubbe, Henry. *An Essay In Defence of the Good Old Cause*. London: n.p., 1659.

Thorpe, Francis Newton, ed. *The Federal and State Constitutions*. 7 vols. Washington, DC: Government Printing House, 1909.

Thucydides. *Eight Bookes of the Peloponnesian Warre*. Edited and translated by Thomas Hobbes. London: n.p., 1629.

Historiae. Vols. I–III. Edited by Giovanni Battista Alberti. Rome: Istituto Poligrafico e Zecca dello Stato, 1972–2000.

The War of the Peloponnesians and the Athenians. Edited and translated by Jeremy Mynott. Cambridge: Cambridge University Press, 2013.

de Tocqueville, Alexis. *Democracy in America.* Edited by J. P. Mayer. New York: Anchor, 1969 [1835].

Democracy in America. Translated by Harvey C. Mansfield and Delba Winthrop. Chicago: University of Chicago Press, 2002.

The Old Regime and the French Revolution. Translated by Stuart Gilbert. New York: Anchor, 1955.

Tucker, Josiah. *A Letter from a Merchant in London to His Nephew in North America.* London: n.p., 1766.

A Letter to Edmund Burke, Esq., in Answer to His Printed Speech. London: n.p., 1775.

A treatise concerning civil government, in three parts. Part I. The notions of Mr. Locke and his followers, concerning the origin, extent, and end of civil government, examined and confuted. . . . London: n.p., 1781.

Tucker, St George. *Blackstone's Commentaries: with notes of reference to the Constitution and laws of the federal government of the United States and of the commonwealth of Virginia.* Philadelphia: n.p., 1803.

Weber, Max. *From Max Weber: Essays in Sociology.* Edited by H. H. Gerth and C. Wright Mills. New York: Oxford University Press, 1946.

Weber, Max. 'Between Two Laws' [1916]. *Weber: Political Writings.* Edited by Peter Lassman and Ronald Speirs, 75–9. Cambridge: Cambridge University Press, 1994.

'Bureaucracy'. *From Max Weber: Essays in Sociology.* Edited by H. H. Gerth and C. Wright Mills, 196–244. New York: Oxford University Press, 1958.

'Capitalism and Rural Society'. *From Max Weber: Essays in Sociology.* Edited by H. H. Gerth and C. Wright Mills, 363–85. New York: Oxford University Press, 1958.

'Class, Status, Party'. *From Max Weber: Essays in Sociology.* Edited by H. H. Gerth and C. Wright Mills, 180–95. New York: Oxford University Press, 1958.

Economy and Society: An Outline of Interpretative Sociology. Edited by G. Roth and C. Wittich. Berkeley: University of California Press, 1978.

'National Character and the Junkers'. *From Max Weber: Essays in Sociology.* Edited by H. H. Gerth and C. Wright Mills, 386–95. New York: Oxford University Press, 1958.

'The Nation State and Economic Policy (Inaugural Lecture)' [1895]. *Weber: Political Writings.* Edited by Peter Lassman and Ronald Speirs, 1–28. Cambridge: Cambridge University Press, 1994.

'On the Situation of Constitutional Democracy in Russia' [1906]. *Weber: Political Writings.* Edited by Peter Lassman and Ronald Speirs, 29–74. Cambridge: Cambridge University Press, 1994.

'Parliament and Government in Germany under a New Political Order' [1917]. *Weber: Political Writings.* Edited by Peter Lassman and Ronald Speirs, 130–271. Cambridge: Cambridge University Press, 1994.

'Politik als Beruf' [1919]. *Gesammelte Politische Schriften*. 5th edn. Edited by J. Winckelmann, 505–60. Tübingen: J. C. B. Mohr (Paul Siebeck), 1988 [1921].

'The President of the Reich' [1919]. *Weber: Political Writings*. Edited by Peter Lassman and Ronald Speirs, 304–8. Cambridge: Cambridge University Press, 1994.

'The Profession and Vocation of Politics' [1919]. *Weber: Political Writings*. Edited by Peter Lassman and Ronald Speirs, 309–69. Cambridge: Cambridge University Press, 1994.

'Religious Rejections of the World and their Directions'. *From Max Weber: Essays in Sociology*. Edited by H. H. Gerth and C. Wright Mills, 267–359. New York: Oxford University Press, 1958.

'Russia's Transition to Pseudo-Democracy' [1917], *The Russian Revolutions*. Edited by G. C. Wells and P. Baehr, 241–60. Cambridge: Polity Press, 1997.

'Science as a Vocation' [1918]. *From Max Weber: Essays in Sociology*. Edited by H. H. Gerth and C. Wright Mills, 129–256. New York: Oxford University Press, 1958.

'Socialism' [1918]. *Weber: Political Writings*. Edited by Peter Lassman and Ronald Speirs, 272–303. Cambridge: Cambridge University Press, 1994.

'Suffrage and Democracy in Germany' [1917]. *Weber: Political Writings*. Edited by Peter Lassman and Ronald Speirs, 80–129. Cambridge: Cambridge University Press, 1994.

von Welcker, Carl Theodor. 'Bund'. *Staats-lexicon, oder Encyclopedie der Staatswissenschaft*. 14 vols. Edited by Carl von Rotteck and Carl Theodor von Welcker. Vol. III, 76–116. Altona: Hammerlich, 1839–48.

'Juste-milieu'. *Staats-lexicon, oder Encyclopedie der Staatswissenschaft*. 14 vols. Edited by Carl Rotteck and Carl Theodor von Welcker. Vol. IX, 3–29. Altona: Hammerlich, 1839–48.

'Moral'. *Staats-lexicon, oder Encyclopedie der Staatswissenschaft*. 14 vols. Edited by Carl Rotteck and Carl Theodor von Welcker. Vol. X, 692–755. Altona: Hammerlich, 1839–48.

Whately, Thomas. *The Regulations Lately Made Concerning the Colonies and the Taxes Imposed Upon Them, Considered*. London: n.p., 1765.

Wigard F., ed. *Stenographischer Bericht über die Verhandlungen der deutschen constituierenden Nationalversammlung*. 9 vols. Leipzig: Teubner, 1848–9.

Williams, David. *Lessons to a Young Prince on the Present Disposition in Europe to a General Revolution*. London: n.p., 1790.

Wilson, James. *Considerations on the Nature and Extent of the Legislative Authority of the British Parliament*. Philadelphia: n.p., 1774.

The Works of the Honourable James Wilson, L.L.D. 3 vols. Edited by Bird Wilson. Philadelphia: n.p., 1804.

The Works of James Wilson. 2 vols. Edited by Robert McCloskey. Cambridge, MA: The Belknap Press of Harvard University Press, 1967.

Woodhouse, A. S. P. ed. *Puritanism and Liberty Being the Army Debates (1647–9) from the Clarke Manuscripts with Supplementary Documents*. 2nd edn. London: J. M. Dent, 1974.

[Xenophon]. *On Government*. Edited by Vivienne J. Gray. Cambridge: Cambridge University Press, 2007.

Historia Graeca [*Hellenica*]. Edited by E. C. Marchant. Oxford: Clarendon Press, 1922.

Mémorables, Livres II–III. Edited by Michele Bandini and Louis-André Dorion. Paris: Les Belles Lettres, 2011.

The '*Old Oligarch*': The '*Constitution of the Athenians*' *Attributed to Xenophon*. Edited by J. L. Marr and P. J. Rhodes. Oxford: Aris & Phillips, 2008.

Zonaras. *Ioannis Zonarae Epitome Historiarum*. 6 vols. Edited by L. Dindorf. Leipzig: Teubner, 1868–74.

Zubly, John Joachim. *An Humble Inquiry into the Nature of the Dependency of the American Colonies*. [Charleston]: n.p., 1769.

SECONDARY SOURCES

Allen, Danielle S. *The World of Prometheus: The Politics of Punishing in Democratic Athens*. Princeton: Princeton University Press, 2000.

Ankersmit, F. R. *Political Representation*. Stanford: Stanford University Press, 2002.

Annas, Julia. 'Plato's *Laws* and Cicero's *De legibus*'. *Aristotle, Plato and Pythagoreanism in the First Century BC*. Edited by Malcolm Schofield, 206–24. Cambridge: Cambridge University Press, 2013.

Arena, Valentina. *Libertas and the Practice of Politics in the Late Roman Republic*. Cambridge: Cambridge University Press, 2012.

Arendt, Hannah. *On Revolution*. New York: Penguin Books, 1963.

Astin, Alan E. 'Censorship in the Late Republic'. *Historia* 34 (1984): 175–99.

'Cicero and the Censorship'. *Classical Philology* 30 (1985): 233–9.

Atkins, E. M. 'Cicero'. *The Cambridge History of Greek and Roman Political Thought*. Edited by Christopher Rowe and Malcolm Schofield, 489–98. Cambridge: Cambridge University Press, 2000.

Bailyn, Bernard. *The Ideological Origins of the American Revolution*. Rev. edn. Cambridge, MA: Harvard University Press, 1992 [1967].

Baker, Keith Michael. *Inventing the French Revolution: Essays on French Political Culture in the Eighteenth Century*. Cambridge: Cambridge University Press, 1990.

Balibar, Étienne. *We, the People of Europe? Reflections on Transnational Citizenship*. Princeton: Princeton University Press, 2004.

Balot, Ryan K., ed. *A Companion to Greek and Roman Political Thought*. Oxford: Blackwell, 2009.

Baraz, Yelena. 'From Vice to Virtue: The Denigration and Rehabilitation of Superbia in Ancient Rome'. *Kakos: Badness and Anti-Value in Classical Antiquity*. Edited by Ineke Sluiter and Ralph M. Rosen, 365–97. Leiden and Boston: Brill, 2008.

Bates, David. 'Political Theology and the Nazi State: Carl Schmitt's Concept of the Institution'. *Modern Intellectual History* 3 (2006): 415–42.

Baume, Sandrine. *Hans Kelsen and the Case for Democracy*. Translated by John Zvesper. Colchester: ECPR Press, 2012.

'On Political Theology: A Controversy between Hans Kelsen and Carl Schmitt'. *History of European Ideas* 35 (2009): 369–81.

Baumstark, Moritz. 'The End of Empire and the Death of Religion: David Hume's Later Political Thought.' *Philosophy and Religion in Enlightenment Britain: New Case Studies.* Edited by Ruth Savage, 231–257. Oxford: Oxford University Press, 2012.

Bayly, C. A. *Recovering Liberties: Indian Thought in the Age of Liberalism and Empire.* Cambridge: Cambridge University Press, 2011.

Becker, Kurt E. 'Der Römische Cäsar mit Christi Seele'. *Max Webers Charisma-Konzept: Eine systematisch kritische Analyse unter Einbeiziehung biographischer Fakten.* Frankfurt-am-Main: Peter Lang, 1988.

Beetham, David. *Max Weber and the Theory of Modern Politics.* London: Allen & Unwin, 1974.

Bell, David. *The Cult of the Nation in France.* Cambridge, MA: Harvard University Press, 2003.

Bell, Duncan. *The Idea of Greater Britain: Empire and the Future of World Order, 1860–1900.* Princeton: Princeton University Press, 2007.

Bellamy, Richard. *Liberalism and Modern Society: A Historical Argument.* University Park: Pennsylvania State University Press, 1992.

Bellomo, Manlio. *Questiones in iure civili disputatae: Didattica e prassi colta nel sistema del diritto comune fra Duecento e Trecento.* Rome: Istituto storico italiano per il Medio Evo, 2008.

Benhabib, Seyla. 'Deliberative Rationality and Models of Democratic Legitimacy'. *Constellations* 1 (1994): 26–53.

Berger, Ben. *Attention Deficit Democracy: The Paradox of Civic Engagement.* Princeton: Princeton University Press, 2011.

Berger, Mark T. 'After the Third World? History, Destiny and the Fate of Third Worldism'. *Third World Quarterly* 25.1 (2004): 9–39.

Bilakovics, Steven. *Democracy without Politics.* Cambridge, MA: Harvard University Press, 2012.

Billanovich, Giuseppe. 'Il preumanesimo padovano'. *Storia della cultura veneta*, vol. II: *Il Trecento*, 19–110. Vicenza: Neri Pozza Editore, 1976.

Bowen, Huw V. 'A Question of Sovereignty? The Bengal Land Revenue Issue, 1765–1767'. *Journal of Imperial and Commonwealth History* 16.2 (January 1988): 155–76.

Bowsky, William M. *Henry VII in Italy: The Conflict of Empire and City-State, 1310–1313.* Lincoln: University of Nebraska Press, 1960.

Boyancé, P. 'Le Platonisme à Rome: Platon et Cicéron'. *Congrès de Tours et de Poitiers*, 195–221. Paris: Les Belles Lettres, 1954.

Breen, T. H. 'Ideology and Nationalism on the Eve of the American Revolution: Revisions Once More in Need of Revising'. *Journal of American History* 84 (1997): 13–39.

Brett, Annabel. '"The Matter, Forme, and Power of a Common-Wealth": Thomas Hobbes and Late Renaissance Commentary on Aristotle's *Politics*'. *Hobbes Studies* 23 (2010): 72–102.

Brunt, P. A. 'Lex de Imperio Vespasiani'. *Journal of Roman Studies* 67 (1977): 95–116.

'Plato's *Academy* and *Politics*'. *Studies in Greek History and Thought*, 282–342. Oxford: Clarendon Press, 1993.

Bull, Hedley, and Adam Watson, eds. *The Expansion of International Society*. Oxford: Clarendon Press, 1984.

Burgess, Glenn. *British Political Thought, 1500–1660: The Politics of the Post-Reformation*. Basingstoke: Palgrave Macmillan, 2009.

The Politics of the Ancient Constitution: An Introduction to English Political Thought, 1603–1642. Basingstoke: Macmillan, 1992.

Burrow, John. *Whigs and Liberals*. Oxford: Clarendon Press, 1988.

Calasso, Francesco. *I glossatori e la teoria della sovranità*. Milan: Giuffrè, 1951.

Caldwell, Peter C. *Popular Sovereignty and the Crisis of German Constitutional Law: The Theory and Practice of Weimar Constitutionalism*. Durham, NC: Duke University Press, 1997.

Calvelli, Lorenzo. 'Pociora legis precepta: Considerazioni sull'epigrafia giuridica esposta in Laterano fra Medioevo e Rinascimento'. *Leges publicae: La legge nell'esperienza giuridica romana*. Edited by J.-L. Ferrary, 593–625. Pavia: IUSS Press, 2012.

Cammack, Daniela. 'Rethinking Athenian Democracy'. Ph.D. thesis, Harvard University, 2013.

Canning, Joseph. *The Political Thought of Baldus de Ubaldis*. Cambridge: Cambridge University Press, 1987.

Carawan, Edwin M. '*Eisangelia* and *Euthyna*: The Trials of Miltiades, Themistocles, and Cimon'. *Greek, Roman, and Byzantine Studies* 28 (1987): 167–208.

Carrington, Dorothy. 'The Corsican Constitution of Pasquale Paoli (1755–1769)'. *English Historical Review* 88 (1973): 481–503.

Cartledge, Paul. *The Greeks: A Portrait of Self and Others*. 2nd edn. Oxford: Oxford University Press, 2002.

Caserta, Marco. *Democrazia e costituzione in Hans Kelsen e Carl Schmitt*. Rome: Aracne, 2005.

Chatterjee, Partha. *Nationalist and the Colonial World: A Derivative Discourse?* London: Zed Books, 1986.

Childers, Christopher. 'Interpreting Popular Sovereignty: A Historiographical Essay'. *Civil War History* 57.1 (2011): 48–70.

Claeys, Gregory. 'Non-Marxian Socialism'. *The Cambridge History of Nineteenth-Century Political Thought*. Edited by Gareth Stedman-Jones and Gregory Claeys, 521–55. Cambridge: Cambridge University Press, 2011.

Clark, Chris. 'After 1848: The European Revolution in Government'. *Transactions of the Royal Historical Society* 22 (2012): 171–97.

'The Wars of Liberation in Prussian Memory'. *Journal of Modern History* 68.3 (1996): 550–76.

Clark, J. C. D. *English Society, 1688–1832: Ideology, Social Structure and Political Practice during the Ancien Regime*. Cambridge: Cambridge University Press, 2000 [1985].

The Language of Liberty, 1660–1832: Political Discourse and Social Dynamics in the Anglo-American World. Cambridge: Cambridge University Press, 1994.

Clemente, G. 'Cicerone, Clodio e la censura: la politica e l'ideale'. *Munuscula: Scritti in ricordo di Luigi Almirante*. Edited by Elio Dovere, 51–73. Naples: Edizioni Scientifiche Italiane, 2010.

Colle, Francesco Maria. *Storia scientifico-letteraria dello studio di Padova I*. Padua: Minerva, 1824.

Connor, W. R. 'Tyrannis [*sic*] Polis'. *Ancient and Modern: Essays in Honor of Gerald F. Else*. Edited by J. H. D'Arms and John William Eadie, 95–109. Ann Arbor, MI: Center for Coordination of Ancient and Modern Studies, 1977.

Cooper, Frederick. *Colonialism in Question: Theory, Knowledge, History*. Berkeley: University of California Press, 2005.

Copland, Ian. *The Princes of India in the Endgame of Empire 1917–1947*. Cambridge: Cambridge University Press, 1997.

Cornell, T. J. 'Cicero on the Origins of Rome'. *Cicero's Republic*. Edited by John A. North and J. G. F. Powell, 41–56. London: University of London Institute of Classical Studies, 2001.

Crahay, Roland, Marie-Thérèse Isaac and Marie-Thérèse Lenger. *Bibliographie critique des éditions anciennes de Jean Bodin*. Gembloux: Académie Royale de Belgique, 1992.

Craiutu, Aurelian. *Liberalism under Siege: The Political Thought of the French Doctrinaires*. Lanham, MD: Lexington, 2003.

Crifó, G. 'Attivitá normative del senato in etá repubblicana'. *Bullettino dell'Istituto di Diritto Romano* 71 (1968): 31–115.

Cromartie, Alan. *The Constitutionalist Revolution: An Essay on the History of England, 1450–1642*. Cambridge: Cambridge University Press, 2006.

Crook, Malcolm. *Elections in the French Revolution*. Cambridge: Cambridge University Press, 2002 [1996].

'The Plebiscite on the Empire'. *Napoleon and his Empire: Europe, 1804–1814*. Edited by Philip Dwyer and Alan Forrest, 16–29. New York: Palgrave Macmillan, 2007.

'The Uses of Democracy: Elections and Plebiscites in Napoleonic France'. *The French Experience from Republic to Monarchy, 1792–1824*. Edited by Maire F. Gross and David Williams, 58–71. New York: Palgrave Macmillan, 2000.

Dahl, Robert A. *A Preface to Democratic Theory*. Chicago: University of Chicago Press, 1956.

Who Governs? New Haven: Yale University Press, 1961.

Darmstaedter, Friedrich. *Bismarck and the Creation of the Second Reich*. New Brunswick, NJ: Transaction Publishers, 2008.

Daubresse, Sylvie. *Le Parlement de Paris ou La Voix de la Raison (1559–1589)*, Travaux d'Humanisme et Renaissance 398. Geneva: Librairie Droz, 2005.

David, Jean-Michel. 'Les Règles de la violence dans les assemblées populaires de la République romaine'. *Politica Antica* 3 (2013): 11–29.

Davidson, Basil. *The Black Man's Burden: Africa and the Curse of the Nation-State*. New York: Times Books, 1992.

De Dijn, Annelien. *French Political Thought from Montesquieu to Tocqueville: Liberty in a Levelled Society?* Cambridge: Cambridge University Press, 2011 [2008].

De Graff, Thelma B. 'Plato in Cicero'. *Classical Philology* 35 (1940): 143–53.

Derman, Joshua. *Max Weber in Politics and Social Thought: From Charisma to Canonization*. Cambridge: Cambridge University Press, 2012.

'Skepticism and Faith: Max Weber's Anti-Utopianism in the Eyes of his Contemporaries'. *Journal of the History of Ideas* 71 (2010): 481–503.

Dexter, H. 'Res Publica'. *Maia* 9 (1957): 247–81 and 10 (1958):3–37.

Diner, Dan, ed. *Hans Kelsen and Carl Schmitt: A Juxtaposition*. Gerlingen: Bleicher, 1999.

Dippel, Horst. 'The Changing Idea of Popular Sovereignty in Early American Constitutionalism: Breaking Away from European Patterns'. *Journal of the History of the Early Republic* 16.1 (1996): 21–45.

Dodwell, Henry. *Dupleix and Clive: The Beginning of Empire*. London: Frank Cass & Co., 1967 [1920].

Dolcini, Carlo. *Introduzione a Marsilio da Padova*. Rome-Bari: Laterza, 1995.

Dolcini, Carlo and Roberto Lambertini, 'Mainardini Marsilio'. *Dizionario Biografico degli Italiani*. LXIII, 569–76. Rome: Istituto dell'Enciclopedia Italiana, 2007.

von Dornum, Deirdre Dionysia. 'The Straight and the Crooked: Legal Accountability in Ancient Greece'. *Columbia Law Review* 97.5 (1997): 1483–1518.

Downs, Anthony. *An Economic Theory of Democracy*. New York: Harper & Row, 1957.

Dunn, John. Legitimacy and Democracy in the World Today'. *Legitimacy and Criminal Justice: An International Exploration*. Edited by Justice Tankebe and Alison Liebling, 7–18. Oxford: Oxford University Press, 2014.

'*Setting the People Free: The Story of Democracy*. London: Atlantic Books, 2006.

Dyck, A. R. *A Commentary on Cicero, De legibus*. Ann Arbor: University of Michigan Press, 2004.

'On the Interpretation of Cicero *De re publica*'. *Classical Quarterly* 48 (1998): 564–8.

Dyzenhaus, David. 'Legal Theory in the Collapse of Weimar: Contemporary Lessons?' *American Political Science Review* 91 (1997): 121–34.

Legality and Legitimacy: Carl Schmitt, Hans Kelsen, and Hermann Heller in Weimar. Oxford: Oxford University Press, 1999.

Eberl, Matthias. *Die Legitimität der Moderne: Kulturkritik und Herrschaftskonzeption bei Max Weber und bei Carl Schmitt*. Marburg: Tectum, 1994.

Eden, Robert. 'Doing without Liberalism: Weber's Regime Politics'. *Political Theory* 10 (1982): 379–407.

Englebrekt, Kjell. 'What Carl Schmitt Picked up in Weber's Seminar: A Historical Controversy Revisited'. *The European Legacy* 14 (2009): 667–84.

Ercole, Francesco. *Da Bartolo all'Altusio*. Florence: Vallecchi, 1932.

Dal Comune al Principato. Florence: Vallecchi, 1929.

Eschenburg, Theodor. *Die improvisierte Demokratie: gesammelte Aufsätze zur Weimarer Republik*. Munich: R. Piper & Co., 1963.

Euben, J Peter. *Corrupting Youth: Political Education, Democratic Culture, and Political Theory*. Princeton: Princeton University Press, 1997.

Fantham, Elaine. 'Aequabilitas in Cicero's Political Theory and the Greek Tradition of Proportional Justice'. *Classical Quarterly* 23 (1973): 285–90.

Farrar, Cynthia. 'Plato, Thucydides, and the Athenian Politeia'. *Politeia in Greek and Roman Philosophy*. Edited by Melissa Lane and Verity Harte, 32–56. Cambridge: Cambridge University Press, 2013.

Ferente, Serena. 'The Liberty of Italian City-States'. *Freedom and the Construction of Europe*. 2 vols. Edited by Quentin Skinner and Martin van Gelderen, 157–75. Cambridge: Cambridge University Press, 2013.

Ferrante, Riccardo. *La difesa della legalità. I sindacatori della Repubblica di Genova*. Turin: Giappichelli, 2005.

Ferrary, Jean-Louis. 'L'Archéologie du *De Re Publica* (2.2.4–37.63): Cicéron entre Polybe et Platon'. *Journal of Roman Studies* 74 (1984): 87–98.

'Le idee politiche a Roma nell'epoca repubblicana'. *Storia delle idee politiche economiche e sociali*. Edited by L Firpo, 724–804. Turin: Unione Tipografico Edizione Torinese, 1982.

'The Statesman and the Law in the Political Philosophy of Cicero'. *Justice and Generosity: Studies in Hellenistic Social and Political Philosophy*. Edited by A. Laks and M. Schofield, 48–73. Cambridge: Cambridge University Press, 1995.

Fitzsimmons, Michael P. 'The Committee of the Constitution and the Remaking of France, 1789–1791'. *French History* 4.1 (1990): 23–47.

The Remaking of France: The National Assembly and the Constitution of 1791. Cambridge: Cambridge University Press, 2002 [1994].

Flaherty, Martin S. 'More Apparent than Real: The Revolutionary Commitment to Constitutional Federalism'. *Kansas Law Review* 45 (1996–7): 993–1014.

Fontanella, Francesca. 'Introduzione al *De legibus* di Cicerone. II'. *Athenaeum* 86 (1998): 181–208.

Forsyth, Murray. *Reason and Revolution: The Political Thought of the Abbé Sieyes*. New York and Leicester: Holmes & Meier/Leicester University Press, 1987.

'Thomas Hobbes and the Constituent Power of the People'. *Political Studies* 29.2 (1981): 191–203.

Unions of States. Leicester: Leicester University Press, 1981.

Foxley, Rachel. *The Levellers: Radical Political Thought in the English Revolution*. Manchester: Manchester University Press, 2013.

'Problems of Sovereignty in Leveller Writings'. *History of Political Thought* 28 (2007): 642–60.

Franklin, Julian. *Jean Bodin and the Rise of Absolutist Theory*. Cambridge: Cambridge University Press, 1973.

Jean Bodin and the Sixteenth-Century Revolution in the Methodology of Law and History. New York and London: Columbia University Press, 1963.

Freund, Julien. 'Schmitt's Political Thought'. *Telos* 102 (1995): 11–42.

Fritz, Christian G. *American Sovereigns: The People and America's Constitutional Tradition before the Civil War*. Cambridge: Cambridge University Press, 2008.

Froehner, Wilhelm. *Les Inscriptions grecques*. Paris: Charles de Mourgues Frères, 1865.

Fröhlich, Pierre. *Les Cités grecques et le contrôle des magistrats (IVe–Ier siècle avant J.-C.)*. Geneva: Droz, 2004.

Fukuda, Arihiro. *Sovereignty and the Sword: Harrington, Hobbes, and Mixed Government in the English Civil Wars*. Oxford: Clarendon Press, 1997.

Furber, Holden. 'Edmund Burke and India'. *Bengal Past and Present: Journal of the Calcutta Historical Society* 76 (1957): 11–21.

Furet, François. *Interpreting the French Revolution*. Cambridge: Cambridge University Press, 1988 [1978].

'La Monarchie et le règlement électoral de 1789'. *The French Revolution and the Creation of Modern Political Culture*. 4 vols. Edited by Keith Michael Baker, 375–86. Oxford: Pergamon, 1987–94.

Penser la revolution française. Paris: Gallimard, 1978.

Garré, Roy. *Consuetudo: Das Gewohnheitsrecht in der Rechtsquellen- und Methodenlehre des späten ius commune in Italien (16.–18. Jahrhundert)*. Frankfurt am Main: Vittorio Klostermann, 2005.

Garsten, Bryan. 'Benjamin Constant's Liberalism and the Political Theology of the General Will'. *The General Will: The Evolution of a Concept*. Edited by James Farr and David Lay Williams, 382–401. Cambridge: Cambridge University Press, 2015.

'Representative Government and Popular Sovereignty'. *Political Representation*. Edited by Ian Shapiro, Susan Stokes, Elisabeth Wood and Alexander Kirshner, 90–110. Cambridge: Cambridge University Press, 2010.

'Seeing "Not Differently, but Further, than the Parties"'. *The Arts of Rule: Essays in Honor of Harvey C. Mansfield*. Edited by Sharon R. Krause and Mary Ann McGrail, 359–76. Lanham, MD: Lexington Books, 2009.

Gentles, Ian. 'The *Agreements of the People* and their Political Context'. *The Putney Debates of 1647: The Army, the Levellers, and the English State*. Edited by Michael Mendle, 148–74. Cambridge: Cambridge University Press, 2001.

Gewirth, Alan. 'John of Jandun and the *Defensor Pacis*'. *Speculum* 23 (1948): 267–72.

von Gierke, Otto. *Political Theories of the Middle Age*. Translated by Frederic William Maitland. Cambridge: Cambridge University Press, 1900.

Giesey, Ralph E. 'Medieval Jurisprudence in Bodin's Concept of Sovereignty'. *Verhandlungen Der Internationalen Bodin Tagung in München*. Edited by Horst Denzer, 167–86. Munich: C. H. Beck, 1973.

Gildenhardt, Ingo. 'Of Cicero's Plato: Fictions, Forms, Foundations'. *Aristotle, Plato and Pythagoreanism in the First Century BC*. Edited by Malcolm Schofield, 225–75. Cambridge: Cambridge University Press, 2013.

Gildersleeve, Basil Lanneau. *Syntax of Classical Greek from Homer to Demosthenes*. New York: American Book Co., 1900.

Girardet, K. M. 'Ciceros Urteilüber die Entstehung des Tribunatesals Instituion der römischen Verfassung'. *Festgabe J. Straub*. Edited by A. Lippold, 179–200. Bonn: Nikolaus Himmelmann, 1977.

Gish, Dustin. 'Defending *Dēmokratia*: Athenian Justice and the Trial of the Arginusae Generals in Xenophon's *Hellenica*'. *Xenophon: Ethical Principles and Historical Enquiry*. Edited by Fiona Hobden and Christopher Tuplin, 161–212. Leiden: Brill, 2012.

Glowacki, Kevin. 'A Personification of Demos on a New Attic Document Relief'. *Hesperia* 72 (2003): 447–66.

Godthardt, Frank. 'The Life of Marsilius of Padua'. *Companion to Marsilius of Padua*. Edited by Gerson Moreno-Riaño and Cary Nederman, 13–55. Leiden: Brill, 2012.

Gordon, Peter E. and John P. McCormick, eds. *Weimar Thought: A Contested Legacy*. Princeton: Princeton University Press, 2013.

Goswami, Manu. 'Imaginary Futures and Colonial Internationalisms'. *American Historical Review* 117.5 (2012): 1461–85.

Green, Jeffrey Edward. *The Eyes of the People: Democracy in an Age of Spectatorship*. Oxford: Oxford University Press, 2011.

'Max Weber and the Reinvention of Popular Power'. *Max Weber Studies* 8 (2008): 187–224.

Greene, J. P. *The Constitutional Origins of the American Revolution*. Cambridge: Cambridge University Press, 2010.

Grilli, Alberto. 'Data e senso del *De legibus* di Cicerone'. *Parola del Passato* 45 (1990): 175–87.

'L'idea di stato dal *De re publica* al *De legibus*'. *Ciceroniana* 7 (1990): 249–62.

'Populus in Cicerone'. *Popolo e potere nel mondo antico*. Edited by Gianpaolo Urso, 123–39. Pisa: ETS, 2005.

Grimm, Dieter. *Souveränität: Herkunft und Zukunft eines Schlüsselbegriffs*. Berlin: Berlin University Press, 2009.

Gross, Michael B. *The War against Catholicism: Liberalism and the Anti-Catholic Imagination in Nineteenth-Century Germany*. Ann Arbor: University of Michigan Press, 2004.

Gross, Raphael. *Carl Schmitt and the Jews: The 'Jewish Question', the Holocaust, and German Legal Theory*. Translated by Joel Golb. Madison: University of Wisconsin Press, 2007.

Guttridge, G. H. *English Whiggism and the American Revolution*. Berkeley: University of California Press, 1966.

Habermas, Jürgen. *Between Facts and Norms: Contributions to a Discourse Theory of Law and Democracy*. Translated by William Rehg. Cambridge, MA: MIT Press, 1996.

'The Horrors of Autonomy: Carl Schmitt in English'. *The New Conservatism: Cultural Criticism and the Historians' Debate*. Edited and translated by Shierry Weber Nicholsen, 128–39. Cambridge, MA: MIT Press, 1989.

'Leadership and Leitkultur'. *The New York Times*, 28 October 2010.

'Popular Sovereignty as Procedure'. *Deliberative Democracy: Essays on Reason and Politics*. Edited by James Bohman and William Rehg, 35–65. Cambridge, MA: MIT Press, 1997.

Hampsher-Monk, Iain. 'The Political Theory of the Levellers: Putney, Property and Professor Macpherson'. *Political Studies* 24 (1976): 397–422.

Handlin, Oscar and Mary Handlin. *The Popular Sources of Political Authority*. Cambridge, MA: Harvard University Press, 1966.

Hansen, Mogens Herman. *The Athenian Assembly in the Age of Demosthenes*. Oxford: Blackwell, 1987.

'The Polis as a Citizen-State'. *Historisk-filosofiske Meddelelser* 67 (1993): 7–29.

Polis and City-State: An Ancient Concept and its Modern Equivalent. Copenhagen: Munksgaard, 1998.

'Seven Hundred *Archai* in Classical Athens'. *Greek, Roman and Byzantine Studies* 21 (1980): 151–73.

'Solonian Democracy in Fourth-Century Athens'. W. R. Connor, M. H. Hansen, K. A. Raaflaub and B. S. Strauss, *Aspects of Athenian Democracy*, 71–99. Copenhagen: Museum Tusculanum Press, 1990.

Hardimon, Stephen. *Hegel's Social Philosophy: The Project of Reconciliation.* Cambridge: Cambridge University Press, 1985.

Hartley, T. E., ed. *Proceedings in the Parliaments of Elizabeth I.* 3 vols. Leicester: Leicester University Press, 1981–95.

Hélie, Faustin-Adolphe. *Les Constititutions de la France.* Paris: Mairesq Aîné, 1880.

Henderson, Jeffrey. 'Demos, Demagogue, Tyrant in Attic Old Comedy'. *Popular Tyranny: Sovereignty and its Discontents in Ancient Greece.* Edited by Kathryn A. Morgan, 155–79. Austin: University of Texas Press, 2003.

Herrera, Carlos–Miguel, ed. *Le Droit, le politique: autour de Max Weber, Hans Kelsen, Carl Schmitt.* Paris: L'Harmattan, 1995.

Hewitson, Mark. *Nationalism in Germany, 1848–1866.* Basingstoke: Macmillan, 2010.

'"The Old Forms are Breaking Up . . . Our New Germany is Rebuilding Itself": Constitutionalism, Nationalism and the Creation of a German Polity during the Revolutions of 1848–49'. *English Historical Review* 75.116 (2010): 1173–1214.

Hinsley, F. H. *Sovereignty.* 2nd edn. Cambridge: Cambridge University Press, 1986.

Hoekstra, Kinch. 'Early Modern Absolutism and Constitutionalism'. *Cardozo Law Review* 34 (2013): 1079–98.

Holmes, Stephen. 'Saved by Danger/Destroyed by Success: The Argument of Tocqueville's *Souvenirs*'. *Archives européennes de sociologie* 50: 2 (2009): 171–99.

Hont, Istvan. 'The Permanent Crisis of a Divided Mankind: "Nation-State" and "Nationalism" in Historical Perspective'. *Jealousy of Trade: International Competition and the Nation-State in Historical Perspective*, 447–528. Cambridge, MA: Harvard University Press, 2005.

Hucko, Elmar. M., ed. *The Democratic Tradition: Four German Constitutions.* Oxford: Berg, 1987.

Hyde, John Kenneth. *Padua in the Age of Dante.* Manchester: Manchester University Press, 1966.

Innes, Joanna and Mark Philp, eds. *Re-imagining Democracy in the Age of Revolutions, 1750–1850.* Oxford: Oxford University Press, 2013.

Isenmann, Moritz. 'From Rule of Law to Emergency Rule in Renaissance Florence'. *The Politics of Law in Late Medieval and Renaissance Italy: Essays in Honour of Lauro Martines.* Edited by Lawrin Armstrong and Julius Kirshner, 55–76. Toronto: University of Toronto Press, 2011.

Legalität und Herrschaftskontrolle (1200–1600). Eine vergleichende Studie zum Syndikatsprozess: Florenz, Kastilien und Valencia. Frankfurt: Klostermann Vittorio GmbH, 2010.

Israel, Jonathan. *Revolutionary Ideas*. Princeton: Princeton University Press, 2014.

Jabloner, Clemens. 'Hans Kelsen'. *Weimar: A Jurisprudence of Crisis*. Edited by Arthur Jacobsen and Bernard Schlink, 67–76. Berkeley and Los Angeles: University of California Press, 2002.

'Kelsen and his Circle: The Viennese Years'. *European Journal of International Law* 9 (1998): 368–85.

Jackson, Robert H. *Quasi-States: Sovereignty, International Relations and the Third World*. Cambridge: Cambridge University Press, 1990.

Jainchill, Andrew. *Reimagining Politics after the Terror: The Republican Origins of French Liberalism*. Ithaca: Cornell University Press, 2008.

Jalal, Ayesha. *The Sole Spokesman: Jinnah, the Muslim League and the Demand for Pakistan*. Cambridge: Cambridge University Press, 1985.

Jaume, Lucien. *Tocqueville: The Aristocratic Sources of Liberty*. Translated by Arthur Goldhammer. Princeton: Princeton University Press, 2013.

Jaurès, Jean. *Histoire socialiste de la Révolution française*. 7 vols. Paris: Editions sociales, 1968–73.

Jennings, Jeremy. *Revolution and the Republic: A History of Political Thought in France since the Eighteenth Century*. Oxford: Oxford University Press, 2013.

Johnson, P. 'Carl Schmitt, Jürgen Habermas, and the Crisis of Politics'. *The European Legacy* 3 (1998): 15–32.

Jones, A. H. M. *The Criminal Courts of the Roman Republic and Principate*. Oxford: Blackwell, 1972.

Judde de la Rivière, Claire and Rosa Salzberg. 'Le Peuple est la cité: l'idée de popolo et la condition des popolani à Venise (XVe–XVIe siècles)'. *Annales HSS* 68 (2013): 1113–40.

Judson, Margaret A. *The Crisis of the Constitution: An Essay in Constitutional and Political Thought in England 1603–45*. New Brunswick, NJ: Rutgers University Press, 1949.

'Henry Parker and the Theory of Parliamentary Sovereignty'. *Essays in History and Political Theory: In Honor of Charles Howard McIlwain*. Edited by Carl Wittke, 138–67. Cambridge, MA: Russell & Russell, 1936.

Kahan, Alan S. *Aristocratic Liberalism: The Social and Political Thought of Jacob Burckhardt, John Stuart Mill, and Alexis de Tocqueville*. New York: Oxford University Press, 1992.

Kallet, Lisa. 'Demos Tyrannos: Wealth, Power and Economic Patronage'. *Popular Tyranny: Sovereignty and its Discontents in Ancient Greece*. Edited by Kathryn Morgan, 117–53. Austin: University of Texas Press, 2003.

Kalyvas, Andreas. *Democracy and the Politics of the Extraordinary: Max Weber, Carl Schmitt, and Hannah Arendt*. Cambridge: Cambridge University Press, 2008.

'Who's Afraid of Carl Schmitt?' *Philosophy and Social Criticism* 25 (1999): 87–125.

Kedourie, Elie. *Nationalism*. London: Hutchinson & Co, 1960.

Nationalism in Asia and Africa. New York and Cleveland: New American Library, 1970.

Kelley, Donald. 'Civil Science in the Renaissance: The Problem of Interpretation'. *The Languages of Political Theory in Early-Modern Europe*. Edited by Anthony Pagden, 57–78. Cambridge: Cambridge University Press, 1987.

Foundations of Modern Historical Scholarship: Language, Law, and History in the French Renaissance. New York and London: Columbia University Press, 1970.

Kelly, Duncan. 'Carl Schmitt's Political Theory of Representation'. *Journal of the History of Ideas* 65 (2004): 113–34.

'Idealism and Revolution: T. H. Green's *Four Lectures on the English Commonwealth*'. *History of Political Thought* 27.3 (2006): 505–42.

The Propriety of Liberty. Princeton: Princeton University Press, 2010.

The State of the Political: Conceptions of Politics and the State in the Thought of Max Weber, Carl Schmitt, and Franz Neumann. Oxford: Oxford University Press, 2003.

Kennedy, Ellen. 'Carl Schmitt's *Parlamentarismus* in its Historical Context'. Carl Schmitt, *Crisis of Parliamentary Democracy.* Translated by Ellen Kennedy, xiii–l. Cambridge, MA: MIT Press, 1988.

Constitutional Failure: Carl Schmitt in Weimar. Durham, NC: Duke University Press, 2004.

Keyes, Clinton Walker. 'Original Elements in Cicero's Ideal Constitution'. *American Journal of Philology* 42 (1921): 309–23.

Kilker, E. 'Max Weber and Plebiscitary Democracy: A Critique of the Mommsen Thesis'. *International Journal of Politics, Culture, and Society* 2 (1989): 429–65.

Kingdon, Robert M. 'Calvinism and Resistance Theory, 1550–1580'. *The Cambridge History of Political Thought, 1450–1700.* Edited by J. H. Burns and Mark Goldie, 193–218. Cambridge: Cambridge University Press, 1991.

Knox, Bernard. *Oedipus at Thebes: Sophocles' Tragic Hero and his Time.* 2nd edn. New Haven: Yale University Press, 1998 [1957].

Koditschek, Theodore. *Liberalism, Imperialism, and the Historical Imagination: Nineteenth-Century Visions of a Greater Britain.* Cambridge: Cambridge University Press, 2011.

Koenen, Andreas. *Der Fall Carl Schmitt: Sein Aufsteig zum 'Kronjuristen des Dritten Reiches'.* Darmstadt: Wissenschaftliche Buchgesellschaft, 1995.

Koenigsberger, H. G. 'Composite States, Representative Institutions and the American Revolution'. *Historical Research* 62.148 (June 1989): 135–53.

'Monarchies and Parliaments in Early Modern Europe: Dominium Regale or *Dominium Politicum et Regale*'. *Theory and Society* 5.2 (1978): 191–217.

Kolb, Eberhard. *The Weimar Republic.* Translated by P. S. Falla. London: Unwin Hyman, 1988.

Korb, Axel-Johannes. *Kelsens Kritker: Ein Beitrag zur Geschichte der Rechts- und Staatstheorie (1911–1934).* Tübingen: Mohr Siebeck, 2010.

Koselleck, Reinhart. *Futures Past.* Translated by Keith Tribe. New York: Columbia University Press, 2004.

'Volk, Nation, Nationalismus, Masse'. *Geschichtliche Grundbegriffe.* 8 vols. Edited by Reinhart Koselleck, Otto Brunner and Werner Conze. Vol. VII, 357–62. Stuttgart: Klett-Cotta, 1978.

Laclau, Ernesto. *On Populist Reason.* London: Verso, 2005.

LaCroix, Alison A. *The Ideological Origins of American Federalism*. Cambridge, MA: Harvard University Press, 2010.

Ladavac, Nicoletta Bersier. 'Hans Kelsen (1881–1973): Biographical Note and Bibliography'. *European Journal of International Law* 9 (1998): 391–400.

Laks, André. 'The Laws'. *Cambridge History of Greek and Roman Political Thought*. Edited by Christopher Rowe and Malcolm Schofield, 278–84. Cambridge: Cambridge University Press, 2005.

Landauer, Matthew. 'The *Idiōtēs* and the Tyrant: Two Faces of Unaccountability in Democratic Athens'. *Political Theory* 42 (2014): 139–66.

Lane, Melissa. 'Claims to Rule: The Case of the Multitude'. *The Cambridge Companion to Aristotle's* Politics. Edited by Marguerite Deslauriers and Pierre Destrée, 247–74. Cambridge: Cambridge University Press, 2013.

'Political Expertise and Political Office in Plato's *Statesman*: The Statesman's Rule (*Archein*) and the Subordinate Magistracies (*Archai*)'. *Plato's* States-man: *Proceedings of the Eighth Symposium Platonicum Pragense*. Edited by Aleš Havlíček, Jakub Jirsa and Karel Thein, 51–79. Prague: OIKOYMENH, 2013.

Langford, Paul. 'New Whigs, Old Tories, and the American Revolution'. *Journal of Imperial and Commonwealth History* 2 (1980): 106–30.

Lawton, Carol L. *Attic Document Reliefs: Art and Politics in Ancient Athens*. Oxford: Oxford University Press, 1995.

Lee, Daniel. '"Office Is a Thing Borrowed": Jean Bodin on Offices and Seigneurial Government'. *Political Theory* 41 (2013): 409–40.

Leunissen, Mariska. 'Teleology and Necessity in Aristotle's Account of the Nat-ural and Moral Imperfections of Women'. Unpublished paper presented at the Classical Philosophy Conference, Princeton University, 2013.

Lévy, Edmond. '*Politeia* et *politeuma* chez Aristote'. *Aristote et Athènes*. Edited by Marcel Piérart, 65–90. Fribourg: Séminaire d'histoire ancienne de l'Université de Fribourg, 1993.

Levy, Jacob T. 'Montesquieu's Constitutional Legacies'. *Montesquieu and his Legacy*. Edited by Rebecca E. Kingston, 115–38. New York: State University of New York Press, 2008.

Lintott, A. W. 'Provocatio: From the Struggle of the Orders to the Principate'. *Aufstieg und Niedergang der römischen Welt* 1.2 (1972): 226–67.

The Roman Constitution. Oxford: Clarendon Press, 1999.

Long, A. A. 'Cicero's Plato and Aristotle'. *Cicero the Philosopher*. Edited by J. G. F. Powell, 37–62. Oxford: Oxford University Press, 1995.

Loughlin, Martin. *Foundations of Public Law*. Oxford: Oxford University Press, 2010.

The Idea of Public Law. Oxford: Oxford University Press, 2003.

McAuley, Alex. 'Officials and Office-Holding'. *A Companion to Ancient Greek Government*. Edited by Hans Beck, 176–90. Chichester: Wiley-Blackwell, 2013.

McConville, Brendan. *The King's Three Faces: The Rise and Fall of Royal America, 1688–1776*. Chapel Hill: University of North Carolina Press, 2006.

McCormick, John P. *Carl Schmitt's Critique of Liberalism: Against Politics as Technology*. Cambridge: Cambridge University Press, 1997.

'Legal Theory and the Weimar Crisis of Law and Social Change'. *Weimar Thought: A Contested Legacy*. Edited by Peter E. Gordon and John McCormick, 55–72. Princeton: Princeton University Press, 2013.

MacCulloch, Diarmuid. *Tudor Church Militant: Edward VI and the Protestant Reformation*. London: Allen Lane, 1999.

McDiarmid, John F., ed. *The Monarchical Republic of Early Modern England: Essays in Response to Patrick Collinson*. Aldershot: Ashgate, 2007.

McGlew, James. F. *Tyranny and Political Culture in Ancient Greece*. Ithaca and London: Cornell University Press, 1993.

McIlwain, Charles Howard. *The American Revolution: A Constitutional Interpretation*. New York: Macmillan, 1923.

Macleod, C. W. 'Reason and Necessity: Thucydides III 9–14, 37–48'. *Journal of Hellenic Studies* 98 (1978): 64–78.

Macpherson, C. B. *The Political Theory of Possessive Individualism: Hobbes to Locke*. Oxford: Oxford University Press, 1962.

Majed Khan, Abdul. *The Transition in Bengal, 1756–1775: A Study of Saiyid Muhammad Reza Khan*. Cambridge: Cambridge University Press, 1969.

Malcolm, Noel. 'Jean Bodin and the Authorship of the "Colloquium Heptaplomeres"'. *Journal of the Warburg and Courtauld Institutes* 69 (2006): 95–150.

Manent, Pierre. *Tocqueville and the Nature of Democracy*. Lanham, MD: Rowman & Littlefield, 1996.

Manin, Bernard. 'On Legitimacy and Political Deliberation'. *Political Theory* 15 (1987): 338–68.

The Principles of Representative Democracy. Cambridge: Cambridge University Press, 1997.

Mantena, Karuna. *Alibis of Empire: Henry Maine and the Ends of Liberal Imperialism*. Princeton: Princeton University Press, 2010.

'On Gandhi's Critique of the State: Sources, Contexts, Conjunctures'. *Modern Intellectual History* 9.3 (2012): 535–63.

Marangon, Paolo. 'Marsilio fra preumanesimo e cultura delle arti'. *Medioevo: Rivista di storia della filosofia medievale* 3 (1977): 89–119.

Margerison, Kenneth. 'P.-L. Roederer: Political Thought and Practice during the French Revolution'. *Transactions of the American Philosophical Society* NS 73.1 (1983): 1–166.

Markle, M. M., III. 'Jury Pay and Assembly Pay at Athens'. *Crux: Essays Presented to G. E. M. de Ste. Croix on his 75th Birthday*. Edited by Paul Cartledge and F. D. Harvey, 265–97. Exeter: Imprint Academic, 1985.

Markovits, Elizabeth. *The Politics of Sincerity: Plato, Frank Speech, and Democratic Judgment*. University Park: Pennsylvania State University Press, 2008.

Marston, Jerrilyn Greene. *King and Congress: The Transfer of Political Legitimacy, 1774–1776*. Princeton: Princeton University Press, 1987.

Mendle, Michael. *Dangerous Positions: Mixed Government, the Estates of the Realm, and the Making of the Answer to the XIX Propositions*. Tuscaloosa: University of Alabama Press, 1985.

Henry Parker and the English Civil War: The Political Thought of the Public's 'Privado'. Cambridge: Cambridge University Press, 1995.

'Parliamentary Sovereignty: A Very English Absolutism'. *Political Discourse in Early Modern Britain*. Edited by Nicholas Phillipson and Quentin Skinner, 97–119. Cambridge: Cambridge University Press, 1992.

Messerschmidt, Wolfgang. *Prosopopoiia: Personifikationen politischen Charakters in spätklassischer und hellenistischer Kunst*. Cologne: Böhlau, 2003.

Metcalf, Thomas. *Ideologies of the Raj*. Cambridge: Cambridge University Press, 1995.

Miethke, Jürgen. 'Die Briefgedichte des Albertino Mussato an Marsilius von Padua'. *Pensiero politico medievale* 6 (2008): 49–65.

Millar, Fergus. 'Imperial Ideology in the Tabula Siarensis'. *Estudios sobre la Tabula Siarensis*. Edited by Julian González and Javier Arce, 11–19. Madrid: CSIC, Centro de Estudios Históricos, 1988.

Miller, David. *National Responsibility and Global Justice*. Oxford: Oxford University Press, 2012.

Mirhady, David C. 'Aristotle, the *Rhetorica ad Alexandrum* and the *Tria Genera Causarum*'. *Peripatetic Rhetoric after Aristotle*. Edited by William W. Fortenbaugh and David C. Mirhady, 54–65. New Brunswick, NJ: Transaction Publishers, 1994.

Moggach, Douglas and Widukind de Ridder. 'Hegelianism in Restoration Prussia, 1841–1848'. *Hegel's Thought in Europe*. Edited by Lisa Herzog, 71–92. Basingstoke: Palgrave, 2013.

Mommsen, Hans. *The Rise and Fall of Weimar Democracy*. Translated by Elborg Forster and Larry Eugene Jones. Chapel Hill: University of North Carolina Press, 1996 [1989].

Mommsen, Wolfgang J. 'The Antinomian Structure of Max Weber's Political Thought'. *Current Perspectives in Social Theory* 4 (1983): 289–311.

Max Weber and German Politics, 1890–1920. Translated by M. S. Steinberg. Chicago: University of Chicago Press, 1984 [1959].

Moreau-Reibel, Jean. *Jean Bodin et le droit public comparé*. Paris: Vrin, 1933.

Moreno-Riaño, Gerson and Cary J. Nederman, eds. *Companion to Marsilius of Padua*. Leiden: Brill, 2012.

Morgan, Edmund S. *Inventing the People: The Rise of Popular Sovereignty in England and America*. New York: Norton, 1988.

Morgan, Kathryn A., ed. *Popular Tyranny: Sovereignty and its Discontents in Ancient Greece*. Austin: University of Texas Press, 2003.

Morrow, Glenn R. *Plato's Cretan City: A Historical Interpretation of the* Laws. Princeton: Princeton University Press, 1960.

Mouffe, Chantal. *The Return of the Political*. London: Verso, 1993.

Mulgan, Richard. 'Aristotle's Sovereign'. *Political Studies* 18 (1970): 518–22.

Nelson, Eric. *The Royalist Revolution: Monarchy and the American Founding*. Cambridge, MA: Harvard University Press, 2014.

Nicolet, C. 'Cicéron, Platon et le vote secret'. *Historia* 19 (1970): 39–66.

La Mémoire perdue: à la recherche des archives oubliées, publiques et privées, de la Rome antique. Paris: La Sorbonne, 1994.

Nozick, Robert. *Anarchy, State, and Utopia*. New York: Basic Books, 1974.

Oakley, Francis. 'Celestial Hierarchies Revisited: Walter Ullmann's Vision of Medieval Politics'. *Past and Present* 60 (1973): 3–48.

Ober, Josiah. *The Athenian Revolution: Essays on Ancient Greek Democracy and Political Theory*. Princeton: Princeton University Press, 1996.

Mass and Elite in Democratic Athens: Rhetoric, Ideology, and the Power of the People. Princeton: Princeton University Press, 1989.

'The Original Meaning of Democracy: Capacity to Do Things, Not Majority Rule'. *Constellations* 15 (2008): 3–9.

'Review Article: The Nature of Athenian Democracy'. *Classical Philology* 84 (1989): 322–34.

Ochoa Espejo, Paulina. *The Time of Popular Sovereignty: Process and the Democratic State*. University Park: Pennsylvania State University Press, 2011.

Ostwald, Martin. *From Popular Sovereignty to the Sovereignty of Law: Law, Society, and Politics in Fifth-Century Athens*. Berkeley: University of California Press, 1986.

Language and History in Ancient Greek Culture. Philadelphia: University of Pennsylvania Press, 2009.

Owen, T. M. *History of Alabama and Dictionary of Alabama Biography*. 4 vols. Chicago: S. J. Clarke, 1921.

Ozouf Marignier, Marie-Vic. *La Formation des départements: la representation du territoire Français à la fin du 18e siècle*. Paris: EHESS, 1989.

Palladini, Fiammetta, ed. *La biblioteca di Samuel Pufendorf: catalogo dell'asta di Berlin del settembre 1697*. Wiesbaden: Harrassowitz, 1999.

Palmer, R. R. *The Age of Democratic Revolution: A Political History of Europe and America, 1760–1800*. 2 vols. Princeton: Princeton University Press, 1959–64.

Parent, Joseph. *Uniting States*. Oxford: Oxford University Press, 2011.

Paret, Peter. *German Encounters with Modernism*. Cambridge: Cambridge University Press, 2001.

Parkin, Jon. *Taming the Leviathan: The Reception of the Political and Religious Ideas of Thomas Hobbes in England, 1640–1700*. Cambridge: Cambridge University Press, 2007.

Pasquino, Pasquale. 'Machiavelli and Aristotle: The Anatomies of the City'. *History of European Ideas* 35 (2009): 397–407.

Sieyès et l'invention de la constitution en France. Paris: Edition Odile Jacob, 1998.

Peltonen, Markku. *Classical Humanism and Republicanism in English Political Thought, 1570–1640*. Cambridge: Cambridge University Press, 1995.

Perelli, L. 'Note sul tribunato della plebe nella riflessione ciceroniana'. *Quaderni di Storia* 10 (1979): 285–303.

Il pensiero politico di Cicerone. Florence: La Nuova Italia, 1990.

Peters, Ronald M. *The Massachusetts Constitution of 1780: A Social Compact*. Amherst: University of Massachusetts Press, 1978.

Pettit, Philip. *On the People's Terms: A Republican Theory and Model of Democracy*. Cambridge: Cambridge University Press, 2012.

Peukert, Detlev. *The Weimar Republic: The Crisis of Classical Modernity*. Translated by R. Deveson. London: Allen Lane, 1991.

Pflanze, Otto. *Bismarck and the Development of Germany*, vol. II: *The Period of Consolidation 1871–1880*. Princeton: Princeton University Press, 1990.

Piccone, Paul and Gary Ulmen. 'Introduction to Carl Schmitt'. *Telos* 72 (1987): 3–14.

Piérart, M., 'Les εὔθυνοι athéniens'. *L'Antiquité Classique* 40 (1971): 526–73.

Pincin, Carlo. *Marsilio*. Turin: Giappichelli, 1967.

Pintard, René. *La Mothe le Vayer – Gassendi – Guy Patin: études de bibliographie et de critique suivies de textes inédits de Guy Patin*. Paris: Boivin, 1943.

Pitkin, Hanna Fenichel. *The Concept of Representation*. Berkeley: University of California Press, 1967.

Pittia, Sylvie. 'La Dimension utopique du traité Cicéronien *De legibus*'. *Utopia e utopie nel pensiero storico antico*. Edited by Chiara Carsana and Maria Teresa Schettino, 27–48. Rome: L'Erma di Bretschneider, 2008.

Pocock, J. G. A. *The Ancient Constitution and the Feudal Law: A Study of English Historical Thought in the Seventeenth Century*. 2nd edn. Cambridge: Cambridge University Press, 1987 [1957].

'Josiah Tucker on Burke, Locke and Price: A Study in the Varieties of Eighteenth-Century Conservatism'. *Virtue, Commerce, and History: Essays on Political Thought and History, Chiefly in the Eighteenth Century*, 157–92. Cambridge: Cambridge University Press, 1985.

The Machiavellian Moment: Florentine Political Thought and the Atlantic Republican Tradition. Princeton: Princeton University Press, 1975.

Pope, M. 'Thucydides and Democracy'. *Historia: Zeitschrift für Alte Geschichte* 37 (1988): 276–96.

Powell, J. G. F. 'Were Cicero's Laws the Laws of Cicero's Republic?' *Cicero's Republic*. Edited by John A. North and J. G. F. Powell, 17–40. London: Institute of Classical Studies, 2001.

Przeworski, Adam. *Democracy and the Limits of Self-Government*. Cambridge: Cambridge University Press, 2010.

'Minimalist Conception of Democracy: A Defence'. *Democracy's Value*. Edited by I. Shapiro and C. Hacker-Cordón, 23–55. Cambridge: Cambridge University Press, 1999.

Pulzer, Peter. *Germany, 1870–1945: Politics, State Formation, and War*. Oxford: Oxford University Press, 1997.

Quillet, Jeannine. 'Community, Counsel and Representation'. *The Cambridge History of Medieval Political Thought c. 350–1450*. Edited by J. H. Burns, 520–71. Cambridge: Cambridge University Press, 1988.

Raaflaub, Kurt. 'The Breakthrough of *Demokratia* in Mid-Fifth-Century Athens'. *Origins of Democracy in Ancient Greece*. Kurt A. Raaflaub, Josiah Ober and Robert W. Wallace, 105–54. Berkeley: University of California Press, 2007.

The Discovery of Freedom in Ancient Greece. Chicago: University of Chicago Press, 2004.

'Stick and Glue: The Function of Tyranny in Fifth-Century Athenian Democracy'. *Popular Tyranny: Sovereignty and its Discontents in Ancient Greece*. Edited by Kathryn Morgan, 59–93. Austin: University of Texas Press, 2003.

Rakove, Jack. *The Beginnings of National Politics: An Interpretive History of the Continental Congress*. New York: Knopf, 1979.

Rao, Riccardo. *Signorie di popolo: Signoria cittadina e società comunale nell'Italia nord-occidentale, 1250–1350*. Milan: Franco Angeli, 2012.

Rawson, E. 'The Interpretation of Cicero's *De legibus*'. *Aufstieg und Niedergang der römischen Welt* 1.4 (1973): 334–56; also published in E. Rawson, *Roman Culture and Society*, 125–48. Oxford: Oxford University Press, 1991.

Recchia, Stefano. 'The Origins of Liberal Wilsonianism: Giuseppe Mazzini on Regime Change and Humanitarian Intervention'. *Just and Unjust Military Intervention*. Edited by Stefano Recchia and Jennifer Walsh, 237–62. Cambridge: Cambridge University Press, 2013.

Reid, John Philip. *Constitutional History of the American Revolution: The Authority of Law*. Madison: University of Wisconsin Press, 1993.

Constitutional History of the American Revolution: The Authority to Legislate. Madison: University of Wisconsin Press, 1991.

Reynolds, Susan. *Kingdoms and Communities in Western Europe, 300–1300*. Oxford: Oxford University Press, 1986.

Rhodes, P. J. 'The "Acephalous" Polis?'. *Historia: Zeitschrift für Alte Geschichte* 44 (1995): 153–67.

A Commentary on the Aristotelian Athenaion Politeia. Oxford: Oxford University Press, 1981.

Euthynai *(Accounting): A Valedictory Lecture Delivered before the University of Durham* (n.p.: n.p., 2005).

Richter, Melvin. 'Toward a Concept of Political Illegitimacy: Bonapartist Dictatorship and Democratic Legitimacy'. *Political Theory* 10.2 (1982): 185–214.

Rihll, T. E. 'Democracy Denied: Why Ephialtes Attacked the Areiopagus'. *Journal of Hellenic Studies* 115 (1995): 87–98.

Ringer, F. 'Max Weber's Liberalism'. *Central European History* 35 (2002): 379–95.

Röben, Betsy Baker. 'The Method behind Bluntschli's "Modern" International Law'. *Journal of the History of International Law* 4 (2002): 249–92.

Roberts, Jennifer Tolbert. *Accountability in Athenian Government*. Madison: University of Wisconsin Press, 1982.

Robinson, Eric W. *Democracy beyond Athens: Popular Government in the Greek Classical Age*. Cambridge: Cambridge University Press, 2011.

Rosanvallon, Pierre. *Democracy Past and Future*. Edited by Samuel Moyn. New York: Columbia University Press, 2006.

Rose, Paul Lawrence. 'The Politique and the Prophet: Bodin and the Catholic League 1589–1594'. *The Historical Journal* 21 (1978): 783–808.

Rudé, George. *Robespierre*. New York: Prentice Hall, 1967.

Ruebel, J. 'The Trial of Milo in 52 BC: A Chronological Study'. *Transactions of the American Philological Association* 109 (1979): 231–49.

Saffon, M. P. and N. Urbinati. 'Procedural Democracy, the Bulwark of Equal Liberty'. *Political Theory* 41 (2013): 441–81.

Salerno, F. *Tacita Libertas: l'introduzione del voto segreto nella Roma repubblicana*. Naples: Edizioni Scientifiche Italiane, 1999.

Salmon, J. H. M. *The French Religious Wars in English Political Thought*. Oxford: Clarendon Press, 1959.

Sanderson, John. *'But the People's Creatures': The Philosophical Basis of the English Civil War*. Manchester: Manchester University Press, 1989.

Sarkar, Sumit. *The Swadeshi Movement of Bengal 1903–1908*. New Delhi: Oxford University Press, 1973.

Saxonhouse, A. W., *Athenian Democracy: Modern Mythmakers and Ancient Theorists*. Notre Dame: University of Notre Dame Press, 1996.

Sbriccoli, Mario. *Crimen laesae maiestatis: I problema del reato politico alle soglie della scienza penalistica moderna*. Milan: n.p., 1974.

Schmidt, P. L. *Die Abfassungzeit der Ciceros Schrift über die Gesetze*. Rome: Centro di Studi Ciceroniani, 1969.

Schmitt, Carl. *Political Theology: Four Chapters on the Concept of Sovereignty*. Translated by George Schwab. Cambridge, MA: MIT Press, 1985.

Schofield, Malcolm. 'Friendship and Justice in the *Laws*'. *The Platonic Art of Philosophy*. Edited by George Boys-Stones, Dimitri El Murr and Christopher Gill, 283–98. Cambridge: Cambridge University Press, 2013.

'The *Laws*' Two Projects'. *Plato's Laws: A Critical Guide*. Edited by Christopher Bobonich, 12–28. Cambridge: Cambridge University Press, 2010.

Saving the City: Philosopher-Kings and Other Classical Paradigms. London and New York: Routledge, 1999.

Scott, David. *Refashioning Futures: Criticism after Postcolonialism*. Princeton: Princeton University Press, 1999.

Scott, James C. *Seeing Like a State: How Certain Schemes to Improve the Human Condition Have Failed*. New Haven: Yale University Press, 1999.

Scurr, Ruth. 'Pierre-Louis Roederer and the Debate on Forms of Government in Revolutionary France'. *Political Studies* 52.2 (June 2004): 251–68.

Shaw, Tamsin. 'Max Weber on Democracy: Can the People Have Political Power in Modern States?'. *Constellations* 15 (2008): 33–45.

Shklar, Judith. *Men and Citizens: A Study of Rousseau's Social Theory*. Cambridge: Cambridge University Press, 1985 [1969].

Shogimen, Takashi. 'Medicine and the Body Politic in Marsilius of Padua's *Defensor Pacis*.' *Companion to Marsilius of Padua*. Edited by Gerson Moreno-Riaño and Cary J. Nederman, 71–115. Leiden: Brill, 2011.

Sinclair, R. K. *Democracy and Participation in Athens*. Cambridge: Cambridge University Press, 1988.

Sinha, Mrinalini. 'The Strange Death of an Imperial Ideal: The Case of *Civis Britannicus*'. *Handbook of Modernity in South Asia: Modern Makeovers*. Edited by Saurabh Dube, 29–42. New Delhi: Oxford University Press, 2012.

'Whatever Happened to the Third British Empire? Empire, Nation Redux'. *Writing Imperial Histories*. Edited by Andrew S. Thompson, 168–83. Manchester: Manchester University Press, 2013.

Skinner, Quentin. 'The Empirical Theorists of Democracy and their Critics: A Plague on Both their Houses'. *Political Theory* 1 (1973): 287–306.

The Foundations of Modern Political Thought, 2 vols. Cambridge: Cambridge University Press, 1978.

'Hobbes on Persons, Authors and Representatives'. *The Cambridge Companion to Hobbes's* Leviathan. Edited by Patricia Springborg, 157–80. Cambridge: Cambridge University Press, 2007.

'Hobbes on Representation'. *European Journal of Philosophy* 13 (2005): 155–84.

Hobbes and Republican Liberty. Cambridge: Cambridge University Press, 2008.
'Rethinking Political Liberty'. *History Workshop Journal* 61 (2006): 156–70.
Visions of Politics, vol. III: *Hobbes and Civil Science.* Cambridge: Cambridge University Press, 2002.

Smith, Amy C. *Polis and Personification in Classical Athenian Art.* Leiden: Brill, 2011.

Smith, Sophie. 'Nature, Knowledge and the City in John Case and the Aristotelian Tradition'. Ph.D. thesis, University of Cambridge, 2014.

Soboul, Albert. *The French Revolution, 1787–1799.* London: Unwin Hyman, 1989 [1962].

Sommerville, Johann P. 'English and European Political Ideas in the Early Seventeenth Century: Revisionism and the Case of Absolutism'. *Journal of British Studies* 35.2 (April 1996): 168–94.

Sonenscher, Michael. *Before the Deluge.* Princeton: Princeton University Press, 2007.

Spitzer, Robert J. *The Presidential Veto: Touchstone of the American Presidency.* Albany: State University of New York Press, 1988.

Stalley, R. F. *An Introduction to Plato's Laws.* Oxford: Blackwell, 1983.

Stammer, Otto (ed.), *Max Weber and Sociology*, trans. Kathleen Morris. Oxford: Basil Blackwell, 1971.

Stein, Katrin. *Die verantwortlichkeitpolitischer Akteure.* Tübingen: J. C. B. Mohr (Paul Siebeck), 2009.

Stokes, Eric. *The English Utilitarians and India.* Oxford: Clarendon Press, 1963.

Suolahti, Jaakko. *The Roman Censors: A Study on Social Structure.* Helsinki: Suomalainen Tiedeakatemia, 1963.

Sutherland, Lucy. 'The City of London in Eighteenth-Century Politics'. *Essays Presented to Sir Lewis Namier.* Edited by Richard Pares and A. J. P. Taylor, 49–74. London: Macmillan, 1956.
'Edmund Burke and the First Rockingham Ministry'. *English Historical Review* 47.185 (January 1932): 46–72.

Syros, Vasileios. *Marsilius of Padua at the Intersection of Ancient and Medieval Traditions of Political Thought.* Toronto: University of Toronto Press, 2012.

Tackett, Timothy. 'Nobles and the Third Estate in the Revolutionary Dynamic of the National Assembly, 1789–1790'. *American Historical Review* 94.2 (April 1989): 271–301.

Tatum, Jeffrey. 'The *Lex Clodia de censoria notione*'. *Classical Philology* 85 (1990): 34–43.
The Patrician Tribune: Publius Clodius Pulcher. Chapel Hill and London: University of North Carolina Press, 1999.

Thomas, Keith. 'The Levellers and the Franchise'. *The Interregnum: The Quest for Settlement, 1646–1660.* Edited by G. E. Aylmer. London: Macmillan, 1974.

Thomas, Peter D. G. *Tea Party to Independence: The Third Phase of the American Revolution, 1773–1776.* Oxford: Clarendon Press, 1991.

Thomas, Yan. 'Cicéron, le Sénat et les tribuns de la plebe'. *Revue Historique de Droit Français et Étranger* 1.5 (1977): 189–210.

Tierney, Brian. '"The Prince is Not Bound by the Laws": Accursius and the Origins of the Modern State'. *Comparative Studies in Society and History* 5 (1963): 378–400.

Todd, Margo. *Christian Humanism and the Puritan Social Order*. Cambridge: Cambridge University Press, 1987.

Topitsch, Ernst. *Gottwerdung und Revolution: Beiträge zur Weltanschauungsanalyse und Ideologiekritik*. Munich: Dokumentation, 1973.

Troiani, L. 'Alcune considerazioni sul voto nell'antica Roma a proposito di Cic. Leg. III.10'. *Athenaeum* 65 (1987): 493–9.

'Sulla lex de suffragiis in Cicerone de legibus III.10'. *Athenaeum* 59 (1981): 180–4.

Tuck, Richard. 'The "Modern" Theory of Natural Law'. *Languages of Political Theory in Early-Modern Europe*. Edited by Anthony Pagden, 99–122. Cambridge: Cambridge University Press, 1987.

Natural Rights Theories: Their Origin and Development. Cambridge: Cambridge University Press, 1979.

Philosophy and Government, 1572–1651. Cambridge: Cambridge University Press, 1993.

The Sleeping Sovereign. Cambridge: Cambridge University Press, forthcoming.

Ullmann, Walter. 'The Development of the Medieval Idea of Sovereignty'. *English Historical Review* 64 (1949): 1–33.

Principles of Government and Politics in the Middle Ages. New York: Barnes & Noble, 1961.

Ulmen, G. L. *Politischer Mehwert: eine Studie über Max Weber und Carl Schmitt*. Weinheim: VCH Acta Humaniora, 1991.

'The Sociology of the State: Carl Schmitt and Max Weber'. *State, Culture and Society* 1 (1985): 3–57.

Urbinati, Nadia. *Representative Democracy: Principles and Genealogy*. Chicago: Chicago University Press, 2006.

Vieira, Mónica Brito and David Runciman. *Representation*. Cambridge: Polity Press, 2008.

Villa, Dana. 'The Legacy of Max Weber in Weimar Political and Social Theory'. *Weimar Thought: A Contested Legacy*. Edited by Peter E. Gordon and John McCormick, 73–97. Princeton: Princeton University Press, 2013.

Vincent, K. Steven. *Benjamin Constant and the Birth of French Liberalism*. New York: Palgrave Macmillan, 2011.

Vinx, Lars. *Hans Kelsen's Pure Theory of Law: Legitimacy and Legality*. Oxford: Oxford University Press, 2007.

Vishnia, Rachel Feig. 'Written Ballot, Secret Ballot and the *Iudicia Publica*: A Note on the Leges Tabellariae (Cicero, *De Legbius* 3.33–39)'. *Klio* 90:2 (2008): 334–46.

Voegelin, E. 'Kelsen's Pure Theory of Law'. *Political Science Quarterly* 42 (1927): 268–76.

Warren, Mark. 'Max Weber's Liberalism for a Nietzschean World'. *American Political Science Review* 82 (1988): 31–50.

Weber, Marianne. *Max Weber: Ein Lebensbild*. Heidelberg: Lambert Schneider, 1950 [1926].

Weichlein, Siegfried. 'Europa und der Föderalismus: Zur Begriffsgeschichte politischer Ordnungsmodelle'. *Historisches Jahrbuch* 125 (2005): 133–52.

Weiss, Roberto. *The Dawn of Humanism in Italy*. London: Haskell House Publishers, 1947.

Weston, C. C. 'English Constitutional Doctrines from the Fifteenth Century to the Seventeenth: II. The Theory of Mixed Monarchy under Charles I and after'. *English Historical Review* 75 (1960): 426–43.

Weston, C. C. and J. R. Greenberg. *Subjects and Sovereigns: The Grand Controversy over Legal Sovereignty in Stuart England*. Cambridge: Cambridge University Press, 1981.

Whatmore, Richard. *Against War and Empire: Geneva, Britain, and France in the Eighteenth Century*. New Haven: Yale University Press, 2012.

Wilder, Gary. *The French Imperial Nation-State: Negritude and Colonial Humanism between the Two World Wars*. Chicago: University of Chicago Press, 2005.

'Untimely Vision: Aimé Césaire, Decolonisation, Utopia'. *Public Culture* 21.1 (2009): 101–40.

Williams, Bernard. *Making Sense of Humanity and Other Philosophical Papers, 1982–1993*. Cambridge: Cambridge University Press, 1995.

Wilson, Stephen. *Feuding, Conflict and Banditry in Nineteenth-Century Corsica*. Cambridge: Cambridge University Press, 1988.

Wirszubski, C. *Libertas* as a Political Idea at Rome. Cambridge: Cambridge University Press, 1950.

Witt, Ronald. *In the Footsteps of the Ancients: The Origins of Humanism from Lovato to Bruni*. Leiden: Brill, 2000.

Wittke, Carl. *The Utopian Communist: A Biography of Wilhelm Weitling*. Baton Rouge: Louisiana State University Press, 1950.

Wokler, R. *Rousseau, the Age of Enlightenment, and their Legacies*, ed. B. Garsten. Princeton: Princeton University Press, 2012.

Wolin, Sheldon S. 'Norm and Form: The Constitutionalizing of Democracy'. *Athenian Political Thought and the Reconstruction of American Democracy*. Edited by J. Peter Euben, John R. Wallach and Josiah Ober, 29–58. Ithaca: Cornell University Press, 1994.

Wolterstorff, N. *Understanding Liberal Democracy: Essays in Political Philosophy*. Edited by T. Cuneo. Oxford: Oxford University Press, 2012.

Wood, Gordon. *The Creation of the American Republic, 1776–1787*. Chapel Hill: University of North Carolina Press, 1998 [1969].

Wootton, David. 'From Rebellion to Revolution: The Crisis of the Winter of 1642/3 and the Origins of Civil War Radicalism'. *English Historical Review* 105 (1990): 654–69.

Yack, Bernard. 'Popular Sovereignty and Nationalism'. *Political Theory* 29.4 (2001): 517–36.

Zabbia, Marino. 'Albertino Mussato'. *Dizionario biografico degli Italiani*, vol. LXXVII, 520–4. Rome: Istituto dell'Enciclopedia Italiana, 2012.

Zaller, Robert. 'Henry Parker and the Regiment of True Government'. *Proceedings of the American Philosophical Society* 135 (1991): 255–85.

Zarone, G. *Crisi e critica dello stato: scienza giuridica e trasformazione sociale tra Kelsen e Schmitt*. Naples: Scientifiche Italiane, 1982.

Ziebarth, E. 'Nomophylakes'. *Realencyclopädie der classischen Altertumswissenschaft* XVII.1 (1936): 832–3.

Zorzi, Andrea. 'The Popolo'. *Italy in the Age of the Renaissance, 1300–1550*. Edited by John M. Najemy, 145–64. Oxford: Oxford University Press, 2004.

Index

Made in the USA
Monee, IL
19 November 2019